Make sure that this is the right book for your Excel version

There are two different Windows versions of Excel in common use: Excel 2019 and Excel 365. This book is designed for use with the Excel 365 version (we publish a different book for Excel 2019 users).

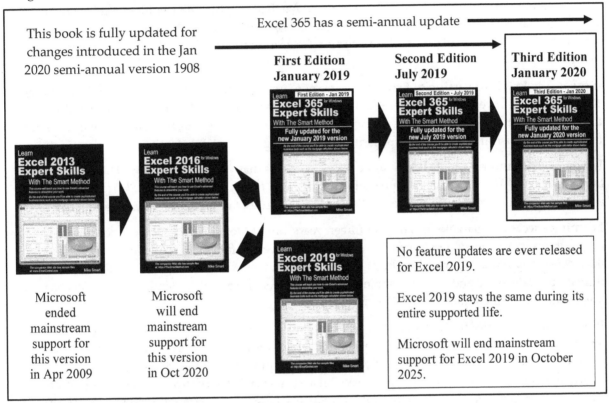

This book is fully updated for changes introduced in the Jan 2020 semi-annual version 1908

Excel 365 has a semi-annual update

First Edition January 2019

Second Edition July 2019

Third Edition January 2020

Microsoft ended mainstream support for this version in Apr 2009

Microsoft will end mainstream support for this version in Oct 2020

No feature updates are ever released for Excel 2019.

Excel 2019 stays the same during its entire supported life.

Microsoft will end mainstream support for Excel 2019 in October 2025.

What is the difference between Excel 2019 (perpetual) and Excel 365 (subscription)?

Excel 2019 (even when first purchased) had fewer features than Excel 365 and some features worked in a different way. This will always be the case because (unlike Excel 365), Excel 2019 is never updated with new features. For this reason we only need one book to support Excel 2019 learners: *Learn Excel 2019 Expert Skills with The Smart Method*.

Excel 365 is the latest version of Excel. Every six months (in January and July) Microsoft bring out a new major semi-annual update to Excel 365. This update adds new features to Excel and also often changes or retires older features. For this reason we bring out a new edition of our Excel 365 books in January and July each year so that the latest edition of our book always supports the latest version of Excel 365.

How to tell which version you are using

Excel 2019 is a "pay once and use forever" product. Excel 365 is a subscription product (pay monthly or pay annually). When you start Excel, a splash screen showing the words "Office 2019" or "Office 365" is briefly shown on screen. In: *Lesson 1-1: Check that your Excel version is up to date,* you'll learn more about identifying your Excel version.

Why you should use this book to learn Excel 365

- **It provides a thorough coverage of Power Pivot, Power Query, data modeling and DAX.** Power Pivot is an advanced professional tool for designing OLAP multi-dimensional databases. It is impossible to effectively use Power Pivot without first acquiring the relational modeling and OLAP theory needed to use it. This book will not only teach you DAX but will also give you all the OLAP data modeling skills you need in order to use Power Pivot and Get & Transform/Power Query effectively.

- **It is up-to-date.** A new Excel 365 semi-annual version is released every six months* (in January and July) and automatically updated on your computer. We then publish a new edition of this book to support the latest update. This means that new features are covered and the screen grabs will exactly match what you see on your screen. It can be very frustrating to try to learn Excel 365 using an out-of-date book.

- **It covers the Excel 365 version of Excel.** There are now two current Windows versions of Excel: **Excel 2019** (the pay-once version) and **Excel 365** (the subscription version that has more features and a different user interface). This book is specifically written for the *Excel 365 Jan 2020 semi-annual* version. It can be very frustrating to attempt to learn Excel 365 using an Excel 2019 book.

- **It won't waste your time by teaching basic Excel 365 skills that you already know.** This isn't a beginner's book. If you are an absolute beginner, you need our *Excel 365 Essential Skills* book. By assuming that you are already able to use Excel's basic features, far more ground can be covered.

- **Learning success is guaranteed.** For over fifteen years, Smart Method® courses have been used by large corporations, government departments and the armed forces to train their employees. This book has been constantly refined (during hundreds of classroom courses) by observing which skills students find difficult to understand and then developing simpler and better ways of explaining them. This has made the book effective for students of all ages and abilities.

- **It is the book of choice for teachers.** As well as catering for those wishing to learn Excel by self-study, Smart Method® books have long been the preferred choice for Excel teachers as they are designed to teach Excel and not as reference books. Books follow best-practice adult teaching methodology with clearly defined objectives for each learning session and an exercise to confirm skills transfer. With single, self-contained lessons, the books cater for any teaching or self-learning period (from minutes to hours).

- **Smart Method® books are #1 best sellers.** Every paper printed Smart Method® Excel book (and there have been twelve of them starting with Excel 2007) has been an Amazon #1 best seller in its category. This provides you with the confidence that you are using a best-of-breed resource to learn Excel.

- **It teaches to true Expert level.** This *Expert Skills* book teaches Excel to an extremely high level of competence that is very rarely found in the workplace (even amongst top professionals). At Expert level your skills will be greater and broader than almost all other Excel users and you will understand (and be able to effectively use) absolutely every Excel and Power Pivot feature. You'll have a complete mastery of skills that are often even a mystery to Excel power users.

Master Excel expert skills by setting aside just a few minutes each day

This book makes it easy to learn at your own pace because of its unique presentational style. The book contains short self-contained lessons and each lesson only takes a few minutes to complete.

You can complete as many, or as few, lessons as you have the time and energy for each day. Many learners have developed expert-level skills by setting aside just a few minutes each day to complete a single lesson.

---

* Excel 365 Version 1908 was released to the *Semi-Annual* update channel in Jan 2020. An earlier build of the same version was released earlier to the *Monthly* update channel. You'll learn more about update channels, builds and versions in: *Lesson 1-1: Check that your Excel version is up to date.*

Who Is This Book for?

This book isn't for absolute beginners

If you're just starting out with Excel, you need to complete the lessons in our *Essential Skills* book to learn all of Excel's basic features.

The full course outline for the *Essential Skills* book can be viewed at the end of this book in: *Appendix B: Skills Covered in the Essential Skills Course.*

This *Expert Skills* book teaches Excel to an extremely high level of competence that is very rarely found in the workplace (even amongst top professionals).

At *Expert* level your skills will be greater and broader than almost all other Excel users and you will understand (and be able to use) absolutely every Excel feature.

This book is intended for competent Excel 365 users who:

- Are already comfortable with Excel 365's basic features (ideally by completing all of the lessons in our *Essential Skills* book).

- Want in-depth coverage of all Excel 365's more powerful and complex features rather than a simple overview.

- Want an in-depth knowledge of multidimensional analysis using the new Power Pivot add-in (now included in all Excel versions).

- Want to master the other OLAP "power" tools now included in all Excel versions, the tools previously known as Power Query (now re-named: Get & Transform) and Power Maps (now re-named: 3D Maps).

- Schools, colleges and universities who wish to provide advanced Excel 365 training courses.

Use of this book as courseware

While this book is effective for self-instruction, the book is also the official courseware for The Smart Method's *Excel 365 Expert Skills* course.

Smart Method courses have been taken by a varied cross-section of the world's leading companies. We've had fantastic feedback from the vast number of professionals we've empowered with Excel skills.

This book is also suitable for use by other training organizations, teachers, schools, colleges and universities to provide structured, objective-led, and highly effective classroom courses.

Every lesson is presented on two facing pages

> Pray this day, on one side of one sheet of paper, explain how the Royal Navy is prepared to meet the coming conflict.
>
> *Winston Churchill, Letter to the Admiralty, Sep 1, 1939*

Winston Churchill was aware of the power of brevity. The discipline of condensing thoughts into one side of a single sheet of A4 paper resulted in the efficient transfer of information.

A tenet of our teaching system is that every lesson is presented on *two* facing sheets of A4. We've had to double Churchill's rule as they didn't have to contend with screen grabs in 1939! If we can't teach an essential concept in two pages of A4 we know that the subject matter needs to be broken into two smaller lessons.

How this book avoids wasting your time

Over the years I have read many hundreds of computer text books and most of my time was wasted. The big problem with most books is that I must wade through thousands of words just to learn one important technique. If I don't read everything I might miss that one essential insight.

Many presentational methods have been used in this book to help you to avoid reading about things you already know how to do, or things that are of little interest to you.

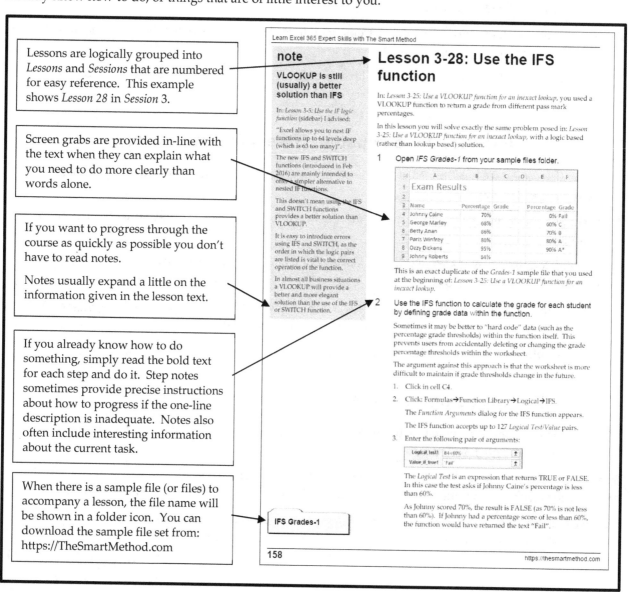

Learning by participation

Tell me, and I will forget. Show me, and I may remember. Involve me, and I will understand.

Confucius, Chinese teacher, editor, politician and philosopher (551-479 BC)

Confucius would probably have agreed that the best way to teach IT skills is hands-on (actively) and not hands-off (passively). This is another of the principal tenets of The Smart Method® teaching method.

Research has backed up the assertion that you will learn more material, learn more quickly, and understand more of what you learn if you learn using active, rather than passive methods.

For this reason, pure theory pages are kept to an absolute minimum with most theory woven into the hands-on lessons, either within the text or in sidebars.

This echoes the teaching method used in Smart Method classroom courses where snippets of pertinent theory are woven into the lessons themselves so that interest and attention is maintained by hands-on involvement, but all necessary theory is still covered.

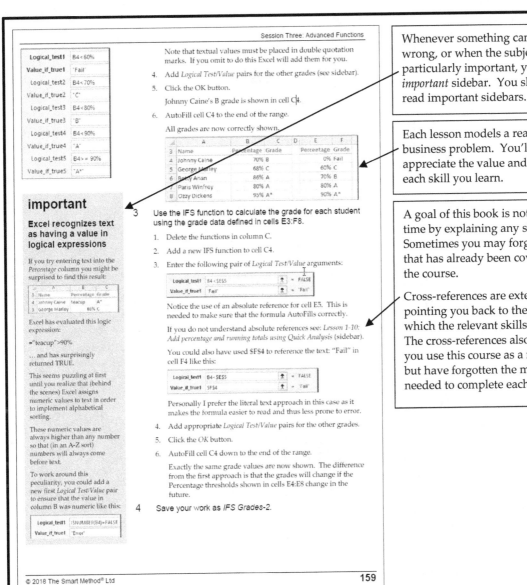

Whenever something can easily go wrong, or when the subject text is particularly important, you will see the *important* sidebar. You should always read important sidebars.

Each lesson models a real-world business problem. You'll immediately appreciate the value and relevance of each skill you learn.

A goal of this book is not to waste your time by explaining any skill twice. Sometimes you may forget something that has already been covered earlier in the course.

Cross-references are extensively used, pointing you back to the lesson in which the relevant skills were learned. The cross-references also help when you use this course as a reference book but have forgotten the more basic skills needed to complete each step.

Learn Excel 365 Expert Skills with The Smart Method

Third Edition: updated for the Jan 2020 Semi-Annual version 1908

Mike Smart

Learn Excel 365 Expert Skills with The Smart Method
Third Edition: updated for the Jan 2020 Semi-Annual version 1908

Published by:

Smart Method Enterprises Ltd
Kemp House
160 City Road
London
EC1V 2NX

The Smart Method® is a trading style of Smart Method Enterprises Ltd.

Tel: +44 (0)845 458 3282

E-mail: Use the contact page at https://thesmartmethod.com/contact
Web: https://thesmartmethod.com

Copyright © 2020 by Mike Smart

All Rights Reserved. No part of the contents of this book may be reproduced or transmitted in any form or by any means, electronic or mechanical, including photocopying, recording, or by any information storage and retrieval system without the prior agreement and written permission of the publisher, except for the inclusion of brief quotations in a review.

The sample files that accompany this book, or that are available for download from the Internet by owners of this book, are protected by copyright. You are granted a single-user license to use the software for your own personal, non-commercial use only. You may not reproduce, circulate, redistribute, resell, or commercially exploit the sample files or any portion of them without the written consent of The Smart Method® Ltd.

We make a sincere effort to ensure the accuracy of all material described in this document. The content is based upon final release software whenever possible, but parts of the book may be based upon pre-release versions supplied by software manufacturers. The Smart Method® Ltd makes no warranty, express or implied, with respect to the quality, correctness, reliability, accuracy, or freedom from error of this document or the products it describes.

The names of software products referred to in this manual are claimed as trademarks of their respective companies. Any other product or company names mentioned herein may be the trademarks of their respective owners.

Unless otherwise noted, the example data, companies, organizations, products, people and events depicted herein are fictitious. No association with any real company, organization, product, person or event is intended or should be inferred. The sample data may contain many inaccuracies and should not be relied upon for any purpose.

International Standard Book Number (ISBN13): 978-1-909253-43-8

The Smart Method® is a registered trademark of The Smart Method Ltd.

4 6 8 10 9 7 5 3 1

Author's Acknowledgements

O would some Power, the gift to give us, To see ourselves as others see us!

Robert Burns, Scottish poet (1759-1796)

Many people will read this book. Some will be confronting advanced concepts, such as pivot tables and macros, for the very first time. Others will be seasoned professionals with an IT background. Readers will include students, office workers, accountants, administrators, doctors, scientists, engineers, bankers and many other professions.

The book aims to communicate how to use Excel's advanced features in a way that is comprehensible to all.

I couldn't have written the original version of this book without the help of many pairs of eyes. I was extremely lucky to have had this help, throughout the writing process, from a wonderful group of international readers who kindly agreed to test drive the course prior to going to print.

I'm very grateful to Nate Barber (from San Antonio, Texas, USA). Nate was already a seasoned Excel power user and provided some wonderful technical insights. He also highlighted many cases where my British English didn't quite make the journey across the Atlantic. His feedback really helped me to improve the book in so many ways.

Many thanks are also due to Valérie Rousseau (from Quebec, Canada). Valérie spotted an embarrassing number of grammatical errors in my writing and managed to discover errors that had been missed by all other reviewers.

Huge thanks also go out to Mark Casey (from London, England). Mark provided clear and concise feedback that caused me to completely re-write some of the lessons. His excellent command of the written word enabled me to eloquently re-phrase some of my clumsier sentences.

I'd like to show great appreciation to Lorna Henderson (from Auckland, New Zealand). Lorna provided fantastically detailed feedback, resulting in hundreds of improvements to the book. There's hardly a page in the book that has not benefited from her suggestions and comments.

Many thanks also to Heidi Hembree (from Maryville, Tennessee, USA). Heidi highlighted many areas where I hadn't communicated concepts as well as I should have. Her feedback had a significant impact upon every session.

I'm also extremely grateful to Rosalind Johnson (from Pantymwyn, Wales). Rosalind's useful suggestions helped me to improve the readability of many lessons.

Thanks are also due to Jennifer Lashely (from London, England). Jennifer highlighted many potential pitfalls when working through the lessons that I was then able to eliminate from the final copy.

Special thanks are also due to Simon Smart (my son) who took time out of his own busy software development schedule to undertake the original very comprehensive technical proof read.

Huge thanks also to Sue Ferrario (from Douglas, Great Britain) who tirelessly completed the final proofread of the book prior to going to print.

I've also recently received fantastic feedback from Dwayne Roberts (from Arizona, USA). Dwayne provided a huge number of useful ideas as he worked through the entire book between 2018 and 2020. It was wonderful to receive such detailed feedback as the book has changed in so many ways during the last twelve years of updates and regular revisions.

I'd also like to thank the many others that have helped to shape the content of this book that I have not mentioned by name. Your contributions were greatly appreciated.

Contents

Session Three: Advanced Functions 107

Session Four: Using Names and the Formula Auditing Tools 169

Session Five: What If Analysis and Security 207

Session Six: Working with Hyperlinks and Other Applications   243

Session Seven: Forms and Macros   261

Session Eight: Pivot Tables   307

Session Nine: 3D Maps   365

Session Ten: Create Get & Transform queries 399

Introduction to the Data Modeling and Power Pivot sessions — 475

Session Eleven: Power Pivot, Data Modeling, OLAP and Business Intelligence — 477

Session Twelve: An introduction to DAX   527

Appendix A: Power Pivot Rules   555

Appendix B: Skills Covered in the Essential Skills Course   563

Index   569

Introduction

Welcome to *Learn Excel 365 Expert Skills with The Smart Method®*. This book has been designed to enable students to master Excel 365 advanced skills by self-study. The book is equally useful as courseware in order to deliver classroom courses.

Smart Method® publications are continually evolving as we discover better ways of explaining or teaching the concepts presented.

Feedback

At The Smart Method® we love feedback – both positive and negative. If you have any suggestions for improvements to future versions of this book, or if you find content or typographical errors, the author would always love to hear from you.

You can make suggestions for improvements to this book using the online form at:

https://thesmartmethod.com/contact

Future editions of this book will always incorporate your feedback so that there are never any known errors at time of publication.

If you have any difficulty understanding or completing a lesson, or if you feel that anything could have been more clearly explained, we'd also love to hear from you. We've made hundreds of detail improvements to our books based upon reader's feedback and continue to chase the impossible goal of 100% perfection.

Downloading the sample files

In order to use this book, it is sometimes necessary to download sample files from the Internet. The process of downloading the free sample files will be explained later, in: *Lesson 1-4: Apply a simple filter to a range.*

Problem resolution

If you encounter any problem using any aspect of the course you can contact us using the online form at:

https://thesmartmethod.com/contact

We'll do everything possible to quickly resolve the problem.

The Excel version and locale that were used to write this book

This edition was written using *Excel 365 semi-annual version 1908*, released on Jan 14 2020 running under the Windows 10 operating system. You'll discover which version your computer is running in: *Lesson 1-1: Check that your Excel version is up to date.*

This book was written using English (United States) *Region format* settings. The English - US Region format uses the decimal separator for a period and a comma for the thousands separator, producing formatted numbers such as 12,345.67. Dates are formatted as Month/Day/Year. If you are situated in a different region it is possible to change your region format (in Windows settings) but there is no need to do so. Just be aware that some of the screen grabs in this book will be formatted differently to what you see on your screen.

Typographical Conventions Used in This Book

This guide consistently uses typographical conventions to differentiate parts of the text.

When you see this	Here's what it means
Click *Line Color* on the left-hand bar and then click *No line.*	Italics are used to refer to text that appears in a worksheet cell, an Excel dialog, on the ribbon, or elsewhere within the Excel application. Italics may sometimes also be used for emphasis or distinction.
Click: Home→Font→Underline.	Click on the ribbon's *Home* tab and then look for the *Font* group. Click the *Underline* button within this group (that's the left-hand side of the button, not the drop-down arrow next to it).
Click: Home→Font→ Underline Drop Down→Double Underline.	Click on the ribbon's *Home* tab and then look for the *Font* group. Click the drop-down arrow next to the Underline button (that's the right-hand side of the button) within this group and then choose *Double Underline* from the drop-down list.
Click: File→Options→ Advanced→General→ Edit Custom Lists→Import	This is a more involved example. 1. Click the *File* tab on the ribbon, and then click the *Options* button towards the bottom of the left-hand pane. The *Excel Options* dialog appears. 2. Choose the *Advanced* list item in the left-hand pane and scroll down to the *General* group in the right-hand pane. 3. Click the *Edit Custom Lists…* button. Yet another new dialog pops up. 4. Click the *Import* button.
Type **European Sales** into the cell.	Whenever you are supposed to actually type something on the keyboard it is shown in bold faced text.
Press <Ctrl> + <Z>.	You should hold down the **Ctrl** key and then press the **Z** key.
	When a lesson tells you to click a button, an image of the relevant button will often be

shown either in the page margin or within the text itself.

note

Power Pivot tables support up to two thousand million rows. This enables Excel to analyze *Big Data*.

If you want to read through the book as quickly as possible, you don't have to read notes.

Notes usually expand a little on the information given in the lesson text.

important

Do not click the *Delete* button at this point as to do so would erase the entire table.

Whenever something can easily go wrong, or when the subject text is particularly important, you will see the *important* sidebar.

You should always read important sidebars.

tip

Moving between tabs using the keyboard

You can also use the <Ctrl>+<PgUp> and <Ctrl>+<PgDn> keyboard shortcuts to cycle through all of the tabs in your workbook.

Tips add to the lesson text by showing you shortcuts or time-saving techniques relevant to the lesson.

The bold text at the top of the tip box enables you to establish whether the tip is appropriate to your needs without reading all of the text.

In this example you may not be interested in keyboard shortcuts so do not need to read further.

anecdote

I ran an Excel course for a small company in London a couple of years ago...

Sometimes I add an anecdote gathered over the years from my Excel classes or from other areas of life.

If you simply want to learn Excel as quickly as possible you can ignore my anecdotes.

trivia

The feature that Excel uses to help you out with function calls first made an appearance in Visual Basic 5 back in 1996 ...

Sometimes I indulge myself by adding a little piece of trivia in the context of the skill being taught.

Just like my anecdotes, you can ignore these if you want to. They won't help you to learn Excel any better!

The World's Fastest Cars

When there is a sample file (or files) to accompany a lesson, the file name will be shown in a folder icon. You can download the sample files from: *https://thesmartmethod.com*. Detailed instructions are given in*: Lesson 1-4: Apply a simple filter to a range.*

© 2020 The Smart Method® Ltd

How to use this course

This course utilizes some of the tried and tested techniques developed after teaching Excel to vast numbers of students during many years of Smart Method classroom courses.

In order to master Excel as quickly and efficiently as possible you should use the recommended learning method described below. If you do this there is absolutely no doubt that you will master the advanced Excel skills taught in this book.

Three important rules

#1 Complete the course from beginning to end

It is always tempting to jump around the course completing lessons in a haphazard way.

We strongly suggest that you start at the beginning and complete lessons sequentially.

That's because each lesson builds upon skills learned in the previous lessons and one of our goals is not to waste your time by teaching the same skill twice. If you miss a skill by skipping a lesson you'll find the later lessons more difficult, or even impossible to follow. This, in turn, may demoralize you and make you abandon the course.

#2 If possible, complete a session in one sitting

The book is arranged into *sessions* and *lessons*.

You can complete as many, or as few, lessons as you have the time and energy for each day. Many learners have developed Excel skills by setting aside just a few minutes each day to complete a single lesson.

If it is possible, the most effective way to learn is to lock yourself away, switch off your telephone, and complete a full session, without interruption, except for a 15 minute break each hour. The memory process is associative and we've ensured that the lessons in each session are very closely coupled (contextually) with the others. By learning the whole session in one sitting, you'll store all of that information in the same part of your memory and will find it easier to recall later.

The experience of being able to remember all of the words of a song as soon as somebody has got you "started" with the first line is an example of the memory's associative system of data storage.

#3 Rest at least every hour

In our classroom courses we have often observed a phenomenon that we call "running into a wall". This happens when a student becomes overloaded with new information to the point that they can no longer follow the simplest instruction. If you find this happening to you, you've studied for too long without a rest.

You should take a 15-minute break every hour (or more often if you begin to feel overwhelmed) and spend it relaxing rather than catching up with your e-mails. Ideally you should relax by lying down and closing your eyes. This allows your brain to use all of its processing power to efficiently store and index the skills you've learned. We've found that this hugely improves retention of skills learned.

How to work through the lessons

At the end of each session, complete the session exercise

Keep attempting the exercise at the end of each session until you can complete it without having to refer to lessons in the session. Don't start the next session until you can complete the exercise from memory.

At the end of each session, review the objectives

The session objectives are stated at the beginning of each session.

Read each objective and ask yourself if you have truly mastered each skill. If you are not sure about any of the skills listed, revise the relevant lesson(s) before moving on to the next session.

You will find it very frustrating if you move to a new session before you have truly mastered the skills covered in the previous session. This may demoralize you and make you abandon the course.

How to best use the incremental sample files

Many lessons in this course use a sample file that is incrementally improved during each lesson. At the end of each lesson an interim version is always saved. For example, a sample file called Sales-1 may provide the starting point to a sequence of three lessons. After each lesson, interim versions called Sales-2, Sales-3 and Sales-4 are saved by the student.

A complete set of sample files (including all incremental versions) are provided in the sample file set. This provides three important benefits:

- If you have difficulty with a lesson it is useful to be able to study the completed workbook (at the end of the lesson) by opening the finished version of the lesson's workbook.

- When you have completed the book, you will want to use it as a reference. The sample files allow you to work through any single lesson in isolation, as the workbook's state at the beginning of each lesson is always available.

- When teaching a class one student may corrupt their workbook by a series of errors (or by their computer crashing). It is possible to quickly and easily move the class on to the next lesson by instructing the student to open the next sample file in the set (instead of progressing with their own corrupted file or copying a file from another student).

The time you spend learning Excel will be hugely worthwhile

If you persevere with this course there is no doubt that you will master Excel expert skills. A substantial amount of time and effort is needed but the skills you'll acquire will be hugely valuable for the rest of your life.

Enjoy the course.

Session One: Tables, and Ranges

> As a general rule the most successful man in life is the man who has the best information.
>
> *Benjamin Disraeli, British Politician (1804-1881)*

In this session you'll learn all about tables, how they differ from ranges, and how to use them effectively to manage data.

This session also introduces *structured table references* that provide a completely new way to reference dynamic table data. This has eliminated the need for the complex workarounds required to work with dynamic ranges.

Session Objectives

By the end of this session you will be able to:

- Understand update channels
- Check that automatic updates are enabled
- Change the Office Theme
- Apply a simple filter to a range
- Apply a top 10 and custom filter to a range
- Apply an advanced filter with multiple OR criteria
- Apply an advanced filter with complex criteria
- Apply an advanced filter with function-driven criteria
- Extract unique records using an advanced filter
- Add totals using Quick Analysis
- Add percentage and running totals using Quick Analysis
- Convert a range into a table and add a total row
- Format a table using table styles and convert a table into a range
- Create a custom table style
- Sort a range or table by rows
- Sort a range by columns
- Sort a range or table by custom list
- Name a table and create an automatic structured table reference
- Create a manual structured table reference
- Use special items in structured table references
- Understand unqualified structured table references

important

Update Channels

Update channels determine *when* users will receive the latest Excel version.

Excel 365 home users

If you have a subscription version of Excel 365 that is targeted at home users, you are required to receive monthly updates

This is called the *Monthly Channel*.

You will potentially receive new or improved features every month.

Excel 365 business users

New features added in the *Monthly Channel* may have bugs, as they will not yet have been extensively tested by real-world use.

If you have an Excel 365 version that is targeted at business users (usually called *Excel Pro Plus*), you will (by default) have a different update channel (the *Semi-annual Channel*). The *Semi-annual Channel* only updates Excel twice each year (in January and July).

The Semi-annual Channel allows new features to be thoroughly tested before release to business users (as Monthly Channel users will report any bugs encountered).

It is possible (though difficult) for Excel Pro-Plus users to change their update channel to the *Monthly Channel*.

This book was written using the *Jan 2020 Semi-Annual Version 1908*.

Excel 2019 perpetual users

Perpetual license users (the pay-once version of Excel) do not receive any feature updates, so do not have an update channel. Even upon first release the Excel 2019 version of Excel had fewer features than Excel 365.

Lesson 1-1: Check that your Excel version is up to date

Automatic Updates

Normally Excel will look after updates without you having to do anything. By default, automatic updates are enabled. This means that updates are downloaded from the Internet and installed automatically.

It is possible that automatic updates have been switched off on your computer. In this case there is a danger that you may have an old, buggy, unsupported and out of date version of Excel installed.

This lesson will show you how to make sure that you are using the latest (most complete, and most reliable) version of Excel.

1   Start Excel and open a new blank workbook (if you have not already done this).

2   Make sure that automatic updates are enabled.

1.   Click the *File* button at the top-left of the screen.

This takes you to *Backstage View*. Backstage View allows you to complete an enormous range of common tasks from a single window.

2.   Click: *Account* [Account] in the left-hand list.

Your account details are displayed on screen. Notice the *Office Updates* button displayed in the right-hand pane.

If all is well, and automatic updates are switched on, you will see a button similar to this:

If automatic updates have been switched off, you will see a similar button to this.

In this case you will need to switch automatic updates on (see next step).

3   Switch on automatic updates if necessary.

Click: Update Options→Enable Updates.

note

Version number and Build

If you have a subscription version of Excel 365 that is targeted at home users, you will receive a new Excel version every month.

Each new version may add new features to Excel 365.

If bugs or security issues are found in a new version, Microsoft will fix them and publish a new *build* of the same version.

It is quite normal for there to be several new builds of each new monthly version during the month that it is released.

4   If there are updates waiting to install, apply them.

Sometimes Excel will download updates but will not install them automatically.

In this case you will see an update button similar to the following:

If you see this type of button you should apply the update.

Click: Update Options→Apply Updates.

You may be asked to confirm that you want to apply the update, and to close any open programs to apply the update.

5   Notice your version number and update channel.

note

Perpetual license versions have different features

Perpetual license holders still receive monthly updates, but these only include security updates and bug fixes (not new features).

A perpetual license holder running version 1908 will thus see different features than a subscription license holder running the same Excel version.

You will see a product information section displayed. If you see the number *365* or the words *Subscription Product*, you will know that you are using the subscription version (Excel 365) that this book teaches. This is the case for products B and C above. Otherwise you are using the *perpetual license* version (this is the case for product A above). This is not the correct book for learning the perpetual version (we also publish an Excel 2019 book).

Notice also the *update channel* and *version numbers* (see sidebars).

6   Click the *Back* button 🔙 to leave *Backstage View* and return to the worksheet.

7   Click the *Close* button ⊠ in the top-right corner of the Excel screen to close Excel.

Lesson 1-2: Change between touch mode and mouse mode

Both Excel and Windows allow you to operate in one of two modes: Touch Mode and Mouse Mode. Excel tries to figure out which mode you want to use and then sets it for you automatically. This lesson will enable you to set the mode you prefer manually.

Touch Mode: In Touch Mode the icons are spaced further apart so that they are easier to tap with your finger.

Mouse Mode: This is the mode preferred by most Excel users. In Mouse Mode the icons are displayed closer together. Unless you have a very large screen you will usually also see more icons on your screen when in Mouse Mode. This means that you can often execute a command with one click rather than two.

For this reason, it is usually more efficient to work with Excel in Mouse Mode (using a mouse to select commands) than to use Touch Mode (using your finger to select commands).

1   Open Excel and open a new blank Excel workbook.

2   Enable the *Touch/Mouse Mode* button on the *Quick Access Toolbar*.

At the top left of the screen you will see several icons. This strip of icons is called the *Quick Access Toolbar.* .

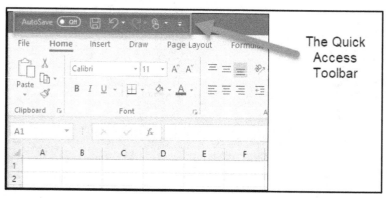

The Quick Access Toolbar

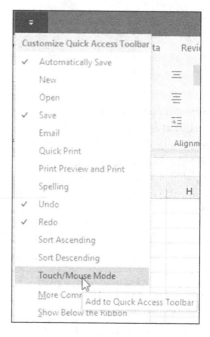

You may already see the *Touch/Mouse Mode* button on the *Quick Access Toolbar*. If you do you can progress to the next step.

If you don't see the *Touch/Mouse Mode* button click the drop-down arrow to the right of the *Quick Access Toolbar* and then click *Touch/Mouse Mode* on the drop-down menu (see sidebar).

The *Touch/Mouse Mode* button is then added to the *Quick Access Toolbar*.

3   Set Excel to use *Touch Mode*.

If you are using a tablet device, you may find that Excel is already using touch mode.

1.   Click on the *Touch/Mouse Mode* button. Two options appear on the drop-down menu:

note

Windows 10 also has a touch and mouse mode

In Windows 10 *Touch Mode* is called *Tablet Mode.*

Tablet Mode makes all applications run at full screen and shows a different screen when Windows starts.

To enable *Tablet* mode:

1. Click the Windows button:

… on the bottom left of the screen.

2. Click *Settings* on the pop-up menu.

3. Click *System.*

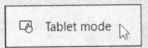
System
Display, sound, notifications, power

4. Click the *Tablet Mode* button:

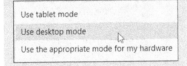
Tablet mode

5. Select the option you prefer:

Use tablet mode
Use desktop mode
Use the appropriate mode for my hardware

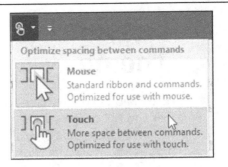

Optimize spacing between commands

Mouse
Standard ribbon and commands.
Optimized for use with mouse.

Touch
More space between commands.
Optimized for use with touch.

2. Click the *Touch* option.

Notice that fewer icons are now displayed. You are now using Excel in *Touch Mode.*

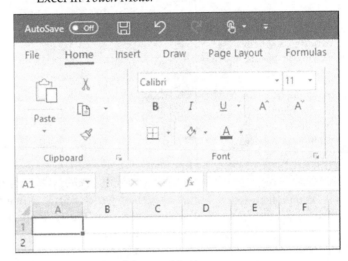

4   Set Excel to use *Mouse Mode.*

Now do the same thing but this time select *Mouse Mode.*

Notice that the icons are now closer together:

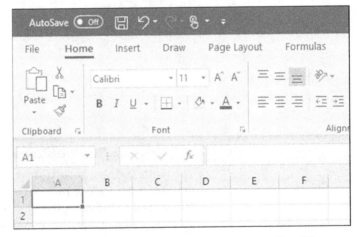

If you decide that you prefer *Touch Mode,* you'll still have no difficulty working through all of the lessons in this book.

note

Themes and Backgrounds affect every Office application on all of your devices

When you set a theme or background in Excel you are actually changing the theme and background for the entire Office suite.

This means that you will have a consistent experience when using other Office applications such as *Word* and *PowerPoint*.

If you are logged in to a *Microsoft Account*, the theme you select will also magically appear on all of your devices (such as a work computer, home computer, laptop, tablet and smartphone). This is part of Microsoft's comprehensive support for cloud computing.

Cloud computing is extensively covered in the *Essential Skills* book in this series, in which a whole session is dedicated to Excel's cloud computing features.

Lesson 1-3: Change the Office Theme

Excel allows you to change the colors of screen elements (such as the title bar and ribbon) by selecting a *theme*. There are four themes available: *Colorful, White, Dark Gray* and *Black*.

Colorful

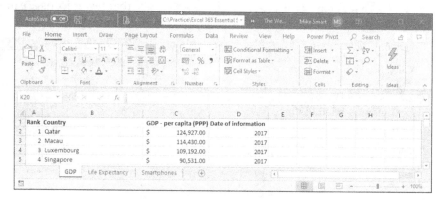

Excel 365 uses the *Colorful* theme as the default. The colorful theme makes it clear which of the Office applications you are using as Word, Excel, PowerPoint, Outlook and other Office applications each have their own unique color.

White

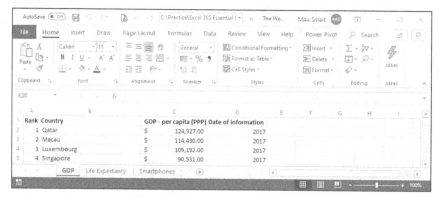

The *White* theme has very low contrast and shading. Some designers feel that this gives Excel a modern and "minimalist" appearance. This was introduced as the default theme for Excel 2013, but was widely criticized by some users for causing eye strain and being difficult to work with.

In 2016 the default was changed to the (much better) colorful theme.

note

You can also personalize Excel by changing the background

Background customization can only be done if you are connected to the Internet and logged into a Microsoft Account.

If you are logged into your Microsoft Account, you will see an *Office Background* drop-down list (above the *Office Theme* setting) that enables backgrounds to be set:

When you choose a background a "tattoo" is added to the area above the Ribbon with your chosen design:

note

Audio cues

If you enable *Audio Cues* a different sound will be played whenever you complete common Excel actions (such as cut and paste).

The idea is that you will subconsciously link sounds with actions so that when you make a mistake it will "sound wrong".

To enable Audio cues, click:

File→Options→
Ease of Access→
Feedback options→
Provide feedback with sound.

You are also able to choose between two different *Sound Schemes*.

Dark Gray and Black

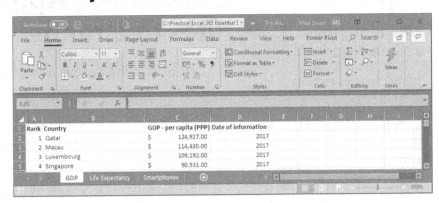

The *Dark Gray* and *Black* themes provide high contrast between different screen elements. It has been suggested that these themes would be particularly useful for users with impaired vision.

1   Open Excel and open a new blank Excel workbook.

2   Change the *Office Theme*.

    1. Click the *File* button [File] at the top-left of the screen.

    2. Click the *Options* button [Options] near the bottom of the left-hand menu bar.

        The *Excel Options* dialog box appears.

        In the *Personalize your copy of Microsoft Office* section, you'll see an *Office Theme* drop-down list. Click the drop-down arrow to see the different themes available.

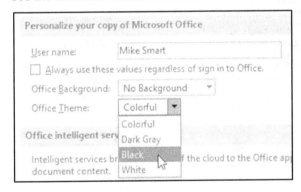

    3. Click the *Dark Gray* theme.

    4. Click *OK* to return to the Excel screen.

        Experiment with each theme until you discover the one you prefer. All of the screen grabs in this book were made using the *Colorful* theme. If you choose a different theme the screen grabs in the book may look slightly different to what you see on your computer screen.

3   Close Excel.

important

Organizing your sample files folder

When you complete a lesson that involves a sample file that is changed, you will be instructed to save the file with a suffix.

By the time you've completed the course you'll have sample files such as:

Sales-1
Sales-2
Sales-3
Sales-4 ... etc

The first file is the sample file that you downloaded and the others (with the number suffix) are interim versions as you complete each lesson.

The sample file set includes the starting sample file and all interim versions.

The interim versions are provided for three reasons:

1. If your work-in-progress becomes unusable (for example after a system crash) you can continue without starting at the beginning again.

2. If a lesson doesn't seem to give the results described, you can view the example to get some clues about what has gone wrong.

3. When you have completed the course you will use this book as a reference. The interim versions allow you to work through any of the lessons in isolation if you need to remind yourself how to use a specific Excel feature.

It is a good idea to place the sample files in a different folder to your saved work. If you don't do this you'll be over-writing the sample interim files (such as Sales-1, Sales-2 etc) with your own finished work.

Inventory-1

Lesson 1-4: Apply a simple filter to a range

1 Download the sample files (if you haven't already done so).

    1. Open your web browser and type in the URL:

       https://TheSmartMethod.com

    2. Click the *Sample Files* link on the top menu bar of the home page.

    3. Download the sample files for *Excel 365 Expert Skills Third Edition* (also see sidebar: *Organizing your sample files folder*).

       While we provide the sample files in both .EXE and .ZIP file format it is strongly recommended that you download the sample files as a self-extracting .EXE file. This avoids the Protected View issue discussed on the facing page sidebar.

2 Open *Inventory-1* from your sample files folder.

This workbook contains a list showing all goods in stock.

3 Add a filter to the range.

    1. Click anywhere inside the range.

    2. Click: Data→Sort & Filter→Filter.

Notice that small drop-down arrow buttons have appeared in the range header row:

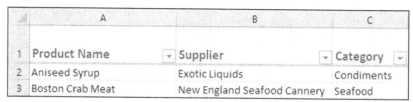

4 Use the filter to display products in the *Seafood* category.

    1. Click the drop-down arrow to the right of *Category* in cell C1.

    2. Uncheck the *(Select All)* check box.

    3. Check the *Seafood* checkbox.

    4. Click the *OK* button.

Only Seafood products are now displayed:

	A	B	C
1	Product Name	Supplier	Category
3	Boston Crab Meat	New England Seafood Cannery	Seafood
5	Carnarvon Tigers	Pavlova, Ltd.	Seafood

note

Potential problem when downloading sample files

Protected View is a security feature that was first introduced in Excel 2010. It is designed to protect you from potential viruses by treating all files downloaded from the Internet as being suspicious.

Any workbooks that are downloaded from the Internet, or are sent by e-mail attachment, will open in *Protected View* by default.

The user then has to click an *Enable Editing* button to use the file as normal:

Enable Editing

While some users may find it useful to be reminded about the origin of their files, others may find this feature annoying.

To avoid seeing this message whenever you open a sample file, we provide the sample files as a digitally-signed self-extracting download. This means that the sample files will open without warnings.

We also offer an alternative zip file method to download (the link to this page is in the FAQ section at the bottom of the web page).

The alternative zip file has been provided because some companies (or anti-virus products) block the download of executable files.

If you download using the zip file option, you'll have to click the *Enable Editing* button every time you open a sample file.

Notice that the filter button next to *Category* in cell C1 has changed to show that a filter condition is in effect.

Notice also that the row numbers along the left of the worksheet are now shaded blue and are no longer sequential.

5 Add a second filter condition to show items in the *Seafood* category with an inventory value greater than 1,000.

1. Click the drop-down arrow to the right of *Value* in cell F1.

2. Click: Number Filters→Greater Than... from the drop-down menu.

3. Type **1000** into the text box.

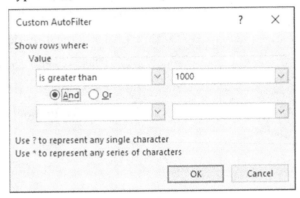

4. Click the *OK* button.

Only rows that are in the *Seafood* category and exceed a value of 1,000 are now shown.

	A	B	C	D	E	F
				Unit	In	
1	Product Name	Supplier	Category	Price	Stoc	Value
3	Boston Crab Meat	New England Seafood Cannery	Seafood	18.40	123	2,263.20
5	Carnarvon Tigers	Pavlova, Ltd.	Seafood	62.50	42	2,625.00
26	Inlagd Sill	Svensk Sjöföda AB	Seafood	19.00	112	2,128.00
51	Röd Kaviar	Svensk Sjöföda AB	Seafood	15.00	101	1,515.00
59	Spegesild	Lyngbysild	Seafood	12.00	95	1,140.00

6 Remove the filter from the range.

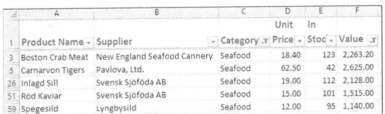

1. Click anywhere inside the range.

2. Click: Data→Sort & Filter→Filter.

Notice that the small drop-down handles have disappeared from the range header row and that all rows are now displayed.

7 Use *Filter by selection* to only show rows in the *Dairy Products* category.

1. Right-click any cell in the *Category* column containing the text: *Dairy Products*

2. Click: Filter→Filter by Selected Cell's Value from the shortcut menu.

Notice that only rows that are in the *Dairy Products* category are now displayed.

8 Remove the filter from the range.

Lesson 1-5: Apply a top 10 and custom filter to a range

Filter

1   Open *Inventory-1* from your sample files folder (if it isn't already open).

2   Add a filter to the range.

Click anywhere inside the range and then click:

Data→Sort & Filter→Filter

3   Apply a top ten filter to identify the ten items that have the most expensive inventory.

1.   Click the drop-down arrow to the right of *Value* in cell F1.

2.   Click: *Number Filters.*

3.   Click: *Top 10...* from the fly-out menu.

The *Top 10 AutoFilter* dialog is displayed:

It is possible to use this dialog to filter to a number other than 10 or to filter to the *Bottom* values (if you wanted to show the items with the least expensive inventory).

4.   Click the *OK* button.

The ten items with the most expensive inventory are shown. Note that they are still sorted alphabetically, in ascending order, by *Product Name.* You'd probably want to sort the rows by value in descending order. Sorting will be covered later, in: *Lesson 1-15: Sort a range or table by rows.*

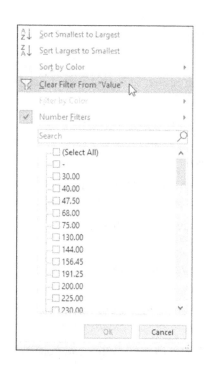

4   Clear the filter condition from the *Value* column.

1.   Click the button to the right of *Value* in cell F1.

2.   Click *Clear Filter From "Value"* from the shortcut menu.

The filter condition is removed and all items in the list are shown.

5   Use a custom filter to show items that have a value between 1,000 and 3,000.

1.   Click the drop-down arrow to the right of *Value* in cell F1.

2.   Click: Number Filters→Custom Filter on the drop-down menu.

Inventory-1

note

Filtering by color

The *Filter by Color* option is only enabled when at least one cell in the column has a font color or background color.

You can then click the filter arrow at the top of the column and choose *Filter by Color*. This displays a fly-out menu listing every color in the column:

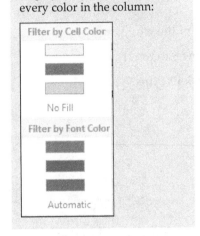

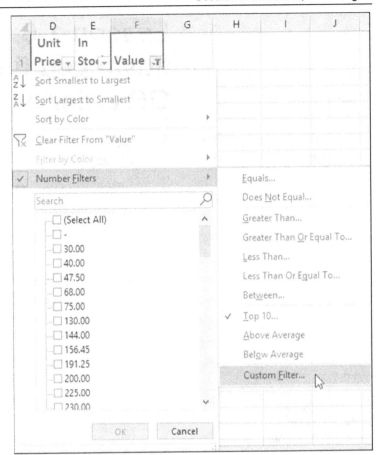

The *Custom AutoFilter* dialog is displayed.

3. Set the filter condition to: *is greater than or equal to 1000* **And** *is less than or equal to 3000*.

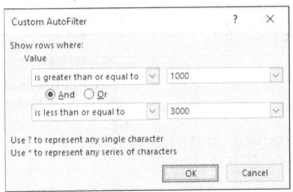

4. Click the *OK* button.

Only products with a value between 1,000 and 3,000 are shown.

6   **Remove the filter from the range.**

1. Click anywhere inside the range.

2. Click: Data→Sort & Filter→Filter.

Notice that the small drop-down arrows have disappeared from the range header row and that all rows are now displayed.

Lesson 1-6: Apply an advanced filter with multiple OR criteria

note

The criteria range can appear anywhere on the worksheet and does not have to be complete

It is quick and convenient to place the criteria above the range to be filtered.

You may, however, place the criteria anywhere in the workbook – even on a different worksheet.

In this example, all of the fields in the range are listed by making a complete duplicate of the range headers. The advanced filter will work just as well if the header list is not complete.

Example:

To filter down to the *Seafood* category you could simply type **Category** into cell J1 and **Seafood** into cell J2 and then set the criteria range to J1:J2.

note

The criteria range can span any number of rows

In this example a criteria range of four rows is used (A1:F4).

You can use as many rows as you need in your criteria range.

It is crucial that you leave at least one blank row between the criteria range and any other range on the worksheet.

1   Open *Inventory-1* from your sample files folder (if it isn't already open).

2   Create the criteria range.

The criteria range is the area on your worksheet where you define the advanced filter criteria.

1.   Insert five blank rows at the top of the worksheet.

2.   Copy the range headers from row 6 to row 1.

Your worksheet should now look like this:

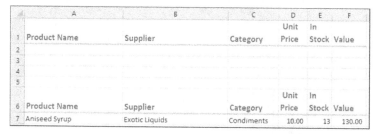

Each of the rows 2-4 can now be used to define the criteria needed for each column in the range.

3   Add filter criteria to show all products in the *Condiments*, *Seafood* and *Confections* categories.

This is an example of a filter with three OR criteria. The filter can be defined as:

Condiments OR Seafood OR Confections.

Add the three filter criteria by typing (or copy and pasting) the three category names into cells C2:C4.

4   Apply the criteria using an advanced filter.

1.   Click anywhere in the range to be filtered (any cell in the range A6:F75).

2.   Click: Data→Sort & Filter→Advanced.

The *Advanced Filter* dialog is displayed with the range already defined. Because you clicked within the range in step one you have saved yourself the trouble of manually selecting the range.

Inventory-1

note

Using wildcards in criteria

Sometimes you will want to filter using a subset of the letters in a text column.

In this case, you can use the wildcard characters – the asterisk (*) and the question mark (?).

The asterisk means that any number of wildcard letters can occur between the letters.

The question mark means that only one wildcard letter can occur between the letters.

Here are some examples:

C*g   Finds **Containing**
         Finds **Citing**
         Doesn't find **Chair**

S?d   Finds **Sid**
         Finds **Sad**
         Doesn't find **Said**
         Doesn't find **Send**

note

Text filters are inexact by default

This lesson's example works just fine but it would have worked just as well if you had entered the filter expression **Cond** instead of **Condiments.**

For the same reason, the filter expression **Dairy** would return the category **Dairy Products.**

Sometimes this isn't what you want and you need an exact match. In this case, you need to enter the filter conditions like this:

="=Seafood"

="=Dairy Products"

Unlike **Con**, The filter condition

="=Con"

... doesn't return the *Condiments* category.

3. Click in the *Criteria range*: text box.

4. Select the range A1:F4 with the mouse.

   The criteria range appears as: A1:F4.

5. Click the *OK* button.

   The range is now filtered to display only *Condiments, Seafood* and *Confections*.

	Product Name	Supplier	Category	Unit Price	In Stock	Value
6						
7	Aniseed Syrup	Exotic Liquids	Condiments	10.00	13	130.00
8	Boston Crab Meat	New England Seafood Cannery	Seafood	18.40	123	2,263.20
10	Carnarvon Tigers	Pavlova, Ltd.	Seafood	62.50	42	2,625.00
14	Chef Anton's Cajun Seasoning	New Orleans Cajun Delights	Condiments	22.00	53	1,166.00
15	Chocolade	Zaanse Snoepfabriek	Confections	12.75	15	191.25

5   Remove the advanced filter from the range.

1. Click anywhere inside the range.

2. Click: Data→Sort & Filter→Clear.

   The advanced filter is cleared and all records are displayed.

6   Save your work as *Inventory-2.*

Lesson 1-7: Apply an advanced filter with complex criteria

1   Open *Inventory-2* from your sample files folder (if it isn't already open).

2   Create complex advanced filter criteria.

This time you are going to create a filter with both AND and OR criteria. This is an example of a filter that is beyond the scope of a simple filter. Here are the criteria that you are going to apply:

WHERE

Category equals Condiments

OR

(Category equals Seafood AND Value is greater than 2,000)

OR

Value is greater than 3,000

This will list everything in the *Condiments* category.

It will also list products in the *Seafood* category, but only if their value is greater than 2,000.

It will also list all products that have a value greater than 3,000 irrespective of which category they are in.

1. Set the criteria range as follows:

	C	D	E	F
		Unit	In	
1	Category	Price	Stock	Value
2	Condiments			
3	Seafood			>2000
4				>3000

2. Apply the advanced filter using the skills learned in: *Lesson 1-6: Apply an advanced filter with multiple OR criteria.*

3. If you select cells A1:F4 with the mouse (the fastest and easiest way), you may see the following values in the *Advanced Filter* dialog:

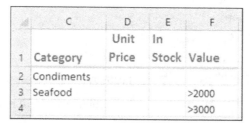

List range:	$A$6:$F$75
Criteria range:	Inventory!Criteria

You may wonder why the *Criteria range* displays as *Inventory!Criteria* instead of *Inventory!$A$1:$F$4*.

The reason is that Excel has created something called a *Range Name* behind the scenes. You'll learn all about Range Names

Inventory-2

later, in: *Session Four: Using Names and the Formula Auditing Tools.*

Now you can audit the results:

	A	B	C	D	E	F
6	Product Name	Supplier	Category	Unit Price	In Stock	Value
7	Aniseed Syrup	Exotic Liquids	Condiments	10.00	13	130.00
8	Boston Crab Meat	New England Seafood Cannery	Seafood	18.40	123	2,263.20
10	Carnarvon Tigers	Pavlova, Ltd.	Seafood	62.50	42	2,625.00
14	Chef Anton's Cajun Seasoning	New Orleans Cajun Delights	Condiments	22.00	53	1,166.00
16	Côte de Blaye	Aux joyeux ecclésiastiques	Beverages	263.50	17	4,479.50
21	Genen Shouyu	Mayumi's	Condiments	15.50	39	604.50
24	Grandma's Boysenberry Spread	Grandma Kelly's Homestead	Condiments	25.00	120	3,000.00
27	Gula Malacca	Leka Trading	Condiments	19.45	27	525.15
31	Inlagd Sill	Svensk Sjöföda AB	Seafood	19.00	112	2,128.00
38	Louisiana Fiery Hot Pepper Sauce	New Orleans Cajun Delights	Condiments	21.05	76	1,599.80
39	Louisiana Hot Spiced Okra	New Orleans Cajun Delights	Condiments	17.00	4	68.00
45	Northwoods Cranberry Sauce	Grandma Kelly's Homestead	Condiments	40.00	6	240.00
47	Original Frankfurter grüne Soße	Plutzer Lebensmittelgroßmärkte	Condiments	13.00	32	416.00
52	Queso Manchego La Pastora	Cooperativa de Quesos 'Las Cabr	Dairy Products	38.00	86	3,268.00
53	Raclette Courdavault	Gai pâturage	Dairy Products	55.00	79	4,345.00
61	Sir Rodney's Marmalade	Specialty Biscuits, Ltd.	Confections	81.00	40	3,240.00
63	Sirop d'érable	Forêts d'érables	Condiments	28.50	113	3,220.50
73	Vegie-spread	Pavlova, Ltd.	Condiments	43.90	24	1,053.60

- All eleven *Condiments* products are listed irrespective of their value.

- Only three *Seafood* products are shown – only the items with a value greater than 2,000.

- Items such as *Sir Rodney's Marmalade* are listed even though they do not appear in the *Condiment* or *Seafood* categories. This is because their value is greater than 3,000.

3   Remove the advanced filter from the range.

1. Click anywhere inside the range.

2. Click: Data→Sort & Filter→Clear.   [▽x Clear]

The advanced filter is cleared, and all records are displayed.

4   Save your work as *Inventory-3*.

tip

Using the ROW function to remove the need to add a counter column

In the example, you inserted a new column with the row number in it and then used the formula:

=MOD(A7,5)=0

The same problem could have been solved without inserting the new column by using the ROW function.

ROW returns the row number of a reference:

=ROW(A1)

Returns the number 1

=ROW(A2)

Returns the number 2

With this knowledge it is clear that the filter formula would work just as well if it were written:

=MOD(ROW(A7)-6,5)=0

This would work even if column A was deleted.

This works because row 7 originally contained the number 1 in column A.

ROW(A7) brings back a value of 7, so subtracting six from it also results in the value 1 for the first data row in the range.

Remember that you must have a blank space above a formula in order to use it within an advanced filter.

The formula can be placed anywhere on the worksheet.

Lesson 1-8: Apply an advanced filter with function-driven criteria

When a company conducts a physical stock check of its inventory there will always be some errors in the count. Auditors have to verify the accuracy of a stock check. To do this they extract some random samples in order to establish the likely margin of error.

In this lesson, you'll take the *Inventory* workbook and extract an auditing sample by using an advanced filter in conjunction with a MOD (Modulus or Remainder) function.

Excel's MOD function returns the remainder after a number is divided by a divisor. It is often used in conjunction with the INT (integer) function to convert minutes into hours and minutes. For example, to convert 170 minutes into 2 hours 50 minutes you would use the functions like this:

=INT(170/60)   This returns 2, as the whole number part of 2.83 is 2.

=MOD(170,60)   This returns 50, because 60 only divides evenly into 170 twice (120) leaving 50 over.

You're going to use the MOD function in conjunction with an advanced filter to show one transaction in every five, so that you can sample one in five (20%) of the products to check during the audit.

1   Open *Inventory-3* from your sample files folder (if it isn't already open).

2   Add a column to the left of the range, head it with the text: **No,** format the column header to match the style in the other header columns, and fill the column with incremental numbers.

	A	B	C
6	No	Product Name	Supplier
7	1	Aniseed Syrup	Exotic Liquids
8	2	Boston Crab Meat	New England Seafood Cannery
9	3	Camembert Pierrot	Gai pâturage
10	4	Carnarvon Tigers	Pavlova, Ltd.

3   Add a MOD function to cell A2 that will return TRUE when the value in cell A7 is divisible by five.

1.   Type the following function into cell A2:

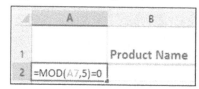

2.   Press the **<Enter>** key.

The cell contains the value: *FALSE.*

Inventory-3

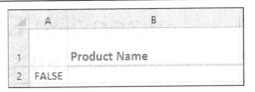

note

Using a function-driven criteria to implement a case sensitive filter

Filters are case insensitive by default.

The filters:

Category=Seafood

And

Category=SEAFOOD

… will produce exactly the same result.

You can implement a case sensitive filter by using the EXACT function.

The filter condition:

=EXACT(D7, "Seafood")

… would extract the *Seafood* records in this table.

The filter condition:

=EXACT(D7, "SEAFOOD")

… would not extract any records.

note

Selecting every fifth item is not a truly random sample

In this lesson you select every fifth row to audit.

In a true auditing scenario this would not be a robust approach as a client (who knew your method) could deliberately mislead you by placing false values in other rows.

You could make a truly random selection by using the function:

=RANDBETWEEN(1,5)=1

The formula generates a value between one and five and compares it with one. This returns TRUE in approximately 20% of cases.

This is because the number in cell A7 (the value: 1) is not evenly divisible by five.

Here's how the MOD function works:

- The value in cell A7 is divided by five and the remainder is returned. In this case the remainder is 1 because the number 1 is not evenly divisible by 5.

- The expression 1=0 is not true so the cell displays a result of FALSE.

- If cell A7 had contained a value that is evenly divisible by 5 (such as 5 or 10) the MOD function would have returned zero (because the remainder is zero). This would result in the cell displaying a TRUE result because the expression 0=0 is true.

4 Apply an advanced filter using the *Criteria range* A1:A2.

Notice that you didn't type the word **No** into cell A1 (a copy of the text header appearing in cell A6).

For a function-driven filter you must leave the cell above the formula blank. This tells the advanced filter to work directly upon the result of the function.

1. Apply an advanced filter in the same way as you did in: *Lesson 1-6: Apply an advanced filter with multiple OR criteria,* using A1:A2 as the *Criteria range*. The *Advanced Filter* dialog should look like this:

2. Click the *OK* button.

6	No	Product Name	Supplier
11	5	Chai	Exotic Liquids
16	10	Côte de Blaye	Aux joyeux ecclésiastiques
21	15	Genen Shouyu	Mayumi's

Note that the numbers in column A now read 5,10,15,20...

The list now contains the 20% sample needed for the audit.

5 Save your work as *Inventory-4*.

note

You'll learn other ways to extract unique records later

Later, in: *Lesson 2-13: Remove duplicate values from a table,* you'll learn a more powerful way to extract unique records using *Excel's Remove Duplicates* feature.

In *Session Eight: Pivot Tables* you'll also discover an extremely fast way to extract unique records using a pivot table.

tip

Use this technique to find spelling mistakes

You'll often encounter a cell range that contains spelling mistakes.

For example, a cost center column could contain the common spelling error *Stationary* (not moving) instead of *Stationery* (writing materials). The spell checker won't help you find the errors because both are real words.

You can use the *Unique records only* feature to extract all unique values from the list. You can then A-Z sort the extracted unique list to see if any words appear that have two different spellings.

Sorting will be covered in: *Lesson 1-15: Sort a range or table by rows.*

Inventory-4

Lesson 1-9: Extract unique records using an advanced filter

1   Open *Inventory-4* from your sample files folder (if it isn't already open).

2   Click: Data→Sort & Filter→Clear to show all items in the range.

Notice that one supplier often provides multiple products. For example, *Specialty Biscuits, Ltd.* supplies four different products:

A	B	C
54	Scottish Longbreads	Specialty Biscuits, Ltd.
55	Sir Rodney's Marmalade	Specialty Biscuits, Ltd.
56	Sir Rodney's Scones	Specialty Biscuits, Ltd.
61	Teatime Chocolate Biscuits	Specialty Biscuits, Ltd.

In this lesson you'll extract a list of suppliers from the workbook using an advanced filter. The advanced filter's *Unique records only* feature will be used to ensure that each supplier is only listed once.

You will be amazed at how often you'll find this feature useful in your day-to-day business use of Excel.

3   Delete rows 1-5 (the cells that were previously used to define the advanced filter criteria condition).

After deleting these rows your worksheet should look like this:

	A	B	C
1	No	Product Name	Supplier
2	1	Aniseed Syrup	Exotic Liquids
3	2	Boston Crab Meat	New England Seafood Cannery
4	3	Camembert Pierrot	Gai pâturage
5	4	Carnarvon Tigers	Pavlova, Ltd.

4   Bring up the *Advanced Filter* dialog.

Click: Data→Sort & Filter→Advanced.

5   Set the *List range* to all cells in column C within the range.

1.   Click in the *List range* text box.

2.   Click into cell C1.

3.   Press: **<Ctrl>+<Shift>+<DownArrow>**

The range C1:C70 appears in the *List range* text box.

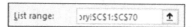

6   Leave the *Criteria Range* box blank and check the *Unique records only* check box.

7   Click the *Copy to another location* option button.

tip

Extracting data to a different worksheet

A very common question in my courses is: "can we use the advanced filter to extract records to another worksheet"?

This is possible but, due to a quirk in Excel, you have to do it in a rather special way.

If you select the source sheet, display the *Advanced Filter* dialog, and then click into a different worksheet to set the *Copy to:* cell reference, Excel will display the error message:

"You can only copy filtered data to the active sheet".

But Excel isn't telling the whole truth!

Excel will happily let you set the *List range* and *Criteria range* from a different worksheet. It only has a problem with the *Copy to* reference.

The trick is to display the *Advanced Filter* dialog from the destination (and not the source) worksheet.

Here's how it's done:

1. Select the destination sheet by clicking its sheet tab.

2. Click: Data→Sort & Filter→ Advanced.

3. Set the *List range, Criteria range* and *Copy to* cell references.

You'll then find that the advanced filter will happily extract the filtered cells to the destination sheet.

8 Click in the *Copy to:* box and then click once in cell I1.

The dialog should now look like this:

9 Click the *OK* button.

A list of suppliers appears in column I:

In Stock	Value		Supplier
13	130.00		Exotic Liquids
123	2,263.20		New England Seafood Cannery
19	646.00		Gai pâturage
42	2,625.00		Pavlova, Ltd.
39	702.00		Aux joyeux ecclésiastiques
17	323.00		New Orleans Cajun Delights

Notice that there are no duplicate entries in the list. The *Unique records only* feature has ensured that each supplier is only listed once.

10 Delete column I.

11 Save your work as *Inventory-5*.

Lesson 1-10: Add totals using Quick Analysis

Quick Analysis provides a simple way to do simple things. All of the features provided by Quick Analysis are also available (usually with more options and features) by using the ribbon.

You'll find yourself using Quick Analysis a lot, to save time when adding simple totals to ranges.

1   Open *Hours Worked-1* from your sample files folder (if it isn't already open).

2   Select every cell in the range A3:F8.

    1.   Click anywhere inside the range A3:F8.

    2.   Press the **<Ctrl>+<A>** keys.

    Notice that the *Quick Analysis* button has appeared at the bottom-right corner of the selected range.

3   Understand the Quick Analysis totals options.

    1.   Click the *Quick Analysis* button.

    Five tabs are shown across the top of the Quick Analysis palette:

    Formatting, Charts and *Sparklines* were extensively covered in the *Essential Skills* book in this series.

    The *Tables* quick analysis options will be covered later, in *Lesson 1-12: Convert a range into a table and add a total row (sidebar)* and *Lesson 8-1: Create a one-dimensional pivot table report from a table (sidebar).*

    For this lesson you are only concerned with the *Totals* option.

    2.   Click the *Totals* tab.

    There are ten icons. You need to use the scroll-right arrow to view all of them:

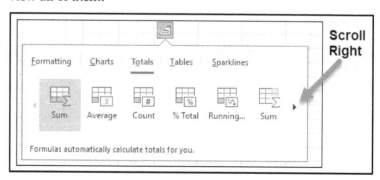

The first five icons will add totals to the bottom of the range. The second five icons will add totals to the right-hand side of the range.

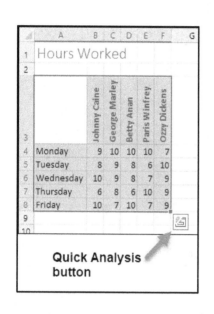

Quick Analysis button

Hours Worked-1

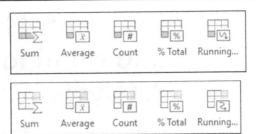

Add totals to bottom of range.

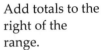

Add totals to the right of the range.

The *Running Total* icon can cause confusion as it has no real purpose when added to the bottom of a range.

4   Click both *Quick Analysis Sum* buttons to show total hours worked for each employee, and total hours worked for each day.

Notice that, as you hover the mouse cursor over each icon, a preview of the result is shown on the worksheet.

	A	B Johnny Caine	C George Marley	D Betty Anan	E Paris Winfrey	F Ozzy Dickens	G Sum
4	Monday	9	10	10	10	7	46
5	Tuesday	8	9	8	6	10	41
6	Wednesday	10	9	8	7	9	43
7	Thursday	6	8	6	10	9	39
8	Friday	10	7	10	7	9	43
9	Sum	43	43	42	40	44	

5   Delete the contents of column G and row 9.

6   Use the *Quick Analysis Average* buttons to show average hours worked for each employee, and average hours worked for each day.

	A	B Johnny Caine	C George Marley	D Betty Anan	E Paris Winfrey	F Ozzy Dickens	G Average
4	Monday	9	10	10	10	7	9.2
5	Tuesday	8	9	8	6	10	8.2
6	Wednesday	10	9	8	7	9	8.6
7	Thursday	6	8	6	10	9	7.8
8	Friday	10	7	10	7	9	8.6
9	Average	8.6	8.6	8.4	8	8.8	

7   Delete the contents of column G and row 9.

8   Close the workbook without saving.

Lesson 1-11: Add percentage and running totals using Quick Analysis

As you saw in: *Lesson 1-10: Add totals using Quick Analysis,* the Quick Analysis feature provides a simple and easy way to add simple SUM and AVERAGE functions to rows and columns. The COUNT function can be used in the same way to return the number of cells containing values present in a row or column.

Quick Analysis is also able to add some more complex functions to compute *Running Total* and *% Total.*

1 Open *Hours Worked-1* from your sample files folder (if it isn't already open).

2 Select every cell in the range A3:F8.

　1. Click anywhere inside the range A3:F8.

　2. Press the **<Ctrl>+<A>** keys.

　　Notice that the *Quick Analysis* button has appeared at the bottom-right corner of the selected range.

3 Click the Quick Analysis button.

4 Use both Quick Analysis *% Total* buttons to add percentage totals for each row and column.

　You learned how to do this in: *Lesson 1-10: Add totals using Quick Analysis.*

	A	B	C	D	E	F	G
4	Monday	9	10	10	10	7	21.70%
5	Tuesday	8	9	8	6	10	19.34%
6	Wednesday	10	9	8	7	9	20.28%
7	Thursday	6	8	6	10	9	18.40%
8	Friday	10	7	10	7	9	20.28%
9	% Total	20.28%	20.28%	19.81%	18.87%	20.75%	

5 Understand how % Totals are calculated.

　The *% Total* figures look interesting, but it may not be clear precisely what they relate to.

　1. Click on cell B9 and examine the formula (shown in the formula bar):

```
fx    =SUM(B4:B8)/SUM($B$4:$F$8)
```

　This formula represents:

　Hours worked by Johnny Caine (43)
　divided by
　Hours worked by all employees (212)

　In other words: *of all of the hours worked, by all employees, this week, Johnny Caine worked 20.28% of the total (43/212=0.2028).*

　2. Click on cell G4 and examine the formula:

Hours Worked-1

You can see that the formula is calculating:

Hours worked on Monday (46)
divided by
Hours worked on every day of the week (212)

In other words: *of all of the hours worked, by all employees, this week, 21.70% of them were worked on Monday (46/212=0.2169).*

6 Delete the contents of column G and row 9.

7 Use the Quick Analysis *Column Running Total* button to add a running total to cells G4:G8.

Make sure that you use the *column running total* icon and not the *row running total* (see sidebar).

8 Re-format the running total to show as a number.

Column G was formatted using the percentage style when you added *% Totals* earlier. You'll need to return the formatting of these cells to the default *General* format.

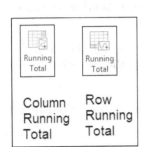

1. Select cells G4:G8.

2. Click: Home→Number→
   Number Format Drop-Down→General.

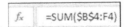

Cell formatting was covered extensively in the *Essential Skills* book in this series.

	A	B	C	D	E	F	G
4	Monday	9	10	10	10	7	46
5	Tuesday	8	9	8	6	10	87
6	Wednesday	10	9	8	7	9	130
7	Thursday	6	8	6	10	9	169
8	Friday	10	7	10	7	9	212

You can now see that 46 hours were worked on Monday, and that 87 hours were worked on both Monday on Tuesday.

9 Understand how *Running Totals* are calculated.

Click on cell G4 and examine the formula (shown in the formula bar):

=SUM($B$4:F4)

You can see that Quick Analysis has used an absolute reference for cell $B$4 and used a SUM function to add all of the values in row 4.

Because an absolute reference was used, the formula will correctly adjust when AutoFilled down to G8, maintaining a running total for all hours worked during the week to date.

10 Save your work as *Hours Worked-2.*

note

You can also convert a range into a table by using the Quick Analysis button

When you select an entire range you'll see the *Quick Analysis* button 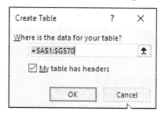 appear on the bottom right-hand corner of the selected range.

You can also use this button to convert the range into a table by clicking:

Quick Analysis Button→ Tables→Table.

tip

You can also convert a range into a table using the keyboard shortcut:

<Ctrl>+<T>

note

Slicers can be used to visually filter tables

You will learn about slicers later, in: *Lesson 8-7: Filter a pivot table visually using slicers*

Slicers can also be used with normal tables (such as the one used in this lesson) in exactly the same way they are used with pivot tables.

Lesson 1-12: Convert a range into a table and add a total row

This lesson introduces tables (originally added to Excel in the Excel 2007 version). While tables have now been with us for twelve years, they remain a mystery to many professional Excel users.

Tables provide a completely new way to work with tabular data and are particularly powerful when dealing with dynamic data. A table is very similar to a range but incorporates several very useful extra features.

You can freely convert a table into a range, or a range into a table. The key difference between ranges and tables is that table references shrink and grow dynamically.

For example, if you create a chart from a table and then add more rows to the table, the chart's source data will automatically adjust to include the new rows. This doesn't happen with a range.

1   Open *Inventory-5* from your sample files folder (if it isn't already open).

2   Convert the range into a table.

   1.   Click anywhere inside the range

   2.   Click: Insert→Tables→Table.

      The *Create Table* dialog is displayed:

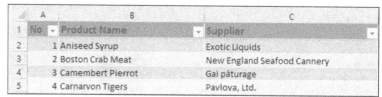

   3.   Click the *OK* button.

   The range is converted into a table. The appearance of the range changes and filter arrows appear in the header row.

	A	B	C
1	No	Product Name	Supplier
2	1	Aniseed Syrup	Exotic Liquids
3	2	Boston Crab Meat	New England Seafood Cannery
4	3	Camembert Pierrot	Gai pâturage
5	4	Carnarvon Tigers	Pavlova, Ltd.

3   Scroll down the table and notice the "sticky" column headers.

   1.   Click inside the table

   2.   Scroll down the table until the headers disappear from the top row.

      In a range you would have to freeze panes in order to continue to view the range headers (freeze panes was covered in the Essential Skills book in this series). Tables are much easier to work with. The table headers and filter buttons are always visible as they replace the column letters when scrolled off the screen:

Inventory-5

No	Product Name	Supplier
19	18 Grandma's Boysenberry Spread	Grandma Kelly's Homestead
20	19 Gravad lax	Svensk Sjöföda AB
21	20 Gudbrandsdalsost	Norske Meierier
22	21 Gula Malacca	Leka Trading

note

Excel's use of the quirky SUBTOTAL function

When Excel adds a total row, the quirky SUBTOTAL function is used. The SUBTOTAL function has a very odd syntax. It is:

SUBTOTAL(function_num, ref1, [ref2], ...)

The *function_num* argument can cause confusion as it has been implemented in a very unusual way.

The *function_num* can be a value from 1 to 11, each corresponding to a different function. For example, function_num 9 is the SUM function and function_num 1 is the AVG function.

The *function_num* argument also supports the same numbers with 100 added to them (ie 101-111) and these correspond to the same functions. For example, function_num 9 is the SUM function and so is function_num 109.

So why does the SUBTOTAL's *function_num* argument accept the values 109 and 9 if they both mean the SUM function?

The reason is that a 109 SUM function ignores any rows that are hidden, while a 9 SUM function will include any hidden rows. (You'll learn about hidden rows later, in: *Lesson 5-7: Hide and unhide worksheets, columns and rows*).

By default, the total row ignores hidden rows meaning that (in this lesson's example) the function used to total (or sum) the column is:

=SUBTOTAL(109,[Value])

Sometimes you might want to include any hidden rows in the total. In this case you would have to change the formula to:

=SUBTOTAL(9,[Value])

4 **Add a total row.**

Tables have a built-in ability to add total rows.

1. Click anywhere inside the table.

   The *Table Tools* tab appears on the ribbon.

2. Click: Table Tools→Design→Table Style Options→Total Row.

   A total row appears at the bottom of the table.

	Category	Unit Price	In Stock	Value
69	Grains/Cereals	33.25	22	731.50
70	Confections	9.50	36	342.00
71				69,598.25

3. Re-size the *Value* column if needed to view the total.

   By default, the total row contains the SUM of all values in the right-most column. Excel uses the SUM function indirectly via the rather quirky SUBTOTAL function (see sidebar).

   Note that you can do nearly the same thing by using the *Quick Analysis* feature (used in: *Lesson 1-10: Add totals using Quick Analysis*) to add a SUM total row. The only difference is that a *Quick Analysis* sum is added to every column (rather than only to the right-most column).

5 **Change the total from SUM to AVERAGE and add a total for the *In Stock* column.**

1. Click cell G71 (the cell containing the total).

   A drop-down arrow appears next to the total.

2. Click the drop-down arrow and choose *Average* from the function list.

3. Click on cell F71 at the bottom of the *In Stock* column (the cell in the dark blue total row).

   A drop-down arrow appears next to the empty cell.

4. Click the drop-down arrow and then click *Sum* from the function list.

   The sum of units in stock is now also displayed.

6 **Change the AVERAGE in cell G71 back to a SUM.**

	E	F	G
69	33.25	22	731.50
70	9.50	36	342.00
71		3018	69,598.25

7 **Save your work as *Inventory-6*.**

note

Formatting mayhem when converting tables into ranges and back

When you convert a table into a range, all of the formatting applied to the table remains.

The biggest problem occurs if you need to convert a formatted range back into a table again.

Because each cell contains formatting information, Excel politely refuses to change any of the colors. This makes it impossible to change the table style using the table styles gallery.

The table's appearance then becomes very strange when you add rows to the table. The added rows will use the table style, while the rows imported from the range will keep their old formatting (because Excel thinks that the formatting has been manually applied).

The simple solution is to always obey the important rule:

Apply the None style before converting a table into a range, except when you are sure that you will never want to convert the range back into a table again.

See facing page sidebar for techniques to clean things up after conversion if you didn't apply this rule.

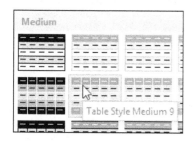

Inventory-6

Lesson 1-13: Format a table using table styles and convert a table into a range

When you have formatted your data as a table, you can customize the appearance of the table using Excel's powerful *table styles* feature.

You can either apply a table style from the *table styles gallery* or you can create your own custom table styles.

All of the pre-defined styles in the *table styles gallery* follow best practice by restricting color choices to theme colors. Themes are covered in great depth in the *Essential Skills* book in this series.

In this lesson you will explore the simpler of the two options by applying some of the standard pre-defined table styles. Later, in *Lesson 1-14: Create a custom table style,* you'll create your own custom-designed table style.

1 Open *Inventory-6* from your sample files folder (if it isn't already open).

2 Apply the *Berlin* theme to the workbook.

   Click: Page Layout→Themes→Themes→Berlin.

   The *Berlin* theme is applied and the colors used in the table change.

   The reason the colors change is that Microsoft used best practice when creating the built-in table styles and restricted their color and font choices to theme colors and theme fonts.

3 Change the theme back to the default *Office* theme.

4 Choose a new table style from the *Table Styles Gallery*.

   1. Click anywhere inside the table.

   2. Click: Table Tools→Design→Table Styles→More.

      The *More* button is located on the right hand side of the *Table Styles* group:

      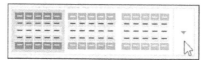

      The table styles gallery is displayed.

   3. Click any of the table styles that you find attractive.

      The chosen table style is applied.

   4. Restore the table style to the default *Table Style Medium 9*.

5 Change the table's appearance using *Table Style Options*.

   1. Click inside the table.

   2. Click the Table Tools→Design tab and focus upon the *Table Style Options* group.

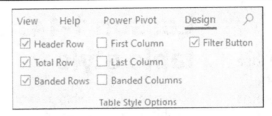

note

Solutions to range and table formatting issues after conversion

The previous page sidebar discusses how to avoid formatting issues when converting tables to ranges (and ranges to tables).

Sometimes you may accidentally convert a richly formatted table or range.

Here are some simple techniques for removing all existing formatting from a range or table:

To remove all formatting information from a range

1. Select all cells in the range (the easiest way is click inside the range and then press the **<Ctrl>+<A>** keys).

2. Click: Home→Styles→ Cell Styles→Normal.

To remove all formatting information from a table

1. Click inside the table.

2. Click: Table Tools→ Design→Table Styles→More, to open the *Table Styles Gallery*.

3. Right-click any style and then select: *Apply and Clear Formatting* from the shortcut menu.

4. Apply the *None* style.

tip

How to quickly identify tables and ranges

A quick way to tell tables from ranges is to click inside the table/range.

If you see the *Table Tools* tab on the ribbon, you will immediately know that you are looking at a table.

The easiest way to understand the options is to experiment by switching each option on and off. The function of each option will then be obvious.

6 Apply the *None* quick table style to remove all table style formatting.

The *None* style is extremely useful.

In a moment you're going to convert the table back into a range. You'll nearly always want to remove table style formatting prior to conversion (see sidebar for more on this).

1. Click anywhere inside the table.

2. Click: Table Tools→Design→Table Styles→ More→None.

The *None* style is the one in the top left corner of the gallery.

The table now looks more like a range but it is still a table and still provides all table features.

7 Set the *None* style as the default.

I always like to work with the *None* style as the default. Excel's default table styles are a little too colorful for me. Note that this sets the default style only for this workbook. When you open a different workbook, the default table style will revert to *Table Style Medium 9*.

1. Click inside the table.

2. Click: Table Tools→Design→Table Styles→More.

3. Right-click on the *None* style and click *Set As Default* from the shortcut menu.

Every time you create new tables in the *Inventory-6* workbook they will now display with the *None* style.

8 Convert the table back into a range.

1. Click anywhere inside the table.

2. Click: Table Tools→Design→Tools→Convert to Range.

3. Click the *Yes* button.

The table has now been converted back into a range.

9 Save your work as *Inventory-7*.

note

Why it is a good idea to restrict custom style colors to theme colors

If you restrict your color choice to the 60 *Theme Colors*, your worksheet design will be compatible with documents that use other themes.

If you use non-theme colors, your worksheets will not seamlessly integrate (from a design point of view) with PowerPoint presentations, Word documents, and other Office documents that use a different theme.

Example

John creates a worksheet using the default *Office* theme.

Mary wants to use this in her PowerPoint presentation that uses the *Berlin* theme. John e-mails the worksheet to her and then she simply pastes the required cells into her presentation and changes the theme to *Berlin*.

Joe sees the presentation and wants to use the same worksheet in his Word report that uses the *Circuit* theme. Mary e-mails the presentation to him and then he simply pastes the required slides into his Word document and changes the theme to *Circuit*.

The same worksheet has been used without modification and it blends perfectly into both Joe and Mary's work because John followed best practice and restricted his color choices to theme colors.

Themes are covered in great depth in the *Essential Skills* book in this series.

Lesson 1-14: Create a custom table style

Perhaps none of the huge selection of styles in the *table styles gallery* is suitable for your requirements. In this case you can create a custom table style from scratch.

Another great feature of a custom table style is that you can set it as the default for this workbook. This saves you from continually reapplying a style every time you create a table.

1   Open *Inventory-7* from your sample files folder (if it isn't already open).

   Notice that this range, (created from a table with a total row in: *Lesson 1-13: Format a table using table styles and convert a table into a range*), has totals in row 71.

2   Convert the range into a table.

   You learned how to do this in: *Lesson 1-12: Convert a range into a table and add a total row.*

3   Convert the *range total row* to a *table total row*.

   If you click Table Tools→Design you will see that the *Total Row* check box is unchecked.

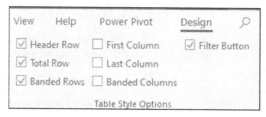

   Why then does the table appear to have a total row in row 71?

	D	E	F	G
69	Grains/Cereals	33.25	22	731.50
70	Confections	9.50	36	342.00
71			3018	69,598.25

   The reason is that row 71 is the total row defined in the range and has nothing to do with the total row that is available as a table feature.

   1.   Check: Table Tools→Design→Table Style Options→ Total Row.

   A second total row appears beneath the first. This is the *table total row*:

	D	E	F	G
69	Grains/Cereals	33.25	22	731.50
70	Confections	9.50	36	342.00
71			3018	69,598.25
72				69,598.25

   2.   Delete row 71 to remove the range total row.

4   Create a custom table style based upon an existing style.

Inventory-7

1. Click anywhere inside the table.

2. Click: Table Tools→Design→Table Styles→More.

   The *More* button is located on the bottom right hand corner of the Table Styles group:

   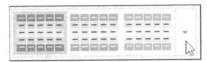

   The table styles gallery is displayed.

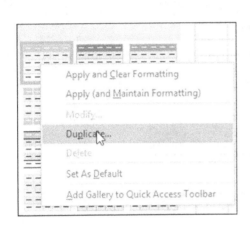

3. Right-click one of the existing styles and then click *Duplicate* from the shortcut menu.

   The *Modify Table Style* dialog is displayed:

4. Name the new table style: **TSM**

   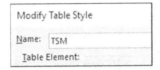

   Each of the table's elements are listed on the left of the dialog.

   Each element that has been formatted (in the style you chose to duplicate) is shown in bold face type.

5. Choose a table element and then click the *Format* button to set the *Font, Border* and *Fill* formatting.

   To follow best practice, you should restrict your color and font choices to theme colors and theme fonts (see sidebar on facing page).

6. Customize as many other elements as you wish.

7. Click the *OK* button.

5 **Apply your new custom style to the table**.

1. Click on any cell inside the table.

2. Click: Table Tools→Design→Table Styles→More.

3. Notice the new *Custom* section at the top of the gallery containing your new style.

4. Hover the mouse cursor over your new style. The style name appears in a tip.

5. Click the style to apply it to the worksheet.

6. Change the style back to *None*.

6 **Save your work as *Inventory-8*.**

Lesson 1-15: Sort a range or table by rows

1   Open *Inventory-8* from your sample files folder (if it isn't already open).

2   Sort the categories from Z-A.

     1.   Click anywhere in the *Category* column.

     2.   Click: Data→Sort & Filter→Z-A.

        The categories are now sorted in reverse alphabetical order:

	Category	Unit Price	In Stock	Value
13	Seafood	12.00	95	1,140.00
14	Produce	10.00	4	40.00
15	Produce	53.00	20	1,060.00
16	Produce	23.25	35	813.75

3   Sort the categories from A-Z.

     1.   Click anywhere in the *Category* column.

     2.   Click: Data→Sort & Filter→A-Z.

        The categories are now sorted in alphabetical order:

	Category	Unit Price	In Stock	Value
11	Beverages	14.00	111	1,554.00
12	Beverages	18.00	20	360.00
13	Condiments	10.00	13	130.00
14	Condiments	22.00	53	1,166.00

4   Sort by both Category and Supplier.

There's a small problem with the existing sort. It can be seen that one category often has many suppliers:

	C	D	E
55	Tokyo Traders	Produce	10.00
56	G'day, Mate	Produce	53.00
57	Mayumi's	Produce	23.25
58	Grandma Kelly's Homestead	Produce	30.00

In the above example it would be nice to also have the suppliers listed in alphabetical order. This can be achieved with a two-column sort.

     1.   Click: Data→Sort & Filter→Sort.

        The *Sort* dialog appears:

     2.   Click the *Add Level* button to add a second sort that will sort the *Supplier* column from A-Z.

Inventory-8

note

You can also sort from the Home tab

The *Home* tab also has a *Sort & Filter* menu button in the *Editing* group.

This is one of the unusual cases where a feature is repeated on two different ribbon tabs.

It doesn't matter which you use as the functionality is identical.

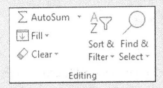

tip

Sort with a right-click

The fastest sort method of all is to right-click any cell and select *Sort* from the shortcut menu.

The fly-out menu then provides every sort option available from the ribbon.

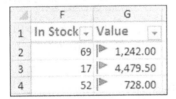

note

Sort by font color or cell color

Note that there is also a *Cell Color* and *Font Color* option (in the *Sort On* drop-down list).

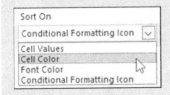

These work in exactly the same way as the other options.

3. Click the *OK* button.

   The table is now sorted first by *Category* and then by *Supplier*.

5 **Select all of the data cells in column G.**

   1. Scroll to the top of the table so that row 1 is visible.

   2. Hover the mouse cursor over the top of cell G1 until you see a black down-arrow. Note that the arrow *must* overlap the bottom of the column header button. If you hover inside the button, you'll still see the black arrow but your selection will then include every cell in column G (rather than the value cells within the table).

   3. When you see the arrow, click once to select cells G2:G70.

6 **Add a *Three Flags* conditional format icon set to column G.**

   Conditional formatting was covered in depth in the *Essential Skills* book in this series.

   1. Click: Home→Styles→Conditional Formatting→Icon Sets→ 3 Flags.

   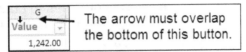

   2. If necessary, widen column G to make room for the flags.

      Values in column G have red, yellow or green flags added depending upon their value.

7 **Sort by icon so that the green flagged cells appear first, the yellow flagged second and the red flagged last.**

   1. Click any value in column G.

   2. Click: Data→Sort & Filter→Sort.

   3. Click the *Delete Level* button twice to remove existing sort conditions.

   4. Add the following three sort conditions to sort by flag.

   5. Click the *OK* button.

8 **Save your work as *Inventory-9*.**

Lesson 1-16: Sort a range by columns

Students often come to my classes with long "wish lists". Usually by the end of the course they have ticked all of their requirements off and don't have to ask any of the questions they had arrived with.

An item that seems to be on everybody's wish list is a way to sort data by columns. This lesson will teach you a simple technique to achieve this.

Note that this technique will work for ranges but not for tables. If you need to sort a table by columns, you'll have to convert it to a range first. That's exactly what you'll do in this lesson.

1   Open *Inventory-9* from your sample files folder.

2   Convert the table into a range.

   You learned how to do this in: *Lesson 1-13: Format a table using table styles and convert a table into a range.*

3   Add a blank row at the top of the range.

4   Add numbers to enable a column sort order of: *No, Category, Supplier, Product Name, Unit Price, In Stock, Value.*

   The blank row that you have just added is a dummy row to set the sort order.

   Type numbers into row 1 that numerically describe the desired sorted position for each column:

	A	B	C	D	E	F	G
1	1	4	3	2	5.00	6	7
2	No	Product Name	Supplier	Category	Unit Price	In Stock	Value

   Note that the value in cell E1 only appears to be different to the others because it has inherited the two decimal place format from the *Price* field in the table.

5   Sort the range by reference to row one.

   1.   Click anywhere inside the range.

   2.   Press **<Ctrl>+<A>** to select every cell in the range (including the dummy header row).

   3.   Click: Data→Sort & Filter→Sort.

      Notice that row 1 is no longer included in the selected range. This is because the *My data has headers* box is checked.

   4.   Uncheck the *My data has headers* check box.

      The entire range (including row 1) is now selected.

   5.   Remove any existing sort condition(s) by clicking the *Delete Level* button.

Inventory-9

6. Click the *Options...* button.

The *Sort Options* dialog is displayed.

7. Click the *Sort left to right* option button.

8. Click the *OK* button.

9. Click the *Add Level* button.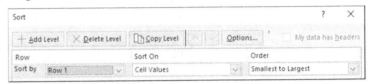

10. Set a new sort to sort using *Row 1, Cell Values, Smallest to Largest*.

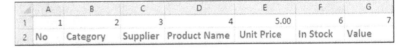

11. Click the *OK* button.

The worksheet is now sorted in the same order as the dummy sort row.

	A	B	C	D	E	F	G
1	1	2	3	4	5.00	6	7
2	No	Category	Supplier	Product Name	Unit Price	In Stock	Value

6 Delete row 1.

7 Convert the range back into a table.

You learned how to do this in: *Lesson 1-12: Convert a range into a table and add a total row.*

8 Save your work as *Inventory-10*.

Lesson 1-17: Sort a range or table by custom list

Sometimes you need a sort order that is not alphabetical.

For example, you might run a support desk and be given support incidents marked as *Low, Medium, High, Urgent* and *Critical*. You would want to sort such a list in order of priority, but these priorities do not lend themselves to an alphabetical sort.

If you create a custom sort list with each incident listed in order of importance, you can then use the list to sort a range or table. This lesson will show you how.

1   Open *Help Desk-1* from your sample files folder.

This worksheet lists several support incidents sent to the help desk and prioritized from *Low* to *Critical*.

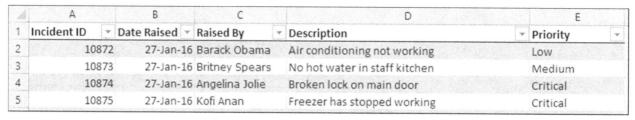

	A	B	C	D	E
1	Incident ID	Date Raised	Raised By	Description	Priority
2	10872	27-Jan-16	Barack Obama	Air conditioning not working	Low
3	10873	27-Jan-16	Britney Spears	No hot water in staff kitchen	Medium
4	10874	27-Jan-16	Angelina Jolie	Broken lock on main door	Critical
5	10875	27-Jan-16	Kofi Anan	Freezer has stopped working	Critical

2   Create a custom list.

1. Click: File→Options→Advanced→General→ Edit Custom Lists.

The *Custom Lists* dialog is displayed.

2. Type each of the support incident priority levels followed by the **<Enter>** key into the *List entries* box in the following order:

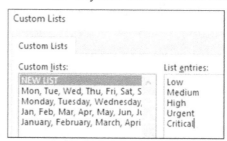

3. Click the *OK* button twice to close both dialogs.

3   Sort the table using the custom list.

1. Click anywhere in column E.

2. Click: Data→Sort & Filter→Sort.

The *Sort* dialog appears.

3. Select *Priority* from the *Sort by* drop down.

4. Select *Custom List…* for the *Order:*

Help Desk-1

The *Custom Lists* dialog appears showing all defined custom lists.

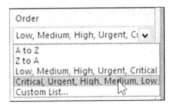

5. Click on your newly added custom list and then click the *OK* button twice to close both dialogs.

    The worksheet is now sorted in order of priority from lowest to highest.

4   **Reverse the sort order to show the higher priority incidents first.**

    1. Click anywhere inside the range.

    2. Click: Data→Sort & Filter→Sort.

    3. Click the drop-down arrow next to *Order*.

        Notice that your custom sort order is shown twice as *Low to Critical* and as *Critical to Low*.

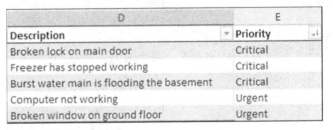

    4. Click *Critical to Low*.

    5. Click the *OK* button.

        The worksheet is now sorted with higher priority incidents listed first.

D	E
Description	Priority
Broken lock on main door	Critical
Freezer has stopped working	Critical
Burst water main is flooding the basement	Critical
Computer not working	Urgent
Broken window on ground floor	Urgent

5   **Save your work as *Help Desk-2*.**

© 2020 The Smart Method® Ltd

important

Because structured table references were only introduced in Excel 2007, this feature will not work if you have saved a workbook in *Excel 97-2003 Workbook* format to maintain compatibility with earlier versions.

note

If this feature doesn't work for you, somebody may have switched it off

Excel allows structured references to be switched off.

You really wouldn't ever want to do this, as structured references are one of the most useful features of tables.

If you simply want to maintain compatibility with Excel 2003 you can save the workbook in *Excel 97/2003 Workbook* format. The structured reference feature will then be automatically disabled.

You can check that this feature is enabled by clicking:

File→Options→
Formulas→
Working with formulas→
Use table names in formulas

When the check box is checked the feature is switched on (the default).

Lesson 1-18: Name a table and create an automatic structured table reference

One of the key differences between a range and a table is that tables shrink and grow dynamically.

The table's ability to shrink and grow wouldn't be useful without a way to enter a cell reference into a formula that points to all of the rows in a table column (no matter how many rows the table contains).

Consider the following range:

⊿	A	B	C	D	E	F	G
1	Sales						
2							
3	Month	Net	Tax	Total		Total Sales	
4	Jan	15,249.00	2,287.35	17,536.35			
5	Feb	18,320.00	2,748.00	21,068.00			
6	Mar	21,260.00	3,189.00	24,449.00			

To calculate the total sales in cell G3 you could use the formula:

=SUM(D4:D6)

A recurring problem with data ranges is that when you add a new row to the range for April's sales, the SUM formula has to be adjusted (to D4:D7).

In order to exploit the power of dynamic tables, the Excel designers had to figure out a whole new way of referencing cell ranges. They needed a cell reference that would mean:

=SUM(All of the cells in column D that are inside this table)

Because there may be several tables on a single worksheet, the cell reference needs to indicate which table the range is in. This has been solved by adding the ability to name tables. If the table in this example was called *Sales* and the column was called *Total*, the formula would be:

=SUM(Sales[Total])

This type of reference is called a *structured reference.*

In this lesson, you'll use structured references to create some formulas that will always give the correct result, no matter how many rows you add or remove from a table.

1   Open *Sales Summary-1* from your sample files folder.

2   Convert the range into a table.

   1.   Click anywhere inside the range (A3:D6).

   2.   Click: Insert→Tables→Table.

       The *Create Table* dialog is displayed.

   3.   Click *OK* to accept the automatically detected range A3:D6.

Sales Summary-1

tip

Don't abbreviate your table names

It may seem like a good idea to abbreviate your table names. For example, why not call the table SL instead of Sales?

On a simple worksheet such as this one, you would always know which table SL was referencing. But imagine a workbook with a hundred tables. Your abbreviations would make the structured references very difficult to understand.

There's no good argument for ever abbreviating table names.

important

Unlike ranges, an Excel table will assume that calculated fields remain consistent throughout a column.

When you added a row to the table, Excel automatically added formulas to cells C7 and D7.

This saves a lot of time compared to ranges (where you have to manually AutoFill your formulas to the remainder of the column).

tip

If the table doesn't automatically expand, somebody has switched the feature off

If this is the case, switch it back on again by clicking:

File→Options→ Proofing→ AutoCorrect Options→ AutoFormat As You Type→ Include new rows and columns in table.

3   Set the table name to: **Sales**

1. Click anywhere inside the table.

   Notice that a *Table Tools* tab has appeared on the ribbon.

2. Click: Table Tools→Design→Properties→Table Name.

3. Type **Sales** into the table name text box).

4. Press the **<Enter>** key.

4   Add a SUM function to cell G3 using a structured reference.

1. Click in cell G3 and type:

   =SUM(

2. Hover the mouse cursor over the top of cell D3 until you see a black down-arrow.

3. When you see the arrow, click once to select cells D4:D6 (all of the data cells in the column).

4. Note the structured reference that has been automatically entered:

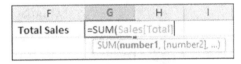

5. Press the **<Enter>** key.

   There's no need to close the bracket, Excel is clever enough to add this for you automatically.

   The structured reference means:

   The sum of all values in the Total column in the Sales table.

5   Add another row to the Sales table by entering the value: 24,400 in cell B7.

| 6 | Mar | 21,260.00 | 3,189.00 | 24,449.00 |
| 7 | Apr | 24,400.00 | 3,660.00 | 28,060.00 |

You only have to enter a value in cell B7. Cells C7 and D7 will automatically calculate as Excel automatically adds formulas to new table rows (see *important* sidebar for more on this).

Notice that the total in cell G3 has updated to include April's sales figure. You can now appreciate the power of structured table references.

6   Save your work as *Sales Summary-2*.

Lesson 1-19: Create a manual structured table reference

In the last lesson you created a structured reference automatically by selecting a range inside a table.

In this lesson you'll appreciate the powerful tools that are built into Excel to make the creation of manual structured references very easy and intuitive.

1 Open *Sales Summary-2* from your sample files folder (if it isn't already open).

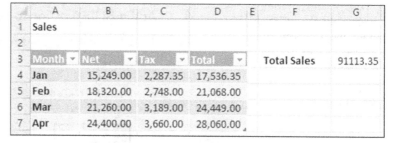

2 Add a formula to cell G4 that will calculate average sales using a manual structured reference.

1. Type the words **Average Sales** into cell F4.

2. Press the **<Tab>** key to move to cell G4.

3. Type:

   =AVERAGE(Sa

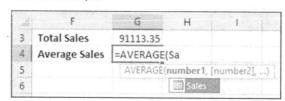

   Notice that a small icon of a table has appeared with the name *Sales*. If there was more than one table on any worksheet in this workbook that began with **Sa** you'd see them all listed here. It doesn't matter whether you type **Sa, sa** or **SA**. Table names are not case sensitive.

4. Press the **<Tab>** key.

   The remaining letters in the table name are entered into the formula.

   The table name references all of the data in a table excluding the header and totals row.

   In this case, and at this time, it will reference cells A4:D7.

   As rows are added and removed from the table, the cells referenced by the table name will dynamically adjust to continue to reference all of the data in the table.

5. Open a square bracket after the word *Sales*.

Sales Summary-2

This time something interesting happens. Excel lists all of the columns in the table:

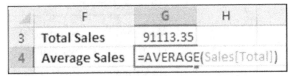

There are also some items that begin with a hash (#). These are called *special items*. You'll learn about special items later, in: *Lesson 1-20: Use special items in structured table references.*

6. Use the **<Down Arrow>** key to move the highlight to the *Total* field.

7. Press the **<Tab>** key.

8. Type the closing square bracket.

9. Type the closing curved bracket

The formula should now look like this:

	F	G	H
3	Total Sales	91113.35	
4	Average Sales	=AVERAGE(Sales[Total])	

In a similar way to the table name, the column name will reference all of the data in the *Total* column excluding the header and total rows.

In this case, and at this time, it will reference cells D4:D7.

As rows are added and removed from the table, the cells referenced by the table name and column name will dynamically adjust to continue to reference all of the data in the column.

10. Press the **<Enter>** key to view the result of the formula.

Average sales during the period Jan-Apr were 22,778.34.

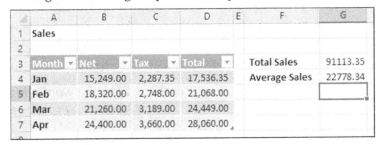

3   Save your work as *Sales Summary-3*.

note

Automatic name changing in formulas

If you change a table name or a column name, any formulas that reference the table will automatically change.

Unfortunately, this will not be the case if you have macros that reference table names (macros will be covered later in: *Session Seven: Forms and Macros*).

For this reason, it is a good idea to name your tables as soon as they are created and to avoid changing table and column names.

Lesson 1-20: Use special items in structured table references

You may have wondered what the items beginning with the hash symbol (#) meant in the last lesson:

These are called *special items*. They can be used to reference different parts of a table.

The #Data special item is rarely used because it is the default and doesn't have to be explicitly stated. In the last lesson you created the structured reference:

Average Sales =AVERAGE(Sales[Total])

You could have entered the same formula in a different (and needlessly complex) way by adding the #Data special item like this:

=AVERAGE(Sales[[#Data],[Total]])

The #Data special item simply means:

All of the data excluding the header and totals row.

1   Open *Sales Summary-3* from your sample files folder (if it isn't already open).

2   Add a total row to the table.

You learned how to do this in: *Lesson 1-12: Convert a range into a table and add a total row.*

3   Change the total at the bottom of column D so that it displays the maximum sales in any one month (using the *Max* option).

1. Click in cell D8.

2. Click the drop-down arrow next to the cell and select *Max* from the shortcut menu.

4   Type the words: **Max Sales** into cell F5 and then press the **<Tab>** key to move to cell G5.

Sales Summary-3

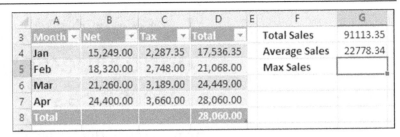

This time you're going to reference the value in cell D8 using the special item: *#Totals*.

5   Add an automatic structured reference to cell G5 that will reference the total at the bottom of the *Sales* table.

   1. Press the equals key (=) to start the formula.

   2. Click in cell D8.

       An automatic structured reference is created that uses the special item *#Totals* to point to the *Total* row.

       This means:

       Reference the value in the Totals row of the Sales table that is at the bottom of the Total column.

   3. Press the **<Enter>** key to save the formula to the cell.

       The *Max Sales* figure is displayed.

6   Apply the comma style to cells G3:G5.

   1. Select cells G3:G5.

   2. Click: Home→Number→Comma Style.

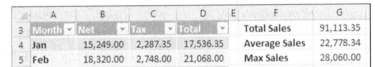

7   Understand all of the special items.

   Here's what the other special items mean:

Special item	What it references
#All	Every cell in the table (this includes the header and total rows).
#Data	The entire contents of the table excluding the header and total rows (this is the default).
#Headers	The header row.
#Totals	The total row.
@ - This Row	Covered in the next lesson.

8   Save your work as *Sales Summary-4*.

Lesson 1-21: Understand unqualified structured table references

A qualified structured reference is a reference that includes the table name such as:

=Sum(Sales[Net])

An unqualified structured reference may be used in formulas within the table itself. In this case you do not have to use the table name as well as the field name because it is obvious.

For example, if you wanted to add *Net sales* and *Tax*, you could use the qualified structured reference:

=Sales[Net]+Sales[Tax]

… but it would be easier and more readable to use the unqualified structured reference:

=[Net]+[Tax]

This reference works because the @ (meaning *This Row*) special item is the default when entering structured references into tables.

You could have entered the same formula in a different way by adding the @ (meaning *This Row*) special item like this:

=[@Net]+[@Tax]

The @ special item is useful when you want to place a formula *alongside* a table and then want to AutoFill the formula to reference each row in the table.

tip

You can also convert a table into a range by right-clicking anywhere in the table and then clicking:

Table→Convert to Range

… from the shortcut menu.

The shortcut menu method is much faster than using the ribbon.

note

When working with tables you don't *have* to convert the old-style A1 references into structured references, but it does make the formulas easier to read if you do.

Sales Summary-4

1   Open *Sales Summary-4* from your sample files folder (if it isn't already open).

2   Convert the A1 style references within the table to unqualified structured references.

1. Double-click in cell C4 and note the existing A1 style reference:

The formula is calculating sales tax as 15% of the net sales value.

2. Delete this formula and replace it with the unqualified structured reference:

=[Net]*0.15

3. Press the **<Enter>** key.

4. Double-click in cell D4 and note the existing A1 style reference:

important

Be careful that you don't accidentally switch Calculated Columns off

The *Calculated Columns* feature is switched on by default. You can easily switch off this amazingly useful feature forever by accident.

When you add any formula to an empty table column a calculated column is created and Excel shows a Smart Tag next to the table.

If you click on the Smart Tag you'll see these options:

The dangerous option is: *Stop Automatically Creating Calculated Columns*.

If you click this option, you will switch off the *Calculated Columns* feature.

On all future occasions, when you add a formula to an Excel table, you'll see a Smart Tag with a single option:

The option this time is: *Overwrite all cells in this column with this formula*. It isn't clear from this description that Excel really means that it will create a calculated column.

I strongly recommend that you leave the *Calculated Columns* feature switched on. If you've switched it off by accident, you'll have to do this:

1. Click: File→Options→ Proofing→ AutoCorrect options→ AutoCorrect Options...→ AutoFormat As You Type.

2. Check the checkbox: *Fill formulas in tables to create calculated columns.*

The formula is adding the sales tax to the net value.

5. Delete this formula and replace it with the unqualified structured reference:

   =[Net]+[Tax]

6. Press the **<Enter>** key.

7. Click: Formulas→Formula Auditing→Show Formulas to view the formulas in each cell:

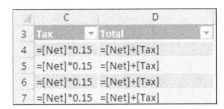

Notice that, even though you didn't AutoFill the formulas in cells C4 and D4, Excel has automatically converted all of the formulas in columns C and D into structured references.

This has happened because Excel now regards column D as being a *Calculated Column*. This provides a major advantage of tables over ranges.

Unfortunately, there's a huge potential pitfall that you can encounter by accidentally switching off the *Calculated Columns* feature (see important sidebar).

8. Click: Formulas→Formula Auditing→Show Formulas once again to display values.

3 Convert the table back to an unformatted range.

1. Click anywhere inside the table.

2. Click: Table Tools→Design→Table Styles→More→None.

   The formatting is removed from the table. In: *Lesson 1-13: Format a table using table styles and convert a table into a range,* you learned why this step is essential before converting a table into a range.

3. Click: Table Tools→Design→Tools→Convert to Range.

4. Click the *Yes* button.

   Notice that the filter buttons have now disappeared.

   Notice also that the structured references have now changed into (rather verbose) A1 style references.

4 Convert the range back to a table.

1. Click anywhere inside the range.

2. Click: Insert→Tables→Table.

3. Click the *OK* button to accept the data range A3:D8.

Notice that the filter buttons have now re-appeared. Notice also that the A1 style references remain. They are not converted into structured references when you convert a range into a table.

5 Save your work as *Sales Summary-5*.

Session 1: Exercise

1   Open *Land Speed Records* from your sample files folder.

2   Convert the range A1:F13 into a table.

3   Name the table *SpeedRecord*.

4   Use a simple filter to only show speed records achieved at Bonneville Salt Flats.

5   Remove the filter to show all speed records.

6   Use an advanced filter to show speed records:

- At Bonneville Salt Flats that are greater than 575 mph.

- Together with all records held by Tom Green (irrespective of location and top speed).

Another way of expressing this is:

Where Location = Bonneville Salt Flats AND MPH > 575
OR where Driver = Tom Green.

Here's the result set you should see:

	A	B	C	D	E	F
5	Date	Location	Driver	Vehicle	Power	MPH
7	05-Oct-64	Bonneville Salt Flats	Tom Green	Wingfoot Express	Turbojet	413.199
13	07-Nov-65	Bonneville Salt Flats	Art Arfons	Green Monster	Turbojet	576.553
14	15-Nov-65	Bonneville Salt Flats	Craig Breedlove	Spirit of America - Sonic 1	Turbojet	600.601
15	23-Oct-70	Bonneville Salt Flats	Gary Gabelich	Blue Flame	Rocket	622.407

7   Remove the advanced filter to show all records and remove any rows that you may have added for the advanced filter criteria.

8   Sort the table A-Z, first by *Location* and then by *Driver*.

9   Add a total row to the table and use the MAX function to display the maximum value in column F.

10   Type **Km/h** into cell G1.

11   Use a formula containing a structured reference to show speeds in kilometers per hour in column G.

12   Save your work as *Land Speed Records-1*.

	A	B	C	D	E	F	G
1	Date	Location	Driver	Vehicle	Power	MPH	Km/h
2	15-Oct-97	Black Rock Desert	Andy Green	ThrustSSC	Turbofan	766.000	1232.758
3	04-Oct-83	Black Rock Desert	Richard Noble	Thrust2	Turbojet	633.000	1018.715
4	07-Oct-64	Bonneville Salt Flats	Art Arfons	Green Monster	Turbojet	434.022	698.4907
5	27-Oct-64	Bonneville Salt Flats	Art Arfons	Green Monster	Turbojet	536.710	863.751
6	07-Nov-65	Bonneville Salt Flats	Art Arfons	Green Monster	Turbojet	576.553	927.8721
7	05-Sep-63	Bonneville Salt Flats	Craig Breedlove	Spirit of America	Turbojet	407.447	655.7224
8	13-Oct-64	Bonneville Salt Flats	Craig Breedlove	Spirit of America	Turbojet	468.719	754.3301
9	15-Oct-64	Bonneville Salt Flats	Craig Breedlove	Spirit of America	Turbojet	526.277	846.9607
10	02-Nov-65	Bonneville Salt Flats	Craig Breedlove	Spirit of America - Sonic 1	Turbojet	555.485	893.9665
11	15-Nov-65	Bonneville Salt Flats	Craig Breedlove	Spirit of America - Sonic 1	Turbojet	600.601	966.5736
12	23-Oct-70	Bonneville Salt Flats	Gary Gabelich	Blue Flame	Rocket	622.407	1001.667
13	05-Oct-64	Bonneville Salt Flats	Tom Green	Wingfoot Express	Turbojet	413.199	664.9793
14	Total					766.000	

If you need help slide the page to the left

Land Speed Records

Session 1: Exercise Answers

These are the four questions that students find the most difficult to answer:

Q 11	Q 8	Q 6	Q 2
1. Click in cell G2. 2. Type: = 3. Click on cell F2. 4. Type: / 5. Click on cell B17. 6. Press the **<F4>** key to change the reference to cell B17 into an absolute reference. Absolute references are covered in depth in the *Essential Skills* book in this series. The formula should now read: **=[@MPH]/$B$17** 7. Press the **<Enter>** key. You learned how to do this in: *Lesson 1-21: Understand unqualified structured table references.*	1. Click anywhere inside the table. 2. Click: Data→ Sort & Filter→Sort. 3. Set the *Sort by* drop-down list to: *Location* 4. Set the *Sort On* drop-down list to: *Cell Values* 5. Set the *Order* drop-down list to: *A to Z* 6. Click *Add Level.* 7. Set the *Then by* drop-down list to: *Driver* 8. Set the *Sort On* drop-down list to: *Cell Values* 9. Set the *Order* drop-down list to: *A to Z* 10. Click the *OK* button. You learned how to do this in: *Lesson 1-15: Sort a range or table by rows.*	1. Insert four blank rows at the top of the worksheet. 2. Copy the table headers from row 5 to row 1. 3. In cell F2, type : **>575** 4. In cell B2 type: **Bonneville Salt Flats** 5. In cell C3 type: **Tom Green** 6. Click anywhere inside the table and then click: Data→Sort & Filter→ Advanced. 7. Set the *Criteria Range* to A1:F3. 8. Click the *OK* button. You learned how to do this in: *Lesson 1-7: Apply an advanced filter with complex criteria.*	1. Click anywhere inside the range. 2. Click: Insert→Tables→Table You learned how to do this in: *Lesson 1-12: Convert a range into a table and add a total row.*

If you have difficulty with the other questions, here are the lessons that cover the relevant skills:

3   Refer to: *Lesson 1-18: Name a table and create an automatic structured table reference*.

4   Refer to: *Lesson 1-4: Apply a simple filter to a range.*

5   Refer to: *Lesson 1-4: Apply a simple filter to a range.*

7   Refer to: *Lesson 1-6: Apply an advanced filter with multiple OR criteria.*

9   Refer to: *Lesson 1-12: Convert a range into a table and add a total row.*

2

Session Two: Data Integrity, Subtotals and Validations

> The longer I live the more I see that I am never wrong about anything, and that all the pains I have so humbly taken to verify my notions have only wasted my time.
>
> *George Bernard Shaw, Irish dramatist & socialist (1856 - 1950)*

In an ideal world all data entry personnel would be just like George Bernard Shaw and never make any mistakes. Unfortunately, the world is not ideal and you will have to give users of your worksheets a little help by validating their input.

In this session you will learn how to validate cells and entire columns in order to restrict the values that users are able to enter. As well as simple validations you'll learn several advanced Excel validation techniques.

Excel's ability to automatically add subtotals never fails to elicit a gasp of amazement during my courses. In this session you'll find out why, when you add sophisticated grouped multi-level subtotals with just a few clicks of the mouse.

Session Objectives

By the end of this session you will be able to:

- Split fixed width data using Text to Columns
- Split delimited data using Text to Columns
- Automatically subtotal a range
- Create nested subtotals
- Consolidate data from multiple data ranges
- Use data consolidation to generate quick subtotals from tables
- Validate numerical data
- Create user-friendly messages for validation errors
- Create data validation input messages
- Add a formula-driven date validation and a text length validation
- Add a table-based dynamic list validation
- Use a formula-driven custom validation to enforce complex business rules
- Remove duplicate values from a table
- Use a custom validation to add a unique constraint to a column

trivia

Dr Codd and his amazing "third normal form" rules

Dr E.F. Codd (1923-2003) is a cult figure to every database designer worthy of the name.

He was not only the inventor of the relational database (while working for IBM) but he also wrote the rulebook for excellence in database design.

Codd's books are essential (and even exciting) reading for anybody who designs relational databases for a living. I have read all of them and hung on every word.

Codd defined a set of rules that are collectively called third normal form (or 3NF for short).

Codd's rules are broken into three parts: First Normal Form, Second Normal Form and Third Normal Form.

Each set of rules builds upon the earlier set so that a database design cannot conform to 2NF unless it first conforms to 1NF (and a 3NF design must first conform to 2NF).

Keeping data atomic is one of the most basic rules that must be applied to comply with 1NF; Codd's least strict definition of a correctly designed data table.

I've worked with many hundreds of database designs over the years and you'd be amazed how many do not conform to Codd's rules.

I've noticed that when one of Codd's rules is broken, the database will always bite back eventually.

As you can see in this lesson, Dr Codd can teach us a thing or two about designing Excel tables too!

Sales Analysis

Lesson 2-1: Split fixed width data using Text to Columns

Over the years, students have brought some very interesting workbooks to my classes from many diverse areas of business and commerce.

Often the workbook has become extremely complex and unmanageable with convoluted formulas that are difficult to audit.

Many times, all of the problems can be traced to the workbook designer breaking one simple golden rule of data table design:

"Keep data atomic"

This is one of Dr Codd's rules for efficient database design (see sidebar) that is equally relevant to Excel tables and ranges. In the same way that the atom is the smallest basic unit you can divide matter into, a column should contain the smallest possible amount of data.

Here's a simple example to illustrate the concept:

	A	B
1	Name	Age
2	Mr John Smith	42
3	Ms Jane Johnson	28

In the example above it wouldn't be easy to sort or filter column A by first name or last name. If you had observed the *keep data atomic* rule you would have split the data into multiple columns like this:

	A	B	C	D
1	Title	First Name	Last Name	Age
2	Mr	John	Smith	42
3	Ms	Jane	Johnson	28

The benefits provided by this simple example are obvious. It is not as easy to see the problem when a general ledger code or part number contains many different pieces of data. Here's an example:

	A	B	C	D
1	Part Number	Units	Unit Price	Ext Price
2	GB480Z	2	42.70	85.40
3	EU522S	3	22.50	67.50

The error isn't so easy to see here. In this particular example the *Part Number: GB480Z* is actually made up of three pieces of data:

1. GB: Where the product is made (GB=Great Britain, EU=Rest of Europe, US=USA).

2. 480: Product ID.

3. Z: Sales tax rate (Z=Zero rated, S=Standard rated, E=Exempt).

When you see this type of number in your data you should immediately break it up into its constituent parts.

Excel now provides three different ways to split text:

1. **Flash Fill:** This incredibly useful feature is covered comprehensively in Session 2 of the *Essential Skills* book in this series. It is the simplest way to split text.

anecdote

How one company fell into the atomic data trap

A couple of years ago I ran an Excel VBA programming course for an engineering company.

They had designed an incredibly complex system to manage their workflow using Excel and they thought that they needed VBA skills to cater for new requirements that they believed Excel was unable to implement.

The workbook contained huge formulas making extensive use of the MID, LEFT, RIGHT and FIND functions, often nested inside IF functions. As soon as I saw the first function I knew that they had fallen into the atomic data trap.

The system was based upon *Job Id* numbers, each containing about ten data elements. Once this data had been split into columns, the entire workbook became very simple to work with. In fact, they found that they didn't need any custom VBA coding to elegantly implement all of their business requirements!

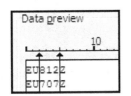

2. **Using Functions:** You can use the MID, LEFT, RIGHT and FIND functions to split text. (You'll learn about these functions later in: *Lesson 3-20: Extract text from fixed width strings using the LEFT, RIGHT and MID functions*). This is the most complex technique but is the only method that will automatically update when the source text changes.

3. **Using the *Text to Columns* tool**: This is the method used in this lesson.

1 Open *Sales Analysis* from your sample files folder.

The table contains a list of products sold during March, April and May 2016. But there's a problem with this list. Column B contains part numbers that break the atomic data rule.

	A	B	C	D	E
1	Date	Part Number	Units	Unit Price	Ext Price
2	01-Mar-16	EU812Z	3	72.00	216.00
3	01-Mar-16	EU707Z	4	60.00	240.00
4	01-Mar-16	EU522S	3	22.50	67.50

2 Insert two blank columns to the left of column C.

These columns, along with the original column, will receive the new atomic values.

	B	C	D	E
1	Part Number	Column1	Column2	Units
2	EU812Z			3

3 Split column B into atomic data elements.

1. Select all of the values in column B of the table (B2:B54).

2. Click: Data→Data Tools→Text to Columns.

3. Click *Fixed width* (you'll learn about delimited data in *Lesson 2-2: Split delimited data using Text to Columns*).

Original data type
Choose the file type that best describes your data:
○ Delimited - Characters such as commas or tabs separate each field.
● Fixed width - Fields are aligned in columns with spaces between each field.

4. Click *Next*.

5. Click in the *Data preview* window to break up each data element within the part number (see sidebar).

6. Click the *Finish* button.

The part number is split into atomic data

4 Rename the columns B, C and D as **Region, Part Number** and **Tax**.

	A	B	C	D	E
1	Date	Region	Part Number	Tax	Units
2	01-Mar-14	EU		812 Z	3
3	01-Mar-14	EU		707 Z	4

5 Save your work as *Sales Analysis-2*.

Lesson 2-2: Split delimited data using Text to Columns

Fixed width data

In *Lesson 2-1: Split fixed width data using Text to Columns*, you worked with data that can be split into its constituent parts by reference to the character position of each piece of information.

Several accounting packages export data in a similar fixed width format:

Mr	John	Smith	19-Mar-14	2,220.24	2	4,440.48
Ms	Susan	Phillips	22-Mar-14	125.45	1	125.45
Mrs	Jennifer	Scott	23-Mar-14	1,145.60	2	2,291.20

This type of data is easy to recognize because all of the data elements "line up".

Delimited data

You'll often encounter delimited data. This type of data uses a special character (such as a comma or semicolon) to split each data element. This type of data will be structured like this:

```
Mr;John;Smith;19-Mar-14;2,220.24;2;4,440.48
Ms;Susan;Phillips;22-Mar-14;125.45;1;125.45
Mrs;Jennifer;Scott;23-Mar-14;1,145.60;2;2,291.20
```

In the above example the semicolon (;) is used as the delimiter.

1   Open *US Labor Force-1* from your sample files folder.

	A	B
1	US Labor Force - by occupation:	
2		
3	farming, forestry, and fishing: 0.7%	
4	manufacturing, extraction, transportation, and crafts: 20.3%	
5	managerial, professional, and technical: 37.3%	
6	sales and office: 24.2%	
7	other services: 17.6%	
8	note - figures exclude the unemployed (2009)	

This worksheet contains some data that has been cut and pasted from the *CIA World Fact book* web site.

When you cut and paste information from other documents, (such as web pages), the information often isn't in a format that is "Excel friendly".

In this lesson you'll split this data into a structured table so that you can display the division of labor as a pie chart.

2   Split the data in column A into text and percentages.

1.   Insert a row above row 8.

It is always a good idea to have a blank row separating a range from other data.

US Labor Force-1

2. Select cells A3:A7.

3. Click: Data→Data Tools→Text to Columns.

4. Click *Delimited*.

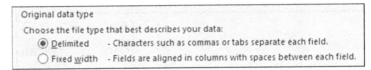

Original data type

Choose the file type that best describes your data:

⦿ <u>D</u>elimited — Characters such as commas or tabs separate each field.

◯ Fixed <u>w</u>idth — Fields are aligned in columns with spaces between each field.

5. Click the *Next >* button.

6. Set the delimiter to a colon (see sidebar).

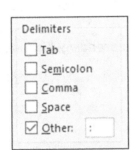

Delimiters

☐ <u>T</u>ab

☐ Se<u>m</u>icolon

☐ <u>C</u>omma

☐ <u>S</u>pace

☑ <u>O</u>ther: :

You can see that there is a colon before each percentage value in column A. By setting this as a delimiter you can extract the percentages.

7. Click: *Next >*.

8. Click: *Finish.*

The percentages are moved to their own column.

	A	B
1	US Labor Force - by occupation:	
2		
3	farming, forestry, and fishing	0.70%
4	manufacturing, extraction, transportation, and crafts	20.30%
5	managerial, professional, and technical	37.30%
6	sales and office	24.20%
7	other services	17.60%
8		
9	note: figures exclude the unemployed (2009)	

3 **Create a pie chart to display the data visually.**

1. Select cells A3:B7.

2. Click:

Insert→Charts→Recommended Charts→Pie Chart

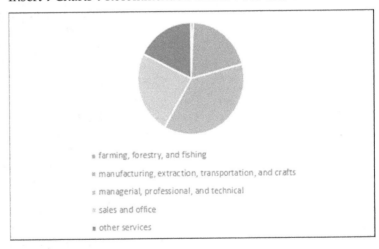

3. Click the *OK* button.

Charting is covered in depth in the *Essential Skills* book in this series.

4 **Save your work as *US Labor Force-2*.**

Lesson 2-3: Automatically subtotal a range

1   Open *Inventory-10* from your sample files folder.

2   Remove conditional formatting from the table.

  1. Click anywhere inside the table.

  2. Click: Home→Styles→Conditional Formatting→Clear Rules→ Clear Rules from This Table.

3   Sort the table by *Category* in ascending order (A-Z).

  You learned how to do this in: *Lesson 1-15: Sort a range or table by rows.*

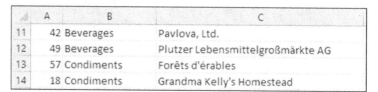

	A	B	C
11	42	Beverages	Pavlova, Ltd.
12	49	Beverages	Plutzer Lebensmittelgroßmärkte AG
13	57	Condiments	Forêts d'érables
14	18	Condiments	Grandma Kelly's Homestead

4   Convert the table into a range.

  You learned how to do this in: *Lesson 1-13: Format a table using table styles and convert a table into a range.*

  You must convert the table into a range because you cannot add subtotals to tables.

5   Delete the total row (row 71).

6   Add subtotals to the *In Stock* and *Value* columns for each category.

  1. Click anywhere inside the range.

  2.   Click: Data→Outline→Subtotal.

    The *Subtotal* dialog appears:

Inventory-10

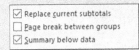

note

Other subtotal options

Note the three subtotal options:

☑ Replace current subtotals
☐ Page break between groups
☑ Summary below data

You can use the first option to add different types of subtotal to different columns.

For example, if you wanted to view both the average and the sum at the same time you could add a second subtotal by unchecking this box.

The new subtotal is then shown above the old one:

Beverages Average
Beverages Total

note

Copying subtotals to another location

A very common request in my courses is:

"How can I copy the subtotals only (ie the level two outline) to another worksheet. When I copy the subtotals and paste I get the detail rows as well – but I just want the subtotals".

The secret here is to only select the visible cells on the worksheet before copying.

Here's how it is done:

1. Display level two subtotals by clicking the ② button.

2. Click: Home→Editing→ Find & Select→Go To Special→ Visible cells only, and then click OK.

OR

Select the range and then press the <Alt>+<;> keys.

4. Copy.

5. Paste to the destination cells.

3. Tell Excel which column of repeating data you wish to add subtotals to by choosing *Category* in the *At each change in:* drop down.

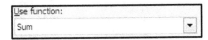

4. Make sure that the *Sum* function is selected.

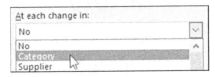

5. Click the check boxes to add subtotals to the *In Stock* and *Value* columns:

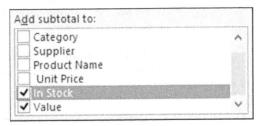

6. Click the *OK* button.

The worksheet is now subtotaled and Excel has added an outline bar to the left hand side:

1 2 3		A	B	C	D	E	F	G
	55	64	Grains/Cereals	PB Knäckebröd AB	Tunnbröd	9.00	61	549.00
	56	68	Grains/Cereals	Plutzer Lebensmitte	Wimmers gute Semme	33.25	22	731.50
	57		**Grains/Cereals Total**				282	5,230.50
	58	43	Meat/Poultry	Ma Maison	Pâté chinois	24.00	115	2,760.00
	59	63	Meat/Poultry	Ma Maison	Tourtière	7.45	21	156.45
	60		**Meat/Poultry Total**				136	2,916.45

7 Collapse and expand the entire outline.

Notice the small 1 2 3 buttons in the top left corner of the worksheet.

- When you click button 1 only the grand total is shown.

- When you click button 2 each category subtotal is shown.

- When you click button 3 all items are shown.

8 Collapse and expand categories within the outline.

Note the + and − buttons in the left-hand sidebar.

Experiment by clicking them and notice how you can selectively expand and collapse any group within the outline.

9 Remove the subtotals from the range.

1. Click anywhere within the range.

2. Click: Data→Outline→Subtotal→Remove All.

10 Save your work as *Inventory-11*.

Lesson 2-4: Create nested subtotals

Sometimes you'll find a need for more than one level of subtotal.

Consider this data:

	Category	Supplier	Product Name
4	Beverages	Bigfoot Breweries	Sasquatch Ale
5	Beverages	Bigfoot Breweries	Laughing Lumberjack Lager
6	Beverages	Bigfoot Breweries	Steeleye Stout
7	Beverages	Exotic Liquids	Chai
8	Beverages	Exotic Liquids	Chang

In the example above both *Bigfoot Breweries* and *Exotic Liquids* supply more than one product in the *Beverages* category.

As well as wishing to know subtotals for each *category* you may also wish to know subtotals for each *supplier* within each *category*. In other words:

What is the value of Bigfoot Breweries inventory in each category?

By nesting subtotals, you can quickly cater for this requirement.

1   Open *Inventory-11* from your sample files folder (if it isn't already open).

2   Apply a two-level A-Z sort, first by *Category* and then by *Supplier*.

You learned how to do this in: *Lesson 1-15: Sort a range or table by rows*.

Column		Sort On		Order	
Sort by	Category	Cell Values		A to Z	
Then by	Supplier	Cell Values		A to Z	

3   At each change in *Category* use the *Sum* function to add subtotals to the *In Stock* and *Value* columns.

You learned how to do this in:
Lesson 2-3: Automatically subtotal a range.

At each change in:
Category

Use function:
Sum

Add subtotal to:
☐ Category
☐ Supplier
☐ Product Name
☐ Unit Price
☑ In Stock
☑ Value

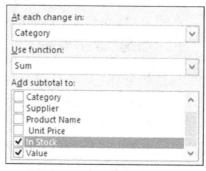

		Meat/Poultry Total		
60				
61	34	Produce	G'day, Mate	Manjimup Dried Apples
62	65	Produce	Grandma Kelly's Homestead	Uncle Bob's Organic Dried Pears
63	62	Produce	Mayumi's	Tofu
64	31	Produce	Tokyo Traders	Longlife Tofu

Inventory-11

4   Add a nested subtotal to show totals by *Supplier* within each category.

1. Click anywhere within the range.

2. Click: Data→Outline→Subtotal.

3. Uncheck the *Replace current subtotals* check box.

   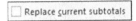
   ☐ Replace current subtotals

   This is the secret when creating nested subtotals. If you didn't uncheck this box, the new subtotal would simply replace the old one. By keeping the current subtotal you'll add a nested subtotal.

4. At each change in *Supplier* add a *Sum* function to subtotal the *In Stock* and *Value* columns:

5. Click the *OK* button.

   Nested subtotals are now shown by category/by supplier:

   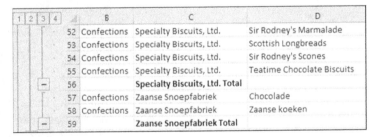

   Notice that there's an extra level button too:

   The fourth level is the nested subtotal, allowing you to collapse and expand the *Supplier* subtotals.

5 Save your work as *Inventory-12*.

Lesson 2-5: Consolidate data from multiple data ranges

Totaling data from multiple worksheets onto a summary sheet is a very common business requirement. Excel can automatically consolidate data if each worksheet has an identical structure.

If you use this technique, it is a good idea to use templates for each of the worksheets that will be consolidated in order to ensure that they are identical. (Templates are covered in depth in the *Essential Skills* book in this series).

1   Open *Sales and Profit by Employee-1* from your sample files folder.

This worksheet shows each employee's sales, cost and profit data for the first three months in the quarter.

The *January, February, March* and *Summary* worksheets have an identical structure. This makes the consolidation feature very easy to use.

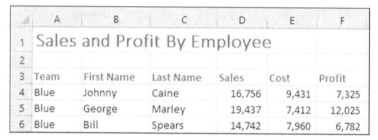

	A	B	C	D	E	F
1	Sales and Profit By Employee					
2						
3	Team	First Name	Last Name	Sales	Cost	Profit
4	Blue	Johnny	Caine	16,756	9,431	7,325
5	Blue	George	Marley	19,437	7,412	12,025
6	Blue	Bill	Spears	14,742	7,960	6,782

2   Consolidate data for the first three months into the summary sheet.

1. Click into the destination cell for the consolidated data. This is cell D4 on the *Summary* sheet.

2. Click: Data→Data Tools→Consolidate.

The *Consolidate* dialog appears.

3. Make sure that the *Function* drop-down displays the *Sum* function because you want to add together the values in the *January, February* and *March* worksheets:

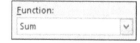

4. Click in the *Reference* box.

5. Click the *January* worksheet tab and select cells D4:F17:

Reference:

January!$D$4:$F$17

Sales and Profit by Employee-1

6. Click the *Add* button to add the reference to the list of references to be consolidated:

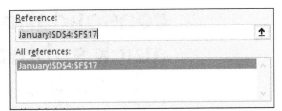

7. Click the *February* worksheet tab. This time the same range (on the *February* worksheet) is automatically displayed in the dialog.

8. Click the *Add* button to add the *February* range to the list of references to be consolidated.

9. Repeat the same operation for the *March* range.

    The dialog should now look like this:

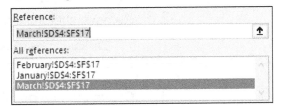

10. Click the *OK* button to display the consolidated totals on the summary sheet:

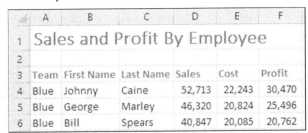

3   Create a data consolidation that is linked to the source data.

In the previous operation the consolidated values were not linked to the source worksheets. If a value on a source worksheet changes, the summary worksheet will not update.

1. Delete the range D4:F17 on the *Summary* worksheet.

2. Click in cell D4 on the *Summary* worksheet.

3. Click: Data→Data Tools→Consolidate.

4. Check the *Create links to source data* check box:

5. Click the *OK* button.

This time the data consolidation links to the source data and also displays a grouped outline similar to an automatic subtotal, enabling you to view each of the source data values for the consolidation.

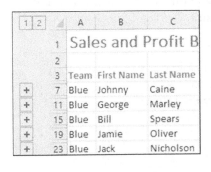

4   Save your work as *Sales and Profit by Employee-2*.

Lesson 2-6: Use data consolidation to generate quick subtotals from tables

In: *Lesson 2-3: Automatically subtotal a range* you used Excel's fantastic *Automatic Subtotal* feature to quickly add subtotals to a range. Unfortunately, automatic subtotals do not work with tables.

Another problem with automatic subtotals is that you have little control over the formatting of the subtotal data.

Data consolidation can overcome both of these problems by allowing full control of formatting, along with the ability to work with both ranges and tables.

1   Open *Inventory-12* from your sample files folder.

2   Remove subtotals from the range.

    1.   Click anywhere inside the range.

    2.   Click: Data→Outline→Subtotal→Remove All.

3   Convert the range into a table.

    You learned how to do this in: *Lesson 1-12: Convert a range into a table and add a total row.*

4   Add quick subtotals by category using data consolidation.

    1.   Click in cell I1.

    2.   Click: Data→Data Tools→Consolidate.

        The *Consolidate* dialog is displayed:

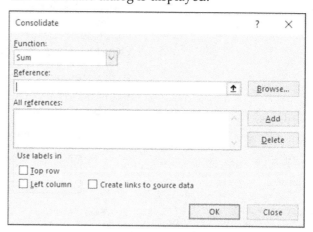

    3.   Make sure that *Sum* is shown in the *Function* box. This should be the case as *Sum* is the default.

    4.   Click in the *Reference* box and select the range B1:G70.

        A quick way to do this is to click in cell B1, press **<Ctrl>+<Shift>+<DownArrow>**, and then press **<Ctrl>+<Shift>+<RightArrow>**.

Inventory-12

Reference:

$B$1:$G$70

note

Consolidated subtotals cannot be linked to source data on the same worksheet

In: *Lesson 2-5: Consolidate data from multiple data ranges*, you learned how to create consolidated totals that are linked to source data.

You did this by checking the *Create links to source data* checkbox.

This is really useful as linked consolidated totals will update whenever an existing row in the source data is changed or deleted.

The consolidated totals will not, however, update when new rows are added to the source data.

Unfortunately, the option to link only works when the consolidated data is on a different worksheet to the source data.

If you try to link consolidated totals on the same worksheet as the source data, you will see this dialog:

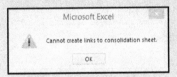

If you need to display linked consolidated totals on the same worksheet there's a simple work-around.

1. Create linked consolidated totals on a different worksheet.

2. Create cross-worksheet formulas that reference the values on the worksheet containing the linked consolidated totals.

5. Check the two check boxes: *Use labels in Top row, Left column.*

6. Click the *OK* button.

Subtotals appear beginning in cell I1 for every column.

	Supplier	Product N	Unit Price	In Stock	Value
Beverages			451.25	539	######
Condiments			255.40	507	######
Confections			327.08	386	######
Dairy Products			287.30	393	######

5 Delete columns J:L.

Subtotals are impossible on the text columns: *Supplier* and *Product Name.* They are also of no interest for the *Unit Price* column.

6 Re-size columns I, J and K.

Useful subtotals are now displayed:

	I	In Stock	Value
2	Beverages	539	12,390.25
3	Condiments	507	12,023.55
4	Confections	386	10,392.20
5	Dairy Products	393	11,271.20
6	Grains/Cereals	282	5,230.50
7	Meat/Poultry	136	2,916.45
8	Produce	74	2,363.75
9	Seafood	701	13,010.35

7 Add averages alongside the totals using the same technique.

1. Click in cell L1.

2. Do exactly the same thing you did for the *Sum* but choose the *Average* function in the consolidate dialog:

3. Click the *OK* button.

4. Delete columns L:O.

5. Change the label in L1 to: **Average In Stock**

6. Change the label in M1 to: **Average Value**

7. Change the number of decimal places shown for the values in column L to zero.

8. Re-size columns L and M.

	I	In Stock	Value	Average In Stock	Average Value
2	Beverages	539	12,390.25	49	1,126.39
3	Condiments	507	12,023.55	46	1,093.05

8 Save your work as *Inventory-13.*

tip

Clearing validation from selected cells

In this lesson you may have noticed that the validation applied to "all of column E" has also been applied to cells E1:E6.

This would prevent you from editing the column header in cell E6.

To quickly clear validation rules from these cells:

1. Right-click on any cell on the worksheet that has no data validation rules.

2. Click: *Copy* from the shortcut menu.

3. Select cells E1:E6.

4. Right-click inside the selected range and select: *Paste Special…* from the shortcut menu.

5. Click the *Validation* option button.

6. Click the *OK* button.

Health Club Bookings-1

Lesson 2-7: Validate numerical data

In the next lessons you'll explore the power of Excel's data validation features. You can prevent a huge number of data entry errors by catching them when they are entered and then politely informing your users that they have made a mistake.

1   Open *Health Club Bookings-1* from your sample files folder.

This worksheet manages all of the treatments sold in a health club.

There are several rules that must not be broken when entering data (see sidebar). These types of rules are often referred to as *business rules* when designing data systems.

At the moment the worksheet doesn't police these rules itself but relies upon all personnel understanding and applying them.

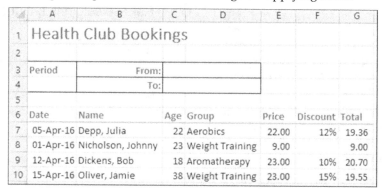

2   Apply the Age rule (see sidebar) to column C.

1. Select all of column C by clicking the column header.

You need to select the entire column when you want to add data validation to every cell in the column.

2. Click: Data→Data Tools→Data Validation.

The data validation dialog appears.

3. Click the *Settings* tab.

At the moment Excel is allowing *Any value*. This is the default, meaning that the user is free to type anything at all into any cell in column C.

4. Choose *Whole number* from the *Allow* drop-down list.

Whole number will not allow the user to enter decimal values such as 22.8. As ages cannot have decimal places this is a good validation rule for a column containing age data.

Criteria now appear that are relevant to whole numbers.

5. Click in the *Data* box and select *between*:

6.   Click in the *Minimum* box and then click on cell J5.

7.   Make J5 into an absolute reference.

8.   Click in the *Maximum* box and then click on cell J6.

9.   Make J6 into an absolute reference.

The dialog should now look like this:

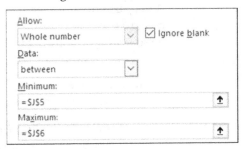

10. Click the *OK* button.

3   Test the data validation.

Data validation will now ensure that any new values entered into column C are valid. It will not change any existing invalid values in the column. (See sidebar for a quick way to find existing invalid values).

Enter an invalid value (such as an age of 101 or 15) into any cell in column C.

A rather unfriendly error message appears advising that an error has occurred:

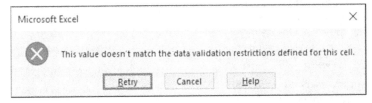

In the next lesson you'll discover how to make this message a little friendlier.

4   Add another data validation.

Use the same technique to apply the business rule: *Prices must be between 10.00 and 100.00* (stated in cells I16:J17) to column E.

Notice that cell E8 now violates the validation criteria. When you apply a new validation rule to a cell, any values that already exist will remain without any error warnings. It will, however, be impossible to change the value to another that violates the validation criteria.

5   Save your work as *Health Club Bookings-2*.

---

note

How to quickly find invalid values

The *Data Validation* button on the ribbon is a split button. If you click the small arrow on the:

Data→Data Tools→
Data Validation

… button you'll see some more options:

Click: *Circle Invalid Data* to show red circles around all invalid values on this worksheet:

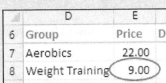

When you have reviewed the invalid data you can use the *Clear Validation Circles* command to remove the circles.

Lesson 2-8: Create user-friendly messages for validation errors

anecdote

Be careful what you write in your error messages

One of my programmer friends once got fired from his job for writing "inappropriate error messages" in his software.

I can't repeat his error messages in this book, but I thought his employers were a bit hard on him because they were quite funny!

Around 1990 I wrote a mass-market accounting program that sold well in the garage trade.

Sometimes I would put little error messages at break points to amuse me when I was testing the code. One day I compiled a release version and forgot to take one out.

One of my users reported that his point of sale terminal was displaying the message:

"Come on Mike, you're supposed to be at the pub by now".

Fortunately, I owned the company so I didn't get fired.

A very useful design goal when developing computer software is to create a user interface that requires no user training. The interface should be so simple, and the features so obvious, that users can train themselves by experimentation and discovery.

For this reason, a user needs to be provided with an informative error message whenever they do something that is not allowed.

1 Open *Health Club Bookings-2* from your sample files folder (if it isn't already open).

2 Add an error message to column C.

1. Select all of column C.

2. Click: Data→Data Tools→Data Validation.

3. Click the *Error Alert* tab.

4. Type: **Invalid Age** into the *Title* box.

5. Click in the *Error message* box and type:

    Age must be at least 17 and no more than 100.

    Your dialog should now look like this:

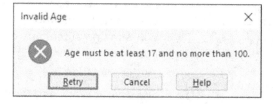

6. Click the *OK* button.

3 Test the error message.

When you enter an invalid age into any cell in column C, you will see the error message:

Health Club Bookings-2

4 Change the validation from mandatory to advisory.

This validation is called *mandatory* because there is absolutely no possibility of the user entering an invalid value (other than by copying and pasting a value into the cell).

Sometimes this restriction is too strict. You may want to tell the user that an age of over 100 is unusual, but if the user is really sure that the client is over 100 they can still continue.

1. Select all of column C.

2. Click: Data→Data Tools→Data Validation.

3. Change the error message to read: **Age is usually between 17 and 100. Are you sure this is correct?**

4. Change the style of the error message from *Stop* to *Warning*.

    The dialog should now look like this:

5. Click the *OK* button.

5 Test the error message.

When you enter an invalid age into any cell in column C you will now see a different style of error message:

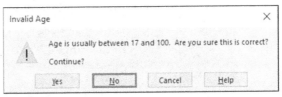

You then have the opportunity to click the *Yes* button and over-ride the validation.

6 Add an informative error message to column E.

Use the same technique to add an error message to column E.

7 Save your work as *Health Club Bookings-3*.

note

The Stop, Warning and Info error alert styles

Windows users are conditioned to understand the meaning of three different icons.

Stop

Something terrible has happened!

Warning

Something quite bad has happened.

Information

We just thought you'd like to know.

Each of these styles produces a slightly different error message dialog.

The *Warning* dialog shows four buttons (see text) and the *Information* dialog shows just three buttons: OK, Cancel and Help.

The only important difference between them is that the *Stop* style is mandatory while the *Information* and *Warning* styles are advisory.

Lesson 2-9: Create data validation input messages

In the last lesson: *Lesson 2-8: Create user-friendly messages for validation errors*, you discovered how to provide an informative error message whenever the user breaks a business rule.

Users can become frustrated if they can only discover business rules by first making mistakes and then being informed of the error. To make applications more efficient and user-friendly, it is sometimes better to inform the user of the business rules before they attempt to enter a value.

In this lesson you'll use data entry input messages to provide a better user experience.

1   Open *Health Club Bookings-3* from your sample files folder (if it isn't already open).

2   Add a data validation input message to column C.

In *Lesson 2-7: Validate numerical data*, you added a validation to column C to ensure that ages are entered as whole numbers between 17 and 100.

You will now use the *Input Message* feature to inform the user of this business rule before an attempt is made to enter an age.

1.   Select all of column C by clicking the column header.

You must select the entire column when you want to add an input message to every cell in the column.

2.   Click: Data→Data Tools→Data Validation.

The data validation dialog appears.

3.   Click the *Input Message* tab.

4.   In the *Title* box, type: **Age**

5.   In the *Input message* box, type: **Ages must be whole numbers in the range 17-100.**

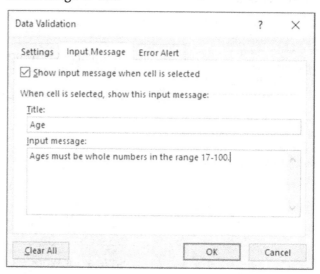

Health Club Bookings-3

note

Data validation input messages can be annoying on columns of data

The sample workbook used in this lesson isn't a good candidate for data validation input messages.

The little yellow box may have been welcome the first time the user saw it. Once the business rule is known to the user, however, it becomes very irritating.

I've found that the best use for this feature is on one-time forms.

In this scenario each message is added to only one cell and provides useful information to aid completion of the form.

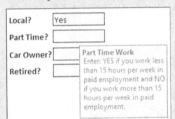

6. Click the *OK* button.

3 Test the data validation input message.

Click any cell in column C. The input message is displayed:

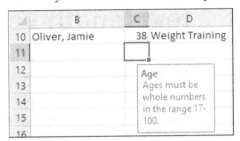

4 Use the same technique to add a data validation input message to column E.

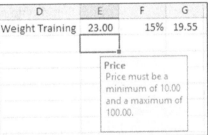

5 Save your work as *Health Club Bookings-4*.

© 2020 The Smart Method® Ltd

Lesson 2-10: Add a formula-driven date validation and a text length validation

Validation parameters do not have to be simple values. They can also be set to the value returned by a formula.

In this lesson you'll use Excel's TODAY function to add a validation that will not allow a date to be entered that is in the past.

1 Open *Health Club Bookings-4* from your sample files folder (if it isn't already open).

2 Add a validation to column A that will not allow dates that are in the past to be entered.

   1. Select all of column A.

   2. Click: Data→Data Tools→Data Validation.

   3. Click the *Settings* tab.

   4. Set the *Allow:* box to *Date*.

   5. Set the *Data:* box to *greater than or equal to*.

   6. Add a TODAY function to the *Start Date* text box by typing:

      =TODAY()

      The TODAY function returns today's date. The TODAY function will be covered in depth later in: *Lesson 3-8: Understand common date functions.*

      Your dialog should now look like this:

3 Add an appropriate error alert message.

   1. Click the *Error Alert* tab.

   2. Type: **Date Error** into the *Title* box.

   3. Type: **Dates cannot be in the past** into the *Error message* box.

   4. Click the *OK* button.

Health Club Bookings-4

4   Test the validation.

Attempt to enter a date that is in the past.

An error message is displayed:

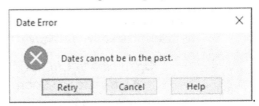

5   Apply a text length validation to column B to enforce the rule: *Minimum name length = 2 characters, Maximum name length = 20 characters*

The validation dialog will look like this:

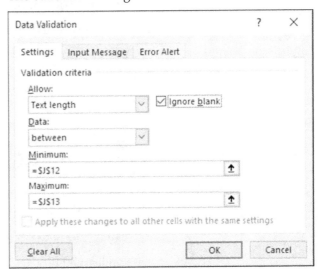

Note that it is important to use the absolute references $J$12 and $J$13 rather than the relative references J12 and J13. Absolute, Relative and Mixed cell references are covered in depth in the *Essential Skills* book in this series.

6   Add an appropriate *Error Alert* for this validation.

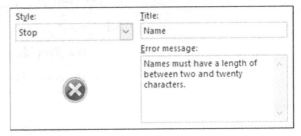

7   Test the validation.

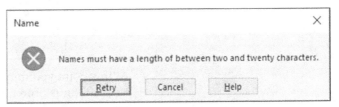

8   Save your work as *Health Club Bookings-5*.

Lesson 2-11: Add a table-based dynamic list validation

List validations prevent the user from entering any value into a cell that is not contained within a pre-defined list.

1   Open *Health Club Bookings-5* from your sample files folder (if it isn't already open).

2   Create a table (with a header) in cells I24:I30 containing a list of the valid groups: *Yoga, Aerobics, Weight Training, Aromatherapy, Massage* and *Aquarobics.*

    1.   Type **Group** into cell I24.

    2.   Type the valid group names (shown below) into cells I25:I30.

    3.   Convert cells I24:I30 into a table.

        You learned how to do this in: *Lesson 1-12: Convert a range into a table and add a total row.*

    4.   Name your new table: **ValidGroups**

        You learned how to do this in: *Lesson 1-18: Name a table and create an automatic structured table reference.*

3   Add a validation to column D that will only allow groups defined in the *ValidGroups* table (cells I24:I30) to be entered.

    1.   Select all of column D.

    2.   Click: Data→Data Tools→Data Validation.

    3.   Click the *Settings* tab.

    4.   In the *Allow* drop down click *List.*

    5.   Click in the *Source* box and then select cells I25:I30 with the mouse.

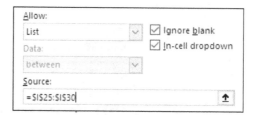

At this point you may wonder why you don't simply type: **=ValidGroups** into the *Source* box. While this makes perfect sense, Excel won't allow it. (See the important sidebar for more on this).

Health Club Bookings-5

important

There are five ways to define validation list source data

1. Type values directly into the source box.

When you do this you need to type a comma in between each value:

2. Define values as a range.

Simply select a regular range to define the values:

3. Define values as a table.

Convert the source values from a range to a table before setting the source data.

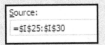

This seems to be the same as method 2. It differs because Excel treats source cells that are in a table differently from source cells that are in a range (but only when the table is on the same worksheet as the cells to be validated).

When the source cells originate in a table on the same worksheet, Excel will automatically grow and shrink the range as items are added and removed from the table.

4. Define values as a named range.

You'll learn all about named ranges in: *Session Four: Using Names and the Formula Auditing Tools*.

5. Define values as a named range that references a table.

This is the best method of all as the validation table can then reside on any worksheet. You'll use this technique, in: *Lesson 4-7: Create table-based dynamic range names*.

6. Add an appropriate *Error Alert*.

You learned how to do this in: *Lesson 2-8: Create user-friendly messages for validation errors*.

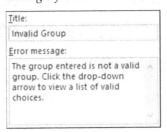

7. Click the *OK* button.

4 Test the validation.

1. Click anywhere in column D.

Notice that a drop down arrow appears on the right-hand side of the cell.

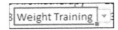

2. Click the drop-down arrow.

A list of all valid groups is displayed:

3. Click any of the valid groups.

The selected value is displayed in the cell.

5 Add *Circuit Training* as a valid group.

1. Click in cell I31.

2. Type: **Circuit Training**.

3. Press the **<Enter>** key.

The new item is added to the table.

6 Test the validation again.

Click on the drop-down arrow to the right of any cell in column D.

Note that *Circuit Training* is now a valid item in the list.

This only happened because you converted the source cells I24:I30 into a table. If you hadn't done this, *Circuit Training* would not have been valid (see the important sidebar for more on this).

7 Save your work as *Health Club Bookings-6*.

Lesson 2-12: Use a formula-driven custom validation to enforce complex business rules

The simple dialog-driven validations have served all of your requirements up to now.

Sometimes you will have to implement a validation that is too complex for any of the dialog-driven validations to handle. In this case you will have to write a formula-driven custom validation.

In the sample file you have been working with, there is a requirement (listed in the business rules) that states:

Discounts	
Minimum price for discount	20.00

This means that the value in column F will depend upon the value in column E.

	E	F	G
6	Price	Discount	Total
7	22.00	12%	19.36
8	9.00		9.00
9	23.00	10%	20.70
10	23.00	15%	19.55

In cell F8 above it is prohibited to enter a discount because the price is less than 20.00. Right now there's nothing to stop a user doing this. You need to enforce this business rule with a formula-driven custom validation.

1   Open *Health Club Bookings-6* from your sample files folder (if it isn't already open).

2   Add a validation to column F that will enforce the business rule: *Minimum price for discount = 20.00*.

   1.   Select all of column F.

   2.   Click: Data→Data Tools→Data Validation→Data Validation…

   3.   Click the *Settings* tab.

   4.   Select *Custom* from the *Allow* drop-down list.

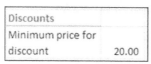

Allow:
Custom

Custom validations require a formula. The validation will only allow a value to be entered if the formula returns a value of TRUE.

   5.   Click in the *Formula* text box and type the following text:

=E1>=$J$20

Health Club Bookings-6

important

Excel's validation mechanism is easily defeated

Excel's validation rules are not very robust.

A user is able to copy and paste any value into any cell to bypass validation rules.

This formula will return FALSE if the value in cell E1 is less than the value in cell J20, and TRUE if the value in cell E1 is greater than or equal to the value in cell J20.

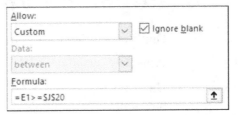

Note that E1 is a relative cell reference (ie it does not have the dollar prefixes $E$1). This is because you want it to adjust to the current row.

For example, when the user enters a percentage into cell F11 you want to check the value in cell E11 against the value in J20. E1 adjusts to E11 as it is relative but $J$20 is always fixed as it is an absolute reference.

6. Add an appropriate *Error Alert*:

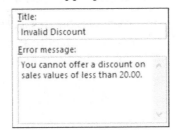

7. Click the *OK* button.

3 Test the validation.

1. Enter a discount into cell F8. Because the value in cell E8 is only 9.00 an error alert is displayed:

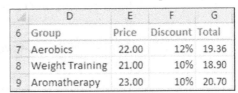

2. Click the *Cancel* button.

3. Change the value in cell E8 to: **21.00**

4. Enter a discount of 10% in cell F8.

    This time the value is accepted.

	D	E	F	G
6	Group	Price	Discount	Total
7	Aerobics	22.00	12%	19.36
8	Weight Training	21.00	10%	18.90
9	Aromatherapy	23.00	10%	20.70

4 Save your work as *Health Club Bookings-7*.

trivia

Spot the famous hybrid names

The names in the *Employees-1* workbook were generated by using Excel's RANDBETWEEN function.

I used this function to randomly mix the first and last names of some of the world's most famous people.

See how many famous half-names you can spot.

Some of them would make really good names for the film stars of the future, while others are definite non-starters.

Lesson 2-13: Remove duplicate values from a table

Duplicate entries are a common problem in data systems of all types.

When tables contain duplicate entries they are said to be corrupt.

Unfortunately, just about every corporate database I've ever worked with has contained corrupt data. You'll almost certainly have to clean up data sets containing duplicate values at some point in your Excel career.

This lesson will show you how to quickly weed out duplicate entries from tables.

Note that the technique taught in this lesson will only work with tables. If you have a range that needs to have duplicate values removed, you will need to first convert it into a table using the skills learned in: *Lesson 1-12: Convert a range into a table and add a total row.*

1   Open *Employees-1* from your sample files folder.

The table contains a list of employees along with their *EmployeeID* (a unique identification number). Every employee should only be listed once but you suspect that the list contains duplicate entries.

	A	B	C
1	EmployeeID	First Name	Last Name
2	362281	Brad	Cruise
3	324794	Ian	Dean
4	998783	Paris	Smith

2   Sort by *EmployeeID* from smallest to largest.

If the list was very short you could manually identify duplicate *EmployeeID* rows by simply sorting column A. This skill was covered in: *Lesson 1-15: Sort a range or table by rows.*

When the numeric EmployeeID values are sorted, part of the problem is instantly revealed:

	A	B	C
1	EmployeeID	First Name	Last Name
2	117362	Johnny	Caine
3	117362	Johnny	Caine
4	118657	George	Marley
5	118657	George	Marley
6	128947	Bill	Spears

Johnny Caine and George Marley clearly have duplicate entries in the table.

3   Automatically remove employees with duplicate *EmployeeID* values.

1.   Click any cell inside the table.

Employees-1

note

A formula-driven approach to identifying duplicate values

Imagine that the problem posed in this lesson occurred in a real-life business scenario involving a large amount of data.

The primitive "sort and look" or "remove duplicates without review" features discussed in this lesson wouldn't provide a reasonable solution.

Here's one way that you could solve the problem.

1. Close the workbook without saving.

2. Re-open the *Employees-1* sample file (this will still contain duplicate Employee ID numbers).

2. Sort *EmployeeID* (column A) from *Smallest to Largest*.

3. Insert a new column to the left of column B.

4. Type: **Duplicate** into cell B1 (the new column's column header).

5. Enter this formula into cell B2:

= A2=A1

The function only returns TRUE if the value in column A is the same as the value above (ie a duplicate entry).

6. Filter column B so that only TRUE values are shown.

The duplicate entries are now revealed:

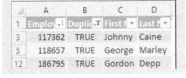

2. Click: Table Tools→Design→Tools→Remove Duplicates.

The *Remove Duplicates* dialog is displayed:

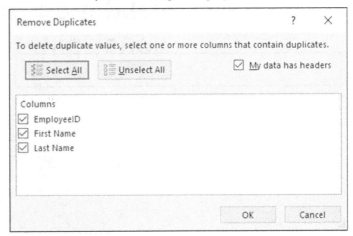

Notice that, by default, Excel has selected every field in the table.

3. Click the *OK* button twice to close both dialogs.

All of the duplicate entries are deleted.

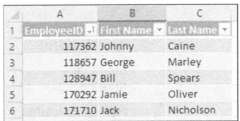

This is a very fast method but not very sophisticated as there's no opportunity to review the values that have been deleted.

In: *Lesson 2-14: Use a custom validation to add a unique constraint to a column,* you'll discover how to catch duplicate entries at the point of entry.

4   Save your work as *Employees-2*.

Lesson 2-14: Use a custom validation to add a unique constraint to a column

You'll often find yourself working with a table or range that contains a column that must have unique values.

For example, consider this list of employees:

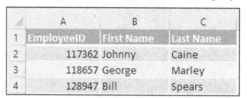

The *EmployeeID* column should never contain the same number listed twice. If it does, an error has occurred because no two employees can have the same *EmployeeID*.

In cases such as this, it would be very useful to refuse to let the user add duplicate values to column A. This type of restriction is called a *unique constraint* and is a fundamental feature of database products such as Microsoft Access, SQL Server and Oracle.

Excel doesn't provide an easy way to apply unique constraints directly (hopefully it will in a later version). Fortunately, there's an easy way to leverage upon the custom validation feature to add this functionality to Excel 365 tables.

1 Open *Employees-2* from your sample files folder (if it isn't already open).

In this table, each employee should have a unique *EmployeeID*. At the moment the table does not enforce this rule.

2 Add a duplicate EmployeeID.

1. Press the **<Ctrl>+<End>** keys to move to the end of the table (cell C120).

2. Press the **<Tab>** key.

If you press the **<Tab>** key in the last cell of a table, a new row is added to the table.

	A	B	C
119	997371	Michal	Marley
120	998783	Paris	Smith
121			

3. Add a duplicate entry for *Paris Smith*.

	A	B	C
119	997371	Michal	Marley
120	998783	Paris	Smith
121	998783	Paris	Smith

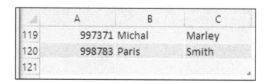

Employees-2

Notice that Excel allows the duplicate entry. In a moment you'll add a unique constraint to make this impossible.

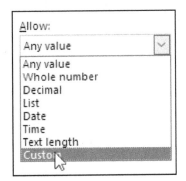

note

The COUNTIF function

The COUNTIF function will be covered in depth later, in: *Lesson 3-6: Use the SUMIF and COUNTIF functions to create conditional totals.*

If you are curious about how it works in this lesson, here's a quick explanation.

COUNTIF(range, criteria)

The COUNTIF function returns the number of cells in a *range* that meet a stated condition (the *criteria* argument).

In this lesson, **A:A** is used for the *range* argument. This means all of the cells in column A.

The relative reference **A2** is used for the *criteria* argument.

The COUNTIF function compares the value in the current row within column A to every other value in column A. It should always result in finding only one value (the value you have entered).

If your entry is unique, the COUNTIF function will return 1. If it is not unique, the function will return a number greater than 1.

As 1=1 is TRUE, the function returns TRUE (passing the validation) when the value is unique and FALSE (failing the validation) when the value is not unique.

3   Delete the duplicate EmployeeID (row 121).

4   Add a unique constraint to column A.

1.   Select all of the table cells in column A except the header row.

A quick way to do this is to click in cell A2 and then press:

<Ctrl>+<Shift>+<DownArrow>

2.   Click: Data→Data Tools→Data Validation.

3.   Click the *Settings* tab.

4.   In the *Allow* drop-down, select *Custom.*

5.   Type the following function into the *Formula* box:

=COUNTIF(A:A,A2)=1

See sidebar for a discussion of the COUNTIF function.

6.   Add an appropriate error alert.

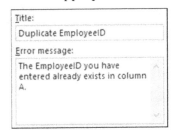

7.   Click the *OK* button.

5   Test the unique constraint.

1.   Attempt to change the *EmployeeID* in row 3 so that it is the same as any existing *EmployeeID*.

Note that you must type the values in. If you copy and paste, the entry is not validated.

2.   Attempt to add a new row at the end of the table with a duplicate ID:

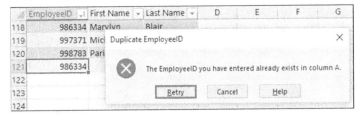

6   Save your work as *Employees-3.*

Session 2: Exercise

1   Open *Sales Performance Analysis-1* from your sample files folder.

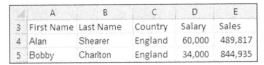

2   Using *Text to Columns*, break the data in the *Salesman* column into two columns: *First Name* and *Last Name*.

Make sure that you also type the column labels **First Name** and **Last Name** into cells A3 and B3.

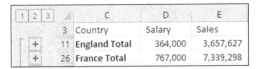

3   Automatically subtotal by *Country,* showing subtotals for *Salary* and *Sales.*

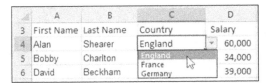

4   Remove the subtotals.

5   Add a validation to column C so that the country may only be entered as *England, France* or *Germany.*

6   Add a user-friendly Error Alert to column C.

Country Error	✕
❌ Invalid Country. Click the drop-down arrow next to the country to see a list of valid entries.	
Retry Cancel Help	

7   Add an input message to column C to inform users which countries are valid.

	A	B	C	D	E
3	First Name	Last Name	Country	Salary	Sales
4	Alan	Shearer	England	▾ 60,000	489,817
5	Bobby	Charlton	England	00	844,935
6	David	Beckham	England	00	766,277
7	Gary	Lineker	England	00	330,707
8	Gordon	Banks	England	00	700,950
9	Kevin	Keegan	England	00	334,433

Country — Country must be France, England or Germany.

8   Save your work as *Sales Performance Analysis-2.*

Sales Performance Analysis-1

If you need help
slide the page to
the left ➡

Session 2: Exercise Answers

These are the four questions that students find the most difficult to answer:

Q 6	Q 5	Q 3	Q 2
1. Select all of column C. 2. Click: Data→ Data Tools→ Data Validation. 3. Click the *Error Alert* tab. 4. In the *Title* box, enter the text: **Country Error** 5. In the *Error message* box, enter the text: **Invalid Country. Click the drop-down arrow next to the country to see a list of valid entries.** 6. Click the *OK* button. You learned how to do this in: *Lesson 2-8: Create user-friendly messages for validation errors.*	1. In cell G3 type the text: **Valid Countries** 2. Type the text: **France, England** and **Germany** into cells G4, G5 and G6. 3. Select all of column C. 4. Click: Data→ Data Tools→ Data Validation. 5. Click the *Settings* tab. 6. Set up the dialog as follows: 7. Click the *OK* button. You learned how to do this in: *Lesson 2-11: Add a table-based dynamic list validation.*	1. Click on any of the countries in column C. 2. Click: Data→Sort & Filter→ A-Z …to sort column C in ascending order. 3. Click: Data→Outline→Subtotal 4. Set up the dialog as follows: 5. Click the *OK* button. You learned how to do this in: *Lesson 2-3: Automatically subtotal a range.*	1. Insert a column to the left of column B. 2. Select cells A4:A34. 3. Click: Data→ Data Tools→ Text to Columns. 4. Leave the data type as *Delimited* and click the *Next* button. 5. Select *Space* in the *Delimiters* option group. 6. Click *Finish*. 7. Type: **First Name** and **Last Name** in cells A3 and B3. You learned how to do this in: *Lesson 2-2: Split delimited data using Text to Columns.*

If you have difficulty with the other questions, here are the lessons that cover the relevant skills:

4   Refer to: *Lesson 2-3: Automatically subtotal a range.*

7   Refer to: *Lesson 2-9: Create data validation input messages.*

3

Session Three: Advanced Functions

> All animals are equal, but some animals are more equal than others.
>
> *George Orwell, "Animal Farm"*
> *English essayist, novelist, & satirist (1903 - 1950)*

There are 477 functions in the Excel 365 function library and more are usually added with each new semi-annual version . This would be a very large book if I tried to cover all of them.

In this session, I'll cover the most important Excel functions and put them into context by demonstrating real-world examples of how they can be used.

With the insights that you'll gain from using these functions, you'll be able to confidently explore the vast array of other functions in Excel's huge library should you ever need them.

Session Objectives

- Understand precedence rules and use the Evaluate feature
- Use common functions with Formula AutoComplete
- Use the Insert Function dialog and the PMT function
- Use the PV and FV functions to value investments
- Use the IF logic function
- Use the SUMIF and COUNTIF functions to create conditional totals
- Understand date serial numbers
- Understand common date functions
- Use the DATEDIF function
- Use date offsets to manage projects using the scheduling equation
- Use the DATE function to offset days, months and years
- Enter time values and perform basic time calculations
- Perform time calculations that span midnight

- Understand common time functions and convert date serial numbers to decimal values
- Use the TIME function to offset hours, minutes and seconds
- Use the AND and OR functions to construct complex Boolean criteria
- Understand calculation options (manual and automatic)
- Concatenate strings using the concatenation operator (&)
- Use the TEXT function to format numerical values as strings
- Extract text from fixed width strings using the LEFT, RIGHT and MID functions
- Extract text from delimited strings using the FIND and LEN functions
- Use a VLOOKUP function for an exact or inexact lookup
- Use an IFERROR function to suppress error messages
- Use the SWITCH, MATCH, INDEX and IFS functions

tip

PEMDAS, BEDMAS, BODMAS and BIDMAS

Maths teachers often use acronyms to help their students to remember the rules of precedence.

In the United States the commonest acronym is **PEMDAS** (often expanded to the mnemonic "Please Excuse My Dear Aunt Sally").

P: Parenthesis first
E: Exponents (ie powers and root extraction)
MD: Multiplication and Division (left-to-right)
AS: Addition and Subtraction (left-to-right)

Canada and New Zealand prefer the term *Brackets* instead of *Parenthesis* producing the acronym: **BEDMAS** (Brackets, Exponents, Division/Multiplication, Addition/Subtraction).

In the UK, Australia and India the terms *Brackets* and *Order* are often preferred producing the acronym: **BODMAS** (Brackets, Order, Division/Multiplication, Addition/Subtraction).

The UK also sometimes prefers the term *Indices* instead of *Exponents* or *Order* producing the acronym: **BIDMAS** (Brackets, Indices, Division/Multiplication, Addition/Subtraction).

The use of these acronyms can cause confusion as students can misinterpret the acronym to suggest that addition has precedence over subtraction. For example, for the expression:

11-2+3

The correct answer is 12 and not 6.

Payroll-1

Lesson 3-1: Understand precedence rules and use the Evaluate feature

Here are Excel's precedence rules:

Operator	Description
Parentheses (brackets)	Any expression in brackets is always evaluated first. **(6+2)*3=24**
Exponent	Exponents are always evaluated next. Exponents tend to be used in engineering/scientific scenarios and are rarely seen in accounting scenarios. **(1+1)*6^2=72**
Multiply and Divide	Multiplication and Division operators have the same precedence and are evaluated from left to right.
Add and Subtract	Addition and Subtraction operators have the same precedence and are evaluated from left to right.

If you only ever work with accounting scenarios, all you really need to remember is:

- Brackets are evaluated first.

- Multiplication and Division are evaluated next.

- Addition and Subtraction are evaluated last.

1   Open *Payroll-1* from your sample files folder.

This worksheet contains some simple formulas required to compute *Net Pay* from *Hours Worked* (see *Payroll Rules* grab on facing page).

Most tax regimes have more complicated rules than those defined in this simple example. Employees are paid the same hourly rate for all hours worked. A different percentage of gross pay is then deducted for Tax, Social Security and Pension contributions.

2   Evaluate the formula in cell B17.

Cell B17 contains the simple formula:

f_x =B15*B4

There's really not much that can go wrong with such a simple formula, but you can see how it works using Excel's evaluation feature.

1.   Click on cell B17.

2.   Click: Formulas→Formula Auditing→Evaluate Formula.

	A	B
1	Payroll	
2		
3	Payroll Rules	
4	Hourly rate	12.00
5	Tax	32%
6	Social Security	8%
7	Pension	5%
8		
9	Day	Hours Worked
10	Monday	10
11	Tuesday	8
12	Wednesday	12
13	Thursday	7
14	Friday	9
15	Total	46
16		
17	Gross	552.00
18	Tax	176.64
19	Social Security	44.16
20	Pension	27.60
21	Net Pay	303.60
22		
23	Net Pay	303.60

The *Evaluate Formula* dialog appears. You can see that the first part of the formula that will be evaluated is **B15**. This is indicated by an underline:

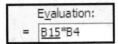

3. Click the *Step In* button. This will show the formula behind cell B15.

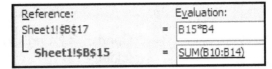

4. Click the *Step Out* button.

   The value in cell B15 now replaces the cell reference:

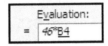

5. Click the *Evaluate* button. The value in cell B4 now replaces the cell reference:

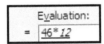

6. Click the *Evaluate* button again. You can now see the result of the evaluation:

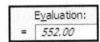

   The *Evaluate* button has now changed its caption to *Restart*. If you wanted to, you could click this button to start the evaluation process all over again.

7. Click the *Close* button.

3 **Evaluate the formula in cell B23.**

To better illustrate precedence rules, a formula that uses a rather long winded way of calculating *Net Pay* has been inserted into cell B23:

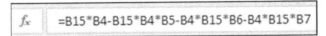

Because of the rules of precedence, the formula works correctly. It could also have been written with parentheses like this:

The parentheses are not needed because the precedence rules state that multiplication happens before subtraction. I still prefer the formula with redundant parentheses (see sidebar).

4 **Save your work as *Payroll-2*.**

tip

Use parentheses to make formulas more readable

I often use parentheses even when they are not needed.

There are two reasons for this:

1. The formula is easier to read.

2. Errors caused by precedence–related mistakes are eliminated.

trivia

The feature that Excel uses to help you out with function calls first made an appearance in Visual Basic 5 back in 1996 and had the wonderful name: *IntelliSense*. The Excel implementation is called *Formula AutoComplete*.

In 1996, I was working in Switzerland developing a ski-school management application. I was extremely impressed by *IntelliSense* as I didn't have to remember hundreds of function names any more. I was even slightly worried that just about anybody could now program (but, of course, I was wrong).

Recently, I was in London being driven by a Hackney cab driver. (Hackney cab drivers know every shortcut and back street in London). He was worried that satellite navigation would now mean that anybody could become a London cabbie.

Of course, he really had nothing to worry about either.

note

If AutoComplete doesn't work

As with so many other features, Microsoft allows you to turn this very useful feature off.

You'd never want to do this, but you may work on a machine that has had *Formula AutoComplete* switched off and need to turn it on again. To do this, click:

File→Options→Formulas→ Working with formulas

…and make sure that the *Formula AutoComplete* box is checked.

The World's Tallest Buildings-1

Lesson 3-2: Use common functions with Formula AutoComplete

The functions most often seen in workbooks are: SUM, AVERAGE, COUNT, MAX and MIN. In this lesson, you'll use Excel's *Formula AutoComplete* feature to add these formulas to a workbook.

1   Open *The World's Tallest Buildings-1* from your sample files folder.

This worksheet contains information about the world's 20 tallest buildings. You'll use the SUM, MAX, MIN, AVERAGE and COUNT functions to populate cells B25:B29.

2   Click into cell B25 and type **=S** into the cell.

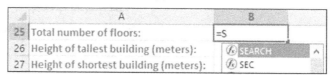

A list appears showing every function in the Excel function library beginning with S. This feature (introduced in Excel 2007) is called *Formula AutoComplete*. (If this didn't work for you, see the sidebar).

3   Continue typing: **=SU**

Notice that the list now only shows functions beginning with SU. You can see the SUM function, three down in the list.

4   Select the SUM function.

There are two methods for selecting the SUM function:

Press the **<Down Arrow>** key twice.

OR

Click on the function name with the mouse.

The SUM function now displays a tip telling you what the function does:

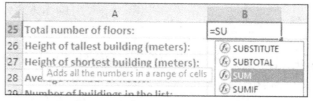

5   Display detailed help for the SUM function.

The tip tells you a little about the SUM function but to get the full story press the **<F1>** key while *SUM* is still highlighted in the dropdown list.

The Excel help system opens, showing detailed help for the SUM function (this will only work if your are connected to the Internet).

This will not work if you are not connected to the Internet as the help system in Excel 365 is only available online.

note

The Syntax box

The Syntax box tells you which arguments (sometimes called parameters) the function needs.

Arguments in square brackets are optional.

In the case of the SUM function, the first argument does not have square brackets, meaning that you can't leave it out.

For such a simple function as SUM, the syntax box is hardly needed, but later you'll discover functions that require several arguments and then the syntax box will be invaluable.

trivia

How the foot got shorter in 1959

This workbook uses the foot-to-meter conversion factor of 0.3048. Before 1959, a foot was slightly longer at 0.3048006096012 meters!

In 1893, the US Office of Weights and Measures (now the National Bureau of Standards) fixed the value of the US foot at 0.3048006096012 Meters. Unfortunately, the rest of the world used a slightly different factor.

Because this caused problems, an international agreement was reached in 1959 to re-define the standard conversion factor at exactly 0.3048 meters, making a post-1959 foot slightly shorter than a pre-1959 foot!

Because the new standard upset existing survey data, it was further agreed that, for geodetic purposes only, the old conversion factor would remain valid. To avoid confusion, survey data is now defined in a new unit called the *US Survey Foot*.

Read the help text if you are interested and then close the help window.

Complete the formula so that you see: **=SUM(**

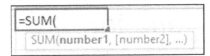

Notice that a little box has appeared beneath the function call. This is the *Syntax box* (see sidebar for more information).

6   Select the cells that you need to sum (cells F4:F23) with the mouse or keyboard.

You can select the cells with the keyboard using the following technique:

1.   Erase the current contents of cell B25 (to start again).

2.   Type: **=SUM(**

3.   Press the **<Up Arrow>** and **<Right Arrow>** keys until you reach cell F4.

4.   Press **<Ctrl>+<Shift>+<Down Arrow>** to select cells F4:F23.

7   Press the **<Enter>** key to finish the formula.

There's no need to type the closing bracket as Excel is clever enough to enter it for you. The total number of floors in all 20 buildings is now displayed in cell B25.

8   Use the same technique to add a MAX function to cell B26.

1.   Click in cell B26.

2.   Type **=MA**

3.   Press the **<Down Arrow>** key once to move the cursor over the MAX function.

4.   Press the **<Tab>** key to automatically enter the MAX function into cell B26.

5.   Select the range D4:D23 using either the mouse or the keyboard.

The formula should now be: **=MAX(D4:D23**

6.   Press the **<Enter>** key.

There's no need to type the closing bracket as, once again, Excel helps you out by entering it automatically.

9   Use the same technique to add MIN, AVERAGE and COUNT functions to cells B27:B29.

	A	B
25	Total number of floors:	=SUM(F4:F23)
26	Height of tallest building (meters):	=MAX(D4:D23)
27	Height of shortest building (meters):	=MIN(D4:D23)
28	Average number of floors:	=AVERAGE(F4:F23)
29	Number of buildings in the list:	=COUNT(D4:D23)

10   Save your work as *The World's Tallest Buildings-2.*

Lesson 3-3: Use the Insert Function dialog and the PMT function

In this lesson, you'll use a complex function with five parameters that will calculate the monthly repayments on a mortgage loan.

1 Open *Mortgage Repayments-1* from your **sample files folder**.

This worksheet contains details of mortgages for loans from 50,000 to 300,000 with a 25-year term and an interest rate of 6.7%. You will use the PMT function to calculate the monthly repayments.

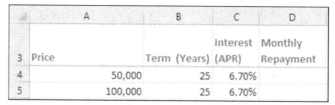

	A	B	C	D
3	Price	Term (Years)	Interest (APR)	Monthly Repayment
4	50,000	25	6.70%	
5	100,000	25	6.70%	

2 Calculate the monthly repayments using the PMT function and the *Insert Function* dialog.

1. Click in cell D4.

2. Click the *Insert Function* button at the left of the formula bar:

The *Insert Function* dialog appears.

3. Type **Loan** into the *Search for a function* text box and then click the *Go* button:

A list of functions is shown in the *Select a function* list. Excel's second best guess is the PMT function. Click once on the PMT function and look at the help text below the list. You can see what the PMT function is used for:

PMT(rate,nper,pv,fv,type)
Calculates the payment for a loan based on constant payments and a constant interest rate.

While the help lets you know what the function does, it is unclear (at this stage) what the arguments mean. Note also that there is a hyperlink pointing to the help page for this function.

Help on this function

The help page provides detailed information about each argument. It is, however, more convenient to obtain interactive help as each argument is entered.

Mortgage Repayments-1

note

What are the Fv and Type arguments used for?

Fv

Fv is the Future Value. It is an amount that will still be owed, or a cash bonus that will be paid to the borrower at the end of the loan. This is sometimes called a balloon payment.

If a positive amount is entered into the Fv box, this amount will be paid to the borrower at the end of the loan.

If a negative amount is entered, it will represent an amount still owed at the end of the loan.

This type of loan is common in vehicle loan agreements and can also be used to model *interest only* mortgages.

Example:

A car is sold for 10,000 across three years. At the end of the three years, the borrower is able to buy the car for 3,000 or to hand it back to the dealer.

To model this loan, the Pv would be 10,000 and the Fv would be -3,000.

Type

Most loans require the repayment to be made at the end of the period (in this example, at the end of each month). Some insurance-backed loans require the repayment to be made at the beginning of the period.

Payments for this type of loan can be calculated by setting the *Type* argument to 1.

	C	D
3	Interest (APR)	Monthly Repayment
4	6.70%	343.88
5	6.70%	687.76
6	6.70%	1,031.64
7	6.70%	1,375.51
8	6.70%	1,719.39
9	6.70%	2,063.27

4. Click the *OK* button.

The *Function Arguments* dialog is displayed.

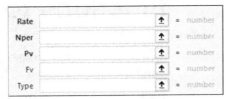

The arguments shown in bold face are required (**Rate, Nper** and **Pv**). The last two arguments are optional (Fv and Type). You won't be using the Fv and Type arguments, but if you are interested in their purpose see the sidebar for more information.

5. Click in the first box (*Rate*). Notice that help is provided at the bottom of the dialog:

> **Rate** is the interest rate per period for the loan. For example, use 6%/4 for quarterly payments at 6% APR.

6. Click in cell C4 and then type **/12**. You need to divide the annual interest rate by twelve to calculate the monthly interest rate.

7. Complete the next two arguments by studying the help text for each. Your dialog should now look like this:

Rate	C4/12	↑	= 0.005583333
Nper	B4*12	↑	= 300
Pv	A4	↑	= 50000

8. Click the *OK* button.

The monthly repayment is now shown in cell D4 but the amount shown is negative. The number is shown as negative because it represents money going out of your account (a negative cash flow).

The PMT function automatically formats the repayment with a currency prefix matching the currency locale on your computer.

9. Click in cell D4 and add a minus operator to the front of the formula:

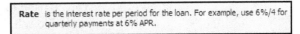

10. Press the **<Enter>** key.

The value is now displayed as a positive number, which is more visually pleasing:

	A	B	C	D
3	Price	Term (Years)	Interest (APR)	Monthly Repayment
4	50,000	25	6.70%	343.88

11. AutoFill the formula to the end of the list to show monthly repayments for all six loan amounts.

3 Save your work as *Mortgage Repayments-2*.

Lesson 3-4: Use the PV and FV functions to value investments

> Compound interest is the eighth wonder of the world. He who understands it, earns it … he who doesn't … pays it
>
> *Albert Einstein, theoretical physicist (1879-1955)*

Present Value

Present Value is the total amount that a series of future payments is worth now.

Present Value can be used to value an existing loan. This would be useful if you wanted to sell the loan to another party.

In this lesson, you will explore the following scenario:

I have loaned my friend John $20,000 to buy a car. John has agreed to repay $1,000 per month for two years (making me $4,000 in interest on the deal). I want to sell the loan on to my other friend Bill. Bill says he is happy to buy it from me, but he needs a return of 12% on his investment. I can use the PV function to work out what the loan is worth today based upon Bill's requirement for a 12% return.

Future Value

Future value is used to work out how much capital will accumulate if a fixed amount is saved each month at a specified compound interest rate.

In this lesson, you will also explore the following scenario:

I save $100 each month towards my retirement fund. If I save for 30 years and the interest rate during this time will be 10%, how much money will I have in my fund upon retirement?

1 Open *Investments-1* from your sample files folder.

This worksheet contains details of the retirement fund and car loan scenarios described above.

2 Use the FV function to calculate the retirement fund value.

In the last lesson, you discovered how to use the *Insert Function* button 𝑓ₓ to access functions in Excel's vast function library.

You can also access the library by using the *Function Library* buttons on the ribbon.

1. Click in cell B7.

2. Click: Formulas→Function Library→Financial→FV.

Notice that when you hover the mouse cursor over the FV option a tip appears showing a short description of the function:

Investments-1

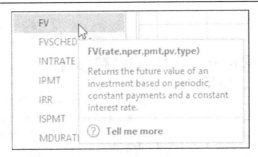

3. Add the correct values to the *Function Arguments* dialog:

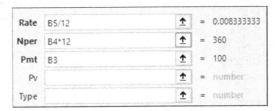

4. Click the *OK* button. The retirement fund is shown as a negative because it represents money leaving your account.

5. Add a minus sign in front of *FV* in the formula bar to convert it to a more visually pleasing positive value:

Although only 36,000 was paid into the retirement fund, compound interest has boosted the amount saved to 226,048.79.

You can now appreciate why Einstein described compound interest as the eighth wonder of the world.

3 **Use the PV function to calculate the value of the car loan.**

1. Click in cell B15.

2. Click: Formulas→Function Library→Financial→PV.

3. Add the correct values to the *Function Arguments* dialog:

4. Click the *OK* button.

5. Add a minus sign in front of *PV* in the formula bar to convert it to a positive value:

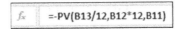

6. Press the **<Enter>** key. The result is 21,243.39 so you turned a profit on the deal!

(The *Fv* and *Type* arguments are discussed in: *Lesson 3-3: Use the Insert Function dialog and the PMT function*).

4 **Save your work as *Investments-2*.**

tip

Eliminating divide by zero errors with the IF function

I'm often asked how it is possible to avoid the unsightly divide by zero errors in worksheets:

#DIV/0!

The IF function provides an easy solution. By testing the divisor for a zero value, the error can be eliminated.

Here's an example:

You wish to divide A1 by B1 but the formula:

=A1/B1

... gives divide by zero errors when B1=0.

Replace the formula with:

=IF(B1=0,0,A1/B1)

This time no attempt is made to divide by zero when B1=0, eliminating divide by zero errors.

You could also use the IF function to provide a custom error message like this:

=IF(B1=0,"Divide by Zero Error",A1/B1)

This technique is very useful when you only want to test for a divide by zero error.

Later in this session (in: *Lesson 3-24: Use an IFERROR function to suppress error messages*) you'll learn a different technique to suppress all types of error messages, including divide by zero errors.

Earnings Summary-1

Lesson 3-5: Use the IF logic function

The IF function is one of Excel's most widely used and useful functions. It is also a function that often confuses my students, so I'll begin this lesson by explaining the concept of the logical test. Later, you'll construct a worksheet containing three examples of the IF function at work.

The IF function requires a *logical test* and then performs one action if the test returns TRUE and a different action if the test returns FALSE.

Here are some examples of logical tests:

Expression	Returns	Why?
6=2	FALSE	Because six does not equal two.
100<90	FALSE	Because 100 is not less than 90.
6+2 = 4+4	TRUE	Because eight does equal eight.

In this lesson, you'll use three different logical tests in order to calculate several employees' earnings during a week.

1 Open *Earnings Summary-1* from your sample files folder.

Notice the *Payroll Rules* section:

	A	B	C	D	E	F
3	Payroll Rules:					
4	All hours up to 35 hours per week paid at hourly rate					
5	All hours over 35 hours per week paid at time and a half (150% of hourly rate)					
6	Bonus of 5% paid on all sales above target					

Logical tests will be constructed to calculate *Standard Pay, Overtime Pay* and *Bonus*:

	A	B	C	D	E	F	G	H	I
8	Name	Sales	Target	Hourly Rate	Hours Worked	Standard Pay	Overtime Pay	Bonus	Total
9	Brad Cruise	22,000	10,000	15.00	40				

2 Use an IF function to calculate standard pay.

In the case of *Standard Pay*, the logical test will be:

"Did this employee work more than 35 hours this week?"

The formula for the logical test is: **E9<=35** (cell E9 is less than or equal to 35).

If this returns *TRUE*, then standard pay will be:

*Hours Worked * Hourly Rate*, (E9*D9)

…because the employee worked for 35 hours or less.

If this returns **FALSE**, then standard pay will be:

*35*Hourly Rate* (35*D9)

… because the employee worked more than 35 hours (and the first 35 hours of this time will be paid at standard rate).

tip

Avoid nesting IF functions

Here's an example of a two-level nested IF function:

=IF(A31="Apples",10%,IF(A31="Lemons",20%,0))

This would return 10% if the value in A31 was *Apples*, 20% if the value was *Lemons* and zero if the value was anything else. Note that the words *Apples* and *Lemons* are enclosed in quotation marks. You must refer to text in this way within Excel formulas.

Whenever you see nested IF functions be aware that there is almost surely a better, less complex, less error-prone and more elegant solution.

Excel allows you to nest IF functions up to 64 levels deep (which is 63 too many).

Most problems that you will find solved with a nested IF function could be better solved using a VLOOKUP function. This function will be covered later, in: *Lesson 3-22: Use a VLOOKUP function for an exact lookup.*

The above problem could also be better solved using either a SWITCH or IFS function. These functions will be covered later, in:

Lesson 3-23: Use the SWITCH function

… and

Lesson 3-28: Use the IFS function.

1. Click in cell F9.

2. Click: Formulas→Logical→IF.

   The *Function Arguments* dialog appears.

3. Complete the dialog as follows:

Logical_test	E9<=35	↑	=	FALSE
Value_if_true	E9*D9	↑	=	600
Value_if_false	35*D9	↑	=	525

   If you do not completely understand why the above formulas are used, read the introduction to this lesson again.

4. Click the *OK* button.

   Standard Pay is correctly displayed in cell F9 (525.00).

3   Use an IF function to calculate overtime pay in cell G9.

It should now be clear to you why the correct arguments for the IF function, this time, are:

Logical_test	E9<=35	↑	=	FALSE
Value_if_true	0	↑	=	0
Value_if_false	(E9-35)*D9*1.5	↑	=	112.5

(The *Value_if_false* argument would have worked in exactly the same way if you had used a value of 150% instead of 1.5 as Excel recognizes both as having the same value but different formats).

4   Use the IF function to calculate the bonus in cell H9.

Once again, it should be clear to you why the correct arguments for the IF function this time are:

Logical_test	B9>C9	↑	=	TRUE
Value_if_true	(B9-C9)*5%	↑	=	600
Value_if_false	0	↑	=	0

5   Add a formula to cell I9 to calculate total pay.

The correct formula could be either of the following:

=F9+G9+H9
=SUM(F9:H9)

6   AutoFill the formulas in cells F9:I9 to cells F10:I17.

The payroll worksheet is now complete.

	A	B	C	D	E	F	G	H	I
8	Name	Sales	Target	Hourly Rate	Hours Worked	Standard Pay	Overtime Pay	Bonus	Total
9	Brad Cruise	22,000	10,000	15.00	40	525.00	112.50	600.00	1,237.50
10	Ian Dean	9,000	8,000	13.00	35	455.00	-	50.00	505.00
11	Paris Smith	10,000	12,000	15.00	42	525.00	157.50	-	682.50

7   Save your work as *Earnings Summary-2*.

Lesson 3-6: Use the SUMIF and COUNTIF functions to create conditional totals

note

The SUMIFS and COUNTIFS functions

The SUMIFS and COUNTIFS functions work in exactly the same way as the SUMIF and COUNTIF functions used in this lesson but they accept multiple criteria.

For example, if you needed to know the combined total salary for Male employees in the *Sales* department, you'd set the SUMIFS arguments as follows:

SUMIFS	
Sum_range	C4:C17
Criteria_range1	D4:D17
Criteria1	"Sales"
Criteria_range2	B4:B17
Criteria2	"M"

tip

Quickly make a range reference absolute

Many users type in those little dollar signs by hand, which is very time consuming.

Here's a great time saver:

1. Select the entire range reference (for example **D4:D17**).

2. Press the **<F4>** key once. The range is then converted to absolute (for example **$D$4:$D$17**).

If you press the **<F4>** key more than once, you'll cycle through all possible mixed cell references for the range.

Headcount & Salaries-1

In the previous lesson, you used the IF logical function to return different values based upon a logical test that returned TRUE or FALSE.

SUMIF and COUNTIF are similar functions but are used to sum or count values within a range based upon a similar logical test.

This lesson's sample workbook lists all of an organization's employees along with their gender and department:

	A	B	C	D
3	Name	Sex	Salary	Department
4	Johnny Caine	M	37,864	Sales
5	George Marley	M	26,148	Purchasing
6	Betty Anan	F	26,345	Logistics
7	Paris Winfrey	F	23,562	Sales

You'll use the SUMIF and COUNTIF functions to list the total salary and headcount for each department, along with the total salary and headcount for each gender.

1   Open *Headcount & Salaries-1* from your sample files folder.

2   Use the SUMIF function to calculate the total salary for each department.

    1.   Click in cell B21.

    2.   Click: Formulas→Function Library→Math & Trig→SUMIF.

      The *Function Arguments* dialog appears.

      There are three arguments for the SUMIF function:

      The *Range* argument defines the range in which to look for the department name. In this case, it is the range D4:D17 (the cells containing the *Departments*).

      The *Criteria* argument is the thing to look for within the stated range. In this case, it is the word "Sales" contained in cell A21.

      The *Sum_range* argument is the range containing numerical data that needs to be added up when the criteria is true. In this case, it is the range C4:C17 (the cells containing *Salary* values).

    3.   Complete the dialog with the following arguments:

Range	$D$4:$D$17	⬆
Criteria	A21	⬆
Sum_range	$C$4:$C$17	⬆

note

Using wildcards in logical criteria

Sometimes you will only have a partial idea of what you need to find.

In this case, you can use the wildcard characters – the asterisk (*) and the question mark (?). It is easiest to explain how wildcards work with a few examples:

C*g	Finds **Containing**
	Finds **Citing**
	Finds **Changing**
S?d	Finds **Sid**
	Finds **Sad**
	Finds **Syd**
	Finds **Sud**

In the above examples, you can see that the first search finds all words that begin with C and end with g. The second example only finds three letter words that begin with S and end with d.

Later in this session, in: *Lesson 3-18: Concatenate strings using the concatenation operator (&),* you'll learn about concatenating strings. After this lesson, you will understand the following examples:

Imagine you have a range containing the values:

22 Cherry Walk
144 Cherry Road
Cherry Tree House
Cherry Tree Lodge

... and you want to construct a COUNTIF or SUMIF function based upon the partial string contained in cell A1 (for this example, let's imagine that the word *Cherry* is in cell A1).

The criteria would be:

"*" & A1 & "*"

This would find all four values.

To find values that begin with the word *Cherry*, you would use the criteria:

A1 & "*"

This would find two values.

Note the use of absolute references for each range. This will allow you to AutoFill the function for the *Purchasing* and *Logistics* totals.

4. Click the *OK* button.

5. AutoFill cell B21 to cells B22:B23 to display the total salaries for the *Purchasing* and *Logistics* departments.

3   **Use the COUNTIF function to calculate the headcount for each department.**

COUNTIF works in exactly the same way as SUMIF but returns a count of all cells that match the criteria.

1. Click in cell C21.

2. Click: Formulas→Function Library→ More Functions→Statistical→COUNTIF.

3. Complete the dialog with the following arguments:

Range	$D$4:$D$17	↑
Criteria	A21	↑

4. Click the *OK* button.

5. AutoFill cell C21 to cells C22:C23 to display the headcount for the *Purchasing* and *Logistics* departments.

4   **Use SUMIF and COUNTIF functions to calculate the salary and headcount for male and female employees in cells B27:C28.**

Use exactly the same technique as you did for *Salary* and *Headcount by Department*. The correct arguments for cells B27 and C27 are:

Range	$B$4:$B$17	↑
Criteria	A27	↑
Sum_range	$C$4:$C$17	↑

And:

Range	$B$4:$B$17	↑
Criteria	A27	↑

	A	B	C
20	Department	Salary	Headcount
21	Sales	179,898	6
22	Purchasing	137,557	5
23	Logistics	73,601	3
24	Total:	391,056	14
25			
26	Gender	Salary	Headcount
27	M	253,587	9
28	F	137,469	5
29	Total:	391,056	14

5   **Save your work as *Headcount & Salaries-2*.**

trivia

The Julian and Gregorian calendars

When you work with very old dates, you can run into a problem with the Julian and Gregorian calendars.

In 1582 it was noticed that the seasons had drifted by 10 days because the Julian system (named after Julius Caesar who adopted it in 45 BC) had incorrectly miscalculated a year as being 365 ¼ days. A year is actually slightly shorter than this.

Pope Gregory XIII decreed that, in order to put things right, the world had to lose 10 days to make up for all of those extra leap years.

The reformed Gregorian calendar also adopted a new leap year rule to keep things on track in future years.

It took nearly 200 years for everybody to get on board with the Gregorian calendar. The Catholic countries of Spain, Italy and Portugal adopted it at once, but England and parts of America didn't convert until September 14th 1752.

This means that in Spain the dates October 5th 1582 to October 14th 1582 never actually existed. In England it was the dates Sept 3rd 1752 to September 14th 1752.

The strangest case of all was Sweden who decided to "phase it in gradually" between 1700 and 1740, meaning that their calendar was out of step with the rest of the world for 40 years.

If you work with historical data from this era you have to be very careful indeed.

Lesson 3-7: Understand date serial numbers

This lesson was included in the *Essential Skills* book in this series and has also been included in this book as a recap. A full understanding of the date serial number concept is essential in order to understand the date and time functions that will be introduced in later lessons.

Excel stores dates in a very clever way. Understanding Excel's date storage system empowers you to use date arithmetic. You can use date arithmetic to compute the difference between two dates (in days) or to shift date ranges by a given time interval.

How Excel stores dates

Dates are stored as simple numbers called *date serial numbers*. The serial number contains the number of days that have elapsed since 1st January 1900 (where 1st January 1900 is 1).

The world began in 1900

An interesting shortcoming of Excel is its inability to easily work with dates before 1900. Excel simply doesn't acknowledge that there were any dates before this time. If you work with older dates, you will have to work-around this limitation.

In Excel, every time is a date, and every date is a time

You've already realized that 5th January 1900 is stored as the number 5. What would the number 5.5 mean? It would mean midday on 5th January 1900.

It is possible to format a date to show only the date, only the time, or both a time and a date.

When you enter a time into a cell without a date, the time is stored as a number less than one. Excel regards this as having the non-existent date of 00 January 1900!

When you enter a date into a cell without a time, the time is stored as midnight at the beginning of that day.

1 Create a new blank workbook and put the numbers 1 to 5 in cells A1:A5.

2 Type the formula **=A1** into cell B1 followed by the **<Enter>** key, and then AutoFill the formula to the end of the list.

	A	B
1	1	1
2	2	2
3	3	3
4	4	4
5	5	5

https://thesmartmethod.com

trivia

The peculiar case of the Excel date bug and Lotus 1-2-3

Here's the Gregorian leap year rule as defined in 1582 by Pope Gregory XIII:

Every year that is exactly divisible by four is a leap year, except for years that are exactly divisible by 100; the centurial years that are exactly divisible by 400 are still leap years.

This means that the year 1900 wasn't a leap year, but 2000 was (causing many millennium software bugs).

The designers of Lotus 1-2-3 weren't paying enough attention to Pope Gregory's rules. Their DATE() function thought that 1900 was a leap year and thus recognized the mythical date February 29th 1900.

Because Excel needed to be compatible with Lotus 1-2-3, Microsoft had to replicate the Lotus bug when they designed Excel.

Try entering 29th Feb 1900 into a worksheet and Excel will gladly accept it.

This bug has the effect of introducing a one-day error into any date arithmetic you may do that spans 29th February 1900.

3 Apply a date format to column A that will show a four-digit year.

	A	B
1	Sunday, January 1, 1900	1
2	Monday, January 2, 1900	2

This reveals that the numbers 1 to 5 represent the dates 1-Jan-1900 to 05-Jan-1900.

4 Set a custom format of **dd mmm yyyy hh:mm** for the dates in column A (to show both dates and times).

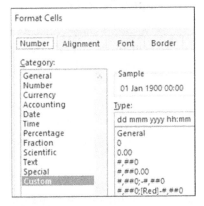

Notice that when you enter a date without a time, the time is set to midnight at the beginning of that day.

	A	B
1	01 Jan 1900 00:00	1
2	02 Jan 1900 00:00	2

5 Change the time in cell A2 to: **12:00:00 PM**

Notice that the number in cell B2 has changed to 2.5, showing that times are stored by Excel as the decimal part of a number.

	A	B
1	01 Jan 1900 00:00	1
2	02 Jan 1900 12:00	2.5

6 Compute the number of days that occurred between 01 Jan 1900 and 01 Jan 2000.

Now that you have a good grasp of Excel's serial numbers, this task is easy.

1. Enter the two dates in cells A7 and A8, one beneath the other.

2. Subtract one date from the other by entering the formula: **=A8-A7** into cell A9.

3. Format cell A9 to display numeric (rather than date) values.

7	Sunday, January 1, 1900
8	Saturday, January 1, 2000
9	36,525.00

You now know that 36,525 days occurred during the last century (actually 36,524 due to the Lotus 1-2-3 bug – see sidebar).

7 Close the workbook without saving.

Lesson 3-8: Understand common date functions

Excel's primary date functions are TODAY, DAY, MONTH and YEAR. In the previous lesson, you gained an understanding of how Excel stores dates as serial numbers. You can now use this knowledge in conjunction with the above date functions to create some very useful date related formulas.

1   Open *Resources-1* from your sample files folder.

   This worksheet contains a list of Employees along with their dates of birth.

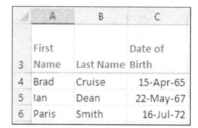

2   Use the YEAR function to calculate the year in which each employee was born.

   1.   Click in cell D4.

   2.   Click: Formulas→Function Library→Date & Time→Year.

      The *Function Arguments* dialog is displayed.

   3.   Click in cell C4.

      Because you know that all dates are represented by a serial number, and because cell C4 contains a date, this reference will cause the YEAR function to return 1965 (the year Brad Cruise was born).

      Notice that the dialog previews the result as = *1965* and also lets you know that the date serial number for 15th April 1965 is *23,847*.

   4.   Click the *OK* button.

      The year in which Brad Cruise was born is now displayed in cell D4.

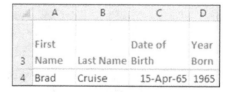

3   Use the DAY function to place the day when Brad Cruise was born into cell E4.

https://thesmartmethod.com

4   Use the MONTH function to calculate the month when Brad Cruise was born into cell F4.

	D	E	F
3	Year Born	Day Born	Month Born
4	=YEAR(C4)	=DAY(C4)	=MONTH(C4)

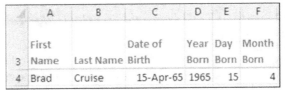

	A	B	C	D	E	F
3	First Name	Last Name	Date of Birth	Year Born	Day Born	Month Born
4	Brad	Cruise	15-Apr-65	1965	15	4

5   Use the TODAY function to place a volatile current date into cell G4.

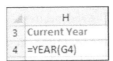

	G			G
3	Today		3	Today
4	=TODAY()		4	26-Jun-19

The TODAY function returns the current date. The date is volatile. This means that if you were to open this worksheet again tomorrow, you would see tomorrow's date in cell G4.

6   Use the YEAR function to place the current year into cell H4.

By using the value in cell G4 as the argument for the YEAR function, it is possible to insert the current year into cell H4.

Because the value in cell G4 is volatile, the value in H4 is also volatile. This means that if this worksheet was opened again in the year 2020, you would see the value 2020 in cell H4.

	H			H
3	Current Year		3	Current Year
4	=YEAR(G4)		4	2019

7   Add a formula to cell I4 to calculate the employee's maximum age this year.

Calculating the employee's current age from their date of birth using the YEAR, MONTH and DAY functions is quite a feat (although it can be done). You'll discover an easy way to do this in the next lesson using a different technique.

In this lesson, you'll simply calculate what the employee's maximum age will be this year with a simple subtraction of the year born from the current year.

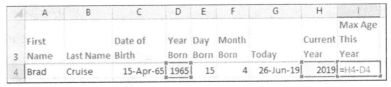

	A	B	C	D	E	F	G	H	I
3	First Name	Last Name	Date of Birth	Year Born	Day Born	Month Born	Today	Current Year	Max Age This Year
4	Brad	Cruise	15-Apr-65	1965	15	4	26-Jun-19	2019	=H4-D4

8   AutoFill cells D4:I4 down to row 12.

9   Save your work as *Resources-2*.

© 2020 The Smart Method® Ltd

---

tip

Entering a non-volatile current date

The TODAY function is very useful, but it inserts a volatile date. In other words, the date will change each day to reflect the current date.

You'll often want to place the current date into a worksheet in a non-volatile way. For example, where you want to include a *Date Created* cell at the top of the worksheet, but you never want this date to change.

The easiest way to do this is to use the **<Ctrl>+<;>** (Control + semicolon) shortcut key.

note

Calculating max age this year from date of birth with a single formula

The example in this lesson is deliberately laborious as the goal is to introduce each of the common date functions one at a time.

In a real world worksheet, you could alternatively calculate the *maximum age this year* from date of birth with a single formula like this:

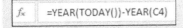

| f_x | =YEAR(TODAY())-YEAR(C4) |

note

Why calculating age from date of birth is so difficult

I've seen some weird and wonderful attempts to calculate age from date of birth in my student's worksheets.

At first, it doesn't seem such a big deal. The first solution that occurs is to simply convert each date to days and then divide by 365. Like this:

(TODAY() – BirthDate)/365

If it wasn't for leap years, this would work. To overcome the leap year issue, I've seen solutions based upon the assumption that a year is, on average, 365.25 days long. So why won't this work?

(TODAY() – BirthDate)/365.25

There are two reasons why.

The first reason is that the date may belong to a child who has not yet lived through a leap year.

The second reason is caused by the Gregorian leap year rule that skips a leap year in centurial years (see: *Lesson 3-7: Understand date serial numbers*, sidebar).

Lesson 3-9: Use the DATEDIF function

Three may keep a secret, if two of them are dead.

Benjamin Franklin (1706 - 1790)

One of the most useful date-related functions available in Excel is the DATEDIF function. For some reason this is a secret, and you'll find nothing about this wonderful function anywhere in the Excel 365 documentation. Some have speculated that this may be for legal reasons as the function was originally included for compatibility with Lotus 1-2-3.

Microsoft documented the function in Excel 2000 so, in their spirit of backward compatibility, they continue to support it in Excel 365 and can be expected to also support it in all future Excel versions.

DATEDIF is able to calculate the difference between two dates for several intervals. In this lesson, you'll use it to calculate an age from a date of birth. This is hugely complex using the YEAR, MONTH and DAY functions (see sidebar).

Because you probably don't have a copy of the Excel 2000 manual, here is the syntax for the function:

=DATEDIF(StartDate, EndDate, Interval)

StartDate: The first date.

EndDate: The second date.

Interval: The interval to return, such as the number of months or years between the two dates.

The interval arguments are:

"m"	Months between two dates.
"d"	Days between two dates.
"y"	Years between two dates.
"ym"	Months between two dates, ignoring the year (ie as if both dates were the same year).
"yd"	Days between two dates, ignoring the year.
"md"	Days between two dates, ignoring the months and years.

1   Open *Resources-2* from your sample files folder (if it isn't already open).

2   Change the text in cell I3 to: **Age (Years)**

Resources-2

note

Calculating age from date of birth using the YEARFRAC and INT functions

Excel is also able to calculate an age from a date of birth using the INT and YEARFRAC functions.

YEARFRAC returns the number of years between two dates expressed as a fraction.

The syntax is:

YEARFRAC(start_date,end_date,basis)

In this lesson's sample file, you would use the function (in cell I4) like this:

=YEARFRAC(C4, G4, 1)

The last argument (basis) tells Excel to take leap years into account when calculating the fractional part of the year.

In this lesson's sample file YEARFRAC produced these results (on 26th June 2019):

	A	B	I
3	First Name	Last Name	Age (Years)
4	Brad	Cruise	54.198
5	Ian	Dean	52.096

This means that Brad Cruise was 53.198 years old.

In: *Lesson 1-8: Apply an advanced filter with function-driven criteria*, you learned about the INT function. This returns the whole number portion of a number. For example, **=INT(25.99)** would return the whole number **25**.

In the example above, the formula:

=INT(I4)

… would return **54** (Brad Cruise's age).

You could also combine the two functions like this:

=INT(YEARFRAC(C4, G4, 1))

---

3 Delete cells I4:I12.

	C	D	E	F	G	H	I
3	Date of Birth	Year Born	Day Born	Month Born	Today	Current Year	Age (Years)
4	15-Apr-65	1965	15	4	26-Jun-19	2019	
5	22-May-67	1967	22	5	26-Jun-19	2019	
6	16-Jul-72	1972	16	7	26-Jun-19	2019	

4 Add the following formula to cell I4:

=DATEDIF(C4,TODAY(),"y")

Notice that *Formula AutoComplete* doesn't even want to admit that this function exists.

The function works by comparing the date of birth (in cell C4) with today's date (returned by the TODAY function) and returns the interval between the date of birth, and today's date, in years.

5 Calculate each resource's precise age in years, months and days.

This requirement illustrates the use of the "ym" and "md" arguments.

1. Type the text: **Age (Months)** into cell J3.

2. Type the text: **Age (Days)** into cell K3.

3. Match the formatting of cells J3 and K3 to that in cell I3.

   (Formatting is an elementary skill covered in the *Essential Skills* book in this series).

	E	F	G	H	I	J	K
3	Day Born	Month Born	Today	Current Year	Age (Years)	Age (Months)	Age (Days)
4	15	4	26-Jun-19	2019	54		

(You will probably see a different age depending upon whatever today's date is at the time you read this book).

4. Add the following formula to cell J4:

   =DATEDIF(C4,TODAY(),"ym")

5. Add the following formula to cell K4:

   =DATEDIF(C4,TODAY(),"md")

6. AutoFill cells I4:K4 to the end of the range.

	A	B	C	D	I	J	K
3	First Name	Last Name	Date of Birth	Year Born	Age (Years)	Age (Months)	Age (Days)
4	Brad	Cruise	15-Apr-65	1965	54	2	11
5	Ian	Dean	22-May-67	1967	52	1	4

The above was calculated on 26th June 2019. They'll all be a little older by the time you complete this exercise.

6 Save your work as *Resources-3*.

---

note

Project Management and Excel

Excel is often misused to manage projects.

Project Management involves scheduling tasks and assigning resources to complete each task. For example, to build a house you would have tasks such as *lay bricks* and *fit windows*.

Each task has a *start* and *end* date, along with one or more *dependencies* (for example you cannot fit the windows until you have laid the bricks).

Each task also has one or more *resources* assigned to it (for example you may assign Bill and Bob to lay the bricks and Colin to fit the windows).

The best way to illustrate a project plan is the Gantt chart, named after Henry Gantt (1861–1919). It is quite easy to produce a primitive Gantt chart using Excel (but not a true Gantt chart showing inter-task dependencies).

Now that you understand Excel's date functions, you might think that Excel is a great tool for managing projects – but there's a far, far better way.

Microsoft Project is a tool designed specifically to manage projects and produce excellent Gantt charts.

If you have complex workbooks that seek to manage the type of scenario described above, you really should check out Microsoft Project – it is a superb tool.

Many students that attend my Project Management courses have first tried hard and failed using Excel.

Lesson 3-10: Use date offsets to manage projects using the scheduling equation

In this lesson, you'll use date offsets in conjunction with the scheduling equation to create a worksheet that will manage a small project.

In order to understand project management, you need to first understand the scheduling equation:

Time = Work/Units

Let's pose the age-old primary school math problem:

"If it takes one man ten days to dig a hole, how long will it take two men to dig the same hole"?

The answer is, of course, five days (in mathematics, if not in reality).

To use the scheduling equation, each unit can be described (in this example) as being a man and the work can be defined in days.

In the first example:

10 days = 10 days/1 Man

In the second example:

5 days = 10 days/2 Men

If you increase your estimate of 10 days work, then the time will increase. If you add more men to the task, then the time will decrease, as the equation will always balance.

In this lesson, you'll learn how to create formulas that will enable task lengths to dynamically re-scale as you either add more resources to each task, or revise your estimate for the amount of work needed to complete each task.

1   Open *Project-1* from your sample files folder.

The worksheet contains a simple project plan consisting of four linked tasks:

	A	B	C	D
3	Task Name	Start date	Work (Man-Days)	Units
4	Dig Foundations	15-Jun-16	3	3
5	Pour Footings		2	1
6	Lay Bricks to DPC		8	4
7	Pour floor slab		2	1

Each task has a *start to finish dependency*. This means that each task must complete before the following task can begin.

2   Calculate the *End Date* for the first task.

Enter the formula: **=B4+C4/D4-1** into cell E4.

Note that, because of the rules of precedence, this is the equivalent of **=B4+(C4/D4)-1**

Project-1

important

Refining the example worksheet

The example presented in this lesson is very simple as its aim is to teach the use of date offsets (rather than to create a useful project management system).

Here are some of the worksheet's shortcomings:

1. If you assign more units to a task than there is work, the task will finish in the past.

This could be overcome by adding a MAX function to column E as follows:

=MAX(B4+C4/D4-1,B4)

This would ensure that the *End Date* of a task could never be earlier than the *Start Date*.

2. The worksheet can only deal with whole days.

With the refinement suggested above:

(a) When a task ends early in the day all workers are assumed to stop work for the day (rather than move to the next task).

(b) Where *Work/Units* does not result in a whole number the *End Date* will not be accurately calculated.

For example, if 7 men were allocated to a 8 man-day task, the worksheet would assume that the task would be completed in one day (as 0.875 is not a whole number).

This could be overcome by adding a formula-driven custom validation to column D that would only allow *Units* to be entered when *Work/Units* produced a whole number result.

Formula-driven validations were covered in: *Lesson 2-10: Add a formula-driven date validation and a text length validation.*

(Precedence was covered in: *Lesson 3-1: Understand precedence rules and use the Evaluate feature*).

One day is subtracted because a job of one day's duration will begin and end on the same day. The formula calculates the *End Date* using the scheduling equation discussed at the beginning of this lesson (see sidebar for a more in-depth discussion).

	A	B	C	D	E
			Work		
3	Task Name	Start date	(Man-Days)	Units	End Date
4	Dig Foundations	15-Jun-16	3	3	15-Jun-16
5	Pour Footings		2	1	
6	Lay Bricks to DPC		8	4	
7	Pour floor slab		2	1	

The *End Date* is 15-Jun-16 because three men have been assigned to a task that has three man-days' work. The task thus takes one day to complete and so begins and ends on the same day.

3 **Test the scheduling equation.**

If you were to take two men off the job, the single remaining man would take three days to complete the task.

1. Change the value in cell D4 to 1.

   Notice that the task now takes three days to complete.

	A	B	C	D	E
			Work		
3	Task Name	Start date	(Man-Days)	Units	End Date
4	Dig Foundations	15-Jun-16	3	1	17-Jun-16

2. Revise your estimate of the work to 8 Man-Days and assign two men to the task.

   This time, the task takes four days to complete.

	A	B	C	D	E
			Work		
3	Task Name	Start date	(Man-Days)	Units	End Date
4	Dig Foundations	15-Jun-16	8	2	18-Jun-16

4 **Add a formula to show the start date for the *Pour Footings* task.**

The start date of the *Pour Footings* task will be the day after the end date of the *Dig Foundations* task.

Enter the formula: **=E4+1** into cell B5.

5 **AutoFill cells B5 and E4 to the end of the range.**

You now have a dynamic project plan that will adjust the end date of the project based upon your work estimates and the number of resources that you assign to each task.

	A	B	C	D	E
			Work		
3	Task Name	Start date	(Man-Days)	Units	End Date
4	Dig Foundations	15-Jun-16	8	2	18-Jun-16
5	Pour Footings	19-Jun-16	2	1	20-Jun-16
6	Lay Bricks to DPC	21-Jun-16	8	4	22-Jun-16
7	Pour floor slab	23-Jun-16	2	1	24-Jun-16

6 **Save your work as *Project-2*.**

Lesson 3-11: Use the DATE function to offset days, months and years

Now that you understand the TODAY, DAY, MONTH and YEAR functions, you will be able to use the DATE function to dynamically manage more sophisticated date offsets.

1   Open *Service Schedule-1* from your sample files folder.

In this example, the service schedule requires that vehicles are inspected 20 days after first supply, 3 months after the 20-day inspection, and then every year thereafter.

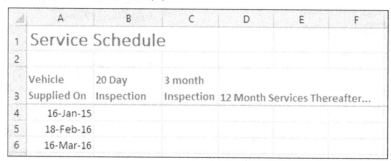

	A	B	C	D	E	F
1	Service Schedule					
2						
3	Vehicle Supplied On	20 Day Inspection	3 month Inspection	12 Month Services Thereafter...		
4	16-Jan-15					
5	18-Feb-16					
6	16-Mar-16					

2   Put a formula in cell B4 that will calculate the date for the 20-day inspection based upon the date in cell A4.

1. Type **=D** into cell B4.

The DATE function is the first in the drop-down list:

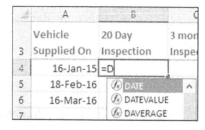

	A	B	C
3	Vehicle Supplied On	20 Day Inspection	3 mor Inspe
4	16-Jan-15	=D	
5	18-Feb-16	*fx* DATE	
6	16-Mar-16	*fx* DATEVALUE	
7		*fx* DAVERAGE	

2. Press the **<Tab>** key to enter the formula into the cell.

3. Click the *Insert Function* button on the left of the formula bar:

fx =DATE(

The *Function Arguments* dialog is displayed.

The DATE function demands three numerical arguments: *Year, Month* and *Day.* For example:

=DATE(2019,11,26)

... would return 26th November 2019.

Because the DATE function requires numerical arguments, you need to use the YEAR, MONTH and DAY functions to convert each part of the date into numbers.

tip

You can also use the keyboard shortcut:

<Ctrl>+<A>

...to bring up the *Function Arguments* dialog when you are entering a function.

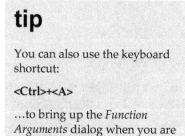

Service Schedule-1

4. Complete the dialog as follows:

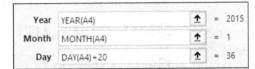

Notice that in the *Day* argument, the number 20 has been added to 16 create 36 for the day argument. You can see from the argument result values on the right of the above grab that you are requesting the date: *36th January 2015*. This is not, of course, a valid date.

Fortunately, Excel is intelligent enough to understand that you really require the date: *5th February 2015*.

5. Click the *OK* button.

A date is shown that is 20 days after 16th January 2015:

3 Put a DATE formula in cell C4 that will calculate a date that is three months later than the 20-day inspection date.

This time your dialog should look like this:

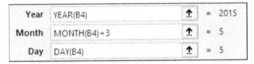

4 Put a DATE formula in cell D4 that will calculate a date that is one year later than the 3-month inspection date.

This time your dialog should look like this:

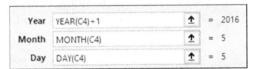

5 AutoFill the formula in cell D4 to cells E4:G4.

6 AutoFill the formulas in cells B4:G4 to the end of the range.

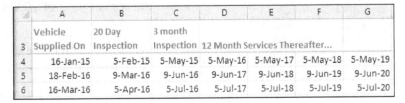

7 Save your work as *Service Schedule-2*.

important

Why do my times and dates look different from the ones in the screen grabs?

The default formats for times and dates are based upon the *Region Settings* set up in Windows. To view your regional settings:

Type: *Region settings* into the Windows 10 search box and then click *Region settings*.

Windows then displays your current Regional format data:

Short date:	6/26/2019
Long date:	Wednesday, June 26, 2019
Short time:	5:26 PM
Long time:	5:26:30 PM
Change data formats	

The above settings are the default regional formats for the *United States* region. These are the settings used for all of the screen grabs in this book.

Short date:	26/06/2019
Long date:	26 June 2019
Short time:	17:24
Long time:	17:24:45
Change data formats	

The above settings are the default regional formats for the *United Kingdom* region.

There's also a *Change Data Formats* hyperlink that allows you to change the formats if you wish.

These are, of course, only the defaults and you will normally apply a specific format to times as you do at the end of this lesson.

If your region format is set to another country there is no need to change it. Just be aware that some of the screen grabs in this book will be formatted differently to those on your screen.

Time Sheet-1

Lesson 3-12: Enter time values and perform basic time calculations

Serial number recap

In: *Lesson 3-7: Understand date serial numbers,* you learned how Excel combines time and date information in a single date serial number.

Excel represents dates by counting from 1st January 1900 to the present day. For example, the date serial number 2.0 represents midnight (00:00) on 2nd January 1900.

Excel represents time using the decimal part of the serial number. For example, the date serial number 3.5 represents midday on 3rd January 1900.

Excel also allows you to work with pure time values (times that do not have an associated date). In this case, the non-existent date of 0 Jan 1900 is used. For example, the date serial number 0.3333 represents the time 08:00 but does not represent any date.

In this lesson, you'll focus on entering time values into a worksheet without any associated date and learn how to avoid the mistakes commonly made when working with time values.

1 Open *Time Sheet-1* from your sample files folder.

This worksheet contains details of the hours worked by an employee during a single week.

2 Add a start time of 08:00 and finish time 17:00 for Monday.

24-hour notation is the best way to enter times as it is the least error prone and easiest to read.

Type **08:00** into cell B8 and **17:00** into cell C8.

	A	B	C
7	Day	Start	Finish
8	Monday	8:00	17:00

3 Add a start time of 10:00 AM and finish time 6:00 PM for Tuesday.

AM/PM notation is preferred by some users, but is more error prone than the recommended 24-hour notation.

Type **10:00 AM** into cell B9 and **6:00 PM** into cell C9. Make sure that you leave a space between the time and the AM/PM indicator, otherwise Excel will interpret the value as text rather than time.

	A	B	C
7	Day	Start	Finish
8	Monday	8:00	17:00
9	Tuesday	10:00 AM	6:00 PM

4 Complete the rest of the time sheet as follows:

	A	B	C
7	Day	Start	Finish
8	Monday	8:00	17:00
9	Tuesday	10:00 AM	6:00 PM
10	Wednesday	21:00	3:00
11	Thursday	10:00 PM	4:00 AM
12	Friday	8:00	17:00

Depending upon your *Windows Region settings*, your dates and times may display differently to those shown above. See the sidebar on the facing page for more information about how your regional settings affect the default format of dates and times.

5 Examine the date serial numbers in cells B8:C12.

1. Select cells B8:C12.

2. Right-click the selected cells and click *Format Cells...* from the shortcut menu.

3. Click *General* in the *Category* list.

4. Click the *OK* button.

Notice that all of the time values begin with zero. This is because no date is associated with them. Understanding this is very important when creating time formulas.

Notice that the time in cell B8 is 0.333333. This is because at 08:00 approximately 33.333333% of the day has elapsed, as eight hours is approximately 33.333333% of 24.

6 Add a formula to cell D8 that will calculate the number of hours worked.

Add the formula **=C8-B8** to cell D8.

	A	B	C	D
7	Day	Start	Finish	Hours Worked
8	Monday	0.333333	0.708333	0.375

The result shows that Frank worked for 37.5% of the day on Monday.

7 Format cells B8:D12 to show times in the 24-hour format.

1. Select cells B8:D12.

2. Right-click the selected cells and click *Format Cells...* from the shortcut menu.

3. From the *Custom* category, set the format to: **hh:mm**

4. Click the *OK* button.

The number of hours and minutes worked is now shown in cell D8.

	A	B	C	D
7	Day	Start	Finish	Hours Worked
8	Monday	8:00	17:00	9:00
9	Tuesday	10:00	18:00	

8 Save your work as *Time Sheet-2*.

---

tip

You can also return to *General* format using the shortcut key:

<Ctrl>+<Shift>+<~>

(Control + Shift + Tilde)

tip

Converting time serial numbers to decimal values

In this lesson, you subtracted 08:00 from 17:00, giving a result of 0.375, representing 9 hours as 37.5% of one 24-hour day.

Sometimes, it is convenient to express times as simple decimal numbers (in this case as 9.0). In order to convert a time serial number to a numeric value representing hours, you simply multiply the serial number by 24:

24*37.5% = 9.0 hours

tip

You can also open the *Format Cells* dialog using the shortcut key:

<Ctrl>+<1>

	A	B	C
7	Day	Start	Finish
8	Monday	8:00	17:00
9	Tuesday	10:00	18:00
10	Wednesday	21:00	3:00
11	Thursday	22:00	4:00
12	Friday	8:00	17:00

Lesson 3-13: Perform time calculations that span midnight

1   Open *Time Sheet-2* from your sample files folder (if it isn't already open).

2   AutoFill the formula in cell D8 to cells D9:D12.

	A	B	C	D
7	Day	Start	Finish	Hours Worked
8	Monday	8:00	17:00	9:00
9	Tuesday	10:00	18:00	8:00
10	Wednesday	21:00	3:00	#############
11	Thursday	22:00	4:00	#############
12	Friday	8:00	17:00	9:00
13	Total:			

A problem is now revealed. On Wednesday and Thursday, Frank's working times spanned midnight. A row of hashes is shown to signify an error as Excel cannot display a time value that is negative (Frank's Wednesday hours would result in minus 18 hours worked).

3   Correct the formulas in cells D8:D12 so that time is correctly calculated, even when the times span midnight.

Fortunately, it is very easy to correct the formula using the IF logic function covered in: *Lesson 3-5: Use the IF logic function.*

1. Change the formula in cell D8 to the following:

   =IF(C8>B8, C8-B8, C8+1-B8)

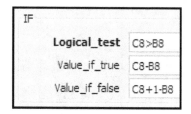

   The formula works by adding the number one (representing one day) to the finish time when the finish time is earlier than the start time.

2. AutoFill the formula from cell D8 to cells D9:D12.

   The times are now correctly calculated:

	A	B	C	D
7	Day	Start	Finish	Hours Worked
8	Monday	8:00	17:00	9:00
9	Tuesday	10:00	18:00	8:00
10	Wednesday	21:00	3:00	6:00
11	Thursday	22:00	4:00	6:00
12	Friday	8:00	17:00	9:00

4   Add a formula to show the total hours worked this week in cell D13.

Add a SUM function to cell D13 to sum the values in cells D8:D12.

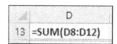

	D
13	=SUM(D8:D12)

Time Sheet-2

The formula doesn't return an error but it seems to produce the wrong answer:

	A	B	C	D
7	Day	Start	Finish	Hours Worked
8	Monday	8:00	17:00	9:00
9	Tuesday	10:00	18:00	8:00
10	Wednesday	21:00	3:00	6:00
11	Thursday	22:00	4:00	6:00
12	Friday	8:00	17:00	9:00
13	Total:			14:00

tip

Another way to sum time serial numbers that exceed 24 hours

In this lesson, you use the **[h]:mm** custom format to display the time data correctly.

The value of **1.5833** then correctly displayed as **38:00**.

The value 1.5833 actually means 158.33% of a 24-hour day, so another method of correcting the result would be to multiply it by 24:

=SUM(D8:D12)*24

...and then to format cell D13 as a number.

The advantage of this method is that it is often easier to work with numerical values than with date serial numbers if you need to perform further mathematical calculations.

You'll see this technique in action in: *Lesson 3-14: Understand common time functions and convert date serial numbers to decimal values.*

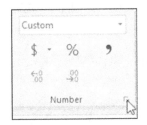

tip

You can also open the Format Cells dialog using the shortcut key:

<Ctrl>+<1>

The value in cell D13 is actually correct. The problem lies in the way in which cell D13 is formatted.

Remember that the date serial numbers in cells D8:D12 contain the percentage of each 24-hour day that was worked. When they are added together they will add up to more than one. Because cell D13 is formatted to show times, it will ignore the whole number part of the date/time serial number, believing that this represents a date.

The actual value in cell D13 is 1.583333 and that represents 14:00 on 1st January 1900.

5 **Display the value in cell D13 correctly by adjusting the format.**

There are two ways to solve this problem. In this lesson a custom format is used. The other potential method is discussed in the sidebar.

Because adding time values is a common requirement, Excel provides a special custom format to display times that exceed 24 hours.

1. Click on cell D13.

2. Click: Home→Number→Dialog Launcher.

   The *Format Cells* dialog appears.

3. Click the *Custom* category.

   Notice that the current format is: **hh:mm**

4. Manually type in the new custom format: **[h]:mm**

   The square brackets around the [h] means that where there is a whole number in the date serial number it should be regarded as time data.

   For example, the date serial number 2.0 will be interpreted as meaning 48 hours and not midnight on 2nd January 1900. The serial number 1.5 will be interpreted as 36 hours and not midday on 1st January 1900.

5. Click the *OK* button.

   The *total hours worked* in cell D13 now displays correctly:

	A	B	C	D
11	Thursday	22:00	4:00	6:00
12	Friday	8:00	17:00	9:00
13	Total:			38:00

6 **Save your work as *Time Sheet-3*.**

Lesson 3-14: Understand common time functions and convert date serial numbers to decimal values

Excel's primary time functions are NOW, HOUR, MINUTE and SECOND. In this lesson, you'll learn how to use all of them along with some important techniques that are useful when performing calculations with time values.

1   Open *Time Sheet-3* from your sample files folder (if it isn't already open).

2   Add formulas to cells E8:E12 to calculate earnings.

This isn't as straightforward as it first seems.

The actual values in cells D8:D12 represent the percentage of each day that was worked. For example, cell D9 actually contains the value 0.333333, as eight hours are approximately 33.3333% of one 24-hour day.

In order to calculate the correct earnings figure, it is necessary to multiply the date serial number in column D by 24 to convert the date serial number into hours.

1.   Type the formula: **=D8*24*$B$5** into cell E8.

Note the absolute reference for cell B5. This will enable the formula to be AutoFilled to the cells below without adjusting the reference to cell B5.

2.   AutoFill the formula in cell E8 down to cells E9:E12.

3.   Select cells E8:E13.

4.   Click: Home→Number→Comma Style 🔢 to show two decimal places.

The correct earnings figure is now shown in every case.

5.   Use a SUM function to show total earnings for the week in cell E13.

	A	B	C	D	E
5	Hourly Rate:	15.00			
6					
7	Day	Start	Finish	Hours Worked	Earnings
8	Monday	8:00	17:00	9:00	135.00
9	Tuesday	10:00	18:00	8:00	120.00
10	Wednesday	21:00	3:00	6:00	90.00
11	Thursday	22:00	4:00	6:00	90.00
12	Friday	8:00	17:00	9:00	135.00
13	Total:			38:00	570.00

3   Add a NOW function to cell B15 to display the current date and time.

Time Sheet-3

1.   Type **Current Date and Time** into cell A15.

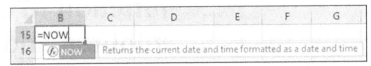

tip

Entering a non-volatile current time

The NOW function is very useful but it inserts a volatile date and time. This means that the date and time will change to reflect the current date and time whenever the worksheet opens or is recalculated.

You'll often want to place the current date and time into a worksheet in a non-volatile way. For example, where you want to include a *Date and Time Created* cell at the top of the worksheet, but you never want this date and time to change.

To enter the current time into a cell, press the keys:

<Ctrl>+<Shift>+<;>

(Control plus Shift plus semicolon)

To place the current date into a cell press the keys:

<Ctrl>+<;>

(Control plus semicolon)

tip

Recalculate the workbook or a single sheet using a shortcut key

To recalculate the entire workbook, press:

<F9>

If you have a very large workbook with multiple pages and hundreds of formulas, it can take a significant time to recalculate. In this case, you can recalculate only the currently selected worksheet by pressing:

<Shift>+<F9>

2. Click on cell B15.

3. Type **=NOW**

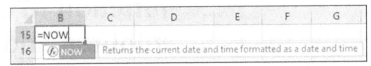

The tip advises that this function returns the current date and time. This is a little like the TODAY function encountered in *Lesson 3-8: Understand common date functions* except that it returns the current date *and* time rather than midnight on the current date.

The current date and time is the time that the worksheet was last recalculated (you'll learn how to recalculate the worksheet later in this lesson).

4. Press the **<Tab>** key twice. Notice that Excel has added brackets for you to create the formula: **=NOW()**

5. If necessary, widen columns A and B so that they are wide enough to see all of their contents.

	A	B
15	Current Date and Time	6/26/2019 18:01

4 Add a TIME function to cell B16 to display the current time.

The TIME function works in a similar way to the DATE function encountered in: *Lesson 3-10: Use date offsets to manage projects using the scheduling equation.*

1. Type **Current Time** into cell A16.

2. Click in cell B16.

3. Click: Formulas→Function Library→Date & Time→TIME.

The *Function Arguments* dialog is displayed.

4. Enter the following values for each argument:

5. Click the *OK* button.

The current time appears in cell B16.

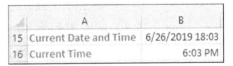

5 Re-calculate the worksheet to update the current time.

Click: Formulas→Calculation→Calculate Sheet.

Provided that at least a minute has passed since you created the NOW and TIME functions, you will see the time update to the current time.

6 Save your work as *Time Sheet-4*.

Lesson 3-15: Use the TIME function to offset hours, minutes and seconds

In this lesson, you will use the TIME function in conjunction with the HOUR, MINUTE and SECOND functions to offset time data.

You'll construct a train timetable that will run a service every 10 minutes before 09:00 and every hour thereafter.

1 Open *Train Timetable-1* from your sample files folder.

The formulas in this worksheet will be constructed so that the entire timetable can be automatically updated by simply changing the *First Train* times in column B.

This will work because all of the subsequent journeys will be defined as offsets from the first train's arrival time using the TIME function.

	A	B	C	D	E	F	G
3	Trains run every 10 minutes before 09:00 and every hour at other times.						
4							
5	Route	First Train	Further trains at...				
6	Northern	8:30					
7	Jubilee	8:20					

2 Put formulas into cells C6:K6 that will calculate the arrival times of subsequent trains on the Northern line.

You know that trains arrive every 10 minutes before 09:00 so would expect trains at 08:40, 08:50 and 09:00. After that, you would expect trains each hour at 10:00, 11:00, 12:00...

1. Click in cell C6.

2. Click: Formulas→Function Library→Date & Time→TIME.

The *Function Arguments* dialog appears.

3. Enter the following values for each argument:

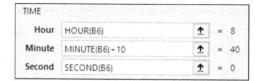

4. Click the *OK* button.

The correct time of the next train appears in cell C6.

	A	B	C	D
5	Route	First Train	Further trains at...	
6	Northern	8:30	8:40	

5. AutoFill the formula in cell C6 to cells D6:K6.

Unsurprisingly, the formula applies an offset of 10 minutes to each cell:

Train Timetable-1

	A	B	C	D	E	F
5	Route	First Train	Further trains at...			
6	Northern	8:30	8:40	8:50	9:00	9:10

Unfortunately, that isn't what is needed. After the 09:00 train there shouldn't be another until 10:00.

To fix the formula, you need to add an IF function that will check the time of the previous train. If the time is later than or equal to 09:00, the increment should be one hour and not 10 minutes (the IF function was covered in: *Lesson 3-5: Use the IF logic function*).

6. Copy the function from cell C6 *excluding the = sign* by clicking in cell C6, selecting the function in the formula bar (but not the = sign) and then copying (by pressing **<Ctrl>+<C>** or by right-clicking and then selecting *Copy* from the shortcut menu).

7. Press the **<ESCAPE>** key to exit cell edit mode

8. Click cell C6 again and then press the **<Delete>** key to remove the existing formula from the cell.

9. Click: Formulas→Function Library→Logical→IF.

   The *Function Arguments* dialog is displayed.

10. Paste the function (previously copied) into the **Value_if_true** and **Value_if_false** text boxes.

    The dialog should now look like this:

11. Set the Logical_test argument to:

    HOUR(B6)>=9

12. Edit the *Value_if_true* argument so that it offsets the previous train time by one hour rather than ten minutes:

    TIME(HOUR(B6)+1,MINUTE(B6),SECOND(B6))

13. Click the *OK* button.

14. AutoFill cell C6 to cells D6:K6.

3 AutoFill cells C6:K6 down to cells C7:K10 to complete the timetable.

The timetable is now complete and correct:

	A	B	C	D	E	F	G
5	Route	First Train	Further trains at...				
6	Northern	8:30	8:40	8:50	9:00	10:00	11:00
7	Jubilee	8:20	8:30	8:40	8:50	9:00	10:00
8	Circle	8:27	8:37	8:47	8:57	9:07	10:07

4 Save your work as *Train Timetable-2*.

note

The NOT logical function

This session introduces the two Excel logical functions:

AND
OR

There's another logical function that can sometimes make your formulas easier to read (though it is never actually necessary).

This is the NOT function that will invert a logical result.

In other words, it will change TRUE to FALSE and FALSE to TRUE.

The rule:

If Sales > Target AND Years Service > 2

OR

Years Service > 5

Could also be written as:

If Sales > Target AND NOT Years Service < 2

OR

Years Service NOT < 5

Lesson 3-16: Use the AND and OR functions to construct complex Boolean criteria

When using logical functions such as IF, COUNTIF and SUMIF, you need to construct a logical test (sometimes also called Boolean criteria) that will return TRUE or FALSE.

You've already used simple Boolean criteria such as:

E9<=35

This Boolean expression returns TRUE if the value in cell E9 is less than or equal to 35, otherwise it returns FALSE.

In this lesson, you'll use the logical functions AND and OR to create more complex Boolean criteria.

The sample file for this lesson computes bonuses for employees, based upon the following rules:

Bonus rules
A bonus of 2% of sales will be paid to employees who meet the following criteria:
1/ Sales are above target.
2/ Have worked for the company for more than two years.
Note: *Employees with more than five years service will receive the bonus even if sales are below target.*

Here are the bonus figures for the first three employees:

	A	B	C	D	E
9	Name	Years service	Sales	Target	Bonus
10	Johnny Caine	2	11,000	9,000	-
11	George Marley	7	7,000	9,000	140
12	Betty Anan	3	13,000	5,000	260

- You can see that Johnny Caine exceeded his target but received no bonus because he only has two years' service.

- George Marley has over five years' service and thus receives a bonus even though he didn't reach his sales target.

- Betty Annan has three years' service and she has also exceeded her sales target, so she receives a bonus.

Another way of expressing the logical test that governs when bonus will be paid is:

If Sales > Target AND Years Service > 2
OR
Years Service > 5

A logical expression can be created to implement the rules using Excel's AND and OR functions.

Here's how you can use the AND function to test that Johnny Caine's sales are above his target AND that he has more than two years' service:

Bonus Calculator-1

=AND(C10>D10, B10>2)

The AND function will return TRUE only if both expressions evaluate TRUE. In Johnny's case, it will return FALSE because Johnny only has two years' service.

You also need to check whether the employee has over five years' service. Here's how you can use the OR function to do this:

=OR(B10>5, AND(C10>D10, B10>2)**)**

The OR function will return TRUE if either of the arguments return TRUE. In Johnny's case, this will still return FALSE as he also has less than five years' service, but in George's case it would return TRUE since George has seven years' service.

Now that you understand how to construct the logical test for the bonus calculation, you can create the IF function for the sample file.

1   Open *Bonus Calculator-1* from your sample files folder.

    1. Click in cell E10.

    2. Click: Formulas→Function Library→Logical→IF.

    3. Enter the following values into the dialog (see text above for explanation):

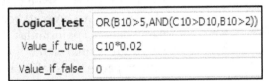

Logical_test	OR(B10>5,AND(C10>D10,B10>2))
Value_if_true	C10*0.02
Value_if_false	0

    4. Click the *OK* button.

    5. AutoFill the formula from cell E10 to the end of the range.

	A	B	C	D	E
9	Name	Years service	Sales	Target	Bonus
10	Johnny Caine	2	11,000	9,000	-
11	George Marley	7	7,000	9,000	140
12	Betty Anan	3	13,000	5,000	260
13	Paris Winfrey	1	11,000	10,000	-
14	Ozzy Dickens	5	9,000	9,000	-
15	Johnny Roberts	2	6,000	7,000	-
16	Charles Monroe	8	10,000	5,000	200

2   Save your work as *Bonus Calculator-2*.

note

Gross profit and mark up

Newcomers to the retail business often confuse mark up with gross profit.

In general business, gross profit is the more widely accepted metric when discussing profits.

Here's an example of mark up:

Bob buys a watch for $500 and marks it up by 50%. This means that he adds 50% to the cost price and sells it for $750. In this case, the formula is:

Selling Price = Cost Price * (1+MarkUp)

$750 = $500 * 1.5

Here's an example of gross profit:

Bill buys a hard disk for $100. His company needs to make 50% gross profit on all goods sold. This means that they need to sell the hard drive for $200, making 50% of the selling price ($100) in profit. In this case, the formula is:

Selling Price = Cost Price/ (1-Gross Profit%)

$200 = $100/(1-0.5)

You can see from the above example that a gross profit of 50% is the same as a mark up of 100%.

Terminology

I use the terms *Gross Profit* when discussing both cash amounts and percentages.

There's a lot of controversy about correct terminology. Some purists would argue that the correct terms are *Gross Margin* (or simply *Margin*) for *% Gross Profit*, and *Gross Profit* for a Gross Profit cash value.

Classic Watches-1

Lesson 3-17: Understand calculation options (manual and automatic)

It is possible to change the calculation mode used by Excel. The three modes available are:

1. *Automatic:* Whenever you change the value in a cell, all values that reference that cell are automatically recalculated. This is the default.

2. *Automatic except for data tables:* This is similar to *Automatic*, but data tables will only be recalculated when the **<F9>** key is pressed. (you will learn about data tables later, in*: Lesson 5-1: Create a single-input data table*).

3. *Manual:* Calculation will only take place when the **<F9>** key is pressed.

Most users are unaware that the calculation options exist and leave Excel set to the default *Automatic* at all times.

So why would you ever need the other two options? The answer is that Excel worksheets can be very large indeed (over a million rows and over 16,500 columns). A workbook could contain many millions (or even many billions) of formulas. Such a workbook is very unusual, but could take a substantial amount of time to recalculate. You wouldn't want to have to pause for recalculation every time you edited any cell in such a workbook, so you would switch to one of the other two calculation modes under those circumstances.

1   Open *Classic Watches-1* from your sample files folder.

This worksheet calculates the selling prices for a classic watch dealer.

	A	B	C	D	E
5			Gross Profit	33%	
7	Description	Date	Cost price	Selling Price	Profit
8	Breitling Duograph 18K	1948	11,500.00	17,164.18	5,664.18
9	Cartier Tank 18K	1974	3,200.00	4,776.12	1,576.12
10	Rolex Tudor Oyster	1966	300.00	447.76	147.76

The dealer makes 33% Gross Profit (sometimes also called *Margin, Gross Margin* or *Gross Profit Margin*) on all watch sales (see sidebar for a discussion of the difference between gross profit and mark up).

The formula in column D:

=C8/(1-$D$5)

... calculates the selling price based upon the gross profit stated in cell D5.

2   Change the gross profit to 25%.

When the value in cell D5 is changed to 25%, the worksheet recalculates to show the new selling prices.

important

Calculation mode is set at application level

It would be quite reasonable to assume that the calculation mode could be set for a specific worksheet or workbook. Unfortunately, Excel doesn't work in this way, causing great confusion amongst users who begin to believe that Excel is randomly changing the calculation mode.

You can't set the calculation mode for a single worksheet or workbook. When you change the calculation mode, it also changes for all other worksheets and all other open workbooks.

Consider the following scenario:

1/ You create a workbook and set the calculation mode to *Manual*.

2/ You then open another workbook without closing the first one. The second workbook is also in manual calculation mode because only one calculation mode can exist for all open workbooks.

Things become even more confusing because the calculation mode is saved with the workbook.

Suppose that you had two workbooks called *Manual* and *Automatic*. The first was saved in manual calculation mode and the second saved in automatic calculation mode.

If you open the *Manual* workbook followed by the *Automatic* workbook, then both workbooks will be set to *Manual* calculation mode, as this was the mode of the first workbook opened.

If you open the *Automatic* workbook followed by the *Manual* workbook, then both workbooks will be set to *Automatic* calculation mode.

	A	B	C	D	E
5			Gross Profit	25%	
7	Description	Date	Cost price	Selling Price	Profit
8	Breitling Duograph 18K	1948	11,500.00	15,333.33	3,833.33
9	Cartier Tank 18K	1974	3,200.00	4,266.67	1,066.67
10	Rolex Tudor Oyster	1966	300.00	400.00	100.00

This is exactly what you would expect because this workbook is using the default *automatic* calculation mode.

3   Change the calculation mode to manual.

Click: Formulas→Calculation→Calculation Options→Manual.

4   Change the gross profit to 30%.

This time nothing happens to the other values, because the worksheet will only recalculate when you explicitly request a recalculation.

	A	B	C	D	E
5			Gross Profit	30%	
7	Description	Date	Cost price	Selling Price	Profit
8	Breitling Duograph 18K	1948	11,500.00	15,333.33	3,833.33
9	Cartier Tank 18K	1974	3,200.00	4,266.67	1,066.67
10	Rolex Tudor Oyster	1966	300.00	400.00	100.00

5   Manually recalculate the workbook.

EITHER

Press the <F9> key.

OR

Click: Formulas→Calculation→Calculate Now.

The workbook recalculates to show the new selling prices at 30% gross profit.

	A	B	C	D	E
5			Gross Profit	30%	
7	Description	Date	Cost price	Selling Price	Profit
8	Breitling Duograph 18K	1948	11,500.00	16,428.57	4,928.57
9	Cartier Tank 18K	1974	3,200.00	4,571.43	1,371.43
10	Rolex Tudor Oyster	1966	300.00	428.57	128.57

Note that you can also click:

Formulas→Calculation→Calculate Sheet

You would use this option to save calculation time when other worksheets in the workbook contained large numbers of formulas. In the case of this simple workbook (that contains only one worksheet), there is no calculation time difference between using *Calculate Now* and *Calculate Sheet*.

6   Change the calculation mode back to automatic.

Click: Formulas→Calculation→Calculation Options→Automatic.

7   Save your work as *Classic Watches-2*.

note

ASCII

ASCII (pronounced Askey) is an acronym for: *American Standard Code for Information Interchange.*

In 1968, the US President (Lyndon B. Johnson) ordered that all computers purchased by the United States Federal Government must support ASCII.

ASCII defines a number (between 0 and 127) for the numbers **0-9**, lowercase letters **a** to **z**, uppercase letters **A** to **Z**, basic punctuation symbols, the space character, and 33 non-printable control characters (many of which are now obsolete).

For example, the ASCII code for an upper-case **A** character is 65.

Excel has two ASCII related functions:

CHAR(number)

This function returns an ASCII character from the corresponding ASCII code. For example:

=CHAR(65)

... would result in an upper-case **A** character appearing in the cell.

CODE(text)

This function returns an ASCII code number from a character. For example:

=CODE("A")

... would return the number 65 (the ASCII code number for an upper-case A).

Lesson 3-18: Concatenate strings using the concatenation operator (&)

About strings

In the world of computers, letters, numbers, spaces, punctuation marks and other symbols are referred to as *characters*.

When several characters are grouped together (perhaps to spell out words), they are referred to as a *string*.

Here are some examples of strings:

Abc123

John Smith

Strings may be of any length, from a single character to thousands of words.

The concatenation operator (&)

When numbers are added together, the addition operator (+) is used to return the sum of the numbers. For example, the formula:

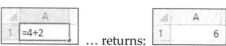 ... returns:

The concatenation operator joins two strings together. For example, the formula:

 ... returns:

Concatenation is rarely used with numbers. It is more likely that you may wish to concatenate *Title*, *First Name* and *Last Name* cells to produce a full name. For example:

 ... returns:

Note the use of double quotation marks to indicate that each value is a string.

In this example, it would be nice to have spaces between each of the words. To do this, you would concatenate a string containing only a space between each word. Here's how it's done:

 ... returns:

1   Open *Classic Watches-2* from your sample files folder (if it isn't already open).

Classic Watches-2

note

Using a control code to add a line break

In the (previous page) sidebar, it was stated that there are 33 non-printable control characters defined by ASCII, many of which are now obsolete.

Two of these control codes can sometimes be very useful when you need to create a formula that outputs multiple-line text. These are:

Line Feed (ASCII 10)
and
Carriage Return (ASCII 13)

The term *Carriage Return* comes from the age of mechanical typewriters. In computer terms it is a control code that is used to move the cursor to the first position on the same line. A *Carriage Return* control code is often used with a *Line Feed* control code in order to begin a new line. This sequence is often referred to as CRLF (or, in Excel terms, =CHR(10) & CHR(13).

To force a line break in a cell Excel only requires a line feed.

Here's an example of concatenating an ASCII 10 control code (in a cell with word-wrap enabled) in order to force a line break:

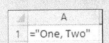

Results in:

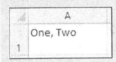

... While

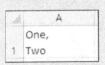

Results in:

	A
1	One, Two

2   Type **Classified Ad** into cell F7 and apply the *Heading 3* style.

To apply the *Heading 3* style, select cell F7 and then click:

Home→Styles→Style Gallery→Titles and Headings→Heading 3

Cell styles were covered in depth in Session 4 of the *Essential Skills* book in this series.

Cells F8:F17 will contain text to be included in a classified ad listing in the local newspaper. You want to show the description of the watch, the year of manufacture and the selling price.

	A	B	C	D	E
7	Description	Date	Cost price	Selling Price	Profit
8	Breitling Duograph 18K	1948	11,500.00	16,428.57	4,928.57

3   Round the values in cells D8:D17 to the nearest five dollars.

The Breitling Duograph is priced at $16,428.57. It would be cleaner to round all of the prices up (or down) to the nearest five dollars. This can easily be achieved using the MROUND (multiple round) function.

1.   Change the formula in cell D8 from:

=C8/(1-$D$5)

TO

=MROUND(C8/(1-$D$5),5)

2.   AutoFill the formula to the end of the range.

4   Use the concatenation operator to place the classified ad into cell F8 in the format:
Breitling Duograph 18K (1948) -$16,430

As described in the introduction to this lesson, this can easily be achieved using the concatenation operator. The correct formula is:

f_x	=A8 & " (" & B8 & ") -$" & D8

This very nearly provides the required result:

	E	F	G	H	I
7	Profit	Classified Ad			
8	4,930.00	Breitling Duograph 18K (1948) -$16430			

The only thing that isn't correct is the comma thousand separator in the cash price of the watch ($16430 should be $16,430). In the next lesson, you'll discover how to solve this problem using the TEXT function.

5   AutoFill the formula in cell F8 to cells F9:F17.

	E	F	G	H	I
7	Profit	Classified Ad			
8	4,930.00	Breitling Duograph 18K (1948) -$16430			
9	1,370.00	Cartier Tank 18K (1974) -$4570			
10	130.00	Rolex Tudor Oyster (1966) -$430			

6   Save your work as *Classic Watches-3*.

Lesson 3-19: Use the TEXT function to format numerical values as strings

Custom format strings recap

The TEXT function allows numbers to be explicitly formatted as strings. The *Essential Skills* book in this series extensively covers the (rather cryptic) formatting codes available in Excel.

Zeroes are used in formatting codes to define the number of decimal places that are required, along with leading and trailing zeroes. Here are some examples (reproduced from the *Essential Skills* book).

Custom Format String	Value	Display
0	1234.56	1235
0.0	1234.56 1234.5 .5	1234.6 1234.5 0.5
0.00	1234.56 1234.5 .5	1234.56 1234.50 0.50
00.000	4.56	04.560
0.000	1234.56	1234.560

The hash symbol (#) is mainly used to add comma separators to thousands and millions. Here are some examples (once again, reproduced from the *Essential Skills* book).

Custom Format String	Value	Display
#	123.4500	123
#.##	123.45 123.50	123.45 123.5
#,#	1234.56	1,235
#,#.##	1234.56 1234.50 12341234.56	1,234.56 1,234.5 12,341,234.56

Because the hash symbol can be used in conjunction with zeroes, it is also possible to indicate that you want both thousand separators *and* a specific number of leading or trailing zeroes.

Custom Format String	Value	Display
#,#0.00	12341234.5	12,341,234.50

Classic Watches-3

note

The TEXTJOIN function

The (hugely useful) TEXTJOIN function is unfamiliar to most Excel 365 users as it was only added in February 2016.

The TEXTJOIN function syntax is:

TEXTJOIN(delimiter, ignore_empty, text1, [text2], …)

This new function makes it very easy to add spaces or commas between text strings. Here is an example:

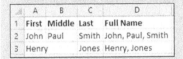

In the above example a TEXTJOIN function has been placed in cell D2 and then AutoFilled down to cell D3.

The argument values used were:

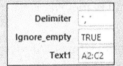

The *Delimiter* argument has been specified as a comma followed by a space.

The *Ignore_empty* argument prevents two commas from being added between *Henry* and *Jones*.

The TEXTJOIN function's ability to simply concatenate a range will solve many concatenation problems that would previously have been very tedious using the CONCAT (or older CONCATENATE) functions.

1 Open *Classic Watches-3* from your sample files folder (if it isn't already open).

2 Delete the contents of cells F8:F17.

3 Use the CONCAT function to place the classified ad into cell F8 in the format:
Breitling Duograph 18K (1948) - $16,430

The concatenation operator (&) used in the last lesson provides a quick and easy way to concatenate text:

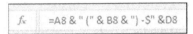

It would be possible to use the TEXT function in conjunction with the concatenation operator (&) to construct the formula, but this approach would result in the formula:

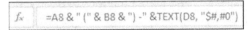

... which is difficult to read and prone to error. Instead, you'll use the CONCAT function.

1. Click in cell F8.

2. Click: Formulas→Function Library→Text→CONCAT.

3. Populate the dialog as follows:

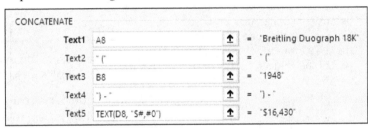

Note that each string is enclosed in double quotation marks to denote text.

Note also the use of the TEXT function with a reference to cell D8 followed by the custom format string:

"$#,#0"

This format string means "show a leading dollar sign, show a comma after thousands and show only whole numbers (no decimal places)".

4. Click the *OK* button.

The text is displayed as specified:

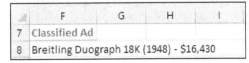

4 AutoFill cell F8 to the end of the range (cells F9:F17).

5 Save your work as *Classic Watches-4.*

important

Allow for formatting characters when using the LEFT RIGHT and MID functions

Consider a cell that contains the value 28 in cell A1 and has been formatted as *currency* using the dollar currency prefix. The cell would display the value:

$28.00

But the actual value in the cell (and displayed on the formula bar) would be:

28

If you were to extract the first character using the LEFT function

=LEFT(A1, 1)

...you would extract 2 and not $ because the $ character is simply displayed as a result of the cell's formatting and is not part of the value in the cell.

Lesson 3-20: Extract text from fixed width strings using the LEFT, RIGHT and MID functions

In *Lesson 2-1: Split fixed width data using Text to Columns*, you learned how to extract fixed width data using Excel's *Text to Columns* feature.

It is also possible to split data using Excel's Flash Fill feature (covered extensively in the *Essential Skills* book in this series).

While these methods work well, you'll often need to extract data dynamically using a formula. In this lesson, you'll use the LEFT, RIGHT and MID functions to do just that.

1   Open *Best Selling Books-1* from your sample files folder.

This worksheet lists some of the bestselling fiction books of all time:

	A	B	C	D	E
3	Title	Author	Year	Copies (millions)	ISBN-13
4	A Tale of Two Cities	Charles Dickens	1859	200	978-0141439600
5	The Lord of the Rings	J.R.R. Tolkein	1954	150	978-0618640157

For this lesson, the interesting data is in column E: the *International Standard Book Number* (ISBN-13).

ISBN numbers are a good example of fixed-width strings. At first they simply seem to be a jumble of numbers but they actually contain four discrete pieces of data:

	A	B	C	D
17	Anatomy of an ISBN Number			
18	Digits 1-3	EAN (European Article Number)		
19	Digit 4	Group Identifier (country or language code)		
20	Digits 5-12	publisher prefix and title identifier		
21	Digit 13	Check digit (proves accuracy)		

2   Use a LEFT function to extract the EAN from the ISBN code.

You know that the leftmost three digits represent the EAN. The LEFT function extracts a given number of characters from the left part of a string.

1.   Click in cell F4.

2.   Click: Formulas→Function Library→Text→LEFT.

3.   Complete the dialog as follows:

Text	E4	↑	=	ˈ978-0141439600ˈ
Num_chars	3	↑	=	3
			=	ˈ978ˈ

4.   Click the *OK* button.

Best Selling Books-1

tip

Converting a textual result to a numerical result

In this lesson, you extract several numeric codes from an ISBN number.

Notice that the results are left aligned in each cell. This tells you that they are textual, rather than numeric values.

Often you will wish the results to be numeric values. There are many ways to do this in Excel.

Multiply by a numeric value

To convert the textual return value of a formula to a true number, simply multiply the result of the formula by 1.

For example, to return the EAN as a numeric value you would use the following formula:

=LEFT(E4,3)*1

Use a mathematical operator upon the textual value

It is interesting to note that there are many other mathematical operations that will achieve the same result, such as adding 0 (+0), dividing by 1 (/1) adding two negative signs in front of the number (--) and even raising to the power of 1 (^1).

Use the VALUE function

There's also a function-based method using the VALUE function. You could wrap the LEFT function with a VALUE function like this:

=VALUE(LEFT(E4,3))

The EAN is extracted into cell F4.

3   Use a RIGHT function to extract the Check Digit from the ISBN code.

You know that the rightmost single digit represents the *Check Digit*. The RIGHT function extracts a given number of digits from the right part of a string.

1.   Click in cell I4.

2.   Click: Formulas→Function Library→Text→RIGHT.

3.   Complete the dialog as follows:

4.   Click the *OK* button.

The *Check Digit* is extracted into cell I4.

4   Use a MID function to extract the Group from the ISBN code.

The MID function extracts text from within a string. You know that digit 4 is the *Group Identifier* that indicates the language that the book is written in. Because the ISBN has a hyphen between the third and fourth digits, you'll have to extract a single character from position five in the string.

1.   Click in cell G4.

2.   Click: Formulas→Function Library→Text→MID.

3.   Complete the dialog as follows:

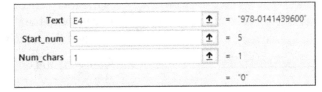

4.   Click the *OK* button.

The *Group* is extracted into cell G4.

5   Use a MID function to extract the *Publisher and Title* code from the ISBN code.

This time, the correct arguments for the dialog will be:

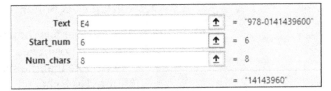

6   AutoFill the formulas in cells F4:I4 to cells F15:I15.

You can now see from the Group (country or language code) that *Le Petit Prince* was published in French.

7   Save your work as *Best Selling Books-2*.

Lesson 3-21: Extract text from delimited strings using the FIND and LEN functions

Here are two examples of international telephone numbers.

+44 (0)113-4960227 (a UK telephone number)
+356 (0)2138-3393 (a Maltese telephone number)

The *country code* (or international dialing code) is shown as a + symbol followed by one or more numbers. The *NDD* (National Direct Dialing prefix) is shown in brackets. This is the access code used to make a call within the relevant country but it is omitted when calling from outside the country. The *Area Code* consists of the numbers after the closing bracket but before the hyphen.

In this lesson, you'll use the FIND and LEN functions, in combination with the LEFT and MID functions, to extract the country code, area code and phone number from an international telephone number.

1   Open *Phone Book-1* from your sample files folder.

2   Insert a FIND function into cell C4 to find the first occurrence of an opening bracket within the telephone number.

    1.   Click in cell C4.

    2.   Click: Formulas→Function Library→Text→FIND.

        The FIND function demands three arguments. The first is the character to find (in this case the opening bracket), the second is the text to search within (in this case the telephone number in cell B4). There's also an optional argument that allows you to begin the search at a specified position within the string.

    3.   Complete the dialog as follows:

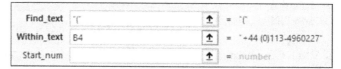

        Note that you don't have to manually type the quotation marks around the text in the *Find_text* argument. Excel will helpfully add them for you automatically.

    4.   Click the *OK* button.

        The number 5 is shown in cell C4. This is because the opening bracket is positioned five characters from the left of the string **+44 (.** Note that the space before the opening bracket is counted as a character.

3   Insert a FIND function into cell D4 to find the first occurrence of a closing bracket within the telephone number.

    Repeat *Step 2,* but use a closing bracket for the *Find_text* argument.

4   Insert a FIND function into cell E4 to find the first occurrence of a hyphen within the telephone number.

Phone Book-1

note

Avoid leading and trailing spaces with the TRIM function

In *Step 6* you extracted the country code using the LEFT function. This could result in strings with a trailing space such as:

"+44 "
"+356 "

Because you can't see the trailing space, this doesn't seem to matter.

Trailing spaces cause many problems when comparing data because strings that appear to be the same visually are, in fact, different:

="+44 " = "+44"
(returns FALSE)

="+44" = "+44"
(returns TRUE)

For this reason, it is good practice to always remove leading and trailing spaces using the TRIM function.

You could have used the TRIM function in *Step 6* like this:

=TRIM(LEFT(B4,C4-1))

If this seems a little too complex, you could also have placed the trimmed country code in a different column and then used the untrimmed result as an argument like this:

=TRIM(G4)

Repeat *Step 2,* but use a hyphen ("-") for the *Find_text* argument.

5 Insert a LEN function into cell F4 to find the total number of characters in the telephone number.

1. Click in cell F4.

2. Click: Formulas→Text→LEN.

3. Click cell B4 for the single argument for this function.

4. Click the *OK* button.

   The length of the telephone number string (18 characters) is displayed in cell F4.

6 Insert a LEFT function into cell G4 to extract the country code.

The correct arguments are:

Text	B4	= "+44 (0)113-4960227"
Num_chars	C4-1	= 4

Note that C4-1 is used for the number of characters to avoid returning the opening bracket. This could result in a trailing space (see sidebar for a way to remove trailing spaces).

7 Insert a MID function into cell H4 to extract the area code.

The MID function was covered in: *Lesson 3-20: Extract text from fixed width strings using the LEFT, RIGHT and MID functions.*

The correct arguments are:

Text	B4	= "+44 (0)113-4960227"
Start_num	D4+1	= 8
Num_chars	E4-D4-1	= 3

8 Insert a MID function into cell I4 to extract the phone number.

The correct arguments are:

Text	B4	= "+44 (0)113-4960227"
Start_num	E4+1	= 12
Num_chars	F4-E4	= 7

9 AutoFill cells C4:I4 into cells C5:I18.

	A	B	C Position of opening bracket (	D Position of closing bracket)	E Position of Hyphen	F Length of entire string	G Country Code	H Area Code	I Phone Number
3	Company	Telephone							
4	Books A Million	+44 (0)113-4960227	5	7	11	18	+44	113	4960227
5	Maltese Books	+356 (0)2138-3393	6	8	13	17	+356	2138	3393

10 Hide columns C:F.

Select columns C:F, right click the mouse and then click *Hide* from the shortcut menu.

11 Save your work as *Phone Book-2.*

note

The MATCH function can be used to make a VLOOKUP more resilient

The syntax for the MATCH function is:

MATCH(lookup_value, lookup_array, [match_type])

The MATCH function is very similar to the VLOOKUP function but returns a number relating to the position of a matched cell in a range.

You can use a MATCH function to feed the correct column number to a VLOOKUP. The following function will return the value of 2 (the correct column number for the *Description* in the *Stock* table):

MATCH("Description", Stock[#Headers], FALSE)

Note the use of a structured reference in the above function (you learned about this type of structured reference in: *Lesson 1-20: Use special items in structured table references*).

The above function could be used in place of the number 2 (used for the third argument of the VLOOKUP in this lesson's example).

The VLOOKUP would then continue to work correctly even if one or more new columns were added to the left of column B in the *Stock* table.

You'll learn more about the MATCH function later, in: *Lesson 3-26: Use a MATCH function for an exact lookup.*

Lesson 3-22: Use a VLOOKUP function for an exact lookup

Consider the following worksheet:

	A	B	C	D	E
5	Code	Description	Date	Cost price	Selling Price
6	BR48	Breitling Duograph 18K	1948	11,500.00	16,430.00
7	CA74	Cartier Tank 18K	1974	3,200.00	4,570.00
8	RO66	Rolex Tudor Oyster	1966	300.00	430.00

The retailer has created a stock code to save time when creating invoices. The code is made up of the first two letters of the watch description, along with the last two numbers of the date of manufacture.

When provided with a stock code, the VLOOKUP function can scan all of the codes in column A until a match is found and then return a value from the same row for any of the other columns.

1   Open *Invoice-1* from your sample files folder.

	A	B	C
5	Code	Description	Price
6	CA74		
7			
8			
9		Total:	-

In this lesson, you will create a VLOOKUP formula that will automatically return the *Description* of any watch into column B when the user enters a stock code into column A.

2   Convert the range A5:G15 on the *Stock* worksheet into a table named: **Stock**

This was covered in: *Lesson 1-12: Convert a range into a table and add a total row* and *Lesson 1-18: Name a table and create an automatic structured table reference.*

When working with the VLOOKUP function it is best practice to use a table for the *Table_array* argument (see sidebar on facing page).

Using a table will make the data dynamic. In other words, the VLOOKUP function will still work correctly if you add and remove rows from the *Stock* table.

3   Insert a VLOOKUP function into cell B6 on the *Invoice* worksheet to find the description that matches the *Code* in cell A6 on the *Stock* worksheet.

1.   Click in cell B6 on the *Invoice* worksheet.

2.   Click: Formulas→Function Library→ Lookup & Reference→VLOOKUP.

The VLOOKUP *Function Arguments* dialog appears. It can be seen that the VLOOKUP function has three required arguments (shown in bold face) and one optional argument:

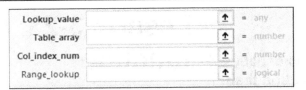

important

It is best practice to use tables with your VLOOKUP functions

In this lesson I've shown you how to construct a VLOOKUP function that uses a table for the *Table_array* argument.

This has been best practice since the release of Excel 2007, but it wasn't possible in Excel 2003 as the (fantastically useful) table feature wasn't available.

In worksheets constructed using pre-2007 versions of Excel it is common to see absolute range references for *Table_array* arguments like this:

More sophisticated users of pre-2007 Excel versions learned how to use *Range Names*. (You'll learn all about Range Names in: *Session Four: Using Names and the Formula Auditing Tools*).

When you see a *Range Name* reference, it looks the same as a table reference. This example shows the use of a *Range Name* also called *Stock*:

Table_array	Stock

While *Range Names* were best practice in pre-2007 Excel versions, they have a fatal flaw as they are not truly dynamic.

Users of earlier versions had to resort to a complex work-around to make their Range Names dynamic. You'll learn about this workaround in: *Lesson 4-6: Create dynamic formula-based range names using the OFFSET function*.

This information is provided so that you will understand any older Excel worksheets you may inherit, (or worksheets that were created by users that haven't yet learned how to use tables).

4 Set the *Lookup_value* argument to: **A6**

This is the cell on the *Invoice* worksheet that provides the value to be searched for in column A of the *Stock* worksheet. You want to look up the description for the watch that has the code *CA74*. This is contained in cell **A6**.

5 Set the *Table_array* argument to: **Stock**

The table array is the *range, table* or *name* (see sidebar) you will search for a match to the value in cell A6. VLOOKUP always searches the left-most column of the *range, table* or *name*.

Type: **Stock** into the *Table_array* text box.

It is best practice to use a table for the *Table_array* argument (see sidebar).

6 Set the *Col_index_num* argument to: **2**

	A	B	C	D	E
5	Code	Description	Date	Cost price	Selling Price
6	BR48	Breitling Duograph 18K	1948	11,500.00	16,430.00
7	CA74	Cartier Tank 18K	1974	3,200.00	4,570.00

Counting from left to right, the *Col_index_num* argument is the column that contains the value you want to return. In this case, it is the *Description* column, so you want to return column **2**.

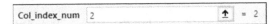

7 Set the *Range_lookup* argument to: **FALSE**

Beginners often overlook this vital argument because it is optional.

If it is left blank, VLOOKUP will return an inexact match. Later, in *Lesson 3-25: Use a VLOOKUP function for an inexact lookup*, you'll find out why that might be useful, but in this case you want an error to be returned if the stock code is not found, so it is vital to set this argument to **FALSE**.

8 Click the *OK* button.

The description of the *Cartier Tank 18K* is returned to cell B6.

	A	B
6	CA74	Cartier Tank 18K

9 Save your work as *Invoice-2*.

note

VLOOKUP is usually a better solution than SWITCH

The SWITCH function is mainly intended to offer a simpler and more elegant alternative to many common uses of nested IF functions.

This doesn't mean that using the SWITCH function provides a better solution than VLOOKUP.

You could have completed this lesson by using a VLOOKUP function like this:

1. Make the range A27:B32 into a table and name it: **Category**

2. Add this VLOOKUP function into cell E4:

=VLOOKUP(
D4, Category, 2,FALSE)

3. AutoFill to the end of the range.

This solution would allow users to add or edit rows in the Category table.

Lesson 3-23: Use the SWITCH function

In: *Lesson 3-22: Use a VLOOKUP function for an exact lookup,* you used a VLOOKUP function to return price information from a watch retailer's constantly changing stock list.

When you need to lookup values from this type of dynamically changing table VLOOKUP is always the best approach.

A very useful SWITCH function was added to Excel in February 2016. This may be a better solution when you have lookup data that is not expected to change (or at least rarely changes). This type of data is often called *static data* by IT professionals.

In this lesson you will use the maximum wind speeds defined by the *Saffir-Simpson Hurricane Wind Scale* for category 1 to 5 hurricanes. The defined SSHS maximum wind speeds are extremely unlikely to change in the future, so it is reasonable to describe this as static data.

1   Open *Biggest Atlantic Hurricanes-1* from your sample files folder.

The sample file for this lesson lists some of the biggest Atlantic hurricanes from 1870 to present. Each hurricane is categorized (from 1-5).

	A	B	C	D	E
3	Name	Start Date	Damage (USD Millions)	Category*	Max Wind Speed
4	San Marcos	October 5, 1870	12	3	
5	Sea Islands	August 15, 1893	1	3	
6	Chenier Caminanda	September 27, 1893	5	4	
7	San Ciriaco	August 3, 1899	20	4	

2   Use the SWITCH function to calculate the maximum wind speed for each hurricane.

The maximum wind speed for each hurricane category is shown at the bottom of the list:

	A	B
27	Hurricane Category	Max Wind Speed (mph)
28	5	157 and over
29	4	156
30	3	129
31	2	110
32	1	95

With the skills you learned in*: Lesson 3-22: Use a VLOOKUP function for an exact lookup,* you could easily have calculated the maximum wind speed by looking up the *Hurricane Category* in cells A28:B32 (see sidebar).

By using a SWITCH function instead, there will be no danger of a user editing the contents of cells A28:B32 causing the worksheet to become inaccurate.

1.   Click in cell E4.

Biggest Atlantic Hurricanes-1

2. Click: Formulas→Function Library→Logical→SWITCH.

   The *Function Arguments* dialog appears.

3. Click in the *Expression* box.

4. Click once on cell D4.

5. In the *Value1* box enter the value: **1**

6. In the *Result1* box enter the value: **95**

   You have now defined a *Value/Result* pair for a *Category 1* hurricane.

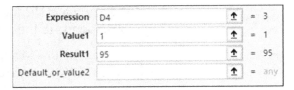

7. Continue to define pairs of values for category 2 to 5 hurricanes (see sidebar).

   The SWITCH function allows you to add up to 127 *Value/Result* pairs.

8. In the final *Default_or_value6 box*, type: **"Error"**

   This text will be displayed in the event that a category cell is out of range or empty.

   See sidebar for all of the values that you should have entered.

9. Click the OK button.

3 AutoFill the formula in cell E4 down to the end of the range.

   The maximum wind speed is now shown for each hurricane.

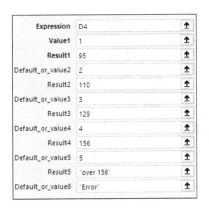

	A	B	C	D	E
1	Strongest Atlantic Hurricanes				
2					
3	Name	Start Date	Damage (USD Millions)	Category*	Max Wind Speed
4	San Marcos	October 5, 1870	12	3	129
5	Sea Islands	August 15, 1893	1	3	129
6	Chenier Caminanda	September 27, 1893	5	4	156

4 Save your work as *Biggest Atlantic Hurricanes-2.*

---

note

The IFS function is more sophisticated than SWITCH

Many common uses of nested IF functions can be solved using a SWITCH function.

In February 2016 a more sophisticated function called IFS was added to Excel 365.

The IFS function is able to replace **all** uses of nested IF functions.

You'll learn to use the IFS function later, in:

Lesson 3-26: Use a MATCH function for an exact lookup

Lesson 3-24: Use an IFERROR function to suppress error messages

1   Open *Invoice-2* from your sample files folder (if it isn't already open).

2   Select the *Invoice* worksheet.

3   Add a VLOOKUP formula to cell C6 to return the price that corresponds to the *Code* in cell A6.

You learned how to add a VLOOKUP function in *Lesson 3-22: Use a VLOOKUP function for an exact lookup*. This time, the correct arguments are:

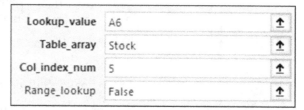

Lookup_value	A6
Table_array	Stock
Col_index_num	5
Range_lookup	False

4   AutoFill cells B6:C6 to cells B7:C8.

	A	B	C
5	Code	Description	Price
6	CA74	Cartier Tank 18K	4,570.00
7		#N/A	#N/A
8		#N/A	#N/A
9		Total:	#N/A

This is nearly what is needed. The invoice will work just fine when all three lines are populated:

	A	B	C
5	Code	Description	Price
6	CA74	Cartier Tank 18K	4,570.00
7	RO66	Rolex Tudor Oyster	430.00
8	BR43	Breitling Chronomat 18K	3,070.00
9		Total:	8,070.00

But you need to cater for customers that only wish to purchase one watch. To make this work, you need to suppress the error messages when some invoice lines have no stock code.

Fortunately, the IFERROR function is designed precisely for this purpose.

5   Wrap each VLOOKUP function with an IFERROR function to return a blank space when an error is encountered.

The IFERROR function can return the value of your choice whenever a formula returns an error.

1.   Click in cell B6.

Look at the formula in the formula bar:

Invoice-2

This is the VLOOKUP function that returns the description. You're going to use this formula as the *value* argument for the IFERROR function. When one function is used inside another function in this way, the outside function is sometimes referred to as a *wrapper*.

2. Click just to the right of the equals sign in the formula bar.

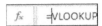

3. Type **IFERROR(**

Notice the tip that has appeared. The entire VLOOKUP function is now being used as the *value* argument for the IFERROR function.

4. Click to the extreme right of the formula in the formula bar and add a comma:

You are now ready to add the second argument for the IFERROR function. This argument defines what will be displayed if the VLOOKUP function returns an error.

5. Add an empty string to the IFERROR function.

    Type *""*. This is an empty string and tells Excel to keep the cell blank when an error is returned.

6. Close the bracket to complete the formula.

7. Press the **<Enter>** key.

8. Do the same thing for the *Price* formula in cell C6.

    f_x =IFERROR(VLOOKUP(A6,Stock,5,FALSE), "")

6   AutoFill the formulas in cells B6:C6 to cells B7:C8.

The invoice now works correctly, even when some stock codes are left blank.

▲	A	B	C
5	Code	Description	Price
6	CA74	Cartier Tank 18K	4,570.00
7			
8	PA83	Patek Phillipe Jumbo Nautilus	20,355.00
9		Total:	24,925.00

7   Save your work as *Invoice-3*.

---

tip

AutoFill a range of cells in one operation

I've noticed in my classes that many students will respond to the instruction:

"AutoFill the formulas in cells B6:C6 to cells B7:C8"

... by performing two AutoFill operations:

1. Select cell B6.

2. AutoFill cell B6 down to row 8.

3. Select cell C6.

4. AutoFill cell C6 down to row 8.

A quicker way to do this is to AutoFill both cells at the same time:

1. Select cells B6:C6.

2. AutoFill both cells down to row 8.

---

note

The HLOOKUP function works in the same way as the VLOOKUP function

In the VLOOKUP function, V is an abbreviation of *Vertical*. This means that you search for a matching value in a (vertical) column and return a value from any column in that row.

In the HLOOKUP function, H is an abbreviation of Horizontal. This means that you can search for a matching value in a (horizontal) row and return a value from any row in that column.

You'll see the VLOOKUP function used far more often than HLOOKUP but you may find a scenario where it is useful.

Lesson 3-25: Use a VLOOKUP function for an inexact lookup

In: *Lesson 3-22: Use a VLOOKUP function for an exact lookup,* you set the fourth argument of the VLOOKUP to FALSE in order to achieve an *exact* lookup. Most of the time, that's exactly what you want to do.

Sometimes you don't want to search for an exact match but are interested in a close match. This is called an *inexact* lookup. Consider the following exam grades:

	E	F
3	Percentage	Grade
4	0%	Fail
5	60%	C
6	70%	B
7	80%	A
8	90%	A*

An *exact* VLOOKUP for a student with a mark of 80% would correctly return a grade of A.

An *exact* VLOOKUP for a student with a mark of 77% would result in an error because there is no exact value of 77% in column E.

If you ask VLOOKUP to perform an *inexact* lookup, it will return an exact match if one is found. If an exact match is not found, it will return the largest value *that is less than* the lookup value.

For VLOOKUP to work with inexact matches, it is vital that the lookup column is sorted in ascending order (from the lowest to the highest value).

In the above example, an inexact search for 68% would find row 5 (a C grade) because 60% is the largest value that is less than 68%.

1 Open *Grades-1* from your sample files folder.

	A	B	C	D	E	F
1	Exam Results					
2						
3	Name	Percentage	Grade		Percentage	Grade
4	Johnny Caine	70%			0%	Fail
5	George Marley	68%			60%	C
6	Betty Anan	86%			70%	B
7	Paris Winfrey	80%			80%	A
8	Ozzy Dickens	95%			90%	A*
9	Johnny Roberts	84%				

2 Convert cells E3:F8 into a table named: **Grade**

This was covered in: *Lesson 1-12: Convert a range into a table and add a total row* and *Lesson 1-18: Name a table and create an automatic structured table reference.*

When working with the VLOOKUP function it is best practice to use a table for the *Table_array* argument.

Grades-1

This will make the data dynamic. In other words, the VLOOKUP function will still work correctly if you add and remove grades from the *Grade* table.

3   Add an inexact VLOOKUP to cell C4 to return the grade that corresponds to the percentage mark in cell B4.

You learned how to add an exact VLOOKUP in *Lesson 3-22: Use a VLOOKUP function for an exact lookup*. An inexact lookup is done in exactly the same way, except that the *Range_lookup* argument is set to TRUE (or omitted, as the default is TRUE).

This time, the correct arguments are therefore:

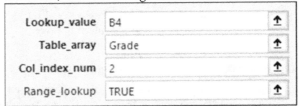

Lookup_value	B4	⬆
Table_array	Grade	⬆
Col_index_num	2	⬆
Range_lookup	TRUE	⬆

4   AutoFill cell C4 to cells C5:C17.

The correct grades are now shown for each student.

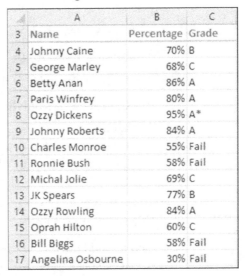

	A	B	C
3	Name	Percentage	Grade
4	Johnny Caine	70%	B
5	George Marley	68%	C
6	Betty Anan	86%	A
7	Paris Winfrey	80%	A
8	Ozzy Dickens	95%	A*
9	Johnny Roberts	84%	A
10	Charles Monroe	55%	Fail
11	Ronnie Bush	58%	Fail
12	Michal Jolie	69%	C
13	JK Spears	77%	B
14	Ozzy Rowling	84%	A
15	Oprah Hilton	60%	C
16	Bill Biggs	58%	Fail
17	Angelina Osbourne	30%	Fail

5   Save your work as *Grades-2*.

Lesson 3-26: Use a MATCH function for an exact lookup

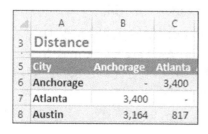

1   Open *Bus Fare Calculator-1* from your sample files folder.

In the next two lessons you will create a fare calculator for a long-distance bus company.

There are two tables in the sample file. The *Distance* table (see sidebar) shows the distance between major US cities. You can see at a glance that the distance between Austin and Atlanta is 817 miles. The second table shows the *Fare*. As more passengers share the vehicle it is possible to charge a lower fare per passenger.

When the worksheet is completed, the operator will select a *From* and *To* destination and enter the *Min Passengers* (minimum number of passengers who will travel). The worksheet will then automatically calculate the *Distance* and *Fare*.

In this lesson you will use the MATCH function to identify the cell in the *Distance* table that contains the correct distance value for the selected *From* and *To* cities.

2   Unhide all rows between row 53 and 60.

1. Select rows 53 to 60

2. Right click on one of the selected column headers.

3. Click: *Unhide* from the shortcut menu.

   Several new rows are now revealed. These are often called helper cells. They will make the formulas more readable. Later, when the worksheet is complete, you will hide these cells again.

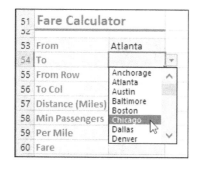

3   Add a list validation to cells B53 and B54 to show a drop-down list of all cities.

You learned how to do this in: *Lesson 2-11: Add a table-based dynamic list validation.*

You can use cells A6:A35 as the source of both lists as the row and column City names in the *Distance* table are (and always will be) identical.

4   Select **Atlanta** as the *From* city and **Chicago** as the *To* city.

5   Use a MATCH function to find which row in the *City* column of the *Distance* table contains the text: *Atlanta*

1. Click in cell B55.

2. Click: Formulas→Function Library→ Lookup & Reference→MATCH.

   The *Function Arguments* dialog for the MATCH function appears.

3. Click in the *Lookup_value* box.

4. Click on cell B53.

Bus Fare Calculator-1

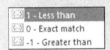

note

The MATCH function offers three different match types

MATCH(lookup_value, lookup_array, [match_type])

MATCH offers a choice of three values for the *match_type* argument:

```
1 - Less than
0 - Exact match
-1 - Greater than
```

For a **Less than** match the list must be sorted in ascending order.

For a **Greater than** match the list must be sorted in descending order.

For an **Exact match** the list does not have to be sorted in any particular order.

Here is a table named *Price*:

	A	B
1	Qty	Price
2	5	$ 10.00
3	10	$ 9.00
4	15	$ 8.00

MATCH(13, Price[Qty], 1)

In this case **10** is the largest value that is less than, or equal to **13**. For this reason, the function returns 2 (the second data row in the table).

MATCH(13, Price[Qty], 0)

This would return an error as there is no *Qty* value that is exactly equal to 13.

MATCH(13, Price[Qty], -1)

Remember that, to use this match type, the *Qty* column would have to be sorted in descending order.

In this case **15** is the largest value that is greater than, or equal to **13**. For this reason, the function returns 1 (the first data row in the table after the table has been sorted in descending order).

5. Click in the *Lookup_array* box

6. Select the range A6:A35 in the distance table.

   Note that this results in the structured reference: *Distance[City]*.

7. Click in the *Match_type* box.

   The *Match_type* is very similar to the *Exact Match* and *Inexact Match* arguments of the VLOOKUP function. See sidebar for a discussion of the three possible arguments. Enter a value of **0** (meaning an *Exact Match*).

   The dialog should now look like this.

Lookup_value	B53
Lookup_array	Distance[City]
Match_type	0

8. Click the *OK* button.

   A value of 2 is returned to cell B55. Notice that *Atlanta* is the second city listed in the *Distance* table.

6   Insert a MATCH function into cell B56 to define the column in the *Distance* table that contains the header text: **Chicago**

This time the function arguments should be:

Lookup_value	B54
Lookup_array	Distance[#Headers]
Match_type	0

	A	B
51	Fare Calculator	
52		
53	From	Atlanta
54	To	Chicago
55	From Row	2
56	To Col	7
57	Distance (Miles)	
58	Min Passengers	
59	Per Mile	
60	Fare	

A value of 7 is returned to cell B56. Notice that the text **Chicago** appears in the seventh row of the *Distance* table.

	A	B	C	D	E	F	G
5	City	Anchorage	Atlanta	Austin	Baltimore	Boston	Chicago
6	Anchorage	-	3,400	3,164	3,351	3,366	2,849
7	Atlanta	3,400	-	817	576	935	587
8	Austin	3,164	817	-	1,346	1,693	977

In the next lesson you will use these row and column references within an INDEX function to return the correct *Distance (Miles)* value from the *Distance* table.

7   Save your work as *Bus Fare Calculator-2*.

note

A combined INDEX and MATCH formula can be used to emulate a VLOOKUP

In this lesson you use this simple VLOOKUP function to calculate the *Fare Per Mile*:

=VLOOKUP(B58, Fare, 2,TRUE)

You could emulate this single function using a combined INDEX and MATCH formula like this:

=INDEX(Fare[PerMile],MATCH(B58,Fare[Min Passengers],1))

With your understanding of the INDEX and MATCH functions you should understand how this formula works.

I'm sure that you will agree that this approach seems pointless but if you search the web you might find arguments that this is a "better" approach.

In almost every case it isn't (though in older versions of Excel it used to execute a little faster).

One argument for the INDEX/MATCH approach is that the function cannot be broken by a user inserting or deleting a column in the lookup table. If this robustness is required it is better achieved by using a MATCH function in combination with a VLOOKUP function. See: *Lesson 3-22: Use a VLOOKUP function for an exact lookup*, (sidebar) for an example of this technique.

It is still useful to understand how the above INDEX/MATCH approach works as you may have to maintain an older workbook that has used this function combination.

Bus Fare Calculator-2

Lesson 3-27: Use the INDEX function

In: *Lesson 3-26: Use a MATCH function for an exact lookup* you determined row and column co-ordinates to identify a value within a range.

Specifically, you identified that the driving distance from Atlanta to Chicago was contained in row 2 and column 7 of the *Distance* table.

	A	B	C	D	E	F	G
5	City	Anchorage	Atlanta	Austin	Baltimore	Boston	Chicago
6	Anchorage	-	3,400	3,164	3,351	3,366	2,849
7	Atlanta	3,400	-	817	576	935	587
8	Austin	3,164	817	-	1,346	1,693	977

The INDEX function can be used to retrieve a value from a range or table when the numerical co-ordinates are known.

1   Open *Bus Fare Calculator-2* from your sample files folder.

2   Place an INDEX function in cell B57 that will return the value in the *Distance* table that is identified by the row and column references in cells B55 and B56.

1.   Click in cell B57.

2.   Click: Formulas→Function Library→ Lookup & Reference→INDEX.

   A *Select Arguments* dialog appears

   The INDEX function is quite unusual because it is said to be *overloaded*. An overloaded function can accept different sets of arguments.

   The function decides the form it will take by examining the arguments provided. See sidebar (facing page) for examples of the different sets of arguments that can be used.

3.   Click the first set of arguments (the set beginning with *array*) and click the *OK* button. This is the more commonly used form of the INDEX function.

4.   Click in the *Array* box.

5.   Type: **Distance** to reference the *Distance* table.

6.   Click in the *Row_num* box.

7.   Click on cell B55 (this identifies the row in the table that has *Atlanta* in the *City* column).

8.   Click in the *Column_num* box.

9.   Click on cell B56 (this identifies the column in the table that has *Chicago* in the header row).

   The *Function Arguments* dialog should now look like this:

Array	Distance	↑
Row_num	B55	↑
Column_num	B56	↑

note

There are many ways to use the INDEX function

Using this lesson's sample file:

INDEX(Distance, 2, 7)

This was used in this lesson (by referencing the values in cells B55 and B56) to return the single value of 587 miles (the distance from Atlanta to Chicago).

INDEX(Distance, 2)

This example returns an array of all of the values in the Atlanta row.

INDEX(Distance,,7)

This example returns an array of all of the values in the Chicago column.

INDEX(A7:AE7,,7)

This example references the seventh column in the *Atlanta row* (cells A7:AE7). 587 miles is returned (the distance from Atlanta to Chicago).

=INDEX(Distance[Chicago],2)

This example references the second row in the Chicago column. 587 miles is returned (the distance from Atlanta to Chicago).

=INDEX((Distance,Fare),2,7,1)

This example uses the lesser-used *reference* form of the INDEX function. You won't often see this form in real-world workbooks.

In this example both the *Distance* and *Fare* tables have been referenced, followed by the usual row and column references (2 and 7).

The last argument is the *Area_num*. It identifies which table to use for the lookup (in this case the first table: *Distance*).

587 miles is returned (the distance from Atlanta to Chicago).

---

10. Click the *OK* button

    Notice that the distance from Atlanta to Chicago is now shown in cell B57 (587 miles).

3   Type: **14** into cell B58 (to define a test value for *Min Passengers*).

4   Add a VLOOKUP formula to cell B59 to retrieve the *Fare per mile* from the *Fare* table.

As more passengers share the vehicle it is possible to charge a lower fare per passenger. The *Fare* table defines the cost per mile based upon a minimum number of passengers.

In: *Lesson 3-25: Use a VLOOKUP function for an inexact lookup* you learned how to find the correct value in the *Fare* table. Here are the correct arguments for the VLOOKUP:

Lookup_value	B58	↥
Table_array	Fare	↥
Col_index_num	2	↥
Range_lookup	TRUE|	↥

5   Add a function to cell B60 to calculate the fare for this journey.

This is simply the distance multiplied by the fare per mile:

=B57*B59

6   Hide rows 55, 56 and 59.

It is always a good idea to hide helper cells when a worksheet is completed. This keeps the worksheet simple and clear.

1. Select rows 55, 56 and 59.

2. Right click on one of the selected row headers and click *Hide* from the shortcut menu.

7   Test the bus fare calculator

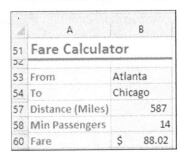

	A	B
51	Fare Calculator	
52		
53	From	Atlanta
54	To	Chicago
57	Distance (Miles)	587
58	Min Passengers	14
60	Fare	$ 88.02

Later, in: *Lesson 5-11: Restrict the cells users are allowed to change*, you will learn how to lock cells B57 and B60 to prevent users from over-writing the formulas by mistake.

8   Save your work as *Bus Fare Calculator-3*.

---

note

VLOOKUP is still (usually) a better solution than IFS

In: *Lesson 3-5: Use the IF logic function* (sidebar) I advised:

"Excel allows you to nest IF functions up to 64 levels deep (which is 63 too many)".

The new IFS and SWITCH functions (added to Excel 365 in Feb 2016) are mainly intended to offer a simpler alternative to nested IF functions.

This doesn't mean using the IFS and SWITCH functions provides a better solution than VLOOKUP.

It is easy to introduce errors using IFS and SWITCH, as the order in which the logic pairs are listed is vital to the correct operation of the function.

In this lesson the arguments are ordered correctly (as shown on the facing page sidebar).

If you were to state the grades in reverse order like this:

Logical_test1	B4<90%
Value_if_true1	"A"
Logical_test2	B4<80%
Value_if_true2	"B"

… most students would have a Grade A pass:

3	Name	Percentage	Grade
4	Johnny Caine	70%	A
5	George Marley	68%	A
6	Betty Anan	86%	A

This happens because the first logical test is applied and, because most students have a grade of less than 90%, a grade A pass is returned.

In almost all business situations a VLOOKUP will provide a better and more elegant solution than the use of the IFS or SWITCH function.

IFS Grades-1

Lesson 3-28: Use the IFS function

In: *Lesson 3-25: Use a VLOOKUP function for an inexact lookup*, you used a VLOOKUP function to return a grade from different pass mark percentages.

In this lesson you will solve exactly the same problem posed in: *Lesson 3-25: Use a VLOOKUP function for an inexact lookup*, with a logic based (rather than lookup based) solution.

1   Open *IFS Grades-1* from your sample files folder.

	A	B	C	D	E	F
1	Exam Results					
2						
3	Name	Percentage	Grade		Percentage	Grade
4	Johnny Caine	70%			0%	Fail
5	George Marley	68%			60%	C
6	Betty Anan	86%			70%	B
7	Paris Winfrey	80%			80%	A
8	Ozzy Dickens	95%			90%	A*
9	Johnny Roberts	84%				

This is an exact duplicate of the *Grades-1* sample file that you used at the beginning of: *Lesson 3-25: Use a VLOOKUP function for an inexact lookup*.

2   Use the IFS function to calculate the grade for each student by defining grade data within the function.

Sometimes it may be better to "hard code" data (such as the percentage grade thresholds) within the function itself. This prevents users from accidentally deleting or changing the grade percentage thresholds within the worksheet.

The argument against this approach is that the worksheet is more difficult to maintain if grade thresholds change in the future.

1.   Click in cell C4.

2.   Click: Formulas→Function Library→Logical→IFS.

The *Function Arguments* dialog for the IFS function appears.

The IFS function accepts up to 127 *Logical Test/Value* pairs.

3.   Enter the following pair of arguments:

| Logical_test1 | B4<60% |
| Value_if_true1 | "Fail" |

The *Logical Test* is an expression that returns TRUE or FALSE. In this case the test asks if Johnny Caine's percentage is less than 60%.

As Johnny scored 70%, the result is FALSE (as 70% is not less than 60%). If Johnny had a percentage score of less than 60%, the function would have returned the text "Fail".

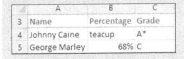

Logical_test1	B4<60%
Value_if_true1	"Fail"
Logical_test2	B4<70%
Value_if_true2	"C"
Logical_test3	B4<80%
Value_if_true3	"B"
Logical_test4	B4<90%
Value_if_true4	"A"
Logical_test5	B4>= 90%
Value_if_true5	"A*"

Note that textual values must be placed in double quotation marks. If you omit to do this Excel will add them for you.

4. Add *Logical Test/Value* pairs for the other grades (see sidebar).

   It is vital that these arguments are added in the correct order (see facing page sidebar for the reason for this).

5. Click the OK button.

   Johnny Caine's B grade is shown in cell C4.

6. AutoFill cell C4 to the end of the range.

   All grades are now correctly shown.

	A	B	C	D	E	F
3	Name	Percentage	Grade		Percentage	Grade
4	Johnny Caine	70%	B		0%	Fail
5	George Marley	68%	C		60%	C
6	Betty Anan	86%	A		70%	B
7	Paris Winfrey	80%	A		80%	A
8	Ozzy Dickens	95%	A*		90%	A*

3 Use the IFS function to calculate the grade for each student using the grade data defined in cells E3:F8.

1. Delete the functions in column C.

2. Add a new IFS function to cell C4.

3. Enter the following pair of *Logical Test/Value* arguments:

Logical_test1	B4<$E$5	↑	= FALSE
Value_if_true1	"Fail"	↑	= "Fail"

Notice the use of an absolute reference for cell E5. This is needed to make sure that the formula AutoFills correctly.

You could also have used $F$4 to reference the text: "Fail" in cell F4 like this:

Logical_test1	B4<$E$5	↑	= FALSE
Value_if_true1	$F$4	↑	= "Fail"

Personally I prefer the literal text approach in this case as it makes the formula easier to read and thus less prone to error.

4. Add appropriate *Logical Test/Value* pairs for the other grades.

5. Click the *OK* button.

6. AutoFill cell C4 down to the end of the range.

   Exactly the same grade values are now shown. The difference from the first approach is that the grades will change if the Percentage thresholds shown in cells E4:E8 change in the future.

4 Save your work as *IFS Grades-2*.

important

Excel recognizes text as having a value in logical expressions

If you try entering text into the *Percentage* column you might be surprised to find this result:

	A	B	C
3	Name	Percentage	Grade
4	Johnny Caine	teacup	A*
5	George Marley	68%	C

Excel has evaluated this logic expression:

="teacup">90%

… and has surprisingly returned TRUE.

This seems puzzling at first until you realize that (behind the scenes) Excel assigns numeric values to text in order to implement alphabetical sorting.

These numeric values are always higher than any number so that (in an A-Z sort) numbers will always come before text.

To work around this peculiarity, you could add a new first *Logical Test/Value* pair to ensure that the value in column B was numeric like this:

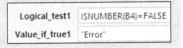

Logical_test1	ISNUMBER(B4)=FALSE
Value_if_true1	"Error"

Session 3: Exercise

1   Open *Employee Summary-1* from your sample files folder.

	A	B	C	D	E	F	G
3	Full Name	Last Name	First Name	Department	Date Started	Year Started	Bonus
4	Johnny Caine				16-Jan-04		
5	George Marley				18-Feb-08		

2   Using the RIGHT, LEFT, LEN and FIND functions, split the *Full Name* in column A into *Last Name* and *First Name* in columns B and C.

	A	B	C
3	Full Name	Last Name	First Name
4	Johnny Caine	Caine	Johnny

3   Use an exact VLOOKUP to return the *Department* for each employee (departments are listed on the *Departments* worksheet).

	A	B	C	D
3	Full Name	Last Name	First Name	Department
4	Johnny Caine	Caine	Johnny	Sales

4   Use a COUNTIF function to return the headcount for each department in cells B20:B22.

	A	B
19	Department	Headcount
20	Sales	6
21	Purchasing	5
22	Logistics	3

5   Use the YEAR function to populate column F with the year each employee started.

	A	B	C	D	E	F
3	Full Name	Last Name	First Name	Department	Date Started	Year Started
4	Johnny Caine	Caine	Johnny	Sales	16-Jan-04	2004
5	George Marley	Marley	George	Purchasing	18-Feb-08	2008

6   Each employee in the *Sales* department receives a 10% bonus, while all other employees receive a 5% bonus. Use an IF function to populate column G with the correct bonus percentage.

	A	B	C	D	E	F	G
3	Full Name	Last Name	First Name	Department	Date Started	Year Started	Bonus
4	Johnny Caine	Caine	Johnny	Sales	16-Jan-04	2004	10%
5	George Marley	Marley	George	Purchasing	18-Feb-08	2008	5%

7   Save your work as *Employee Summary-2*.

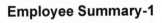

Employee Summary-1

If you need help slide the page to the left

Session 3: Exercise Answers

These are the four questions that students find the most difficult to answer:

Q 6	Q 4	Q 3	Q 2
1. Click in cell G4. 2. Click: Formulas→ Function Library→ Logical→IF. 3. Add the following arguments: Logical_test — D4="Sales" Value_if_true — 10% Value_if_false — 5% 4. Click the *OK* button. 5. AutoFill the formula in cell G4 to cells G5:G17. This was covered in: *Lesson 3-5: Use the IF logic function.*	1. Click in cell B20. 2. Click: Formulas→ Function Library→ More Functions→ Statistical→ COUNTIF. 3. Add the following arguments: Range — $D$4:$D$17 Criteria — A20 4. Click the *OK* button. 5. AutoFill the formula in cell B20 to cells B21:B22. This was covered in: *Lesson 3-6: Use the SUMIF and COUNTIF functions to create conditional totals.*	1. Select the *Departments* worksheet. 2. Convert the range A3:B17 into a table named: **Department** 3. Select the *Employees* worksheet. 4. Click in cell D4. 5. Click: Formulas→ Function Library→ Lookup & Reference→ VLOOKUP. 6. Add the following arguments: Lookup_value — A4 Table_array — Department Col_index_num — 2 Range_lookup — False 7. Click the *OK* button. 8. AutoFill the formula in cell D4 to cells D5:D17. This was covered in: *Lesson 3-22: Use a VLOOKUP function for an exact lookup.*	The easiest way to do this is to use the LEFT and RIGHT functions to return a specified number of characters from the left and right hand side of the *Full Name* string. The formula for the *First Name* (in cell C4) is quite easy. You can simply use the FIND function to find the first space and return that number of characters from the left hand side of the string: **=LEFT(A4, FIND(" ",A4)-1)** The *Last Name* is a little more involved. You also need to use the LEN function to return the total number of characters in the string: **=RIGHT(A4,LEN(A4)-FIND(" ",A4))** This was covered in: *Lesson 3-21: Extract text from delimited strings using the FIND and LEN functions.*

If you have difficulty with the other questions, here are the lessons that cover the relevant skills:

5   Refer to: *Lesson 3-8: Understand common date functions.*

4

Session Four: Using Names and the Formula Auditing Tools

> To make no mistakes is not in the power of man; but from their errors and mistakes, the wise and good learn wisdom for the future.
>
> *Plutarch (46 AD - 120 AD)*

This session introduces Excel's ability to apply a name to a range of cells, a single cell, a formula, a constant or a table. Some problems are almost impossible to solve without names. In this session, you'll use name-based techniques to address several common business scenarios.

This session also introduces Excel's superb formula auditing tools. These will allow you to check your work for mistakes or track down errors when you know that something is wrong. As Plutarch asserts, you *will* make errors when working with Excel (assuming that you are human of course).

By the end of this session, you'll be able to use all of the auditing tools to track down and repair workbook errors.

Session Objectives

By the end of this session you will be able to:

■ Automatically create single-cell range names

■ Manually create single cell range names and named constants

■ Use range names to make formulas more readable

■ Automatically create range names in two dimensions

■ Use intersection range names and the INDIRECT function

■ Create dynamic formula-based range names using the OFFSET function

■ Create table based dynamic range names

■ Create two linked drop-down lists using range names

■ Understand the #NUM!, #DIV/0! and #NAME? error values

■ Understand the #VALUE!, #REF! and #NULL! error values

■ Understand background error checking and error checking rules

■ Manually check a worksheet for errors

■ Audit a formula by tracing precedents

■ Audit a formula by tracing dependents

■ Use the Watch Window to monitor cell values

■ Use Speak Cells to eliminate data entry errors

Lesson 4-1: Automatically create single-cell range names

The sample worksheet for this lesson contains prices that need to be expressed in different currencies. When you have this type of data, a separate exchange rate worksheet makes the exchange rates easy to maintain.

Here's how the exchange rates will be defined:

	A	B
3	GBP/USD	1.45427
4	EUR/USD	1.0923
5	JPY/USD	0.00852

A range name will then be automatically created for each of the values in column B. Excel will choose range names for column B based upon the values in column A. For the exchange rate in cell B3, it will automatically create the range name:

GBP_USD

You can then use the range name to make your formulas more readable.

	A	B	C	D
3	Description	Year	US Dollars	British Pounds
4	Chateau Lafite	1787	160000	=C4/USD_GBP

note

About names

A name can be applied to a range of cells, a single cell, a formula, a constant or a table.

When a name has been applied, it can be referred to within a formula in place of the item that it represents. For example, if the range A5:A45 was given the name *Sales*, the formulas:

=SUM(A5:A45)

and

=SUM(Sales)

…would produce exactly the same result.

tip

You can also bring up the *Create Names from Selection* dialog using the keyboard shortcut:

<Ctrl>+<Shift>+<F3>

1   Open *Vintage Wines-1* from your sample files folder.

2   Automatically create a range name for each of the exchange rates.

1.   Click the *ExchangeRates* worksheet tab.

2.   Select the range A3:B5.

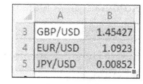

3.   Click: Formulas→Defined Names→Create from Selection.

The *Create Names from Selection* dialog appears:

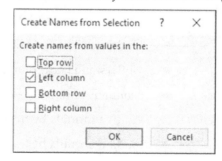

Notice that Excel has correctly guessed that the labels for each exchange rate are in the left column.

4.   Click the *OK* button.

Vintage Wines-1

note

Syntax rules for Range Names

Range names cannot contain spaces and may only begin with a letter, an underscore character (_), or a backslash (\).

Only letters, numbers, periods, question marks and underscores can be included within a name.

Range names are not case sensitive, so the name **SALES** or **Sales** can be used to reference a range name defined as **sales**.

Range names cannot be the same as any valid cell reference.

Good:
Boeing737
Boeing_737
_Boeing737
\Boeing.737

Bad:
737Boeing (number at start)
Boeing 737 (contains space)
BOE737 (same as a cell reference)

Excel uses range names for some of its own features. For this reason, you should never use any of the following range names:

Print_Area
Sheet_Title
Consolidate_Area
Print_Titles
Criteria

My preferred naming convention is to always spell out names in full, using mixed case with no underscores:

Good:
SalesTarget

Bad:
Sales_Target (underscore)
SlsTgt (abbreviation)

Nothing seems to have happened, but Excel has actually created a range name for each of the values in cells B3:B5.

3 Click the drop-down arrow on the right of the *Name* box to view the range names.

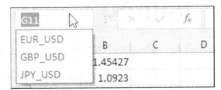

Notice that Excel hasn't used the exact names shown in column A, but has changed each forward slash to an underscore. This is because a forward slash isn't valid syntax for a range name (see sidebar for more on range name syntax).

4 Use formulas containing a range name to calculate prices in Great Britain Pounds, Euros and Japanese Yen.

1. Click the *Prices* worksheet tab.

2. Click in cell D4.

3. Type =**C4/** to begin the formula.

4. Click: Formulas→Defined Names→Use in Formula.

   A drop-down list appears containing all defined range names.

5. Click: *GBP_USD* to insert the range name.

6. Press the **<Enter>** Key.

7. Use the same technique to enter a formula to calculate the *Euro* and *Japanese Yen* prices in cells E4 and F4.

5 AutoFill the formulas in cells D4:F4 to cells D5:F11.

	C	D	E	F
3	US Dollars	British Pounds	Euros	Japanese Yen
4	$160,000.00	£ 110,020.84	€ 146,479.90	¥18,779,342.72
5	$ 43,500.00	£ 29,911.91	€ 39,824.22	¥5,105,633.80

6 Save your work as *Vintage Wines-2*.

note

Qualified and Unqualified range name references

An unqualified reference means that the range name is used on its own. For example:

=C4*KilometerToMile

Qualified references state the worksheet name, then an exclamation mark, and then the *range name*. For example:

ConversionFactors! KilometerToMile

Range Name scope

Scope means the places in your workbook where an *unqualified* range name may be used. There are two possible scopes:

Workbook Scope – The name may be used within any of the worksheets in the workbook.

Worksheet Scope – The name may only be used within a specified worksheet.

Scope mayhem

Excel confusingly allows a *workbook scope* and a *worksheet scope* range name to share the same name. If this is done, the *worksheet scope* name takes precedence within the specified worksheet and the *workbook scope* name has precedence everywhere else.

Lesson 4-2: Manually create single cell range names and named constants

1 Open *Distances-1* from your sample files folder.

2 Manually create a range name for the *Kilometer to Mile* conversion factor using the *Name* box.

1. Click the *ConversionFactors* worksheet.

	A	B	C
3	From	To	Multiply By
4	Kilometer	Mile	0.621371192
5	Meter	Foot	3.28083

This time you are unable to automatically create range names because the values in column B are not descriptive enough to easily identify each conversion factor.

2. Click in cell C4.

3. Type **KilometerToMile** into the *Name* box.

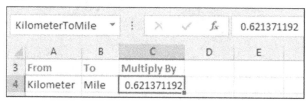

4. Press the **<Enter>** key.

3 Manually create a range name for the Meter to Foot conversion factor using the *Define Name* dialog.

This is an alternative method of defining range names.

1. Click in cell C5.

2. Click: Formulas→Defined Names→Define Name.

The *New Name* dialog appears.

3. Type the name **MeterToFoot** into the *Name* box.

Leave the scope as *Workbook* (see sidebar for an explanation of scope).

4. Click the *OK* button.

4 Use formulas containing range names to calculate distances in miles on the *Distances* worksheet.

	A	B	C	D
3	From	To	Km	Miles
4	London	Paris	343	

1. Click in cell D4 on the *Distances* worksheet.

2. Type: **=C4***

Distances-1

You now need to insert the conversion factor to convert Kilometers to Miles.

3. Click: Formulas→Defined Names→Use in Formula.

    A drop-down list appears showing all currently defined range names.

4. Click *KilometerToMile*.

    f_x =C4*KilometerToMile

5. Press the **<Enter>** key.

5 AutoFill cell D4 to cells D5:D11.

	A	B	C	D
3	From	To	Km	Miles
4	London	Paris	343	213.13
5	New York	Sydney	15,989	9,935.10

6 Given that one Kilometer = 0.539956803 Nautical Miles, create a named constant that will convert Kilometers into Nautical Miles.

Constants are used for values that will rarely change. Named constants are useful because they are difficult to change and are thus less likely to be changed accidentally.

When you create a named constant, there is no cell on the worksheet that contains the constant value.

1. Click: Formulas→Defined Names→Define Name.

2. Type **KilometerToNauticalMile** into the *Name* box:

    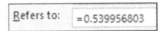
    Name: KilometerToNauticalMile

3. Type: **=0.539956803** into the *Refers to* box.

    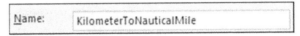
    Refers to: =0.539956803

4. Click the *OK* button.

7 Use the *KilometerToNauticalMile* named constant to add a formula to cell E4 that will calculate the distance from London to Paris in nautical miles.

1. Click in cell E4.

2. Type **=C4*** to start the formula.

3. Click: Formulas→Defined Names→Use in Formula to see the list of defined names.

4. Click *KilometerToNauticalMile* from the drop-down list.

    f_x =C4*KilometerToNauticalMile

5. Press the **<Enter>** Key.

8 AutoFill cell E4 to cells E5:E11.

9 Save your work as *Distances-2.*

---

tip

You can also use the **<F3>** shortcut key to display a list of all currently defined names.

This is very useful when creating formulas that incorporate names.

note

When to use constants rather than range names

You should use single-cell range names when a value may possibly change in the future.

This was the case in: *Lesson 4-1: Automatically create single-cell range names* because you were dealing with currency exchange rates that fluctuate.

Constants are more appropriate when a value is never expected to change. For this reason, constants would be more appropriate for the conversion factors used in this lesson.

Lesson 4-3: Use range names to make formulas more readable

1   Open *Sales and Profit-1* from your sample files folder.

	A	B
3	Sales	10,000.00
4	Cost	8,000.00
5	Gross Profit	2,000.00
6	Commission	100.00
7	Tax	200.00
8	Net Profit	1,700.00

2   Show formulas instead of values within the worksheet.

Click: Formulas→Formula Auditing→Show Formulas.

	A	B
3	Sales	10000
4	Cost	8000
5	Gross Profit	=B3-B4
6	Commission	=B5*5%
7	Tax	=B5*10%
8	Net Profit	=B5-B6-B7

It is reasonably clear from the formulas that:

Gross Profit = Sales - Cost

... and that five percent commission and ten percent tax are being deducted.

You can make the formulas a lot easier to read using range names.

3   Create automatic range names for all of the values in cells B3:B8.

This was covered in depth in: *Lesson 4-1: Automatically create single-cell range name.*

1.   Select cells A3:B8.

2.   Click: Formulas→Defined Names→Create from Selection.

3.   Click *OK*.

4   View the range names created by Excel.

The easiest way to view the range names is to click the drop-down arrow to the right of the *Name* box:

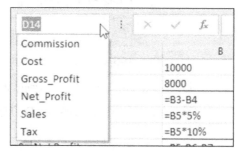

tip

The *Name* box is re-sizable.

Just click and drag the right-hand edge to make it as wide or as narrow as you want.

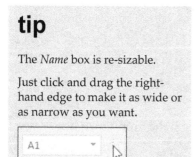

Sales and Profit-1

5 **Apply the new range names to the existing formulas.**

1. Make sure that cells A3:B8 are still selected.

2. Click: Formulas→Defined Names→
Define Name (Drop-down arrow)→Apply Names…

The *Apply Names* dialog appears.

3. Click the *OK* button.

The formulas should now show range names instead of cell references, making them a lot easier to read (but see next step for a potential Excel bug):

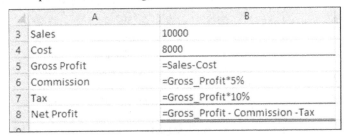

	A	B
3	Sales	10000
4	Cost	8000
5	Gross Profit	=Sales-Cost
6	Commission	=Gross_Profit*5%
7	Tax	=Gross_Profit*10%
8	Net Profit	=Gross_Profit - Commission -Tax

6 **Correct a possible Excel 365 bug.**

In Excel 2007, the range names would display as shown in the screen grab above. A bug was introduced in Excel 2010 that was still present in Excel 365 semi-annual version 1908, released on Jan 14 2020 (though it may have been repaired by the time you read this book).

If this bug still exists in your copy of Excel 365, you may see some unusual error dialogs (though the range names are still correctly applied).

You may also see an incorrect formula:

	A	B
8	Net Profit	=Gross_Profit Commission

Or you may find that cell B8 has not updated at all.

If this is the case, manually change cell B8 to:

	A	B
8	Net Profit	=Gross_Profit - Commission -Tax

7 **Show values instead of formulas within the worksheet.**

Click: Formulas→Formula Auditing→Show Formulas.

Values are now displayed rather than formulas:

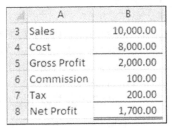

	A	B
3	Sales	10,000.00
4	Cost	8,000.00
5	Gross Profit	2,000.00
6	Commission	100.00
7	Tax	200.00
8	Net Profit	1,700.00

8 **Save your work as *Sales and Profit-2*.**

Lesson 4-4: Automatically create range names in two dimensions

1   Open *Earnings Summary-2* from your sample files folder.

	A	B	C	D	E	F	G	H	I
8	Name	Sales	Target	Hourly Rate	Hours Worked	Standard Pay	Overtime Pay	Bonus	Total
9	Brad Cruise	22,000	10,000	15.00	40	525.00	112.50	600.00	1,237.50
10	Ian Dean	9,000	8,000	13.00	35	455.00	-	50.00	505.00
11	Paris Smith	10,000	12,000	15.00	42	525.00	157.50	-	682.50
12	Gordon Ramsay	12,000	14,000	17.00	45	595.00	255.00	-	850.00
13	Barack Brown	15,000	9,000	13.00	35	455.00	-	300.00	755.00
14	Johnny Nicholson	18,000	14,000	17.00	40	595.00	127.50	200.00	922.50
15	Tony Blair	9,000	10,000	15.00	42	525.00	157.50	-	682.50
16	Jack Nicholson	10,000	9,000	13.00	30	390.00	-	50.00	440.00
17	Bob Clinton	9,000	11,000	15.00	35	525.00	-	-	525.00
18	Totals:	114,000	97,000		344	4,590.00	810.00	1,200.00	6,600.00

This worksheet was previously created in Session 3.

2   Create automatic range names based upon the labels in column A and row 8.

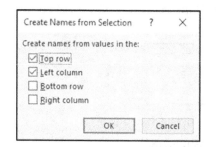

1.   Select the range A8:I17.

2.   Click: Formulas→Defined Names→Create from Selection.

Excel correctly guesses that the labels are in the *Top row* and *Left column*.

3.   Click the *OK* button.

3   View the range names created using the *Name Manager*.

1.   Click: Formulas→Defined Names→Name Manager.

The *Name Manager* dialog appears.

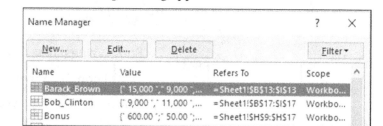

The *Name Manager* is fantastically useful when working with names. It lists all currently defined names and allows you to edit them. Note the *Filter* drop-down that allows you to show a subset of names. This is useful when working with workbooks that contain large numbers of names.

You can see that you have created a range name for each employee (named in column A) and for each of the columns (named in row 8).

2.   Click the *Close* button.

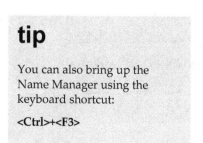

tip

You can also bring up the Name Manager using the keyboard shortcut:

<Ctrl>+<F3>

Earnings Summary-2

https://thesmartmethod.com

4   Type **Average Sales** into cell A20.

5   Type **Average Bonus** into cell A21.

6   Add a formula to cell B20 that uses a range name to calculate the average sales.

This time, you'll use Excel's *formula AutoComplete* feature to insert the range name into an AVERAGE formula.

1.   Click in cell B20 and type:

=AVERAGE(S

Notice that *Formula AutoComplete* shows both functions and defined names beginning with S:

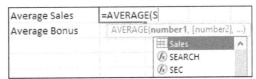

2.   Press the **<Tab>** key to insert the *Sales* range name.

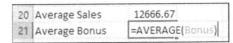

3.   Press the **<Enter>** key (the closing bracket is automatically added).

7   Add a formula to cell B21 that uses a range name to calculate the average bonus.

The correct formula is:

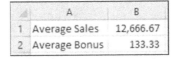

8   Apply the *Comma Style* to cells B20:B21.

1.   Select cells B20:B21.

2.   Click: Home→Number→Comma Style.

9   Widen column B slightly so that both values are visible.

10   Add a new worksheet (you can leave it at the default name of *Sheet2*).

11   Copy cells A20:B21 from the Sheet1 worksheet and then paste into cells A1:B2 on the *Sheet2* worksheet.

	A	B
1	Average Sales	12,666.67
2	Average Bonus	133.33

You can now appreciate one of the great advantages of range names. The formula on *Sheet2* is exactly the same as that on *Sheet1* and still works correctly.

Without the use of range names, it wouldn't have been possible to copy and paste the formulas between worksheets. You would have had to re-write the formula as:

=AVERAGE(Sheet1!B9:B17)

12   Save your work as *Earnings Summary-3*.

Lesson 4-5: Use intersection range names and the INDIRECT function

1   Open *Distance Chart-1* from your sample files folder.

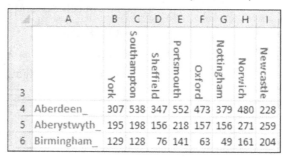

The chart allows you to quickly find the distance between two UK locations. For example, it is clear that the distance from Birmingham to Oxford is 63 miles.

2   Create automatic range names based upon the labels in column A and row 3.

1. Select the range A3:X26.

2. Click: Formulas→Defined Names→Create from Selection.

    Excel correctly guesses that the labels are in the *Top row* and *Left column*.

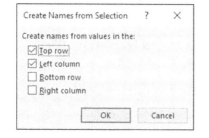

3. Click the *OK* button.

3   View the range names created using the *Name Manager*.

1. Click: Formulas→Defined Names→Name Manager.

    The *Name Manager* dialog appears.

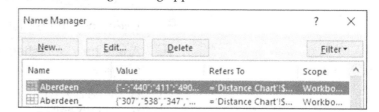

It is now clear why trailing underscores were used for the labels in column A. Without them, there would have been a naming conflict as each place name appears for both a row and a column.

2. Click the *Close* button.

4   Type **From** into cell A30.

5   Type **To** into cell A31.

6   Type **Miles** into cell A32.

7   Merge cells B30:E30, B31:E31 and B32:E32 (see sidebar if you are unable to do this).

tip

You can also bring up the Name Manager using the keyboard shortcut:

\<Ctrl\>+\<F3\>

Note

Merging cells

Merging cells is a basic skill covered in depth in *Lesson 4-6* of the *Essential Skills* book in this series.

To merge the cells:

1. Select cells B30:E30.

2. Click:

Home→Alignment→ Merge & Center→ Merge Across

Distance Chart-1

Note

The indirect function converts text to references

Consider this worksheet:

	A	B
1	Item	Cell Reference
2	Sales Total	A19
3	Cost Total	A35
4	**Profit**	

In this example the *Sales Total* value is present in cell A19 and the *Cost Total* value is present in cell A35.

If you placed this formula into cell B4:

=B2-B3

… the formula would fail:

	A	B
1	Item	Cell Reference
2	Sales Total	A19
3	Cost Total	A35
4	**Profit**	#VALUE!

The formula fails because Excel sees the values in cells B2 and B3 as simple text.

The correct formula would be:

=INDIRECT(B2)-INDIRECT(B3)

This formula succeeds:

	A	B
1	Item	Cell Reference
2	Sales Total	A19
3	Cost Total	A35
4	**Profit**	6,895.00

… because you have instructed Excel to regard the values in cells B2 and B3 as cell references rather than values.

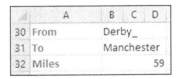

	A	B	C	D
30	From	Derby_		
31	To	Manchester		
32	Miles			59

8 Add a list validation to cell B30 that will restrict the cell to the items appearing in cells A4:A26.

This was covered in: *Lesson 2-11: Add a table-based dynamic list validation.*

9 Add a list validation to cell B31 that will restrict the cell to the items appearing in cells B3:X3.

10 Click in cell B30 and choose *Birmingham_* from the drop down list.

11 Click in cell B31 and choose *Oxford* from the drop down list.

Your worksheet should now look like this:

	A	B	C	D
30	From	Birmingham_		
31	To	Oxford		
32	Miles			

12 Use the intersection operator to create a formula in cell B32 that will show the distance from Birmingham to Oxford.

1. Click in cell B32.

2. Type the formula:

   =Birmingham_ Oxford

   Note that there is a space between the words *Birmingham_* and *Oxford*.

3. Press the **<Enter>** key.

The space is the intersection operator. The correct mileage is displayed in cell B32 (63 miles).

13 Use the INDIRECT function and the intersection operator (space) to show the correct distance in cell B32 based upon the values in cells B30 and B31.

This is more difficult than it first seems.

You could be forgiven for thinking that the formula:

=B30 B31

…would work.

Unfortunately, you can't refer to range names in this way. Excel provides the INDIRECT function to solve this problem (see sidebar).

1. Type the following formula into cell B32:

   Note that there is a space between *=INDIRECT(B30)* and *INDIRECT(B31)*.

2. Press the **<Enter>** key.

   The correct mileage is now shown in cell B32 for any journey that you select in cells B30 and B31.

14 Save your work as *Distance Chart-2.*

important

Tables are a better way to implement a dynamic name

You may wonder why I am wasting time teaching a technique that you shouldn't use!

The reason is that there are two scenarios where you may need to use dynamic formula-based range names:

1. You may have to work with a legacy workbook that was originally created before 2007 (or by an author who didn't understand tables).

2. You may need to use *Custom Views.* This feature doesn't work if a table exists anywhere in the workbook. You'll learn about *Custom Views* later, in *Lesson 5-8: Create custom views.*

Some Excel features (such as validations) are not yet compatible with tables. You still shouldn't waste time using formula-based range names as it is easier to create a dynamic range name based on a table. This will be covered later in: *Lesson 4-7: Create table-based dynamic range names.*

Lesson 4-6: Create dynamic formula-based range names using the OFFSET function

The technique shown in this lesson is a work-around that, in most cases, hasn't been needed since 2007 when the *table* feature was introduced. (You learned about tables in: *Session One: Tables, and Ranges*).

Feel free to skip this lesson if it is not relevant to you (see sidebar).

The range referred to by a range name is already dynamic to a point. If the range has rows or columns added or removed *inside the range,* the range name will automatically adjust. Problems occur when a new value is added to a blank row immediately below a range. In this case, the range name does not automatically adjust.

1 Open *Human Resources-1* from your sample files folder.

This is a simple workbook containing two worksheets. One worksheet lists employees and the other lists all of the company's current offices and departments.

2 Create automatic range names for cells A4:A6 and C4:C7 on the *Validations* worksheet.

1. Select the *Validations* worksheet.

2. Select cells A3:A6 (to include the range header).

3. Click: Formulas→Defined Names→Create from Selection.

Note that the actual range name will be A4:A6. Cell A3 was only included in order to define the automatic name: *Offices.*

4. Click the *OK* button.

5. Repeat for the range C3:C7.

3 Create list validations for columns B and C on the *Employees* worksheet.

1. Select all of the cells in column B on the *Employees* worksheet.

2. Click: Data→Data Tools→Data Validation.

3. Select *List* in the *Allow* drop-down list.

4. Type **=Offices** into the *Source* box.

5. Click the *OK* button.

6. Use the same technique to add a list validation for *Departments* to column C.

4 Use the drop-down lists to add some random *Offices* and *Departments* for Brad Cruise, Ian Dean and Paris Smith.

5 Type **Rome** into cell A7 on the *Validations* worksheet.

6 Select the *Employees* worksheet.

7 Add an office for Gordon Ramsay.

	A	B	C
3	Name	Office	Department
4	Brad Cruise	London	Purchasing
5	Ian Dean	Paris	Credit Control
6	Paris Smith	New York	Sales

Human Resources-1

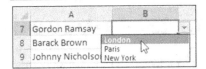

Notice that the new *Rome* office can't be added. That's because the range name does not adjust itself when a new value is added to a blank row immediately below a range.

8   Convert the *Offices* range name into a formula-based name that is able to automatically re-size.

To do this you need to use the OFFSET function. This returns a range reference that is a given number of rows or columns from a specified cell, or from an offset from a specified cell.

In this case, the specified cell will be A4 (on the *Validations* worksheet) as this contains the first *Office*, but how can you automatically detect how many offices there are?

The answer is to use the COUNTA function to return the number of cells in column A that are not empty. COUNTA needs a range to examine for non-blank cells. You'll use the range A4:A200 on the basis that you're unlikely to ever have more than 197 offices.

=COUNTA(Validations!$A$4:$A$200) will thus return 4: the current number of offices in the range.

To convert the *Offices* range name into a formula-based range name, you will need to use the *Name Manager*.

1.   Click: Formulas→Defined Names→Name Manager.

2.   Click the *Offices* range name.

3.   Click the *Edit* button.

Note that this name currently refers to the range:

Refers to: =Validations!$A$4:$A$6

4.   Type the following formula into the *Refers to* box:

=OFFSET(Validations!$A$4,0,0,COUNTA(Validations!$A$4:$A$200))

The four arguments specify where the range will begin, the number of rows to offset the start of the range by, the number of columns to offset the start of the range by, and the number of rows in the range.

5.   Click the *OK* button.

9   Convert the *Departments* range name into a formula-based range name that is able to automatically re-size.

Do this in exactly the same way as for the *Offices* range. This time, the formula in the *Refers to* box will be:

=OFFSET(Validations!$C$4,0,0,COUNTA(Validations!$C$4:$C$200))

10   Test the validation by adding *Offices* and *Departments*.

When you add a new *Office* or *Department*, the range names now dynamically expand to include the new item. Note that there should never be any blank entries within the list.

11   Save your work as *Human Resources-2*.

Lesson 4-7: Create table-based dynamic range names

In the last lesson: *Lesson 4-6: Create dynamic formula-based range names using the OFFSET function,* you used a complex method based on the OFFSET and COUNTA functions to implement a dynamic formula-based range name.

You'll be pleased to know that (since 2007) there has been a much simpler way to achieve the same thing using a table-based range name. The technique described in this lesson is also more elegant and less prone to error.

1 Open *Human Resources-2* from your sample files folder (if it isn't already open).

This is a simple workbook containing two worksheets. One worksheet lists employees and the other lists all of the company's current offices and departments.

2 Delete the existing range names for *Departments* and *Offices.*

1. Click: Formulas→Defined Names→Name Manager.

2. Select *Departments* and *Offices* and then click the *Delete* button.

3. Click *OK* to confirm that you want to delete.

4. Click the *Close* button to close the *Name Manager.*

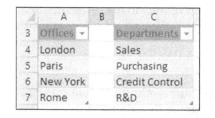

3 Convert the ranges A3:A7 and C3:C7 on the *Validations* worksheet into tables.

This was covered in depth in: *Lesson 1-12: Convert a range into a table and add a total row.*

1. Click anywhere in the range A3:A7 on the *Validation* worksheet.

2. Click: Insert→Tables→Table.

3. Click the *OK* button.

4. Do exactly the same thing for the *Departments* range.

4 Name the two new tables *Office* and *Department.*

1. Click anywhere inside the range A3:A7.

2. Click Table Tools→Design→Properties→Table Name.

3. Type **Office** into the text box.

4. Do exactly the same thing to name the *Department* table.

Human Resources-2

5   Create range names called *OfficeTable* and *DepartmentTable* based upon the two new tables.

Unfortunately, Excel doesn't accept a table name for a list validation. Fortunately, it is happy to accept a range name associated with a table.

1. Select all of the values in the *Office* table (cells A4:A7), being careful not to include the header row.

2. Click: Formulas→Defined Names→Define Name.

   The *New Name* dialog appears.

3. Type **OfficeTable** in the *Name* text box.

   Note that the *Refers to* box now contains the structured reference:

   This means that the structured reference refers to all of the data in the *Office* table. In other words, it is a dynamic named range that will shrink and grow with the *Office* table.

4. Click the *OK* button.

5. Create a *DepartmentTable* range name in exactly the same way.

6   Edit the list validation on columns B and C in the *Employees* worksheet to reference the *OfficeTable* and *DepartmentTable* range names.

1. Select column B on the *Employees* worksheet.

2. Click: Data→Data Tools→Data Validation.

3. Delete *=Offices* from the *Source* text box.

4. Press the **<F3>** key to bring up a list of range names.

   This is the fastest way to bring up the *Paste Name* dialog. The slower ribbon method is to click:

   Formulas→Defined Names→Use In Formula→Paste Names

5. Click: *OfficeTable*.

6. Click the *OK* button.

7. Click the OK button on the *Data Validation* dialog.

8. Use the same method to edit the list validation for column C.

7   Test the validations.

As items are added and deleted from the tables in the *Validations* worksheet, the changes are reflected in the contents of the drop-down validation lists on the *Employees* worksheet.

8   Save your work as *Human Resources-3*.

Lesson 4-8: Create two linked drop-down lists using range names

In this lesson, you're going to push Excel's validation feature into bold new territory by addressing a common business requirement.

Here's the sample worksheet for this session:

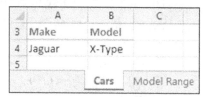

You want to add a validation to columns A and B (to allow users to select a *Make* and *Model*) for each row.

The *Make* validation is easy to implement as a simple list validation.

The *Model* validation is not so simple. The values that are valid need to change depending upon the selected *Make*.

Here's what you want to see:

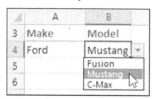 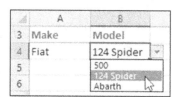

- When the Make is *Ford,* valid models are *Fusion, Mustang* and *C-Max*.

- When the Make is *Fiat*, valid models are *500, 124 Spider* and *Abarth*.

This lesson provides a solution to the problem by dynamically selecting the correct *Model* range name that matches the selected *Make*.

1   Open *New Car Model Range-1* from your sample files folder.

2   Create an automatic range name for the *Make* table on the *Model Range* worksheet.

   1. Select the *Model Range* worksheet.

   2. Select cells A5:A8.

   3. Click: Formulas→Defined Names→Create From Selection.

   4. Click the *OK* button.

3   Create automatic range names for each *Model* on the *Model Range* worksheet.

   1. Select cells A12:C15.

   2. Click Formulas→Defined Names→Create from Selection.

   3. De-select the *Left column* check box because you only want the range names to use the labels from the *Top row*.

   4. Click the *OK* button.

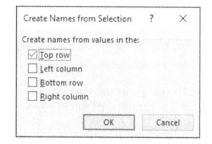

New Car Model Range-1

4   Apply a list validation to column A of the *Cars* worksheet that uses the *Make* range name as its source.

1.   Select column A on the *Cars* worksheet.

2.   Click: Data→Data Tools→Data Validation.

3.   Enter the following values into the dialog:

4.   Click the *OK* button.

5   Use the drop-down list to select a car make in cell A4.

6   Apply a list validation to cell B4 that will display a list of models based upon the make displayed in cell A4.

1.   Click in cell B4.

2.   Click: Data→Data Tools→Data Validation.

3.   Enter the following values into the dialog:

It is very important that the reference to cell A4 is relative (A4) and not absolute ($A$4) because you are going to copy the validation to the other cells in column B in a moment.

4.   Click the *OK* button.

7   Copy and paste the validation to all of the cells in column B.

1.   Copy the contents of cell B4.

2.   Select all of column B.

3.   Right-click inside the selected range and click *Paste Special...* from the shortcut menu.

4.   Select *Validation* from the *Paste Special* dialog.

5.   Click the *OK* button.

8   Test the validation.

The valid choices for *Model* now change based upon the *Make* selected in column A.

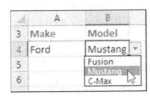

9   Save your work as *New Car Model Range-2.*

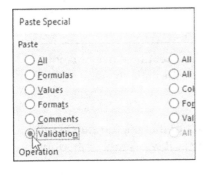

tip

Removing validation from the label row

It is quick and convenient to add validation to an entire column because you are never sure how many entries will ultimately be added to the range.

An unfortunate side-effect of this is that the validation drop-down arrows also appear when you click in the header and label rows (in this example rows 1 to 3).

To solve this problem:

1. Click on any empty cell in the worksheet *that contains no validation constraint.*

2. Press **<Ctrl>** + **<C>** to copy.

3. Select the cells that you want to remove validation from, and then click:

Home→Clipboard→Paste→ Paste Special→Validation

...to clear the validation.

Lesson 4-9: Understand the #NUM!, #DIV/0! and #NAME? error values

note

The #N/A error value

Sometimes Excel can't figure out exactly why an error has occurred.

In this case it displays the:

"I don't know what the specific problem is"

…error value.

#N/A

So why call it #N/A?

The official explanation is that this error displays when a value is *not available* to a function or formula.

Excel has six specific error values that it is able to display in cells containing formulas. It's important that you understand the type of problem that causes Excel to display each of these errors.

The error values are:

#DIV/0!, #NAME?, #NULL!, #NUM!, #REF! and **#VALUE!**

There's also a nonspecific error value called **#N/A** (see sidebar).

The sample worksheet for this lesson has faulty formulas that produce all six errors.

1   Open *Errors-1* from your sample files folder.

This worksheet has a lot of problems. You can see each of the six error messages appearing in different cells.

2   Diagnose and solve the problem causing the #NUM! error in cell D4.

	A	B	C	D
3	Month	Sales	Target	Above/Below Target
4	Jan	$ 5,210.00	$ 3,500.00	#NUM!
5	Feb	$ 5,650.00	$ -	$ 5,650.00

The #NUM! error is usually caused by a formula that returns a number that is too large, or too small for Excel to handle.

Another possible cause is a non-numeric value entered as an argument for a function that expects a numeric value.

1.   Examine the formula in cell D4:

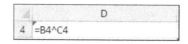

Here lies the problem. Excel is trying to calculate B4 *exponent* C4, which results in a huge number that Excel isn't capable of handling.

2.   Correct the formula.

As you need to calculate how far sales are above or below target you will need to correct the formula to:

The problem then vanishes. Notice that the formula in cell D10 now also displays correctly as it was simply inheriting the #NUM! error from cell D4.

Errors-1

https://thesmartmethod.com

3   Diagnose and solve the problem causing the #DIV/0! error in cell E5.

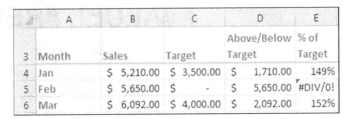

	A	B	C	D	E
				Above/Below	% of
3	Month	Sales	Target	Target	Target
4	Jan	$ 5,210.00	$ 3,500.00	$ 1,710.00	149%
5	Feb	$ 5,650.00	$ -	$ 5,650.00	#DIV/0!
6	Mar	$ 6,092.00	$ 4,000.00	$ 2,092.00	152%

Dividing by zero causes Excel's "Divide by Zero" error to be displayed.

1. Examine the formula in cell E5.

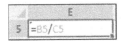

	E
5	=B5/C5

You know that the zero value must be in cell C5. Sure enough, no sales target was entered for February.

2. Enter a sales target of **3,250** for February.

The problem is solved.

If you didn't know the target for February and wanted to suppress the error message, you could use the IFERROR function as described in: *Lesson 3-24: Use an IFERROR function to suppress error messages.*

4   Diagnose and solve the problem causing the #NAME? error in cell C10.

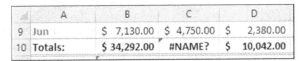

	A	B	C	D
9	Jun	$ 7,130.00	$ 4,750.00	$ 2,380.00
10	Totals:	$ 34,292.00	#NAME?	$ 10,042.00

The #NAME? error means that Excel has encountered a name it doesn't understand. The most likely cause is that you've used a range name that doesn't exist.

1. Examine the formula in cell C10.

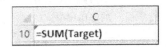

	C
10	=SUM(Target)

Because there was a #NAME? error you know that there is no range name called *Target.*

2. Select cells C3:C9.

3. Click: Formulas→Defined Names→Create from Selection.

4. Click the *OK* button.

The problem is now solved.

5   Save your work as *Errors-2.*

© 2020 The Smart Method® Ltd

Lesson 4-10: Understand the #VALUE!, #REF! and #NULL! error values

1   Open *Errors-2* from your sample files folder (if it isn't already open).

2   Diagnose and solve the problem causing the #VALUE! error in cell F8.

	A	B	C	D	E	F
3	Month	Sales	Target	Above/Below Target	% of Target	Exceeded Target?
4	Jan	$ 5,210.00	$ 3,500.00	$ 1,710.00	149%	Yes
5	Feb	$ 5,650.00	$ 3,250.00	$ 2,400.00	174%	Yes
6	Mar	$ 6,092.00	$ 4,000.00	$ 2,092.00	152%	Yes
7	Apr	$ 3,955.00	$ 4,250.00	$ -295.00	93%	No
8	May	$ 6,255.00	$ 4,500.00	$ 1,755.00	139%	#VALUE!

The #VALUE! error means that a function contains an invalid argument.

1. Examine the formula in cell F8.

    fx   =IF("B8>C8", "Yes", "No")

    The IF function was covered in: *Lesson 3-5: Use the IF logic function.*

    The first argument of an IF function demands a logical expression that evaluates TRUE or FALSE.

    There's nothing wrong with the logical expression: **B8>C8**. The problem is caused by the quotation marks that cause Excel to interpret it as text.

2. Correct the formula in cell F8 by removing the quotation marks from the expression **B8>C8** (the IF function's first argument).

    fx   =IF(B8>C8, "Yes", "No")

    The problem is solved.

3   Diagnose and solve the problem causing the #REF! error in cell B11.

	A	B	C
10	Totals:	$ 34,292.00	$ 24,250.00
11	GBP Totals:	#REF!	

The #REF! error means that a formula refers to a cell that isn't valid. This happens when you reference a cell from a formula and then delete the row or column that used to contain the referenced cell.

Errors-2

1. Examine the formula in cell B11

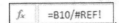

Because this cell needs to convert the dollar sales figure in cell B10 to Great Britain Pounds (GBP), the missing reference is the USD/GBP exchange rate.

2. Replace the #REF! part of the formula with **1.62** (the USD/GBP exchange rate when this lesson was first written).

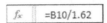

3. Press the **<Enter>** key.

The problem is solved.

4   Diagnose and solve the problem causing the #NULL! error in cell B16.

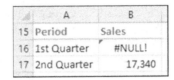

The #NULL! error occurred because Excel is confused by the use of the intersection (space) operator. It usually simply means that you've incorrectly typed one of a function's arguments.

1. Examine the formula in cell B16.

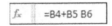

It is clear that there is a missing addition (+) operator between B5 and B6.

Excel has interpreted the missing operator as an attempt to reference the intersection of cells B5 and B6. It is, of course, impossible to have an intersection between two single cell references.

The intersection operator was covered in: *Lesson 4-5: Use intersection range names and the INDIRECT function.*

2. Correct the formula in cell B16 by adding the missing addition operator.

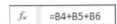

3. Press the **<Enter>** key.

The problem is solved.

5   Save your work as *Errors-3*.

Lesson 4-11: Understand background error checking and error checking rules

Excel is constantly working in the background, automatically checking for errors. Whenever Excel thinks you've made a mistake, it will politely let you know. Of course, Excel isn't always correct. It can only guess that you've made a mistake and it is often wrong.

1   Open *Daily Profit Report-1* from your sample files folder.

This workbook contains two errors. Excel has automatically detected them and indicates each by a small green triangle in the top left hand corner of each cell containing a suspected error.

If you don't see the green triangles on your computer, somebody has switched automatic error checking off. See the sidebar for instructions on how to switch it back on.

	A	B	C	D
3	Date	Sales	Costs	Profit
4	18-Sep-16	20,000	12,000	8,000
5	19-Sep-16	21,000	12,500	8,500
6	20-Sep-16	22,800	12,600	35,400
7	21-Sep-16	23,500	13,000	10,500
8	Total:	87,300	50,100	62,400

2   Understand error checking rules.

1. Click: File→Options→Formulas.

Note that Excel monitors for nine different error conditions by default. There's a tenth that is switched off by default but can be enabled if required:

☑ Cells containing formulas that result in an error ⓘ
☑ Inconsistent calculated column formula in tables ⓘ
☑ Cells containing years represented as 2 digits ⓘ
☑ Numbers formatted as text or preceded by an apostrophe ⓘ
☑ Formulas inconsistent with other formulas in the region ⓘ

☑ Formulas which omit cells in a region ⓘ
☑ Unlocked cells containing formulas ⓘ
☐ Formulas referring to empty cells ⓘ
☑ Data entered in a table is invalid ⓘ
☑ Misleading number formats ⓘ

2. Click the *Cancel* button.

3   Remove the error warning from cell A5.

1. Click on cell A5. Notice that an *Error Smart Tag* has appeared to the right of the cell.

2. Hover the mouse cursor over the *Smart Tag*.

note

Why can't I see any green triangles?

If you don't see the green triangles, somebody has switched off automatic error checking.

To switch it back on, check the check box:

File→Options→Formulas→Error Checking→Enable background error checking

Daily Profit Report-1

trivia

Why the world was predicted to end in the year 2000

As the year 2000 approached, many computer experts predicted world chaos caused by computer systems crashing due to the "Y2K bug".

The theory was that dates containing only two digits for the year would confuse computer systems, causing them to fail.

As media hype moved into gear, experts were lined up to predict the failure of air traffic control systems and the world's financial markets.

One widely reported theory was that every elevator (lift) in the world would stop working, as their control software would assume that it was 1900 and that they all were overdue for a service!

There was even a theory that nuclear missiles would launch themselves as their control software went haywire.

All of this hype was really good for sales of such things as bottled water and candles as the new millennium approached.

Governments worried that public fears would cause a massive run on the banks, making the Y2K problem a self-fulfilling prophecy.

1st January 2000 came and went with hardly any problems, proving that you shouldn't believe everything that you read in the newspapers.

A tip appears showing the rule that Excel believes has been violated:

5	19-Sep-16	!	▾ 21,000	12,500	8,500
6	20-Sep-16				
7	21-Sep-16		23,500	15,000	10,500

This cell contains a date string represented with only 2 digits for the year.

3. Click the down arrow on the Smart Tag.

	A	B	C	D
3	Date	Sales	Costs	Profit
4	18-Sep-16	20,000	12,000	8,000
5	19-Sep-16 !	▾ 21,000	12,500	8,500
6	20-Sep-16	Text Date with 2-Digit Year		35,400
7	21-Sep-16			10,500
8	Total:	Convert XX to 19XX		62,400
9		Convert XX to 20XX		
10		Ignore Error		
11		Edit in Formula Bar		
12		Error Checking Options...		
13				

Excel is worried because the date (unlike the other dates in the column) has been entered as a text value with two digits for the year. This is a throw-back to the problems caused in the year 2000 when such dates were predicted to bring about the end of the world (see sidebar).

A date can be entered in this way by preceding the date by an apostrophe to indicate that the entry is a textual value:

'19-Sep-16

Notice that two of the options in the *Smart Tag list* offer to convert the date to 2016 or to 1916.

4. Click *Ignore Error*.

The green triangle vanishes.

4 Correct the error in cell D6.

1. Click on cell D6 and hover the mouse cursor over the *Smart Tag*.

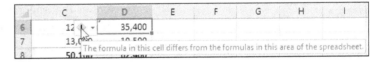

This time Excel has found a real error. It has noticed that the formula in cell D6 is inconsistent with the other formulas in column D. The formula is adding costs to sales when it should be subtracting them.

2. Click the down arrow on the *Smart Tag* and click *Copy Formula From Above* from the shortcut menu.

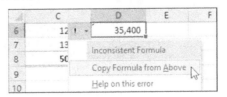

The error is corrected.

5 Save your work as *Daily Profit Report-2*.

© 2020 The Smart Method® Ltd

Lesson 4-12: Manually check a worksheet for errors

Sometimes those little green triangles can be annoying. Excel often picks up "errors" that are not really errors at all.

Some Excel users would prefer to switch off background error checking and instead run a manual error check when the worksheet is complete.

In this lesson, you'll switch off Excel's background error checking and then manually scan a worksheet for errors.

1   Open *Operating Expenses-1* from your sample files folder.

This workbook contains three errors. Excel has automatically detected them and indicates each by a small green triangle in the top left-hand corner of each cell containing a suspected error.

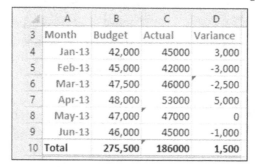

	A	B	C	D
3	Month	Budget	Actual	Variance
4	Jan-13	42,000	45000	3,000
5	Feb-13	45,000	42000	-3,000
6	Mar-13	47,500	46000	-2,500
7	Apr-13	48,000	53000	5,000
8	May-13	47,000	47000	0
9	Jun-13	46,000	45000	-1,000
10	Total	275,500	186000	1,500

2   Switch off background error checking.

1.   Click: File→Options→Formulas.

2.   Clear the *Enable background error checking* check box:

Error Checking

☐ Enable background error checking

3.   Click the *OK* button.

Notice that the green triangles have now vanished, even though the error conditions remain.

3   Manually check the worksheet for errors.

1.   Click: Formulas→Formula Auditing→Error Checking.

Cell D6 is selected (the first cell in the worksheet containing a suspected error) and the *Error Checking* dialog appears:

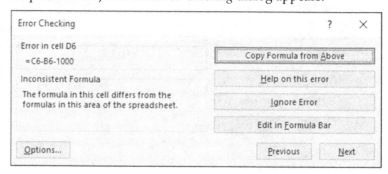

Error Checking	? ×
Error in cell D6	Copy Formula from Above
=C6-B6-1000	
Inconsistent Formula	Help on this error
The formula in this cell differs from the formulas in this area of the spreadsheet.	Ignore Error
	Edit in Formula Bar
Options...	Previous Next

Operating
Expenses-1

The dialog indicates that Excel has detected an inconsistent formula. This means that the formula in cell D6 is not consistent with the other formulas in column D.

2. Click: Formulas→Formula Auditing→Show Formulas.

The formulas behind the cells are now displayed:

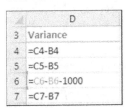

	D
3	Variance
4	=C4-B4
5	=C5-B5
6	=C6-B6-1000
7	=C7-B7

The error is now apparent. For some reason an extra 1,000 has been deducted from the variance for March 2016.

3. Click: Formulas→Formula Auditing→Show Formulas.

Values are once again shown in all cells.

4. Click the *Resume* button on the *Error Checking* dialog.

5. Click *Copy Formula from Above* to correct the error.

The error is corrected, and the active cell moves to cell C8. Cell C8 is the next cell in the worksheet that contains a suspected error.

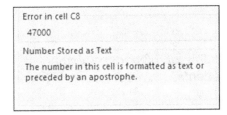

This time, the error is caused by a number being stored as text. This can happen when a numeric cell is formatted as text or when a value is typed into a cell preceded with an apostrophe like this:

'47000

6. Click *Convert to Number*.

The error is corrected, and the active cell moves to cell C10. Cell C10 is the next cell in the worksheet that contains a suspected error.

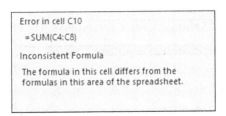

This time the error is another inconsistent formula. The formula in cell C10 is incorrectly adding the values in cells C4:C8 instead of C4:C9. Excel has noticed that this is inconsistent with the formulas in cells B10 and D10.

7. Click *Copy Formula from Left* to correct the error.

8. Click the *OK* button to end the error check.

Re-enable background error checking.

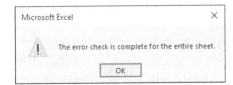

1. Click: File→Options→Formulas.

2. Check the *Enable background error checking* check box.

3. Click the *OK* button.

Notice that there are no longer any green triangles as you've corrected all of the errors.

5 Save your work as *Operating Expenses-2*.

Lesson 4-13: Audit a formula by tracing precedents

When you have a worksheet with cross-worksheet formulas and range names, there is a lot of scope for error. Ranges and formulas can often reference the wrong cells.

Excel's *trace precedents* tool provides an easy way to quickly audit cell references in order to confirm the integrity of your workbook.

1   Open *Profit Analysis-1* from your sample files folder.

This workbook summarizes data from the *January, February* and *March* worksheets into a *First Quarter Summary*. The workbook also makes extensive use of range names.

	A	B	C	D	E	F	G	H
1	First Quarter Summary							
2								
3		Sales	Cost	Profit				
4	Jan	89,199	45,318	43,881				
5	Feb	99,197	42,510	56,687				
6	Mar	87,194	45,025	42,169				
7	Totals:	275,590	132,853	142,737				
8								

First Quarter Summary | January | February | March

2   Audit the formula in cell D7 of the *First Quarter Summary* worksheet using *Trace Precedents*.

1. Click into cell D7.

    Notice that it isn't possible to immediately see which cells are referenced by the *Profit* range name.

    fx   =SUM(Profit)

2. Click: Formulas→Formula Auditing→Trace Precedents.

    The cells referenced by the *Profit* range name are now apparent.

	A	B	C	D
3		Sales	Cost	Profit
4	Jan	89,199	45,318	43,881
5	Feb	99,197	42,510	56,687
6	Mar	87,194	45,025	42,169
7	Totals:	275,590	132,853	142,737

You might think that this isn't very impressive. You could have done the same thing by pressing the **<F2>** key, or by clicking the word *Profit* in the formula bar. But there's more to come!

3. Click: Formulas→Formula Auditing→Trace Precedents again.

    This time the next level of precedents is shown:

Profit Analysis-1

https://thesmartmethod.com

	A	B	C	D
3		Sales	Cost	Profit
4	Jan	89,199	45,318	43,881
5	Feb	99,197	42,510	56,687
6	Mar	87,194	45,025	42,169
7	Totals:	275,590	132,853	142,737

note

Use Trace Error to quickly find the first error in a chain

When a cell shows an error condition (such as **#DIV/0!**), it is often caused by an error in a precedent cell.

It is possible to click:

Formulas→
Formula Auditing→
Trace Precedents

... several times in order to trace the cell causing the error.

Excel also provides a way of tracing all precedents in a single click when a cell shows an error condition, allowing you to save a few mouse clicks.

When the active cell contains an error condition, you can click:

Formulas→
Formula Auditing→
Error Checking→
Trace Error

This shows all precedents, at all levels, with a single click.

You can see that the value in cell D4 is calculated from the values in cells B4 and C4. You can also see that the value in cell D7 is calculated from the range D4:D6.

But where are the values in cells B4:C6 coming from?

4. Click: Formulas→Formula Auditing→Trace Precedents again.

	A	B	C	D
2				
3		Sales	Cost	ofit
4	Jan	89,199	45,318	43,881
5	Feb	99,197	42,510	56,687
6	Mar	87,194	45,025	42,169
7	Totals:	275,590	132,853	142,737

The icons pointing to cells B4:C6 indicate that their values come from different worksheets in this (or even another) workbook.

5. Double-click the dotted line joining cell B4 and the icon.

The *Go To* dialog appears, showing the source of the value in cell B4.

6. Select the item shown in the *Go To* window and then click the *OK* button.

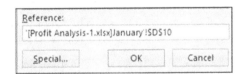

7. Click: Formulas→Formula Auditing→Trace Precedents again.

Now you can see the precedents of cell D10 in the *January* worksheet (see sidebar).

8. Click: Formulas→Formula Auditing→Remove Arrows.

The precedent arrows are removed from the *January* worksheet.

9. Select the *First Quarter Summary* worksheet.

10. Click: Formulas→Formula Auditing→Remove Arrows.

The precedent arrows are removed from the *First Quarter Summary* worksheet.

	D	E	
3	Sales	Cost	
4	16,756	9,431	
5	19,437	7,412	
6	14,742	7,960	
7	15,881	6,214	
8	11,835	8,714	
9	10,548	5,587	
10	89,199	45,318	

You are taken to the cell in the *January* worksheet that provides the value shown in cell B4 on the *First Quarter Summary* worksheet.

Lesson 4-14: Audit a formula by tracing dependents

1   Open *Profit Analysis-1* from your sample files folder (if it isn't already open).

2   Select the *January* worksheet.

3   Audit the formula in cell D6 using *Trace Dependents*.

1.   Click cell D6 to make it the active cell.

2.   Click: Formulas→Formula Auditing→Trace Dependents.

The direct dependents are shown for cell D6. These cells have formulas that directly reference cell D6.

	A	B	C	D	E	F
3	Team	First Name	Last Name	Sales	Cost	Profit
4	Blue	Johnny	Caine	16,756	9,431	7,325
5	Blue	George	Marley	19,437	7,412	12,025
6	Blue	Bill	Spears	14,742	7,960	6,782
7	Red	Gordon	Depp	15,881	6,214	9,667
8	Red	Tom	Marley	11,835	8,714	3,121
9	Red	Charles	Blair	10,548	5,587	4,961
10	Totals:			89,199	45,318	43,881
11						
12	Team			Average Sales	Average Cost	Average Profit
13	Blue			16,978	8,268	8,711
14	Red			12,755	6,838	5,916

You can see that:

• The *Profit* in cell F6 depends upon *Sales* in D6 (because Profit = Sales-Cost).

• The *Total Sales* in cell D10 depends upon the *Sales* in D6.

• The *Average Sales* for the *Blue* team also depends upon the value in D6 because Bill Spears is in the *Blue* team.

3.   Click: Formulas→Formula Auditing→Trace Dependents again.

	A	B	C	D	E	F
3	Team	First Name	Last Name	Sales	Cost	Profit
4	Blue	Johnny	Caine	16,756	9,431	7,325
5	Blue	George	Marley	19,437	7,412	12,025
6	Blue	Bill	Spears	14,742	7,960	6,782
7	Red	Gordon	Depp	15,881	6,214	9,667
8	Red	Tom	Marley	11,835	8,714	3,121
9	Red	Charles	Blair	10,548	5,587	4,961
10	Totals:			89,199	45,318	43,881
11						
12	Team			Average Sales	Average Cost	Average Profit
13	Blue			16,978	8,268	8,711
14	Red			12,755	6,838	5,916

The next level of dependents is shown. You can now see that:

Profit Analysis-1

- The *Total* in cell F10 depends upon the *Profit* value in cell F6.

- The Blue Team's *Average Profit* in cell F13 depends upon the *Average Sales* in cell D13.

There is also an icon pointing to cell D10 indicating that there is a dependent value in a different worksheet in this (or even another) workbook.

4. Double-click the dotted line joining cell D10 and the icon.

The *Go To* dialog appears showing the source of the value in cell D10.

5. Select the item shown in the *Go To* window and then click the *OK* button.

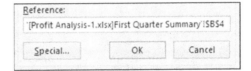

You are taken to cell B4 in the *First Quarter Summary* worksheet as this cell depends upon the value in cell D10 on the *January* worksheet.

6. Click: Formulas→Formula Auditing→Trace Dependents again.

You can now see the cells whose formulas directly depend upon the value in cell B4.

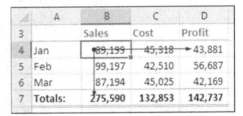

7. Click: Formulas→Formula Auditing→Trace Dependents again.

The final level of dependents is shown:

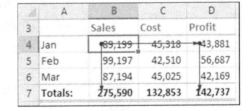

8. Click: Formulas→Formula Auditing→Remove Arrows.

The dependent arrows are removed from the *First Quarter Summary* worksheet.

9. Select the *January* worksheet.

10. Click: Formulas→Formula Auditing→Remove Arrows.

The dependent arrows are removed from the *January* worksheet.

Lesson 4-15: Use the Watch Window to monitor cell values

The *Watch Window* is useful when developing workbooks that contain cross-worksheet formulas. You'll often want to monitor one or more result cells on a summary worksheet as you edit values in source worksheets.

1 Open *Profit Analysis-1* from your sample files folder (if it isn't already open).

2 Select the *First Quarter Summary* worksheet.

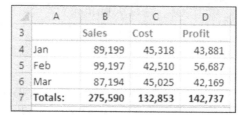

	A	B	C	D
3		Sales	Cost	Profit
4	Jan	89,199	45,318	43,881
5	Feb	99,197	42,510	56,687
6	Mar	87,194	45,025	42,169
7	Totals:	275,590	132,853	142,737

3 Set up a *Watch Window* to monitor the values in cells B7, C7 and D7.

1. Click cell B7 to make it the active cell.

2. Click: Formulas→Formula Auditing→Watch Window.

   The *Watch Window* appears.

3. Click the *Add Watch…* button.

   The *Add Watch* dialog appears:

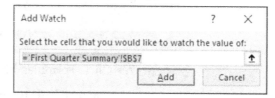

4. Click the *Add* button.

   The watchrd cell's details appear in the *Watch Window*.

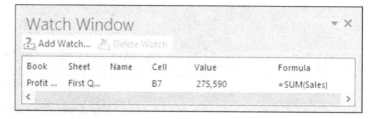

5. Click the *Add Watch…* button again.

6. Click on cell C7.

7. Click the *Add* button.

   A second watch appears in the *Watch Window*.

8. Add a watch for cell D7 in the same way.

   The *Watch Window* now contains three watched cells.

Profit Analysis-1

4   Dock the *Watch Window* to the top of the screen.

Drag the *Watch Window* to the top of the screen. It then snaps into place above the formula bar:

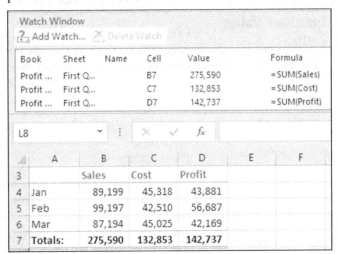

5   Convert the watch window into a floating dialog box.

1. Click the drop down menu at the top right corner of the *Watch Window* and then click *Move* from the shortcut menu.

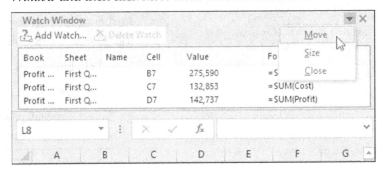

2. Move the cursor into the worksheet grid.

The window is converted back into a floating dialog box.

(You can also do this simply by dragging the top window downward).

6   Change some values on the *February* worksheet while monitoring the values defined in the Watch Window.

1. Click on the *February* worksheet tab.

2. Change Johnny Caine's sales (in cell D4) to 20,000 and press the **<Enter>** key.

Note that the values in the *Watch Window* have changed to reflect the new value.

Book	Sheet	Name	Cell	Value
Profit ...	First Quarter Summary		B7	276,841
Profit ...	First Quarter Summary		C7	132,853
Profit ...	First Quarter Summary		D7	143,988

3. Close the *Watch Window*.

7   Save your work as *Profit Analysis-2*.

note

Access Excel's hidden features using Tell Me help.

Tell Me help is covered in depth in *Lesson 1-19* of the *Essential Skills* book in this series.

Tell Me help is different from all previous versions of Excel help, as it allows you to both access help topics and execute Excel commands directly from the help system. This feature enables you to execute all of the *Commands Not in the Ribbon* that you saw listed in this lesson.

There are over 250 of these "secret" Excel commands and now, for the first time, you can execute any of them instantly using *Tell Me help*.

Here's how you could access the (very useful) *Speak Cells* hidden feature using *Tell Me help*:

1. Select some cells that have numbers, text or dates in them.

2. Click on the *Search* box in the menu bar:

3. Type: **Speak Cells** into the *Search* box.

A menu appears showing all of the *Speak Cells* commands:

4. Click on the *Speak Cells* menu item.

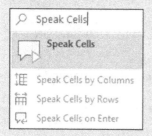

Excel will then read the selected cells to you.

Lesson 4-16: Use Speak Cells to eliminate data entry errors

One of my favorite Excel features is its ability to read the workbook to me via the *Speak Cells* facility. When I need to input lots of numbers from a sheet of paper and want to check them, I get Excel to read them to me as I tick each off my list. This is much faster and nicer than continuously looking first at the screen, and then at the paper, for each entry.

This is one of those "secret" features that most Excel users will never discover because you won't find it anywhere on the ribbon or standard Excel dialogs.

In pre-2016 versions of Excel, you had to add some custom buttons to the Quick Access Toolbar or ribbon in order to use this feature (you'll learn how to create a custom ribbon tab later in: *Lesson 7-20: Create a custom ribbon tab*). The *Tell Me help* system (accessed via the *Search* box at the top right of the menu bar) now provides a new way of accessing Excel's hidden features (discussed in the sidebar).

1 Open *Profit Analysis-2* from your sample files folder (if it isn't already open).

2 Add custom buttons to the Quick Access Toolbar for all of the *Speak Cells* commands.

    1. Click: File→Options→Quick Access Toolbar.

    The *Customize the Quick Access Toolbar* pane appears.

    2. Select *Commands Not in the Ribbon* from the *Choose commands from* drop-down list:

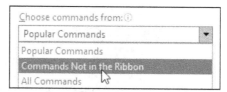

    3. Click the *Speak Cells* command in the list of commands:

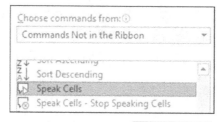

    4. Click the *Add* button. [Add >>]

    5. Click the *Add* button four more times to add all *Speak Cells* commands to the Quick Access Toolbar.

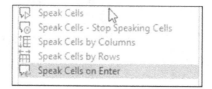

Profit Analysis-2

6.   Click the *OK* button.

3   Type **Bonus** into cell G3 on the *January* worksheet.

4   If necessary, apply the *Heading 3* cell style to cell G3.

5   Click in cell G4.

6   Click the *Speak Cells on Enter* button that you added to the Quick Access Toolbar.

You should hear the words "Cells will now be spoken on enter". If you don't hear this, your speakers are either muted or not working.

7   Add the following values to column G without looking at the Excel screen.

	E	F	G
3	Cost	Profit	Bonus
4	9,431	7,325	700
5	7,412	12,025	1200
6	7,960	6,782	600
7	6,214	9,667	900
8	8,714	3,121	300
9	5,587	4,961	400
10	45,318	43,881	

Notice that Excel speaks the number back to you every time that you press the **<Enter>** key. This means that you can be sure that you added the correct value without having to continually look from paper to screen.

8   Select cells G4:G9.

9   Click the *Speak Cells* button that you added to the Quick Access Toolbar.

This time Excel speaks each value in the column in sequence. This is an alternative way to double-check that figures have been entered correctly.

10   Click the *Speak Cells on Enter* button that you added to the Quick Access Toolbar.

You should hear the words "Turned off speak on enter". If you don't do this, Excel will continue to speak to you when you remove the toolbar buttons!

11   Remove the *Speak Cells* buttons from the Quick Access Toolbar.

Right-click on each *Speak Cells* button in turn and then click *Remove from Quick Access Toolbar*.

12   Save your work as *Profit Analysis-3*.

note

Excel won't stop talking!

You may delete your *Quick Access Toolbar* buttons and then find that Excel continues to talk to you.

It's easy to run into this problem, as you would reasonably expect the *Stop Speaking Cells* button to switch off the voice.

However, Excel will continue speaking as long as the *Speak Cells on Enter* button is pressed.

Session 4: Exercise

1 Open *Excel Quiz-1* from your sample files folder.

2 Select cells A5:E9 on the *Choices* worksheet.

	A	B	C	D	E
4					
5	1	64,000	128,000	512,000	1,048,576
6	2	1985	1992	1995	1997
7	3	Excel 7	Excel 12	Excel 9	Excel 16
8	4	Lotus 1-2-3	SuperCalc	VisiCalc	Multiplan
9	5	256	512	16,384	22,256

3 Create range names from the selected cells, using the value in the left column to name each range.

4 Apply a list validation to cell C4 on the *Quiz* worksheet that will show a list of all valid answers to the first question by referencing the range name matching the value in cell A4 on the *Quiz* worksheet using the INDIRECT function.

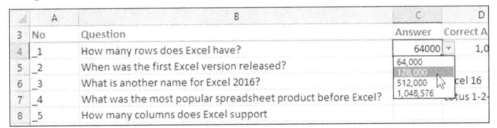

5 Copy and paste the validation from cell C4 to cells C5:C8.

6 Put an IF function into cell E4 that will show the text "CORRECT" if the answer in cell C4 equals the correct answer in cell D4, and a blank space if the answer is not correct.

	C	D	E
3	Answer	Correct Answer	Correct?
4	1048576	1,048,576	CORRECT

7 AutoFill cell E4 down to cells E5:E8.

8 Hide columns A and D.

9 Save your work as *Excel Quiz-2*.

	B	C	E
3	Question	Answer	Correct?
4	How many rows does Excel have?	1048576	CORRECT
5	When was the first Excel version released?	1985	CORRECT
6	What is another name for Excel 2016?		
7	What was the most popular worksheet before Excel?	Excel 7 / Excel 12	
8	How many columns does Excel support	Excel 9 / Excel 16	
9			

Excel Quiz-1

If you need help slide the page to the left

Session 4: Exercise Answers

These are the four questions that students find the most difficult to answer:

Q 6	Q 5	Q 4	Q 3
The correct function is: **=IF(D4=C4, "CORRECT", "")** This was covered in: *Lesson 3-5: Use the IF logic function.*	1. Click in cell C4. 2. Click: Home→ Clipboard→Copy. 3. Select the range C5:C8. 4. Click: Home→ Clipboard→ Paste→ Paste Special… 5. Select *Validation* in the *Paste Special* dialog. 6. Click the *OK* button. This was covered in: *Lesson 4-8: Create two linked drop-down lists using range names.*	1. Click in cell C4 on the *Quiz* worksheet. 2. Click: Data→ Data Tools→ Data Validation. 3. Complete the Data Validation dialog like this: The INDIRECT function allows you to use the value in column A to reference the range name (with the same name) that contains the correct multiple-choice answers. This was covered in: *Lesson 4-8: Create two linked drop-down lists using range names.*	1. Click: Formulas→ Defined Names→ Create from Selection. 2. Make sure that only the *Left column* is checked in the *Create Names from Selection* dialog. 3. Click the *OK* button. This was covered in: *Lesson 4-1: Automatically create single-cell range names.*

If you have difficulty with the other questions, here are the lessons that cover the relevant skills:

8 In order to hide a column, right-click the column header and select *Hide* from the shortcut menu.

This skill is covered in: *Lesson 3-27: Use the INDEX function.*

5

Session Five: What If Analysis and Security

> The superior man, when resting in safety, does not forget that danger may come. When in a state of security, he does not forget the possibility of ruin. When all is orderly, he does not forget that disorder may come. Thus his person is not endangered, and his States and all their clans are preserved.
>
> *Confucius (551 BC - 479 BC)*

The concept of "What If" is very simple. A business may wish to know what will happen in a given set of circumstances (called a scenario). For example, a simple scenario might be: "What if I reduced my profit margins by 5% and this caused my sales to increase by 20%?" Excel provides several tools that are geared to more complex scenarios. In this session you'll learn how to use these tools effectively.

Sometimes you'll want to keep the contents of a workbook secure. This session will show you how to prevent unauthorized users from opening or changing your workbooks. You'll also learn how to restrict the cells that a user is able to edit within a workbook. This session will also show you how to hide rows and columns and then create multiple custom views of the worksheet – each view hiding and showing different information.

Session Objectives

By the end of this session you will be able to:

- Create a single-input data table
- Create a two-input data table
- Define scenarios
- Create a scenario summary report
- Use Goal Seek
- Use Solver
- Hide and unhide worksheets, columns and rows
- Create custom views
- Prevent unauthorized users from opening or modifying workbooks
- Control the changes users can make to workbooks
- Restrict the cells users are allowed to change
- Allow different levels of access to a worksheet with multiple passwords
- Create a digital certificate
- Add an invisible digital signature to a workbook
- Add a visible digital signature to a workbook

Lesson 5-1: Create a single-input data table

Don't be fooled by the name. A *data table* has nothing to do with a regular Excel table. Data tables are another of those wonderful Excel features that are a complete mystery to virtually all Excel users.

In this lesson you'll use a data table to list the monthly repayments for a loan at different interest rates.

1   Open *Mortgage-1* from your sample files folder.

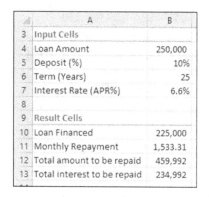

This is a simple worksheet that calculates four result values from four input values. When performing what-if analysis, it is a good idea to separate the input values from the result values on your worksheet.

The worksheet uses the PMT function that was covered in: *Lesson 3-3: Use the Insert Function dialog and the PMT function.*

During the last 25 years, mortgage interest rates have never dropped below 2.5% or increased to more than 15.5%.

Based upon the assumption that future rates will stay in this range, you will create a data table to show how potential changes in interest rates will affect monthly payments.

2   Create a single input data table to display all result cells for interest rates between 2.5% and 15.5% in half percent increments.

1.   Type **Interest %** into cell D3.

2.   Type **Monthly Payment** into cell E3.

3.   Type **Total Payments** into cell F3.

4.   Type **Total Interest** into cell G3.

5.   AutoSize columns D, E, F and G so that all of the headers are readable.

6.   Select cells D3:G3.

7.   Click: Home→Styles→Cell Styles→Heading 3.

8.   Type **2.5%** into cell B7.

When you create a data table, you should always put the lowest input value into the relevant input cell. You'll see why in a moment.

9.   Add formulas to cells D4:G4 that refer to the relevant input and result cells. The correct formulas are shown below:

	D	E	F	G
3	Interest %	Monthly Payment	Total Payments	Total Interest
4	=B7	=B11	=B12	=B13

10.   Type **=D4+0.005** into cell D5 (the formula **=D4+0.5%** would produce an identical result).

11.   AutoFill cell D5 down to cell D30 (15.5%).

note

Single-input data tables can have the input cells along rows or columns

It is also possible to place the result cells along the left of the data table and the input cells along the top.

In this case, you would specify a *Row input cell* rather than a *Column input cell* in the *Data Table* dialog.

Mortgage-1

trivia

What is the TABLE function?

If you look at the function behind each cell in the data table, you'll see a strange syntax:

{=TABLE(,B7)}

This often confuses users, because you'll find no reference to a TABLE function in the Excel help.

You'll also find that you are unable to manually create a TABLE function.

The TABLE function is simply Excel's "behind the scenes" way of implementing data table functionality. The only way that you can insert a TABLE function into a worksheet is by creating a data table.

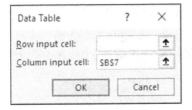

note

Data tables are read only

You cannot change or delete a cell in a data table.

If you try to do this, Excel will produce an error message.

If you need to remove a cell from a data table, you must delete the entire table.

12. Select cells D4:D30.

13. Use the Home→Number→Decrease Decimal and Home→Number→Increase Decimal buttons, to show interest rates to only one decimal place.

Your worksheet should now look like this:

	D	E	F	G
3	Interest %	Monthly Payment	Total Payments	Total Interest
4	2.5%	1,009.39	302,816	77,816
5	3.0%			

14. Convert cells D4:D30 from formulas to values.

Excel data tables have a problem with certain formulas in the left-hand column. For this reason, you need to *Copy* the values in cells D4:D30 and then *Paste Special* them back to the same location as *Values.*

Another work-around for this limitation is discussed in: *Lesson 7-8: Add a single input data table to a form.*

You are now ready to create your data table.

15. Select cells D4:G30.

16. Click: Data→Forecast→What-If Analysis→Data Table...

The *Data Table* dialog appears.

17. Click once in the *Column input cell* text box.

18. Click on cell B7.

This sets the *Column input cell* to the absolute cell reference: $B$7.

Because the interest rates are shown in column D, Excel must change the input value in cell B7 (to each value in column D) in order to calculate result values for columns E, F and G.

19. Click the *OK* button.

The data table is populated to show all result cells for all interest rates.

20. Select cells E4:G30.

21. Click: Home→Styles→Cell Styles→Comma[0].

	D	E	F	G
3	Interest %	Monthly Payment	Total Payments	Total Interest
4	2.5%	1,009	302,816	77,816
5	3.0%	1,067	320,093	95,093

You are now able to change the *Loan Amount, Deposit* or *Term* input values to update the data table.

3 Save your work as *Mortgage-2*.

Lesson 5-2: Create a two-input data table

A two-input data table is similar to a one-input data table.

However, in a two-input data table, input cells are arranged along both the top and the left-hand side of the table.

In this lesson you'll use a two-input data table to show monthly repayments for different loan amounts and different interest rates.

1   Open *Mortgage-2* from your sample files folder (if it isn't already open).

2   Create a new worksheet and name it: **Variable Interest and Capital**

3   Copy cells A1:B13 from the *Variable Interest* worksheet and paste them into the same cells in the *Variable Interest and Capital* worksheet.

4   AutoSize columns A and B so that they are wide enough to display all values.

5   Create rows for your data table in cells E3:L3, showing capital amounts from 125,000 to 300,000 in increments of 25,000.

1.   Type **125,000** into cell E3.

2.   Type **150,000** into cell F3.

3.   Select cells E3:F3 and AutoFill across to cell L3.

	E	F	G	H
3	125,000	150,000	175,000	200,000

6   Create row labels for your data table in cells D4:D30, showing interest rates from 2.5% to 15.5% in increments of 0.5%.

1.   Type **2.5%** into cell D4.

2.   Type **3%** into cell D5.

3.   Select cells D4:D5 and AutoFill down to cell D30 (15.5%).

7   Format cells D4:D30 to show one decimal place.

1.   Select cells D4:D30.

2.   Click: Home→Number→Decrease Decimal.

8   Add a formula to cell D3 that will reference the *Monthly Repayment* result cell.

	D	E	F	G
3	=B11	125000	150000	175000

9   If necessary, AutoSize column D so that it is wide enough to display all values.

10   Apply the *Note* cell style to cells D3:D30 and cells E3:L3.

1.   Select cells D3:D30 and cells E3:L3.

Mortgage-2

https://thesmartmethod.com

tip

Hiding values with the three-semicolon custom format

You will often want to hide numbers or text in specific cells.

A common way of doing this is to format the cell as white text upon a white background.

A better solution is to create a custom format consisting of three semicolons. This is better because the cell contents will remain hidden no matter which background and foreground colors are set for the cell.

Here's how you would hide the value in cell D3:

1. Right-click cell D3.

2. Click *Format Cells...* from the shortcut menu.

3. Click the *Custom* category.

4. Type three semicolons into the *Type* box.

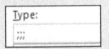

5. Click the *OK* button.

The value in cell D3 has now become invisible:

	D	E
3		125000
4	2.5%	504.69
5	3.0%	533.49

Custom formats are covered in depth in the *Essential Skills* book in this series.

2. Click: Home→Styles→Cell Styles→Note.

Your worksheet should now look like this:

	C	D	E	F	G
2					
3		1,009.39	125000	150000	175000
4		2.5%			
5		3.0%			
6		3.5%			
7		4.0%			

You are now ready to create your two-input data table.

11 Create a two-input data table to show monthly payments for each capital amount and interest rate.

1. Select cells D3:L30.

2. Click: Data→Forecast→What-If Analysis→Data Table...

The *Data Table* dialog appears.

The *Row input cell* is the *Loan Amount* in cell B4.

The *Column input cell* is the *Interest Rate* in cell B7.

Note that you could take the view that the amount financed in cell B10 is the correct row input cell. You're using cell B4 as it represents how much capital you would have available if your lender demands a 10% deposit.

3. Enter these values into the dialog and then click the *OK* button.

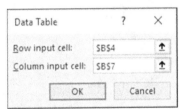

4. Select cells E4:L30.

5. Click: Home→Number→Comma Style.

The numbers are formatted with a thousand comma separator and two decimal places.

The two-input data table is complete.

	C	D	E	F	G
2					
3		1,009.39	125000	150000	175000
4		2.5%	504.69	605.63	706.57
5		3.0%	533.49	640.19	746.88
6		3.5%	563.20	675.84	788.48
7		4.0%	593.82	712.58	831.34

The value in cell D3 looks a little untidy. See the sidebar tip if you'd like it to become invisible.

12 Save your work as *Mortgage-3*.

Lesson 5-3: Define scenarios

When you create a set of input values, it is referred to as a scenario.

For example, here's a scenario:

Forecasted sales for next month are: 1,500 Grommets, 4,300 Sprockets, 3,100 Widgets and 2,800 Flugel Valves.

You enter the scenario's values into the input cells:

	A	B
3	Input Cells	Units
4	Grommets	1,500
5	Sprockets	4,300
6	Widgets	3,100
7	Flugel valves	2,800

… and the result cells display the result:

	A	B
15	Result Cells	
16	Sales	842,280.00
17	Cost	643,230.00
18	Profit	199,050.00
19	Gross Profit Pct	23.6%

Sometimes, you will have several different scenarios that you want to compare side-by-side. For example, you may ask your salesmen for *"worst case, expected case* and *best case"* scenarios.

	A	B	C	D
21	Scenarios			
22	Product	Worst Case	Expected Case	Best Case
23	Grommets	750	1,500	2,200
24	Sprockets	4,100	4,300	4,350
25	Widgets	2,000	3,100	3,750
26	Flugel valves	2,400	2,800	2,950

Excel's *Scenario Manager* is designed to enable you to easily compare these scenarios side-by-side.

1 Open *Profit Forecast-1* from your sample files folder.

Notice that this worksheet has been grouped to show four sets of values:

- Input Cells (referred to as *changing cells* in Excel scenarios).

- Constants (cells that do not, or rarely, change their values).

- Result Cells (cells that change when input cells change).

- Scenarios (values for best, worst and expected case).

2 Create single-cell range names for the input and result cells.

This was covered in depth in: *Lesson 4-1: Automatically create single-cell range names.*

As you'll see later, in: *Lesson 5-4: Create a scenario summary report,* the *Scenario Manager* expects you to define range names for input

note

The scenario manager can only handle 32 changing cells

If you try to define more than 32 changing cells, Excel will display an error message.

Profit Forecast-1

tip

View your scenarios from the Quick Access Toolbar

Excel is able to display a drop-down list of defined scenarios from the Quick Access Toolbar.

This is another of those features that cannot be used unless you customize the Quick Access Toolbar or ribbon, as it doesn't appear anywhere on the standard ribbon.

Here's how to add it:

1. Right-click on the Quick Access Toolbar.

2. Click *Customize Quick Access Toolbar...* from the shortcut menu.

3. Select *Commands Not in the Ribbon* in the left-hand drop-down list.

4. Select *Scenario* in the left-hand list box.

5. Click the *Add>>* button.

6. Click the *OK* button.

You now have a new icon on the Quick Access Toolbar.

When you click the icon, a drop-down list of all currently defined scenarios appears:

You can then choose a scenario to display the result cells on the worksheet.

Excel 365 version 1908 build 11929.20562 had a bug that could prevent users from changing scenarios from the quick access toolbar. This may have been repaired (via a build update) by the time you read this book.

and result cells in order to correctly display scenario summary reports.

1. Select cells A4:B7.

2. Click: Formulas→Defined Names→Create from Selection.

3. Click the *OK* button.

4. Repeat for cells A16:B19.

3 **Define the scenarios listed in cells A22:D26.**

1. Click: Data→Forecast→What-If Analysis→ Scenario Manager...

   The *Scenario Manager* dialog appears.

2. Click the *Add* button to add a new scenario.

3. Type **Worst Case** into the *Scenario name* box.

4. Click in the *Changing cells* box and select cells B4:B7 with the mouse.

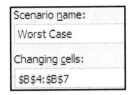

The *Scenario Manager* uses the term *Changing cells* to refer to *Input Cells*.

5. Click the *OK* button.

6. Enter the following values for the *Worst Case* scenario:

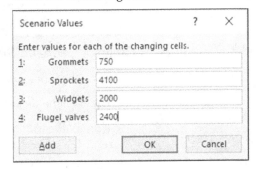

7. Click the *Add* button and then use the same technique to add the *Expected Case* and *Best Case* scenarios.

8. Click OK when finished.

4 **Use the Scenario Manager to view result cells for each scenario.**

1. Select one of the cases in the *Scenarios* list.

2. Click the *Show* button to display the scenario on the worksheet.

3. Select a different case and click the *Show* button.

4. Click the *Close* button to close the Scenario Manager.

5 **Save your work as** *Profit Forecast-2*.

note

Merging scenarios

Excel allows you to merge scenarios from one or more other workbooks.

Imagine that you send a worksheet out to three salesmen: Tom, Dick and Harry. Your salesmen are well trained in Excel and know how to define a scenario.

You instruct each of them to forecast their sales by completing the input cells on their worksheet. They then name a scenario with their own name which references the input cells.

When you receive their workbooks, you merge them with your summary workbook like this:

1. Make sure that the *Tom, Dick, Harry,* and *Summary* workbooks are open (they are in the sample files if you want to follow through).

2. Make sure that you are viewing the *Summary* workbook.

3. Click: Data→Forecast→ What-If Analysis→ Scenario Manager.

You should see the *Tom, Dick* and *Harry* scenarios listed.

4. Click the *Merge...* button.

5. Select *Sheet1* of the *Tom* workbook.

6. Click the *OK* button.

7. Do the same for *Dick* and *Harry.*

8. Close the *Tom, Dick* and *Harry* workbooks.

The three merged scenarios *Tom, Dick* and *Harry* are now available in the *Summary* workbook. (You may also see duplicate scenarios listed and can delete them if you wish)

Profit Forecast-2

Lesson 5-4: Create a scenario summary report

When scenarios have been defined, it is possible to display a neatly formatted report or pivot table, showing each scenario side-by-side.

1 Open *Profit Forecast-2* from your sample files folder (if it isn't already open).

2 Open the Scenario Manager.

Click: Data→Forecast→What-If Analysis→Scenario Manager…

The *Scenario Manager* dialog is displayed:

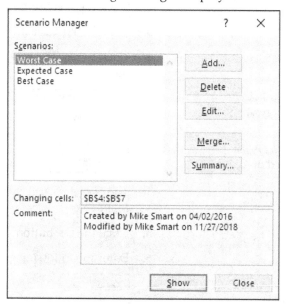

3 Create a *Scenario Summary* Report.

1. Click the *Summary…* button.

   The *Scenario Summary* dialog is displayed.

   This dialog asks which result cells should be displayed on the report.

2. Delete the current contents of the *Result cells* box.

3. Select cells B16:B19 with the mouse:

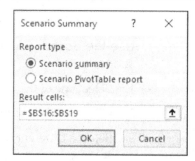

Note that it is possible to show the report as either a *Scenario summary* or as a *Scenario PivotTable report.* You'll learn about PivotTable reports later, in: *Session Eight: Pivot Tables.*

4. Click the *OK* button.

The *Scenario Summary* report is displayed on its own worksheet.

	Current Values:	Worst Case	Expected Case	Best Case
Scenario Summary				
Changing Cells:				
Grommets	1,500	750	1,500	2,200
Sprockets	4,300	4,100	4,300	4,350
Widgets	3,100	2,000	3,100	3,750
Flugel_valves	2,800	2,400	2,800	2,950
Result Cells:				
Sales	842,280.00	661,725.00	842,280.00	950,415.00
Cost	643,230.00	519,680.00	643,230.00	715,235.00
Profit	199,050.00	142,045.00	199,050.00	235,180.00
Gross_Profit_Pct	23.6%	21.5%	23.6%	24.7%

Notes: Current Values column represents values of changing cells at time Scenario Summary Report was created. Changing cells for each scenario are highlighted in gray.

Notice that the report is shown as an outline and that it is possible to collapse and expand the outline by clicking on the plus and minus buttons or on the number buttons in the top left corner.

You can now see how important it was to define named ranges for the input and result cells. Without these, the report would show cell references rather than descriptive names such as *Flugel_valves*.

4 Save your work as *Profit Forecast-3*.

Lesson 5-5: Use Goal Seek

It is very easy to view result values by changing input values. You simply type the new values into the input cells.

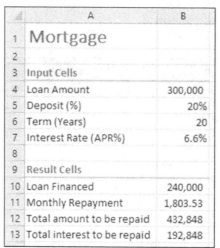

In the above worksheet, I wanted to know the monthly repayment for a 300,000 loan with a 20% deposit over 20 years at 6.6% interest. I simply typed the values into the input cells and viewed the results in the result cells.

Consider the case where you want to know the maximum *Loan Amount* if you can only afford a monthly payment of 1,000. This is more difficult because the result cells contain formulas rather than values.

By using Goal Seek, Excel will change one (and only one) input cell so that the desired value is shown in one result cell.

There's a much more complex tool called Solver. You'll learn about this later in: *Lesson 5-6: Use Solver*. Solver is a more advanced goal seek tool, able to automatically set multiple input cells.

For now, you'll examine the simple and extremely useful Goal Seek tool.

1   Open *Mortgage-3* from your sample files folder.

2   Create a new worksheet called: **Goal Seek**

3   Copy cells A1:B13 from the *Variable Interest and Capital* worksheet into the same cells on the *Goal Seek* worksheet.

4   AutoSize columns A and B so that all text and values are visible.

5   Use *Goal Seek* to find the maximum *Loan Amount* available if you can afford only 1,000 per month.

   1.   Click in cell B11 (the *Monthly Repayment* cell).

Mortgage-3

2. Click: Data→Forecast→What-If Analysis→Goal Seek…

The *Goal Seek* dialog appears:

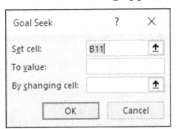

You want to set the *Monthly Repayment* (B11) to the value 1,000 by changing the *Loan Amount* (B4).

3. Complete the dialog as follows:

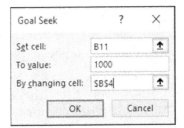

4. Click the *OK* button.

Goal Seek advises you that it has found a solution:

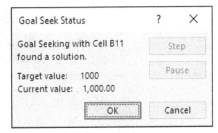

5. Click the *OK* button.

The solution to the problem is shown on the worksheet:

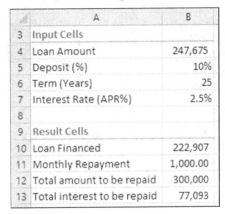

	A	B
3	Input Cells	
4	Loan Amount	247,675
5	Deposit (%)	10%
6	Term (Years)	25
7	Interest Rate (APR%)	2.5%
8		
9	Result Cells	
10	Loan Financed	222,907
11	Monthly Repayment	1,000.00
12	Total amount to be repaid	300,000
13	Total interest to be repaid	77,093

The maximum *Loan Amount* I could raise will be 247,675 if I can only afford 1,000 per month. I could, of course, have also used Goal Seek to change any of the other input cells. The key limitation of Goal Seek is that it can only change one input cell.

6 Save your work as *Mortgage-4.*

Lesson 5-6: Use Solver

important

Feel free to skip this lesson

Most of the business people that take my courses have no use for Solver.

The tiny percentage that do often get wildly excited about the potential of this tool.

Because Solver is really an external tool (installed as an add-in) rather than a core part of Excel, this book doesn't explore some of the more exotic features of this remarkable tool.

There are a huge number of tutorials covering some extremely advanced uses of Solver at:

http://www.solver.com

You'll find all you could ever want to know about Solver there.

What is Solver?

Conceptually, Solver is similar to Goal Seek. While Goal Seek can only change one input cell to set a value in one result cell, Solver can change any number of input cells. This makes the tool a lot more complex.

You can also define a set of rules (called constraints) that Solver needs to observe when finding a solution.

1   Open *Bicycle Manufacturing Schedule-1* from your sample files folder.

This worksheet models a bicycle manufacturing company. The company manufactures four different types of bicycle but has a limited number of parts available.

- Cells B4:E4 are the input cells (or changing cells) for the worksheet. They define how many bicycles of each model will be manufactured.

- The parts needed to manufacture each type of bicycle are shown in cells B7:E11. For example, a *Street Bike* needs 2 wheels, 1 steel chassis and 1 set of derailleur gears.

- Column I shows how many parts are available.

- Cells B14:F14 show the profit for each bicycle type, along with the total profit for all bicycle types.

	A	B	C	D	E	F	G	H	I
3		Mountain Bike	Street Bike	Racing Bike	Commuter Bike		Input (Changing) Cells		
4	Qty To Manufacture	20	20	20	20				
5								Constraints	
6	Parts List						Parts needed	Operator	Parts Available
7	Wheels	2	2	2	2		160	<=	180
8	Alloy Chassis	1		1			40	<=	40
9	Steel Chassis		1		1		40	<=	60
10	Hub Gears	1			1		40	<=	50
11	Derailleur Gears		1	1			40	<=	40
12									
13	Profit Analysis		Profit Per Unit			Total Profit			
14		$ 45	$ 60	$ 55	$ 50	$ 4,200			

(labels on figure: Constraints; Result (Target) Cell)

Your challenge is to maximize profit by manufacturing the optimum number of each type of bicycle.

2   Install the Solver add-in (if it is not already installed).

1. Click: File→Options→Add-ins.

2. Click the *Go…* button.

3. Check the *Solver Add-in* check box and click the *OK* button.

Bicycle Manufacturing Schedule-1

note

The SUMPRODUCT function

This worksheet uses the SUMPRODUCT function to calculate the *Parts Needed* in column G and the *Total Profit* in cell F14.

SUMPRODUCT is an array function. Array functions accept ranges as arguments and then perform calculations using each value in the range.

In cell G7 you will find the function:

= SUMPRODUCT($B$4:$E$4, B7:E7)

This will perform the calculation:

B4*B7+C4*C7+D4*D7+E4*E7

trivia

Solver wasn't developed by Microsoft

Solver is a product developed by Frontline Systems who have now distributed over a billion copies of their product to users.

As well as Excel's Solver, Frontline also developed the solvers included in Lotus 1-2-3 and Quattro Pro.

Every copy of Excel sold since 1990 has included Frontline's Solver.

Frontline also produce a more advanced version of Solver (available at extra cost) called *Premium Solver*. There's also a *Risk Solver* product that enables Excel to model Monte Carlo simulations.

Solver now appears on the ribbon's *Data* tab in a new *Analyze* group.

3   Open Solver.

Click: Data→Analyze→Solver.

Solver appears.

4   Let Solver know which are the *Changing* (Input) cells and which is the *Objective* (Result) cell.

Complete the dialog as follows:

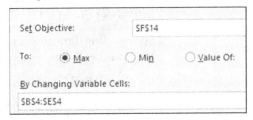

You are telling Solver to maximize the profit (shown in cell F14) by changing the *Input Cells* (or *Changing Cells*) B4:E4.

5   Define the constraints for the problem.

1.   Click the *Add* button next to the *Subject to the Constraints* list box.

2.   Complete the dialog as follows:

This tells Solver that it cannot manufacture a negative number of bicycles.

3.   Click the *Add* button.

4.   Set up a second constraint as follows:

This tells Solver that it cannot use more parts than are available.

5.   Click the *OK* button.

6   Solve the problem.

1.   Click the *Solve* button.

2.   Click the *OK* button.

Solver has solved the problem.

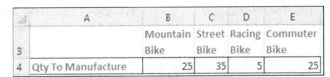

	A	B	C	D	E
3		Mountain Bike	Street Bike	Racing Bike	Commuter Bike
4	Qty To Manufacture	25	35	5	25

This mix of bicycles maximizes profits to $4,750.

7   Save your work as *Bicycle Manufacturing Schedule-2*.

note

Hiding and unhiding a worksheet using the ribbon

The right-click method is much faster than using the ribbon but here's how it can be done:

To hide a worksheet:

Click: Home→Cells→ Format→Hide & Unhide→ Hide Sheet.

To Unhide a worksheet:

Click: Home→Cells→ Format→Hide & Unhide→ Unhide Sheet.

Then select the sheet that you want to hide/unhide from the dialog and click the *OK* button.

important

Don't rely on hidden worksheets for security

There is no password associated with hiding and unhiding a worksheet, row or column. A knowledgeable user can easily unhide any hidden item.

If you need to hide items more securely, it is possible to protect the structure before distributing a workbook.

When this is done, it isn't possible to unhide and view the hidden items unless you know the password.

Protecting the structure of a workbook will be covered in: *Lesson 5-10: Control the changes users can make to workbooks.*

Human Resources-1

Lesson 5-7: Hide and unhide worksheets, columns and rows

1 Open *Human Resources-1* from your sample files folder.

2 Hide the *Headcount & Salaries* worksheet.

The *Payroll* worksheet depends upon the *Headcount & Salaries* worksheet in order to calculate each employee's hourly rate.

Because this data is sensitive, you may decide to hide the entire *Headcount & Salaries* worksheet.

1. Select the *Headcount & Salaries* worksheet.

2. Right-click the worksheet tab.

3. Click *Hide* from the shortcut menu.

The worksheet disappears.

3 Unhide the *Headcount & Salaries* worksheet.

1. Right-click on any worksheet tab (at the moment the only visible worksheet tab is *Payroll*).

2. Click *Unhide* from the shortcut menu.

   The *Unhide* dialog is displayed, listing all currently hidden worksheets.

3. Click the *OK* button.

   The *Headcount & Salaries* worksheet reappears.

   You can see that this is not a good way to hide confidential information, as any knowledgeable user can simply unhide the worksheet (see sidebar).

4 Hide rows 3:6, rows 19:23 and row 9 on the *Payroll* worksheet.

Perhaps you would like to print out the *Payroll* worksheet for the floor manager so that each employee's hours can be reviewed.

This might be a problem if the salaries had to be kept confidential.

For this reason, you are going to hide the confidential rows on the *Payroll* worksheet before printing.

1. Select the *Payroll* worksheet.

2. Select rows 3 to 6.

3. Right-click anywhere within the selected cells.

4. Click *Hide* from the shortcut menu.

note

Sharing information using screenshots

A screenshot is a little like a photograph of all, or part of a worksheet.

You will often want to paste a read-only depiction of part of a worksheet into an e-mail, Word document, PowerPoint presentation or other Office document.

To take a screenshot:

1. Select the cells that you want to take a screenshot of.

2. Click:
Home→Clipboard→Copy→ Copy as Picture…

You'll then see the *Copy Picture* dialog with two sets of option buttons:

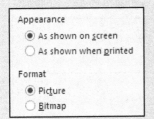

If you choose: *As shown on the screen,* you are able to choose a *Picture* or *Bitmap.*

The main difference between these options is that a *Picture* will have a transparent background and a *Bitmap* will have a white background (unless you have set a background color for the cells that you are copying).

tip

A faster way to hide a single row or column

A hidden column is simply a column that has its width set to zero.

You can quickly hide a row or column by dragging its border to make it so narrow that it is no longer visible.

The rows disappear.

5. Do the same to hide rows 19:23.

6. Do the same to hide row 9.

The payroll no longer shows any financial values. It would now be possible to print the worksheet (or take a screenshot of the worksheet – see sidebar) without showing the hidden rows.

5 Hide columns E:O on the *Payroll* worksheet.

This is very similar to hiding rows.

1. Select columns E:O.

2. Right-click anywhere in the selected area.

3. Click *Hide* from the shortcut menu.

The columns disappear.

	A	B	C	D
1	Payroll			
2				
8		Johnny Caine	George Marley	Betty Anan
11	Hours Worked			
12	Monday	9	10	10
13	Tuesday	8	9	8
14	Wednesday	10	9	8
15	Thursday	6	8	6
16	Friday	10	7	10
17	Total	43	43	42

6 Unhide columns E:O on the *Payroll* worksheet.

1. Select columns D:P (the columns that are on either side of the hidden columns).

2. Right-click anywhere in the selected area.

3. Click *Unhide* from the shortcut menu.

The columns re-appear.

7 Unhide all hidden rows on the *Payroll* worksheet.

1. Click the *Select All* button (in the top left corner of the worksheet) to select every cell.

2. Right-click any of the row headers (the numbered buttons on the left of the worksheet).

3. Click *Unhide* from the shortcut menu.

4. All hidden rows re-appear.

There is no need to save this workbook as it has not been changed in any way.

important

Custom views don't work if there is a table anywhere in the workbook

In *Excel 365 version 1908 Jan 2020*, custom views could not be used in any workbook that contains a table (though I expect that this will be fixed in a future version).

If there's a table anywhere in the workbook, the *Custom Views* button will be grayed out for all worksheets.

You can work-around this limitation by using range names in place of tables when you really need the *Custom Views* feature.

In: *Lesson 4-6: Create dynamic formula-based range names using the OFFSET function*, there's a description of a technique that allows you to create range names that have the same dynamic features as tables.

Lesson 5-8: Create custom views

In: *Lesson 5-7: Hide and unhide worksheets, columns and rows*, you learned how useful it can be to hide columns and rows when printing (or taking a screenshot from) a worksheet.

Sometimes you may find that you are continuously hiding and unhiding the same rows and columns in order to print selected parts of a worksheet. When you notice that this is happening, you have an ideal candidate for a custom view.

Custom views allow you to save and recall worksheet layouts that have hidden columns and rows.

1   Open *Human Resources-1* from your sample files folder (if it isn't already open).

2   Select the *Payroll* worksheet.

3   Save the current view as *HR*.

    1.   Click: View→Workbook Views→Custom Views.

       The *Custom Views* dialog appears:

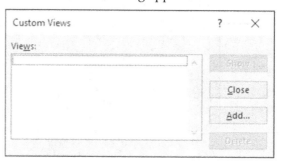

    2.   Click the *Add…* button.

       The *Add View* dialog appears.

    3.   Type **HR** into the *Name* box.

Human Resources-1

Notice that custom views don't only save hidden rows and columns.

Custom views also save all of the following:

- *Print settings*, including any *Page Layout* settings.
- Any filters that are currently applied to the worksheet.
- The zoom factor.
- Window sizes and positions.
- The currently active cell.
- The current worksheet view (*Normal, Page Layout* or *Page Break Preview*).

4. Click the *OK* button.

Nothing seems to have happened, but you have, in fact, stored a view with all rows and columns visible.

4   Hide rows 3:6, rows 19:23 and row 9 on the *Payroll* worksheet.

This was covered in: *Lesson 5-7: Hide and unhide worksheets, columns and rows.*

5   Save the current view as: **Hours Worked**

Do this in the same way that you saved the HR custom view earlier.

6   Hide columns B,C,F,G,H,I,J,K,L and N.

7   Save the current view as: **Hours Worked (Female)**

8   Show the *Hours Worked* view.

1. Click: View→Workbook Views→Custom Views.

The *Custom Views* dialog is displayed, showing the three saved views:

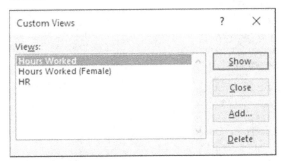

2. Click the *Hours Worked* view in the *Views* list.

3. Click the *Show* button.

The worksheet changes to show the *Hours Worked* view.

9   Show the *Hours Worked (Female)* view.

10   Show the *HR* view.

11   Save your work as *Human Resources-2*.

important

Secure passwords

Hacking tools (freely available on the Internet) commonly use five methods to discover passwords:

1. Dictionary attack

In a matter of seconds, the tool tries every word in the dictionary. For this reason, your password should never be a real word such as *London*.

2. Dictionary + numbers

The tool makes several passes through the dictionary, appending a sequential number to the front or back of the password. For this reason, your password should never be a real word with leading or trailing numbers, such as *London99* or *99London*.

3. Reverse words

The tool tries every word in the dictionary spelled backwards.

4. Words with the letter O replaced with a zero

5. *Brute force* attack

The tool tries every possible combination of the letters of the alphabet. A 2017 test showed that it takes less than 10 minutes for an Intel core i5-6600K dual-core Pentium to crack a seven letter single-case password such as: *xcoekfh*

For ultimate security against brute force attacks, include upper and lower case letters, numbers, and symbols in your passwords. The best approach is to create a password from a phrase such as: "I like to ride my Honda motorcycle at 100 MPH". This gives the extremely secure password: *IltrmHm@100MPH*

This password would take up to 5 million years to crack using an Intel i5.

Human Resources-2

Lesson 5-9: Prevent unauthorized users from opening or modifying workbooks

There are two levels of password protection available when you save a workbook. You can:

• Prevent users from opening the workbook.

• Prevent users from changing a workbook once they have opened it.

In this lesson you'll implement both types of protection.

1 Open *Human Resources-2* from your sample files folder (if it isn't already open).

2 Protect the workbook with a password that will prevent other users from opening it.

1. Click: File→Save As→Browse.

   The *Save As* dialog is displayed.

2. Click: Tools→General Options at the bottom-right of the dialog.

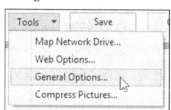

3. Type a password in the *Password to open* box.

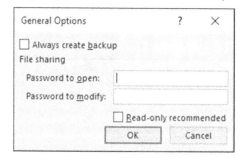

See the *secure passwords* sidebar for important information about choosing an appropriate password.

See the facing page sidebar for a discussion of the *Always create backup* and *Read-only recommended* check box options.

4. Click the *OK* button.

   Excel reminds you not to forget the password and prompts for it again to protect against accidental typing errors.

5. Type the password again.

6. Click the *OK* button.

note

Excel passwords do not provide 100% security

Even if you choose a secure password that is nine or more characters long, there are tools freely available on the Internet that can crack most Excel 365 worksheet protection passwords in minutes. Currently, only the *password to open* is not easily cracked.

The *password to open* is encrypted using the AES 128 standard.

This encryption standard is approved by the US government to encrypt classified documents up to SECRET level. This suggests that it is extremely secure.

note

General Options check boxes

The *Always create backup* check box provides you with an escape route if you need to return to the previous version of the workbook. A copy of the old workbook is saved every time you save, so that you always have two copies of each workbook. One copy is a *Microsoft Excel Backup* file with the file extension .xlk.

If you check the *Read-only recommended* check box, the user is presented with a dialog when opening a protected workbook. The dialog suggests that the workbook be opened read-only.

If the user ignores this suggestion, a read/write copy will be opened. As you discovered in this lesson, this copy cannot be used to over-write the protected file but can be used to create a new file with a different name.

7. Click the *Save* button.

8. If necessary, click *Yes* to overwrite the existing file.

3 Close the *Human Resources-2* workbook and then try to re-open it.

You are unable to open the workbook without the password.

4 Enter the password and click OK to open the workbook.

5 Remove the password from the workbook.

1. Click: File→Save As→Browse.

2. Click: Tools→General Options at the bottom-right of the dialog.

3. Remove the password from the *Passsword to open* box.

4. Click the *OK* button.

5. Click the *Save* button.

6. Click *Yes* to overwrite the existing file.

6 Protect the workbook with a password that will prevent other users from changing it.

Follow the same procedure as you did when adding a *Password to open*, but this time specify a *Password to modify*.

7 Save and Close the workbook.

8 Open *Human Resources-2* read only.

1. Click: File→Open→Human Resources-2.

2. The *Password* dialog appears.

3. Click the *Read Only* button without entering a password.

   This doesn't have the effect you might expect. You've opened the workbook without a password and are able to change it.

9 Attempt to save the workbook.

Surprisingly, Excel will only prevent you from saving the workbook with the same name as the password-protected workbook. Excel is quite happy for you to make a copy and even prompts you to do so when you attempt to save the file.

10 Save the workbook as *Human Resources-3*.

This workbook no longer has password protection.

trivia

Protect Windows is a throwback to Excel 2010

In older versions of Excel, it was possible to open several *workbook windows* within one *application window*. This way of working is called MDI (Multiple Document Interface).

One of the big changes in Office 2013 was a change to SDI (Single Document Interface) and this change remains in Excel 365.

For me this is a very welcome change as I now find it much easier to work when several different workbooks (or other Office documents) are open.

The *Protect Structure and Windows* dialog should more properly now read *Protect Structure* as there are no longer any windows to protect.

The *Windows* checkbox in the *Protect Structure and Windows* dialog is always grayed out in Excel 365 and no longer has any function.

By the time you read this book it is possible that Microsoft will have updated Excel 365 with a revised dialog that no longer includes a *Windows* check box.

Lesson 5-10: Control the changes users can make to workbooks

Sometimes you are quite happy for any user to open your workbook, but you need to prevent them from inserting, deleting, renaming, moving, hiding or unhiding any of the worksheets.

This is called protecting the *Structure* of a workbook.

1 Open *Human Resources-3* from your sample files folder (if it isn't already open).

2 Display the *Hours Worked (Female)* custom view.

This was covered in: *Lesson 5-8: Create custom views.*

3 Hide the Headcount & Salaries worksheet

This was covered in: *Lesson 5-7: Hide and unhide worksheets, columns and rows.*

4 Protect the structure of the workbook.

1. Click: Review→Protect→Protect Workbook.

The *Protect Structure and Windows* dialog is displayed.

In Excel 365, it is no longer possible to protect windows, making the *Windows* option redundant (see sidebar).

2. Check the *Structure* check box (if necessary) and add a password.

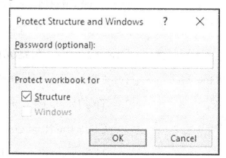

3. Click the *OK* button.

4. Enter the password again when prompted and click *OK*.

Because you checked the *Structure* check box you are now unable to add, delete, rename, move, hide or unhide any of the worksheets in this workbook.

5 Attempt to unhide the Headcount & Salaries worksheet.

Right-click on the *Payroll* worksheet tab.

Human Resources-3

important

Do not rely upon Protect Structure to hide confidential data

Protect Structure is not a secure method to hide confidential data.

Protect Structure does its job well only if the Excel file is opened (in Excel) in the normal and intended way.

I managed to hack this protected worksheet in less than a minute using only common tools found on every desktop computer. Most users with basic IT skills could figure out how to do the same thing.

note

Protection options are also available from File→info→ Protect Workbook

The features demonstrated in: *Lesson 5-9: Prevent unauthorized users from opening or modifying workbooks, Lesson 5-10: Control the changes users can make to workbooks* and *Lesson 5-11: Restrict the cells users are allowed to change* can also be accessed from File→Info→Protect Workbook.

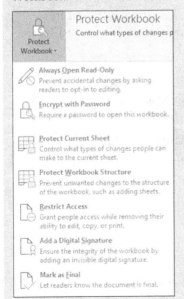

Before Protection / **After Protection**

Notice that the *Unhide* option is grayed out and unavailable. This has happened because you have protected the structure of the workbook.

Notice also that the *Insert, Delete, Rename, Move or Copy, Tab Color* and *Hide* options are now unavailable.

6   **Remove password protection from the structure**.

1. Click: Review→Protect→Protect Workbook.

   You are prompted for the password to remove protection:

2. Enter the password and click the *OK* button.

   Protection is removed.

7   **Unhide the *Headcount & Salaries* worksheet**.

This time you are permitted to unhide the worksheet as the structure is no longer protected.

8   **Display the *HR* custom view**.

There's no need to save the workbook as it has not changed.

tip

Use cell locking to make forms more user-friendly

Excel is often used to create forms (such as booking forms). The form is sent to the user by e-mail and the user completes and returns it.

This type of form becomes much easier to use if you do the following:

1. Unlock the cells that the user should type data into.

2. Protect the worksheet making sure that only the *Select unlocked cells* option is checked.

When this is done, the user can use the **<Tab>** key to navigate through all of the cells in the form that need to be completed.

note

Cells can also be locked and unlocked using the Ribbon

To do this you need to first select the cell(s) to be locked or unlocked and then click:

Home→Cells→Format→ Lock Cell

You might have thought that the menu option would show the text: *Lock Cell* or *Unlock Cell* depending upon whether the range selected was already locked.

Confusingly, the icon always displays *Lock Cell* but is highlighted in gray if the selected range is locked.

Lesson 5-11: Restrict the cells users are allowed to change

1   Open *Human Resources-3* from your sample files folder (if it isn't already open).

2   Display the *Hours Worked* custom view.

This was covered in: *Lesson 5-8: Create custom views.*

3   Hide the *Headcount and Salaries* worksheet.

This was covered in: *Lesson 5-7: Hide and unhide worksheets, columns and rows.*

4   Re-size columns B:O so that they are just wide enough to display their contents:

A	Johnny Caine	George Marley	Betty Anan	Paris Winfrey	Ozzy Dickens	Johnny Roberts	Charles Monroe	Ronnie Bush	Michal Jolie	JK Spears	Ozzy Rowling	Oprah Hilton	Bill Biggs	Angelina Osbourne
Payroll														
Hours Worked														
Monday	9	10	10	10	7	7	7	7	7	7	7	10	8	6
Tuesday	8	9	8	6	10	10	10	7	6	10	7	8	7	9
Wednesday	10	9	8	7	9	8	6	8	7	8	8	6	6	8
Thursday	6	8	6	10	9	7	6	6	7	8	8	6	6	9
Friday	10	7	10	7	9	10	9	8	8	10	8	9	10	6
Total	43	43	42	40	44	42	38	36	35	43	38	39	37	38

The challenge this time will be to prevent the user from changing any value other than those in the yellow shaded cells (cells B12:O16).

You will solve this problem by *unlocking* these cells and then *protecting* the worksheet. This will only allow the user to enter values into the *unlocked* cells.

5   Unlock cells B12:O16.

All cells on a worksheet are (by default) *locked*. You are able to type values into them because the worksheet is not yet *protected*.

In order to prevent the user from changing any cell except cells B12:O16 you need to do two things:

• Unlock the cells that you want the user to be able to change.

• Protect the worksheet.

Here's how to unlock the cells:

1.   Select cells B12:O16.

2.   Right click anywhere in the selected area.

note

You can keep your formulas secret with the Hidden attribute

If you set the *Hidden* attribute on the *Format Cells* dialog's *Protection* tab, users cannot see any of your formulas.

Even if a cell is unlocked, the formula does not display in the formula bar when the cell is selected. This could be used if the formula used to calculate a value was a "trade secret".

This will only take effect when the worksheet is protected.

tip

Leave all cells locked to distribute a read-only workbook

If you protect a workbook without unlocking any cells, you have effectively created a read-only workbook.

To prevent the user from copying and pasting the contents, you should also un-check the *Select locked cells* check box. Note that the user will still be able to click:

Insert→Illustrations→Screenshot

… from any another Office application to copy an image of the worksheet.

3. Click *Format Cells…* from the shortcut menu.

4. Click the *Protection* tab.

5. Uncheck the *Locked* check box.

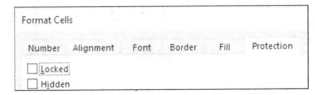

See sidebar for more about the *Hidden* attribute.

6. Click the *OK* button.

6   Protect the *Payroll* worksheet so that the user is unable to change or select any of the locked cells.

When you protect a worksheet, it is no longer possible to change the contents of a *locked* cell.

1. Click: Review→Protect→Protect Sheet.

   The *Protect Sheet* dialog appears

   The default settings allow the user to select (but not change) the contents of locked cells. This normally makes sense as you want the user to be able to copy and paste any part of the worksheet.

   In this case, however, it creates a huge security problem as the user can easily copy the entire worksheet, paste it into a new worksheet, and then unhide the hidden rows.

   For this reason, you want to prevent the user from selecting locked cells.

2. Uncheck the *Select locked cells* check box.

   Notice that, by default, the user is prevented from doing many more things to the worksheet (such as formatting cells). You can selectively allow these actions by checking the appropriate check boxes.

3. Enter a password.

4. Click the *OK* button, confirm the password and then click the *OK* button once more.

7   Test the protected worksheet.

You are unable to change (or even select) any of the locked cells but you can select and change any of the unlocked cells.

8   Unprotect the worksheet.

1. Click: Review→Protect→Unprotect Sheet.

2. Enter the password, and then click the *OK* button.

9   Lock cells B12:O16.

Do this in the same way that you unlocked the cells, but this time check the *Locked* check box (instead of un-checking it).

10   Save your work as *Human Resources-4*.

note

You can allow access based upon the Windows log-in password or user group

You can also use your existing Windows passwords and user groups to allow access to specific ranges of cells.

To use Windows permissions, click:

Review→Protect→ Allow Edit Ranges→ New...→Permissions...

Lesson 5-12: Allow different levels of access to a worksheet with multiple passwords

Sometimes you will want different users to be able to change different ranges in your worksheet. In this lesson, you'll set the following levels of access to the *Hours Worked* worksheet.

	A	B	C	D	E
3	Payroll Rules				
4	Tax	32%			
5	Social Security	8%			
6	Pension	5%			
7					
8		Johnny Caine	George Marley	Betty Anan	Paris Winfrey
9	Hourly Rate	18.20	12.57	12.66	11.32
10					
11	Hours Worked				
12	Monday	9	10	10	10
13	Tuesday	8	9	8	6
14	Wednesday	10	9	8	7
15	Thursday	6	8	6	10
16	Friday	10	7	10	7
17	Total	43	43	42	40

Group	Permission	Password
Human Resources	Access to cells B4:B6, B9:O9 and B12:O16. This allows the HR department to change *Tax, Social Security, Pension, Hours Worked* and *Hourly Rate* values.	cat
Floor Manager	Access to cells B12:O16 only. Floor managers can only change the *Hours Worked* values.	dog
Administrator	All rights (this is the unprotect password).	cow

I have deliberately used very insecure passwords in order to save you the effort of typing longer (and more secure) ones. If security was important, you would use secure passwords (see sidebar in: *Lesson 5-9: Prevent unauthorized users from opening or modifying workbooks*, for details of how to construct a secure password).

1   Open *Hours Worked-1* from your sample files folder.

2   Set up the *Human Resources* password and permissions.

   1.   Select cells B4:B6.

Hours Worked-1

2. Hold down the **<Ctrl>** key and select cells B9:O9 and cells B12:O16.

3. Click: Review→Protect→Allow Edit Ranges.

   The *Allow Users to Edit Ranges* dialog appears.

4. Click the *New...* button

5. Type **Human Resources** as the *Title.*

6. Type **cat** as the *Range password.*

7. Click the *OK* button.

8. Type the password again when prompted and click the *OK* button.

3 Set up the *Floor Manager* password and permissions.

1. Click the *New...* button.

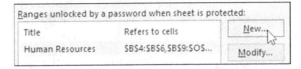

2. Type **Floor Manager** as the *Title.*

3. Click in the *Refers to cells* box and delete the current contents.

4. Select cells B12:O16.

5. Type **dog** as the *Range password.*

6. Click the *OK* button.

7. Type the password again when prompted and click the *OK* button.

8. Click the *OK* button to close the dialog.

4 Protect the worksheet.

1. Click: Review→Protect→Protect Sheet.

2. Type the administrator password: **cow** into the *Password to unprotect sheet* box.

3. Click *OK,* re-enter the password when prompted and click *OK.*

5 Test the worksheet.

1. Try to change any of the numbers in cells B12:O16.

   A dialog appears asking for a password.

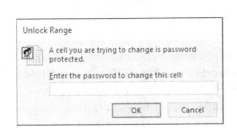

2. Type **dog** as the password.

   You are now able to freely change any value in cells B12:O16 for as long as the workbook stays open.

3. Try to change any of the values in cells B4:B6 or cells B9:O9.

   In each case, a dialog appears asking for a password.

4. Type **cat** as the password.

   You are now able to freely change any value in cells B4:B6, B9:O9 or B12:O16 for as long as the workbook stays open.

6 Save your work as *Hours Worked-2.*

Lesson 5-13: Create a digital certificate

Why digital certificates are needed

If you receive a workbook via e-mail, you cannot be sure where it has really come from. It is remarkably easy to send an e-mail that appears to have been sent by a different person.

You may also worry that the workbook may have been altered by somebody since the author sent it to you.

The solution to both of these problems is to digitally sign your workbooks.

If a workbook is digitally signed, it confirms the identity of the author. Excel will also warn the recipient if the workbook has been changed since the author signed it.

Digital certificates are of great use when you need to distribute workbooks that contain macros within an organization. (You'll learn all about macros in: *Session Seven: Forms and Macros*). Macros can contain destructive macro viruses and you wouldn't ever want to open a workbook containing macros without being absolutely sure of its origin.

Self-certification and third-party certification

There are two ways to create a digital certificate in Excel 365:

1. Create your own digital certificate. This isn't very secure, as it is easy to forge a self-certified digital certificate. When another user opens a workbook with a self-certified signature it will display the message:

This isn't likely to inspire a great deal of confidence in the recipient. In fact, I'd go so far as to say that a self-certified digital certificate has no value as it doesn't really increase security at all.

The terminology *recoverable signature* isn't very descriptive (see sidebar). In this case it means that the certificate issuer isn't trusted. You'll learn more about trusted issuers later, in: *Lesson 7-13: Implement macro security.*

2. Buy a certificate from a trusted third party such as VersiSign. Third-party certificates provide a high level of security as they are certified to be genuine by an outside agency. When a user opens a workbook, Excel will confirm that the certificate is genuine by contacting the third-party's server. Most third-party subscriptions cost between US$100 and US$500 per year.

In this lesson, you'll create your own digital certificate. Although this doesn't really improve security, it will give you all of the skills you need to effectively use digital certificates should you eventually purchase a third-party subscription.

1   Open the Windows digital certificate dialog.

note

What is a recoverable signature?

A recoverable signature means that the signature isn't valid but might be valid in the future.

Causes of this error are:

1. You are offline.

You need an Internet connection to enable Excel to confirm that the signature is genuine.

2. The certificate has expired.

You need to maintain a subscription to a digital certification authority. If your subscription has lapsed the certificate will expire.

3. The certificate issuer isn't trusted.

In this lesson the certificate has been self-certified so the issuer is not trusted.

It is actually possible to trust a self-certified digital certificate on the machine upon which it was created. I cannot think of any circumstances where this would be useful, as there are better ways to certify your own work.

You'll learn about them in: *Lesson 7-12: Understand macro security, Lesson 7-13: Implement macro security* and *Lesson 7-14: Understand trusted documents.*

As mentioned in the introduction, the ability to create a self-certified digital certificate is a contradiction in terms.

Microsoft also must have thought it a pointless feature as they still allow you (but have recently made it rather difficult) to create a self-certified digital certificate.

If you do want to work through the remainder of this lesson here's how it can be done (at least how it could be done at time of writing in Jan 2020).

1. Navigate to:

   C:\Program Files\Microsoft Office\root\Office16

   Or for some users:

   C:\Program Files (x86)\Microsoft Office\root\Office16

   In this folder you should find an application called:

   SELFCERT.exe

2. Double-click *SELFCERT.exe* to open it.

2 Create a self-certified digital certificate.

The *Create Digital Certificate* dialog should now be shown:

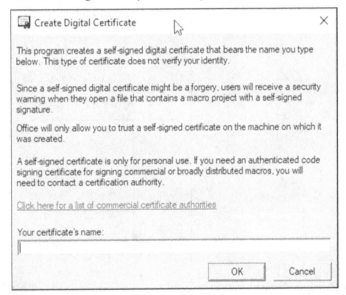

The dialog refers to macros because workbooks containing macros present the most serious security threat. You'll learn more about macros in: *Session Seven: Forms and Macros.*

Notice that there is a hyperlink on this dialog that will direct you to several commercial certificate authorities should you wish to purchase a third-party certificate.

1. Type a name for your certificate into the *Your certificate's name* box.

2. Click the *OK* button.

   A dialog appears confirming that the certificate has been created.

Lesson 5-14: Add an invisible digital signature to a workbook

As discussed in: *Lesson 5-13: Create a digital certificate*, a self-certified digital certificate has little value as it doesn't increase security at all. As you'll see in this lesson, Microsoft go out of their way to warn the user of this.

Should your organization purchase a "real" digital certificate this lesson will give you all of the skills you need to effectively attach certificates to workbooks.

1 Open *Salary Increase-1* from your sample files folder.

This worksheet details salary increases for the coming year:

You want your HR department to be confident that this workbook was really created by you and that nobody has changed any of the salary increases since it was sent out.

This can be achieved by adding a digital certificate.

2 Add an invisible digital signature.

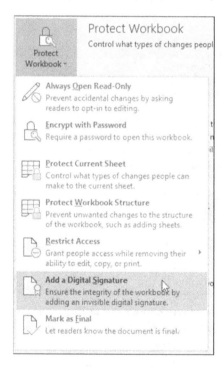

1. Click: File→Info→Protect Workbook→Add a digital signature.

   The *Sign* dialog appears.

2. Use the *Commitment Type* drop-down to add a *Commitment Type* of: *Created and approved this document*.

3. Enter a *Purpose for signing this document* into the text box:

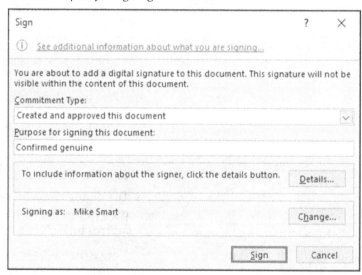

4. Click the *Sign* button.

5. You are warned that a self-certified certificate cannot be verified. Click *Yes* to confirm that you really do want to use the self-certified certificate.

   The document is now digitally signed.

   Notice that Excel warns you (in a rather cryptic way) that a self-certified signature cannot be relied upon as it cannot be

Salary Increase-1

verified. Recoverable signatures are discussed in: *Lesson 5-13: Create a digital certificate (sidebar).*

Recoverable Signatures

One or more of the digital signatures in this workbook is recoverable or could not be verified. A recoverable signature may indicate that an error occurred when the workbook was signed.

6. Click the *Back Button* to return to the worksheet.

Notice that two things have changed on the worksheet.

There is a warning at the top of the worksheet that it has been marked as final (by adding the certificate):

MARKED AS FINAL   An author has marked this workbook as final to discourage editing.   Edit Anyway

There is also an icon at the bottom left corner showing that the workbook contains a digital signature:

Ready

This document contains signatures.

3   Close the workbook.

You don't have to save the workbook. It is automatically saved when you add a signature.

4   Close Excel.

5   Re-open Excel.

6   Re-open the *Salary Increase-1* workbook.

Note the two status bars at the top of the screen:

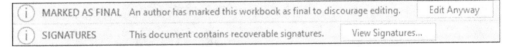

MARKED AS FINAL   An author has marked this workbook as final to discourage editing.   Edit Anyway

SIGNATURES   This document contains recoverable signatures.   View Signatures...

You can see that a self-certified digital signature is presented to the user as *recoverable* by Microsoft. This is Microsoft's way of saying "the signature is not verified by a third-party agency and cannot be relied upon".

Note also that the top status bar indicates that the workbook has been opened as read-only.

Salary Increase-1 - Read-Only - Excel

Lesson 5-15: Add a visible digital signature to a workbook

1 Open *Salary Increase-1* from your sample files folder (if it isn't already open).

2 Remove the invisible digital signature.

   1. Click the signature icon at the bottom-left of the screen.

   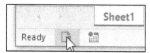

   The *Signatures* pane appears.

   2. Click the certificate issuer name in the task pane.

   A drop-down arrow appears to the right of the certificate issuer.

   3. Click the drop-down arrow and then click *Remove Signature* from the menu.

   The *Remove Signature* dialog appears.

   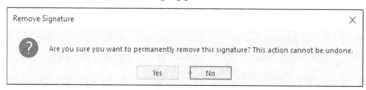

   4. Click *Yes*.

   This *Signature Removed* dialog may appear.

   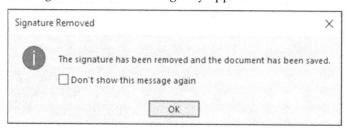

   5. Check the *Don't show this message again* check box to prevent this dialog from displaying in future.

   6. Click the *OK* button.

3 Add a visible signature.

   1. Click: Insert→Text→Signature Line→ Microsoft Office Signature Line.

   The *Signature Setup* dialog appears.

   2. Enter a *Name, Title* and *E-mail Address* into the relevant boxes:

Salary Increase-1

3. Click the *OK* button.

   A graphic appears on the worksheet with a blank space for the signature. This graphic may be freely dragged to any location on the screen.

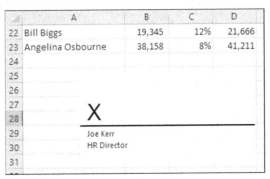

4. Double-click the signature graphic.

   The *Sign* dialog appears.

   The *Sign* dialog allows you to either select a signature image (created from a scan of your handwritten signature) or to type a name into the box.

5. Type a name into the box.

6. Click the *Sign* button.

   A signature confirmation dialog appears, warning you that your self-certified digital signature cannot be verified.

7. Click the *Yes* button.

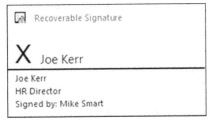

8. If a confirmation dialog appears, click the *OK* button.

   Microsoft flags the signature as *recoverable* because it is self-certified, easily forged, and thus not of any real use as a security measure.

4 Close the *Salary Increase-1* workbook without saving.

Session 5: Exercise

1   Open *Selling Price Calculator-1* from your sample files folder.

	A	B
3	Input Cells	
4	Cost	$ 4.50
5	Retail Price	$ 17.95
6	Wholesale Discount	60%
7	Annual Units	2,000.00
8		
9	Result Cells	
10	Sales (at wholesale price)	$14,360.00
11	Total Cost	$ 9,000.00
12	Gross Profit	$ 5,360.00
13	Gross Profit Percent	37%

2   Create an attractively formatted single input data table in cells D3:F18 to display the *Gross Profit* and *Gross Profit Percent* that would result from a *Retail Price* of $17.95 to $24.95 in increments of $0.50.

	D	E	F
3	Retail Price	Gross Profit	Gross Profit Percent
4	$ 17.95	$ 5,360.00	37%
5	$ 18.45	$ 5,760.00	39%
6	$ 18.95	$ 6,160.00	41%

3   Hide columns D:F.

4   Use *Goal Seek* to calculate the *Retail Price* that would be needed to produce a *Gross Profit Percent* of exactly *50%*.

5   Create range names for cells B4:B7 and cells B10:B13 using the names in cells A4:A7 and A10:A13.

6   Use the scenario manager to create three scenarios:

Worst Case: 2,000 Annual Units
Expected Case: 3,500 Annual Units
Best Case: 5,000 Annual Units

7   Create a *Scenario Summary* report to show *Sales (at wholesale price), Total Cost, Gross Profit* and *Gross Profit Percent* values for each scenario.

Scenario Summary				
	Current Values:	Worst Case	Expected Case	Best Case
Changing Cells:				
Annual_Units	2,000.00	2,000.00	3,500.00	5,000.00
Result Cells:				
Sales__at_wholesale_price	$ 17,998.98	$ 17,998.98	$ 31,498.22	$ 44,997.45
Total_Cost	$ 9,000.00	$ 9,000.00	$ 15,750.00	$ 22,500.00
Gross_Profit	$ 8,998.98	$ 8,998.98	$ 15,748.22	$ 22,497.45
Gross_Profit_Percent	50%	50%	50%	50%

8   Protect the *Selling Price Calculator* worksheet so that only cells B4:B7 (the cells shaded yellow) can be changed.

9   Save your work as *Selling Price Calculator-2*.

Selling Price Calculator-1

If you need help slide the page to the left ▶

Session 5: Exercise Answers

These are the four questions that students find the most difficult to answer:

Q 6	Q 5	Q 4	Q 2
1. Click: Data→Forecast→ What-If Analysis→ Scenario Manager… 2. Click the *Add…* button. 3. Type **Worst Case** into the *Scenario name* box. Scenario name: Worst Case 4. Click in the *Changing cells* box and then click on cell B7. Changing cells: $B$7 5. Click the *OK* button. 6. Type **2000** into the value box. $B$7 2000 7. Click the *OK* button. 8. Click the *Add…* button. 9. Complete the same steps for the *Expected Case* and *Best Case* scenarios. This was covered in: *Lesson 5-3: Define scenarios.*	1. Select cells A4:B7. 2. Click: Formulas→ Defined Names→ Create from Selection. 3. Click the *OK* button. 4. Repeat for cells A10:B13. This was covered in: *Lesson 4-1: Automatically create single-cell range names.*	1. Click: Data→ Forecast→ What-If Analysis→ Goal Seek… 2. Complete the dialog as follows: Set cell: $B$13 To value: 50% By changing cell: $B$5 3. Click *OK* and *OK* again. This was covered in: *Lesson 5-5: Use Goal Seek.*	1. Type **Retail Price, Gross Profit** and **Gross Profit Percent** into cells D3, E3 and F3. 2. AutoSize columns D:F so that all text is visible. 3. Enter the formula: **=B5** into cell D4, **=B12** into cell E4 and **=B13** into cell F4. 4. Enter the formula: **=D4+0.5** into cell D5. 5. AutoFill cell D5 to cells D6:D18. 6. Copy cells D5:D18 and then paste them back into the same location using *Paste Values.* 7. Select cells D4:F18. 8. Click: Data→Forecast→ What-If Analysis→ Data Table… 9. Set the *Column input cell* to: $B$5 and click the *OK* button. 10. Use the *Format Painter* to attractively format each column and the column headers. This was covered in: *Lesson 5-1: Create a single-input data table.*

If you have difficulty with the other questions, here are the lessons that cover the relevant skills:

3   Refer to: *Lesson 5-7: Hide and unhide worksheets, columns and rows.*

7   Refer to: *Lesson 5-4: Create a scenario summary report.*

8   Refer to: *Lesson 5-11: Restrict the cells users are allowed to change.*

6

Session Six: Working with Hyperlinks and Other Applications

> Every generation brings something new to the workplace, and millennials are no exception. As a group, they tend to be highly educated, love to learn, and grew up with the Internet and digital tools in a way that can be highly useful when leveraged properly.
>
> *Kathryn Minshew (1985-)*
> *CEO and co-founder of The Muse*

Anybody who opens an Excel workbook these days will have also spent many hours navigating the Internet using a web browser. Navigating web sites by clicking on hyperlinks will feel natural and intuitive to them.

In this session you'll discover how you can also implement a hyperlink-based navigation system in large workbooks so that even users with no Excel skills will immediately feel at home when viewing your work.

This session will also show you how to embed Excel objects into other Office applications such as Word, PowerPoint and Outlook.

Session Objectives

By the end of this session you will be able to:

- Hyperlink to worksheets and ranges
- Hyperlink to other workbooks and the Internet
- Hyperlink to an e-mail address and enhance the browsing experience
- Embed an Excel worksheet object into a Word document
- Embed an Excel chart object into a Word document
- Link an Excel worksheet to a Word document

Lesson 6-1: Hyperlink to worksheets and ranges

Because just about everybody uses a web browser, the "point and click" method of doing things comes naturally to most users.

It is possible to give users the same browser-like experience by adding hyperlinks to your workbooks in order to mimic web browser navigation. This isn't just a presentational gimmick. Hyperlink browsing is the most efficient way to quickly navigate to specific parts of long multi-page documents.

note

Adding screen tips to hyperlinks

When you hover the mouse cursor over a hyperlink, a screen tip is displayed showing additional information about the hyperlink's destination.

The default screen tip is rather verbose so it is better to define your own custom screen tips.

To add a screen tip:

1. Select the cell containing the hyperlink that you want to add a screen tip to.

2. Click:

Insert→Links→Link

3. Click the *ScreenTip* button.

4. Add the screen tip text to the box and then click *OK* and *OK* again.

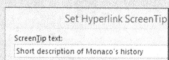

When you hover the mouse cursor over the hyperlink, the tip is displayed.

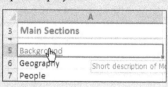

1 **Open *Monaco-1* from your sample files folder.**

This worksheet has a lot of information about Monaco (the second smallest independent state in the world at only 2 sq km).

2 **Create a worksheet hyperlink from cell A5 in the *Main Menu* worksheet to the *Background* worksheet.**

1. Select cell A5 on the *Main Menu* worksheet.

2. Click: Insert→Links→Link.

The *Insert Hyperlink* dialog appears.

3. Select *Place in this Document* from the left-hand navigation bar.

4. Select *Background* from the *Or select a place in this document* tree view.

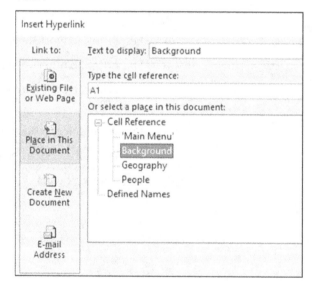

5. Click the *OK* button.

The text in cell A5 has been changed into a hyperlink:

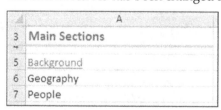

It is also possible to define a screen tip for the hyperlink (see sidebar).

Monaco-1

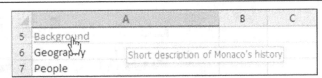

3   Create worksheet hyperlinks from cells A6 and A7 to the *Geography* and *People* worksheets.

Do this in the same way that you created the *Background* hyperlink.

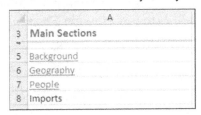

4   Create a range name called *Climate* for cells A32:A33 on the *Geography* worksheet.

   1. Select cells A32:A33 on the *Geography* worksheet.

   2. Click: Formulas→Defined Names→Create from Selection.

   3. Click the *OK* button.

5   Create range names called *Population* and *Life expectancy at birth* for cells A3:A5 and A50:A54 on the *People* worksheet.

Note that the range name: *Life_expectancy_at_birth* will be created with underscores, as range names cannot contain spaces.

6   Make cells A12, A13 and A14 on the *Main Menu* worksheet into hyperlinks pointing to the range names that you created.

   1. Select cell A12 on the *Main Menu* worksheet.

   2. Click: Insert→Links→Link.

       The *Insert Hyperlink* dialog appears.

   3. Select *Place in this Document* from the left-hand navigation bar.

   4. Select *Climate* from the *Or select a place in this document* tree view (*Defined Names* section).

   5. Click the *OK* button.

   6. Do the same for *Population* and *Life Expectancy*.

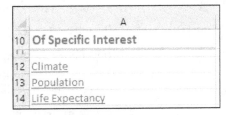

7   Test your hyperlinks.

When you click upon any of the six defined hyperlinks, you are taken to the relevant defined worksheet or range.

8   Save your work as *Monaco-2*.

Lesson 6-2: Hyperlink to other workbooks and the Internet

1   Open *Monaco-2* from your sample files folder (if it isn't already open).

2   Create a hyperlink from cell A8 in the *Main Menu* worksheet to the *Monaco Economy-1* workbook.

    1. Select cell A8.

    2. Click: Insert→Links→Link.

    3. Click: *Existing File or Web Page* in the left-hand navigation bar.

    4. Select *Current Folder* and then the *Monaco Economy-1* file in the central window.

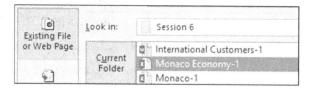

    5. Click the *OK* button.

    6. Click the *Imports* hyperlink in cell A8.

    The *Monaco Economy-1* workbook opens. Note that the hyperlink took you to cell A1 but the *Imports* data is actually in cells A74:A77.

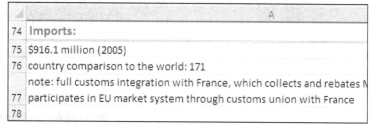

	A
74	Imports:
75	$916.1 million (2005)
76	country comparison to the world: 171
	note: full customs integration with France, which collects and rebates N
77	participates in EU market system through customs union with France
78	

3   Expand the hyperlink to include cells A74:A77.

Once Excel has done the hard work of constructing a hyperlink to a different workbook it is easy to expand it to point to a range if required.

    1. Click: View→Window→Switch Windows→Monaco-2.

    You are returned to the *Monaco-2* workbook.

    2. If not already selected, move the cursor to cell A8 using the keyboard arrow keys (if you simply click the cell you will execute the hyperlink).

    3. Click: Insert→Links→Link.

    The hyperlink address is visible in the *Address* box.

    Notice that a hyperlink must have a %20 code in place of any spaces.

tip

Selecting a hyperlink cell with the mouse

In this lesson, you used the keyboard arrow keys to select a cell containing a hyperlink.

There's also a way to do this using the mouse.

If you click and hold the mouse button down for a second or two, you can select a hyperlinked cell without activating the hyperlink.

Monaco-2

Session Six: Working with Hyperlinks and Other Applications

note

You can also hyperlink to non-Excel files such as Word documents

When you set the *Link to* type to *Existing File or Web Page*, you are able to link to any file on your computer.

Windows knows which application is used to open most file types, so if you link to a Word document, the document will open in Word when you click the hyperlink.

This opens up a huge range of possibilities. You could create a hyperlink on a worksheet that will:

• Play an MP3 sound file.
• View an MP4 video.
• Open a Word document.

... and do anything else that any application installed on your computer is capable of.

4. Edit the hyperlink to reference the range A74:A77 on the *Economy* worksheet by changing the *Address* to the following:

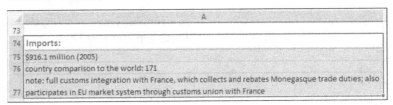

5. Click the *OK* button.

4 Test the hyperlink.

When you click the *Imports* hyperlink, you are taken to the *Economy* worksheet in the *Monaco Economy-1* workbook with cells A74:A77 selected.

A
73
74 Imports:
75 $916.1 million (2005)
76 country comparison to the world: 171
77 note: full customs integration with France, which collects and rebates Monegasque trade duties; also participates in EU market system through customs union with France

5 Return to the *Monaco-2* workbook.

Click: View→Window→Switch Windows→Monaco-2.

6 Make cell A17 on the *Main Menu* worksheet into a *Web Page* hyperlink pointing to the *Monaco Tourist Office* website at: www.visitmonaco.com

1. Select cell A17 on the *Main Menu* worksheet.

2. Click: Insert→Links→Link.

3. Click *Existing File or Web Page* in the *Link to* navigation bar.

4. Type **http://www.visitmonaco.com** into the *Address* box.

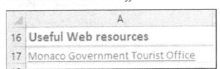

5. Click the *OK* button.

Cell A17 is converted into a hyperlink pointing to the *Monaco Government Tourist Office* website.

A
16 Useful Web resources
17 Monaco Government Tourist Office

7 Save your work as *Monaco-3*.

Lesson 6-3: Hyperlink to an e-mail address and enhance the browsing experience

By now you've probably noticed a big problem when creating Excel hyperlinks. The links take you to the desired destination without problems, but how do you get back to the main menu? Excel has sold you a one-way ticket!

In a regular web browser, you have a *Back Button, Forward Button* and *Document Location Box:*

This lesson will show you how to add the same controls to Excel.

You may also want to allow your users to quickly send you e-mail feedback. The easiest way to do this is to add a clickable e-mail link to the worksheet.

1   Open *Monaco-3* from your sample files folder (if it isn't already open).

2   Add a *Back* button to the *Quick Access Toolbar.*

This is another of those really useful Excel features that can only be accessed by customizing the *Quick Access Toolbar* or the ribbon. You'll learn how to create a custom ribbon tab later in: *Lesson 7-20: Create a custom ribbon tab.*

1. Click the drop-down arrow on the right of the *Quick Access Toolbar.*

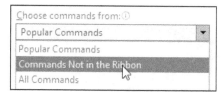

2. Click *More Commands...* from the drop-down menu.

The *Customize the Quick Access Toolbar* dialog appears.

3. Click *Commands Not in the Ribbon* from the *Choose commands from* drop-down list.

A list appears showing all of the commands that are not normally available in Excel.

4. Select the *Back* command from the commands list.

5. Click the *Add>>* button to add the *Back* command to the *Quick Access Toolbar.*

Monaco-3

6. Click the *OK* button.

A back button is now displayed on the *Quick Access Toolbar*.

3   Add a *Forward* button to the *Quick Access Toolbar*.

Do this in the same way that you added the back button.

4   Add a *Document Location* box to the *Quick Access Toolbar*.

5   Click the *OK* button to close the dialog.

6   Test the new navigation controls.

Your Quick Access Toolbar now has familiar browser-like controls.

Click on an Excel hyperlink and then use the *Back* button to return to the *Main Menu* worksheet.

7   Add an e-mail hyperlink to cell A20 on the *Main Menu* worksheet.

1. Type your e-mail address into cell A20 on the *Main Menu* worksheet.

2. Press the **<Enter>** key.

When you press the **<Enter>** key, the e-mail address changes into a hyperlink.

8   Edit the hyperlink to show a subject line for any generated e-mails.

1. If not already selected, move the cursor to cell A20 using the keyboard arrow keys (if you simply click the cell you will execute the hyperlink).

2. Click: Insert→Links→Link.

3. Type **Feedback from Monaco Excel workbook** into the *Subject* box.

4. Click the *OK* button.

9   Test the hyperlink.

When you click the hyperlink, you are taken to your default e-mail application with the destination e-mail address and subject lines already completed.

10   Save your work as *Monaco-4.*

Lesson 6-4: Embed an Excel worksheet object into a Word document

Microsoft Office is an object-orientated application. Simply put, this means that everything you work with in Office is an object.

An Excel cell, an Excel range of cells, an Excel table, an Excel chart, a Word document and a PowerPoint slide are all objects.

The wonderful thing about this object-orientated architecture is that you can freely embed objects inside other objects. For example, you can embed an Excel range into a Word document, or an Excel chart into a PowerPoint presentation.

In this lesson you'll embed an Excel worksheet into a Word document.

1   Open Microsoft Word.

2   Use Word to open *The World's Best Selling Cars-1* (Word document) from your sample files folder.

This file contains the beginning of a Word document:

> The World's Best Selling Cars
>
> Some cars sell well, others hardly sell at all. Once every few years a car comes along that is demonstrably better than its competition. The car may beat the competition on price, performance, reliability, style or a combination of these factors.
>
> Here is a list of the world's most successful cars to date:

3   Embed an Excel worksheet at the end of the word document.

1. Click just to the right of the sentence *"Here is a list of the world's most successful cars to date:"*.

2. Press the **<Enter>** key to move to the next line.

3. Click: Insert→Text→Object→Object...

   The *Object* dialog appears.

4. Select *Microsoft Excel Worksheet* from the *Object type* list.

5. Click the *OK* button.

   An empty Excel worksheet is embedded into the Word document.

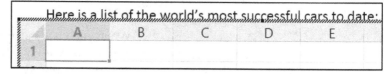

   Notice that something has happened to the ribbon. The Word ribbon has been replaced by the Excel ribbon.

4   Enter the following data into the worksheet:

The World's Best Selling Cars-1

	A	B	C
1	Make	Model	Sales (Million)
2	Ford	Escort	18
3	Volkswagen	Beetle	23.5
4	Volkswagen	Golf	27.5
5	Ford	F Series	35
6	Toyota	Corolla	40

(When you have entered the data, AutoSize each column so that each is wide enough to display the contents).

5   Return to Word.

Click anywhere in the Word document's text (outside the Excel object).

Notice that the appearance of the worksheet has changed and that the Excel ribbon has changed back to the Word ribbon.

6   *Print Preview* the document.

Click: File→Print.

Notice that the worksheet looks just as it would in Excel. The worksheet is too big, however, as there are many empty cells.

7   Return to Excel.

1.   Click the *Back Button*.

2.   Double click anywhere in the Excel object.

Notice that the Excel ribbon has returned.

8   Size the worksheet window so that it is the same size as the data entered.

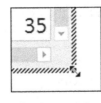

1.   Hover the mouse cursor over the sizing handle in the bottom right corner of the worksheet until you see the double-headed arrow cursor shape.

2.   Click and drag upwards and to the left to re-size the worksheet object so that it is the same size as its contents.

9   Return to Word.

Click anywhere in the Word document's text (outside the Excel object).

Here is a list of the world's most successful cars to date:		
Make	Model	Sales (Million)
Ford	Escort	18
Volkswagen	Beetle	23.5
Volkswagen	Golf	27.5
Ford	F Series	35
Toyota	Corolla	40

10   Save your work as *The World's Best Selling Cars-2*.

Lesson 6-5: Embed an Excel chart object into a Word document

1   Open Microsoft Word.

2   Use Word to open *The World's Best Selling Cars-2* (a Word document) from your sample files folder (if it isn't already open).

3   Convert the range into a table.

1. Double-click the Excel object to return to Excel.

   The Excel ribbon replaces the Word ribbon.

2. Click inside the range.

3. Click: Insert→Tables→Table.

4. Click *OK* to accept the automatically detected range.

   The range is converted into a table.

4   Remove the AutoFilter from the table.

The AutoFilter buttons don't look good in a Word document.

Click: Data→Sort & Filter→Filter.

The filter buttons vanish.

5   Sort the table from bestselling to least selling.

1. Click anywhere in column C.

2. Click: Data→Sort & Filter→Sort Largest to Smallest.

6   Format the values in column C so that they display one decimal place.

1. Select the values in column C.

2. Click Home→Number→Increase Decimal.

7   Add the text **... and here is the same data as a chart** to the end of the document.

1. Click anywhere in the document's text to return to Word.

2. Click slightly to the right of the table.

3. Press the **<Enter>** key to move to the next line.

4. Type the text: **... and here is the same data as a chart.**

5. Press the **<Enter>** key to move to the next line.

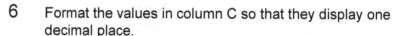

Make	Model	Sales (Million)
Toyota	Corolla	40.0
Ford	F Series	35.0
Volkswagen	Golf	27.5
Volkswagen	Beetle	23.5
Ford	Escort	18.0

... and here is the same data as a chart.

The World's Best Selling Cars-2

note

Use the same technique to embed objects into (and from) PowerPoint and other applications

The mechanism that allows you to embed and link documents is called OLE (Object Linking and Embedding).

Any application that supports OLE is happy to work with any other OLE compatible application.

Applications supporting OLE include (of course) the entire Office suite along with many Adobe and other third-party applications.

You'll find OLE fantastically useful to add Excel ranges and charts to Word documents and PowerPoint presentations, but there's no need to stop there.

8   Copy the Excel object to the end of the document.

1. Click the Excel object once to select it. Be careful to only click once. If you double-click you will go back into Excel.

2. Copy the Excel object.

3. Click on the line after the text: **... and here is the same data as a chart**.

4. Paste.

   An identical Excel object now appears in both places.

9   Convert the duplicated Excel object into a chart.

1. Double-click the lower Excel object to go back into Excel.

2. Select cells A1:C6.

3. Click: Insert→Charts→Insert Pie or Doughnut Chart→ 2-D Pie→Pie.

   The worksheet now contains a pie chart.

4. Right-click just inside the top-left corner of the pie chart.

5. Click *Move Chart...* from the shortcut menu.

6. Click the *New Sheet* option button.

7. Click the *OK* button.

   A portion of the pie chart is now visible in the Excel object.

10   Re-size the Excel chart object to an attractive size.

This was covered in: *Lesson 6-4: Embed an Excel worksheet object into a Word document.*

11   Return to Word.

Click anywhere in the document's text.

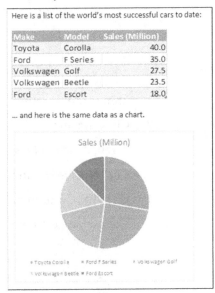

12   Save your work as *The World's Best Selling Cars-3*.

Lesson 6-6: Link an Excel worksheet to a Word document

1   Open Microsoft Word.

2   Open *International Customers-1* from your sample files folder.

This file contains the beginning of a document:

> **Information for International Customers**
>
> We are happy to supply our products to any world location and to bill you in your own currency.
>
> We convert our prices using the following exchange rates:

important

It is very easy to break documents that contain links

Links don't automatically update.

If you do any of the following, you will break the link and your embedded objects will no longer work.

1. Change the name of a linked file.

2. Change the name of the folder that a linked file is stored in.

3. Move a linked file into a different folder.

4. E-mail the parent document to somebody else without including the linked documents.

If you think that you will want to share a set of linked documents in the future, it is a good idea to keep them all in the same folder.

You can then copy the entire folder to another location (or e-mail the entire contents of the folder as a zip file) and your links will then continue to work at the new location.

3   Insert the *International Customer Rates-1* Excel Workbook at the end of the document as a linked object.

The *International Customer Rates-1* workbook contains exchange rates for eleven currencies. They will all have changed by the time you read this book.

1. Click just to the right of the sentence: *We convert our prices using the following exchange rates:*

2. Press the **<Enter>** key to move down to the next line.

3. Click: Insert→Text→Object→Object.

    The *Object* dialog is displayed.

4. Click the *Create from File* tab.

5. Check the *Link to file* check box.

6. Notice the help text that has appeared:

    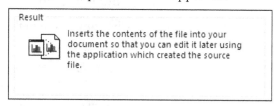

This means that any changes to the Excel worksheet will immediately appear in the linked Excel object.

7. Click the *Browse...* button.

8. Navigate to the *International Customer Rates-1* workbook.

9. Click the *Insert* button.

10. Click the *OK* button.

    The exchange rates are now displayed inside the Word document.

International Customers-1

note

Link and embed objects using drag and drop

You can simply drag and drop a range of cells from Excel to Word. Make sure that you <Ctrl>-click-drag if you want to copy the range. If you simply click and drag, you'll remove the range from the workbook.

To drag and drop, you'll need to arrange your screen so that you can see both the Excel and Word document windows at the same time.

When you drag and drop, Word has to guess whether you want to link or embed.

If you drag and drop a chart, Word will link. If you drag and drop a range of cells, Word will embed.

Because of this limitation, the other methods are preferable when you need to control linking and embedding.

We convert our prices using the following exchange rates:

Exchange Rates		
Country	Multiply GBP Price by:	To get price in:
USA	1.44662	US Dollar
Australia	2.04065	Australian Dollar
Canada	2.01132	Canadian Dollar
Euro	1.29759	Euro
Hong Kong	11.267	Hong Kong Dollar
Indonesia	19,681.80	Indonesian Rupiah
Japan	168.69	Japanese Yen
Singapore	2.0333	Singapore Dollar
Sweden	12.2389	Swedish Krona
Switzerland	1.43485	Swiss Franc
Thailand	51.3285	Thai Baht

4   Test the link by changing values in the Excel workbook.

Linked objects work in a different way to embedded objects.

When you double-click an embedded object, you are able to edit it inside the Word document.

When you double-click a linked object, Excel will open and display the linked file.

1.   Double-click the Excel object.

   Excel opens with the *International Customer Rates-1* workbook.

2.   Re-size the Excel and Word windows so that you can see both documents.

3.   Change one of the exchange rates in the *International Customer Rates-1* workbook.

4.   Click once in the Word document window to make it the active window.

5.   Right-click the Excel linked object in the *International Customers-1* Word document.

6.   Click *Update Link* from the shortcut menu.

   Notice that the values update to match those in the workbook.

   Values are normally only updated when you open the Word document. The *Update Link* command tells Word to refresh the data it is displaying.

5   Close the Excel window without saving.

6   Save the Word document as *International Customers-2*.

Session 6: Exercise

1   Open the *Spectrum Car Sales-1* Excel workbook from your sample files folder.

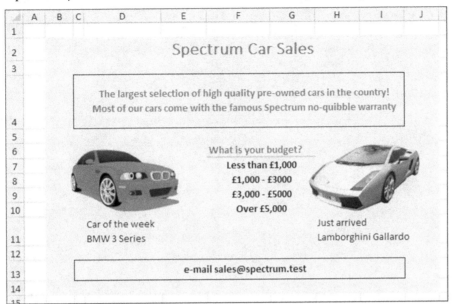

2   Hyperlink the *What is your budget?* cells (F7, F8, F9 and F10) to the relevant worksheets.

3   Hyperlink the *Car of the week BMW 3 Series* text (cell D11) to the *£1,000 - £3,000* worksheet.

4   Hyperlink the *Just arrived Lamborghini Gallardo* text (cell H11) to the *Over £5,000* worksheet.

5   Make the *e-mail sales@spectrum.test* text in cell D13 into an e-mail hyperlink that will send an e-mail to the e-mail address: *sales@spectrum.test* with the subject: *Car sales enquiry*.

6   Save the workbook as *Spectrum Car Sales-2* and close Excel.

7   Open the *Stock List-1* sample file in Microsoft Word.

8   Place a linked object after the text in the *Stock List-1* Word document that will show the contents of the *Over £5,000* worksheet in the *Spectrum Car Sales-2* workbook.

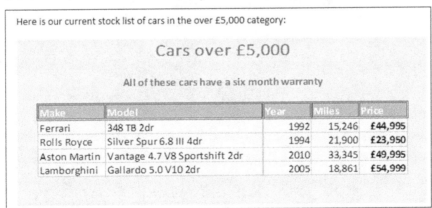

9   Save the Word document as *Stock List-2*.

Spectrum Car Sales-1   Stock List-1   If you need help slide the page to the left

Session 6: Exercise Answers

These are the five questions that students find the most difficult to answer:

Q 8	Q 5	Q 2, 3, 4
1. Open the *Spectrum Car Sales-2 workbook* in Excel. 2. Select the *Over £5,000* worksheet. 3. Save and close the *Spectrum Car Sales-2* workbook. 4. Open the *Stock List-1* document in Microsoft Word. 5. Click just to the right of the *... £5,000 category:* text. 6. Press the **<Enter>** key to move to the next line. 7. Click: Insert→Text→Object→ Object. 8. Select the *Create from File* tab. 9. Click the *Browse* button and select the *Spectrum Car Sales-2* workbook. 10. Click the *Insert* button. 11. Check the *Link to File* check box. 12. Click the *OK* button. This was covered in: *Lesson 6-6: Link an Excel worksheet to a Word document.*	1. Select cell D13 on the *Home* worksheet. 2. Click: Insert→Links→ Link. 3. Click *E-mail Address* on the left-hand selection bar. 4. Complete the dialog as follows: E-mail address: mailto:sales@spectrum.test Subject: Car sales enquiry 5. Click the *OK* button. This was covered in: *Lesson 6-3: Hyperlink to an e-mail address and enhance the browsing experience.*	1. Click in cell F7. 2. Click: Insert→Links→ Link. 3. Click: *Place in This Document* in the left-hand menu bar. 4. Click on *'Under £1,000'* in the central pane. Place in This Document — Cell Reference, Home, Under £1,000, '£1,000-£3,000' 5. Repeat the same steps to add hyperlinks to cells F8, F9, F10, D11 and H11. This was covered in: *Lesson 6-1: Hyperlink to worksheets and ranges.*

© 2020 The Smart Method® Ltd   **259**

Session Seven: Forms and Macros

You don't need to know how an engine works to drive a car.

Proverb, unknown authors

You can design Excel applications for users who have no Excel skills.

When you create this type of application, you need to provide a simple and intuitive form-based user interface. The user interface should be so simple that the application can be used without any training or assumed Excel skills.

In this session you'll create a powerful, form-based, Excel application with a simple and intuitive user interface.

You'll also learn how to record and run macros. Macros allow you to provide users with simple form controls that execute a complex sequence of Excel actions.

Session Objectives

By the end of this session you will be able to:

- Add group box and option button controls to a worksheet form
- Add a combo box control to a worksheet form
- Set form control cell links
- Connect result cells to a form
- Add a check box control to a worksheet form
- Use check box data in result cells
- Add a temperature gauge chart to a form
- Add a single input data table to a form
- Improve form appearance and usability
- Understand macros and VBA
- Record a macro with absolute references
- Understand macro security
- Implement macro security
- Understand trusted documents
- Record a macro with relative references
- Use shapes to run macros
- Run a macro from a button control
- Show and hide ribbon tabs
- Add custom groups to standard ribbon tabs
- Create a custom ribbon tab

Lesson 7-1: Add group box and option button controls to a worksheet form

1 Open *Mortgage Calculator-1* from your sample files folder.

2 Add the *Developer* tab to the ribbon.

Because form controls are an advanced feature of Excel, Microsoft hides them from normal users. You must add the *Developer* tab to the ribbon in order to reveal them.

1. Click: File→Options→Customize Ribbon.

2. Check the *Developer* check box in the right-hand pane.

3. Click the *OK* button.

The *Developer* tab is now visible on the ribbon.

3 Delete row 5 and then insert two new blank rows so that there are four blank rows between *Property Price* and *Arrangement Fee*.

4 Add a *Group Box* control so that it completely fills cells B5:D6.

1. Click: Developer→Controls→Insert→Form Controls→ Group Box (Form Control).

2. Hold down the <**Alt**> key. This will make the group box snap to the corners of the selected cells.

3. Carefully position the black cross cursor near the top left corner of cell B5.

4. Click and drag to the bottom right corner of cell D6 and release the mouse button.

A group box appears.

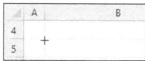

5 Change the caption of the group box to: **Deposit:**

1. Click on a blank area of the worksheet to de-select the group box.

2. Double click the *Group Box 1* caption on the border of the group box.

3. Delete the existing *Group Box 1* text and then type: **Deposit:**

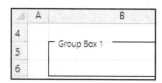

6 Add six option button controls to the group box.

1. Click: Developer→Controls→Insert→Form Controls→ Option Button (Form Control).

2. Click and drag inside the group box to add an option button. Keep the button small, as you need space for six buttons and they should not overlap. Be careful to keep the border of each option button inside the group box.

3. Repeat for the other five buttons. It is important that you add them in sequence from left to right.

Mortgage Calculator-1

note

Why are there two sets of form controls?

When you click:

Developer→Controls→Insert

...you are confronted with two sets of similar controls:

The Form Controls are designed to be used without any understanding of the Visual Basic for Applications (VBA) programming language.

The ActiveX controls are intended to be used as part of the Visual Basic programming environment.

Unless you have Visual Basic programming skills, you will probably not find a use for ActiveX controls.

You'll learn a little more about VBA's relationship with Excel in: *Lesson 7-10: Understand macros and VBA.*

7 Change the option button captions to **5%** to **30%** (reading left to right).

1. Right-click the first option button to select it.

    A box appears around the option button, along with a shortcut menu.

2. Press the **<Esc>** key or click once again inside the control to close the shortcut menu (an even faster way to do steps one and two in a single operation is to double right-click the control).

3. Double-click the text next to the option button.

4. Delete the existing text and type: **5%**

5. Do the same for the **10%** to **30%** option buttons.

8 Move and re-size the option buttons so that they are evenly spaced inside the group box.

1. Select an option button and close the shortcut menu.

2. Use the arrow keys on the keyboard to move the option button to its new position.

3. Click and drag one of the white circles (sizing handles) on the border of the option button to re-size if necessary.

4. Hover over the border of the selected option button control (but not on one of the white circles until you see the four-headed arrow cursor shape).

5. Click and drag to move the option button control.

6. Your option group should now look like this:

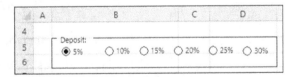

9 Add another set of option buttons to show terms from 5 to 30 years.

1. Delete row 12 and then insert three new rows.

2. Add a group box form control so that it completely fills cells B12:D14.

3. Add the caption and option buttons. It is important that you add them in sequence (in ascending order).

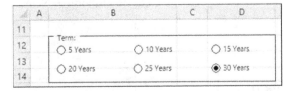

10 Save your work as *Mortgage Calculator-2.*

Lesson 7-2: Add a combo box control to a worksheet form

1   Open *Mortgage Calculator-2* from your sample files folder (if it isn't already open).

2   Delete the contents of cell D16.

3   Remove the black border from cell D16.

   1.   Select cell D16.

   2.   Click: Home→Font→Borders→No Border.

4   Place a combo box control in cell D16.

   1.   Select cell D16.

   2.   Click: Developer→Controls→Insert→Form Controls→ Combo Box (Form Control).

   3.   Hold down the **<Alt>** Key. This will make the control fit perfectly in the cell.

   4.   Click just inside the top left border of cell D16 and drag to just inside the bottom right border.

   5.   Release the mouse button.

   The control is inserted into the cell (and fits perfectly).

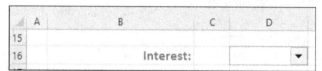

5   Create a new worksheet called *Data* to provide interest rate data from 2% to 15% in increments of 0.5%.

   1.   Create a new worksheet called *Data*.

   2.   Select the *Data* worksheet.

   3.   Type: **Interest Rates** into cell A1.

   4.   Type: **2.0%** into cell A2.

   5.   Type the formula: **=A2+0.5%** into cell A3.

   6.   AutoFill cell A3 into cells A4:A28.

6   Format cells A2:A28 so that only one decimal place is shown.

   1.   Select cells A2:A28.

   2.   Click: Home→Number→Decrease Decimal.

	A	B
1	Interest Rates	
2	2.0%	
3	2.5%	
4	3.0%	

Mortgage Calculator-2

7   Create a range name for the interest rate values in cells A2:A28.

Range names were extensively covered in: *Session Four: Using Names and the Formula Auditing Tools.*

1. Select cells A1:A28.

2. Click: Formulas→Defined Names→Create from Selection.

3. Click the *OK* button.

8   Set the combo box's *Input Range* to reference the interest rate data.

1. Select the *Mortgage Calculator* worksheet.

2. Right-click inside the combo box control.

3. Click *Format Control…* from the shortcut menu.

4. Select the *Control* tab.

5. Click in the *Input Range* box.

6. Type **Interest_Rates** into the *Input range* box.

7. Click the *OK* button.

9   Test the combo box control.

1. Click away from the control to de-select it.

2. Click the drop-down arrow on the combo box.

Notice that the combo box displays all of the interest rates defined by the *Interest_Rates* range name.

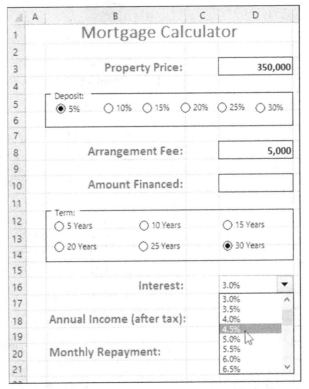

10   Save your work as *Mortgage Calculator-3*.

Lesson 7-3: Set form control cell links

When working with forms, it is useful to separate the user interface from the input and result cells. The user interface is the part of the worksheet where the user enters values and views results. In this lesson's worksheet the user interface comprises of cells B3:D20.

Calculations are done in a different section of the worksheet where you will define *Input Cells* and *Result Cells*. You'll recognize this method of working from the lessons in: *Session Five: What If Analysis and Security*.

In this lesson's worksheet the *Input Cells* and *Result Cells* are shown in cells B23:D36. Later you will hide these rows from the user.

In this lesson you'll connect the *User Interface* with the *Input Cells*.

1   Open *Mortgage Calculator-3* from your sample files folder (if it isn't already open).

2   Link the user interface's *Property Price, Arrangement Fee,* and *Annual Income (after tax)* cells to the relevant *Input Cells*.

This is extremely easy, as it can be done using simple cell references:

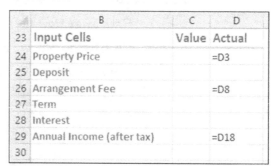

	B	C	D
23	Input Cells	Value	Actual
24	Property Price		=D3
25	Deposit		
26	Arrangement Fee		=D8
27	Term		
28	Interest		
29	Annual Income (after tax)		=D18
30			

3   Connect the data from the *Deposit* group box to cell C25.

1. Right-click the *5% Deposit* option button.

2. Select *Format Control...* from the shortcut menu.

3. Click the *Control* tab.

4. Click in the *Cell link* box.

5. Click in cell C25.

Cell link: $C$25

6. Click the *OK* button.

4   Test the cell link.

1. Click away from the option buttons to de-select.

2. Left-click each option button in turn.

3. Notice that numbers from 1 to 6 appear in cell C25 as each option button is clicked. Option 5% results in 1, option 10% results in 2... and so on.

Mortgage Calculator-3

If you find that the wrong numbers are appearing, it is because you added the option buttons in the wrong order. In this case you'll have to move the buttons around and change their captions, until you have the correct number associated with each button.

5 **Add a formula to cell D25 so that it displays the correct percentage for each option.**

1. Type =**C25*0.05** into cell D25.

2. Test again. This time the actual percentage of the selected option button should display in cell D25.

6 **Connect the data from the *Term* group box to cell C27.**

Do this in exactly the same way that you connected the *Deposit* group box to cell C25.

7 **Add a formula to cell D27 to show the actual term.**

1. Type =**C27*5** into cell D27.

2. Test the *Term* option buttons.

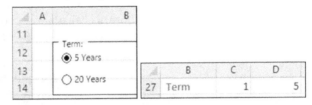

8 **Connect the data from the *Interest* combo box to cell C28.**

1. Right-click the combo box control.

2. Click *Format Control…* from the shortcut menu.

3. Click the *Control* Tab.

4. Click in the *Cell link* box.

5. Click in cell C28.

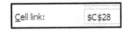

6. Click the *OK* button.

9 **Test the *Interest* combo box cell link.**

Just like the option button controls, the value returned from the combo box is a number representing which option was selected. 2% returns the number 1, 2.5% returns the number 2… and so on.

10 **Add a formula to cell D28 so that it displays the correct interest rate.**

Type the formula =**(C28*0.5+1.5)/100** into cell D28.

11 **Test the combo box.**

12 **Save your work as *Mortgage Calculator-4*.**

Lesson 7-4: Connect result cells to a form

In the previous lessons you created a user interface using Excel's form controls.

The form now collects data from the user, and uses this data to update the input cells.

In this lesson you'll use the input cells to calculate the result cells, and then use the result cells to update the form.

1   Open *Mortgage Calculator-4* from your sample files folder (if it isn't already open).

2   Add a formula to cell D32 that will calculate the *Amount Financed*.

Amount Financed = Property Price – Deposit + Arrangement Fee

To perform this calculation, you need to type the following formula into cell D32:

=D24-(D24*D25)+D26

3   Add a formula to cell D33 to calculate the *Monthly Repayment*.

For this calculation you will use the PMT function that was covered in: *Lesson 3-3: Use the Insert Function dialog and the PMT function.*

The function arguments will be:

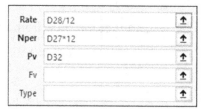

4   Convert the negative *Monthly Repayment* into a positive value.

The easiest way to do this is to place a minus operator in front of the function:

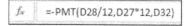

5   Add a formula to cell D34 to calculate the *Total Repaid* amount.

Total Repaid = Monthly Repayment * 12 * Term

To perform this calculation, you need to type the following formula into cell D34:

=D33*12*D27

6   Add a formula to cell D35 to calculate the *Total Interest*.

Total Interest = Total Repaid – Amount Financed

Mortgage Calculator-4

To perform this calculation, you need to use the following formula into cell D35:

=D34-D32

7   Add a formula to cell D36 to calculate the *Repayment as % of Income*.

Repayment as % of Income =
Monthly Repayment * 12/Annual Income (after tax)

To perform this calculation, you need to type the following formula into cell D36:

=D33*12/D29

8   Connect the *Amount Financed* result cell (D32) to the *Amount Financed* form cell (D10).

Enter the following formula into cell D10:

=D32

9   Connect the *Monthly Repayment* result cell (D33) to the *Monthly Repayment* form cell (D20).

Enter the following formula into cell D20:

=D33

10   Test the form.

Enter the values shown below into the form. The result cells should match those shown:

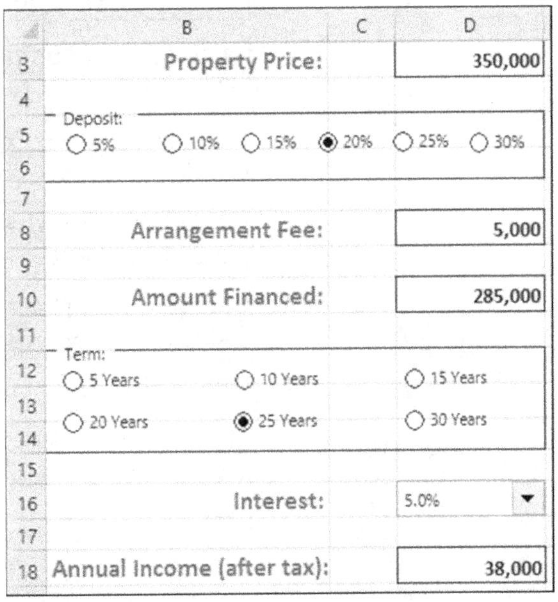

	B	C	D
3	Property Price:		350,000
4			
5	Deposit: ○ 5% ○ 10% ○ 15% ◉ 20% ○ 25% ○ 30%		
6			
7			
8	Arrangement Fee:		5,000
9			
10	Amount Financed:		285,000
11			
12	Term: ○ 5 Years ○ 10 Years ○ 15 Years		
13	○ 20 Years ◉ 25 Years ○ 30 Years		
14			
15			
16	Interest:	5.0%	▼
17			
18	Annual Income (after tax):		38,000

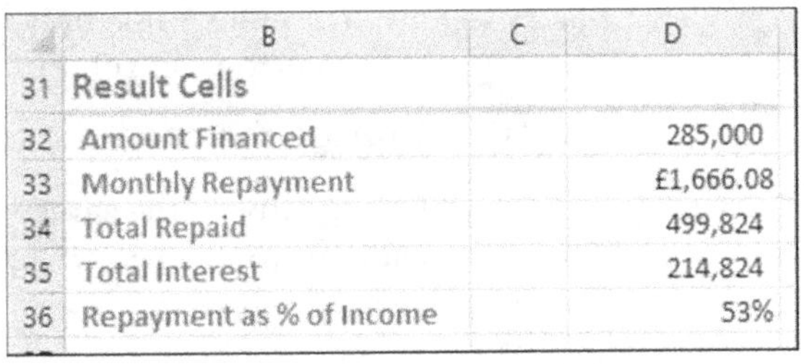

	B	C	D
31	Result Cells		
32	Amount Financed		285,000
33	Monthly Repayment		£1,666.08
34	Total Repaid		499,824
35	Total Interest		214,824
36	Repayment as % of Income		53%

11   Save your work as *Mortgage Calculator-5*.

Lesson 7-5: Add a check box control to a worksheet form

In this lesson you will improve the form to model interest-only mortgages.

1   Open *Mortgage Calculator-5* from your sample files folder (if it isn't already open).

2   Left-align the text in cell B16.

   1.   Select cell B16.

   2.   Click: Home→Alignment→Align Left.

3   Move the combo box so that it appears directly after the *Interest:* text in cell B16.

   1.   Right-click the combo box.

      If a shortcut menu appears either press the **<Esc>** key or click once again inside the control to close it.

   2.   Use the arrow keys on the keyboard to move the combo box to its new position.

      Your combo box should now look like this:

4   Add a check box control so that it completely fills cells C16:D16.

   1.   Click: Developer→Controls→Insert→ Check Box (Form Control).

   2.   Hold down the **<Alt>** key. This will make the control fit perfectly in the cells.

   3.   Click just inside the top left border of cell C16 and drag to just inside the bottom right border of cell D16.

   4.   Release the mouse button.

      The control is inserted into the cells (and aligns perfectly).

      Your check box may have a different caption, such as *Check Box 20* as the control number is not consistently applied.

5   Change the check box caption to: **Interest Only Loan**

   Change this in the same way that you changed the option button captions in: *Lesson 7-1: Add group box and option button controls to a worksheet form.*

Mortgage Calculator-5

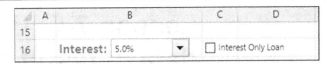

6   Add an input cell to link to the new check box.

1.   Insert a row above row 29.

2.   Type the text **Interest Only?** into cell B29.

	B	C	D
28	Interest	7	5.0%
29	Interest Only?		
30	Annual Income (after tax)		38,000

7   Connect the data from the *Interest Only Loan* check box to cell D29.

1.   Right-click the *Interest Only Loan* check box.

2.   Select *Format Control...* from the shortcut menu.

3.   Click the *Control* tab.

4.   Click in the *Cell link* box.

5.   Click in cell D29.

6.   Click the *OK* button.

8   Test the cell link.

1.   Click away from the check box to de-select it.

2.   Click the *Interest Only Loan* check box a few times.

When the box is checked, TRUE appears in cell D29. When the box is unchecked, FALSE appears in cell D29.

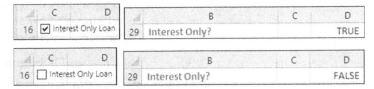

9   Save your work as *Mortgage Calculator-6*.

Lesson 7-6: Use check box data in result cells

1   Open *Mortgage Calculator-6* from your sample files folder (if it isn't already open).

2   Correct the formula in the *Monthly Repayment* result cell (D34) to allow for interest only loans.

   1. Click in cell D34.

   2. Click the *Insert Function* button to the left of the formula bar.

   3. The *Function Arguments* dialog appears.

       The capital owed at the end of an interest only loan (Excel's terminology for this is: *Future Value*) will be a negative number that is the same as the *Amount Financed*. The *Future Value* will thus be:

       Amount Financed * -1

       A normal capital and repayment loan will have been fully repaid by the end of the term, so there will be no future value.

       In order to make the PMT function return the correct value for both types of loan, you will have to use an IF logic function to set the future value. The IF function was covered in: *Lesson 3-5: Use the IF logic function.*

   4. Type the following formula into the *Fv* argument box:

       This will set the *Future Value* to be the same as the **Amount Financed*-1** for an interest only loan, and to **zero** for a capital and repayment loan.

   5. Click the *OK* button.

3   Correct the *Total Interest* result cell (D36) to allow for interest only loans.

   A capital and repayment loan will incur interest of:

   Total Repaid – Amount Financed.

   Every payment in an *interest only* loan consists only of interest. This means that the *Total Interest* will be the same as the *Total Repaid.*

   In order to correct the *Total Interest* result cell, you will, once again, have to use an IF logic function.

   1. Click in cell D36.

   2. Delete the previous formula.

   3. Add an IF function. The function arguments are:

Mortgage Calculator-6

Logical_test	D29	↑
Value_if_true	D35	↑
Value_if_false	D35-D33	↑

4   Test the check box.

I tested with the following form values:

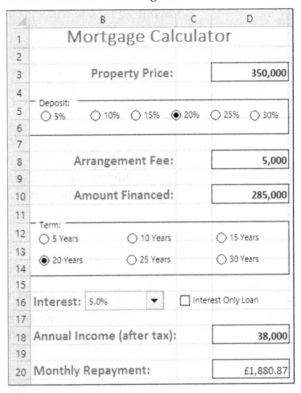

When the *Interest Only Loan* box was unchecked, the *Result Cells* were:

	B	C	D
32	Result Cells		
33	Amount Financed		285,000
34	Monthly Repayment		£1,880.87
35	Total Repaid		451,410
36	Total Interest		166,410
37	Repayment as % of Income		59%

When the *Interest Only Loan* box was checked, the *Result Cells* were:

	B	C	D
32	Result Cells		
33	Amount Financed		285,000
34	Monthly Repayment		£1,187.50
35	Total Repaid		285,000
36	Total Interest		285,000
37	Repayment as % of Income		38%

5   Save your work as *Mortgage Calculator-7*.

Lesson 7-7: Add a temperature gauge chart to a form

Charting is covered in depth in session 5 of the *Essential Skills* book in this series. Excel doesn't have a temperature gauge chart in its pre-defined range of charts. It is possible, however, to create this type of chart by formatting a regular bar chart in a special way.

1   Open *Mortgage Calculator-7* from your sample files folder.

2   Add a column chart to the worksheet with the single data value of *Repayment as % of Income.*

    1.   Select cell D37.

    2.   Click: Insert→Charts→Column or Bar Chart→2-D Column→ Clustered Column.

    3.   Right-click the center of the chart and then click *Select Data…* from the shortcut menu.

    4.   Click the *Edit* button above the *Legend Entries (Series)* list box.

    5.   Remove all of the text from the *Series values* box.

    6.   Click in the *Series values* box and then click cell D37.

    7.   Click *OK* and then *OK* again.

    You now have a chart with a single bar showing the loan affordability as a percentage of income.

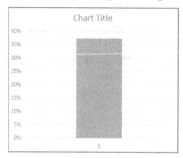

3   Change the vertical axis so that it begins at 0% and ends at 100%.

    1.   Click the chart to activate it.

    2.   Right click on the *Vertical (Value Axis)* (one of the percentages).

    3.   Click *Format Axis:* from the shortcut menu.

    4.   Set the *Minimum* and *Maximum* values to **0** and **1**.

4   Remove the gap from the left hand side of the column.

    1.   Right-click on the chart column and then click *Format Data Series…* from the shortcut menu.

    The *Format Data Series* task pane appears.

    2.   Change the *Gap Width* to *0%*.

5   Remove the *Horizontal Axis* and *Chart Title* elements from the chart.

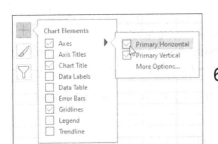

1. Click on the chart to activate it.

2. Click the *Chart Elements* button just outside the top right of the chart.

3. Clear the *Chart Title* check box.

4. Click the *Axes* flyout menu

5. Clear the *Primary Horizontal* check box.

6 Apply a thin black line around the Plot Area.

1. Right-click in the center of the chart (but not on the bar or a gridline).

2. Click *Format Plot Area...* from the shortcut menu.

   The *Format Plot Area* task pane appears.

3. Click on the *Border* fly-out menu.

4. Click the *Solid Line* option button.

5. Click the *Color* button and select *Black*.

7 Re-size the chart so that it resembles a temperature gauge that is the same height as the form.

1. Click on the chart to select it.

2. Click and drag the bottom right-hand corner sizing handle to size as required.

3. Click and drag anywhere on the border of the chart that is not a sizing handle to move it to the required position (see the cover of this book for an idea of roughly where that should be).

8 Remove the border around the chart.

1. Click on the chart to select it.

2. Right-click on the border of the chart.

3. Click *Format Chart Area...* from the shortcut menu.

   The *Format Chart Area* task pane appears.

4. Click: Border→No Line.

9 Add an oval shape to mimic the bulb at the bottom of a thermometer.

1. Click away from the chart to de-select it.

2. Click: Insert→Illustrations→Shapes→Basic Shapes→Oval.

3. Click and drag to draw an oval at the bottom of the chart.

4. Right-click the oval shape and select *Format Shape...* from the shortcut menu.

5. Click Line→No Line in the *Format Shape* task pane.

6. Click the *Close* button ⊠ at the top right of the *Format Shape* task pane.

   Your chart should now look similar to the sidebar.

10 Save your work as *Mortgage Calculator-8.*

Lesson 7-8: Add a single input data table to a form

important

Be careful not to refer to the column input cell when creating data table column formulas

Excel data tables have a strange and subtle quirk that can easily cause your data table to show invalid results.

In step 6.2 you used the formula:

=(C28*0.5+1.5)/100

... to calculate the interest rate when it seems far more logical to use the simpler reference:

=D28

But if you were to refer to cell D28, the data table would show some results correctly and other results incorrectly.

After some time struggling with this problem I discovered the reason.

If you refer to the same cell as the *Column Input Cell* in a column formula, Excel will become confused.

You can see that the *Column Input Cell* was set to cell D28 in step 11.3. It is therefore vitally important that you do not refer to cell D28 in any of the formulas in the left-most column of the data table.

It is easy to work around this by calculating the value of the *Interest Rate* input cell from cell C28.

You covered single-input data tables in: *Lesson 5-1: Create a single-input data table*. In this lesson you'll recap this skill by adding a single-input data table to the form to show how repayments could increase if interest rates were to rise by up to 4% more than the current rate.

1   Open *Mortgage Calculator-8* from your sample files folder (if it isn't already open).

2   Add titles for each of the data table's columns.

Type labels into cells H2:L2 so that they are the same as the following:

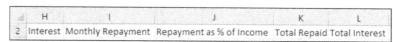

3   Merge cells H1:H2, I1:I2, J1:J2, K1:K2 and L1:L2.

   1.   Select cells H1:H2.

   2.   Click: Home→Alignment→Merge & Center→Merge Cells.

   3.   Repeat for the other cell pairs.

4   Switch text wrapping on for cells H1:L1.

   1.   Select cells H1:L1.

   2.   Click: Home→Alignment→Wrap Text.

5   Arrange the labels so that they appear on two lines where necessary.

   1.   Double-click just before the word *Repayment* in cell I1 (*Monthly Repayment*).

   2.   Hold down the **<Alt>** key.

   3.   Press the **<Enter>** key.

   4.   Repeat for the other column labels.

   5.   Re-size each column.

      Your column headers should now look like this:

      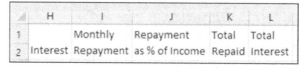

6   Add a formula to cell H3 that will show the interest rate selected on the form.

   1.   Click in cell H3.

   2.   Add the formula: **=(C28*0.5+1.5)/100**

      You need to refer to cell C28 rather than D28 to work-around an odd quirk in Excel data tables (see sidebar).

Mortgage Calculator-8

7   Add a formula to cell H4 that will show an interest rate 1% higher than the rate in cell H3.

1. Click in cell H4.

2. Add the formula: **=H3+0.01**

8   AutoFill the formula in cell H4 to cells H5:H7.

9   Format the formulas in cells H3:H7 so that they are formatted as percentages and display one decimal place.

1. Select cells H3:H7 and click: Home→Number→Percent Style.

2. Click: Home→Number→Increase Decimal.

10   Add formulas to cells I3:L3 that will reference the relative result cells.

The correct formulas are:

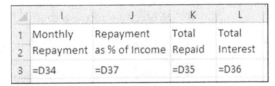

	I	J	K	L
1	Monthly	Repayment	Total	Total
2	Repayment	as % of Income	Repaid	Interest
3	=D34	=D37	=D35	=D36

11   Add a single input data table to cells H3:L7.

1. Select cells H3:L7.

2. Click: Data→Forecast→What-If Analysis→Data Table...

The *Data Table* dialog appears.

3. Click in the *Column input cell* box.

4. Click in cell D28.

5. Click the *OK* button.

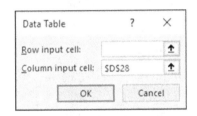

12   Copy the formats in cells I3:L3 to cells I4:L7.

1. Select cells I3:L3.

2. Click: Home→Clipboard→Copy.

3. Select cells I4:L7.

4. Click: Home→Clipboard→Paste→Paste Special...

5. Select the *Formats* option button.

6. Click the *OK* button.

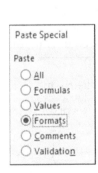

13   Resize the columns if necessary.

Your data table should now look like this:

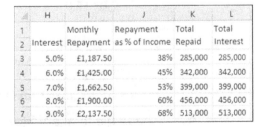

	H	I	J	K	L
1		Monthly	Repayment	Total	Total
2	Interest	Repayment	as % of Income	Repaid	Interest
3	5.0%	£1,187.50	38%	285,000	285,000
4	6.0%	£1,425.00	45%	342,000	342,000
5	7.0%	£1,662.50	53%	399,000	399,000
6	8.0%	£1,900.00	60%	456,000	456,000
7	9.0%	£2,137.50	68%	513,000	513,000

The actual values shown on your worksheet may differ depending upon the values selected in your form.

14   Save your work as *Mortgage Calculator-9.*

Lesson 7-9: Improve form appearance and usability

An elegant form-based user interface enables you to create utilities for users with no Excel skills. The form should be so intuitive that staff training is not needed. In its present form the Mortgage Calculator might intimidate non-technical users. You need to do a few more things to make this into a really professional form. They are:

- Improve the appearance of the form.

- Hide irrelevant worksheets and cells. In this case you need to hide the *Input Cells, Result Cells* and the *Data* worksheet.

- Protect the form so that users cannot alter the functionality or layout.

1   Open *Mortgage Calculator-9* from your sample files folder.

2   Add a pie chart to show the *Amount Financed* and *Total Interest*.

    1.   Click in cell D33, hold down the **<Ctrl>** key and click cell D36.

    2.   Click: Insert→Charts→Insert Pie or Doughnut Chart→ 3-D Pie→3-D Pie.

    3.   Move and re-size the chart so that it fills cells H9:L20.

    4.   Right-click on the center of the pie chart.

    5.   Click *Select Data...* from the shortcut menu.

    6.   Click the *Edit* button at the top of the *Horizontal (Category) Axis Labels* list box.

    7.   Click on cell B33, hold down the **<Ctrl>** key and click on cell B36.

    8.   Click *OK*, and then click *OK* again.

3   Surround the form area with two narrow padding columns.

It is useful for a form to be clearly delineated from the worksheet. This is best achieved by adding two narrow padding columns to each border of the form (see the screen grab on the front cover of this book).

The borders can then be shaded to clearly mark the form edges.

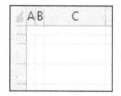

    1.   Add two narrow columns (about 9 pixels wide) to the left of column A.

    2.   Add two narrow rows (about 9 pixels deep) above row 1.

    3.   Add two narrow rows (about 9 pixels deep) above row 24.

    4.   Resize columns P and Q so that they are about 9 pixels wide.

4   Shade the form area (excluding controls and cells that the user will enter data into) light yellow.

    1.   Click in cell D22.

    2.   Set the background color to very light yellow.

Mortgage Calculator-9

3.   Double-click: Home→Clipboard→Format Painter.

4.   Click once in each cell in the range: C4:G23 that should be yellow (see cover of this book for guidance).

You may have to move the checkbox control in order to shade the cells behind it, and then move it back again.

5.   Click: Home→Clipboard→Format Painter to switch the format painter off.

5   **Use a similar technique to format the worksheet to match the design shown (in color) on the cover of this book.**

You will have to add a padding column to the left of the temperature gauge chart. Sample file *Mortgage Calculator-10* has the end result as shown on the book cover. You can use different formatting and colors if you think that they look better.

6   **Switch off the gridlines.**

The gridlines are spoiling the appearance of the group boxes.

Click: View→Show→Gridlines.

note

Charting data in hidden rows and columns

By default, a chart cannot use source data that is in a hidden row or column.

To chart data in hidden rows and columns:

1. Right-click in the center of the chart.

2. Click *Select Data...* from the shortcut menu.

3. Click the *Hidden and Empty Cells* button.

4. Check the *Show data in hidden rows and columns* check box.

☑ Show data in hidden rows and columns

5. Click *OK* and *OK* again.

Charting was covered in depth in the *Essential Skills* book in this series.

Allow all users of this worksheet to:
☐ Select locked cells
☑ Select unlocked cells

7   **Unlock cells F5, F10, F20, E29, E31, E32 and F33.**

In a moment you will protect the workbook. At this point it will only be possible to change unlocked cells. Notice that you have to unlock cells E29, E31, E32 and F33 because a control cannot change a value in a locked cell.

1.   Select all of the cells to be unlocked.

2.   Right-click one of the selected cells.

3.   Click *Format Cells...* from the shortcut menu.

4.   Click the *Protection* tab and clear the *Locked* check box.

Cell locking and protection were covered in: *Lesson 5-11: Restrict the cells users are allowed to change.*

8   **Configure the charts to use data in hidden rows and columns.**

See sidebar if you are unsure how to do this.

9   **Hide the *Data* worksheet, *Input Cells* and *Result Cells* (rows 27:41).**

1.   Right-click the Data tab and click *Hide* from the shortcut menu.

2.   Select rows 27:41, right-click in the selected area and click *Hide* from the shortcut menu.

10   **Protect the worksheet.**

1.   Click: Review→Protect→Protect Sheet.

2.   Add a password if you want greater security.

3.   Check the *Select unlocked cells* check box.

4.   Uncheck the *Select locked cells* check box.

5.   Click the *OK* button.

11   **Save your work as *Mortgage Calculator-10*.**

note

VBA is a programming language that can be used to write custom extensions to Excel

Microsoft Office is written in a very special way. It consists of several hundred objects all "glued" together with programming code. In: *Lesson 7 8: Embed an Excel chart object into a Word document,* you saw how easy it was to place one object inside another object.

Microsoft has documented all of the objects that make up Office, so that programmers can use Office objects in their own applications.

VBA also makes it possible to add new functions and features to Excel that Microsoft didn't anticipate you would want.

Excel is now such a well-featured application that very few reasonable business requirement now need custom VBA programming to implement.

Custom functions are, perhaps, the most likely candidates for the use of VBA programming skills. I have taught VBA classes to oil industry engineers who needed some very specialized functions that were not available within the Excel function library. Of course, only one of the engineers really needed to learn VBA while everybody could use the functions he had created.

VBA isn't an Excel-specific skill. The Visual Basic language can be used to add functionality to Excel, Word, PowerPoint, Visio, Project... and many other Microsoft and third party applications.

Lesson 7-10: Understand macros and VBA

Macros are a very misunderstood concept. Most books cause terrible confusion by mixing up the twin subjects of macros and the VBA (Visual Basic for Applications) programming language.

You don't need to know anything about the VBA programming language to use macros.

Macros record keystrokes and mouse-clicks

The macro recorder is able to record (and play back) every mouse click or key stroke that you make. Here's how I would record a simple macro:

1. Start the recorder to record a macro called *TypeMikeIntoCellA5.*

2. Click into cell A5 to make it the active cell.

3. Type: **Mike** into cell A5.

4. Press the **<Enter>** key.

5. Stop the recorder.

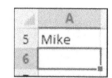

This would record a macro that I would be able to play back in future. The macro recorded the following key presses:

Move to cell A5, Press the **<M>** key, press the **<i>** key, press the **<k>** key, press the **<e>** key, press the **<Enter>** key.

If I wanted to play back the *Mike* macro in the future I would simply run the *TypeMikeIntoCellA5* macro.

The word *Mike* would then magically appear in cell A5 and the cursor would move down to cell A6. The macro would have effectively pressed all of the keys for me automatically.

The actual method that Excel uses, to save and play back your key presses and mouse clicks, is to automatically write VBA code. But you don't need to know anything about those technicalities in order to record and play macros.

1 Open a new blank workbook.

2 Begin recording a macro called *MyName* with a shortcut key of **<Ctrl>+<m>**.

　1. Click: View→Macros→Macros→Record Macro.

　2. Type **MyName** into the *Macro name* box.

　　Note that macro names cannot contain spaces.

　3. Type a lower case **m** into the *Ctrl+* box.

　4. Select *This Workbook* from the *Store macro in* drop-down list.

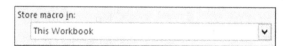

The other options for this setting will be explained later.

note

A little knowledge is a dangerous thing
Alexander Pope, poet
(1688-1744)

While I can teach you all you need to know about macros in less than an hour, I'd need several days to teach you to be a competent and professional Visual Basic programmer.

I run my Excel VBA programming courses across two to five days and still don't have enough time to cover really advanced topics (such as user defined classes). VBA is one of those subjects that it isn't useful to know a tiny bit about, so I am not going to attempt to teach you even a tiny bit in this book.

Of the hundreds of students that I've taught in my Excel VBA programming courses, a large number found that the skills were not useful. Many of them would have benefited far more from this *Expert Skills* course.

Most of the problems that they had imagined needed custom VBA coding could be better (and more easily) solved by the correct use of the Excel features you've learned about in this book.

5. Describe your macro in the *Description* box.

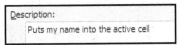

6. Click the *OK* button – but do nothing else!

    You are now recording your macro. There's no time element to a macro recording, so you can be relaxed. The macro will record every key press and every mouse click, so it is important that you do not press any keys or click anywhere with the mouse.

3   Record a macro that will put your name into the active cell.

Remember that every click and keystroke are recorded, so be careful not to move to any other cell. If you did, your name would always appear in the cell you had moved to when the macro was played.

1. Type your name into the currently active cell.

2. Press **<Ctrl>+<Enter>**.

    When you press **<Ctrl>+<Enter>** you save the value into the cell without moving to the next line. This keystroke combination is very useful when recording macros.

4   Stop the macro recording.

You can do this in two ways:

Click: View→Macros→Macros→Stop Recording.

<u>OR</u>

Click the *Stop* button at the bottom left of the screen.

It is a common error to forget to stop a macro recording. I've seen Excel crash in my classes when a student had forgotten and then accidentally continued to record for a long period.

5   Test the macro.

1. Click in any blank cell.

2. Click: View→Macros→Macros→View Macros.

    The *Macro* dialog appears, listing only the *MyName* macro (as you have only recorded one macro so far).

3. Click the *Run* button.

    Your name appears in the currently active cell.

4. Click in another blank cell and press: **<Ctrl>+<m>**

    Once again your name appears in the currently active cell.

6   Close the workbook without saving.

note

Choosing where to store your macros

There are three possible places to store a macro:

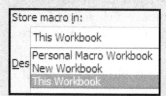

Macros stored in *This Workbook* are also available to other workbooks – but only if the workbook containing the macro is open!

The *Personal Macro Workbook* is a special workbook called *Personal.xlsb*. This is stored in a folder called XLSTART buried deep in the file system where nobody is likely to find and change it.

Whenever you open Excel, the Personal Macro Workbook opens in the background (but it is hidden so you never see it). Because it is always open, every workbook has access to its macros at all times. The only purpose of the Personal Macro Workbook is to act as a container to store macros that you want to be available to every workbook.

Remember that if you store macros in the Personal Macro Workbook, they will only work on your machine. If you e-mail a workbook that depends upon one of these macros, it will not work on the recipient's machine. In this type of scenario, you'd want to store the macro in *This Workbook*.

You'll rarely want to use the *New Workbook* option. If you record a macro in a new workbook, you would have to always make sure that it was open before you could access its macros.

Expenses Claim-1

Lesson 7-11: Record a macro with absolute references

1   Open *Expenses Claim-1* from your sample files folder.

Imagine this is a form that you need to fill in every week. Every time you make an expenses claim, you have to add your *Employee Number* and other details. This isn't very efficient, so you decide to record a macro that will automatically complete part of the form.

2   Begin recording a macro.

Click: View→Macros→Macros→Record Macro.

The *Record Macro* dialog appears.

3   Name the macro *FillInExpenseForm*.

Type **FillInExpenseForm** into the *Macro name* box.

Note that macro names cannot contain spaces. Always use mixed case for macro names and do not abbreviate. (For example, don't use names such as **FillExpFrm** – they will only confuse).

4   Assign a shortcut key of **<Ctrl>+<e>** to the macro.

Type a lower case **e** into the *Ctrl+* box.

See the sidebar on facing page for more about choosing macro shortcut keys.

5   Store the macro in *This Workbook*.

Note that there are three possible places to store a macro

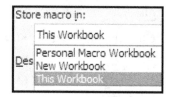

Normally you'll simply want to choose between *This Workbook* (when the macro is only useful in one workbook) and the *Personal Macro Workbook* (when the macro may be used by all workbooks). See the sidebar for more details.

This macro will only ever be used in the *Expenses Claim-1* workbook, so the most appropriate location is in *This Workbook*.

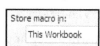

If there were many expense claim forms that all had the same data in cells B3, B5, B7, B9 and B11, you'd want to store the macro in the *Personal Macro Workbook* to make it available to all workbooks on your computer.

6   Add a *Description* to the macro.

It is good practice to describe your macros so that other users will understand what they are used for. The description is displayed in the *Macro* dialog when the user runs the macro.

important

Choosing macro shortcut keys

Excel has many built-in shortcut keys (such as <Ctrl>+<c> to copy).

If you were to define <Ctrl>+<c> as your macro shortcut key, you would override Excel's shortcut key and you'd no longer be able to use <Ctrl>+<c> to copy (as this would run the macro instead).

There are several strategies to avoid causing clashes with the built-in shortcut keys:

1. Use capital letters for shortcut keys. This will result in a shortcut key of:

<Ctrl>+<Shift>+<c>

You will then still be able to copy using the normal:

<Ctrl>+<c>

2. Only run macros from the ribbon.

Click:

View→Macros→Macros→ View Macros

You can also use the shortcut key: **<Alt>+<F8>**

This is quite an awkward way to access your macros.

3. Provide the user with buttons to run macros. You'll learn how to do this in: *Lesson 7-17: Run a macro from a button control.*

4. Add a button to the *Quick Access Toolbar* or *ribbon* to run each macro. You'll learn how to do this later, in: *Lesson 7-17: Run a macro from a button control (sidebar).*

Describe your macro in the *Description* box.

Description:
Fill in the Name, Department, Employee Number, Bank Account No and Sort Code in the Expenses Claim form

7 Record the macro.

1. Click the *OK* button.

2. Make cell B3 the active cell.

   This is a potential pitfall. If B3 is already the active cell (when you begin recording the macro) and you simply type your name, the recorder will place your name into whichever cell is the active cell when the macro is run. This may not be B3.

   For this reason, if B3 was active when you began recording you would have to click into a different cell, and then back again into cell B3 to explicitly record your intention to move the cursor to cell B3.

3. Fill in each box (with fictitious details). Here's the ones I used:

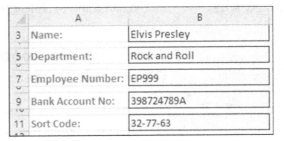

3. Click in cell A16, as this is the most likely cell that the user would want to enter text into after the macro has run.

4. Click: View→Macros→Macros→Stop Recording.

8 Test the macro.

1. Delete the contents of cells B3:B11.

2. Click: View→Macros→Macros→View Macros.

   The macro dialog appears, listing only the *FillInExpenseForm* macro (as you have only recorded one macro so far).

3. Click the *Run* button.

   All of the details that you previously recorded appear in the relevant cells.

4. Delete the contents of cells B3:B11.

5. Press <Ctrl>+<e>.

   Once again the form is completed with the recorded details.

9 Don't save your work yet but keep the workbook open.

You need to understand more about security and workbook formats before you can save. You'll save this workbook in the next lesson: *Lesson 7-12: Understand macro security.*

trivia

The Love Letter macro virus

The *Love Letter* virus was a most ingenious macro virus that preyed upon human curiosity.

It is estimated to have caused $15 Billion of damage in the US alone.

An e-mail would be received that appeared to be from somebody that the recipient knew. The subject line was: *I Love You.*

The e-mail had no message but an attachment named: *LOVE-LETTER-FOR-YOU.*

The attachment contained a macro virus. If the recipient opened the attachment, the macro virus would send the same e-mail and attachment to everybody in the recipient's own Outlook address book.

The virus would then damage the recipient's machine by over-writing random files.

I was working for a dotcom start up when the virus hit (on May 4th 2000) and was amazed how many knowledgeable IT staff (who should have known better) couldn't resist opening the attachment.

The virus also had the effect of bringing e-mail systems to a standstill as millions of e-mail messages were generated.

Within 10 days over fifty million infections were reported, affecting an estimated 10% of the world's Internet-connected computers.

You must begin this sequence of two lessons at: Lesson 7-11

Lesson 7-12: Understand macro security

Why is security needed?

Macros are a wonderful Excel feature but they can also be dangerous. It is possible to record a macro that will damage your computer in many ways.

Macro security provides several methods to identify which macros you can trust and which you can't.

You shouldn't trust any macro enabled workbook that is sent to you across the Internet (unless it is digitally signed). You learned about digital signatures in: *Lesson 5-14: Add an invisible digital signature to a workbook.* Without a digital signature it is impossible to be sure of an e-mail sender's identity. It is extremely easy to send an e-mail with a forged name and e-mail address.

The Excel Workbook and Excel Macro Enabled Workbook formats

There are two commonly used Excel formats:

- Excel Workbook (.xlsx file extension).

  This type of workbook can always be trusted, because it is incapable of storing a macro.

- Excel Macro Enabled Workbook (.xlsm file extension).

  You must ensure that you can trust the origin of this type of workbook as it is capable of carrying destructive macro viruses.

Four ways to trust a macro enabled workbook

Excel 365 provides four mechanisms for recognizing a trusted workbook.

- Make the workbook a *trusted document.* When a workbook becomes a trusted document you will no longer receive a warning when opening it. In: *Lesson 7-14: Understand trusted documents,* you'll learn about trusted documents in depth.

  This is probably the easiest and best way to manage macro security.

- Place the workbook in a trusted folder.

  Excel allows you to designate a folder as a trusted location. You are then able to open macro enabled workbooks that are saved to this location without warnings or restrictions.

  You'll learn about trusted folders in: *Lesson 7-13: Implement macro security.*

- Digitally sign the macro.

trivia

The Melissa macro virus

The Melissa virus was probably the most infamous macro virus.

The virus caused e-mail servers all over the world to crash in early 1999.

Melissa was hidden in a Word document called *List.doc* which was e-mailed to unsuspecting computer users.

When *List.doc* was opened, a macro would automatically run (you'll learn how to automatically run a macro in: *Lesson 7-17: Run a macro from a button control - sidebar*).

The macro e-mailed a message to all of the users in the recipient's Outlook address list. The e-mail included the virus-infected *List.doc* as an attachment.

Different variants of Melissa used different enticing e-mail subjects such as:

Extremely urgent: to all e-mail users.

This announcement is for all e-mail users. Please take note that our e-Mail Server will be down and we recommend that you read the attached document.

The writer of the virus was tracked down, sentenced to 20 months in a federal prison, and fined $5,000. After his arrest he was reported to have assisted the FBI in tracking down other virus writers.

A variant of the Melissa virus copied Excel documents to a distant server and then deleted them. The virus then asked for a ransom of $100 to be paid into an offshore account to return the deleted files.

You learned about digital signatures in: *Lesson 5-14: Add an invisible digital signature to a workbook.*

Excel can be configured to run digitally signed macros from trusted publishers without warnings or restrictions. You'll discover how to do this in: *Lesson 7-13: Implement macro security.*

- Warn the user before enabling macros.

Excel warns you that a workbook contains macros and asks whether you wish to enable them. You'll see this working in: *Lesson 7-13: Implement macro security.*

1 *Expenses Claim-1* should still be open from the previous lesson.

In the previous lesson you recorded a macro within this workbook.

The workbook is currently an anomaly – a regular Excel Workbook that contains a macro. Excel cannot allow such a workbook to be saved.

2 Attempt to save the workbook.

Excel warns you (in a rather cryptic way) that you cannot save this workbook as a regular (macro free) workbook.

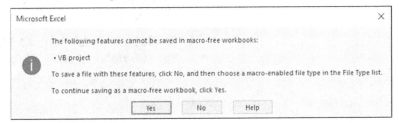

3 Click the *No* button to close the dialog.

The *Save As* dialog opens.

4 Save the workbook as an *Excel Macro Enabled* Workbook named *Expenses Claim-2*.

1. Navigate to the folder that you wish to save the file to.
2. Change the *Save as type* to: *Excel Macro-Enabled Workbook.*
3. Change the file name to: *Expenses Claim-2.*

4. Click the *Save* button.

You have now saved your first macro enabled workbook.

5 Close *Expenses Claim-2*.

Lesson 7-13: Implement macro security

1   Open *Expenses Claim-2* from your sample files folder.

    Remember that this is a macro-enabled workbook. When you open it, one of three things will happen:

    - The workbook opens without warnings and macros are enabled.

    - Excel displays a security warning (this is the default setting). The warning is sometimes not shown if the user is the same user who last saved the workbook (as it is illogical to distrust yourself).

! SECURITY WARNING Macros have been disabled.	Enable Content

    - The workbook opens without warnings, but the macros are disabled.

    It doesn't matter which is the case on your computer at the moment. This lesson will show you how to set up the macro security options to any one of the above.

2   Set the Trust Center's Macro Settings to: *Disable all macros with notification.*

    1.   Click: File→Options→Trust Center.

    2.   Click the *Trust Center Settings…* button.

    3.   Click *Macro Settings* in the left-hand selection bar.

         Macro settings are displayed.

    4.   Click the option: *Disable all macros with notification.*

         This is the default setting for Excel, so it will probably already be selected. This option displays a warning when a workbook containing macros is opened (unless it is digitally signed by a trusted publisher or opened by its own author – see facing page sidebar). It is the best setting for an informed user.

         Macro Settings

         ○ Disable all macros without notification
         ⦿ Disable all macros with notification
         ○ Disable all macros except digitally signed macros
         ○ Enable all macros (not recommended; potentially dangerous code can run)

    5.   Click *OK* and *OK* again.

3   Test macro security.

    As you are the user who last saved the *Expenses Claim-2* workbook you will often not see a warning when you open it.

    To test security, you will open a workbook that I created containing a simple macro. This will always cause Excel to display a warning.

Created by Mike Smart

Expenses Claim-2

note

Controlling macro security using digital certificates

In: *Lesson 5-14: Add an invisible digital signature to a workbook,* you learned that it is possible to obtain a digital certificate by paying a third-party authority for an annual subscription.

By signing a workbook with a digital signature, it is possible to confirm that you are the *publisher* of the workbook.

In order for Excel to suppress the normal security warning, five conditions must be met:

1. The workbook must be signed with a digital signature.

2. The macro must not have been changed since the digital certificate was issued.

3. The digital certificate must not have expired.

4. The digital certificate must have been issued by a certificate authority recognized as reputable by Microsoft.

5. The publisher must appear in your trusted publishers list.

When you open a workbook with a valid digital certificate, you are prompted with the name of the publisher and asked whether you want to add the publisher to your trusted publishers list.

To view publishers currently appearing on your trusted publisher list:

1. Click: File→ Options→Trust Center→ Trust Center Settings...

2. Click *Trusted Publishers* on the left-hand selection bar.

You will then see a list of all trusted publishers and are able to view details of their digital certificates or remove them from the list.

1. Open the *Created by Mike Smart* workbook from your sample files folder.

2. Notice the warning that is displayed:

> SECURITY WARNING Macros have been disabled.   Enable Content

3. Do not click the *Enable Content...* button (if you did this you would create a trusted document). Trusted documents will be covered later, in: *Lesson 7-14: Understand trusted documents.*

4. Close the *Created by Mike Smart* workbook.

4 Set a trusted folder for your macro-enabled workbooks.

If you designate a folder for your trusted macro-enabled workbooks, Excel will know that they are trusted and not bother you with any warnings in future.

For extra security, the trusted folder should always be a non-shared folder on your local hard drive (not a network drive).

1. Create a folder for your trusted macro-enabled workbooks.

   I created a folder called: **C:\Trusted Files** on my own computer just to illustrate how this works.

2. Open a new blank workbook in Excel.

3. Click: File→Options→Trust Center.

4. Click the *Trust Center Settings...* button.

5. Click *Trusted Locations* on the left-hand selection bar.

6. Click the *Add new location...* button.

7. Click the *Browse...* button.

8. Navigate to the folder that your trusted files will be placed in.

9. Click the *OK* button.

10. Click *OK* and *OK* again to close the dialogs.

5 Test the trusted folder.

1. Copy the *Created by Mike Smart* workbook into the trusted folder.

2. Open the *Created by Mike Smart* workbook from the trusted folder.

   This time the workbook opens without warnings.

3. Click in a blank cell.

4. Run the *Test* macro contained within this workbook.

   The word: *Test* appears in the cell, proving that macros are enabled.

6 Close the *Expenses Claim-2* workbook.

7 Close the *Created by Mike Smart* workbook (without saving).

Lesson 7-14: Understand trusted documents

In Excel 2007 (and earlier versions) it was only possible to open a macro-enabled workbook without a security prompt if it was either placed in a trusted document folder or digitally signed.

Most users had to deal with this prompt every time they opened a macro-enabled workbook:

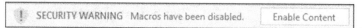

The Excel designers realized that showing the prompt every time didn't really add any security. If you had decided to trust the workbook the first time you opened it, you were hardly likely to change your mind the next time. For this reason, it was decided that Excel would remember which documents you have already trusted and open them without prompts forever more.

Despite the name, Excel does not make the workbook itself "trusted". Excel stores the *location* (also called *path*), *file name* and *file creation time* in a table that is linked to your user name. This means that the macro-enabled workbook will no longer be trusted in any of the following cases:

- A different user logs onto your machine and tries to open the workbook (in this case the user name will be different).

- You change the file name or move the file to a different directory.

- A malicious user deletes the old file and replaces it with another of the same name (in this case the file creation time will not be correct).

1 Open *Created by Mike Smart* from your sample files folder.

   Note that this file must be opened from your sample files folder and not from the trusted folder that you created in: *Lesson 7-13: Implement macro security.*

   Because you have never clicked the *Enable Content* button for this file, the security message bar appears:

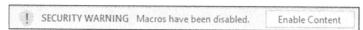

2 Click the *Enable Content* button to allow macros to run.

3 Run the *Test* macro to prove that macros are enabled.

   (You learned how to do this in: *Lesson 7-11: Record a macro with absolute references*).

   The macro runs as intended because you have previously clicked the *Enable Content* button.

4 Close the *Created by Mike Smart* file and re-open it.

   This time the file opens without showing the security message bar because Excel knows that you have previously trusted the file.

   In other words, *Created by Mike Smart* has become a *trusted document*.

5 Run a macro to prove that they are enabled.

Created by Mike Smart

Expenses Claim-2

Run the *Test* macro.

The macro runs as intended because this is now a trusted document.

6 Close *Created by Mike Smart.*

7 Clear your trusted documents list.

As mentioned in the introduction to this lesson, no information is saved in the workbook file when you approve it. Instead a trusted files list is maintained by Excel.

Sometimes you may want to clear the trusted files list. When you do this, all macro-enabled files will once again display the security message bar the first time they are opened (unless, of course, they are in a trusted folder or have a digital certificate).

1. Open Excel and create a new blank workbook.

2. Click: File→Options→Trust Center→
   Trust Center Settings…→Trusted Documents.

   The *Trusted Documents* pane appears.

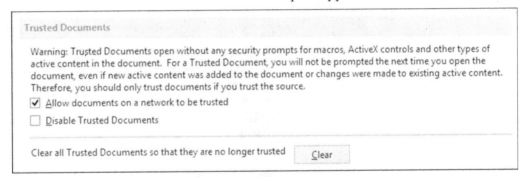

You can see that this pane can also be used to permanently disable the *Trusted Documents* feature for network drives only or for all file locations.

3. Click the *Clear* button.

4. Click *Yes, OK* and *OK* again to clear the dialogs.

   All trusted documents in the trusted documents list are now cleared. This means that all macro-enabled workbooks (including ones you created yourself) will now display the security message bar the first time they are opened.

8 Open *Expenses Claim-2* from your sample files folder.

Notice that the security message bar is shown because *Expenses Claim-2* is no longer a trusted document.

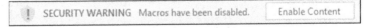

9 Click the *Enable Content* button.

Expenses Claim-2 has once again become a trusted document. This means that the security message bar will not display the next time that you open it.

Lesson 7-15: Record a macro with relative references

1   Open *Company List-1* from your sample files folder.

This workbook contains a list of 88 companies. The list will be used to perform a mail merge (using Microsoft Word).

In order to perform a mail merge, the data needs to be converted into a format that Word can understand. Instead of:

	A
3	Contact Name
4	Alejandra Camino
5	Romero y tomillo
6	Gran Vía, 1
7	Madrid
8	28001
9	Spain
10	
11	
12	
13	Alexander Feuer
14	Morgenstern Gesundkost
15	Heerstr. 22
16	Leipzig
17	4179
18	Germany
19	

The data needs to be re-formatted like this:

	A	B	C	D	E	F
3	Contact Name	Company Name	Address	City	Post Code	Country
4	Alejandra Camino	Romero y tomillo	Gran Vía, 1	Madrid	28001	Spain
5	Alexander Feuer	Morgenstern Gesundkost	Heerstr. 22	Leipzig	4179	Germany

To do this manually would take a long time, but you can convert all 88 records in less than five seconds by creating a macro recorded with relative references.

Relative reference macros record an offset from the active cell. Imagine that the active cell is A4 (Alejandra Camino). The relative macro that you are about to record will record the actions:

- Move one cell down.
- Cut.
- Move one cell up and one cell to the right.
- Paste.

... and so on until all of Alejandra's details are moved to row 4. The macro will then delete the blank rows and be ready to start again with Alexander Feuer.

Company List-1

2   Set up the macro recorder to use relative references.

Click: View→Macros→Macros→Use Relative References.

3   Make cell A4 the active cell.

When recording a relative reference macro, it is vital that you select the active cell <u>before</u> beginning the recording.

4 Record a macro with the name *MoveAddress* and save it in *This Workbook* with the shortcut key <Ctrl>+<m>.

1. Click: View→Macros→Macros→Record Macro.

2. Type **MoveAddress** into the *Macro name* box.

3. Type a lower case **m** into the *Shortcut key* box.

4. Select *This Workbook* from the *Store macro in* drop-down list.

5. Click *OK* to begin recording the macro.

6. Click in cell A5 and cut.

7. Click in cell B4 and paste.

8. Continue until the complete address is pasted into row 4.

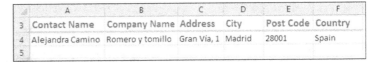

9. Select rows 5:12.

10. Right-click inside the selected cells.

11. Click *Delete* from the shortcut menu.

12. Click in cell A5 to make it the active cell.

The macro will be run multiple times to convert all of the addresses. By placing the cursor in cell A5 before you stop recording, it will be in the right position to convert the next address.

13. Click: View→Macros→Macros→Stop Recording.

5 Convert the other 87 addresses by running the macro multiple times.

1. Make sure that A5 is the active cell.

2. Press: <Ctrl>+<m>

3. The next address is converted.

4. Hold down the <Ctrl>+<m> keys and let the keyboard automatically repeat.

If this macro runs very slowly see sidebar for more details.

6 Save your work as a macro enabled workbook called: *Company List-2.*

note

Version 1908 is a lot slower than the previous semi-annual version

When this lesson's macro was recorded with *the July 2019 semi-annual release 1902* all 87 addresses converted in under five seconds.

This book was written using Semi-annual version 1908 build 11929.20562. This version took almost two minutes to complete the same task (in other words it was more than 20 times slower).

By the time you read this book a new build may have been released that will restore macro performance to that of the earlier version.

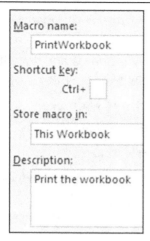

Lesson 7-16: Use shapes to run macros

1   Open *Mortgage Calculator-10* from your sample files folder.

2   Record a macro in *This Workbook* called *PrintWorkbook*.

1.   Click: View→Macros→Macros→Record Macro.

2.   Type **PrintWorkbook** in the *Macro name* box.

3.   Describe what the macro does in the *Description* box (see sidebar).

4.   Click the *OK* button.

5.   Click: File→Print→Print.

     The worksheet will print out on your default printer.

6.   Click: View→Macros→Macros→Stop Recording.

3   Save the workbook as a macro enabled workbook called *Mortgage Calculator-11*.

1.   Click: File→Save As→This PC→Browse.

2.   Navigate to the folder that you wish to save the file in.

3.   Select *Excel Macro-Enabled Workbook* from the *Save as type* dropdown list.

4.   Type: **Mortgage Calculator-11** in the *File Name* box.

5.   Click the *Save* button.

4   Record a macro in *This Workbook* called *SaveWorkbook*.

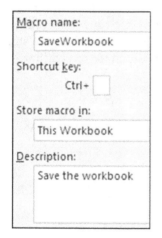

1.   Click: View→Macros→Macros→Record Macro.

2.   Type **SaveWorkbook** in the *Macro name* box.

3.   Describe what the macro does in the *Description* box (see sidebar).

4.   Click the *OK* button.

5.   Click: File→Save.

6.   Click: View→Macros→Macros→Stop Recording.

5   Add three shape controls to the worksheet.

1.   If the worksheet is protected:

     Click: Review→Protect→Unprotect Sheet.

2.   Re-size the pie chart to make space for a row of buttons underneath.

3.   Click: Insert→Illustrations→Shapes→Rectangles→ Rectangle: Rounded Corners.

4.   Click and drag on the worksheet to draw the button.

5.   Click: Drawing Tools→Format→Shape Styles→ More→Intense Effect – Blue, Accent 1.

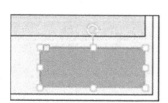

Mortgage Calculator-10

6. Click: Drawing Tools→Format→Shape Styles→Shape Effects→Bevel→Round.

7. Right-click on the button and click *Edit Text* from the shortcut menu.

8. Type: **Save Quote** to add a caption to the shape.

9. Click: Home→Alignment→Middle Align.

10. Click: Home→Alignment→Center.

11. Copy and paste the shape twice.

12. Change the captions on the other two shapes to read **Print Quote** and **Go To Website**.

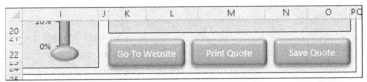

6   Connect the *Save Quote* and *Print Quote* shapes to the *SaveWorkbook* and *PrintWorkbook* macros.

1. Right-click the *Save Quote* shape.

2. Click *Assign Macro...* from the shortcut menu.

3. Select the *SaveWorkbook* macro.

4. Click the *OK* button.

5. Follow the same procedure to assign the *PrintWorkbook* macro to the *Print Quote* shape.

7   Connect the *Go To Website* shape to the website at https://TheSmartMethod.com.

1. Right-click the *Go To Website* shape.

2. Click: *Link* from the shortcut menu.

3. Click: *Existing File or Web Page* on the left hand selection bar.

4. Type **https://TheSmartMethod.com** into the *Address* box.

5. Click the *OK* button.

8   Protect the worksheet.

1. Click: Review→Protect→Protect Sheet.

2. Click the *OK* button.

9   Save your work as *Mortgage Calculator-11*.

10 Test the shapes.

1. Close and re-open the workbook.

   Note that you may need to enable macros after re-opening (see: *Lesson 7-14: Understand trusted documents*).

2. Click upon each shape.

   The relevant macro or hyperlink executes.

Lesson 7-17: Run a macro from a button control

note

You can also run macros from the Quick Access Toolbar

If you have general-purpose macros (saved in the Personal Macro Workbook) that you would like to run with a single click, you can add them to the Quick Access Toolbar.

1. Click: File→Options→ Quick Access Toolbar.

2. Select *Macros* in the *Choose commands from* drop-down list.

3. Select the macro that you want to add to the Quick Access Toolbar.

4. Click the *Add>>* button.

5. Select the macro in the right-hand pane.

6. Click the *Modify...* button to change the icon and tip text for the macro.

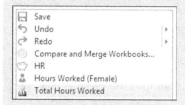

7. Click the *OK* button.

The macros can then be run from the *Quick Access Toolbar* with a single click.

You can also add macro buttons to the ribbon in a similar way. You'll learn how to do this in: *Lesson 7-20: Create a custom ribbon tab.*

Human Resources-2

1 Open *Human Resources-2* from your sample files folder.

This is the workbook created in: *Lesson 5-8: Create custom views.* The workbook contains three custom views:

- Hours Worked

- Hours Worked (Female)

- HR

It is not obvious that the workbook contains custom views. You can make users more aware of the feature, and make the feature easier to use, by adding button controls to move between the custom views.

2 Record macros in *This Workbook* that will show each custom view.

1. Click: View→Macros→Macros→Record Macro.

2. Type **ShowHoursWorkedView** in the *Macro name* box.

3. Describe what the macro does in the *Description* box.

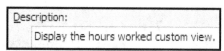

4. Click the *OK* button to begin recording the macro.

5. Click: View→Workbook Views→Custom Views.

6. Select the *Hours Worked* view.

7. Click the *Show* button.

8. Click: View→Macros→Macros→Stop Recording.

9. Create a **ShowHoursWorkedFemaleView** macro that will display the *Hours Worked (Female)* custom view.

10. Create a **ShowHRView** macro that will display the *HR* custom view.

3 Add a button control to cell A8 with the caption *Hours Worked* that will run the *ShowHoursWorkedView* macro.

1. If the *Developer* tab is not shown in the ribbon, click: File→Options→Customize Ribbon and check the *Developer* check box in the right-hand pane.

2. Click: Developer→Controls→Insert→ Form Controls→Button (Form Control).

3. Click and drag in the top of cell A8 to add a button.

4. The *Assign Macro* dialog appears.

note

Create a macro that runs automatically when a workbook is opened

In this lesson's workbook you might want the opening view to always be the HR view, no matter which view was selected when the workbook was last saved.

You are able to do this by creating a macro that automatically runs when the workbook is opened.

To do this, simply record a macro named *Auto_open* that selects the HR view.

The name of the macro tells Excel to run it automatically when the workbook is opened.

5. Select the *ShowHoursWorkedView* macro.

6. Click the *OK* button.

7. Click on the face of the button, delete the existing text and type: **Hours Worked**.

	A	B	C	D
6	Pension	5%		
	Hours Worked			
8		Johnny Caine	George Marley	Betty Anan
9	Hourly Rate	18.20	12.57	12.67

4   Add another button control to cell A8 with the caption *Hours Worked (Female)* that will run the *ShowHoursWorkedFemaleView* macro.

5   Add another button control to cell A8 with the caption *HR* that will run the *ShowHRView* macro.

	A	B	C	D	E	F	G
1	Payroll						
2							
	Hours Worked						
	Hours Worked (Female)						
8	HR	Johnny Caine	George Marley	Betty Anan	Paris Winfrey	Ozzy Dickens	Johnny Roberts
11	Hours Worked						
12	Monday	9	10	10	10	7	7
13	Tuesday	8	9	8	6	10	10

6   Test the workbook.

Click on each of the command buttons. The workbook should display each custom view as the command buttons are clicked.

7   Save your work as a macro-enabled workbook with the name *Human Resources-3*.

Lesson 7-18: Show and hide ribbon tabs

Excel 365 allows you to customize both the Quick Access Toolbar and ribbon.

You can:

- Show and hide ribbon tabs.

- Add your own custom command groups to standard ribbon tabs.

- Add your own custom tab(s) to the ribbon and add custom command groups to them.

1   Open *Mortgage Calculator-11* from your sample files folder.

The Mortgage Calculator has a very simple user interface that non-Excel users will find easy and intuitive to use.

The screen still looks intimidating to a non-Excel user (even though most of the ribbon buttons are grayed out).

If you hide all of the standard ribbon tabs, the screen will seem a lot simpler.

2   Hide all of the standard ribbon tabs.

note

Other ways to open the Customize Ribbon dialog

The easiest way to open the *Customize Ribbon* dialog is to right-click anywhere in a blank area of the ribbon and then select *Customize the Ribbon…* from the shortcut menu as described in the lesson text.

It is also possible to do the same thing by clicking:

File→Options→ Customize Ribbon

1.   Right-click anywhere in a blank area of the ribbon and select *Customize the Ribbon…* from the shortcut menu.

The *Excel Options* dialog appears with the *Customize Ribbon* pane selected.

2.   Select *Main Tabs* in the *Customize the Ribbon* drop-down list on the right-hand pane of the dialog:

Customize the Ribbon: ⓘ

Main Tabs	▾

3.   Clear the check boxes next to each of the main tabs:

4.   Click the *OK* button.

The user interface is now a lot cleaner with only the *File* tab displayed:

Mortgage Calculator-11

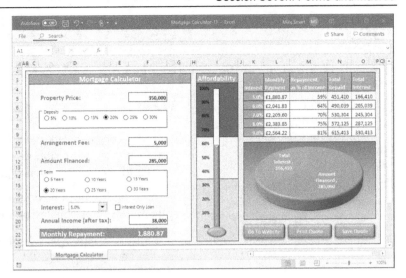

note

Ribbon customizations are set at application level

When you customize the ribbon, you are customizing Excel itself and not the current workbook.

For applications such as the Mortgage Calculator it would be great if you could save customizations that only applied to the current workbook.

Unfortunately, you cannot easily do this but perhaps we'll see this feature in a future Excel release.

3   Bring the tabs back again.

1.   Right-click on the *File* tab and click: *Customize the Ribbon...* from the shortcut menu.

2.   The *Excel Options* dialog appears with the *Customize Ribbon* pane selected.

3.   Check each of the check boxes that you unchecked earlier.

4.   Click the *OK* button.

5.   The standard ribbon tabs are restored.

note

Why it is a bad idea to customize standard ribbon tabs

A common attraction at fairgrounds is the "reverse steering bicycle".

The showman has a bicycle that has special steering. When the handlebars are steered left the bicycle turns right, and when steered right the bicycle turns left.

The showman competently rides the bicycle, demonstrating how easy it is, and challenges the public to ride just five meters to win a prize. Of course, nobody that takes the challenge is able to ride the bicycle.

This works because the showman has learned to ride the bicycle with reverse steering.

Because riding a bicycle is a subconscious process, nobody that has learned to ride a regular bicycle can ride a reverse steering bicycle. In computer terminology, the bicycle has a non-standard user interface.

As a side-effect, the showman will also be unable to ride a normal bicycle.

If you extensively customize standard ribbon tabs, you may find it difficult to work with the unfamiliar standard ribbon on other computers. You may effectively turn yourself into a reverse cyclist!

For this reason, I suggest that you refrain from customizing the standard ribbon tabs but, instead, add any extra functionality you need to a custom ribbon tab.

Passwords-1

Lesson 7-19: Add custom groups to standard ribbon tabs

While I was very pleased when Excel 2010 introduced the ability to add new custom tabs to the ribbon, I was less pleased to find that users can also add and remove command groups on the standard ribbon tabs.

In my opinion it would be best to refrain from doing this (see sidebar). Despite my opinion, this lesson demonstrates this feature.

1   Open *Passwords-1* from your sample files folder.

This workbook has been created so that the user does not forget passwords. Unfortunately, the passwords used are very insecure, in fact they are among the world's top 20 most commonly used passwords. It would be very easy to hack into this user's sites!

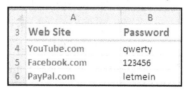

	A	B
3	Web Site	Password
4	YouTube.com	qwerty
5	Facebook.com	123456
6	PayPal.com	letmein

The user has wisely decided to change the passwords to secure ones (secure passwords were discussed in: *Lesson 5-9: Prevent unauthorized users from opening or modifying workbooks*). In order to do this the user has created a secure password generator (see facing page sidebar if you are interested in how this works).

2   Generate a new password and copy it to cell C4.

1.   Press the <F9> key to generate a new password.

2.   Copy the password from cell C21.

3.   Right-click in cell C4.

4.   Click: Paste Options→Values from the shortcut menu.

3   Apply the strikethrough style to the old password.

The strikethrough style is very useful when you have replaced text but still wish to retain it. Unfortunately, this style is not included on the ribbon and it is necessary to use a dialog launcher to access it.

1.   Click in cell B4.

2.   Click: Home→Font→Dialog Launcher.

3.   Check the *Strikethrough* check box. ☑ Strikethrough

	A	B	C
3	Web Site	Password	New Password
4	YouTube.com	~~qwerty~~	Zbx1JhQlQpf%

note

How the secure password generator works

The secure password generator is constructed using skills covered in earlier lessons in this book.

Look at the *Password Characters* worksheet. This contains a table named *Password*. The first column contains sequential numbers and the second contains all of the letters, numbers and special symbols that may be used in the generated password. You learned about tables in: *Session One: Tables, and Ranges.*

Return to the *Passwords* worksheet and unhide rows 23 to 34. You learned how to do this in: *Lesson 5-7: Hide and unhide worksheets, columns and rows.*

Look at the formula in cell A23. This uses the RANDBETWEEN function in conjunction with a VLOOKUP function to return a random letter from the *Password* table. You learned about VLOOKUP in: *Lesson 3-22: Use a VLOOKUP function for an exact lookup.*

Look at the formula in cell C21. This uses the CONCAT function to construct the password from the random characters in cells A23:A34. You learned about the CONCAT function in: *Lesson 3-19: Use the TEXT function to format numerical values as strings.*

It is standard behaviour for a worksheet to recalculate when the **<F9>** key is pressed. Each time this is done, the RANDBETWEEN function generates new random numbers which, in turn, look up new random letters. This is discussed in depth in: *Lesson 3-17: Understand calculation options (manual and automatic).*

4   Add a custom group called *Special Formatting* to the right of the *Font* command group in the *Home* ribbon.

1.   Right-click in a blank area of the ribbon and select *Customize the Ribbon...* from the shortcut menu.

The *Customize the Ribbon* dialog appears.

2.   Click the *Home* tab in the right-hand pane of the dialog.

3.   Click the *New Group* button.

A new group appears within the *Home* tab.

4.   Click the *Rename...* button and type **Special Formatting** into the *Display name* text box.

5.   Click the *OK* button.

6.   Use the up and down arrow buttons to move the group so that it appears after the *Alignment* group.

```
Main Tabs
  ⊞ ☑ Background Removal
  ⊟ ☑ Home
      ⊞ Clipboard
      ⊞ Font
      ⊞ Alignment
         Special Formatting (Custom)
      ⊞ Number
```

5   Add the *Strikethrough* command to the *Special Formatting* custom group.

1.   Select *Commands Not in the Ribbon* from the *Choose commands from* drop-down list at the top of the dialog.

2.   Select the *Strikethrough* command from the left-hand list.

3.   Click the *Add>>* button.

The *Strikethrough* command now appears within the *Special Formatting* custom group.

4.   Click the *OK* button.

The *Home* ribbon now contains a *Special Formatting* custom group with a single *Strikethrough* command.

6   Add a new secure password for *Facebook.com* and strikethrough the old password using the new ribbon command.

	A	B	C
3	Web Site	Password	
4	YouTube.com	~~qwerty~~	2UE5vl@y77e7
5	Facebook.com	~~123456~~	S#yQk1rH#!pS

7   Save your work as *Passwords-2*.

Lesson 7-20: Create a custom ribbon tab

Excel has many really useful features that hardly any user will ever discover. A good example is the Speak Cells feature covered in: *Lesson 4-16: Use Speak Cells to eliminate data entry errors*. The only way to access these features is by adding commands to the Quick Access Toolbar or ribbon or by using *Tell Me help*.

In this lesson you'll create a special ribbon tab containing my own favorite selection of hidden Excel features. You may find that you want to keep this ribbon permanently.

The ribbon tab that you will create is shown in the sidebar.

1   Open a new blank workbook.

2   Create a custom ribbon tab called *Extras.*

   1.   Right-click the ribbon and click: *Customize the Ribbon…* from the shortcut menu.

     The *Customize the Ribbon* dialog appears.

   2.   Click the *New Tab* button at the bottom of the right-hand pane.

     A new custom tab and single new custom group appear in the *Main Tabs* window.

   3.   Select the new tab and click the *Rename…* button.

     Be careful to click the *New Tab* and not the *New Group* item.

     The *Rename* dialog appears.

   4.   Type **Extras** into the *Display Name* text box.

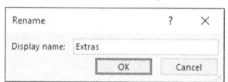

   5.   Click the *OK* button.

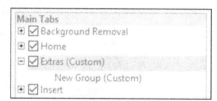

3   Add six more custom groups to the *Extras* tab.

Click the *New Group* button six times.

4   Name the custom groups: *Hyperlinks, Speak, Collaboration, Format, Widgets, Quick Paste* and *File/Print.*

   1.   Select the first *New Group*.

   2.   Click the *Rename…* button.

The *Rename* dialog appears.

Notice that you are able to select a symbol as well as define a name. The symbols will display when the application window is made so narrow that the commands have no room to display... like this:

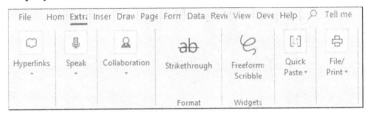

Note that the new *Format* and *Widgets* command groups have only one command, meaning that no symbol is ever shown.

3. Select the cloud symbol and type **Hyperlinks** into the *Display Name* text box.

4. Click the *OK* button.

5. Repeat for the other command groups.

5   Add *Forward* and *Back* commands to the *Hyperlinks* command group.

In: *Lesson 6-3: Hyperlink to an e-mail address and enhance the browsing experience,* you discovered how useful a forward and backward button were when constructing workbooks that had hyperlink-based navigation systems.

1. Select the *Hyperlinks* custom group in the right-hand pane of the *Customize the Ribbon* dialog.

2. Select *Commands Not In the Ribbon* from the drop-down list above the left-hand pane.

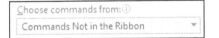

3. Click the *Forward* command in the left-hand pane.

4. Click the *Add>>* button.

5. Repeat for the *Back* command.

6   Add all of the other commands to the relevant ribbon groups.

Use the screen grab on the facing page as a guide. If you don't find a command in the *Commands Not in the Ribbon* group, look in the *All Commands* group.

7   Save your ribbon customizations to a file.

You may wish to share your custom ribbon with other users or to load it onto a different computer.

1. Right-click the ribbon and select *Customize the Ribbon...* from the shortcut menu.

    The *Customize the Ribbon* dialog appears.

2. Click the *Import/Export* button at the bottom of the right-hand pane.

3. Click *Export all customizations* from the drop down list.

4. Name the customizations *Extras Bar* and click *Save.*

Session 7: Exercise

1 Open *Gala Dinner-1* from your sample files folder.

2 Add combo box, group box, option button and check box form controls, so that the user interface looks like this:

3 Add a new worksheet called *Data*.

4 Add a named range to the *Data* worksheet called *Tickets*, containing the numbers 1-10.

5 Set the *Input range* of the combo box control to the *Tickets* range name.

6 Link the combo box and check box controls to the input cells (B19, B20 and B21).

7 Add formulas to the result cells (B24, B25, B26 and B27) to calculate the total cost of the order.

8 Add a formula to cell B13 so that it displays the same value as cell B27 and hide rows 18 to 27.

9 Record a macro named *PrintOrder* in *This Worksheet* that will print the worksheet.

10 Add a button control to the form that will run the *PrintOrder* macro.

11 Save your work as a *Macro-Enabled Workbook* named *Gala Dinner-2*.

Gala Dinner-1

If you need help slide the page to the left

Session 7: Exercise Answers

These are the four questions that students find the most difficult to answer:

Q 9	Q 7	Q 6	Q 3 & 4
1. Click: View→Macros→Macros→Record Macro… 2. Type **PrintOrder** into the *Macro name* box. 3. Select *This Workbook* from the *Store macro in* drop-down list. 4. Click the *OK* button. 5. Click: File→Print. 6. Click the *Print* button. 7. Click: View→Macros→Macros→Stop Recording. This was covered in: *Lesson 7-16: Use shapes to run macros.*	The correct formulas are: *Ticket Cost* (B24): **=B19*22.5** *Water Cost* (B25): **=IF(B20=TRUE, B19*2.5,0)** *Wine Cost* (B26): **=IF(B21=TRUE, B19*5.5,0)** *Total Cost* (B27): **=SUM(B24:B26)** This was covered in: *Lesson 7-6: Use check box data in result cells.*	1. Right-click the combo box. 2. Click *Format Control…* from the shortcut menu. 3. Click the *Control* tab. 4. Click in the *Cell Link* box. 5. Click in cell B19. 6. Click the *OK* button. 7. Follow the same steps for the check boxes, linking the *Water* check box to cell B20 and the *Wine* check box to cell B21. This was covered in: *Lesson 7-3: Set form control cell links.*	1. Click the *New Sheet* button at the bottom left of the screen to insert a new worksheet. 2. Double-click on the new tab and change the worksheet name to: **Data** 3. Select the *Data* worksheet and type **Tickets** into cell A1. 4. Type the numbers 1 to 10 in cells A2:A11. 5. Select cells A1:A11. 6. Click: Formula→Defined Names→Create from Selection. 7. Click the *OK* button. You have now created a named range called *Tickets* that references cells A2:A11. This was covered in: *Lesson 4-1: Automatically create single-cell range names.*

If you have difficulty with the other questions, here are the lessons that cover the relevant skills:

2   Refer to: *Lesson 7-1: Add group box and option button controls to a worksheet form, Lesson 7-2: Add a combo box control to a worksheet form* and *Lesson 7-5: Add a check box control to a worksheet form.*

5   Refer to: *Lesson 7-2: Add a combo box control to a worksheet form.*

8   The correct formula is: **=B27**. To hide the rows, select them, right-click inside the selected range and click *Hide* from the shortcut menu.

10   Refer to: *Lesson 7-17: Run a macro from a button control.*

8

Session Eight: Pivot Tables

> If the only tool you have is a hammer, you tend to see every problem as a nail.
>
> *Abraham Maslow (1908 - 1970)*

I'm constantly amazed at how many highly experienced Excel users are unable to understand pivot tables.

I've seen many cases where a user has spent hours creating a worksheet-based solution that could have been addressed in a few seconds using a pivot table. This session will empower you with a complete mastery of this powerful Excel feature.

Session Objectives

By the end of this session you will be able to:

- Create a one dimensional pivot table report from a table
- Create a grouped pivot table report
- Understand pivot table rows and columns
- Understand the pivot table data cache
- Apply a simple filter and sort to a pivot table
- Use report filter fields
- Filter a pivot table visually using slicers
- Add a timeline control to a pivot table
- Use slicers to create a custom timeline
- Use report filter fields to automatically create multiple pages
- Format a pivot table using PivotTable styles
- Create a custom pivot table style
- Understand pivot table report layouts
- Add/remove subtotals and apply cell styles to pivot table fields
- Display multiple summations within a single pivot table
- Add a calculated field to a pivot table
- Add a calculated item to a pivot table
- Group by text, date and numeric value ranges
- Show row data by percentage of total rather than value
- Use pivot table values in simple formulas
- Use the GETPIVOTDATA function
- Create a pivot chart from a pivot table
- Embed multiple pivot tables onto a worksheet
- Use slicers to filter multiple pivot tables

trivia

Only 10% of Excel users can create a pivot table

An extensive survey of Excel users suggested that only 10% of all Excel users are able to create a pivot table.

Lesson 8-1: Create a one-dimensional pivot table report from a table

In this lesson, you'll create a simple one-dimensional pivot table. There's a huge amount to learn about pivot tables but it will be fun to do some useful work with one straight away.

Here's the sample file that you'll use in this lesson:

	A	B	C	D	E	F	G	H
1	Order No	Order Date	Customer	Employee	Title	Genre	Qty	Total
2	136438	02-Oct-14	Silver Screen Video	Lee,Frank	Lawrence of Arabia	Biography	15	122.76
3	136438	02-Oct-14	Silver Screen Video	Lee,Frank	The Discreet Charm of the Bourgeoisie	Comedy	9	67.46
4	136438	02-Oct-14	Silver Screen Video	Lee,Frank	Berlin Alexanderplatz	Drama	25	250.60
5	136438	02-Oct-14	Silver Screen Video	Lee,Frank	Gone With The Wind	Drama	14	107.72
6	136439	03-Oct-14	Cinefocus DVD	Diamond,Elizabeth	Mouchette	Drama	5	31.77

important

Pivot Tables, Ranges, Named Ranges and Tables

You can create a pivot table that is associated with a *Range*, a *Named Range* or a *Table* but it is best practice to always associate pivot tables with *Tables*.

Ranges and *Named Ranges* share a common problem. If rows are added to either, the pivot table will not be aware of the added rows when it is refreshed. It would be necessary to click:

PivotTable Tools→Analyze→ Change Data Source

… every time a row or column was added to the source data.

Tables are wonderful to use as a data source for pivot tables because you can add and remove rows without affecting the integrity of the pivot table.

You learned everything there is to know about tables in: *Session One: Tables, and Ranges.*

This is the type of worksheet that pivot tables can work well with because the columns contain repeating data.

The sample file contains over 2,000 rows of transactional data listing sales during the 18-month period from October 2014 to March 2016 inclusive.

You can see from the data that the worksheet contains details of orders sold by a DVD wholesaler, along with the titles supplied on each order. Order *136438* was placed on *2nd-Oct-14* and was ordered by *Silver Screen Video*. The order was sold by *Frank Lee* and there were four items on the order. Two of the films ordered were in the *Drama* genre and the other two were in the *Biography* and *Comedy* genres.

A business may wish to ask several questions about sales during this period such as:

- What were my sales by *Genre*?

- How many units did each *Employee* sell?

In this lesson, you'll use a simple pivot table to answer both questions in less than 10 seconds!

1 Open *Transactions-1* from your sample files folder.

This worksheet contains a large table named *Data* (see sidebar for more on using tables with pivot tables).

The table looks like a regular range because the *Filter* buttons have been switched off and the *Table Style* has been set to *None*.

2 Click anywhere inside the table.

3 Click Insert→Tables→PivotTable.

The *Create PivotTable* dialog appears.

Notice that, because you clicked inside the table, the dialog has automatically detected the table's name of *Data*.

Transactions-1

note

You can also create a pivot table using Recommended PivotTables

Instead of creating your pivot table manually (as taught in this lesson), Excel can create a pivot table automatically from a template.

In this lesson you clicked:

Insert→Tables→PivotTable

This created an empty pivot table.

You could also have clicked:

Insert→Tables→ Recommended PivotTables

This option allows you to choose between several ready-made completed pivot tables.

note

Help – my PivotTable Fields task pane has disappeared

Pivot tables are a little like charts in that you cannot work upon their design unless they are activated. To activate, you simply click anywhere inside the pivot table.

When the pivot table is activated, the *PivotTable Fields* task pane appears along with the *PivotTable Tools* tab on the ribbon.

You can also explicitly close the *PivotTable Fields* task pane (by clicking the close button in the top right-hand corner of the task pane). If you do this, it will remain hidden even when the pivot table is activated. To bring back the task pane you will need to:

1. Click inside the pivot table to activate it.

2. Click: PivotTable Tools→ Analyze→Show→Field List.

4   Click the *OK* button.

An empty pivot table is shown on screen and the *PivotTable Fields* task pane appears on the right of the screen.

5   Check the *Genre, Qty* and *Total* check boxes (in that order) in the *PivotTable Fields* task pane.

Simply by clicking on three fields you have answered the first question:

- What were my sales by *Genre*?

6   Format the values shown in column C of the pivot table so that they show two decimal places with a comma separator.

1.   Right-click on any value in column C.

2.   Click *Number Format...* from the shortcut menu.

3.   Click *Number* in the *Category* list.

4.   Click the *Use 1000 Separator* check box.

5.   Click the *OK* button.

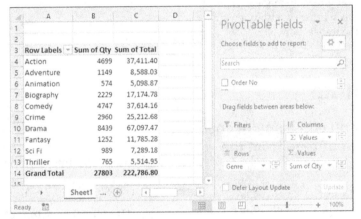

7   Clear all check boxes and then select the *Employee* and *Qty* check boxes.

Once again, with very little effort, you have answered the second question:

- How many units did each *Employee* sell?

8   Name the pivot table: **Transactions**

1.   Click inside the pivot table.

2.   Click: PivotTable Tools→Analyze→PivotTable→ PivotTable Name.

3.   Type **Transactions** into the *PivotTable Name* box.

9   Name the pivot table worksheet tab: **Pivot Table**

10   Save your work as *Transactions-2*.

Lesson 8-2: Create a grouped pivot table report

1 Open *Transactions-2* from your sample files folder (if it isn't already open).

2 Select the *Pivot Table* worksheet (if it isn't already selected).

3 Click inside the pivot table to show the *PivotTable Fields* task pane.

4 Check *Genre* in the *PivotTable Fields* list.

Each Employee's sales for each genre are now shown in the report.

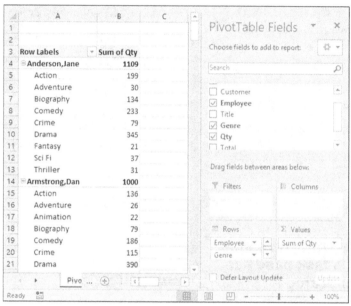

5 Add *Title* information to the pivot table.

Check *Title* in the *PivotTable Field List*.

The report now breaks sales down by *Employee*, *Genre* and *Title*.

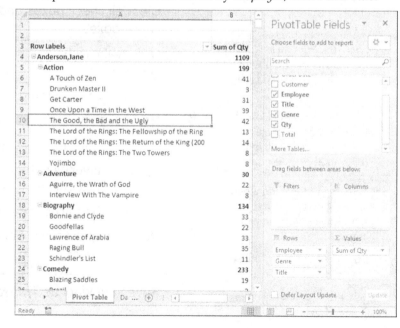

note

Drilling down into pivot table data

Whenever Excel shows a total in a pivot table, it is possible to "drill down" to see the transactions that were used to calculate the total.

When you double-click on a total, (such as the total sales for action movies), a new worksheet opens showing the source transactions.

You'll have to manually delete this worksheet after viewing the transaction list.

note

You can also collapse an outline from the ribbon

The fastest way to collapse and expand an outline is by using the right-click method described in the text.

It is also possible to do this in a less efficient way using the ribbon:

1. Click on a cell (such as the name: *Armstrong, Dan*).

The selected cell becomes the *Active Field*.

2. Click:

PivotTable Tools→Analyze→ Active Field→ Collapse Field

Transactions-2

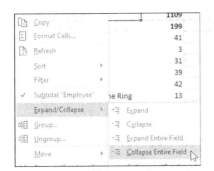

trivia

PivotTable or Pivot Table?

The term *Pivot Table* has been used for a long time to describe the general concept of summarizing data.

One of the earliest implementations of pivot tables was introduced in *Lotus Improv* (released in 1991).

Pivot tables also featured in the 1992 release of *Quattro Pro*. Quattro called this feature *DataPivot*.

Pivot tables first appeared in Excel in the 1994 *Excel 5* release. The Excel pivot table feature was called *PivotTable* (without a space). This name was registered as a trademark by Microsoft in December 1994.

In the ribbon and in most Microsoft documentation you'll see the pivot table spelled as *PivotTable* rather than *pivot table*.

It would be correct to refer to an Excel pivot table both in the more general way (*pivot table*) and also using the Microsoft trademark (*PivotTable*).

In this book I try to consistently use the *PivotTable* terminology only when referring to a feature within the user interface where this spelling is used. At all other times I find *pivot table* (with a space) to be more elegant.

6 Collapse the outline to show only sales by *Employee*.

1. Right-click in cell A4.

    A shortcut menu appears.

2. Click: Expand/Collapse→Collapse Entire Field.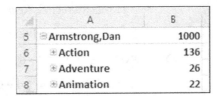

    The pivot table collapses to the level of *Employee*.

	A	B
3	Row Labels	Sum of Qty
4	⊞ Anderson,Jane	1109
5	⊞ Armstrong,Dan	1000
6	⊞ Ashe,Lucille	1116
7	⊞ Bell,Stephen	1409

7 Expand Dan Armstrong's sales to show full details.

Click the small + sign to the left of cell A5.

	A	B
5	⊞ Armstrong,Dan	1000
6	⊞ Ashe,Lucille	1116

Sales are expanded to show full details of Dan's sales.

	A	B
5	⊟ Armstrong,Dan	1000
6	⊟ Action	136
7	A Touch of Zen	24
8	Drunken Master II	22

8 Collapse the outline so that Dan's sales by *Genre* are shown without *Title* details.

1. Right-click in cell A6.

    A shortcut menu appears.

2. Click: Expand/Collapse→Collapse Entire Field.

    The *Title* level of the Pivot Table collapses to show Dan's sales by *Genre* but not by *Title*.

	A	B
5	⊟ Armstrong,Dan	1000
6	⊞ Action	136
7	⊞ Adventure	26
8	⊞ Animation	22

9 Collapse the outline to only show sales by *Employee*.

Click the small minus sign to the left of cell A5.

The outline collapses to show only the *Employee* level.

	A	B
5	⊞ Armstrong,Dan	1000
6	⊞ Ashe,Lucille	1116
7	⊞ Bell,Stephen	1409

10 Save your work as *Transactions-3*.

Lesson 8-3: Understand pivot table rows and columns

1   Open *Transactions-3* from your sample files folder (if it isn't already open).

2   Select the *Pivot Table* worksheet (if it isn't already selected).

3   Click inside the pivot table to display the *PivotTable Fields* task pane.

At the lower right of the screen, you can see four panes:

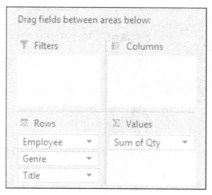

At the moment, you have three columns in the *Rows* list and one in the *Values* list. This creates a pivot table that shows sales grouped first by *Employee,* then grouped by *Genre* and then grouped by *Title.*

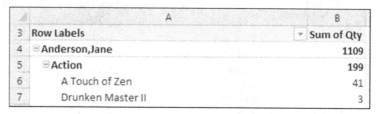

4   Remove the *Genre* and *Title* rows from the Rows list.

1. Click *Genre* in the *Rows* pane of the *PivotTable Fields* task pane and then click *Remove Field* from the shortcut menu.

2. Click *Title* and then click *Remove Field* from the shortcut menu.

5   Add the *Genre* to the pivot table as a *Column Label*.

Instead of checking the *Genre* box in the *PivotTable Fields* task pane, you need to drag it from the *PivotTable Fields* task pane to the *Columns* list below.

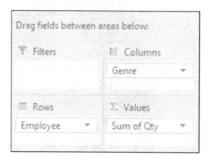

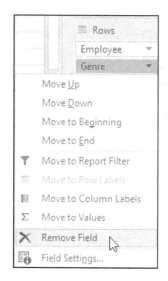

Transactions-3

note

The Defer Layout Update check box

You may have noticed a check box at the bottom left of the *PivotTable Fields* task pane that is labelled: *Defer Layout Update* and a button to the right (that is normally grayed out) labelled *Update*.

This option is useful if you work with very large data sets.

Pivot tables normally update as soon as you add a field to them. On small data sets (such as the 2,155 row data set used in the sample data for this lesson) there is no problem. The pivot table updates in a fraction of a second.

If you find that you have to wait a significant amount of time after adding a field before you can add another, you've found a use for *Defer Layout Update*.

Here's what you need to do:

1. Click the *Defer Layout Update* check box.

The *Update* button will then become enabled.

2. Add all of the fields you need.

3. Click the *Update* button. With a very large data set it could take some time for the pivot table to update.

4. Uncheck the check box.

This is usually a lot faster than adding fields one by one.

It is really important that you remember to uncheck the box. You won't be able to use any of the interactive features of the pivot table (such as filtering, sorting and grouping) until you do.

The pivot table now shows sales for each employee by genre with the genres listed along the top row as column labels:

	A	B	C	D	E
4	Row Labels ▼	Action	Adventure	Animation	Biography
5	Anderson,Jane	199	30		134
6	Armstrong,Dan	136	26	22	79
7	Ashe,Lucille	176	42	23	54

6   Add the *Title* field to the *Columns* list.

Drag the *Title* field from the *PivotTable Fields* task pane to the *Columns* list.

Make sure that you place *Title* below *Genre*.

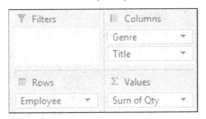

A small + sign is now displayed next to each genre:

	A	B	C	D	E
4		⊞ Action	⊞ Adventure	⊞ Animation	⊞ Biography
5	Row Labels ▼				
6	Anderson,Jane	199	30		134
7	Armstrong,Dan	136	26	22	79
8	Ashe,Lucille	176	42	23	54

7   Expand and collapse the *Action* genre.

1.   Click the small + sign to the left of *Action* in cell *B4.*

The field expands to show each title within the *Action* genre:

	A	B	C	D
4		⊟ Action		
5	Row Labels ▼	A Touch of Zen	Drunken Master II	Get Carter
6	Anderson,Jane	41	3	31

2.   Click the small – sign that has now appeared to the left of *Action* in cell B4.

The outline collapses back to the genre level:

	A	B	C	D
4		⊞ Action	⊞ Adventure	⊞ Animation
5	Row Labels ▼			
6	Anderson,Jane	199	30	
7	Armstrong,Dan	136	26	22

8   Save your work as *Transactions-4.*

Lesson 8-4: Understand the pivot table data cache

Data sources

Your data source will typically be one of the following:

1. **A single table on a single worksheet.**

   This the most common data source for a pivot table and is the type of data source you've been using up until now.

2. **Several tables (on the same, or different worksheets) joined by primary key/foreign key relationships.**

   You'll learn more about primary and foreign keys later in: *Lesson 10-26: Understand primary and foreign keys.*

3. **A table or view residing in an external relational database such as Access, Oracle or SQL Server.**

   You'll learn more about this type of data source later, in: *Lesson 10-30: Load a query directly into the PivotTable cache.*

Pivot tables do not directly use the data source

When you first create a pivot table, a hidden copy of the data source (called the *pivot table data cache*), is created and held in the computer's memory. This is a specially structured version of the data source that includes many pre-computed subtotals as well as all of the source data.

If you change the data source (for example by adding a new row to a table) the change does not appear in the pivot table until you refresh (create a new copy of) the *pivot table data cache.* You'll see how to refresh the cache later in this lesson.

I'm often asked whether Excel has an option to automatically refresh the pivot table whenever the source data changes. Unfortunately, this isn't possible but (as you will see later) you can ask Excel to refresh the cache whenever a workbook is opened.

Pivot tables can work without the data source

When you save a workbook containing a pivot table, the *pivot table data cache* is saved along with the workbook, providing several advantages:

1. If your data source is an external database, your pivot table will still work perfectly when the database is not connected. This means that you could (for example) e-mail the workbook to another user that has no access to the database.

2. If your data source was a worksheet, the pivot table will still work perfectly even if the worksheet is deleted.

The downside is that workbooks containing both the source data and the *pivot table data cache* can have huge file sizes as all data is effectively

Transactions-4

tip

You can refresh a pivot table more quickly using the right-click method

In this lesson you refreshed the pivot table using the ribbon.

If you right-click inside a pivot table, you'll also see a *Refresh* option on the shortcut menu.

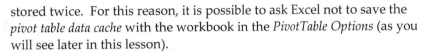

	A	E
4		⊞ Biography
5	Row Labels ▾	
18	Lee,Frank	157

Refresh

	A	E
4		⊞ Biography
5	Row Labels ▾	
18	Lee,Frank	167

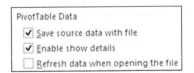

PivotTable Data
- ☑ Save source data with file
- ☑ Enable show details
- ☐ Refresh data when opening the file

stored twice. For this reason, it is possible to ask Excel not to save the *pivot table data cache* with the workbook in the *PivotTable Options* (as you will see later in this lesson).

Workbooks that use external data (such as the one you will create in: *Lesson 10-30: Load a query directly into the PivotTable cache*), are more efficient (in terms of both file size and use of computer memory) as they save only one copy of the data (the *pivot table data cache*) and do not have to hold both the workbook source data and the *pivot table data cache* in memory at the same time.

1   Open *Transactions-4* from your sample files folder.

This pivot table uses the *Data* table on the *Data* worksheet as its data source. Notice that Frank Lee has sold a total of 157 videos in the *Biography* genre.

2   Change the source data to add ten more sales for Frank Lee in the Biography genre.

    1.   Click the *Data* worksheet tab.

    2.   Increase Frank Lee's sale (in cell G2) from 15 units to 25 units.

	D	E	F	G	H
1	Employee	Title	Genre	Qty	Total
2	Lee,Frank	Lawrence of Arabia	Biography	25	122.76

3   Notice that the pivot table does not show any change.

Click the *Pivot Table* worksheet tab. Notice that Frank Lee's *Biography* genre sales remain the same at 157.

4   Refresh the PivotTable data cache and observe the change.

    1.   Click inside the pivot table to activate it.

    2.   Click: PivotTable Tools→Analyze→Data→Refresh.

       Notice that Frank Lee's sales have now updated.

5   Restore Frank Lee's sales (on row 2 of the *Data* table) to the original value (of 15 units) and refresh the pivot table data cache.

6   Examine options relating to the pivot table data cache.

    1.   Click inside the pivot table to activate it.

    2.   Click: PivotTable Tools→Analyze→ PivotTable→Options→Options.

    3.   Click the *Data* tab.

Save source data with file: Unchecking this option prevents Excel from saving the *pivot table data cache*. Doing this can result in greatly reduced file sizes.

Enable show details: This option controls whether you can drill-down to see the transactions that were used to calculate any total. For more on this, see: *Lesson 8-2: Create a grouped pivot table report (sidebar)*.

Refresh data when opening the file: Selecting this option refreshes the pivot table data cache when the workbook is opened.

Lesson 8-5: Apply a simple filter and sort to a pivot table

1   Open *Transactions-4* from your sample files folder (if it isn't already open).

2   Select the *Pivot Table* worksheet (if it isn't already selected).

3   Click inside the pivot table to display the *PivotTable Fields* task pane.

4   Remove the *Genre* and *Title* column fields.

This was covered in: *Lesson 8-3: Understand pivot table rows and columns.*

5   Click the drop-down arrow next to *Row Labels* in cell A3.

Filter options appear.

These are very similar to the options that you learned how to use in: *Lesson 1-4: Apply a simple filter to a range* and *Lesson 1-5: Apply a top 10 and custom filter to a range.*

6   Filter the pivot table so that only female employees are shown.

1. Uncheck the check boxes next to each male employee (see sidebar).

2. Click the *OK* button.

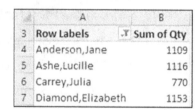

3	Row Labels	⊤ Sum of Qty
4	Anderson,Jane	1109
5	Ashe,Lucille	1116
6	Carrey,Julia	770
7	Diamond,Elizabeth	1153

Notice the filter icon in cell A3 has changed to indicate that the pivot table has been filtered.

This is a very long winded way to filter out the male employees.

In a real-world workbook you'd probably create a *Gender* column in the source data containing the values **M** or **F**.

You could then filter by gender with a single check box.

7   Sort *Employee* names in Z-A order.

At the moment, the names are sorted in A-Z order.

1. Right-click on any of the employee names in column A.

2. Click: Sort→Sort Z to A from the shortcut menu.

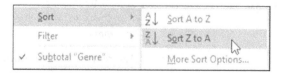

The sidebar checklist:

- ☐ (Select All)
- ☑ Anderson,Jane
- ☐ Armstrong,Dan
- ☑ Ashe,Lucille
- ☐ Bell,Stephen
- ☐ Bradshaw,John
- ☑ Carrey,Julia
- ☐ Davis,Charles
- ☑ Diamond,Elizabeth
- ☐ Goodman,Paul
- ☐ Hawking,Alfred
- ☐ Hicks,Michael
- ☐ Jennings,John
- ☐ Lee,Frank
- ☑ Manning,Marilyn
- ☑ Newhart,Anna
- ☑ Putin,Julia
- ☐ Richards,Andy
- ☑ Sagan,Jessica
- ☑ Silverstone,Gloria
- ☐ Simpson,Howard
- ☑ Simpson,Meryl
- ☑ Spears,Julie
- ☑ Streep,Margaret
- ☐ West,Chuck

Transactions-4

note

Filters are not inherited from source data

If the data associated with a pivot table (whether a table, range or named range) has a filter applied to it (or contains subtotals) this will not be carried forward into the pivot table.

If you need the same filter in your pivot table, you must first create the pivot table and then apply the same filter.

Another way to achieve this is to copy the (filtered) data to a new worksheet and then create the pivot table from this subset of the actual data.

A useful technique for copying and pasting filtered data (visible cells) is described in: *Lesson 2-3: Automatically subtotal a range (sidebar).*

	A	B
3	Row Labels	Sum of Qty
4	Newhart,Anna	1081
5	Diamond,Elizabeth	1153
6	Silverstone,Gloria	1040
7	Anderson,Jane	1109
8	Sagan,Jessica	1407
9	Carrey,Julia	770
10	Putin,Julia	1054
11	Spears,Julie	1314
12	Ashe,Lucille	1116
13	Streep,Margaret	1772
14	Manning,Marilyn	1161
15	Simpson,Meryl	822
16	**Grand Total**	**13799**

The pivot table is sorted in Z-A order.

	A	B
3	Row Labels	Sum of Qty
4	Streep,Margaret	1772
5	Spears,Julie	1314
6	Simpson,Meryl	822
7	Silverstone,Gloria	1040
8	Sagan,Jessica	1407
9	Putin,Julia	1054
10	Newhart,Anna	1081

8 Sort *Employee* names by first name.

It isn't possible to automatically sort by first name. To do this, you would need *First Name* to be a different field to *Last Name*.

If there were a lot of names, you could attend to this in the source data by splitting the *Employee* column into two. (You learned how to do this in: *Lesson 2-1: Split fixed width data using Text to Columns* and in *Lesson 3-21: Extract text from delimited strings using the FIND and LEN functions*).

Because there are only twelve names, it will be quicker to manually sort the list.

1. Right-click on any of the employee names in column A.

2. Click: Sort→More Sort Options… from the shortcut menu.

   The *Sort* dialog appears.

3. Click the *Manual* option button.

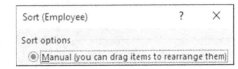

4. Click the *OK* button.

5. Click and drag the border of each *Employee* name to move them to the desired position. Look for the four headed arrow cursor shape before clicking the mouse (sidebar shows sorted order).

11	Manning,Marilyn	1161
12	Diamond,Elizabeth	1153
13	Carrey,Julia	770

9 Remove the filter.

1. Click the filter button at the top right of cell A3.

2. Check the *Select All* check box at the top of the list of names.

3. Click the *OK* button.

10 Save your work as *Transactions-5*.

Lesson 8-6: Use report filter fields

In pre-2007 versions of Excel, report filters were called *Page Fields*.

1   Open *Transactions-5* from your sample files folder (if it isn't already open).

2   Select the *Pivot Table* worksheet (if it isn't already selected).

3   Click inside the pivot table to display the *PivotTable Fields* task pane.

4   Drag the *Genre* field from the field list at the top of the task pane to the *Filters* list below.

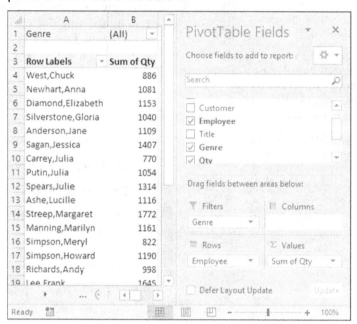

Notice that a filter has appeared at the top left of the pivot table (in cells A1 and B1):

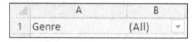

The filter currently shows all sales for all genres.

5   Use the report filter field to display sales for the *Comedy* genre.

1.   Click the drop-down list arrow in cell B1.

2.   Click *Comedy* in the drop-down list.

3.   Click the *OK* button.

Notice that the *Sum of Qty* values now change to only show quantities sold in the *Comedy* genre.

6   Use a report filter field to show sales in the *Comedy* genre for June 2015.

1.   Drag the *Order Date* field from the *PivotTable Fields* task pane down to the *Filters* List.

Transactions-5

2. Click the drop-down arrow in cell B2.

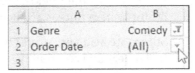

3. Type **jun-15** into the *Search* box.

   (The search text is not case sensitive so exactly the same results would be displayed if you had typed JUN-15).

   The *Search* box filters the entries in the list to dates containing the text *jun-15*.

4. Check the *Select Multiple Items* check box.

   Every June 2015 date is now checked.

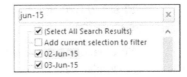

5. Click the *OK* button.

   The total quantities of goods sold in the *Comedy* genre during *June 2015* are now displayed.

	A	B	
1	Genre	Comedy	
2	Order Date	(Multiple Items)	
3			
4	**Row Labels**	**Sum of Qty**	
5	West,Chuck	22	
6	Silverstone,Gloria	22	
7	Anderson,Jane	17	
8	Sagan,Jessica	22	
9	Putin,Julia	40	
10	Spears,Julie	19	
11	Ashe,Lucille	15	
12	Simpson,Meryl	9	
13	Richards,Andy	24	
14	Lee,Frank	6	
15	Bradshaw,John	43	
16	Bell,Stephen	37	
17	**Grand Total**	276	

   Notice that the filter information in cell B2 *(Multiple Items)* gives no information to the user about the filter currently in place. In *Lesson 8-7: Filter a pivot table visually using slicers* you'll discover a much better way of showing the user which multiple item filters are currently active.

7 Save your work as *Transactions-6*.

Lesson 8-7: Filter a pivot table visually using slicers

Unlike report filter fields, slicers show which filters are in place when a multiple-item filter is applied.

Slicers are also very useful for designing touch-screen user interfaces for tablet personal computers.

1   Open *Transactions-6* from your sample files folder (if it isn't already open).

2   Remove all existing fields and filters from the pivot table.

Sometimes you will want to completely clear all filters and fields from a pivot table.

1. Click inside the pivot table to activate it.

2. Click PivotTable Tools→Analyze→Actions→Clear→Clear All.

3   Display the *Total* and *Qty* values for each genre.

Click the check-boxes for *Genre, Qty* and *Total* (in that order) in the field list on the *PivotTable Fields* task pane.

4   Change the number format for the values shown in column C to show two decimal places with a comma thousand separator.

You learned how to do this in: *Lesson 8-1: Create a one-dimensional pivot table report from a table.*

5   Change the number format for the values shown in column B to show no decimal places and a comma thousand separator.

You learned how to do this in: *Lesson 8-1: Create a one-dimensional pivot table report from a table.*

6   Change the text in cell A4 to: **Genre**, in cell B4 to: **Sales Qty** and in cell C4 to: **Total Sales**

Click in each cell and type the new text.

Your pivot table should now look like this:

	A	B	C
4	Genre	Sales Qty	Total Sales
5	Action	4,699	37,411.40
6	Adventure	1,149	8,588.03

7   Add slicers to filter by Genre and Customer.

In *Lesson 8-6: Use report filter fields*, you saw how filtering could be done using report filter fields. This time you'll implement the filters using slicers.

1. Click anywhere in the pivot table to activate it.

2. Click: PivotTable Tools→Analyze→Filter→Insert Slicer.

The *Insert Slicers* dialog appears.

note

Slicers can also be used to visually filter tables

Slicers can be used with tables in exactly the same way that they are used with pivot tables.

Transactions-6

3. Check the *Genre* and *Customer* check boxes.

4. Click the *OK* button.

Two slicers appear on the worksheet.

8 **Move and format the slicers so that they have an attractive appearance.**

1. Click on the *Genre* slicer to select it and then click and drag the border to move it next to the pivot table.

2. Click: Slicer Tools→Options→Buttons→Columns and type **6** into the text box.

3. Re-size the slicer so that all genre names are visible.

4. Click: Slicer Tools→Options→Slicer Styles and select an attractive style.

5. Do the same for the *Customer* slicer, setting the *Columns* to 3.

9 **Test the slicers.**

1. Click the *Action* button on the *Genre* slicer.

Notice that the pivot table is filtered to only show sales values for the *Action* genre.

2. Click the *Cinefocus DVD* button on the *Customer* slicer and then hold down the **<Ctrl>** key and click the *Classic Films* button.

Notice that only sales to the selected customers for the *Action* genre are now shown.

3. Clear the slicer filters by clicking the *Clear Filter* buttons in each slicer's top right corner.

10 **Save your work as *Transactions-7*.**

note

Slicers have a multi-select button

When you want to select more than one item in a slicer you normally hold down the **<Ctrl>** key as you click each item.

This is the preferred technique on a desktop computer but isn't possible on a touchscreen. For this reason, a multi-select button is provided on the top-right corner of slicers.

Click (or touch) the multi-select icon once to enter multi-select mode, select two or more slicer buttons and then click (or touch) the multi-select icon once more to exit multi-select mode.

Lesson 8-8: Add a timeline control to a pivot table

1 Open *Transactions-7* from your sample files folder (if it isn't already open).

2 Add a timeline control to the pivot table.

> ## note
>
> ### You cannot add a timeline control to all pivot tables
>
> Before inserting a timeline control, Excel will make sure that there is at least one column in the source data that contains valid date values that are formatted as dates.
>
> Excel will not allow a timeline control to be added if this is not the case.

1. Click anywhere inside the pivot table to activate it.

2. Click: PivotTableTools→Analyze→Filter→Insert Timeline.

   The *Insert Timelines* dialog appears.

3. Check the *Order Date* check box.

4. Click the *OK* button.

   A *Timeline* control appears on the worksheet.

3 Move the timeline control so that it is neatly placed beneath the two slicers added in the previous lesson.

4 Use the timeline control to show a summary of transactions taking place only in 2014.

1. Click the drop-down arrow in the top right corner of the timeline control.

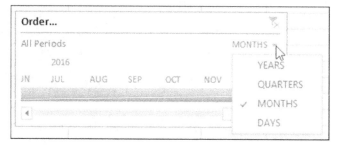

You are now able to select *YEARS, QUARTERS, MONTHS or DAYS*.

2. Select *YEARS*.

   The three years 2014, 2015 and 2016 are shown in the timeline control.

3. Click on the 2014 button to select sales in the year 2014.

Only sales that occurred in 2014 are now shown in the pivot table.

Transactions-7

5   Use the timeline to show a summary of transactions occurring in 2014 and 2015.

Hover the mouse cursor over the 2014 button.

Notice that a sizing handle has appeared on the right-hand side of the button.

Click and drag the right-hand border of the button so that both the 2014 and 2015 buttons are selected.

Only sales that occurred in 2014 or 2015 are now shown in the pivot table.

6   Use the timeline to show a summary of transactions occurring in the period January 2014 to June 2015.

1. Click the drop-down arrow in the top right corner of the timeline control and select *MONTHS* from the drop-down menu.

2. Widen the timeline control so that you can see the months JAN 2014 to JUN 2015.

3. Click on JAN and then drag the right-hand border of the button so that months JAN 2014 to JUN 2015 are selected.

Only sales that occurred between January 2014 and June 2015 are now shown in the pivot table.

7   Use the timeline control to show a summary of all transactions occurring between 1st Jan 2016 and 15th Jan 2016.

Select *DAYS* from the drop-down menu in the top right-hand corner of the timeline and select the days: 1st JAN 2016 to 15th JAN 2016

The pivot table will now only summarize transactions occurring within this date range.

8   Save your work as *Transactions-8.*

note

Customizing the appearance of a timeline control

Just like slicers, timeline controls have their own custom ribbon tab.

When you click on a timeline control you'll see a new:

Timeline Tools→Options

... tab appear on the ribbon.

This ribbon tab includes several customization options, along with a style gallery.

note

Creating Years, Months, Days and Quarters from a date value

Year

The YEAR function is covered in: *Lesson 3-8: Understand common date functions.*

Month as a string

The TEXT function is covered in *Lesson 3-19: Use the TEXT function to format numerical values as strings.*

The custom format code: "mmm" formats a date as a three character text value (such as *Jan*). The *Essential Skills* book in this series extensively covers the (rather cryptic) formatting codes available in Excel.

Day

The DAY function is covered in: *Lesson 3-8: Understand common date functions.*

Quarter

1. The month is first returned as a number (1-12) using the MONTH function (covered in: *Lesson 3-8: Understand common date functions*).

2. The number of the month returned is then divided by three. For example, May would return 5/3 = 2.666.

3. The ROUNDUP function is used to round the number up to the nearest whole number. This returns the correct quarter (1-4).

The completed formula can be seen in the *Data* worksheet:

=ROUNDUP(
MONTH([@Date])/3,0)

Lesson 8-9: Use slicers to create a custom timeline

In *Lesson 8-8: Add a timeline control to a pivot table,* you learned how to use a timeline control. While the timeline control offers a quick and convenient way to add a timeline, you are unable to significantly customize its appearance. In this lesson you'll create the same timeline functionality using slicers to provide a more elegant user interface.

Before you can add a date-driven interface to a pivot table you will need to create fields in the underlying data table for *Year, Month, Day* and *Quarter*. This has already been done in the sample file for this session:

	B	C	D	E	F
1	Date	Year	Month	Day	Quarter
2	02-Jan-13	2013	Jan	2	1
3	01-Jan-13	2013	Jan	1	1

Before beginning this lesson, you may find it useful to study the formulas used to create these fields from the *Date* field. If you do not understand how these formulas work, refer to the sidebar for more information.

1 Open *Executive Summary-1* from your sample files folder (if it isn't already open).

2 Add slicers to the pivot table for *Year, Quarter, Month* and *Day*.

   You learned how to do this in: *Lesson 8-7: Filter a pivot table visually using slicers.*

3 Format the slicers so that they look the same as the screen grab at the bottom of the facing page.

   You learned how to do this in: *Lesson 8-7: Filter a pivot table visually using slicers.*

   Notice that a *Year* slicer has been included even though the underlying data only has a single year (2015).

   When you use slicers to create a timeline, it is good practice to always include a *Year* slicer because you can never be sure that more data will not be added to the underlying data table.

   For example, if 2016 sales data were added to the table, selecting *Jan* would show sales for both Jan 2015 and Jan 2016 if the *Year* slicer was not included.

4 Use the slicers to show sales for the first two quarters of 2015 in the *Action, Animation and Comedy* genres.

   1. Click the *1* button in the *Quarter* slicer and then hold down the <Ctrl> key and click the *2* button.

Quarter			
1	2	3	4

Executive Summary-1

Notice that the months Jan-Jun are now selected in the *Month* slicer.

<u>OR</u>

Click the *Jan* button in the *Month* slicer and then hold down the **<Shift>** key and click the *Jun* button.

Notice that the 1 and 2 buttons are now selected in the *Quarter* slicer

2. Click the *Action* button in the *Genre* slicer and then hold down the **<Ctrl>** key and click the *Animation* and *Comedy* buttons.

Sales are now shown for the first two quarters of 2015 in the *Action, Comedy* and *Animation* genres.

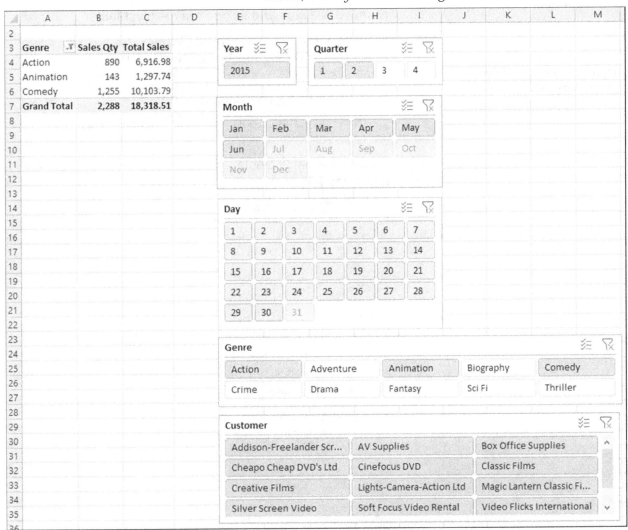

5   Save your work as *Executive Summary-2.*

note

Report filter fields are not supported by OLAP pivot tables

Later, in: *Lesson 11-7: Understand OLAP pivot tables,* you'll learn about a new type of pivot table called an *OLAP pivot table.*

OLAP pivot tables are created in a different way to the regular pivot tables you work with in this session.

Regular pivot tables can do some things that OLAP pivot tables are not capable of. Conversely, OLAP pivot tables have some extra features that regular pivot tables do not have.

Report filter fields are one of those features that are not supported by OLAP pivot tables.

Lesson 8-10: Use report filter fields to automatically create multiple pages

In this lesson, you will cater for the following scenario:

You have been asked to print out a sales listing for each employee. This involves printing a total of 23 separate reports.

It is easy, but time consuming, to print each sheet manually. You would need to perform 23 filter and print operations. Surely there's a better way?

Of course there is. You can use a report filter to automate the whole task and print all 23 reports in one operation.

1 Open *Transactions-8* from your sample files folder.

2 Select the *Pivot Table* worksheet (if it isn't already selected).

3 Remove all filters and fields from the pivot table.

There's a quick way to remove all filters and fields from a pivot table. This is very useful when you want to start again with an empty pivot table.

1. Click inside the pivot table to activate it.

2. Click: PivotTable Tools→Analyze→Actions→Clear→ Clear All.

4 Change the fields displayed by the pivot table so that they match the following:

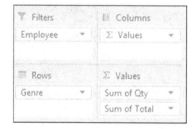

You learned how to do this in: *Lesson 8-3: Understand pivot table rows and columns.* Note that the [Σ Values ▼] field automatically appears in the *Columns* list when you add more than one field to the *Values* list.

Your pivot table now looks like this:

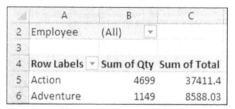

5 Create separate worksheets detailing each employee's sales.

1. Click anywhere within the pivot table.

Transactions-8

2. Click: PivotTable Tools→Analyze→PivotTable→Options→ Show Report Filter Pages…

The *Show Report Filter Pages* dialog appears.

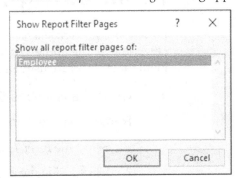

Because there is only one report filter, there's only one choice.

If you had multiple filters, you could choose which filter you wanted to use.

3. Click the *OK* button.

Something amazing happens.

24 worksheets are instantly created, one for each employee.

Here's Jane Anderson's sheet:

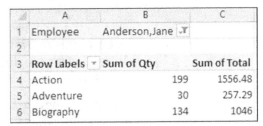

You can see that it contains a copy of the original pivot table with a filter set for *Anderson, Jane.*

6   Print preview all worksheets.

1. Click on the first employee's tab (Anderson, Jane).

2. Use the worksheet scroll bar buttons so that the last employee's tab (West, Chuck) is visible.

3. Hold down the **<Shift>** key.

4. Click on the last employee's tab (West, Chuck).

You have now selected all of the employee worksheets (you don't want to print the *Pivot Table* or *Data* worksheets).

5. Click: File→Print.

Notice that *Print Active Sheets* is selected by default.

Notice the preview pane. All employee sheets will be printed.

6. Click the *Back Button* to return to the worksheet.

7   Save your work as *Multiple Sheets-1.*

Lesson 8-11: Format a pivot table using PivotTable styles

In: *Lesson 1-13: Format a table using table styles and convert a table into a range*, you learned how to use a built-in style to format an Excel table. PivotTable styles are used in a similar way.

1　Open *Transactions-8* from your sample files folder.

2　Remove all existing fields and filters from the pivot table.

    1.　Select the *Pivot Table* worksheet.

    2.　Click inside the pivot table to activate it.

    3.　Click: PivotTable Tools→Analyze→Actions→Clear→ Clear All.

3　Delete the three slicers from the pivot table.

Click on each slicer and then press the **<Delete>** key.

4　Select the fields shown below.

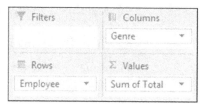

5　Filter to only show the genres: *Action, Adventure* and *Animation* for employees: *Dan Armstrong, Julie Spears* and *Chuck West*.

You learned how to do this in: *Lesson 8-5: Apply a simple filter and sort to a pivot table.*

	A	B	C	D	E
4	Sum of Total	Column Labels			
5	Row Labels	Action	Adventure	Animation	Grand Total
6	Armstrong,Dan	1199.7	195.56	218.1	1613.36
7	Spears,Julie	1032.11	284.58	109.37	1426.06
8	West,Chuck	861.84	44.77	677.02	1583.63
9	Grand Total	3093.65	524.91	1004.49	4623.05

6　Apply the PivotTable style: *Light 17.*

Click: PivotTable Tools→Design→PivotTable Styles→ Light→Light Orange, Pivot Style Light 17.

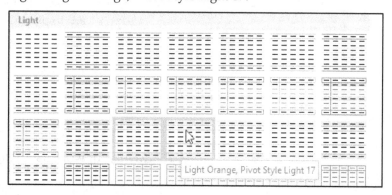

Transactions-8

	A	B	C	D	E
4	**Sum of Total**	**Column Labels** ⫧			
5	**Row Labels** ⫧	**Action**	**Adventure**	**Animation**	**Grand Total**
6	Armstrong,Dan	1199.7	195.56	218.1	1613.36
7	Spears,Julie	1032.11	284.58	109.37	1426.06
8	West,Chuck	861.84	44.77	677.02	1583.63
9	**Grand Total**	**3093.65**	**524.91**	**1004.49**	**4623.05**

7   Enable *Banded Rows.*

Check: PivotTable Tools→Design→PivotTable Style Options→ Banded Rows.

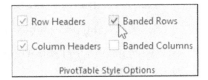

The pivot table changes to show colored shading on alternate rows.

	A	B	C	D	E
4	**Sum of Total**	**Column Labels** ⫧			
5	**Row Labels** ⫧	**Action**	**Adventure**	**Animation**	**Grand Total**
6	Armstrong,Dan	1199.7	195.56	218.1	1613.36
7	Spears,Julie	1032.11	284.58	109.37	1426.06
8	West,Chuck	861.84	44.77	677.02	1583.63
9	**Grand Total**	**3093.65**	**524.91**	**1004.49**	**4623.05**

The colored bands can help the eye to track across rows, especially when a pivot table is printed.

8   Disable *Banded Rows* and enable *Banded Columns.*

Check: PivotTable Tools→Design→PivotTable Style Options→ Banded Columns.

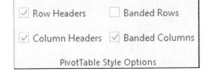

	A	B	C	D	E
4	**Sum of Total**	**Column Labels** ⫧			
5	**Row Labels** ⫧	**Action**	**Adventure**	**Animation**	**Grand Total**
6	Armstrong,Dan	1199.7	195.56	218.1	1613.36
7	Spears,Julie	1032.11	284.58	109.37	1426.06
8	West,Chuck	861.84	44.77	677.02	1583.63
9	**Grand Total**	**3093.65**	**524.91**	**1004.49**	**4623.05**

9   Disable *Banded Columns.*

Clear the *Banded Columns* check box.

10   Understand the two other *PivotTable Style Options.*

The other two options in the *PivotTable Style Options* group are: *Row Headers* and *Column Headers.*

In the *Light 17* style, the column headers are shown in a contrasting color. The *Column Headers* check box allows you to switch this color off.

Some of the other styles also show row headers (cells A6:A8) in a contrasting color. If you were using this type of style, you could switch this color off with the *Row Headers* check box.

11   Save your work as *Transactions-9.*

Lesson 8-12: Create a custom pivot table style

In: *Lesson 1-14: Create a custom table style*, you learned how to create a custom style for an Excel table. Pivot table custom styles are applied in a similar way.

1   Open *Transactions-9* from your sample files folder (if it isn't already open).

2   Remove the existing style.

    1. Click the pivot table to activate it.

    2. Click: PivotTable Tools→Design→PivotTable Styles→ Light→None.

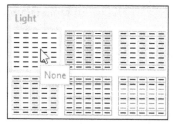

3   Create a custom pivot table style called *Corporate* by duplicating the *Medium8* built in style.

You'll usually find that modifying a duplicate of an existing style is easier than creating a style from scratch.

    1. Right-click on:

        PivotTable Tools→Design→PivotTable Styles→ Medium→White, Pivot Style Medium 8

    2. Click *Duplicate…* from the shortcut menu.

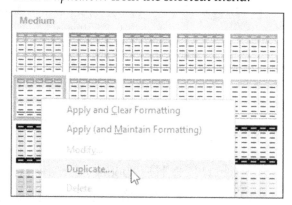

The *Modify PivotTable Style* dialog appears.

Transactions-9

Notice that some of the *Table Elements* are shown in bold face. These are the elements that have had formatting applied to them:

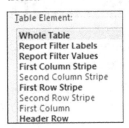

3. Type the name **Corporate** into the *Name* text box.

4. Click the *OK* button to dismiss the dialog.

4 Apply the new *Corporate* style to the pivot table.

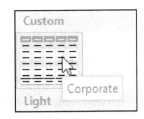

Click: PivotTable Tools→Design→PivotTable Styles→Custom→Corporate.

You'll see the new *Corporate* style at the top of the *PivotTable Styles* gallery in a new group called *Custom*.

5 Modify the *Corporate* style so that it shows the *Grand Total* column in bold face.

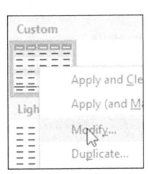

1. Right-click on:

   PivotTable Tools→Design→PivotTable Styles→Custom→Corporate.

2. Click *Modify...* from the shortcut menu.

3. Select *Grand Total Column* from the *Table Element* list.

4. Click the *Format* button.

5. Select the *Font* tab.

6. Select the *Font style:* Bold.

7. Click the *OK* button.

8. Click the *OK* button again.

   The *Grand Total* column is now shown in bold face.

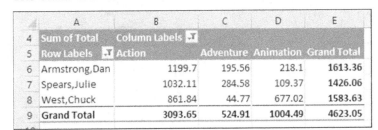

	A	B	C	D	E
4	Sum of Total	Column Labels			
5	Row Labels	Action	Adventure	Animation	Grand Total
6	Armstrong,Dan		1199.7	195.56	218.1	1613.36
7	Spears,Julie	1032.11	284.58	109.37	1426.06
8	West,Chuck	861.84	44.77	677.02	1583.63
9	Grand Total	3093.65	524.91	1004.49	4623.05

6 Save your work as *Transactions-10*.

note

You can change the default Pivot Table report layout

If you would like the default pivot table report layout to be different to the *compact form layout,* you can set a new default like this:

1. Setup the pivot table with the layout options you would like to be the new default and click anywhere inside it.

2. Click: File→Options→ Data→Data options.

3. Click the *Edit Default Layout…* button .

4. Click the *Import* button.

The settings from the existing pivot table will now become the default for any future pivot tables.

Lesson 8-13: Understand pivot table report layouts

1   Open *Transactions-10* from your sample files folder (if it isn't already open).

2   Remove all existing fields from the pivot table by dragging them up into the *PivotTable Fields* list.

This is another way to remove selected fields. You can also drag and drop them onto the worksheet grid area if you wish.

It's important to realize that when you drag a field back to the *PivotTable Fields* list, you do not clear any filter conditions associated with the field. You can still see a filter icon next to each filtered field (see sidebar).

3   Select the fields shown below.

You learned how to do this in: *Lesson 8-3: Understand pivot table rows and columns.*

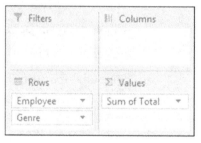

The pivot table is shown in *compact form layout*. This is the default layout.

	A	B
4	Row Labels	Sum of Total
5	Armstrong,Dan	1613.36
6	Action	1199.7
7	Adventure	195.56
8	Animation	218.1
9	Spears,Julie	1426.06
10	Action	1032.11

This layout is useful when you need the report to take up the minimum amount of space on screen or paper.

Subsidiary fields are only slightly indented from their parent field.

Transactions-10

note

The Repeat All Item Labels option

Sometimes you may want to copy and paste values from a pivot table into a regular range. This can be of particular use when you want to create a regular chart from data summarized by a pivot table.

The best way to do this is to use *Tabular Form* layout in conjunction with the *Repeat All Item Labels* option.

Here's how you could achieve this with this lesson's sample file:

1. Click inside the pivot table to activate it.

2. Click: PivotTable Tools→ Design→Layout→ Report Layout→ Show in Tabular Form

3. Click: PivotTable Tools→ Design→Layout→ Report Layout→ Repeat All Item Labels.

4. Click: PivotTable Tools→ Design→Layout→Subtotals→ Do Not Show Subtotals.

5. Click: PivotTable Tools→ Design→Layout→ Grand Totals→ Off for Rows and Columns.

Instead of only showing the *Employee Name* once (in column A) it is now shown on every row in the column.

Subtotals and *Grand Totals* have also been removed.

Employee	Genre
Armstrong,Dan	Action
Armstrong,Dan	Adventure
Armstrong,Dan	Animation
Spears,Julie	Action

You now have a format that is easy to copy and paste into a normal range. The best *Paste Special* option would be: *Paste Values and Number Formats:*

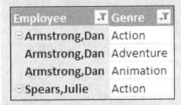

---

4 Change the report layout to *Outline Form*.

Click:

PivotTable Tools→Design→Layout→
Report Layout→Show in Outline Form

	A	B	C
4	Employee	Genre	Sum of Total
5	Armstrong,Dan		1613.36
6		Action	1199.7
7		Adventure	195.56
8		Animation	218.1
9	Spears,Julie		1426.06
10		Action	1032.11

Outline Form is the classic pivot table layout that was the default in pre-2007 versions of Excel.

Outline Form takes up more space but is more readable as each field has its own column label.

5 Change the report layout to *Tabular Form*.

Click:

PivotTable Tools→Design→Layout→
Report Layout→Show in Tabular Form

	A	B	C
4	Employee	Genre	Sum of Total
5	Armstrong,Dan	Action	1199.7
6		Adventure	195.56
7		Animation	218.1
8	Armstrong,Dan Total		1613.36
9	Spears,Julie	Action	1032.11
10		Adventure	284.58
11		Animation	109.37
12	Spears,Julie Total		1426.06
13	West,Chuck	Action	861.84
14		Adventure	44.77
15		Animation	677.02
16	West,Chuck Total		1583.63
17	Grand Total		4623.05

This layout is very easy to read because it is similar to a regular Excel table with totals shown at the bottom of each column.

This layout is also very useful when you want to copy the values in a Pivot Table into a regular range (especially when combined with the *Repeat All Item Labels option* – see sidebar).

6 Save your work as *Transactions-11*.

Lesson 8-14: Add/remove subtotals and apply cell styles to pivot table fields

1 Open *Transactions-11* from your sample files folder (if it isn't already open).

2 Apply a Filter to show only the *Biography* and *Thriller* genres.

You learned how to do this in: *Lesson 8-5: Apply a simple filter and sort to a pivot table.*

3 Add the *Title* field to the pivot table as a third-level row label.

Drag the *Title* field from the *PivotTable Fields* task pane to the *Rows* list.

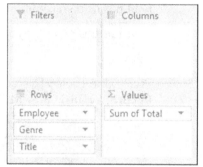

4 If necessary, expand all of the *Genre* fields to show all *Titles*.

You learned how to do this in: *Lesson 8-2: Create a grouped pivot table report.*

Because the pivot table layout is set to *Tabular Form*, subtotals are displayed for all subsidiary groups. Both *Employee* and *Genre* are showing subtotals.

	A	B	C	D
4	Employee	Genre	Title	Sum of Total
5	Armstrong,Dan	Biography	Bonnie and Clyde	96.53
6			Lawrence of Arabia	230.31
7			Raging Bull	329.88
8			Schindler's List	9.14
9		Biography Total		665.86
10		Thriller	Psycho	51.44
11		Thriller Total		51.44
12	Armstrong,Dan Total			717.3

5 Format the *Genre* subtotal fields using the *Total* cell style.

1. Hover the mouse cursor over the left edge of the *Biography Total* label in cell B9.

2. Make sure you see the black arrow cursor shape and then click to select.

	A	B	
9		→Biography Total	
10		Thriller	Psycho

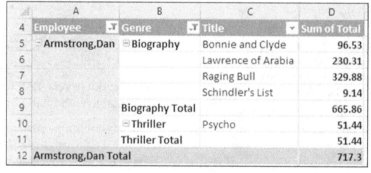

Transactions-11

Notice that when you select the field all *Genre subtotal* cells are selected.

3. Click: Home→Styles→Cell Styles→Total.

The *Total* style is applied to all *Genre subtotal* fields.

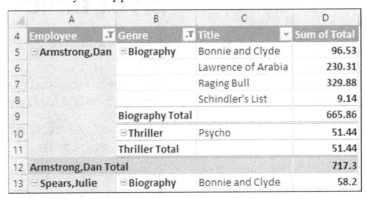

	A	B	C	D
4	Employee	Genre	Title	Sum of Total
5	Armstrong,Dan	Biography	Bonnie and Clyde	96.53
6			Lawrence of Arabia	230.31
7			Raging Bull	329.88
8			Schindler's List	9.14
9		Biography Total		665.86
10		Thriller	Psycho	51.44
11		Thriller Total		51.44
12	Armstrong,Dan Total			717.3
13	Spears,Julie	Biography	Bonnie and Clyde	58.2

6   Remove the *Genre* subtotals.

1. Right-click on any of the genres in column B.

2. Click Subtotal "Genre" from the shortcut menu.

The *Genre* subtotal fields are removed.

7   Remove the *Grand Total.*

Click: PivotTable Tools→Design→Layout→
Grand Totals→Off for Rows and Columns.

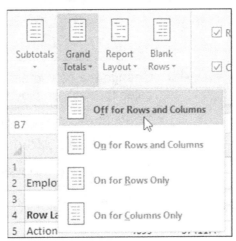

8   Save your work as *Transactions-12.*

note

Switching grand totals on and off with the right-click method

In this lesson, you used the ribbon to enable or disable the *Grand Total.*

It is also possible to do this using the following right-click method:

1. Right click anywhere within the pivot table.

2. Click *PivotTable Options...* from the shortcut menu.

3. Click the *Totals & Filters* tab.

4. Click one, or both of the *Grand Totals* check boxes to enable or disable grand totals.

Grand Totals
☑ Show grand totals for rows
☑ Show grand totals for columns

Lesson 8-15: Display multiple summations within a single pivot table

It is possible to show the same *Value* field many times in the same pivot table.

This is useful when you need to display different summations (such as Average, Sum and Max) on a single pivot table.

1   Open *Transactions-12* from your sample files folder (if it isn't already open).

2   Remove the *Genre* and *Title* fields from the *Rows* list.

3   Add two more *Total* fields to the *Values* list.

Drag the *Total* field from the *PivotTable Fields* pane to the *Values* pane twice.

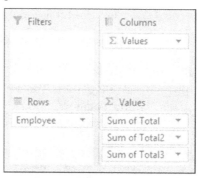

4   Change the new totals to show *Average* sales and *Maximum* sales for each employee.

1.   Right-click anywhere in column C within the pivot table.

2.   Click *Value Field Settings...* from the shortcut menu.

3.   Select *Average* in the *Summarize value field by* list.

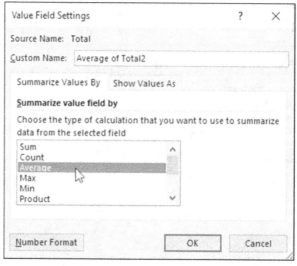

4.   Click the *OK* button.

Transactions-12

5. Use the same technique to make the *Sum of Total3* field display the maximum (*Max*) value.

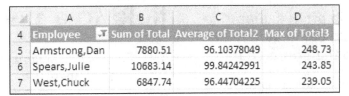

	A	B	C	D
4	Employee	Sum of Total	Average of Total2	Max of Total3
5	Armstrong,Dan	7880.51	96.10378049	248.73
6	Spears,Julie	10683.14	99.84242991	243.85
7	West,Chuck	6847.74	96.44704225	239.05

5 Format the *Average of Total2* field so that it displays two decimal places.

1. Right-click on any value in column C within the pivot table.

2. Click *Number Format…* from the shortcut menu.

3. Select the *Number* category and set two decimal places.

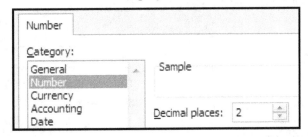

4. Click the *OK* button.

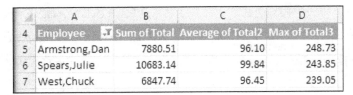

	A	B	C	D
4	Employee	Sum of Total	Average of Total2	Max of Total3
5	Armstrong,Dan	7880.51	96.10	248.73
6	Spears,Julie	10683.14	99.84	243.85
7	West,Chuck	6847.74	96.45	239.05

6 Add a *Grand Total*.

Click anywhere inside the pivot table to activate it.

Click: PivotTable Tools→Design→Layout→
Grand Totals→On for Columns Only.

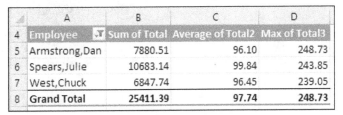

	A	B	C	D
4	Employee	Sum of Total	Average of Total2	Max of Total3
5	Armstrong,Dan	7880.51	96.10	248.73
6	Spears,Julie	10683.14	99.84	243.85
7	West,Chuck	6847.74	96.45	239.05
8	Grand Total	25411.39	97.74	248.73

7 Save your work as *Transactions-13*.

tip

It is often easier to add calculated fields to the source data

When the data source is a worksheet (as is the case in this lesson) it is usually faster and more efficient to add the calculated field to the source data on the worksheet.

You will then see the new field appear in the *PivotTable Fields* list when you refresh the pivot table.

You learned how to refresh a pivot table in: *Lesson 8-4: Understand the pivot table data cache.*

Later, in: *Lesson 10-30: Load a query directly into the PivotTable cache,* you will learn how to connect a pivot table to an Access database.

When working with external data sources, the calculated fields you need may not exist in the data source.

The calculated fields you have learned about in this lesson provide a useful solution to this problem.

Lesson 8-16: Add a calculated field to a pivot table

1   Open *Transactions-13* from your sample files folder (if it isn't already open).

2   Remove the *Average of Total2* and *Max of Total3* fields.

> You learned how to do this in: *Lesson 8-3: Understand pivot table rows and columns.*

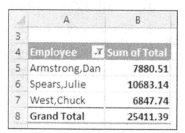

3   Format the *Sum of Total* field to show a comma thousand separator.

1. Right-click any of the values in column B within the pivot table.

2. Click *Number Format…* from the shortcut menu.

3. Click the *Number* category.

4. Check the *Use 1000 Separator (,)* check box.

5. Click *OK.*

4   Add a calculated field called *Bonus* that will calculate 3% of total sales.

1. Click: PivotTable Tools→Analyze→Calculations→ Fields, Items & Sets→Calculated Field…

   The *Insert Calculated Field* dialog appears.

2. Type **Bonus** into the *Name* text box.

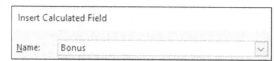

3. Click in the *Formula* text box and remove the zero, leaving only an = sign.

4. Select *Total* in the *Fields* list and then click the *Insert Field* button.

   The word **Total** is added to the formula.

5. Type ***3%** to complete the formula.

Formula: = Total*3%

Transactions-11

note

Calculated fields are not supported by OLAP pivot tables

Later, in: *Lesson 11-7: Understand OLAP pivot tables*, you'll learn about a new type of pivot table called an *OLAP pivot table*.

Calculated fields are not supported by OLAP pivot tables. They provide an alternative (and more powerful) replacement called *calculated measures*.

You'll learn about these later, in: *Lesson 12-3: Create a DAX calculated measure*.

tip

Creating a custom header row

In this lesson, you switched off the field headers in order to remove the filter button from cell A4. This had the side-effect of also removing the word *Employee* from cell A4. It isn't then possible to type any text into cell A4.

If you wanted to keep the *Employee* label but suppress the filter button, you would need to hide row 4 and then re-create the headers in row 3. Here's how you could do this:

1. Copy cells A4:C4 into cells A3:C3.

2. To hide row 4, right-click the row header (the number 4 on the left of the row) and then click *Hide* from the shortcut menu.

3. Type: **Employee** into cell A3.

	A	B
2		
3	**Employee**	**Sales**
5	Armstrong,Dan	7,880.51
6	Spears,Julie	10,683.14
7	West,Chuck	6,847.74
8	**Grand Total**	**25,411.39**

6. Click the *OK* button.

A new field called *Bonus* has now appeared in the *PivotTable Fields* task pane and a *Sum of Bonus* field has appeared in column C.

	A	B	C
4	**Employee** ▼	**Sum of Total**	**Sum of Bonus**
5	Armstrong,Dan	7,880.51	236.42
6	Spears,Julie	10,683.14	320.49
7	West,Chuck	6,847.74	205.43
8	**Grand Total**	**25,411.39**	**762.34**

5 Change the names at the top of columns B and C to *Sales* and *Bonus Due*.

1. Click cell B4.

2. Type the new name: **Sales**

3. Press the **<Tab>** key to save the value and move to cell C4.

4. Type: **Bonus Due** into cell C4.

6 Remove the *Field Header* (this is currently shown in row 4).

The pivot table looks untidy because cell A4 includes a filter button. If you wanted to print the pivot table, you would also want to remove the filter button.

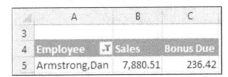

	A	B	C
3			
4	**Employee** ▼	**Sales**	**Bonus Due**
5	Armstrong,Dan	7,880.51	236.42

Click: PivotTable Tools→Analyze→Show→Field Headers.

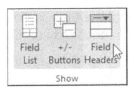

The three items in the *Show* group are toggle buttons which allow you to show and hide different pivot table artefacts.

The pivot table is now well formatted.

	A	B	C
3			
4		**Sales**	**Bonus Due**
5	Armstrong,Dan	7,880.51	236.42
6	Spears,Julie	10,683.14	320.49
7	West,Chuck	6,847.74	205.43
8	**Grand Total**	**25,411.39**	**762.34**

The filter button has disappeared, but so has the *Employee* label.

It is possible to show the *Employee* label without the filter icon. See sidebar for a special technique you can use to make this possible.

7 Save your work as *Transactions-14*.

note

Calculated items are not supported by OLAP pivot tables

Later, in: *Lesson 11-7: Understand OLAP pivot tables,* you'll learn about a new type of pivot table called an *OLAP pivot table.*

Calculated items are not supported by OLAP pivot tables. They provide an alternative (and more powerful) replacement called *calculated measures.*

You'll learn about these later, in: *Lesson 12-3: Create a DAX calculated measure.*

Lesson 8-17: Add a calculated item to a pivot table

One *field* will usually consist of several *items.* For example, the *Genre* field consists of items such as *Drama, Comedy, Action, Biography* etc.

If you wanted to show a sales target of **Sales + 10%**, you'd simply create a calculated field (as described in: *Lesson 8-16: Add a calculated field to a pivot table*).

Sometimes you will want to perform a calculation upon an arbitrary group of items. In this lesson's example, you are interested in combined sales for the *Drama, Comedy* and *Action* genres, as they are your top sellers.

Calculated items provide a solution to this problem. In this lesson, you'll add a calculated item to find the total sales in these genres.

1   Open *Transactions-14* from your sample files folder (if it isn't already open).

2   Clear all filters and fields from the pivot table.

Click: PivotTable Tools→Analyze→Actions→Clear→Clear All.

3   Add the following fields to the pivot table:

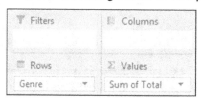

4   Format the *Sum of Total* field to show two decimal places with a thousand comma separator.

1.   Right-click on any of the values in column B within the pivot table.

2.   Click *Number Format* from the shortcut menu.

3.   Click the *Number* category.

4.   Check the *Use 1000 Separator (,)* check box.

5.   Click the *OK* button.

Your pivot table now looks like the one shown in the sidebar.

5   Add a calculated item to show total sales for the genres: *Drama, Comedy and Action.*

1.   Click any pivot table cell in column A.

2.   Click: PivotTable Tools→Analyze→Calculations→ Fields, Items & Sets→Calculated Item…

The *Insert Calculated Item* dialog appears.

This is very similar to the *Insert Calculated Field* dialog. The dialog can be confusing because it shows many fields and items that would not be valid for the *Genre* field. They are not grayed out as you would expect.

	A	B
4		**Sum of Total**
5	Action	37,411.40
6	Adventure	8,588.03
7	Animation	5,098.87
8	Biography	17,174.78
9	Comedy	37,614.16
10	Crime	25,212.68
11	Drama	67,097.47
12	Fantasy	11,785.28
13	Sci Fi	7,289.18
14	Thriller	5,514.95
15	**Grand Total**	**222,786.80**

Transactions-14

3. Name the calculated item: **Drama, Comedy & Action**

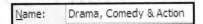

4. Select the *Genre* field and the *Drama* item and then click the *Insert Item* button.

    The formula changes to include the *Drama* item.

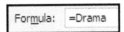

5. Type a + operator into the formula.

6. Add the *Comedy* and *Action* items in the same way so that your formula is the same as the following:

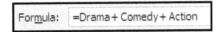

7. Click the *OK* button.

    A total for *Drama, Comedy & Action* appears at the bottom of the pivot table.

	A	B
14	Thriller	5,514.95
15	Drama, Comedy & Action	142,123.03
16	**Grand Total**	**364,909.83**

Notice that this addition has corrupted the *Grand Total* as *Drama, Comedy & Action* are now included in the *Grand Total* twice.

6   Filter the individual *Drama*, *Comedy* and *Action* fields so that they are no longer shown or included in the *Grand Total*.

Because the *Field Headers* are currently switched off, you cannot apply a filter.

1. Click: PivotTable Tools→Analyze→Show→Field Headers.

2. The *Genre* field header appears in cell A4.

	A	B
4	Genre ▼	Sum of Total
5	Action	37,411.40

3. Click the drop-down arrow to the right of cell A4.

4. Remove the individual *Drama*, *Comedy* and *Action* items by un-checking their check boxes.

5. Click: *OK*.

    The *Grand Total* is now correct.

	A	B
11	Thriller	5,514.95
12	Drama, Comedy & Action	142,123.03
13	**Grand Total**	**222,786.80**

7   Save your work as *Transactions-15*.

Lesson 8-18: Group by text

In *Lesson 8-17: Add a calculated item to a pivot table,* you used a calculated item to show a group total for the *Action, Comedy & Drama* genres.

Another solution to this requirement would be to create a *group* for these three genres. The pivot table could then show group totals.

You'll push things a little further in this lesson by placing each of the genres into three groups:

- Action, Comedy & Drama
- Crime, Biography & Fantasy
- Adventure, Sci Fi, Thriller & Animation

1 Open *Transactions-15* from your sample files folder (if it isn't already open).

2 Remove all of the existing fields and filters from the pivot table (including the calculated item added in the last lesson).

You'll often want to remove all items from your pivot table to start again. To do this, click:

PivotTable Tools→Analyze→Actions→Clear→Clear All

3 Add the following fields to the pivot table.

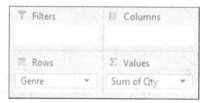

4 Format the *Sum of Qty* field so that it shows 0 decimal places and a comma separator for thousands.

1. Right-click anywhere in column B within the pivot table.

2. Click *Number Format…* from the shortcut menu.

3. Click the *Number* category.

4. Set 0 decimal places with a thousand separator.

5. Click the *OK* button.

5 Add a group for the *Action, Comedy* and *Drama* genres.

1. Click on the *Drama* field in column A (cell A11).

2. Hold down the **<Ctrl>** key and then click on the *Comedy* (A9) and *Action* (A5) fields in column A.

Cells A11, A9 and A5 are now selected.

3. Right-click on any of the selected cells and click *Group* from the shortcut menu.

The fields are grouped:

Transactions-15

note

You can also group selected fields using the Ribbon

The right-click method is usually the fastest way to group but you can also use the Ribbon command:

PivotTable Tools→Analyze→ Group→Group Selection

6 Change the *Genre2* label to: **Category** and the *Group1* label to: **Action, Comedy & Drama**

The default names are not very descriptive. Single-click (be careful not to double-click) on each field (cells A4 and A5) and then type in the new labels.

Category	Genre	Sum of Qty
⊟Action, Comedy & Drama	Action	4,699
	Comedy	4,747

7 Create the *Crime, Biography & Fantasy* group and the *Adventure, Sci Fi, Thriller & Animation* group.

Do this in exactly the same way (this time you will select the *Genres* in column B).

8 AutoSize column A.

Your pivot table should now look like this:

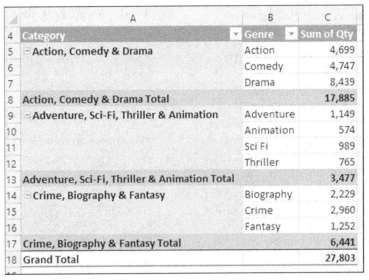

Category	Genre	Sum of Qty
⊟Action, Comedy & Drama	Action	4,699
	Comedy	4,747
	Drama	8,439
Action, Comedy & Drama Total		17,885
⊟Adventure, Sci-Fi, Thriller & Animation	Adventure	1,149
	Animation	574
	Sci Fi	989
	Thriller	765
Adventure, Sci-Fi, Thriller & Animation Total		3,477
⊟Crime, Biography & Fantasy	Biography	2,229
	Crime	2,960
	Fantasy	1,252
Crime, Biography & Fantasy Total		6,441
Grand Total		27,803

Notice how Excel has automatically added subtotals for each group.

9 Collapse all categories.

This was covered in: *Lesson 8-2: Create a grouped pivot table report.*

Your pivot table should now look like this:

Category	Genre	Sum of Qty
⊞Action, Comedy & Drama		17,885
⊞Adventure, Sci-Fi, Thriller & Animation		3,477
⊞Crime, Biography & Fantasy		6,441
Grand Total		27,803

10 Save your work as *Transactions-16.*

note

Excel automatically adds a collection of date related fields

In: *Lesson 8-4: Understand the pivot table data cache,* you learned that a pivot table accesses values stored in its data cache.

In this lesson the data cache is created from the Excel table called *Data* in the *Data* worksheet. This data only has an *Order Date* (in column B).

In: *Lesson 3-7: Understand date serial numbers,* you learned that date serial numbers can contain only a time or both a time and a date.

When the data cache is created Excel doesn't only store the *Order Date* field. It also pre-computes subtotals for seven different values:

Seconds, Minutes, Hours, Days, Months, Quarters and *Years.*

This set of date/time fields are added according to a set of rules.

1. If the source data spans less than one year, Excel will automatically add the *Year* and *Month* fields.

2. If the source data spans more than one year, Excel will automatically add the *Year, Month* and *Quarter* fields (as it did in this lesson).

3. If the data only contains time values, Excel will automatically add the *Seconds, Minutes* and *Hours* fields.

Lesson 8-19: Group by date

Out of all of the skills covered in my classroom *Expert Skills* course, this is surely the star of the show.

Excel's ability to summarize transactional data by daily, monthly, quarterly and yearly totals is extremely difficult to achieve without a pivot table.

1   Open *Transactions-16* from your sample files folder (if it isn't already open).

2   Remove all of the existing fields from the pivot table.

Click:

PivotTable Tools→Analyze→Actions→Clear→Clear All

3   Add the following fields to the pivot table.

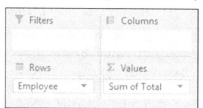

Total sales are now shown for each employee.

	A	B	C
4	Employee	Sum of Total	
5	Anderson,Jane	8833.4	
6	Armstrong,Dan	7880.51	

4   Add the *Order Date* field to the *Columns* pane.

When you do this something unusual happens:

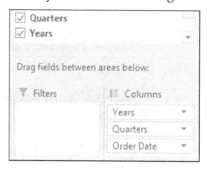

Notice that Excel has created two extra fields: *Quarters* and *Years* (see sidebar for more information about this feature). You can see that the fields are collapsed to show the total sales figure for each year:

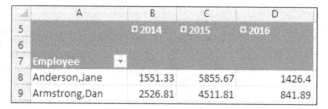

	A	B	C	D
5		2014	2015	2016
6				
7	Employee			
8	Anderson,Jane	1551.33	5855.67	1426.4
9	Armstrong,Dan	2526.81	4511.81	841.89

Transactions-16

https://thesmartmethod.com

note

Problems when grouping pivot tables that share the same data source

In: *Lesson 8-4: Understand the pivot table data cache*, you learned that pivot tables obtain their values from a *pivot table data cache* and not from the original data source.

If you create two pivot tables (in the same workbook) that use the same data source (in this lesson the data source is the *Data* table on the *Data* worksheet), Excel will only create one *pivot table data cache* and share it between the two pivot tables.

Normally this is exactly what you want, as it will result in a lower file size. Unfortunately, this leads to a problem with grouping.

Suppose that you want to create two pivot tables, one showing sales grouped by *Month* and the second showing sales grouped by *Year*. Unfortunately, this won't be possible unless each pivot table has its own *pivot table data cache*. There is a work-around to overcome this problem:

1. Create both pivot tables in your workbook (I'll call this *workbook No. 1*).

2. Leave the workbook open and open a new blank workbook (I'll call this *workbook No 2*).

3. Cut and paste one of the pivot tables in *workbook No.1* into *workbook No. 2*.

4. Copy and paste the pivot table from *workbook No. 2* back again into a new worksheet in *workbook No.1*.

This works because a copy of the PivotTable data cache is copied and pasted along with the pivot table. When the pivot table is pasted back again, the second cache is also pasted.

If you expand each year you can also see totals for each quarter.

Sum of Total	Years	Quarters	Order Date	
	⊟ 2014	⊟ 2015		
	⊟ Qtr4	⊟ Qtr1	⊟ Qtr2	⊟ Qtr3
Employee				
Anderson,Jane	1551.33	2649.27	691.74	1169.35
Armstrong,Dan	2526.81	1714.41	435.63	875.8

You can see that the data only has sales for the fourth quarter of 2014 but has sales for all four quarters in 2015.

Expanding the quarters will display the total for each *Month*.

5 Remove the *Years* and *Quarters* fields from the Columns pane.

You can now see sales rolled up into monthly totals.

Employee	Jan	Feb	Mar
Anderson,Jane	1018.66	632.57	2424.44
Armstrong,Dan	244.03	790.71	1521.56

This seems quite useful at first until you realize that the monthly totals include all years. For example, the *March* totals are the combined sales figures for *March 2015* and *March 2016*.

When you group by *Months* it is really important that you also group by *Years*.

6 Show monthly sales for each employee by *Months* and *Years*.

1. Right-click on any of the months shown in row 5.

2. Click *Group* from the shortcut menu.

   The *Grouping* dialog appears.

3. Select *Months* and *Years*.

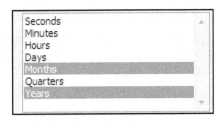

4. Click the *OK* button.

   The pivot table is now grouped by *Year* and by *Month*.

Sum of Total	Years	Order Date		
	⊟ 2014			⊟ 2015
Employee	Oct	Nov	Dec	Jan
Anderson,Jane		1525.91	25.42	495.1
Armstrong,Dan		1453.87	1072.94	244.03
Ashe,Lucille	675.38	281.54	624.23	643.08

7 Save your work as *Transactions-17*.

Lesson 8-20: Group by numeric value ranges

1   Open *Employee Age Profile-1* from your sample files folder.

2   Convert the range A3:C27 into a table named **Data**.

In Excel 365, it is best practice to base pivot tables upon tables (you would have used a named range in pre 2007 Excel versions).

1. Click anywhere in the range A3:C27.

2. Click: Insert→Tables→Table.

3. Click the *OK* button.

4. Type the name **Data** into:

Table Tools→Design→Properties→Table Name

3   Rename the worksheet tab from *Sheet1* to: **Data**

4   Create a pivot table from the *Data* table.

1. Click anywhere inside the table.

2. Click: Insert→Tables→PivotTable.

3. Click the *OK* button.

5   Rename the pivot table worksheet tab to: **Age Profile**

6   Add the following fields to the pivot table:

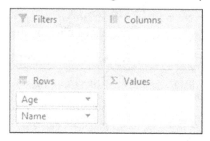

(The order is important. *Age* must come before *Name).*

The pivot table now groups employees by age.

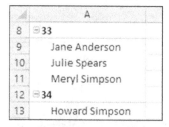

Note that some of the employees may have got a little older by the time you read this book.

Where two or more employees are of the same age, they are grouped together.

The challenge for this lesson will be to group employees into different age bands.

Employee Age Profile-1

7   Group the pivot table into the age bands: *Under 40, 40-49, 50-60* and *Over 60.*

1.   Right-click any of the ages in column A (for example: cell A6).

2.   Click *Group* from the shortcut menu.

The *Grouping* dialog is displayed.

3.   Type the following values into the dialog:

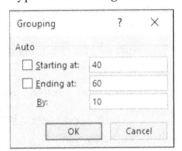

This tells Excel to group into the ages:

- Less than 40

- Over 60

- Between 40 and 60 in bands of 10 years

4.   Click the *OK* button.

Ages are now grouped as defined.

When data is grouped in this way it is sometimes referred to as a *frequency distribution.*

8   Change the *Row Labels* label in cell A3 to: **Age Group**

1.   Click once on cell A3.

2.   Type **Age Group** into the cell.

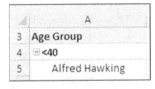

3.   Press the **<Enter>** key.

9   Save your work as *Employee Age Profile-2.*

Lesson 8-21: Show row data by percentage of total rather than value

In this lesson, you will discover which genres each employee is best at selling. This will enable the company to allocate sales leads for each genre to the most competent salesperson in that genre.

This time you're not interested in total sales but the percentage sales by genre for each employee.

As a bonus, you'll see the percentage market share of each genre.

1   Open *Transactions-17* from your sample files folder (if it isn't already open).

2   Remove all of the existing fields and filters from the pivot table.

You'll often want to remove all fields and filters from your pivot table to start again. To do this, click:

PivotTable Tools→Analyze→Actions→Clear→Clear All

3   Add the following fields to the pivot table.

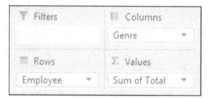

4   Format the *Sum of Total* field to show two decimal places and thousand separators.

This was covered in: *Lesson 8-1: Create a one-dimensional pivot table report* from *a table.*

Sales are now shown for every employee and for every genre.

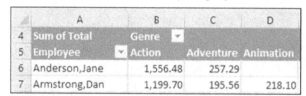

	A	B	C	D
4	Sum of Total	Genre		
5	Employee	Action	Adventure	Animation
6	Anderson,Jane	1,556.48	257.29	
7	Armstrong,Dan	1,199.70	195.56	218.10

5   Show sales values as a percentage of each row total.

1.   Right-click on any of the numerical values in the pivot table.

2.   Click *Value Field Settings* from the shortcut menu.

The *Value Field Settings* dialog is displayed.

Transactions-17

3. Click the *Show Values As* tab.

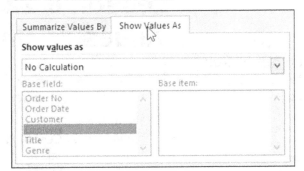

4. Select *% of Row Total* from the *Show values as* drop down list.

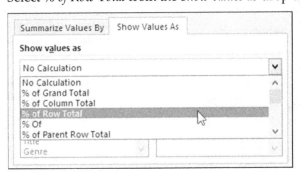

5. Click the *OK* button.

Values are now shown as a percentage of each employee's sales:

	A	B	C	D	E	F	G	H	I	J
5	Employee	Action	Adventure	Animation	Biography	Comedy	Crime	Drama	Fantasy	Sci Fi
6	Anderson,Jane	17.62%	2.91%	0.00%	11.84%	20.93%	7.29%	31.54%	2.37%	3.15%
7	Armstrong,Dan	15.22%	2.48%	2.77%	8.45%	17.37%	11.47%	37.42%	4.09%	0.09%
8	Ashe,Lucille	15.71%	3.84%	2.08%	4.38%	16.87%	12.97%	25.47%	9.70%	1.06%
9	Bell,Stephen	18.34%	7.63%	0.74%	4.52%	18.70%	11.55%	25.14%	7.44%	5.15%
10	Bradshaw,John	16.29%	3.08%	2.20%	10.19%	16.04%	16.16%	29.57%	0.55%	3.69%
11	Carrey,Julia	17.39%	6.06%	0.64%	12.38%	21.05%	12.70%	24.52%	2.81%	1.65%
12	Davis,Charles	23.79%	0.61%	3.50%	5.18%	13.56%	6.44%	31.48%	4.57%	9.17%
13	Diamond,Elizabeth	18.59%	3.62%	5.25%	12.66%	17.38%	5.16%	26.32%	4.21%	4.29%
14	Goodman,Paul	14.57%	3.94%	0.98%	7.17%	15.31%	7.75%	40.02%	4.26%	1.55%
15	Hawking,Alfred	25.86%	4.03%	2.38%	4.57%	16.36%	9.44%	29.77%	2.66%	4.71%
16	Hicks,Michael	12.18%	8.07%	0.00%	9.71%	16.53%	14.92%	31.40%	5.83%	0.00%
17	Jennings,John	16.77%	2.55%	1.76%	4.93%	14.76%	16.04%	31.26%	6.15%	3.35%
18	Lee,Frank	14.50%	2.83%	0.00%	9.12%	19.30%	9.45%	31.79%	9.46%	1.98%
19	Manning,Marilyn	13.37%	7.09%	1.02%	12.65%	15.28%	12.47%	30.31%	3.18%	4.64%
20	Newhart,Anna	16.43%	6.29%	2.81%	3.76%	16.41%	11.90%	23.36%	6.70%	8.56%
21	Putin,Julia	11.78%	3.39%	0.00%	3.48%	25.05%	9.91%	38.17%	4.34%	2.19%
22	Richards,Andy	11.76%	5.50%	0.90%	9.88%	19.06%	17.14%	22.99%	5.47%	3.67%
23	Sagan,Jessica	24.79%	2.32%	7.58%	3.31%	23.17%	4.24%	28.64%	1.90%	3.77%
24	Silverstone,Gloria	21.40%	3.56%	1.02%	9.23%	8.15%	7.86%	23.46%	11.18%	2.98%
25	Simpson,Howard	19.86%	4.61%	1.96%	4.16%	10.04%	10.65%	32.38%	8.44%	4.25%
26	Simpson,Meryl	15.52%	4.01%	3.50%	6.30%	13.78%	6.88%	37.61%	3.41%	5.72%
27	Spears,Julie	9.66%	2.66%	1.02%	11.43%	17.98%	17.54%	32.40%	5.23%	0.00%

You can see at a glance that *Alfred Hawking* does very well with sales in the *Action* genre, and that *Paul Goodman* is our star performer in the *Drama* genre.

You should keep *Michael Hicks* and *Julie Spears* away from *Science Fiction* sales.

6 Save your work as *Transactions-18.*

note

Produce a well formatted report from a pivot table using paste values

Many users work around the formatting limitations of pivot tables like this:

1. Select and copy the cells that you need from the pivot table.

2. Select the destination cell.

3. Click: Home→Clipboard→ Paste Special→ Values and number formats.

4. Format the pasted values in any way you wish.

This works but makes it impossible to refresh the well formatted version.

Lesson 8-22: Use pivot table values in simple formulas

1   Open *Central Park Temperature-1* from your sample files folder (if it isn't already open).

This file contains the average monthly temperatures recorded in New York's Central Park between 2010 and 2015 along with a pivot table that shows the temperatures for April, May and June side by side for the years 2014 and 2015:

	A	B	C
3	Sum of Avg Temp F	Column Labels ⫧	
4	Row Labels ⫧	2014	2015
5	Apr		52.3 54.3
6	May		64 68.5
7	Jun		72.5 71.2

With the skills you have learned in this session so far, you should have no difficulty understanding how this pivot table was created.

It took me less than 30 seconds to create this pivot table, demonstrating the amazing ability of pivot tables to quickly summarize data. It will not, however, win any design competitions.

2   Type: **Increase/Decrease** into cell D4.

3   Add a formula to cell D5 to show the increase/decrease in temperature for each month.

The automatic insertion of GETPIVOTDATA functions confuses and irritates many Excel users because most Excel users would do this:

1.   Click in cell D5.

2.   Press the equals sign: **<=>**

3.   Click on cell C5.

4.   Press the minus key **<->**

5.   Click on cell B5.

6.   Press the **<Enter>** key.

7.   AutoFill cell D5 down to cell D7.

Here's the result of the above actions:

	A	B	C	D
3	Sum of Avg Temp F	Column Labels ⫧		
4	Row Labels ⫧	2014	2015	Increase/Decrease
5	Apr		52.3 54.3	2
6	May		64 68.5	2
7	Jun		72.5 71.2	2

If you examine the formula in cell D5 you'll understand why the calculations return incorrect values. You thought you were asking Excel to create the very simple formula:

=C5-B5

Central Park Temperature-1

Instead, Excel has created a complex formula in all three cells:

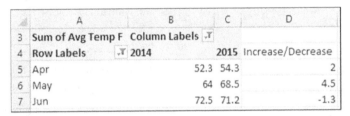

```
=GETPIVOTDATA("Avg Temp F",$A$3,"Month",4,"Years",2015)-GETPIVOTDATA("Avg Temp F",$A$3,"Month",4,"Years",2014)
```

This is an odd thing for Excel to do, as it is inconsistent with the way that Excel normally behaves when creating a formula.

If you really wanted to switch off this behaviour you can do so in the Excel options (see sidebar). But I'd encourage you to leave it switched on.

In: *Lesson 8-22: Use pivot table values in simple formulas,* you'll discover that you can make good use of the GETPIVOTDATA function to make your formulas more resilient to changes in the pivot table layout.

Here's how you can use simple formulas in the above scenario:

1. Delete any formulas in cells D5:D7.

2. Type **=C5-B5** (using the keyboard and not the mouse) into cell D5 (or the formula bar).

3. AutoFill cell D5 down to cell D7.

	A	B	C	D
3	Sum of Avg Temp F	Column Labels ⊤		
4	Row Labels ⊤	2014	2015	Increase/Decrease
5	Apr	52.3	54.3	2
6	May	64	68.5	4.5
7	Jun	72.5	71.2	-1.3

4. Use simple formulas to populate the *Simple Formula Method* range on the *Formatted Report* worksheet.

   1. Delete column D from the *TemperaturePivotTable* worksheet.

   2. Select the *Formatted Report* worksheet.

   3. Enter this formula into cell C7:

   ```
   =TemperaturePivotTable!B5
   ```

   This formula retrieves the value of cell B5 from the *TemperaturePivotTable* worksheet.

   4. AutoFill this formula across to cell D7 and down to cells C8:D9.

   The values from the pivot table are displayed:

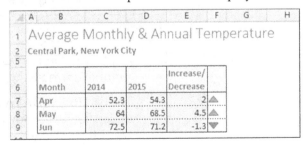

	A	B	C	D	E	F	G	H
1		Average Monthly & Annual Temperature						
2		Central Park, New York City						
5								
6		Month	2014	2015	Increase/Decrease			
7		Apr	52.3	54.3	2 ▲			
8		May	64	68.5	4.5 ▲			
9		Jun	72.5	71.2	-1.3 ▼			

   The table's cells now reference the cell address of the relevant pivot table's cells. It you refresh the pivot table, the values in the formatted report will also update.

5. Save your work as *Central Park Temperature-2.*

note

I really don't like GETPIVOTDATA, how can I switch it off?

Many users do not like the way that Excel automatically inserts GETPIVOTDATA functions when they reference cells within a pivot table.

Students in my classes often ask how they can switch this feature off.

Don't switch it off just yet as you'll be using this feature in the next lesson: *Lesson 8-23: Use the GETPIVOTDATA function.*

If, after completing this lesson, you decide that you would rather Excel didn't automatically insert GETPIVOTDATA functions here's how to switch the feature off:

Uncheck the checkbox:

File→Options→Formulas→ Working with formulas→ Use GetPivotData functions for PivotTable references

There's also a way of doing exactly the same thing from the ribbon:

1. Click inside the pivot table to activate it.

2. Click: PivotTableTools→ Analyze→ Pivot Table→Options (drop-down arrow)→ Generate GetPivotData.

note

A value must be visible on the screen for GETPIVOTDATA to work

If you filter a pivot table, or change it in some other way so that a value is no longer visible, the GETPIVOTDATA function will return an error.

Lesson 8-23: Use the GETPIVOTDATA function

In: *Lesson 8-22: Use pivot table values in simple formulas,* you worked with this pivot table:

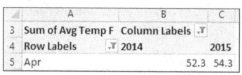

In the previous lesson you used simple formulas to reference the correct cell addresses in the pivot table (for example =B5 was used to return the temperature in April 2014).

Unfortunately, there's a problem with this approach. When a pivot table is filtered, cell addresses move. For example, if I were change the filter to also show 2013 temperatures in the pivot table the pivot table would look like this:

Cell B5 now points to the temperature in April 2013 instead of April 2014, making my formatted report invalid.

To avoid this type of error you can use the GETPIVOTDATA function to make the formulas resilient to pivot table layout changes.

1   Open *Central Park Temperature-2* from your sample files folder.

2   Automatically create a GETPIVOTDATA function that will return the correct pivot table value to cell C14 in the *Formatted Report* worksheet.

   1.   Click in cell C14 on the *Formatted Report* worksheet and press the equals key: **<=>**

   2.   Select the *TemperaturePivotTable* worksheet.

   3.   Click in cell B5 and press the **<Enter>** key.

      A GETPIVOTDATA function is created in cell C14 on the *FormattedReport* worksheet.

```
=GETPIVOTDATA("Avg Temp F",TemperaturePivotTable!$A$3,"Month",4,"Years",2014)
```

3   Adjust the GETPIVOTDATA arguments so that they will AutoFill correctly.

The GETPIVOTDATA function created by Excel is quite difficult to understand. As with all complex functions, things become a lot easier if you launch the function arguments dialog.

   1.   Click in cell C14 on the *FormattedReport* worksheet to make it the active cell.

Central Park Temperature-2

   2.   Click the *Insert Function* button on the left of the formula bar. *fx*

note

The GETPIVOTDATA function works in a different way in regular and OLAP pivot tables

Later, in: *Lesson 11-7: Understand OLAP pivot tables*, you'll learn about a new type of pivot table (introduced in Excel 2013) called an *OLAP pivot table*.

In order to maintain as much similarity as possible between regular pivot tables and OLAP pivot tables, the GETPIVOTDATA function is available in both, but the arguments work in a slightly different way.

An OLAP pivot table also supports a new function that really makes the GETPIVOTDATA function obsolete.

In: *Lesson 11-20: Use the CUBEVALUE function to query a data model*, you'll learn about the new CUBEVALUE function that allows you to bypass an OLAP pivot table entirely and access data directly from the OLAP pivot table's cache.

When you understand how OLAP pivot tables work, you'll realize that the CUBEVALUE function offers a better solution to the problem (solved in this lesson) if you use an OLAP (rather than regular) pivot table.

3. The *Function Arguments* dialog appears:

Data_field	`Avg Temp F`	↥	= `Avg Temp F`
Pivot_table	TemperaturePivotTable!$A$3	↥	= `Sum of Avg Temp F`
Field1	`Month`	↥	= `Month`
Item1	4	↥	= 4
Field2	`Years`	↥	= `Years`
Item2	2014	↥	= 2014

Things are now very easy to understand. The function is returning the *Avg Temp F* value displayed at the intersection of month 4 (April) in the *Month* column and 2014 in the *Years* row displayed in the pivot table.

The pivot table as a whole is identified by any cell within the pivot table (in this case cell A3 is used, but any cell within the pivot table would work).

It should be clear that, no matter how the pivot table layout is changed, the correct result will always be returned. It is vital, however, that the values are always displayed somewhere on the pivot table, otherwise the function will return an error.

4. Fix the formula so that it will AutoFill correctly.

There's a small problem with the *Item1* and *Item2* values. They will not autofill correctly. Make the following small changes:

Field1	`Month`	↥	= `Month`
Item1	MONTH($B14)	↥	= 4
Field2	`Years`	↥	= `Years`
Item2	C$13	↥	= 2014

$B14 and C$13 are mixed cell references (mixed cell references are covered in depth in the *Essential Skills* book in this series). They mean "always look in column B but adjust the row" and "always look in row 13 but adjust the column".

The month value (the *Item1* argument) is returned using the MONTH function (using the month shown in column B as the function's argument).

The MONTH function works because the months shown in column B are actually date serial numbers formatted as months (you learned about date serial numbers in: *Lesson 3-7: Understand date serial numbers*). The year value (the *Item2* argument) is simply obtained from the year value in row 13.

5. Click the *OK* button.

4 AutoFill the GETPIVOTDATA function across to cell D14 and down to cells C15:D16.

5 Test the formatted reports for resilience when the *Year* filter is changed.

Click the *Column Labels* filter button on the pivot table and change the filter to also display 2013 temperatures. Notice that the *GETPIVOTDATA method* formatted report still shows the correct values while the *Simple Formula Method* formatted report now shows incorrect values.

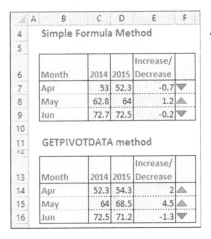

6 Save your work as *Central Park Temperature-3*.

note

Regular charts vs pivot charts

There are two reasons why you might prefer a regular chart to a pivot chart:

1. A worksheet containing a pivot chart also contains the source data, pivot table data cache and a pivot table. This can result in a very large file size.

2. When you distribute a pivot chart you also give the recipient all of the source data that may contain confidential information.

If you prefer a regular chart instead, follow the instructions in: *Lesson 8-13: Understand pivot table report layouts (sidebar)* to export the required values from the pivot table and then create a regular chart from this data.

You may also consider pasting a picture of the pivot chart into a different workbook. To do this, *Copy* the pivot chart and then *Paste Special* as a picture.

Lesson 8-24: Create a pivot chart from a pivot table

Excel is one of the world's most powerful charting tools. Every aspect of charting is covered in the *Essential Skills* book in this series, where a whole session (28 lessons) covers everything there is to know about Excel charts.

This *Expert Skills* book assumes that you already understand normal Excel charts.

When you create a pivot chart from a pivot table, it is important to realize that the chart always matches the data shown in the pivot table.

1   Open *Transactions-18* from your sample files folder (if it isn't already open).

2   Remove all of the existing fields and filters from the pivot table.

Click: PivotTable Tools→Analyze→Actions→Clear→Clear All.

3   Add the following three fields to the pivot table.

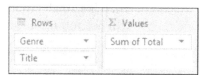

4   Filter the pivot table so that sales are only shown for the *Adventure*, *Animation* and *Sci-Fi* genres.

You learned how to do this in: *Lesson 8-5: Apply a simple filter and sort to a pivot table.*

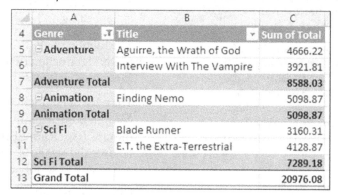

	A	B	C
4	Genre	Title	Sum of Total
5	Adventure	Aguirre, the Wrath of God	4666.22
6		Interview With The Vampire	3921.81
7	Adventure Total		8588.03
8	Animation	Finding Nemo	5098.87
9	Animation Total		5098.87
10	Sci Fi	Blade Runner	3160.31
11		E.T. the Extra-Terrestrial	4128.87
12	Sci Fi Total		7289.18
13	Grand Total		20976.08

5   Collapse the outline so that only the totals are shown.

You learned how to do this in: *Lesson 8-2: Create a grouped pivot table report.*

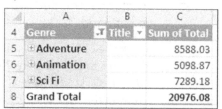

	A	B	C
4	Genre	Title	Sum of Total
5	+Adventure		8588.03
6	+Animation		5098.87
7	+Sci Fi		7289.18
8	Grand Total		20976.08

Transactions-18

note

Advantages of placing charts on chart sheets

In this lesson you embed a chart within an existing worksheet.

While this is sometimes what you want, most of the time you'll want to place your chart into a dedicated *Chart Sheet*. This provides the following advantages:

- They are easier to find, as you can give each sheet a meaningful name.

- They are easier to view, as the chart normally takes up the entire screen. You can re-size a chart on a chart sheet but this isn't often done.

- They are easier to print, as you can simply click the sheet tab and print. You can also print an embedded chart in isolation, but to do so you must first find and activate the chart.

Advantages of embedding charts within worksheets

- You are able to print a chart and worksheet data on the same page.

If you have no need to print worksheet data alongside your chart, it is better to place your charts on chart sheets.

Here's how to move the chart to its own sheet:

1. Click on the chart to activate it.

2. Click: PivotChart Tools→ Design→Location→ Move Chart.

The *Move Chart* dialog appears.

3. Click the *New sheet* option button.

4. Click the *OK* button.

The chart now resides in its own chart sheet.

6   Create a *Clustered Column* pivot chart from the pivot table.

1.   Click anywhere in the pivot table to activate it.

2.   Click: PivotTable Tools→Analyze→Tools→PivotChart.

The *Insert Chart* dialog appears.

3.   Click the *Clustered Column* chart type.

This is usually the default chart type.

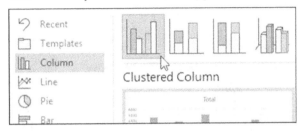

4.   Click the *OK* button.

A clustered column chart is shown embedded in the worksheet.

7   Use the *Expand* and *Collapse* buttons on the chart to show the titles of individual films sold within each genre.

Expand/collapse buttons are shown on any pivot chart that includes grouped fields:

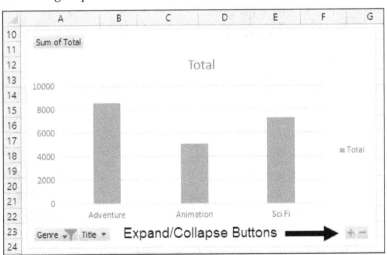

Click the Expand button to show *Titles* in each *Genre*.

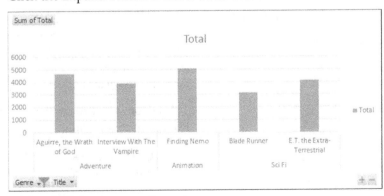

8   Save your work as *Transactions-19*.

Lesson 8-25: Embed multiple pivot tables onto a worksheet

In this lesson, you'll create the following *Sales Summary* worksheet containing three embedded pivot tables:

	A	B	C	D	E	F
1		Sales Summary				
3		Customer ▼	Sales		Employee ▼	Sales
4		Addison-Freelander Screen Agency	17,135.23		Anderson,Jane	8,833.40
5		AV Supplies	15,199.30		Armstrong,Dan	7,880.51
6		Box Office Supplies	22,923.09		Ashe,Lucille	8,755.66
7		Cheapo Cheap DVD's Ltd	20,145.10		Bell,Stephen	11,649.76
8		Cinefocus DVD	22,277.45		Bradshaw,John	9,329.37
9		Classic Films	17,549.80		Carrey,Julia	6,091.91
10		Creative Films	14,637.39		Davis,Charles	6,800.56
11		Lights-Camera-Action Ltd	18,106.20		Diamond,Elizabeth	8,965.29
12		Magic Lantern Classic Film Rental	20,055.78		Goodman,Paul	9,578.01
13		Silver Screen Video	20,757.07		Hawking,Alfred	10,946.28
14		Soft Focus Video Rental	17,870.60		Hicks,Michael	7,091.10
15		Video Flicks International	16,129.79		Jennings,John	11,190.73
16		Grand Total	222,786.80		Lee,Frank	13,488.16
17					Manning,Marilyn	9,064.16
18		Genre ▼	Sales		Newhart,Anna	8,937.66
19		Action	37,411.40		Putin,Julia	8,590.69
20		Adventure	8,588.03		Richards,Andy	8,302.17
21		Animation	5,098.87		Sagan,Jessica	11,004.66
22		Biography	17,174.78		Silverstone,Gloria	8,349.05
23		Comedy	37,614.16		Simpson,Howard	9,370.30
24		Crime	25,212.68		Simpson,Meryl	6,522.80
25		Drama	67,097.47		Spears,Julie	10,683.14
26		Fantasy	11,785.28		Streep,Margaret	14,513.69
27		Sci Fi	7,289.18		West,Chuck	6,847.74
28		Thriller	5,514.95		Grand Total	222,786.80
29		Grand Total	222,786.80			

When several key performance indicators are combined to produce an overview of a business process (in this case Sales) the worksheet is sometimes called a *Dashboard* or *Executive Information System*.

This lesson will also confirm your understanding of many of the skills learned in this session.

1 Open *Transactions-19* from your sample files folder (if it isn't already open).

2 Add a new worksheet and name it: **Summary**

3 Type **Sales Summary** into cell B1.

Transactions-19

4 Apply the *Title* style to cell B1.

Click: Home→Styles→Cell Styles→Titles and Headings→Title.

5 Embed a pivot table starting at cell B3 to show sales value by *Customer*.

1. Click in cell B3.

2. Click: Insert→Tables→PivotTable.

3. Type **Data** into the *Table/Range* box.

4. Click the *OK* button.

5. Check the *Customer* and *Total* fields in the *PivotTable Fields* list.

6 Embed a pivot table starting at cell B18 to show sales value by *Genre*.

7 Embed a pivot table starting at cell E3 to show sales value by *Employee*.

8 Format all values to show two decimal places and thousand separators.

This was first covered in: *Lesson 8-16: Add a calculated field to a pivot table.*

9 Change the *Row Labels* text in cells B3, B18 and E3 to read: **Customer, Genre** and **Employee**

This was first covered in: *Lesson 8-16: Add a calculated field to a pivot table.*

10 Change the *Sum of Total* labels in cells C3, C18 and F3 to read: **Sales**

11 Add a *3 Traffic Lights (Unrimmed)* conditional format to cells C4:C15.

Conditional formatting is covered in depth in the *Essential Skills* book in this series.

1. Select cells C4:C15.

2. Click: Home→Styles→Conditional Formatting→ Icon Sets→3 Traffic Lights (Unrimmed).

12 Add a *Light Blue Data Bar* conditional format to cells C19:C28.

13 Add a *5 Ratings (Icon Set)* conditional format to cells F4:F27.

14 Re-size the column widths to enhance visual appearance.

15 Save your work as *Transactions-20*.

Lesson 8-26: Use slicers to filter multiple pivot tables

Earlier in this session you learned how to use slicers to provide an elegant user interface when filtering pivot tables.

Slicers become even more powerful when used to filter multiple pivot tables (such as the worksheet created in: *Lesson 8-25: Embed multiple pivot tables onto a worksheet*).

In this lesson you'll refine this worksheet to create an overview of sales using slicers to enable the user to filter all of the pivot tables at the same time.

This is a feat that can only be accomplished using slicers. The filter fields that you learned about in: *Lesson 8-6: Use report filter fields* are only capable of filtering a single pivot table.

1   Open *Transactions-20* from your sample files folder (if it isn't already open).

2   Name the pivot tables: **Customer, Employee** and **Genre**

When working with multiple pivot tables it is useful to give each an intuitive name.

   1.   Click on the *Customer* pivot table to activate it.

   2.   Click: PivotTable Tools→Analyze→PivotTable→ PivotTable Name.

   3.   Type **Customer** in the *PivotTable Name* box and press the **<Enter>** key.

   4.   Repeat the process to name the *Employee* and *Genre* pivot tables.

3   Add three slicers that will filter the *Customer* pivot table by *Employee, Customer* and *Genre*.

You learned how to do this in: *Lesson 8-7: Filter a pivot table visually using slicers.*

4   Size and format the slicers so that they provide a compact and attractive user interface.

You learned how to do this in: *Lesson 8-7: Filter a pivot table visually using slicers.*

When you have finished, your user interface should be similar to the screen grab on the facing page.

5   Test your slicers.

Notice that the slicers only affect the *Customer* pivot table. No matter what filter condition you set in the slicers, the values in the *Genre* and *Employee* pivot tables remain unaffected.

6   Connect the slicers to all three pivot tables.

   1.   Click the *Genre* slicer to select it.

   2.   Click: Slicer Tools→Options→Slicer→Report Connections.

Transactions-20

note

How can I stop Excel changing pivot table column widths?

This is caused by a glitch in Excel's *AutoFit* feature.

The easy solution is to switch off AutoFit and size the column widths manually.

To switch off AutoFit:

1. Right-click on each pivot table in turn.

2. Select *PivotTable Options* from the shortcut menu.

3. Click the *Layout & Format* tab.

4. Clear the *Autofit column widths on update* check box.

5. Manually resize each column so that they are wide enough to display their contents correctly.

The *Report Connections* dialog appears.

3. Check the *Employee* and *Genre* check boxes to connect this slicer to all three pivot tables on the *Summary* worksheet.

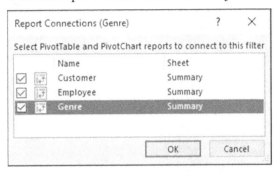

4. Click the *OK* button.

5. Repeat this process for the *Customer* and *Employee* slicers.

7 **Test your slicers.**

Notice that the slicers now work the way you want them to. All three pivot tables are filtered in accordance with the slicer filters that you select.

You may find that the columns are not wide enough to display their values when a filter is applied. See sidebar for a solution to this problem.

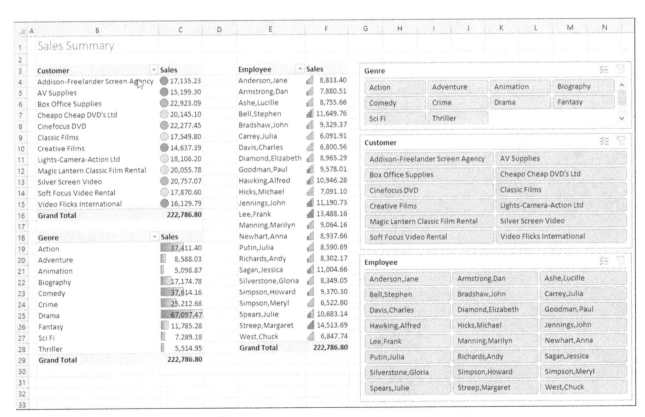

8 Save your work as *Transactions-21*.

© 2020 The Smart Method® Ltd

Session 8: Exercise

1   Open *Film Sales-1* from your sample files folder.

2   Convert the range into a table named *Data*.

3   Create a pivot table from the *Data* table.

4   Add *Row Labels* and *Values* so that your pivot table looks like this:

	A	B	C
3	Row Labels ▾	Sum of Qty	Sum of Total
4	Fedex	6929	55793.38
5	Royal Mail	6606	52965.68
6	TNT	7366	58884.38
7	UPS	6902	55143.36
8	**Grand Total**	**27803**	**222786.8**

5   Re-format the values in the pivot table and change the text in the headers, so that your pivot table looks like this:

	A	B	C
3	Carrier ▾	Units	Cost
4	Fedex	6,929	55,793.38
5	Royal Mail	6,606	52,965.68
6	TNT	7,366	58,884.38
7	UPS	6,902	55,143.36
8	**Grand Total**	**27,803**	**222,786.80**

6   Add a calculated field to calculate the average cost per unit for each carrier formatted to two decimal places with a 1000 comma separator.

	A	B	C	D
3	Carrier ▾	Units	Cost	Cost per Unit
4	Fedex	6,929	55,793.38	8.05
5	Royal Mail	6,606	52,965.68	8.02
6	TNT	7,366	58,884.38	7.99
7	UPS	6,902	55,143.36	7.99
8	**Grand Total**	**27,803**	**222,786.80**	**8.01**

7   Embed a second pivot table starting in cell A10 of the same worksheet that will display sales by studio in an attractive format.

	A	B
10	Studio	▾ Sales
11	20th Century Fox	12,819.76
12	BBC TV	2,891.99
13	Columbia Pictures	11,007.66

8   Save your work as *Film Sales-2*.

Film Sales-1

If you need help
slide the page to
the left ▶

Session 8: Exercise Answers

These are the four questions that students find the most difficult to answer:

Q 7	Q 6	Q 4	Q 2
1. Click in cell A10.	1. Click: PivotTable Tools→Analyze→ Calculations→Fields, Items & Sets→ Calculated Field…	Drag the following fields from the *PivotTable Fields* list to the *Rows* and *Values* lists:	1. Click anywhere inside the range.
2. Click: Insert→Tables→ PivotTable.			2. Click:
3. Type **Data** into the *Table/Range* box.	2. Complete the Calculated field dialog as follows:		Insert→Tables→ Table
4. Click the *OK* button.			3. Click the *OK* button.
5. Drag the following fields from the *PivotTable Fields* list to the *Rows* and *Values* lists:	Name: Cost/Units Formula: = Total/ Qty		4. Click:
	3. Click the *OK* button.	This was covered in: *Lesson 8-3: Understand pivot table rows and columns.*	Table Tools→ Design→Properties→ Table Name
	4. Right-click one of the values in column D.		5. Type **Data** into the *Table Name* box.
	5. Click *Number Format…* from the shortcut menu.		6. Press the **<Enter>** key.
6. Format the values to show two decimal places and a thousand comma separator (as detailed in the question 6 answer).	6. Select the *Number* category.		This was covered in: *Lesson 1-12: Convert a range into a table and add a total row.*
7. Click in cell A10 and type: **Studio**	7. Check the *Use 1000 Separator (,)* check box.		
8. Click in cell B10 and type: **Sales**	8. Click the *OK* button.		
9. Press the **<Enter>** key.	9. Click cell D3 once and type: **Cost per Unit**		
This was covered in: *Lesson 8-3: Understand pivot table rows and columns.*	This was covered in: *Lesson 8-16: Add a calculated field to a pivot table.*		

If you have difficulty with the other questions, here are the lessons that cover the relevant skills:

3   Refer to: *Lesson 8-1: Create a one-dimensional pivot table report from a table.*

5   Refer to: *Lesson 8-1: Create a one-dimensional pivot table report from a table* and *Lesson 8-7: Filter a pivot table visually using slicers.*

Session Nine: 3D Maps

> Regular maps have few surprises: their contour lines reveal where the Andes are, and are reasonably clear. More precious, though, are the unpublished maps we make ourselves, of our city, our place, our daily world, our life; those maps of our private world we use every day.
>
> *Alexander McCall Smith, British writer and professor*
> *(from his book: Love Over Scotland).*

You can use 3D Maps to create stunning video presentations that will amaze, inform, engage and impress your audiences.

The core idea behind 3D Maps is to show visualizations of data upon the surface of a map when data contains geographical locations, but this doesn't begin to describe the huge feature set of this tool.

You can create temporal animations showing how data changes with the passage of time and then position yourself in a "virtual helicopter" above the map to fly your audience around your data in a virtual tour. You are even able to add a narration or musical sound track.

Tours can then be saved in video format, perhaps to publish on YouTube or include inside a PowerPoint presentation. All of this can be done in seconds, with a few clicks of the mouse, and without using any other video editing software.

I can foresee great future demand for 3D Maps skills in the film and TV industries as producers realize the potential of this incredible tool to quickly communicate complex data to audiences in a simple way that anybody can understand.

Session Objectives

By the end of this session you will be able to:

- Understand how 3D Maps use the data model
- Create a simple 3D Map
- Confirm the accuracy of geocoding
- Map using different location fields
- Apply filters to a 3D Map
- Set layer options and customize data cards
- Add a height field to a layer
- Apply different visualization types
- Visualize multiple categories
- Create a visualization with multiple layers
- Add annotations
- Create a video from temporal data
- Set scene options
- Create a tour with multiple scenes

Lesson 9-1: Understand how 3D Maps use the data model

The self-service BI Suite

Since 2010, some versions of Excel (those aimed at enterprise users) were able to install Microsoft's "Power" suite of Business Intelligence (BI) tools. Collectively they are often referred to as the *Self-Service BI suite.*

The suite comprised of four components:

- Power Pivot

- Power Query

- Power Maps

- Power View

Two of these products (*Power Pivot* and *Power Query*) were tools that could only be used by specialized IT staff (with extensive data modeling skills) to create *data models.*

The other two (*Power View* and *Power Maps*) were simple easy-to-learn tools that created visualizations of data within a data model. Excel users could also use a data model as the source data for a pivot table.

The vision behind *self-service BI* was that Excel users with no specialized data modeling skills could make use of the data models created by their IT department to create sophisticated visualizations and reports faster and more easily than was possible with Excel alone.

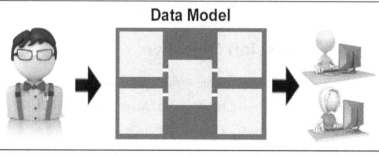

In 2013 the *Power Query* tool was added to Excel and re-named Get & Transform. You'll learn how to use Get & Transform later, in: *Session Ten: Create Get & Transform queries.*

In 2016 *Power Maps* was added to Excel and re-named *3D Maps.* This is the tool that you will learn in this session.

In 2019 *Power Pivot* was added to Excel. You'll learn how to use Power Pivot later, in: *Session Eleven: Power Pivot, Data Modeling, OLAP and Business Intelligence* and *Session Twelve: An introduction to DAX.*

Power View no longer exists as a self-contained product (or add-in) and cannot be added to current versions of Excel. Instead, Power View has evolved into one component of a new desktop and cloud application called *Power BI.*

You can learn and use 3D Maps without learning data modeling

The data modeling skills that are taught in: *Session Eleven: Power Pivot, Data Modeling, OLAP and Business Intelligence* are very challenging to master.

In recognition of this the 3D Maps feature has been designed so that users with no data modeling skills can use 3D Maps by using a single Excel table (or range) as a data source.

Behind the scenes, 3D Maps automatically converts the table (or range) into a one-table data model. The 3D Maps tool then uses this data model as source data.

If you later create advanced data models everything in this session is equally relevant

Data modeling is a very challenging subject that many Excel users may decide not to invest time learning.

If you decide to progress to: *Session Eleven: Power Pivot, Data Modeling, OLAP and Business Intelligence* and *Session Twelve: An introduction to DAX*, you will learn some very advanced data modeling skills.

While well-designed data models are very difficult to create, they are amazingly easy to use. All of the skills you will learn in this session will work in exactly the same way when powered by a hand-crafted multi-dimensional data model.

3D Maps can cause "out of memory" errors

3D Maps needs to hold a data model (that is a duplication of the source data) in your computer's memory.

Data models can require a lot of memory (depending upon the size of the source data).

If you encounter crashes or out-of-memory error warnings while working through this session you will need to consult: *Lesson 11-1: Understand data model memory requirements.* This lesson explains the memory issue (and how to solve this problem) in depth.

important

You must be connected to the Internet in order to use 3D Maps

3D Maps are powered by Microsoft's *Bing Maps* service. Because this service is accessed via the Internet, you cannot create a 3D Map when you are offline.

Lesson 9-2: Create a simple 3D Map

In this lesson you'll create a 3D Map that will show blue squares upon the face of a map. The squares will identify the location of every customer that has made a purchase during 2015.

1   **Open *Sales Summary-1* from your sample files folder and examine the data**.

This workbook contains a large data set showing details of over 16,000 sales made in the year 2015 to customers located all over the USA.

	A	B	C	D	E	F	G
1	Date	Order Number	Customer	Country	State	City	Postal Code
2	01-Jan-15	SO48740	Modular Cycle Systems	US	TX	Austin	78701
3	01-Jan-15	SO48740	Modular Cycle Systems	US	TX	Austin	78701

The data in column A tells you that several items were sold on *1st January 2015*. The inclusion of the date field tells you that this is *temporal data*. *Temporal data* means any data that changes with the passage of time. As you'll see later, in: *Lesson 9-12: Create a video from temporal data*, 3D Maps have some amazing features that visually depict temporal data at different points in time.

Columns B and C identify the Order Number: *S048740* and the Customer: *Modular Cycle Systems*.

Columns D, E, F and G contain geographical location data. Because *Country, State, City* and *Postal Code* are commonly used names for geographical data, 3D Maps will have no difficulty finding the correct geographical location to display on the map for each row. The remaining columns have details for the *Quantity, Price* and *Category* of the products purchased:

	H	I	J	K
1	Qty	Unit Price	Line Total	Category
2	2	$ 469.79	$ 939.59	Bikes
3	3	$ 469.79	$ 1,409.38	Bikes

You can see that the first item ordered was for 2 items at a unit cost of $469.79, making a total price of $939.59. The items ordered were in the category: *Bikes*.

2   **Convert the range into a table named *Sales*.**

You learned how to convert a range into a table in: *Lesson 1-12: Convert a range into a table and add a total row*. You learned how to name a table in: *Lesson 1-18: Name a table and create an automatic structured table reference*.

It would also be possible to create a 3D Map from a range but it is best practice to use a table as source data. By using a table any new rows added to the table in the the future will also used by the 3D Map (when it is refreshed).

3   **Create a 3D Map from the *Sales* table.**

1. Click inside the table.

Sales Summary-1

2. Click: Insert→Tours→3D Map.

3. If you see a dialog asking to enable the *Data Analysis add-ins* click the *Enable* button.

    There will be a short delay as Bing converts the location information contained in your data into longitude and latitude map coordinates.

    An impressive visual of the world (expressed as a globe) then appears.

    Notice that there's a ribbon at the top of the screen and three panes.

    One pane is headed *Tour 1*. This is the *Tour Editor* pane. You'll work with this pane later in: *Lesson 9-14: Create a tour with multiple scenes.*

    The center pane shows a map with a blue square for every city that made a purchase during 2015.

    The right pane shows details about the current Layer. This is the Layer task pane. A layer can be thought of as a transparent layer that sits on top of the map. All of the blue squares are located on this layer. You'll discover more about layers in: *Lesson 9-10: Create a visualization with multiple layers.*

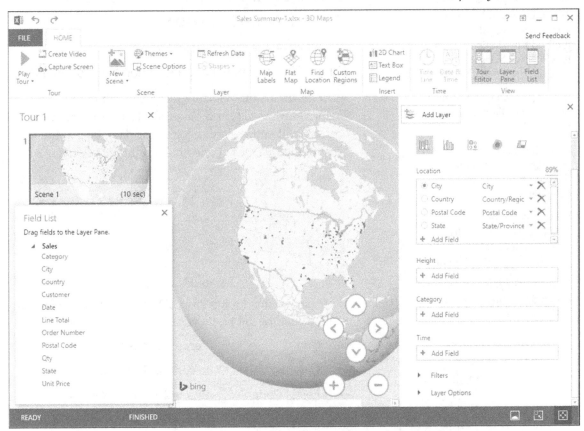

4 Save your work as *Sales Summary-2*

    There's no *Save* button in 3D Maps. When you save a workbook that contains one or more Tours, they are saved with the workbook. You can close the 3D Maps window while working with Excel without losing any changes that you may have made (provided that you save before closing Excel).

trivia

Money sometimes makes things happen

In order for early sailing ships to navigate the world, it was essential to identify the position of the ship when at sea.

Latitude was quite easy to determine (by observing the altitude of the sun, moon or a known star above the horizon).

Determining longitude was a problem that mankind struggled with for centuries.

In 1714 the British government decided that the solution was to offer a reward to any scientist that could solve the problem.

The *Longitude Act* was duly passed into law. The act offered a huge cash prize of 23,000 UK pounds to any scientist who could find a method to establish longitude to at least one degree of accuracy.

23,000 pounds is the equivalent of several million US dollars when adjusted to 2019 values.

John Harrison was 21 years old when the act was passed and devoted his life to solving the problem.

He did eventually succeed (with his H4 sea watch) but was 80 years old before he received his final payment.

Unfortunately, John died at the age of 82 so only had two years to enjoy his reward.

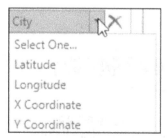

Sales Summary-2

Lesson 9-3: Confirm the accuracy of geocoding

When you first open 3D Maps, place names are converted to points on the map (latitude and longitude). This process is called *geocoding*. The conversion is done (via the Internet) by the *Bing Maps* service.

The geocoding process can fail if your source data contains ambiguous values. For example, there are 235 towns named *San Francisco* in the world. If your data set includes *San Francisco*, then 3D Maps makes a guess and converts the name to the map reference for *San Francisco, California, USA* while your data could really relate to *San Francisco, Mexico*.

For this reason, it is important to confirm that 3D Maps has not incorrectly geocoded any of the locations defined in your source data.

Fortunately, 3D Maps can report any locations that it isn't completely sure of so that you can confirm that all of the guesses are correct.

1   Open *Sales Summary-2* from your sample files folder (if it isn't already open).

2   Open the *Tour 1* tour in the *3D Maps* application.

   1.   Click: Insert→Tours→3D Map.

   2.   Click on the *Open... Tour 1* icon.

3   Check that all fields have been correctly identified.

3D Maps will automatically recognize common column field names (such as *City* and *Country*). To make sure that 3D Maps has correctly identified your geographic data, look at the *Location* pane within the *Layer* task pane (at the right of the screen).

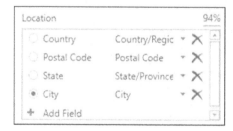

You can see that, in this case, 3D Maps has done a fine job of identifying the data type of each geographic field.

- City   Recognized as *City*.
- Country: Recognized as *Country/Region*.
- Postal Code: Recognized as *Postal Code*.
- State: Recognized as *State/Province*.

Click one of the drop-down arrows to the right of a data type. A list of all valid 3D Maps geographic data types is shown (see sidebar).

Most 3D Maps use *Latitude* and *Longitude* to identify locations. The alternative X and Y coordinates method can be used with a custom

trivia

Before 1884 there were many different prime meridians

If you visit London, there's a wonderful day-trip I'd recommend. You can take a boat trip along the Thames to Greenwich and visit the *Royal Observatory*. There you can see the *Greenwich Meridian* etched into the ground and see John Harrison's H4 Sea Watch (see facing page sidebar). Tourists love to pose for photographs standing astride the meridian.

The Greenwich Meridian is also known as the *Prime Meridian* and defines zero longitude.

The Greenwich Meridian was defined in 1851 and by 1884 over two thirds of all charts and maps were based upon it.

Not everybody agreed that the Greenwich Meridian should be the world standard. Other meridians were used in different countries (often a nation's capital city).

Competing prime meridians included Jerusalem, Rome, Copenhagen, Pisa, Paris, Philadelphia and Washington. This caused widespread confusion.

In 1884 the US government hosted the *International Meridian Conference*. 25 countries sent delegates to finally settle upon a world standard prime meridian.

The Greenwich Meridian was adopted by 22 votes to one. Only San Domingo (now the Dominican Republic) voted against, while France and Brazil abstained.

France continued to use the Paris Meridian for almost three decades after the standard was agreed and only adopted the Greenwich Meridian in 1911.

image. This method will be discussed later, in: *Lesson 9-10: Create a visualization with multiple layers (sidebar)*.

4   Show the *Mapping Confidence* dialog to check that all fields have been correctly geocoded.

Geocoding is the process of converting the geographical data in the fields supplied into latitude and longitude coordinates.

3D Maps provides a confidence rating, letting you know how sure 3D Maps is that the locations have been correctly geocoded. You can see a hyperlink on the top right of the pane advising that 3D Maps is 94% sure that all is well:

Click the 94% hyperlink for more information.

The *Mapping Confidence* dialog is displayed.

Country/Region	State/Province	City	Result
US	FL	Kendall	Kendall, FL
US	NY	Lake George	Lake George, NY
US	NH	Hooksett	Hooksett, NH
US	MO	Jefferson City	Jefferson City, MO
US	NY	New Hartford	New Hartford, NY
US	NH	Tilton	Tilton, NH
US	CO	Westminster	Westminster, CO

A quick review of the locations 3D Maps wasn't sure of shows that all have been correctly geocoded.

If any of these guesses were incorrect, you would have to return to the source data and make corrections. Unfortunately, there is no way to correct badly geocoded locations within 3D Maps itself.

You'll notice that the sample file for this lesson included a *Country* field even though all of the locations are in the US. This wasn't really needed but was done to give 3D Maps as many clues as possible when identifying each location.

5   Close the *Mapping Confidence* dialog.

6   You don't need to save your work as nothing has been changed.

Lesson 9-4: Map using different location fields

The geographic fields provided in the source data for this lesson have four levels of detail: *Country, State, City* and *Postal Code*.

1   Open *Sales Summary-2* from your sample files folder (if it isn't already open).

2   Open the *Tour 1* tour in the *3D Maps* application.

    1.   Click: Insert→Tours→3D Map.

    2.   Click on the *Open… Tour 1* icon.

3   Show a map identifying every state that has been sold to.

At the moment the map is showing every *City* that has at least one sale recorded. You can see that the *City* location field has a selected option button next to it.

Click the *State* option button. A blue spot is now shown on every state that a sale has been made to.

4   Show a flat map (rather than a map shown upon a globe).

Click: Home→Map→Flat Map.

The flat map model used by 3D Maps is a *Mercator Projection* (see sidebar).

5   Display the name upon each state.

Click: Home→Map→Map Labels.

---

note

3D flat maps are created with a Mercator Projection

The flat map displayed by 3D Maps is a *Mercator Projection* (invented by the 16th century Flemish cartographer Gerardus Mercator).

If you wrapped a cylinder of paper around a globe and then projected onto the paper from a light source inside the globe, the result would be a Mercator Projection.

Because the earth is a sphere, distances are not correctly represented on a flat map.

The distortion is most severe at the poles and least severe at the equator. For example, Greenland and Africa seem to be the same size on a Mercator Projection while, in reality, Africa is about fourteen times larger.

Sales Summary-2

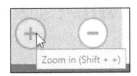

important

Can I control the level of detail shown on the map?

Unfortunately, the only way you can control the level of detail shown on the map is by zooming in and out.

It would be nice to be able to control which artefacts were displayed upon the map (no matter what level of zoom you used).

Perhaps this feature will be added in a future version of 3D Maps.

6   Zoom the map so that only state names are shown.

Notice a set of five buttons at the bottom-right of the map.

Click the plus and minus buttons repeatedly and observe how the map changes.

As you zoom in to the map, the level of detail changes. At first you will only see country names but as you zoom in state names are added, followed by cities. If you zoom in far enough, you'll even see street names.

Zoom so that only state names are shown.

You can now see at a glance the states that have not yet purchased any products (for example, Nebraska and Kansas).

7   Show a map identifying every individual location that has been sold to.

Click: Layer 1→Location→Postal Code.

As each post code has a unique location, you can now see every individual location that a sale has been made to. There are a lot more of them:

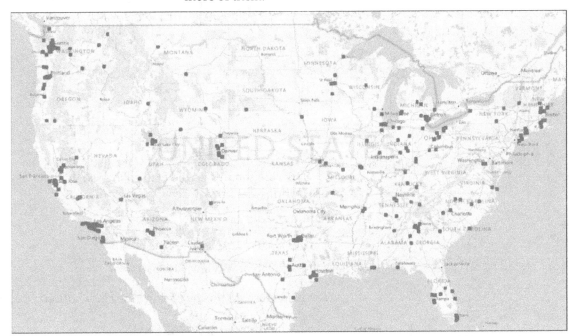

8   Save your work as *Sales Summary-3*.

Lesson 9-5: Apply filters to a 3D Map

In this lesson you'll filter the data points shown on the map so that only data points in Florida are shown.

1 Open *Sales Summary-3* from your sample files folder (if it isn't already open).

2 Open the *Tour 1* tour in the *3D Maps* application.

    1. Click: Insert→Tours→3D Map.

    2. Click on the *Open... Tour 1* icon.

3 Apply a filter so that only data points in Florida are shown.

    1. Click the fly-out menu button shown in front of *Filters* at the bottom of the *Layer* task pane (see sidebar).

    An *Add Filter* button appears.

    2. Click the +*Add Filter* button.

    A field list appears, showing all of the fields in the source data.

    3. Click on the *State* field.

    The *State* field is added as the active filter field. A list showing all states in the data set now appears.

    At present, all states are being shown.

    4. Click the check box next to Florida *(FL).*

    Note that with larger data sets you will not see all filter values in the list (see sidebar facing page).

    The blue squares on the map change so that only locations in Florida (that have purchased any products in 2015) are shown.

4 Hide the *Tour* and *Layer* task panes.

    1. Click: Home →View→Tour Editor.

    2. Click: Home →View→Layer Pane.

    You could also do this by clicking the close button ⊠ at the top right corner of each pane.

Sales Summary-3

important

If there are a large number of unique values in your filter field, you won't see all of them in the list

In this lesson you filtered by *State*.

Because there are only 50 states in the USA, 3D Maps has no difficulty showing all of them in the filter list.

Sometimes you will use a filter value that has hundreds, or even thousands of unique values. In this case it isn't possible for 3D Maps to display all potential filter values in a list.

When 3D Maps is unable to list all values, a subset will be shown in list form with a *Search* box that can be used to find values that do not exist in the list.

For example, if you tried to filter by *City*, the list would be too long and you would see this:

Cities are only listed that begin with A-C. To set a filter for *Orlando*, you'd have to type **Orlando** into the search box.

5 Zoom the map display so that each Florida location is clearly separated.

You can zoom in and out of the display in several ways:

1. Click the plus and minus buttons on the bottom right of the map.

2. Roll the mouse wheel (provided that your mouse has a wheel).

3. Use the plus and minus keys on the keyboard.

4. Double-click on the map to zoom into the map and position the map with the location clicked at the center.

   Unfortunately, it is not possible to zoom out using the double-click method.

6 Position the map so that all of the branches in Florida are visible.

There are two ways to do this:

1. Click and drag the map to re-position it in the map window.

2. Use the arrow keys on the keyboard.

7 Zoom out so that every state is visible on screen.

8 Display the *Tour* and *Layer* task panes.

1. Click: Home → View → Tour Editor.

2. Click: Home → View → Layer Pane.

9 Remove the filter so that data points in all states are shown.

Check the check box next to *All* in the list of states shown in the filter list (see sidebar).

10 Save your work as *Sales Summary-4*.

Lesson 9-6: Set layer options and customize data cards

You can think of a *Layer* as being a sheet of glass laid over the top of the map. Up until now you've only worked with a single layer. Later, in: *Lesson 9-10: Create a visualization with multiple layers,* you'll work with multiple layers stacked on top of each other.

The single layer that you created earlier in this session contains a number of blue squares. Each square marks a single sales location.

If you hover the mouse cursor over any of the location markers, you will see a *data card*:

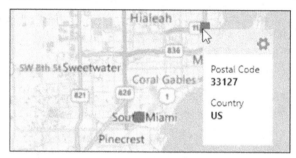

In the example above, the data card simply shows the *Postal Code* and *Country* for the selected location. In this lesson you'll discover how to extensively customize the data card to show other information.

3D Maps also allows you to customize the appearance of each marker. You may want them to be red instead of blue or to be smaller, larger or more transparent. You'll discover how to do all of these things in this lesson.

1   Open *Sales Summary-4* from your sample files folder (if it isn't already open).

2   Open the *Tour 1* tour in the *3D Maps* application.

    1.   Click: Insert→Tours→3D Map.

    2.   Click on the *Open... Tour 1* icon.

3   Change the location field to: *City*

You learned how to do this in: *Lesson 9-4: Map using different location fields.*

4   Zoom in to only show *Florida* locations.

5   Change the color of each location marker to red.

    1.   Click the fly-out button labeled *Layer Options*. This is located at the bottom of the *Layer* task pane.

    2.   Click the *Color* palette and select a red color:

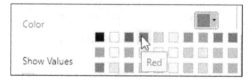

All of the markers on the map are now colored red.

Sales Summary-4

6   Make all of the markers a little smaller so that they are
     clearly separated on the map.

Because some locations are close together, they tend to run into
each other on the map (unless you are using a very large screen).

Adjust the *Size* slider so that no two markers touch each other.

On my own monitor and zoom level, this worked at a size of 70%
but it will be different for you depending upon the size and
resolution of your screen.

7   Reduce the opacity of the markers so that you can still read
     the place names on the map.

If you zoom in to Miami, you'll see that you cannot read the name
as it is obstructed by the marker:

Use the Opacity slider to reduce the opacity of the marker so that it
is reasonably easy to read the text:

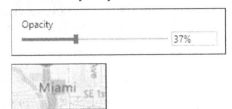

In the above example I've reduced the opacity to 37%.

8   Customize the data card to show the *Postal Code*, *City* and
     State names.

1.   Click: Layer Options→Data Card→Customize at the bottom of
     the *Layer* task pane.

     The *Customize Data Card dialog* is displayed.

2.   Use the +*Add Field* [+ Add Field] and *Remove* [X] buttons to
     add and remove fields so that the dialog looks like the grab
     below. You can also click and drag fields to change their
     position in the list.

3.   Click the *OK* button to dismiss the dialog.

4.   Hover the mouse cursor over any data point to see the new
     data card.

9   Save your work as *Sales Summary-5.*

Lesson 9-7: Add a height field to a layer

The data source for this lesson includes sales values:

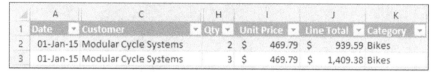

	A	C	H	I	J	K
1	Date	Customer	Qty	Unit Price	Line Total	Category
2	01-Jan-15	Modular Cycle Systems	2	$ 469.79	$ 939.59	Bikes
3	01-Jan-15	Modular Cycle Systems	3	$ 469.79	$ 1,409.38	Bikes

The first row of the data above tells me that *Modular Cycle Systems* purchased two items in the *Bikes* category for a unit price of *$469.79* and a total price of *$939.59*.

3D Maps can summarize these values by geographical location and then display the total sales value (or quantity of units sold) visually as a bar on the layer.

When you use a value field to visually indicate a value, 3D Maps calls the field a *Height* field.

1 Open *Sales Summary-5* from your sample files folder (if it isn't already open).

2 Open the *Tour 1* tour in the *3D Maps* application.

3 Add a *Height* field to visually indicate the total value of sales (SUM of *Line Total*) to each *City* in the *USA*.

1. Click: Layer pane→Height→Add Field.

   A scrolling field list box appears.

2. Click on the *Line Total* field.

   Note that the field added also shows the aggregation method:

   The SUM aggregation method is used by default, but you can use the drop-down button to the right of the field name to show the other aggregation methods that are available:

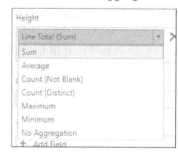

4 Set the layer opacity to 100%.

   You learned how to do this in: *Lesson 9-6: Set layer options and customize data cards.*

Sales Summary-5

Customize Data Card

CHOOSE DATA FIELDS FOR CUSTOM

State

City

Line Total (Sum)

+ Add Field

tip

Three useful buttons

There are three useful buttons on the bottom-right of the 3D Maps window:

The buttons allow you to return to default settings, zoom to selection and to toggle the navigation buttons on and off.

Your *Layer* task pane should now look the same as the one shown in the sidebar.

5 **Zoom out from the map so that only Florida locations are visible.**

You learned how to do this in: *Lesson 9-5: Apply filters to a 3D Map.*

6 **Tilt the map for a more effective visualization.**

Bars are shown that visually represent the total sales for each city. Because you are viewing the map from directly overhead this isn't very effective.

Use the *Tilt and Rotate* buttons at the bottom-right of the map to provide a more effective visualization.

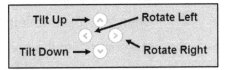

A more intuitive way to tilt and rotate the map is to hold down the **<Alt>** key and then click and drag on the map's surface.

7 **Customize the layer's data card so that it displays the *State*, *City* and *Line Total (Sum)* field values.**

You learned how to do this in: *Lesson 9-6: Set layer options and customize data cards.*

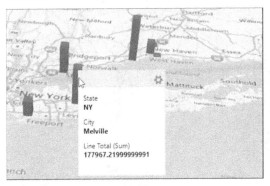

Note the strangely formatted currency value shown in the *Data Card*. This is caused by 3D Maps using a floating point numeric data type internally.

Unfortunately 3D Maps has no option to format the values displayed upon a data card (even rounding in the source data will not work).

In: *Lesson 9-1: Understand how 3D Maps use the data model* you learned that a 3D map uses a data model as the data source. Later, in: *Lesson 11-18: Format values in a data model*, you will learn how to format values within the data model to solve this problem.

8 **Adjust the color, height and opacity of the bars to suit your taste.**

You learned how to do this in: *Lesson 9-6: Set layer options and customize data cards.*

9 **Save your work as *Sales Summary-6*.**

Lesson 9-8: Apply different visualization types

3D Maps supports five different types of visualization.

One layer may only have one visualization type. The maps you have worked with so far have only had one layer. Later, in: *Lesson 9-10: Create a visualization with multiple layers*, you'll work with 3D Maps that have more than one layer. This will allow you show more than one visualization on the same map.

1   Open *Sales Summary-6* from your sample files folder (if it isn't already open).

2   Open the *Tour 1* tour in the *3D Maps* application.

3   Make sure that the *Location* field is set to: *City*.

You learned how to do this in: *Lesson 10 6: Set layer options and customize data cards.*

4   Set the visualization type to: *Clustered Column.*

The visualization type can be selected by clicking on one of the icons at the top of the *Layer* task pane.

Even though there are two column visualizations (*Clustered Column* and *Stacked Column*), both will produce an identical display with the currently selected options.

Later, in: *Lesson 9-9: Visualize multiple categories*, you'll add a *Category* field to the layer and then you'll better understand the difference between the two different column visualization types.

In the above visualization it is easy to see that *Orlando* is generating more sales volume than *Merritt Island*.

5   Set the visualization type to: *Heat Map*

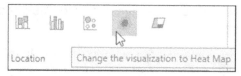

6   Tilt the map so that it is viewed from directly above.

Sales Summary-6

The easiest way to do this is by clicking the *Return the view to its default zoom and pitch levels* button 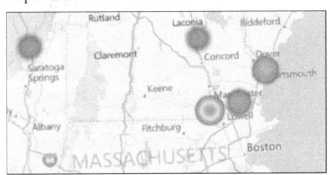 at the bottom-right of the 3D maps window.

The *Heat Map* visualization shows differently colored circles. Blue is the coldest level (lowest sales) and the colors cycle through green, yellow and red as sales increase.

7   Set the visualization type to: *Bubble*

A *Bubble* visualization is similar to a *Heat Map* except that the size of each circle (bubble) indicates the relative sales value of each location.

8   Set the location field to: *State* and the visualization type to: *Region*

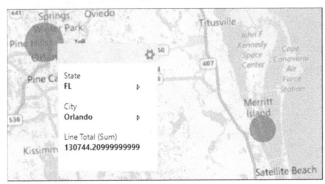

A *Region* visualization indicates sales values by shading in areas. The darkest shaded states indicate the highest sales values. In the above example it is easy to see that *California* is producing a higher sales value than *Arizona.*

9   Save your work as *Sales Summary-7.*

Lesson 9-9: Visualize multiple categories

Up until now, you've only visualized a single data value for each geographical data point.

In this lesson you will visualize multiple data values by displaying *Stacked Column, Clustered Column* and *Pie* charts upon the layer.

1 Open *Sales Summary-7* from your sample files folder (if it isn't already open).

2 Open the *Tour 1* tour in the *3D Maps* application.

3 Replace the layer's *Value* field with the SUM of the *Qty* field.

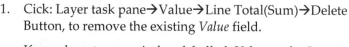

   1. Cick: Layer task pane→Value→Line Total(Sum)→Delete Button, to remove the existing *Value* field.

      If you do not see a window labelled: *Value* on the *Layer* task pane you may have set a different visualization type (see facing page sidebar).

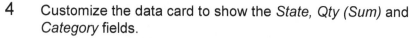

   2. Click: Layer task pane→Value→+ Add Field.

   3. Click on the *Qty* field in the drop-down list.

      The Qty(Sum) field is now displayed in the the *Value* window.

4 Customize the data card to show the *State, Qty (Sum)* and *Category* fields.

   You learned how to do this in: *Lesson 9-6: Set layer options and customize data cards.*

5 Add the *Category* field from the source data as a *Category*.

   The sample data for this lesson has a field called *Category*. This records the product category for each item sold.

   There are only four categories of product: *Accessories, Bikes, Clothing* and *Components.*

   1. Click: Layer task pane→Category→+ Add Field.

      A list appears showing all of the fields in the source data.

   2. Click on the *Category* field.

      The *Category* field is added as the *Category* field for this layer.

6 Select a *Clustered Column* visualization.

   You learned how to do this in: *Lesson 9-8: Apply different visualization types.*

7 Zoom and tilt the map so that it most effectively visualizes sales by *Category.*

   You learned how to do this in: *Lesson 9-7: Add a height field to a layer.*

Sales Summary-7

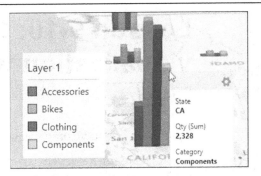

note

The value window is labeled: Value, Size or Height depending upon the current visualization type

3D Maps will show a different label for the Layer task pane's value window depending upon the currently selected visualization type.

Region and *Heatmap* visualization types name the label as: *Value*.

The *Bubble* visualization type names the label as: *Size*.

The *Stacked Column* and *Clustered Column* visualization types name the label as: *Height*.

You are now able to visualize the quantities ordered in different states for each product category.

In this example you can see at a glance that *2328* units in the *Components* category were sold in *California* during 2015.

8   Select the *Stacked Column* visualization.

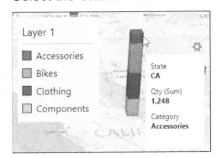

A stacked column visualization shows the same data in a more compact form. Bars are less likely to overlap each other when there is only a single bar.

9   Change the visualization's tilt so that it is viewed from directly overhead.

The easiest way to do this is by clicking the *Return the view to its default zoom and pitch levels* button ▣ at the bottom-right of the 3D Maps window.

Column visualizations are not very effective when viewed from directly overhead.

10   Show a Pie chart visualization to display categorized values for each State.

Change the visualization type to *Bubble*. When you use the *Bubble* visualization with categorized data, pie charts are shown instead of plain bubbles.

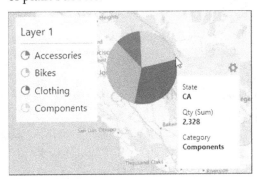

11   Save your work as *Sales Summary-8*.

note

Formatting longitude and latitude values for 3D Maps

There are many ways to format longitude and latitude values but only one is understood by 3D Maps.

The globe is split into 360 equal degrees of longitude. Starting at the *Greenwich Meridian*, longitude is measured in degrees east or west. 3D maps require you to specify *longitude degrees East* as positive values and *longitude degrees West* as negative values.

The globe is also split into 180 equal degrees of *latitude* (each forming a circle called a *parallel*). The central parallel (the equator) represents zero degrees, making the *North Pole* 90 degrees North and the *South Pole* 90 degrees South.

In a similar way to longitude, 3D Maps requires you to specify *latitude degrees North* as positive values and *latitude degrees South* as negative values.

	A	B
1	Longitude	Latitude
2	-96.8892	32.94914

The above example shows correctly formatted coordinates for 3D Maps. You'll often see this formatted as:

32.94914 N 96.8892 W

note

Show/Hide layers

An eyeball icon is shown next to each layer name.

You can click this toggle to hide or show the layer.

US Population-1

Lesson 9-10: Create a visualization with multiple layers

Up until now you've only created visualizations that have a single layer.

If you create several layers (stacked on top of each other) it is possible to create some interesting presentation effects that are not possible with a single-layer visualization.

1   Open *US Population-1* from your sample files folder.

This workbook contains a single worksheet containing a table called: *USPopulation*. This table contains the *Population, Area in Square Miles* and *Population Density* for each major US city.

Notice that nothing has been left to chance for the location of each city, as latitude and longitude coordinates have been defined.

See sidebar for a discussion of how latitude and longitude values need to be defined for 3D Maps to recognize them.

2   Create a 3D Map to show a heat map visualization of population density by city.

1.   Click anywhere in the *USPopulation* table.

2.   Click: Insert→Tours→3D Map.

Notice that Latitude and Longitude have been correctly recognized in the *Location* pane.

3.   Set the *Visualization Type* to: *Heat Map.*

4.   Set the *Location* field to: *City*

5.   Set the *Value* field to: *Population/Square Mile (Sum)*

6.   Click: Home→Map→Flat Map to change the map view from a globe to a flat map.

7.   Click: Home→Map→Map Labels to show names upon the map.

What you have just done demonstrates the incredible power of 3D Maps. In just eight clicks you can clearly visualize which USA cities have the highest population density:

note

Help – one of my layers has disappeared

When you first start to work with multiple layers, you can gain the impression that a layer has disappeared.

This is because layers are shown one beneath the other in the *Layers task pane*. You will often have to scroll down the *Layers task pane* in order to find the other layers.

Layers can also be expanded and collapsed using the triangle shown before the layer name. This is usually easier than scrolling down the task pane.

Expand/Collapse Button

note

It is possible to use the 3D Maps tool without using Bing Maps

Bing Maps converts all location data to longitude and latitude in order to show visualizations on the correct part of a Bing map.

Sometimes you may wish to visualize location-specific data on a custom image instead of a map.

For example, you might want to visually indicate sales values in different shops within a shopping mall.

In this case you would use x and y co-ordinates to refer to pixels in a custom background graphic.

3   Rename the *Layer 1* layer to: **City Population Heat Map**

When working with multiple layers, things are a lot easier if you give each layer a descriptive name.

1. Click the *Rename this layer* icon to the right of the words *Layer 1* at the top of the *Layer* task pane.

2. Type: **City Population Heat Map** into the text box and then press the **<Enter>** key.

4   Create a new layer and name it: **City Population Column**

1. Click the *Add Layer* button at the top of the *Layer* task pane.

2. Click the *Rename this layer* icon to the right of the words *Layer 2* at the top of the *Layer* task pane.

3. Type: **City Population Column** into the text box and then press the **<Enter>** key.

5   Set up the *City Population Column* layer to show *a Clustered Column* visualization of each city's population.

1. Set the *Visualization Type* to: *Clustered Column.*

2. Set the *Location* field to: *City.*

3. Set the *Height* field to: *Population/Square Mile (Sum)*

4. Zoom and tilt the map to most effectively visualize population densities in the *New York* and *Boston* area.

6   Adjust the *Height* and *Thickness* values of the columns and the *Color Scale* and *Radius of Influence* values of the heat map to best visually illustrate population density.

You learned how to do this in: *Lesson 9-6: Set layer options and customize data cards.*

You now have a two-layer visualization that provides more visual information than would be possible with a single layer visualization.

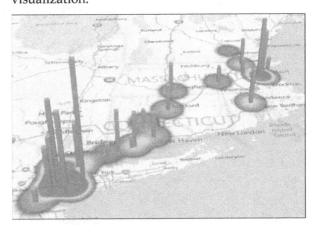

7   Save your work as: *US Population-2.*

Lesson 9-11: Add annotations

In: *Lesson 9-6: Set layer options and customize data cards,* you learned how to control the information that appears on *data cards.*

Data cards appear when you hover the mouse cursor over any of the objects on a 3D Maps layer (see example in sidebar).

Sometimes you may want to add information to a 3D Map that goes beyond what is possible with a data card. In this lesson you'll add *Annotations* to a 3D Map visualization.

Annotations contain information about a specific object on a layer.

1   Open *Popular Names-1* from your sample files folder.

The sample file contains a table called *PopularNames* that lists the most popular male and female names, by state, given to children born in 2014.

	A	B	C
3	State	Male	Female
4	Alabama	William	Ava
5	Alaska	Liam	Emma

You can see that the most popular *Male* name given to children born in 2014 in *Alabama* was *William.*

2   Create a flat map with a *Region* visualization, showing which states had the same most popular *Male* name in 2014.

1. Click anywhere inside the table.

2. Click: Insert→Tours→3D Map.

3. Click: Home→Map→Flat Map.

4. Click the *State* option button in the *Location* pane.

5. Set the *Visualization type* to: *Region.*

6. Set the *Category* field to: *Male.*

7. Zoom into the map to see all of the states except Alaska and Hawaii.

    You can see that states are now colored to show those that shared the same most popular name in 2014.

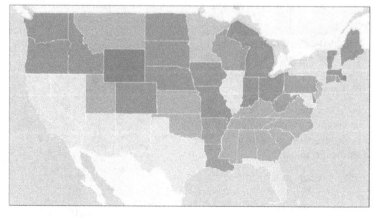

note

You can add an image to an annotation

When you add an annotation to an object, it is possible to add an image instead of custom text or fields.

This opens up a huge range of possibilities as you can create an image that also includes text.

Here's an example:

Popular Names-1

Add Annotation
Choose data fields you would like to add, or type

| Segoe UI | ∨ | 12 | ∨ | **B** | *I* |

TITLE ○ Custom ● State

State: Arizona

DESCRIPTION
○ Custom ● Fields ○ Image

☐ State
☐ Male (Count - Not Blank)
☑ Male

PLACEMENT
○ Left ● Right

note

You can also add text boxes to a map

A text box is similar to an annotation but is not connected to any object. They can be used for titles or freehand notes.

To add a text box to a layer:

1. Right-click on the map.

2. Click: *Add Text Box* from the shortcut menu.

3   Add an annotation to *Arizona* to show the most popular name in this (and similarly colored) states.

1. Right-click on the location of *Arizona* on the map.

2. Click: *Add Annotation* from the shortcut menu.

3. Click the option button to the left of *State* to set the annotation's *TITLE* field to show the state.

4. Set the font size for the *TITLE* field to *12* points.

5. Click on the *Fields* options button underneath *DESCRIPTION* to select a description field to be shown in the annotation.

6. Click the *Male* check box to show the most popular male name in the annotation.

   Note that the *CONTENT PREVIEW* pane now shows how the annotation will look when it is added to the map.

7. Click the *OK* button.

   The annotation is now shown on the map:

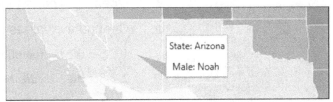

4   Add more annotations, one for each of the nine colors shown on the map.

You may have to select one of the *Left* or *Right* PLACEMENT option buttons at the bottom of the *Add Annotation* dialog to prevent some annotations from overlapping.

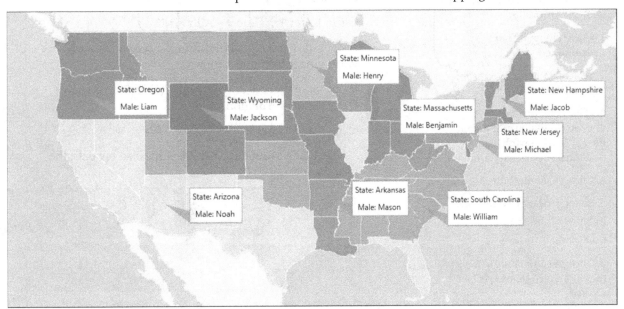

5   Save your work as: *Popular Names-2.*

note

Save a temporal visualization as a movie file

You can use your temporal visualization to create a video in 1080p (full HD), 720p (slightly better than DVD) or 360p (low quality, low file size).

Creating a video uses a lot of processor and memory resources. This means that it can take an older computer a considerable amount of time to render your video.

On a fast, modern i7 computer with solid state hard drive and plenty of memory, it will take less than 30 seconds to create this video in full HD.

If you are using a 32-bit version of Excel with limited memory, it is possible that Excel will be unable to render your video and will report an *Out of Memory* error. If this happens you may find that you are still able to create a video at a lower resolution (the lowest is 360p).

In order to do make a movie of your visualization:

1. Click: Home→Tour→ Create Video.

2. Select the quality you want (1080p, 720p or 360p).

3. Click *Soundtrack Options* if you would like to add a sound file. This will enable you to add music or a voice narration.

4. Click the *Create* button.

5. Select a location to save the video to.

6. Click the *Save* button.

7. Click the *Open* button to view the MP4 video that Excel has created.

Lesson 9-12: Create a video from temporal data

In: *Lesson 9-9: Visualize multiple categories*, you visualized the total sales volume by category during 2015. The total sales volume values were aggregated from over 16,000 individual transactions occurring on different days during the year.

When a data set includes a time dimension, it becomes possible to do some very interesting things with 3D maps. A video presentation can be automatically generated that shows an animation of accumulated sales with the passage of time.

In this lesson you will create a video by adding a *Time* dimension to a 3D Maps layer.

1 Open *Sales Summary-8* from your sample files folder (if it isn't already open).

2 Open the *Tour 1* tour in the *3D Maps* application.

3 Change the values of the fields in the *Layer 1* task pane.

    1. Set the *Location* field to: *City*.

    2. Set the *Visualization Type* to: *Stacked Column*.

    3. Make sure that the *Height* field is set to: *Qty (Sum)*.

    4. Set the *Category* field to: *Category*.

4 Tilt and zoom the map so that the bars are clearly visible.

5 Add the *Date* field from the source data to the layer's *Time* dimension.

    1. Click: Layer 1→Time→+ Add Field.

    A drop-down list of all fields in the source data that contain valid time information appears.

    In this case there is only one field (*Date*) that contains Date/Time information.

    2. Click the *Date* field.

    Notice that a video play bar has appeared beneath the visualization.

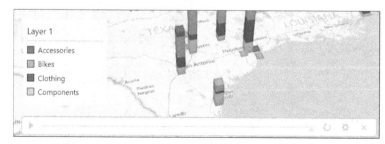

6 Play a video showing sales as they occurred in 2015.

Click the *Play* button.

note

You can use the time scrubber to move to any point in the video

Click and drag the *time scrubber* to move to a specific point in time.

note

Selecting how data should be animated

When you add a *Time* field, a clock icon appears above the selected field:

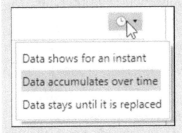

You can see that there are three options.

1. Data accumulates over time.

This is clearly the correct option for this lesson. As each sale is made, you want the total sales to date (a running total) to be visualized.

2. Data stays until it is replaced.

Imagine you are showing how the population of a city has changed over the years. You'd want to replace the previous population figure with the new updated population figure at each census.

3. Data shows for an instant.

In this case, the data disappears as the timeline moves forwards. You might use this to document a road trip when you are only present in one location at one time.

A video plays for ten seconds. Each stacked column gradually grows in height as sales occur during the year. When the video stops playing, a visualization of the total sales for 2015 remains visible.

7   Display only calendar months at the top left of the visualization.

By default, the visualization displays the day, hour and second as it travels through the year.

Perhaps you'd like to keep the display simpler by only displaying the calendar month.

1. Right click on the date and time display at the top left of the visualization.

2. Click *Edit* from the shortcut menu.

    The *Edit Time* dialog is displayed.

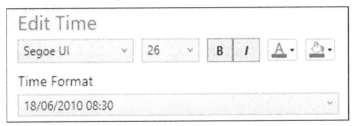

3. Click inside the *Time Format* box.

    A drop-down menu appears listing a huge variety of built-in format types.

4. Select a format that shows only the month and year.

    Notice that you can also customize the font type, font size, font color and background color from this dialog.

5. Click the *Accept* button.

    The time display now only shows the month and year:

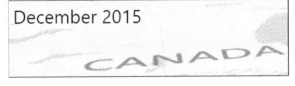

8   Play the video again.

This time the visualization displays each calendar month of 2015 as it animates.

It is possible to save the video you are seeing as an industry-standard MP4 video file (see facing page sidebar). You could then distribute the video or incorporate it into a PowerPoint presentation.

9   Save your work as *Sales Summary-9*.

© 2020 The Smart Method® Ltd

Lesson 9-13: Set scene options

In: *Lesson 9-12: Create a video from temporal data,* you learned how to animate your data. The video that you created was a little uninteresting as it was viewed from a single viewpoint. You could imagine that you were looking down upon the map from a hovering helicopter.

The next time you watch a Hollywood movie, notice that the camera rarely stays still. The viewpoint constantly moves as the camera zooms in and out of the scene and moves around the subject. This adds interest and engages the viewer.

When you create a 3D Maps movie, you can use the same production techniques. You'll find that this creates a more interesting and engaging display.

1　Open *New Jersey Sales-1* from your sample files folder.

This sample file contains a table called *NewJerseySales* containing details of 11,500 sales made by a consumer electronics retailer in the state of *New Jersey* during 2015.

2　Create a flat map with a *City* visualization showing total *Sales Amount* by *City*.

1. Click anywhere inside the table.

2. Click: Insert→Tours→3D Map.

3. Click: Home→Map→Flat Map.

4. Click: Home→Map→Map Labels to show place names on the map.

5. Set the *Location* field to: *City.*

6. Set the *Height* field to: *Sales Amount(Sum).*

7. Zoom and tilt the map to best visualize sales.

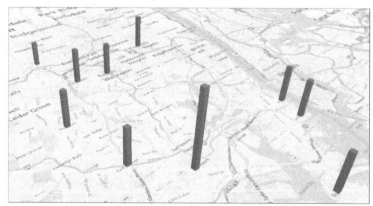

3　Add a *Time* and *Category* field to create a video presentation of 2015 sales by *Category*.

Add the following fields:

New Jersey Sales-1

4 Name the layer: **New Jersey Sales**

1. Click the *Rename this layer* icon at the top right of the *Layer* task pane and type: **New Jersey Sales** into the text box.

2. Press the **<Enter>** key.

5 Name the scene: **Sales by Category**

As you'll discover later in: *Lesson 9-14: Create a tour with multiple scenes,* a *Tour* can have many *Scenes.* The visualization you have created in this lesson only has a single scene. It will still be useful to name it now, so that things don't become confusing if you add another scene in the future.

1. Click: Home→Scene→Scene Options.

   The *Scene Options* dialog appears.

2. Type: **Sales by Category** into the *Scene Name* text box.

3. Close the *Scene Options* dialog.

6 Play the video.

Note that the viewpoint stays still during the video.

7 Add a *Circle* effect to fly around the visualization in a circle.

1. Click: Home→Scene→Scene Options.

2. Click the *Effect* drop-down arrow and set the *Effect* to: *Circle.*

3. Close the *Scene Options* dialog.

8 Play the tour.

Click: Home→Tour→Play Tour.

You won't see the effect if you click the *Play* button at the bottom of the screen.

When you play a *Tour* the display changes to full screen. Notice how much more effective the visualization is as you fly in a partial circle around the visualization.

You will not fly in a full circle. You could achieve this (if required) by changing the *Effect Speed* or *Scene Duration* settings in the *Scene Options dialog.*

Later, in: *Lesson 9-14: Create a tour with multiple scenes,* you'll discover how you can combine scenes and effects to create a stunning presentation. For now, try experimenting with the different effects available in order to become familiar with them.

9 Close full screen view by pressing the **<Escape>** key.

10 Save your work as: *New Jersey Sales-2.*

note

Now that you have mastered all 3D Maps skills, you will be able to create some amazing presentations

The simple tour presented in this lesson completes your 3D Maps skillset.

Try combining multiple layers, multiple scenes, text boxes and annotations in your own presentations. If you have graphics skills, remember that you can also create graphics to include inside annotations.

You can now quickly create presentations that would previously have taken days and involved an entire production team. Your skills are truly cutting-edge.

You can view some stunning 3D Maps tours on YouTube. Many have been produced by Microsoft's in-house designers to push 3D Maps features to their limits. You'll get many ideas for your own presentations by viewing some of these videos.

With the skills you have learned in this session, you'll immediately be able to understand how the designers have implemented their special effects.

Remember that 3D Maps was called *Power Maps* until the release of Excel 2016. The older *Power Maps* work is equally relevant, so you should search for both *Power Maps* and *3D Maps* if you need inspiration.

New Jersey Sales-2

Lesson 9-14: Create a tour with multiple scenes

In this lesson you'll create a tour that begins with a scene that shows total sales by category for each branch (the scene that you created in: *Lesson 9-13: Set scene options*).

This retailer makes most of its income from computer sales. For this reason, you'll then create a second scene showing sales in the *Computers* category for each city.

1 Open *New Jersey Sales-2* from your sample files folder.

2 Open the *Tour 1* tour in the *3D Maps* application.

There is only one scene in the current tour. This scene has only one layer. It would be correct to call this: "The *New Jersey Sales* layer in the *Sales by Category* scene".

3 Change the Visualization type to *Clustered Column.*

Change the visualization from *Stacked Column* to *Clustered Column.*

This will work better for the multi-scene tour.

4 Add a new scene to the Tour called *Computer Sales.*

1. Click: Home→Scene→New Scene (drop-down list)→ Copy Sales by Category.

Notice that a second scene has now appeared beneath the first. There is a green line around this scene to show that it is the active scene.

2. Click: Home→Scene→Scene Options.

The *Scene Options* dialog appears, showing options for the currently active scene.

3. Click in the *Scene Name* box and type the new name: **Computer Sales**

5 Make sure that the *Computer Sales* scene is the active scene.

One scene is always the active scene.

You can see which scene this is in the *Tour Editor* task pane (the task pane shown on the left of the screen). The active scene has a green outline.

If the *Computer Sales* scene is not the active scene, click on it once to select it.

6 Change the layer settings for the *Computer Sales* scene so that only sales in the *Computers* category are displayed.

1. Click: Layer task pane→Filters→+Add Filter.

2. Click the *Category* field from the field list.

3. Check the *Computers* check box in the filter field list.

The visualization changes to only show sales in the *Computers* category.

7 Change the visualization for the *Computer Sales* scene so that the bars are shown at full height for the entire duration of the second scene.

1. Make sure that the *Computer Sales* scene is active (selected).

2. Remove the *Date (None)* field from the *Time* pane in the *Layer* task pane.

   Without a *Time* field, the scene will show total sales for the entire duration of the scene.

8 Remove the transition effect from the *Sales by Category* scene and the *Circle* effect from the *Computer Sales* scene.

It may be overkill to have effects for both scenes.

1. Make sure that the *Sales by Category* scene is active (selected).

2. Click Home→Scene→Scene Options.

3. Set the *Transition Duration (sec)* to: **0.00**

   Transition effects are used to smoothly move to the starting view point of any follow-on scene.

   In the next step, you'll synchronize the starting view point of the *Computer Sales* scene with the ending view point of the Sales by *Category* scene. If you do this well, you won't need a transition effect.

4. Click on the *Computer Sales* scene to activate (select) it.

5. Click Home→Scene→Scene Options.

6. Set the *Effect* to: *No Effect.*

9 Move the starting view point of the *Computer Sales* scene to the approximate finishing location of the *Sales by Category* scene.

Because the view point of the first scene is travelling around the visualization in a circle, the ending view point of the first scene will be in a different position to the starting view point of the second scene.

1. Make sure that the *Computer Sales* scene is active (selected).

2. Use the *Rotate* arrows at the bottom right of the visualization to move around the visualization.

   Avoid clicking the *Tilt Up* and *Tilt Down* arrows to maintain the view point at the same altitude as the previous scene.

3. Play the tour to see how well you did. You may have to do this a few times before you are happy with the effect.

10 Refine and improve your tour.

You may find it useful to compare the New *Jersey Sales-3* sample file (in your sample files folder) to your own work.

11 Save your work as *New Jersey Sales-3.*

Session 9: Exercise

1   Open *European Climate-1* from your sample files folder.

      This workbook contains a single range, showing average monthly temperatures in twelve European cities.

2   Convert the range into a table named: **EuropeanClimate**

3   Create a 3D Maps tour from the table.

4   Review the geocoding to confirm that all locations have been correctly identified.

5   Change the map display so that it shows a *Flat Map* displaying place names (*Map Labels*).

6   Set the *Location, Height* and *Category* fields to display a *Clustered Column* visualization upon each *City* showing the average temperature for each month.

7   Rename the layer to: **Average Temperature** and change the tilt and zoom settings, column *Height* and column *Thickness* to make the visualization as effective and informative as possible.

8   Add a *Fly Over* motion effect to the scene and play the tour.

9   Save your work as *European Climate-2*.

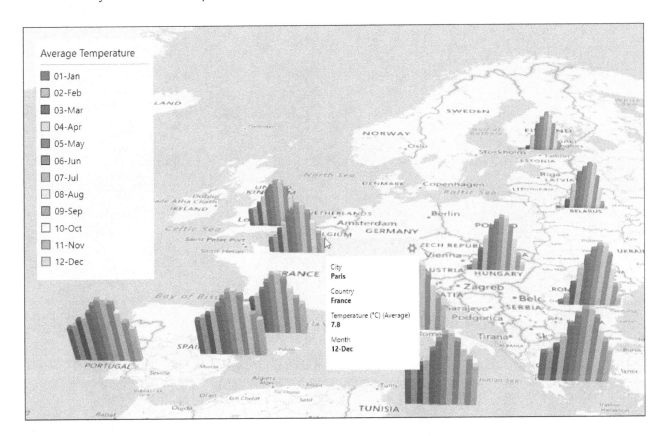

European Climate-1

If you need help slide the page to the left

Session 9: Exercise Answers

These are the three questions that students find the most difficult to answer:

Q 8	Q 7	Q 6
1. Click: Home→Scene→ Scene Options. The *Scene Options* dialog appears. 2. Change the *Effect* to: *Fly Over*. 3. Click: Home→Tour→Play Tour This was covered in: *Lesson 9-13: Set scene options.*	1. Click the *Rename this Layer* icon at the top of the *Layer* task pane and then type: **Average Temperature** into the text box. This was covered in: *Lesson 9-10: Create a visualization with multiple layers.* 2. Use the *Tilt* and *Zoom* buttons to zoom and tilt the map. This was covered in: *Lesson 9-7: Add a height field to a layer.* 3. At the bottom of the *Layer* task pane, click: Layer Options→ Height/Thickness … to change the height and thickness of the bars. This was covered in: *Lesson 9-6: Set layer options and customize data cards*	Set the fields in the *Layer 1* task pane so that they look like this: 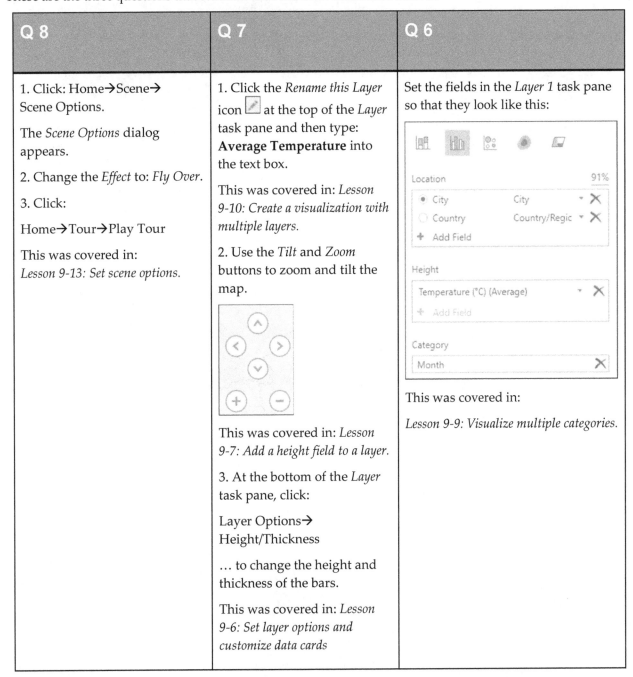 This was covered in: *Lesson 9-9: Visualize multiple categories.*

If you have difficulty with the other questions, here are the lessons that cover the relevant skills:

2   Refer to: *Lesson 1-12: Convert a range into a table and add a total row.*

3   Refer to: *Lesson 9-2: Create a simple 3D Map.*

4   Refer to: *Lesson 9-3: Confirm the accuracy of geocoding.*

5   Refer to: *Lesson 9-4: Map using different location fields.*

10

Session Ten: Create Get & Transform queries

> The goal is to transform data into information, and information into insight.
>
> *Carly Fiorina (1954-),*
> *American former technology business executive and former*
> *Presidential candidate in the 2016 Republican primaries.*

Get & Transform integrates well with both Excel and Power Pivot (an advanced data modeling add-in that is included with Excel). You'll learn more about data modeling with Power Pivot in: *Session Eleven: Power Pivot, Data Modeling, OLAP and Business Intelligence.*

Get & Transform is a powerful and complex professional tool. Entire books have been written to explain how to use Get & Transform. This short session will teach you everything you need to know to use this tool effectively in most business scenarios. By the end of this session you'll have skills that could potentially save an enormous amount of time in your day-to-day work with Excel.

Session Objectives

- Understand Get & Transform and ETL
- Create a simple extract and load web query
- Understand queries and connections
- Move, remove, rename, filter and sort columns
- Split delimited data
- Understand data types
- Create and use a linked data type
- Add a linked data type field using a data card
- Resolve geocoding errors in the Geography linked data type
- Understand Get & Transform data types
- Specify data types
- Understand steps and PQFL
- Remove empty, error and top and bottom rows
- Understand and work with null values
- Transform date and time columns
- Transform number columns
- Add a custom calculated column

- Create an aggregated data query
- Unpivot aggregated data
- Work with multiple queries
- Create an append query
- Understand Column From Examples
- Use Column From Examples with selected source columns
- Use Column From Examples to extract characters from strings
- Understand primary and foreign keys
- Link primary and foreign keys using VLOOKUP
- Efficiently import data using a view
- Understand linked table and Pivot Table refresh
- Load a query directly into the Pivot Table cache
- Understand normal and de-normalized data
- Create a simple two-table merged query
- Create a five-table merged query
- Create a merged query using fuzzy logic

Lesson 10-1: Understand Get & Transform and ETL

Get & Transform is an advanced ETL tool. ETL is an acronym for *Extract, Transform and Load*.

Before Get & Transform was added to Excel, users had to import data into a worksheet and then transform the data inside Excel. The new *Get & Transform* tool enables you to import data (from one or more external sources) and then transform it *before* it is loaded into Excel (or a data model). This provides many advantages.

The diagram below should make it clear what is meant by the terms *Extract, Transform* and *Load*.

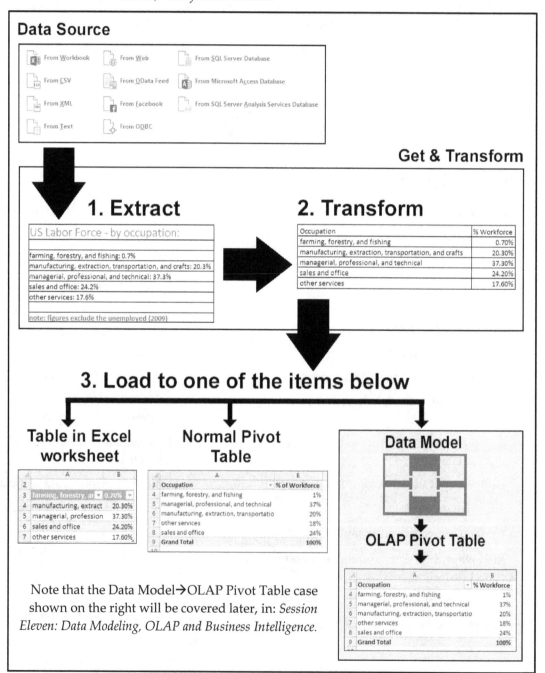

Note that the Data Model→OLAP Pivot Table case shown on the right will be covered later, in: *Session Eleven: Data Modeling, OLAP and Business Intelligence.*

The ETL methodology

Extract: Most data that is analyzed with Excel doesn't start its life in an Excel workbook but is imported from an external data source (often from a database or CSV file). *Extract* simply means moving this data from the external data source into the Get & Transform tool.

Transform: Extracted data often isn't in a form that can be easily analyzed by Excel. There may be unwanted columns, badly named fields, badly formatted fields or corrupted data. The Get & Transform tool includes a vast array of features that enable you to clean your data before loading it into an Excel table or Pivot Table. This cleaning process is called *Data Transformation* (see sidebar).

Load: This simply means exporting the transformed data from the Get & Transform tool to its destination. A Get & Transform query can export (load) transformed data into an Excel table or into an Excel Pivot Table.

Get & Transform can also load data into a special construct called a *Data Model*. Data Modeling will be covered later, in: *Session Eleven: Power Pivot, Data Modeling, OLAP and Business Intelligence.*

Why is ETL better than ELT?

When you add and delete columns, change column headers, re-format columns and add calculated columns to Excel tables you are *transforming* your data. Excel users that do not understand how to use the *Get & Transform* tool use an ELT methodology (*Extract* from data source, *Load* into Excel and *Transform* within Excel). Here are some of the advantages in using Get & Transform to implement an ETL methodology:

1. **Re-usable and sharable queries:** The Get & Transform tool generates a re-usable *Query*. This means that all of the Get & Transform actions that you define can be repeated to refresh the data in a table on your worksheet with a single click. You'll learn more about queries later, in: *Lesson 10-3: Understand queries and connections.*

2. **Automatically refreshed data:** You can configure a query to automatically refresh an Excel table at a timed interval. You'll learn how to automatically refresh data later, in: *Lesson 10-3: Understand queries and connections.*

3. **The ability to transform big data:** Get & Transform does not share Excel's limits (of approximately a million rows of data) so it can be used to transform big data (sending the result directly to the data model, 3D Map, or to an Excel worksheet after aggregation). You'll learn more about pre-aggregating data later, in: *Lesson 10-18: Create an aggregated data query.*

4. **Better tools:** Get & Transform has some advanced transformation tools that are not found in the standard Excel product (for example, the *Unpivot Columns* tool that you'll learn about in: *Lesson 10-19: Unpivot aggregated data*).

5. **The ability to combine data:** Get & Transform enables you to merge queries. This enables you to combine relational data from disparate data sources to create a de-normalized data extract. You'll learn about this later, in: *Lesson 10-31: Understand normal and de-normalized data.*

note

Confusing terminology

In the world of IT, we are very fond of terminology.

The process that I describe as *Data Transformation* is often referred to using the following alternative terminology:

- Data Wrangling
- Data Cleansing
- Data Scrubbing
- Data Shaping
- Data Pre-Processing
- Data Munging

In this session I will exclusively use the term *Data Transformation*.

You can, of course, use the above terminology liberally in meetings. This will make you sound very important and help to confuse your co-workers.

Personally, I'd rather be referred to as a transformer than a munger, scrubber or wrangler.

trivia

Power Query lives on

The *Get & Transform* help advises:

"Power Query is known as Get & Transform in Excel".

In the January 2018 semi-annual Excel release the query editor was called: *Get & Transform Query Editor* as you would have expected.

In the Jul 2018, Jan 2019 and July 2019 and Jan 2020 semi-annual versions it had reverted to the previous name of: *Power Query Editor.*

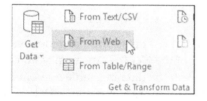

note

Why not use a real currency exchange site?

In earlier versions of this book I directed readers to a "real" exchange rate site that subsequently changed, making the lesson impossible to follow.

For this book I've published my own exchange rate data on the https://TheSmartMethod.com website.

Lesson 10-2: Create a simple extract and load web query

There are many sites on the Internet containing useful data that is constantly changing. Obvious examples are currency exchange rates and stock prices. This type of information is often presented on a web page.

Get & Transform allows you to create a web query that will extract data from a specified table on a specified web page.

When a web query has been created, it is possible to refresh the information in your worksheet (from the source web page) at any time, either manually or automatically (at a specified time interval).

1 Open a new blank workbook.

2 Open your web browser and go to: https://samplefiles.thesmartmethod.com/webquery/ exchangerates

Type the above URL into your web browser's address bar.

A simple web page appears showing eight current (fictitious) currency exchange rates.

Notice that the exchange rates update every five seconds.

3 Create a web query to extract currency exchange rates from: https://samplefiles.thesmartmethod.com/webquery/ exchangerates

1. Return to Excel and select cell A1.

2. Click:

Data→Get & Transform Data→From Web

The *From Web* dialog appears, requesting a URL.

3. Type: https://samplefiles.thesmartmethod.com/webquery/ exchangerates into the *URL* box.

4. Click the *OK* button.

5. If you see a security prompt asking whether to allow access click: *Connect.*

The *Navigator* pane appears, listing a single table and a document.

On a more complicated web page you could see many tables. This is a simple page with only one table.

6. Select the *Table 0* table.

A preview of the table appears in the right-hand pane of the dialog.

Notice that there are three buttons at the bottom of the dialog: *Load, Transform Data* and *Cancel.* The *Transform Data* button would take you to the *Power Query Editor* window where you would be able to transform your data. (You'll use many of Get & Transform's transformation tools later in this session).

For the moment you will use the Get & Transform tool only to *extract* and *load* the data. You've already *extracted* the data and are now ready to *load* it into the worksheet.

4 Load the extracted data into cell A1 on the currently selected worksheet.

1. Click: Load (drop-down arrow)→Load To…

The *Import Data* dialog appears. Notice that the default load location is a table in a new worksheet.

2. Click the *Existing worksheet* option button.

Cell A1 is already selected, so the data will be loaded into a table in cell A1 of the currently selected worksheet. See sidebar for a discussion of the other load options.

3. Click the *OK* button.

The exchange rates are displayed in a table upon the worksheet.

	A	B	C	D	E
1	Place	Currency	Symbol	1 USD	Inverse
2	Atlantis	Orich	ATO	0.8061	1.2406
3	Narnia	Lion	NAL	0.6848	1.4602
4	Middle Earth	Castar	MEC	67.7414	0.0148
5	Hogsmeade Village	Gringott	HOG	1.2182	0.8209
6	Kingdom of Zamunda	Pound	ZAP	0.9407	1.0631
7	El Dorado	Gold Dollar	ELD	1.4877	0.6722
8	Lilliput	Sprug	LIS	125.6879	0.008
9	San Seriffe	Corona	SSC	1.4199	0.7043

Note that this is a rather special table (called a *linked table*). If you click inside the table, you'll see a new *Query Tools* ribbon tab. This tells you that the table is linked to a *Get & Transform* query. The default color of the table (green instead of blue) also provides a visual clue that this is a linked table.

Table Tools	Query Tools
Design	Query

5 Refresh the data shown in the table.

Because the table is linked to a *Get & Transform* query, you can execute the query at any time to update the exchange rates.

1. Click inside the table to select it.

2. Click: Query Tools→Query→Load→Refresh.

Every time you click the *Refresh* button you'll see the values change to show up-to-the-second exchange rates (provided you wait at least five seconds of course).

Later, in: *Lesson 10-3: Understand queries and connections,* you'll learn how to automatically refresh the query at a timed interval (of as little as one minute). The worksheet data will then always be up to date.

6 Save your work as *Exchange Rates-1.*

note

The Import Data dialog options

1. *Table* in *New Worksheet.*

Sends the output to a linked Excel table in a new worksheet.

2. *Table* in *Existing Worksheet.*

Sends the output to an Excel linked table in a specified location in an existing worksheet (the option you used in this lesson).

3. *Only Create Connection.*

This option allows you to save a query to use later. You'll learn how to use saved queries later, in: *Lesson 10-3: Understand queries and connections.*

4. *Add this data to the Data Model.*

If this check box is checked, the data returned by the query will be sent to a table in a special in-memory construct called the data model.

The data model will be covered later, in: *Session Eleven: Power Pivot, Data Modeling, OLAP and Business Intelligence.*

note

Where are queries and connections saved?

When you save an Excel workbook containing a query, the query (that includes both a connection and transformation instructions) is automatically saved as part of the workbook.

Lesson 10-3: Understand queries and connections

A *Get & Transform* query contains two items:

1. A *Connection* that the query uses to connect to a data source and *Extract* raw data.

2. All of the steps needed for the query to *Transform* the data after it is extracted using the connection. Later, in: *Lesson 10-12: Understand steps and PQFL*, you'll learn that these steps are stored in a special language called: *Power Query Formula Language.*

Crucially, the query does not know what to do with the data after transforming it. In other words, it does not contain any *Load* information.

This provides many advantages. You can share a query with other users who can decide where they want to load the resulting query data.

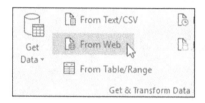

1 Open a new blank workbook.

2 Create a web query to extract currency exchange rates from: https://samplefiles.thesmartmethod.com/webquery/exchangerates.

1. Select cell A1.

2. Click: Data→Get & Transform Data→From Web.

3. Type: https://samplefiles.thesmartmethod.com/webquery/exchangerates into the *URL* box.

4. Click the *OK* button.

5. Select the *Table 0* table.

6. Click: Load (drop-down)→Load To…

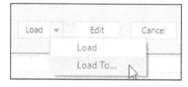

The *Import Data* dialog appears. Notice that the default load location is a table in a new worksheet.

7. Click the *Only Create Connection* option button.

Only Create Connection is rather confusing terminology, as you are actually creating a *Query* that includes both a connection and transformation instructions (and not a simple connection).

8. Click the *OK* button.

note

Unlinking a linked table

When you import a table using a query, the table is linked to the source data.

You may, however, wish to break the link between the source data and the table.

To do this:

1. Right-click on the table.

2. Click:

Table→
Unlink from Data Source

… from the shortcut menu.

3 View query information using the *Queries & Connections* task pane.

1. The *Queries & Connections* task pane should now be visible on the right of your screen. If you have closed it, click:

Data→Queries & Connections→Queries & Connections

… to bring it back again.

2. Hover the mouse cursor over the *Table 0* query.

    A large amount of information about the query is shown in an information box.

4 Give the query a meaningful name.

1. Right-click on the *Table 0* query in the *Queries & Connections* task pane.

2. Click: *Properties* from the shortcut menu.

3. Type: **Currency Exchange Rates** into the *Query name* box.

4. Click the *OK* button.

5 Use the *Currency Exchange Rates* query to provide data to a table on the current worksheet.

1. Right-click on the *Currency Exchange Rates* query in the *Queries & Connections* task pane.

2. Click: *Load To…* from the shortcut menu.

3. Click the *Table* option button.

4. Click the *Existing worksheet* option button.

5. Click the *OK* button.

    The data returned by the query is displayed in a linked table on the current worksheet.

    You learned about linked tables in: *Lesson 10-2: Create a simple extract and load web query.*

6. Click inside the table to select it.

7. Look in the: Table Tools→Design→Properties→Table Name box.

    Notice that Excel has automatically named the table: *Currency_Exchange_Rates.*

    You learned about table names in: *Lesson 1-18: Name a table and create an automatic structured table reference.*

6 Change the connection properties so that the query refreshes every minute.

1. Right-click on the *Currency Exchange Rates* query in the *Queries & Connections* task pane.

2. Click: *Properties* from the shortcut menu.

    The *Query Properties* dialog appears.

3. On the *Usage* tab, check the *Refresh every* check box and set the time interval to 1 minute.

4. Click the *OK* button to close the dialog.

5. Observe the table. Notice that every 60 seconds the currency exchange rates all refresh to show current values.

7 Save your work as *Exchange Rates-2* and close the workbook.

note

The Get & Transform query created in this lesson is re-usable

A CSV (comma separated values) file is typically extracted from a database. In this lesson's example the CSV file would probably have been created from the company's HR system.

In a large company the *Employees* CSV file would change on a regular basis.

If the CSV were to change in the future, you wouldn't have to do any more work to update the *Phone List* generated in this lesson.

Get & Transform has created a linked table. As you discovered in: *Lesson 10-2: Create a simple extract and load web query,* you can manually (or automatically) refresh the linked table at any time without having to recreate the Get & Transform query.

Employees-1 (CSV)

Lesson 10-4: Move, remove, rename, filter and sort columns

1 Open a new blank workbook.

2 Create a *Get & Transform* query to extract the values contained in the *Employees-1* comma separated values (CSV) file.

The CSV file format is often used when exporting data from other applications. If you were to open the *Employees-1* CSV file in *Notepad,* you'd see this:

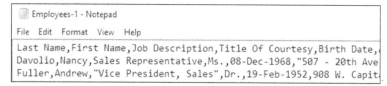

You can see that the first line of the file has column names (sometimes called field names) separated by commas. The second (and subsequent) lines have column values, also separated by commas.

Get & Transform can use a CSV file as a data source.

1. Click:

    Data→Get & Transform Data→From Text/CSV

2. Navigate to the *Employees-1* CSV file in your sample files folder.

3. Either double-click the file name or click once on the file name to select and then click the *Import* button.

    The contents of the *Employees-1* csv file is displayed.

    Notice that, this time, *Get & Transform* didn't ask you to select a table, as a CSV file can only contain a single table.

    You can see that the sample file contains thirteen different fields (columns) with an assortment of information about each employee. In this lesson you will transform this into a compact telephone number listing by removing many of the existing columns.

3 Remove unwanted columns so that only the *Last Name, First Name, Job Description, Title of Courtesy, Country* and *Home Phone* fields remain.

1. Click the *Transform Data* button.

    The *Power Query Editor* appears.

2. Click: Home→Manage Columns→Choose Columns.

3. Click the *(Select All Columns)* check box to uncheck all check boxes.

4. Check the boxes for the fields you want to keep.

5. Click the *OK* button.

   The query editor grid now shows only six columns.

4 Rename the *Title Of Courtesy* field to: **Title**

   1. Double-click on the text: *Title Of Courtesy* in the column header.

   2. Type: **Title** followed by the **<Enter>** key.

5 Change the order of the columns so that they match the screen grab below.

   Click and drag each column header to the required position.

	A^B_C Country	A^B_C Title	A^B_C First Name	A^B_C Last Name	A^B_C Job Description	A^B_C Home Phone
1	USA	Ms.	Nancy	Davolio	Sales Representative	(206) 555-9857
2	USA	Dr.	Andrew	Fuller	Vice President, Sales	(206) 555-9482
3	USA	Ms.	Janet	Leverling	Sales Representative	(206) 555-3412

6 Sort Alphabetically, first by *Country* and then by *Last Name*.

   1. Click on the drop-down arrow to the right of the *Country* column header.

   2. Select *Sort Ascending* from the drop-down list.

   3. Click on the drop-down arrow to the right of the *Last Name* column header.

   4. Select *Sort Ascending* from the drop-down list.

      Notice that this has resulted in a two-level sort. All countries are grouped together, and within each country last names are sorted from A-Z.

7 Filter the list so that only USA telephone numbers are shown.

   1. Click the drop-down arrow to the right of the *Country* column header.

   2. Remove the check from the *UK* check box and click the *OK* button.

8 Close the query editor and load the query result to a table in cell A1 of the worksheet (there is only one worksheet in this workbook).

   1. Click: Home→Close→Close & Load (drop-down arrow)→ Close and Load To…

      The *Import Data* dialog appears.

   2. Select the *Table* and *Existing Worksheet* options.

   3. Make sure that cell **A1** is selected in the *Existing worksheet* cell box.

   4. Click: *OK*.

9 Save your work as *Phone List-1*.

note

Other ways to remove unwanted columns in the Query Editor

1. Select one or more columns by clicking on the column headers. (You can use **<Ctrl>+Click** to select individual columns or **<Shift>+Click** to select an adjacent set of columns).

2. Right-click on any of the selected column headers and (from the shortcut menu) either click *Remove Columns* (to remove the selected columns) or *Remove Other Columns* (to remove the unselected columns).

These shortcut menu options are also available on the ribbon at:

Home→Manage Columns→ Remove Columns (drop-down list)

important

Get & Transform gives Excel the new ability to create multiple views of the same table

In this lesson the Get & Transform query, the source (Get) table, and the target (Load) table reside in the same workbook.

You can also set an automatic refresh interval of as little as one minute for the query.

If you change a value, add a new row (or delete an existing row) in the source table your changes will then update (after a short delay) in the target table.

This means that Excel now has the ability to create different views of the same table within a workbook.

It wasn't possible to implement this before Get & Transform was added to Excel.

This new ability adds huge power to Excel. I can think of hundreds of business requirements that I have encountered over the years that can be simply solved using this new ability.

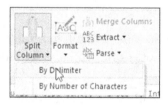

Top 20 Films-1

Lesson 10-5: Split delimited data

1 Open *Top 20 Films-1* from your sample files folder.

The sample file has a single table named: *Top20Films.*

The table is very easy to read for a human but is badly designed from a data perspective. In: *Lesson 2-1: Split fixed width data using Text to Columns,* you learned why you should not have more than one data element in each table column.

In this sample file the *Title* column contains two data elements (*Title* and *Year*). They should be in separate columns.

2 Create a *Get & Transform* query to extract the values contained in the *Top20Films* table.

Up until now you've used *Get & Transform* to connect to external data sources. In this lesson you'll extract data from an Excel table, transform the data, and then load the query result back into the same workbook.

1. Click inside the *Top20Films* table.

2. Click: Data→Get & Transform Data→From Table/Range.

   The *Power Query Editor* appears, showing the contents of the *Top20Films* table.

3 Extract the date from the *Title* column and place it into a new column.

In: *Lesson 2-2: Split delimited data using Text to Columns,* you learned how you could achieve this using Excel's *Text to Columns* tool.

Get & Transform's *Split Column* feature works in a similar way.

1. Click anywhere in the *Title* column.

2. Click: Transform→Text Column→
   Split Column (drop-down list)→By Delimiter.

   Note that there's also a *By Number of Characters* option. You could use this option to split fixed width data (you learned about fixed width data in: *Lesson 2-1: Split fixed width data using Text to Columns*).

   The *Split Column by Delimiter* dialog appears.

3. Select -- *Custom* -- from the *Select or enter delimiter* drop-down list.

4. Type an opening bracket into the text box (if one isn't already there).

5. Click the: *Right-most delimiter* option button.

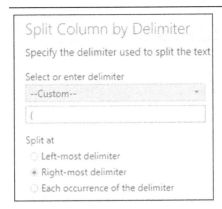

In this data it doesn't really matter which option you select as there is only one opening bracket in each title. The option you have just selected specifies that the split should take place at the right-most occurrence of a bracket character.

6. Click the *OK* button.

The *Title* field now only contains the film title and a new column has been inserted showing the year along with a closing bracket.

4   Rename the *Title.1* column header to: **Title** and the *Title.2* column header to: **Year**.

You learned how to do this in: *Lesson 10-4: Move, remove, rename, filter and sort columns.*

5   Remove the closing bracket from the *Year* column.

1. Click anywhere in the *Year* column.

2. Click: Transform→Any Column→Replace Values.

The *Replace Values* dialog appears.

3. Type a closing bracket into the *Value To Find* box.

4. Leave the *Replace With* box empty.

This will replace any closing brackets found in the column with nothing.

5. Click the *OK* button.

All of the closing brackets are removed from the *Year* column.

6   Close the query editor and load the query result to a table in cell A1 of a new worksheet.

You learned how to do this in: *Lesson 10-2: Create a simple extract and load web query.*

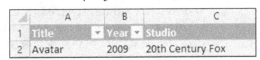

7   Save your work as *Top 20 Films-2*.

note

Solutions to the "penny rounding" problem

Consider the simple addition of two values:

	A			A
1	1.206	1	$	1.21
2	2.206	2	$	2.21
3	**3.412**	3	$	**3.41**

In the examples above, cell A3 has the formula: =A1+A2.

In the right-hand example, the values have been formatted as *currency*.

Best practice

Excel has a ROUND function that can be used to round the result to two decimal places at the point of calculation.

The new formula would become:

=ROUND(A1,2) + ROUND(A2,2)

Changing precision

Click: File→Options→ Advanced.

In the *When calculating this workbook* group, click the *Set precision as displayed* check box.

This alters the default behavior of Excel so that each value in the worksheet is regarded as being precisely the same as its display value when performing calculations.

Using this option can cause data to become inaccurate as it is a global setting, affecting the entire worksheet (and any other worksheets you may open before turning it off).

Use this feature with extreme caution, or better still, don't use it at all!

Lesson 10-6: Understand data types

What are data types?

Excel only supports four native data types: *Number, Text, Logical* and *Error*.

Data Type	Example
Number	22.4567
Text	John Smith
Logical	TRUE or FALSE
Error	#DIV/0, #N/A, #NULL!

Relational database products such as Access and SQL Server have far more data types. For example, Access supports six different numeric data types (such as *Integer* and *Currency*) and SQL server supports eleven.

Excel simulates data types by formatting

In: *Lesson 3-7: Understand date serial numbers*, you learned that Excel uses the *Number* data type to store date and time values. The ingenious use of date serial numbers enables Excel to mimic a *date/time* data type.

You're familiar with using Excel's formatting features to display numbers on a worksheet with a fixed number of decimal places (simulating the *Decimal* data type) or as whole numbers with no decimal places (simulating the *Integer* data type).

Common Excel data type problems

Excel's lack of a *Currency* or *Decimal* data type often causes rounding errors (sometimes referred to as the "penny rounding problem"). The sidebar discusses this problem and some solutions. Because RDBMS (Relational Data Management Systems) such as SQL Server and Access support these data types they do not experience this problem.

Excel's lack of a *Date* data type means that Excel is unable to work with dates that are before 1900. The SQL Server *Date* data type can work with any dates between 1st Jan 0001 and 31st Dec 9999.

You can see that there will often be problems converting values from other data sources into a form that is usable by Excel.

The object data type

All of the data types described so far are called *scalar* data types because they can only hold a single data item.

There are also more complex *non-scalar* data types that can hold many values.

important

Data type terminology used in this book

Scalar data types

Scalar means simple data types like Excel's *Number* and *Text* data types. You can only put one value into an Excel cell and that value is scalar.

Non-scalar data types

Non-scalar data types (such as objects) can contain many values.

Native data types

These are the data types that Excel uses internally to store values.

The *Geography* and *Stocks* linked data types

In this book I'll refer to the *Geography* and *Stocks* data types that reside on Microsoft's servers (and that can be linked to from Excel) as **objects**.

I'll also refer to the collection of values stored inside these objects as **fields** (though some users may describe them as properties).

This book refers to this type of data type as an *object* (see sidebar). The *Geography* and *Stocks* linked data types are objects.

An object can contain many different fields (also sometimes called properties), each of which contains a value. For example, the *Geography* object contains fields for *Population, Longitude* and *Latitude.* You'd obtain the values of these fields using syntax such as:

- City.Population
- City.Longitude
- City.Latitude

Excel does not natively support the object data type but can return field values from remote objects via the Internet using the new *Linked Data Type* feature. You'll learn more about using linked data types later, in: *Lesson 10-7: Create and use a linked data type.*

Linked data types are not native Excel data types

It is important to realize that a linked data type is not an Excel native data type.

Linked data types allow you to return values from an object that resides on a remote server (and not in the Excel workbook) via the Internet. This means that Excel still only has four native data types.

Linked data types will be discussed in depth later, in: *Lesson 10-7: Create and use a linked data type* and *Lesson 10-8: Add a linked data type field using a data card.*

Here is an example of a linked data type:

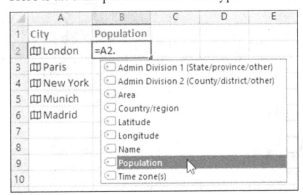

In the above example cells A2:A6 contain text values that define *City* names. The linked data type feature is being used to retrieve the value of the population of *London.*

You could be forgiven for believing that cell A2 contains an object data type with many fields.

In reality the formula has contacted a Microsoft server via the Internet and identified a unique *Geography* object there by using the key text *London.* When the user clicks on the *Population* field, the formula =A1.Population is added to cell B2 and a value representing the population of London is returned to the cell.

important

You need an Internet connection to use this feature

Linked data types allow you to retrieve information via the Internet from objects stored on Microsoft's servers.

This is not possible unless your computer is connected to the Internet.

Lesson 10-7: Create and use a linked data type

1 Open a new blank workbook.

2 Type the following text into the new workbook:

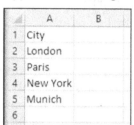

	A	B
1	City	
2	London	
3	Paris	
4	New York	
5	Munich	
6		

3 Convert the range A1:A5 into a table and name it: **City**

You learned how to do this in: *Lesson 1-12: Convert a range into a table and add a total row* and *Lesson 1-18: Name a table and create an automatic structured table reference.*

It isn't necessary to convert a range into a table to use the *linked data types* feature but is recommended best practice.

4 Convert cells A2:A5 into the *Geography* linked data type.

1. Select cells A2:A5.

2. Click: Data→Data Types→Geography.

3. After a short delay, two things happen:

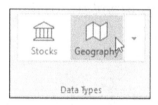

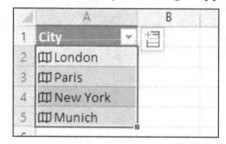

Icons appear to the left of each *City* **name:** The icons confirm that the names in cells A2:A5 are able to identify a single *Geography* object on Microsoft's servers (via the Internet). Be aware that Microsoft is guessing that you mean London, England (there are many more towns and cities in the world named London). You'll learn how to resolve ambiguous names later, in: *Lesson 10-9: Resolve geocoding errors in the geography linked data type.*

An *Add Column* button appears at the top-right of the table.

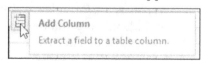

5 Add a non-existent City to cell A6.

note

There are many ways to identify a Geography or Stocks object

A *Geography* object can be identified using a *Country, Province, Territory* or *City* name.

A *Stocks* object can be identified using a *Ticker Symbol, Company Name* or *Fund Name.*

note

The Stocks data type

The *Stocks* linked data type can be used in exactly the same way as the *Geography* linked data type.

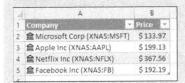

Note that the *Stocks* linked data type icon is different to the *Geography* linked data type icon.

note

Alternative ways to add a field

1. If you begin to type a field name in the header row of the table, this will happen:

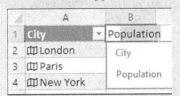

… then when you press the **<Enter>** key the new column is added to the table.

2. If you add a formula to a table column that references a linked data type cell an AutoComplete list will appear enabling you to add a field.

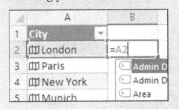

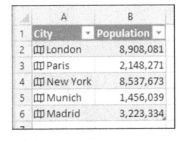

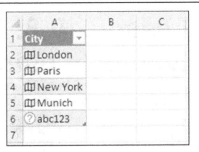

Notice the question mark icon. This informs you that Microsoft is unable to identify a single *Geography* object from the text that you have entered in cell A6.

6   Change the text in cell A6 to: **Madrid**

The icon returns to normal as Microsoft is able to identify a single *Geography* object from the text: *Madrid*.

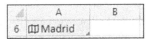

7   Use the *add column* button to retrieve the population of each city.

1.   Click anywhere in the table.

An *Add Column* button appears at the top right of the table.

2.   Click on the *Add Column* button.

Something interesting happens. You can see that Excel now presents a list of fields:

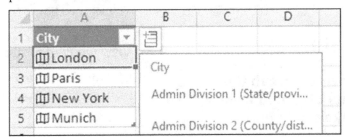

The field list you are seeing is actually provided by a *Geography* object located on a remote Microsoft server. You can select any of them to add a new column that contains the value of the selected field.

3.   Click on the *Population* field.

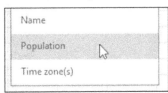

A new *Population* column is added to the table containing up-to-date values for the population of each city.

8   Save your work as *Linked City Data-1*.

important

You need an Internet connection to use this feature

Linked data types allow you to retrieve information via the Internet from objects stored on Microsoft's servers.

This is not possible unless your computer is connected to the Internet.

Lesson 10-8: Add a linked data type field using a data card

Open a new blank workbook.

1   Type the following text into the new workbook:

These are the world's five largest economies (by GDP) along with Tuvalu, the nation with the world's smallest economy.

2   Convert the range A1:A7 into a table and name it: **Country**

You learned how to do this in: *Lesson 1-12: Convert a range into a table and add a total row* and *Lesson 1-18: Name a table and create an automatic structured table reference.*

It isn't necessary to convert a range into a table to use the *linked data types* feature but is recommended best practice.

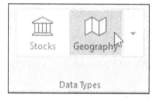

3   Convert cells A2:A7 into the *Geography* linked data type.

You learned how to do this in: *Lesson 10-7: Create and use a linked data type.*

4   View the card for the USA.

Click on the icon to the left of cell A2.

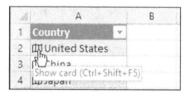

A card is displayed showing information about the United States.

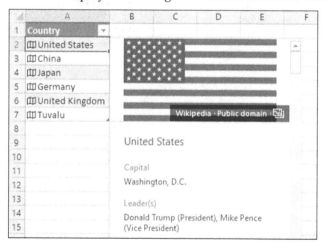

note

How to refresh the data obtained from a linked data type

Linked data types do not automatically refresh. For this reason it is important to manually refresh the data they retrieve from time to time.

To refresh the data, right-click a cell that contains a linked data type and select:

Data Type→Refresh

...from the shortcut menu.

You can also select:

Data→
Queries & Connections→
Refresh All

... from the Ribbon to refresh all data types, data connections and Pivot Tables in the entire workbook.

	A	B
1	Country	Capital
2	United States	Washington, D.C.
3	China	Beijing
4	Japan	Tokyo
5	Germany	Berlin
6	United Kingdom	London
7	Tuvalu	Funafuti

note

Converting a linked data type back into text

1. Right click on a cell containing a linked data type.

2. Click: Data Type→Convert To Text from the shortcut menu.

Wikipedia · CC0

Tuvalu

Capital
Funafuti

Leader(s)
Elizabeth II (Monarch), Enele Sopoaga (Prime Minister), Iakoba Italeli (Governor-general)

Population · 2017
11,192

	A	C
1	Country	Gasoline price
2	United States	$ 0.71
3	China	$ 0.96
4	Japan	$ 1.06
5	Germany	$ 1.39
6	United Kingdom	$ 1.46
7	Tuvalu	Not Available

5 Extract the value of the *Capital* field shown on the card to the table.

   1. Hover over the *Capital* field on the data card.

   Notice that an icon has appeared on the card.

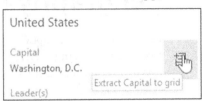

United States

Capital
Washington, D.C.

Extract Capital to grid

Leader(s)

   2. Click on the icon to extract the contents of the *Capital* field to the table for all countries.

6 Extract the value of the *Gasoline Price* field shown on the card to the table.

   1. Click on the icon to the left of cell A2.

   The card for the United States appears.

   2. Hover the mouse over the *Gasoline Price* field and click the *Extract to Grid* button.

   This time one of the field values displays an error.

	A	B	C
1	Country	Capital	Gasolin
2	United States	Washington, D.C.	$ 0.71
3	China	Beijing	$ 0.96
4	Japan	Tokyo	$ 1.06
5	Germany	Berlin	$ 1.39
6	United Kingdom	London	$ 1.46
7	Tuvalu	Funafuti	#FIELD!

As you might expect, the data contained in the *Geography* object for Tuvalu is not as comprehensive as that for the world's five largest economies. You'd need to do further research if you needed to know the *Gasoline Price* in Tuvalu.

7 View the card for Tuvalu.

Notice that this card is much shorter than the USA card and does not contain a *Gasoline* field.

8 Replace the error message in cell C7 with the text: **Not Available**

Edit the formula in cell C2 to the following:

```
=IFERROR([@Country].[Gasoline price], "Not Available")
```

You learned how to use the IFERROR function in: *Lesson 3-24: Use an IFERROR function to suppress error messages.*

9 Save your work as *Linked Country Data-1*.

Lesson 10-9: Resolve geocoding errors in the geography linked data type

When you create a *Stocks* data type it is possible to uniquely identify a stock by specifying a *Ticker Symbol* along with a *Market Identifier Code*. In this example there is no scope for ambiguity:

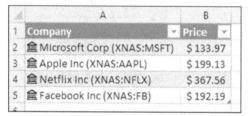

You can see that the *Microsoft Corp* ticker symbol: *MSFT* has been used in conjunction with the *US NASDAQ* Market Identifier Code: *XNAS*.

Geographical data has far more potential for error.

In: *Lesson 10-7: Create and use a linked data type,* you created a geographic linked data type for several cities.

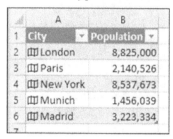

Excel has used the *Bing Maps Service* to guess that the London you are referring to is London UK. There are, however, many different cities in the world also named London. In this lesson you'll create a linked data type to report the population of three different Londons:

- London, England, United Kingdom
- London, Ohio, USA
- London, Kentucky, USA

1   Open a new blank workbook.

2   Type the following text into the new workbook:

3   Convert the range A1:C4 into a table and name it: **London**

You learned how to do this in: *Lesson 1-12: Convert a range into a table and add a total row* and *Lesson 1-18: Name a table and create an automatic structured table reference.*

note

How to refresh the data obtained from a linked data type

Note that it is not possible to automatically refresh data from a linked data type at a timed interval.

While this would be really useful for the Stocks linked data type, Microsoft have probably not implemented this feature to avoid overloading their servers.

You are, however, able to manually refresh the data obtained from a linked data type.

To refresh the data:

1. Right-click a cell that contains a linked data type.

2. Select: Data Type→Refresh from the shortcut menu.

You can also refresh data using the ribbon by clicking:

Data→
Queries & Connections→
Refresh All

This will refresh all data types, data connections and Pivot Tables in the entire workbook.

It isn't necessary to convert a range into a table to use the *linked data types* feature but is recommended best practice.

4   Convert cells A2:A4 into the *Geography* data type.

You learned how to do this in: *Lesson 10-7: Create and use a linked data type.*

5   Add a column to report the population of each city.

You learned how to do this in: *Lesson 10-7: Create and use a linked data type.*

6   Inspect the data card for each row.

You learned how to do this in: *Lesson 10-8: Add a linked data type field using a data card.*

Notice that, in every row, Excel has reported the population of *London, England, United Kingdom.*

7   Correct each row to retrieve the correct population figure.

The Excel terminology for this procedure is *switching out* data.

1. Right-Click on the icon in cell A3.

2. Select: Data Type→Change… from the shortcut menu.

    The *Data Selector* task pane appears.

3. Click on the *Select* button beneath *London, Madison County, Ohio.*

    The figure shown in the *Population* column updates.

4. Use the same method to update row 4 to point to *London, Laurel County, Kentucky.*

    The population figures now display correctly:

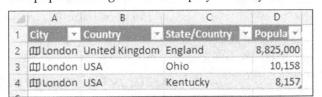

8   Save your work as *Three Londons-1.*

![Data Selector task pane showing City of London, London Laurel County Kentucky, and London Madison County Ohio]

note

You could reasonably argue that the Excel suite consists of five applications rather than three

As well as *Excel, Get & Transform* and *Power Pivot* some might argue that Excel includes two other applications.

3D-Maps

3D Maps was originally a separate application called *Power Maps* before it was added to Excel.

You learned how to use 3D-Maps in: *Session Nine: 3D Maps.*

Visual Basic for Applications (VBA)

You learned about VBA in: *Lesson 7-10: Understand macros and VBA.*

VBA is a programming language that is included with Excel and can be used to program features that are not included in the Excel product.

VBA is actually a port of the Visual Basic 6 language that Microsoft last updated in 1998 and declared a legacy product during 2008. VBA will eventually be retired.

Visual Basic 6 was one of the most widely used business languages in the 1990s and has been used to create many thousands of bespoke business applications (that have no connection with Excel).

Lesson 10-10: Understand Get & Transform data types

The Excel suite includes several different applications

The Excel suite consists of three major applications:

Excel: This is the core Excel product that you've been using in sessions 1-9 of this book. As you discovered in: *Lesson 10-6: Understand data types,* Excel only supports four native data types.

Get & Transform: This is Microsoft's ETL (Extract, Transform and Load) tool that you are learning to use in this session. Get & Transform was originally a separate application called *Power Query*. Because Get & Transform needs to work with data from many different sources it supports twelve different data types.

Power Pivot: This is Microsoft's OLAP (Online Analytical Processing) and data modeling tool. You'll learn how to use Power Pivot later, in: *Session Eleven: Power Pivot, Data Modeling, OLAP and Business Intelligence.* Power Pivot supports five different data types.

Data type conversion (from source)

In order to be able to import (get) data from sources such as SQL Server, Access and Excel, *Get & Transform* must convert source data into one of the data types it supports.

It is often possible for *Get & Transform* to guess the most appropriate data type to convert the source data into. For example, if a source data column contained numeric values with no decimal places, *Get & Transform* might guess that the *Whole Number* data type was most appropriate.

Get & Transform will often play it safe and convert most data into the *Text* data type. You then need to manually set the correct data type using *Get & Transform*. You'll learn how to do this in: *Lesson 10-11: Specify data types.*

Data type conversion (to target)

As well as performing data type conversion during the *Get* and *Transform* operations, data sometimes needs to go through another data type conversion when it is loaded to its final destination.

Later, in: *Session Eleven: Power Pivot, Data Modeling, OLAP and Business Intelligence,* you'll discover that Get & Transform is also the correct tool to use when loading data into a Power Pivot data model.

The *Power Pivot* tool supports more data types than Excel, meaning that fewer data type conversions are needed when loading data into Power Pivot.

Get & Transform supported data types

Data Type	Description
Decimal Number	This corresponds exactly to the Excel Number data type. The Decimal Number data type is a floating-point number that can have decimal places. The largest value that can be represented by a Decimal Number data type is 15 digits long (the decimal separator can occur anywhere in the number).
Currency	The Currency data type allows a maximum of four decimal places.
Whole Number	Numbers that have no decimal places. These are often also called Integers. Whole Numbers can be positive or negative. The largest value that can be represented by a Whole Number data type is 19 digits long.
Percentage	In a similar way to Excel, a percentage value (for example 5%) will be automatically recognized as a percentage value and then converted into a two-digit precision decimal number (in this example 0.05) that can be used for arithmetical operations in the Query Editor, Data Model or a worksheet.
Date/Time	This is stored in the same way as an Excel date/time serial number using a Decimal number type. Valid dates are from 1 Jan 1900 to 31 Dec 9999. Date serial numbers were explained in depth in: *Lesson 3-7: Understand date serial numbers.*
Date	This is stored in the same way as an Excel date/time serial number using a Decimal number type with no decimal places.
Time	This is stored in the same way as an Excel date/time serial number using a Decimal number type with no digits to the left of the decimal place.
Date/Time/Timezone	This represents a UTC Date/Time.
Duration	The Duration data type represents a length of time. This is stored in the same way as an Excel date/time serial number, using a Decimal number type. The Duration data type can be added or subtracted from a Date/Time field with correct results.
Text	A set of Unicode characters. These are often also called Strings. Strings can also represent numbers or dates stored in a text format. The maximum length of a string is 268,435,456 Unicode characters.
True/False	Either a True or False value.
Binary	Binary data is the type of data that is typically stored in a file (such as a picture or video).

Lesson 10-11: Specify data types

In: *Lesson 10-10: Understand Get & Transform data types* you discovered that the *Get & Transform* tool supports twelve different data types. When you import data, *Get & Transform* must convert the source data into one of the data types that it supports.

While *Get & Transform* tries to guess the most appropriate data type to convert the source data into it will often play it safe and convert most data into the *Text* data type.

In this lesson you'll learn how to manually set the correct data type for each column.

1   Open a new blank workbook.

2   Create a *Get & Transform* query to extract the values from the *Invoice* table in the *Invoices-1* Access database.

1.   Click: Data→Get & Transform Data→Get Data→
From Database→From Microsoft Access Database.

2.   Navigate to the *Invoices-1* Access file in your sample files folder and then click the *Import* button.

3.   Select the *Invoice* table and then Click the *Transform Data* button.

The *Power Query Editor* opens.

3   Remove the *InvoiceID* column.

You learned how to do this in: *Lesson 10-4: Move, remove, rename, filter and sort columns.*

4   Correct the *InvoiceDate* and *InvoiceTime* data types.

You can immediately see that the *InvoiceDate* and *InvoiceTime* columns have the wrong data type as they are both displaying both date and time values.

1.   Right-click on the *InvoiceDate* column header.

2.   Hover the mouse cursor over: *Change Type* from the shortcut menu.

A list of data types appears with the *Date/Time* data type checked.

3.   Click: *Date* to change the data type to *Date*.

4.   Repeat this process for the *InvoiceTime* field, changing the data type to *Time*.

Notice the descriptive icons at the top of each column that visually indicate the column's data type.

5   Confirm that the other columns have the most appropriate data type.

You can see that Get & Transform has done a great job on the other columns by identifying the correct data types.

Get & Transform has decided that the safest option is to use the *Text* data type for the *InvoiceNumber* column. You might think that the *Whole Number* data type would be more appropriate as all of the values in this column are whole numbers.

In this case, Get & Transform may have a good argument. Consider an invoice number with leading zeroes (such as 000001). Converting this number to a *Whole Number* data type would remove the leading zeroes and this might make the value more confusing.

6   Close the query editor and load the query result to a table that begins in cell A1 of a new worksheet.

You learned how to do this in: *Lesson 10-4: Move, remove, rename, filter and sort columns.*

7   Save your work as *Invoices-2.*

Lesson 10-12: Understand steps and PQFL

Every transformation that you apply in *Get & Transform* generates a formula that is written in the *Power Query Formula Language* (PQFL). A PQFL formula looks very much like an Excel formula. Unlike Excel formulas, PQFL language formulas are case sensitive.

Get & Transform creates a PQFL formula every time you apply a transformation action.

1 Open *Phone List-1* from your sample files folder.

This is the workbook that you created in: *Lesson 10-4: Move, remove, rename, filter and sort columns.*

2 Click the *Enable Content* button if shown.

3 Display the *Queries & Connections* task pane.

Click: Data→Queries & Connections→Queries & Connections.

The *Queries & Connections* task pane appears.

4 Open the query in the Power Query Editor.

Double-click on the *Employees-1* query (visible in the *Queries & Connections* task pane).

The *Power Query Editor* opens, showing the rows returned by the query.

Notice that there is a *Query Settings* task pane on the right-hand side of the query editor. This should look the same as (or similar to) the one shown in the sidebar.

In the *Applied Steps* list you can see all of the transformations that you applied to this query in: *Lesson 10-4: Move, remove, rename, filter and sort columns.*

Each of the *Applied Steps* contains a PQFL formula.

5 Inspect the PQFL formula for the *Filtered Rows* step.

You may remember that in: *Lesson 10-4: Move, remove, rename, filter and sort columns,* the last transformation you specified was to filter the list to only show USA employees.

This created the *Filtered Rows* step.

1. If the formula bar is not visible check: View→Layout→ Formula Bar.

2. Click on the *Filtered Rows* step in the *Query Settings* task pane.

    Observe the PQFL formula in the formula bar.

    ```
    fx  = Table.SelectRows(#"Sorted Rows", each ([Country] = "USA"))
    ```

    Even without knowing PQFL, you can probably guess broadly how this formula works.

6 Manually edit the PQFL formula for the *Filtered Rows* step so that UK employees are shown instead of USA employees.

Phone List-1

trivia

What's in a name?

The Power Query Formula Language (PQFL)

As you are aware, *Get & Transform* is a re-branding of a product that was originally known as *Power Query*.

The old name lives on in the name of the query language.

The M Language

When PQFL was being developed, Microsoft's original internal code name for the language was "M Language".

The letter *M* comes from the common Business Intelligence term: *Mashup*.

A *Data Mashup* simply means combining data from different data sources.

Much of the PQFL help refers to the language in a rather long-winded way as:

The Power Query Formula Language (informally known as "M").

note

Some steps have arguments

Notice that some steps have a small gear wheel icon next to them, such as the *Source* step shown below:

Source	⚙
Promoted Headers	
Changed Type	

When you see this icon, you know that the step has arguments that you can edit.

If you click on the icon for the *Source* step, you'll find that you are able to edit the file location of the original CSV file.

| File Path |
| C:\Practice\Excel 2016 Expert |

Where you see "USA" in the formula bar, change the text to read "UK" and press the **<Enter>** key.

```
= Table.SelectRows(#"Reordered Columns", each ([Country] = "UK"))
```

The grid changes to show UK employees.

Of course, it would be easier to simply change the filter using the filter button next to *Country*. Country ⧩

This does, however, illustrate the link between the things that you are doing using the ribbon and grid, and the PQFL formula that is generated to implement each of your actions.

7 **Step through the *Applied Steps* one by one.**

1. Click on the *Source* action in the *Query Settings* task pane.

    This was one of two actions that *Get & Transform* automatically created when you first opened the CSV file. You can see the original CSV file just after import. Notice that the column headers have not yet been named.

2. Click on the *Promoted Headers* action.

    This action was also automatically created when you first opened the CSV file.

    Get & Transform intelligently guessed that the first row of the CSV file contained column headers. The term *Promoted* means that the first row is used to define the column names.

3. Click on each of the other actions in turn and watch your data transform as each transformation is applied.

8 **Delete the *Sorted Rows* step.**

You may remember that one of the transformations you applied was to sort the data in A-Z order, first by *Country* and then by *Last Name*.

If you delete the *Sorted Rows* step, the data will be listed in the order that it originally appeared in the CSV file.

1. Click on the *Sorted Rows* step to select it.

    Notice that there is a delete icon on the left-hand side of the step.

2. Click the *Delete* icon.

3. Click the *Delete* button when prompted to confirm the deletion.

    The step is removed.

4. Click on the last *Filtered Rows* step.

    Notice that the *Last Name* column is no longer sorted in alphabetical order.

9 **Close the Power Query Editor (click *Keep* if prompted).**

10 **Save your work as *Phone List-2*.**

Lesson 10-13: Remove empty, error and top and bottom rows

While you can freely remove columns from a query, you need to use different techniques when removing rows.

When you simply need a subset of the rows in the source data, this is normally done by applying a filter.

Sometimes data contains error rows, or top and bottom rows, that need to be removed.

1   Open a new blank workbook.

2   Create a *Get & Transform* query to extract the values from the *Gold-1* CSV file in your sample files folder.

> You learned how to do this in: *Lesson 10-4: Move, remove, rename, filter and sort columns.*
>
> This file contains average monthly spot price of gold (in US dollars) for the period January 2006 to December 2015.

3   Click the *Transform Data* button to enter the Power Query Editor.

4   Use the values in the first row as column headers.

> In: *Lesson 10-4: Move, remove, rename, filter and sort columns,* you worked with a well-structured CSV file and *Get & Transform* was able to automatically detect that the first row should be used as column headers.
>
> The first rows in this CSV file are a little harder to understand:

> You can see that the column header information is contained in both rows 1 and 2.
>
> Click: Transform→Table→Use First Row as Headers.
>
> This solves part of the problem, as the values in row 1 are now used as column headers.

5   Remove row 1.

> You'll often find one or more rows of unwanted header or footer data at the top or bottom of an imported data table.
>
> *Get & Transform* provides a fast way to remove the unwanted rows.
>
> 1.   Click: Home→Reduce Rows→Remove Rows→ Remove Top Rows.

Gold-1 (CSV)

The *Remove Top Rows* dialog appears.

2. Type: **1** into the *Number of rows* box.

3. Click the *OK* button.

6 **Change the data types to appropriate values.**

You learned about data types in: *Lesson 10-6: Understand data types.*

1. Right-click on the *Average Price* column header.

2. Click: Change Type→Currency.

3. Right-click on the *Date* column header.

4. Click: *Change Type* from the shortcut menu.

Notice that the data type is currently set to *Text*.

5. Click: *Date* to change the data type.

Notice that two interesting things have happened.

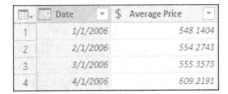

Because there is no information to suggest the correct day of the month, *Get & Transform* has guessed that an appropriate date might be the first day of each month. Later, in: *Lesson 10-15: Transform date and time columns*, you'll find out how you could choose a different day of the month.

There are some values in this column (for example the words: *Average 2007*) that could not be converted to dates. In these cases, Get & Transform is showing the word *Error* in place of a date.

Note that in the above grab the dates are shown in *m/dd/yyyy* format because my Windows *Region format* was set to *English (United States)*. Depending upon your operating system's region format settings, you will see an appropriate format for your geographical location.

7 **Remove error rows.**

Click: Home→Reduce Rows→Remove Rows→Remove Errors.

The error rows are removed from the grid.

8 **Close the Power Query Editor and load the query result to a linked table in cell A1 of the worksheet (there is only one worksheet in this workbook).**

You learned how to do this in: *Lesson 10-4: Move, remove, rename, filter and sort columns.*

9 **Save your work as** *Gold-2*.

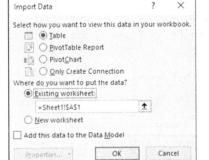

Lesson 10-14: Understand and work with null values

When you see a blank cell in a worksheet, you might interpret this as a value of zero. Computers (and databases) are more sophisticated and support a concept called null. Null is not a value but is the *absence* of a value.

Empty cells often do not contain null values but are left blank because most readers will assume a value that is not stated.

Here's an example:

With nulls

	A	B	C
1	First Name	Last Name	Occupation
2	John	Smith	Electrician
3	Bill	Jones	
4	Arthur	Williams	Bricklayer

Without nulls

	A	B	C
1	First Name	Last Name	Occupation
2	John	Smith	Electrician
3	Bill	Jones	Unemployed
4	Arthur	Williams	Bricklayer

What is the status of Bill Jones in the *With nulls* example above? Is he unemployed, or do you simply not know? Excel would consider the blank cell as having a null value (in other words, you don't know whether Bill has an occupation or not).

Ideally the nulls should be replaced with words similar to: *Not Stated, Withheld, Unemployed, Retired* or *Unknown*.

The issue is far more common (and can cause more errors) with numeric fields. Consider this example:

With nulls

	A	B
1	Item	Quantity
2	Apples	25
3	Oranges	
4	Pears	35
5		

Without nulls

	A	B
1	Item	Quantity
2	Apples	25
3	Oranges	0
4	Pears	35
5		

In the *With nulls* example above, a human might assume that we have zero oranges. Excel would just note the absence of any meaningful data (in other words, a null value) and assume that you have no idea how many oranges you have.

Null values will also affect many of Excel's functions.

In the *With nulls* example above, the formula **=AVERAGE(B2:B4)** returns a value of 30.

In the *Without nulls* example above, the same formula returns a value of 20. A **COUNT** function would also return different results (2 and 3).

The above two examples both illustrate the concept of false null values.

Sometimes (though rarely) you may have real null values (see sidebar for examples). In these special cases it may be better to leave the cells empty.

1   Open a new blank workbook.

note

Examples of real null values

1. A questionnaire may request a date of birth that some respondents refuse to supply.

Clearly the respondent does have a date of birth, you simply don't know what it is. The empty cell contains a real null value.

2. You record the temperature every day in degrees Celsius.

Sometimes you forget to record the temperature.

Clearly a value of 0 degrees is incorrect, so it would be wrong to replace all of the empty cells with a zero.

The empty cells contain real null values. There was a temperature on those days, but you don't know what it was.

Olympics-1 (CSV)

2   Create a *Get & Transform* query to extract the values from the *Olympics-1* CSV file in your sample files folder.

You learned how to do this in: *Lesson 10-4: Move, remove, rename, filter and sort columns.*

3   Click the *Transform Data* button to enter the Power Query Editor.

⊞▾	1²₃ Rank	ABC Country	ABC Continent	1²₃ Summer Olympics	ABC Years (Summer Olympics)	1²₃ Winter Olympics	ABC Years (Winter Olympics)
10	8	Soviet Union/Russia	Europe	1	1980	1	2014
11	8	Greece	Europe	2	1896, 2004	null	
12	8	Australia	Oceania	2	1956, 2000	null	
13	8	Norway	Europe	null		2	1952, 1994
14	8	Austria	Europe	null		2	1964, 1976

note

Why do the Year columns not contain null values?

Get & Transform will represent a null textual value as an *Empty String*.

An empty string can be thought of as a textual value that does not contain any actual text.

For example, the Excel formula:

="Extra" & "" & "terrestrial"

… concatenates an empty string in between the words *Extra* and *terrestrial*.

If you typed the above formula into an Excel cell, the result would be the single word:

Extraterrestrial

Database designers can argue all day about whether a blank textual value should be represented as an empty string or a null value.

In the context of data that will be used by Excel there isn't any real difference, as Excel will regard a cell containing an empty string to be the same as any other empty cell.

In this lesson's data you could, of course, replace the empty text values with meaningful text such as: *Not Applicable*. The resulting data would then produce different results with Excel functions such as COUNTA and COUNTBLANK.

This data contains a list of countries that have hosted one or more Olympic Games.

Notice that there are several null values.

In the above grab you can see that Norway and Austria have a null value in the *Summer Olympics* column.

These are false null values. You actually know that Norway and Austria have never hosted a Summer Olympics. The value should more properly be stated as zero.

Notice also that there are empty values in the *Years* columns when a country has never hosted the Olympics. This is because *Get & Transform* has assigned the *Text* data type to these columns (see sidebar).

4   Correct the null values.

It is generally good practice to remove false null values from data (unless you really intend the value to signify the absence of data).

In this case, the nulls clearly signify zero values

1. Click on the *Summer Olympics* column header to select the entire column.

2. Hold down the **<Ctrl>** key and then click on the *Winter Olympics* column header.

   Both columns are now selected.

3. Click: Home→Transform→Replace Values.

   The *Replace Values* dialog appears.

4. Type **null** into the *Value To Find* box.

5. Type **0** into the *Replace With* box.

6. Click the *OK* button.

   The null values are replaced with zeroes.

5   Close the Power Query Editor and load the query result to a table in cell A1 of the existing worksheet (there is only one worksheet in this workbook).

You learned how to do this in: *Lesson 10-4: Move, remove, rename, filter and sort columns.*

6   Save your work as *Olympics-2*.

note

How can I return day and month names instead of numbers?

When you return day and month numbers instead of names you are able to sort by week or month number and have the days or months appear in the correct order.

This is why the Get & Transform *Day of Week* and *Month* transformations return numbers instead of text.

For example:

1=January, 2=February
and
0=Monday, 1=Tuesday

Sometimes, for display purposes, you'd rather have textual month and day values such as:

Jan, Feb, Mar
and
Mon, Tue, Wed

You can do this by adding a duplicate column and then applying one of the following transformations to it:

Transform→
Date & Time Column→
Date→Month→
Name of Month

Transform→
Date & Time Column→
Date→Day→
Name of Day

Lesson 10-15: Transform date and time columns

When source data contains transactional information (such as a listing of individual sales), you will often want to analyze total sales by *Quarter, Month* or *Year*.

As you learned in: *Lesson 8-19: Group by date*, regular pivot tables have always had the ability to group by *Seconds, Minutes, Hours, Days, Months, Quarters* and *Years*.

This means that you probably won't have to create *Second, Minute, Hour, Day, Month, Quarter* and *Year* fields within your *Get & Transform* queries if you intend to load the query into a pivot table.

While pivot tables can group by these seven different date and time fields, *Get & Transform* supports sixteen additional date and time grouping types. For example:

- You might want to group by the *Week of Year*, to compare this week's sales with the same week's sales last year.

- You might want to group by *Day of Week*, to discover the average sales figure for *Monday*.

In this lesson you'll learn how to add a new *Week of Year* grouping field to a *Get & Transform* query and then use it to analyze sales by week in a pivot table.

1   Open a new blank workbook.

2   Create a *Get & Transform* query to extract the values from the *DVD Sales-1* Excel workbook in your sample files folder.

The *DVD Sales-1* workbook contains a single Excel table called *DVDSales*.

1. Click: Data→Get & Transform Data→Get Data→ From File→From Workbook.

2. Navigate to and select the *DVD Sales-1* Excel workbook file in your sample files folder.

3. Select the *DVDSales* table.

4. Click the *Transform Data* button to open the query in the *Power Query Editor*.

5. Click the *Refresh* button if prompted.

3   Create a duplicate *Date* column named *Week*.

1. Click anywhere in the *Date* column.

2. Click: Add Column→General→Duplicate Column.

A duplicate column is added, named: *Date - Copy*.

DVD Sales-1

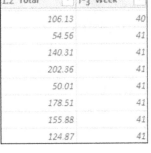

3. Double-click in the column header and type: **Week**

4. Press the **<Enter>** key.

4 Transform the value in the *Week* column so that it displays the week number of each transaction.

1. Click anywhere in the *Week* column to make it the active column.

2. Click: Transform→Date & Time Column→Date→ Week→Week of Year.

   The values in the *Week* column change to show the week number for each transaction.

5 Load the query results directly into a pivot table.

This time you will output the query result directly to a pivot table without loading to a linked table first.

This results in a more compact workbook, both in file size (when you save it) and in memory usage (when it is open).

1. Click: File→Close & Load To…

   The *Import Data* dialog appears.

2. Click the *PivotTable Report* option button.

3. Click the *OK* button.

   You are returned to a new worksheet containing a pivot table.

6 Use the pivot table to show sales by *Customer* for each *Year* and *Week*.

Do this using the same technique you learned in: *Lesson 8-19: Group by date.*

The field settings are:

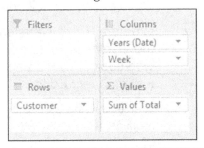

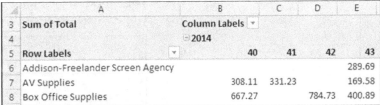

	A	B	C	D	E
3	Sum of Total	Column Labels			
4		2014			
5	Row Labels	40	41	42	43
6	Addison-Freelander Screen Agency				289.69
7	AV Supplies	308.11	331.23		169.58
8	Box Office Supplies	667.27		784.73	400.89

7 Save your work as *DVD Sales-2*.

Lesson 10-16: Transform number columns

You will often find a need to transform the scale and rounding of number columns.

For example, in this table, column C shows numbers using the *Thousand* number scale and percentages as floating-point numbers:

	A	B	C	D
3	From	To	Individuals (thousands)	% In Group
4	0	2,500.00	12,686	5.996350951
5	2,500.00	4,999.00	7,202	3.404203023
6	5,000.00	7,499.00	9,645	4.558947259

You might prefer the *Individuals (thousands)* column to show values without scaling and the *% In Group* column to show values rounded to four decimal places, like this:

	A	B	C	D
1	From	To	Individuals	% In Group
2	0	2500	12686000	5.9964
3	2500	4999	7202000	3.4042
4	5000	7499	9645000	4.5589

You could, of course, do this inside Excel but it is best practice to transform values within Get & Transform.

By transforming the values within *Get & Transform* the linked table will display the correct values as soon as it is created. You are then able to right-click→refresh the table to update and display any future changes that may occur in the data source without having to manually reformat the table after refreshing.

1   Open a new blank workbook.

2   Create a *Get & Transform* query to extract the values from the *IncomeDistribution* table in the *USA Income-1* Excel workbook in your sample files folder and display them in the Power Query Editor.

You learned how to do this in: *Lesson 10-15: Transform date and time columns*.

This workbook contains details of individual incomes in the United States in 2010:

	From	To	Individuals (thousands)	% In Group
21	50000	52499	6320	2.987303958
22	52500	54999	2186	1.033266844
23	55000	57499	3455	1.633091009
24	57500	59999	1876	0.886737694

You can see that *6,320,000* Americans had an income between *$50,000* and *$52,499*, which constituted *2.987303958%* of all individuals.

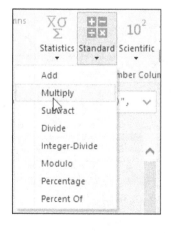

USA Income-1

3   Change the scale of the *Individuals (thousands)* column to show the number without thousand scaling.

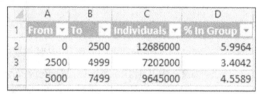

1. Click anywhere in the *Individuals (thousands)* column.

2. Click: Transform→Number Column→Standard→Multiply.

   The *Multiply* dialog appears.

3. Type: **1000** into the *Value* box.

4. Click the *OK* button.

   All values in the *Individuals (thousands)* column are transformed:

	From		To		Individuals (thousands)		% In Group	
1	0		2500		12686000		5.996350951	
2	2500		4999		7202000		3.404203023	
3	5000		7499		9645000		4.558947259	

4 Change the column header of the *Individuals (thousands)* column to: **Individuals**

1. Double-click on the *Individuals (thousands)* column header.

2. Replace the existing text with: **Individuals**

3. Press the **<Enter>** key.

5 Round the values in the *% In Group* column so that values are rounded to four decimal places.

1. Click anywhere in the *% In Group* column.

2. Click: Transform→Number column→Rounding→Round…

   The *Round* dialog appears.

3. Type **4** into the *Decimal Places* box.

4. Click the *OK* button.

   All values in the *% In Group* column are rounded to four decimal places:

	From		To		Individuals		% In Group	
1	0		2500		12686000		5.9964	
2	2500		4999		7202000		3.4042	
3	5000		7499		9645000		4.5589	

6 Close the Power Query Editor and load the query result to a table beginning in cell A1 of the existing worksheet (there is only one worksheet in this workbook).

You learned how to do this in: *Lesson 10-4: Move, remove, rename, filter and sort columns.*

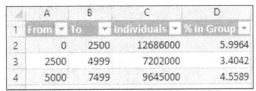

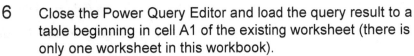

	A	B	C	D
1	From	To	Individuals	% In Group
2	0	2500	12686000	5.9964
3	2500	4999	7202000	3.4042
4	5000	7499	9645000	4.5589

7 Save your work as *USA Income-2.*

Lesson 10-17: Add a custom calculated column

In a few clicks you can add a calculated column to a *Get & Transform* query.

1   Open a new blank workbook.

2   Create a *Get & Transform* query to extract the values from the *Sales* table in the *Bonus-1* Excel workbook in your sample files folder and display them in the Power Query Editor.

    You learned how to do this in: *Lesson 10-15: Transform date and time columns.*

    This workbook contains details of individual sales generated by a DVD wholesaler:

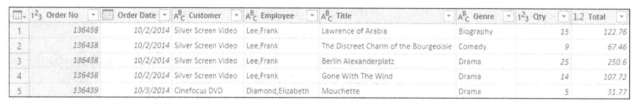

	1²₃ Order No	Order Date	AᴮC Customer	AᴮC Employee	AᴮC Title	AᴮC Genre	1²₃ Qty	1.2 Total
1	136438	10/2/2014	Silver Screen Video	Lee,Frank	Lawrence of Arabia	Biography	15	122.76
2	136438	10/2/2014	Silver Screen Video	Lee,Frank	The Discreet Charm of the Bourgeoisie	Comedy	9	67.46
3	136438	10/2/2014	Silver Screen Video	Lee,Frank	Berlin Alexanderplatz	Drama	25	250.6
4	136438	10/2/2014	Silver Screen Video	Lee,Frank	Gone With The Wind	Drama	14	107.72
5	136439	10/3/2014	Cinefocus DVD	Diamond,Elizabeth	Mouchette	Drama	5	31.77

You can see that *Frank Lee* sold order *136438* to *Silver Screen Video*. The order was for four different DVD titles.

By adding the *Qty* and *Total* field values in rows 1-4 you can see that Frank sold 63 DVDs on this order, for a total price of $548.54.

In this lesson you will calculate a monthly bonus for each employee. The bonus will be calculated as 3% of the total sale value.

3   Add a custom column to the Get & Transform query named: **Bonus** that will calculate 3% of the value shown in the *Total* column.

    1. Click: Add Column→General→Custom Column.

    2. The *Custom Column* dialog appears.

    3. Type: **Bonus** into the *New column name* box.

    4. Click inside the *Custom column formula* box.

    5. Click the *Total* field in the right-hand list.

    6. Click the << *Insert* button to add the *Total* field to the *Custom column formula* box.

        Notice that the field name is shown inside square brackets. This is PQFL syntax for a field name.

    7. Click to the right of the *[Total]* field and type: ***0.03** to complete the formula.

        Multiplying the *Total* field by 0.03 will calculate 3% of the field's value.

Bonus-1

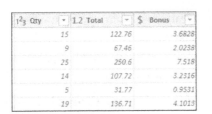

8. Click the *OK* button.

A new custom (calculated) column called *Bonus* is added to the query and shows values that are 3% of the value in the *Total* column:

You can see that *Frank Lee* made $3.68 bonus on his sale of 15 copies of *Lawrence of Arabia*.

4 Set the data type of the *Bonus* field to *Currency*.

You learned how to do this in: *Lesson 10-10: Understand Get & Transform data types*.

5 Load the query results directly into a pivot table.

You did this in: *Lesson 10-15: Transform date and time columns*.

6 Select fields in the pivot table that will show the monthly *Bonus* earned for each *Employee*.

Do this using the same technique you learned in: *Lesson 8-19: Group by date*.

The field settings are:

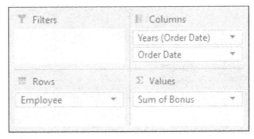

7 Set the *Number Format* for the values shown in the pivot table to *Currency*.

1. Right-click on any value in the pivot table.

2. Select *Number Format…* from the shortcut menu.

3. Set the number format to *Currency*.

4. Click the *OK* button.

You can now see the monthly bonus earned by each *Employee* for each year and month in the period Oct 2014 to Mar 2016.

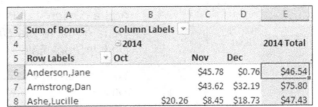

Note that the currency symbol shown in your own pivot table may differ depending upon your Windows region format settings.

8 Save your work as *Bonus-2*.

Lesson 10-18: Create an aggregated data query

Normally you will use *Get & Transform* to transform data and then use a pivot table to aggregate (summarize) the query result.

There may be some special circumstances where you would like the query to aggregate values *before* sending the query results to Excel.

This lesson will bring together many of the skills you have learned so far in this session.

1   Open a new blank workbook.

2   Create a *Get & Transform* query to extract the values from the *Products and Categories View* in the Inventory-1 Access database in your sample files folder and display them in the *Power Query Editor*.

   You will learn more about views later, in: *Lesson 10-28: Efficiently import data using a view.*

   You learned how to connect a *Get & Transform* query to an Access database in: *Lesson 10-11: Specify data types.*

   This view returns inventory details. Each product has been allocated a *Category*.

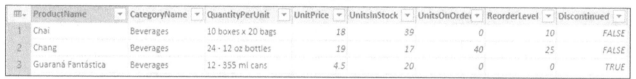

⊞▾	ProductName	▾	CategoryName	▾	QuantityPerUnit	▾	UnitPrice	▾	UnitsInStock	▾	UnitsOnOrder	▾	ReorderLevel	▾	Discontinued	▾
1	Chai		Beverages		10 boxes x 20 bags		18		39		0		10		FALSE	
2	Chang		Beverages		24 - 12 oz bottles		19		17		40		25		FALSE	
3	Guaraná Fantástica		Beverages		12 - 355 ml cans		4.5		20		0		0		TRUE	

Your challenge in this lesson will be to create a *Get & Transform* query that will return aggregated (summarized) values for each *Category*. This is very similar to the results you could obtain using a pivot table (see facing page sidebar for the advantages an aggregated data query).

For each *Category*, the query needs to report the total *Units in Stock, Units on Order, Inventory Value* and *Projected Inventory Value* (the value that would result if all goods on order had already arrived).

3   Set the data type of the *UnitPrice* column to *Currency* (if it isn't already set to *Currency*) and the data type of the *UnitsInStock* and *UnitsOnOrder* columns to *Whole Number*.

   You learned how to do this in: *Lesson 10-11: Specify data types.*

4   Add a custom column named *InventoryValue* that contains a value equal to the *UnitPrice* field multiplied by the *UnitsInStock* field.

   You learned how to do this in: *Lesson 10-17: Add a custom calculated column.*

5   Add a custom column named *ProjectedInventoryValue* that contains a value equal to the *UnitsOnOrder* field multiplied by the *UnitPrice field* added to the (already calculated) *InventoryValue* field.

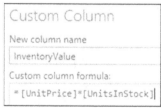

Custom Column

New column name

InventoryValue

Custom column formula:

= [UnitPrice]*[UnitsInStock]

Custom Column

New column name

ProjectedInventoryValue

Custom column formula:

= [UnitsOnOrder]*[UnitPrice]+
[InventoryValue]

Inventory-1

You learned how to do this in: *Lesson 10-17: Add a custom calculated column*.

6   Set the data type of both custom columns to *Currency*.

You learned how to do this in: *Lesson 10-11: Specify data types*.

7   Group the query by *CategoryName* to show aggregated values for the total of the four numeric columns.

1. Click any cell in the *CategoryName* column.

2. Click: Transform→Table→Group By.

    The *Group By* dialog appears.

3. Click the *Advanced* option button.

4. Select *CategoryName* from the *Group by* drop-down list (if it isn't already selected).

5. Type **UnitsInStock** into the *New column name* box.

6. Select: *Sum* from the *Operation* drop-down list.

7. Select *UnitsInStock* from the *Column* drop-down list.

8. Click the *Add aggregation* button to add a second group field for *UnitsOnOrder*.

9. Add three more fields so that your dialog looks like this:

10. Click the *OK* button.

8   Close the Power Query Editor and load the query result to a table in cell A1 of the existing worksheet.

You learned how to do this in: *Lesson 10-4: Move, remove, rename, filter and sort columns*.

	A	B	C	D	E
1	CategoryName	UnitsInStock	UnitsOnOrder	InventoryValue	ProjectedInventoryValue
2	Beverages	559	60	12480.25	13850.25
3	Condiments	507	170	12023.55	14423.55
4	Confections	386	180	10392.2	13009.7

9   Save your work as *Inventory-2*.

note

Advantages of a linked table containing an aggregated query over a pivot table

Automatic refresh capability

You can schedule automatic refreshes with an aggregated query.

In: *Lesson 10-3: Understand queries and connections*, you learned how to automatically refresh a table linked to a *Get & Transform* query every minute.

It isn't possible to automatically refresh data in a pivot table.

Small file and memory size

A worksheet table does not have any associated PivotTable data cache. This can result in a much smaller file size and memory requirement.

Lesson 10-19: Unpivot aggregated data

Recognizing pivoted data

You'll often find data showing rolled-up totals in columns. For example, consider this data:

	A	B	C	D
2	Customer	Jan	Feb	Mar
3	Addison-Freelander Screen Agency	2,195.49	1,673.32	488.52
4	AV Supplies	1,298.66	1,862.95	1,792.25
5	Box Office Supplies	795.39	3,029.79	1,793.12

The data shows aggregated monthly sales.

Data in this format is nicely presented for human readers but is not useful when you need to analyze it using an Excel worksheet or pivot table.

Here is the correct format for easy analysis of the above data:

	A	B	C
2	Customer	Month	Sales
3	Addison-Freelander Screen Agency	Jan	2195.49
4	Addison-Freelander Screen Agency	Feb	1673.32
5	Addison-Freelander Screen Agency	Mar	488.52
6	AV Supplies	Jan	1298.66
7	AV Supplies	Feb	1862.95
8	AV Supplies	Mar	1792.25
9	Box Office Supplies	Jan	795.39
10	Box Office Supplies	Feb	3029.79
11	Box Office Supplies	Mar	1793.12

This transformation would take a substantial amount of time using traditional Excel tools but takes just three clicks in the *Get & Transform* query editor. Many more things can be done when the data is transformed into the correct format for analysis.

- You can create a pivot table from it.

- You can filter by month.

- You can use many of Excel's aggregation functions and features (for example the automatic subtotal feature that you learned to use in: *Lesson 2-3: Automatically subtotal a range*).

1 Open a new blank worksheet.

2 Create a *Get & Transform* query to extract the values from the *MonthlySales* table in the *Sales by Employee-1* Excel workbook in your sample files folder and display them in the Power Query Editor.

You learned how to do this in: *Lesson 10-15: Transform date and time columns.*

This workbook contains monthly total sales figures for each employee.

Sales by Employee-1

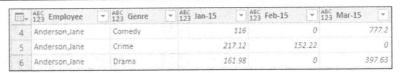

	ABC 123 Employee		ABC 123 Genre		ABC 123 Jan-15		ABC 123 Feb-15		ABC 123 Mar-15	
4	Anderson,Jane		Comedy		116		0		777.2	
5	Anderson,Jane		Crime		217.12		152.22		0	
6	Anderson,Jane		Drama		161.98		0		397.63	

note

Why are there two Month fields shown in the PivotTable Field List

When you add the *Month* pivot table field to the *Columns* box, two different values are shown:

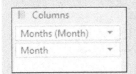

In: *Lesson 10-6: Understand data types*, it was noted that Excel does not support any true *Date* or *Time* data types.

Instead, Excel relies upon formatting numerical values that are regarded as being *date serial numbers*.

Date serial numbers were covered in depth in: *Lesson 3-7: Understand date serial numbers*.

Get & Transform originally assigned the *Text* data type to the *Month* column.

When you changed the data type of the *Month* column to *Date*, Get & Transform assigned the first day of each month to the date values in the column.

The pivot table was not sure whether you wanted date values (such as 01/01/18) or month values (such as *Jan, Feb, Mar*) in the column headers.

For this reason, it helpfully added both *Months (Month)* to show the month name and *Month* (the field name on its own) to show the full date.

You can see that this is a classic example of pivoted data. The *Employee* and *Genre* columns don't have a problem but all of the other columns (*Jan-15* to *Dec-15*) need to be unpivoted.

3 **Unpivot all of the monthly total columns.**

1. Click on the *Jan-15* column header to select it.

2. Hold down the **<Shift>** key.

3. Click on the *Dec-15* column header.

All monthly columns are now selected.

4. Click: Transform→Any Column→Unpivot Columns.

The columns are unpivoted:

	AᴮC Employee		AᴮC Genre		AᴮC Attribute		1.2 Value	
1	Anderson,Jane		Action		Jan-15		0	
2	Anderson,Jane		Action		Feb-15		173.29	
3	Anderson,Jane		Action		Mar-15		409.48	

4 **Rename the *Attribute* column to: Month and the *Value* column to: Sales**

You learned how to do this in: *Lesson 10-4: Move, remove, rename, filter and sort columns.*

5 **Change the data type of the *Month* column to *Date* and the data type of the *Sales* column to *Currency.***

You learned how to do this in: *Lesson 10-11: Specify data types.*

6 **Load the query results directly into a pivot table.**

You did this in: *Lesson 10-15: Transform date and time columns.*

7 **Select fields in the pivot table that will show monthly *Sales* for each *Genre*.**

Do this using the same technique you learned in: *Lesson 8-19: Group by date.*

The field settings are shown in the sidebar.

8 **Set the *Number Format* for the values shown in the pivot table to *Currency*.**

1. Right-click on any value in the pivot table.

2. Select *Number Format…* from the shortcut menu.

3. Set the number format to *Currency*.

4. Click the *OK* button.

	A	B	C	D	E	F
1	Sum of Sales	Column Labels				
2	Row Labels	Jan	Feb	Mar	Apr	May
3	Action	$1,112.11	$1,249.08	$2,630.88	$769.55	$1,001.89
4	Adventure	$246.59	$167.83	$285.65	$379.22	$581.30

9 **Save your work as: *Sales by Employee-2*.**

Lesson 10-20: Work with multiple queries

Up until now you've worked with a single query.

Get & Transform can also combine data from multiple queries. You'll learn how to do this in: *Lesson 10-21: Create an append query*.

Get & Transform also has some features that work well with queries containing related data (you'll learn about relational data later, in: *Lesson 10-26: Understand primary and foreign keys*).

As each query can potentially draw data from a different data source, it is possible to combine data from one or more web queries, CSV files, Excel workbooks and database tables or views.

You could create queries individually (as you have up to now in this session). This lesson will teach you how to work more efficiently by creating multiple queries in a single *Get & Transform* session.

1   Open a new blank workbook.

2   Open the Power Query Editor.

Up until now you've always selected the data source type before entering the query editor. You could do that in this lesson but, for variety, you'll do things a little differently.

Click: Data→Get & Transform Data→Get Data→
Launch Power Query Editor…

The empty query editor opens.

3   Create four queries named *Confections*, *DairyProduce*, *Beverages* and *Condiments* from the four sample files of the same name in the *Session 10/Append* folder in your sample files folder.

The *Session 10/Append* folder contains three Excel sample files and one CSV sample file. Each of the files contains data with the same structure (the same number of columns and the same column header names in each column).

Name	Type	Size
Beverages	Microsoft Excel Comma Separated Values File	1 KB
Condiments	Microsoft Excel Worksheet	10 KB
Confections	Microsoft Excel Worksheet	11 KB
DairyProduce	Microsoft Excel Worksheet	10 KB

1.   Click: Home→New Query→New Source→File→Excel.

2.   Navigate to the *Session 10/Append* folder and double-click the *Condiments* workbook.

3.   Select the *Condiments* table within the workbook.

4.   Click the *OK* button.

The Power Query Editor now shows the contents of the *Condiments* table.

Set of four files in:
Session 10/Append

Notice that the query editor has automatically named the query *Condiments* and that it has appeared in the query list on the left of the screen.

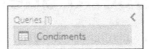

5. Click: Home→New Query→New Source→File→Text/CSV.

6. Navigate to the *Session 10/Append* folder and double-click the *Beverages* CSV file.

   The *Get & Transform* query editor now shows the contents of the *Beverages* CSV file.

7. Click the OK button.

   Notice that the query editor has automatically named the query *Beverages* and that it has appeared underneath the *Condiments* query in the query list on the left of the screen.

8. Repeat the same process for the *Confections* and *DairyProduce* Excel workbooks.

4 **Save the four queries as connection only queries.**

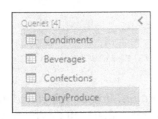

The four queries will be used in the next lesson. For the moment you do not want to load the data returned by the queries anywhere.

1. Click: Home→Close→Close & Load (Drop-down list)→ Close & Load To…

2. Click the *Only Create Connection* option button.

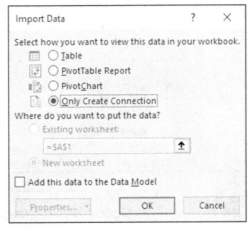

Make sure that the *Add this data to the Data Model* check box is **not** checked.

A *data model* is an in-memory construct that can be analyzed using a new type of pivot table (called an OLAP pivot table). You'll learn about data models later, in: *Session Eleven: Power Pivot, Data Modeling, OLAP and Business Intelligence*.

3. Click the *OK* button.

You are returned to the empty workbook with four *Connection only* queries shown in the *Queries & Connections* task pane.

5 **Save your work as *Multiple Queries-1*.**

Lesson 10-21: Create an append query

You will often find a need to append rows of data from different data sources.

In: *Lesson 10-20: Work with multiple queries,* you created four queries that returned data from three similar workbooks and a CSV file.

This is the data that was returned from the *Condiments* table in the *Condiments* Excel workbook:

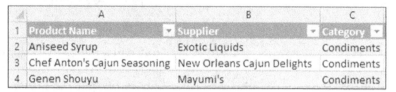

... and here is the data returned from the *Beverages* CSV file:

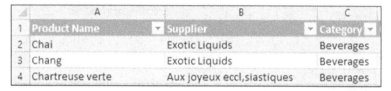

Notice that the column headers (field names) are identical and that each column has the same data type.

You'll often find that you have rows of data residing in different data sources that you need to combine into one table that contains all rows of data. You can do this with a *Get & Transform append query.*

If the above two queries were appended, the resulting table would look like this:

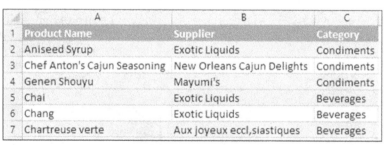

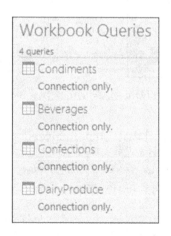

1   Open *Multiple Queries-1* from your sample files folder (if it isn't already open).

This is the workbook that you created in: *Lesson 10-20: Work with multiple queries.*

The workbook is empty apart from four *Connection only* queries that point to four different data sources.

2   Create an append query that will return appended data from the *Condiments, Beverages, Confections* and *DairyProduce* queries.

1.   Click: Data→Get & Transform Data→Get Data→ Combine Queries→Append.

The *Append* dialog appears.

2. Click the *Three or more tables* option button.

3. Select all four tables in the left-hand *Available table(s) list.*

4. Click the *Add >>* button.

    The four tables are displayed in the right-hand *Tables to append* list.

5. Click the *OK* button.

    The Power Query Editor appears, showing the rows from all four queries appended into a single table.

6. Look at the PQFL formula in the formula bar.

```
fx    = Table.Combine({Condiments,Beverages, Confections, DairyProduce})
```

3 Rename your query to: **Full Stock List**

Notice that in the *Query Settings* task pane the query has been named *Append1*.

Double-click the query and type the new query name: **Full Stock List**

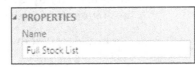

4 Close the Power Query Editor and load the query result to a table in cell A1 of the existing worksheet (there is only one worksheet in this workbook).

You learned how to do this in: *Lesson 10-4: Move, remove, rename, filter and sort columns.*

5 Save your work as *Multiple Queries-2*.

note

PQFL formulas and blank spaces

In this lesson I was careful to name one of the queries: *DairyProduce* (without a space) rather than *Dairy Produce* (with a space).

If you include spaces in query names you will have to refer to them in a special way within PQFL formulas.

To refer to a query called *Dairy Produce* (with a space) you'd need to type:

#"Dairy Produce"

The complete formula would be:

=
Table.Combine({Condiments, Beverages, Confections, #"Dairy Produce"})

Unless you think it likely that you will want to create PQFL code by hand this is unlikely to be of any importance.

Lesson 10-22: Understand Column From Examples

Column from Examples can save you an enormous amount of time when implementing many common transformations.

In: *Lesson 10-5: Split delimited data,* you learned how to transform delimited text using Get & Transform's *Extract* feature. In this lesson you'll split some simple delimited text in a different and far faster way using the *Column from Examples* feature.

1 Open *Column From Examples-1* from your sample files folder.

2 Create a query that will extract the contents of the *Employee* table and open it in the Power Query Editor.

    1. Select the *Employees* worksheet.

    2. Click anywhere inside the *Employee* table.

    3. Click: Data→Get & Transform Data→From Table/Range.

       The query opens in the Power Query Editor.

3 Use the *Column from Examples* feature to extract each Employee's first name into a new column called *First Name*.

    1. Click: Add Column→General→Column From Examples.

       An empty example column appears.

    2. Type: **Jessica**

    3. Press the **<Enter>** key.

       All of the Employees' first names have appeared grayed out in the column (see sidebar).

       The header text at the top of the column has also changed to *Text Before Delimiter*.

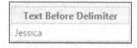

       This lets you know that Get & Transform has intelligently guessed that there is a delimiter (in this case a space) between the first and second names.

    4. Click the *OK* button to apply the transformation and add the column.

    5. Rename the new column: **First Name**

4 Examine the PQFL code that Get & Transform has generated.

    1. If the *Query Settings* task pane is not displayed click:

Column From Examples-1

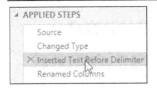

View→Layout→Query Settings.

2. Click on the *Inserted Text Before Delimiter* step in the *Query Settings* task pane.

3. Look at the PQFL code in the formula bar.

```
= Table.AddColumn(#"Changed Type", "Text Before Delimiter", each Text.BeforeDelimiter([Full Name], " "), type text)
```

Even without an in-depth knowledge of PQFL you can see what Get & Transform has done. The code:

Transform: Text.BeforeDelimiter([Full Name], " ")

… is taking each value in the *[Full Name]* column and extracting the text before the space delimiter (" "). This is exactly what you wanted Get & Transform to do.

5   Load the result of the query to a table that begins in cell C1 in the *Employees* worksheet.

1. Click: Home→Close & Load→Close & Load To…

2. Set the *Import Data* settings as follows:

3. Click OK.

6   Set the new linked table to automatically refresh every minute.

You learned how to do this in: *Lesson 10-3: Understand queries and connections.*

7   Add a new name to the *Employees* table and wait one minute.

The new name also appears in the linked table.

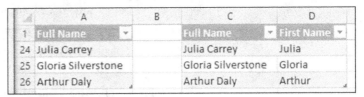

	A	B	C	D
1	Full Name		Full Name	First Name
24	Julia Carrey		Julia Carrey	Julia
25	Gloria Silverstone		Gloria Silverstone	Gloria
26	Arthur Daly		Arthur Daly	Arthur

8   Save your work as *Column From Examples-2*.

Lesson 10-23: Use Column From Examples with selected source columns

The *Jan 2020 Semi-Annual Version 1908* release added the ability to define multiple source columns when working with *Column from Examples*. This enables far more complex transformations to be automatically created.

1   Open *Column From Examples-2* from your sample files folder.

2   Use *Column From Examples* to add a new *Last Name* column to the *Employee* query.

   1.   Open the *Employee* query in the *Power Query* editor.

   2.   Click the column header of the *Full Name* column.

   Every employee's full name is now selected.

   3.   Click: Add Column→General→Column From Examples→ From Selection.

   This instructs *Column From Examples* to only consider the contents of the *Full Name* column when deciding the most appropriate PQFL code to generate.

   4.   Type: **Sagan**

   5.   Press the **<Enter>** key.

   All of the employee last names are shown (grayed out) in the example column (see sidebar).

   6.   Click the OK button

   A new column is added that contains each employee's last name.

   7.   Change the name of the column to: **Last Name**

	A^B_C Full Name	A^B_C First Name	A^B_C Last Name
1	Jessica Sagan	Jessica	Sagan
2	Stephen Bell	Stephen	Bell
3	John Jennings	John	Jennings

3   Use *Column From Examples* to add a new *Initials* column to the *Employee* query.

   1.   Select the *First Name* and *Last Name* columns.

   You need to make *Column From Example's* job as easy as possible by trying to make the method of arriving at your example text clearer.

   2.   Click: Add Column→General→Column From Examples→ From Selection.

   This informs *Column From Examples* to only consider the contents of the *First Name* and *Last Name* columns when figuring out the appropriate PQFL code to generate.

Text After Delimiter

Sagan

Jennings
Simpson
Hawking
Ashe
Putin
Manning
Davis
Diamond
Streep
Simpson
Goodman
Lee
Newhart
Richards
Anderson
Hicks
Armstrong
Bradshaw
West
Spears
Carney
Silverstone
Daly

Column From Examples-2

(If you had asked *Column From Examples* to extract initials from the *Full Name* column it would have failed).

3. Click in the first cell in the *Column1* table.

4. Type: **JS**

5. Press the **<Enter>** key.

   Nothing happens. *Column From Examples* needs another example to understand your requirement.

6. Type: **SB**

7. Press the **<Enter>** key.

   This time *Column From Examples* understands what is needed and all of the employee initials are shown (grayed out) in the example column (see sidebar).

8. Click the *OK* button.

   A new column is added containing all of the Employee initials

9. Change the name of the new column to: **Initials**

4 Use *Column From Examples* to add a new *Reverse Full Name* column to the *Employee* query to show [Last Name], [First Name].

It is common to list names in the form:

Sagan, Jessica

This makes a column of names easy to sort.

1. Select the *First Name* and *Last Name* columns.

2. Use the same technique you used to add the *Initials* column.

   Your first example will look like this:

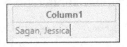

   The *Power Query Editor* window should now look like this:

5 Close the Power Query editor window keeping changes made.

When the window closes you may be asked to click the *Keep* button.

Notice that the linked table has been updated (and will continue to update as you set a timed refresh for it to automatically execute the query in: *Lesson 10-22: Understand Column From Examples*).

6 Save your work as *Column From Examples-3*.

note

You can add an example in any row of the example column

In this lesson you typed the example text in the first row of the example column:

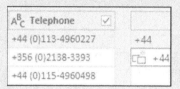

Sometimes you will need to place your example in a different row of the example column.

For example, imagine that you want to capitalize the first letter of the following names:

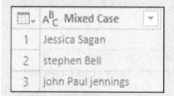

You can see that the first entry is already correct. Get & Transform will not know what you need to do if you simply repeat it in the first row.

Instead you would place your example into the second or third row, as they are incorrect.

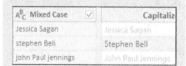

In the above grab, the text: **Stephen Bell** has been typed into the second row of the example column.

This was all Get & Tansform needed understand that you wanted to capitalize each word.

Lesson 10-24: Use Column From Examples to extract characters from strings

In: *Lesson 3-21: Extract text from delimited strings using the FIND and LEN functions* you used Excel formulas to extract the Country Code, NDD and Area Code from some international telephone numbers.

	A	B	G	H	I
3	Company	Telephone	Country Code	Area Code	Phone Number
4	Books A Million	+44 (0)113-4960227	+44	113	4960227
5	Maltese Books	+356 (0)2138-3393	+356	2138	3393
6	Bargain Bookstore	+44 (0)115-4960498	+44	115	4960498
7	Books for Less	+44 (0)116-4960593	+44	116	4960593

This was quite a complex task.

In this lesson you'll use *Column From Examples* to complete the same operation in a fraction of the time.

1 Open *Column From Examples-3* from your sample files folder.

2 Select the *Phone Book (Formatted)* worksheet.

3 Create a query that will extract the contents of the *FormattedPhoneNumbers* table and open it in the Power Query Editor.

　1. Select the *Phone Book (Formatted)* worksheet.

　2. Click anywhere inside the *FormattedPhoneNumbers* table.

　3. Click: Data→Get & Transform Data→From Table/Range.

　　The query opens in the Power Query Editor.

4 Use the *Column from Examples* feature to create a new column containing the Country Code.

You learned how to do this in: *Lesson 10-23: Use Column From Examples with selected source columns.*

Begin by selecting the *Telephone* column as the source.

Your first example will be:

5 Use the *Column from Examples* feature to create a new column containing the Area Code.

Begin by selecting the *Telephone* column as the source.

Your first example will be:

Column From Examples-3

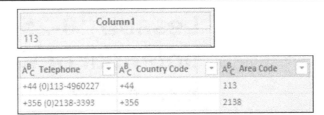

6   Use the *Column from Examples* feature to create a new column containing the Phone Number.

Begin by selecting the *Telephone* column as the source.

Your first example will be:

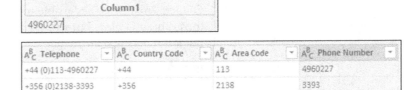

7   Load the result of the query to a table that begins in cell D1 in the *Phone Book (Formatted)* worksheet.

   1.   Click: Home→Close & Load→Close & Load To…

   2.   Set the *Import Data* settings as follows:

8   Set the new linked table to automatically refresh every minute.

You learned how to do this in: *Lesson 10-3: Understand queries and connections.*

9   Add a new company and telephone number to the *FormattedPhoneBook* table and wait one minute.

You may have to begin the number with an apostrophe to indicate that it is a string and prevent Excel from regarding it as a formula.

The new phone number also appears in the linked table.

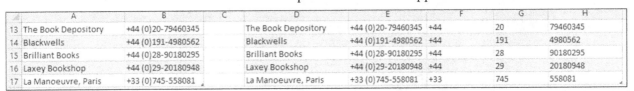

	A	B	C	D	E	F	G	H
13	The Book Depository	+44 (0)20-79460345		The Book Depository	+44 (0)20-79460345	+44	20	79460345
14	Blackwells	+44 (0)191-4980562		Blackwells	+44 (0)191-4980562	+44	191	4980562
15	Brilliant Books	+44 (0)28-90180295		Brilliant Books	+44 (0)28-90180295	+44	28	90180295
16	Laxey Bookshop	+44 (0)29-20180948		Laxey Bookshop	+44 (0)29-20180948	+44	29	20180948
17	La Manoeuvre, Paris	+33 (0)745-558081		La Manoeuvre, Paris	+33 (0)745-558081	+33	745	558081

10   Save your work as *Column From Examples-4*.

Lesson 10-25: Appreciate the potential of Column From Examples

Column From Examples is one of Get & Transform's most useful features.

This lesson gives examples of many common transformations that can be quickly and simply completed using *Column From Examples*. I've also included all of the examples in the sample file: *Column From Examples Samples*.

Column From Examples is able to apply many more transformations than those shown below but the examples may help you to appreciate the potential of this feature.

In each example, *Column From Examples* created the shaded columns.

Split text and extract initials

Full Name	First Name	Last Name	Initials
Jessica Sagan	Jessica	Sagan	JS
Stephen Bell	Stephen	Bell	SB
John Jennings	John	Jennings	JJ

This is similar to the example you created in: *Lesson 10-22: Understand Column From Examples* and *Lesson 10-23: Use Column From Examples with selected source columns.*

Concatenate text

First Name	Last Name	Full Name
Jessica	Sagan	Jessica Sagan
Stephen	Bell	Stephen Bell
John	Jennings	John Jennings

Remove title from names

Full Name	Short Name
Miss Jessica Sagan	Jessica Sagan
Mr Stephen Bell	Stephen Bell
Mr John Jennings	John Jennings

Add commas
(a useful name format for alphabetical sorting)

First Name	Last Name	Sort Name
Jessica	Sagan	Sagan, Jessica
Stephen	Bell	Bell, Stephen
John	Jennings	Jennings, John

Column From Examples Samples

This is similar to the example that you created in: *Lesson 10-23: Use Column From Examples with selected source columns.*

Concatenate text and insert extra text

First Name	Last Name	Full Name
Jessica	Sagan	First Name: Jessica, Last Name: Sagan
Stephen	Bell	First Name: Stephen, Last Name: Bell
John	Jennings	First Name: John, Last Name: Jennings

Change capitalization

Mixed Case	Capitalize Each Word	UPPERCASE	lowercase
jessica elizabeth sagan	Jessica Elizabeth Sagan	JESSICA ELIZABETH SAGAN	jessica elizabeth sagan
stephen Bell	Stephen Bell	STEPHEN BELL	stephen bell
john Paul jennings	John Paul Jennings	JOHN PAUL JENNINGS	john paul jennings

Extract the day, month or year from a date

When using a date as the source column for *Column From Examples* it is important that the data type (within Get & Transform) is set to *Date, Time* or *DateTime*.

Date	Day Name	Day	Month Name	Year	Quarter
1/19/2013	Saturday	19	January	2013	1
8/5/1967	Saturday	5	August	1967	3
9/20/1999	Monday	20	September	1999	3

Extract the domain name and addressee from an e-mail address

E-mail address	Domain	Addressee
Mary@QuiteContrary.com	QuiteContrary.com	Mary
Humpty@Dumpty.com	Dumpty.com	Humpty
Jack@Nimble.com	Nimble.com	Jack

Extract and Format telephone numbers

Company Name	Phone	Area	Exchange	Number	Formatted Number
Great Lakes Food Market	5035557555	503	555	7555	(503)-555-7555
Hungry Coyote Import Store	5035556874	503	555	6874	(503)-555-6874
Lazy K Kountry Store	5095557969	509	555	7969	(509)-555-7969

This is similar to the example you created in: *Lesson 10-24: Use Column From Examples to extract characters from strings.*

In this example it would not be possible to create the *Formatted Number* directly from the *Phone* column.

Column From Examples is first used to extract the *Area, Exchange* and *Number* columns using the *Phone* column as the source.

The *Formatted Number* column is then created using the *Area, Exchange* and *Number* columns as the source.

note

Virtually all of the world's databases work like this

Dr Edgar F Codd (1923-2003) invented the relational database when working for IBM in the 1970's.

The first relational database products came to market in the late 1970's and were quickly adopted by big business.

So good and great was Codd's design that nothing better has been developed in over thirty years.

The entire world of commerce is now powered by relational databases.

You'll usually find a requirement to analyze data from a relational database in all but the very smallest enterprises.

Lesson 10-26: Understand primary and foreign keys

A set of tables that are *related* to each other are referred to as a relational database. Some of Get & Transform's most useful features require an understanding of basic relational database theory.

What is a primary key?

A relational database consists of several tables, each containing data. A database table is conceptually no different to an Excel table except that each row must have a unique *primary key*.

Here's an example of a table from a relational database:

CategoryID	CategoryName	Description
1	Beverages	Soft drinks, coffees, teas, beers, and ales
2	Condiments	Sweet and savory sauces, relishes, spreads, and seasonings
3	Confections	Desserts, candies, and sweet breads

The above example comes from a database table called *Category*. It is good relational database design practice to name a primary key as the table name plus the letters *ID*. This designer has followed best practice and called the primary key *CategoryID*.

The only important quality of a primary key is that all primary key values must be different (unique) within the primary key column. That's because the primary key is used (by a relationship) to identify a single, row in a table. If there were two table rows with the same primary key, a relationship wouldn't be able to correctly identify which single row was being referenced.

In the above example the primary key is a number but primary keys can consist of numbers, letters or both.

What is a foreign key?

Here is an example of two related tables from a relational database:

note

Primary and foreign keys should have the same name

Any database designer worthy of the name will use the same name for the primary key column and the related foreign key column.

I've found that, in the real world of business, I often need to work with a badly designed database where this is not the case. This makes the data a lot more difficult to work with.

CategoryID	CategoryName	Description
1	Beverages	Soft drinks, coffees, teas, beers, and ales
2	Condiments	Sweet and savory sauces, relishes, spreads, and seasonings
3	Confections	Desserts, candies, and sweet breads

ProductID	ProductName	CategoryID	QuantityPerUnit	UnitPrice
1	Chai	1	10 boxes x 20 bags	18.00
3	Aniseed Syrup	2	12 - 550 ml bottles	10.00
16	Pavlova	3	32 - 500 g boxes	17.45
24	Guaraná Fantástica	1	12 - 355 ml cans	4.50
25	NuNuCa Nuß-Nougat-Creme	3	20 - 450 g glasses	14.00
34	Sasquatch Ale	1	24 - 12 oz bottles	14.00

You can see how it is possible to determine that *Aniseed Syrup* is in the *Condiments* category:

- In the *Product* table, *Aniseed Syrup* has a *CategoryID* of 2.

- The item in the *Category* table with a primary key (*CategoryID*) of 2 is *Condiments*.

While *CategoryID* is the primary key column in the *Category* table, it is a *foreign key* column within the *Product* table.

You can think of the *CategoryID* values in the *Product* table as belonging to the *Category* table, making them foreign keys in the *Product* table.

You can probably now see the wisdom of the naming convention for primary keys. It makes it possible to spot which are the primary and foreign keys in a table at a glance.

- The column named with the table name plus *ID* is the primary key.

- Any other column name that is suffixed with *ID* (has *ID* at the end of the name) is a foreign key.

- Any column not suffixed with *ID* is a regular data field containing information.

<table>
<tr><td colspan="5">

anecdote

How meaningful primary keys almost stopped the Welsh from buying cars

Many years ago, I implemented a Europe-wide Business Intelligence solution for a very large automotive finance company.

I was not pleased (but unsurprised) to find that the database designer had used meaningful primary and foreign keys.

The designer had used a concatenation of the customer's last name and date of birth as the primary key for the customer table.

The designer believed that the possibility of having two customers with the same last name and date of birth was extremely unlikely to ever happen.

In fact, it transpired that 13.5% of the Welsh population have a last name of Jones, meaning that it was certain to happen in Wales (and actually very likely to happen everywhere).

The database was, of course, re-designed to use meaningless primary keys.

</td></tr>
</table>

Meaningful and meaningless primary keys

In the above example, the primary key is a *meaningless* number. The number 2 tells you nothing about any attribute of the *Condiments* category. It simply provides a way to find where the correct *Condiments* row is located within the table.

It is also possible to use a *meaningful* primary key (though a professional database designer would never do this). For example, you could argue that because category names are unique, it is fine to use the *CategoryName* column in the above table as the primary key.

If you decided to use the category name as the primary key the tables would look like this:

CategoryID	Description
Condiments	Sweet and savory sauces, relishes, spreads, and seasonings
Beverages	Soft drinks, coffees, teas, beers, and ales
Confections	Desserts, candies, and sweet breads

ProductID	ProductName	CategoryID	QuantityPerUnit	UnitPrice
50	Valkoinen suklaa	Confections	12 - 100 g bars	16.25
1	Chai	Beverages	10 boxes x 20 bags	18.00
77	Original Frankfurter grüne Soße	Condiments	12 boxes	13.00
8	Northwoods Cranberry Sauce	Condiments	12 - 12 oz jars	40.00
68	Scottish Longbreads	Confections	10 boxes x 8 pieces	12.50
70	Outback Lager	Beverages	24 - 355 ml bottles	15.00

From a database design perspective, this is generally a bad idea

You'll often find, however, that you need to create this type of relationship when creating relationships between tables that originate from different databases. In this case, no formal primary key/foreign key relationship will exist.

For example, you may need to join a table from your corporate database containing customer addresses with a table detailing sales tax rates by state that you've downloaded from the Internet. In this case you would need to create a primary key/foreign key relationship between the state columns in each table.

Lesson 10-27: Link primary and foreign keys using VLOOKUP

In: *Lesson 10-26: Understand primary and foreign keys,* you learned how relational databases use primary key/foreign key relationships to relate tables to each other.

In this lesson you'll leverage upon your understanding of primary and foreign keys by using a simple VLOOKUP to retrieve information from a related table.

1   Open *Primary and Foreign Keys-1* from your sample files folder.

Notice the following:

- This workbook contains two worksheets: *Category* and *Product.*

- The *Product* worksheet contains a single table called *Product.*

- The *Category* worksheet contains a single table called *Category.*

- The *Product* table has two fields with the suffix: *ID.* (*ProductID* and *CategoryID*).

- The *Category* table has one field with the suffix: *ID.* (*CategoryID*).

- In: *Lesson 10-26: Understand primary and foreign keys,* you learned that these fields are, in fact, Primary Keys and Foreign Keys.

- In the *Product* table, the *ProductID* field is the primary key and the *CategoryID* field is a foreign key.

- In the *Category* table, the *CategoryID* field is the primary key.

In this lesson you'll use a simple VLOOKUP to add the correct *Category Name* to each row in the *Product* table.

2   Insert a column to the left of the *QuantityPerUnit* column (column D) in the *Product* table.

3   Name the new column: **Category Name**

	B	C	D	E
1	ProductName	CategoryID	Category Name	QuantityPerUnit
2	Chai	1		10 boxes x 20 bags
3	Chang	1		24 - 12 oz bottles

4   Add a VLOOKUP function to cell D2 that will return the *CategoryName* field that matches the *CategoryID* value in cell C2.

You learned how to use the VLOOKUP function in: *Lesson 3-22: Use a VLOOKUP function for an exact lookup.* The correct function arguments in this case are:

Lookup_value	[@CategoryID]
Table_array	Category
Col_index_num	2
Range_lookup	False

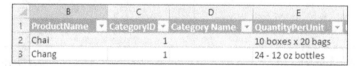

```
fx    =VLOOKUP([@CategoryID],Category,2,FALSE)
```

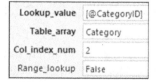

Primary and Foreign Keys-1

Because this is a table, the function should be automatically replicated to all table cells in column D.

If this does not happen for you, somebody has disabled automatic calculated column creation on your machine. Refer to: *Lesson 1-21: Understand unqualified structured table references (sidebar)*, for instructions showing how to switch calculated columns back on.

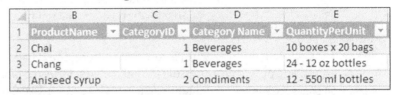

5   Hide the primary and foreign key columns A and C.

The primary key columns are crucial when linking tables in a relational database but the data within them is of no interest.

To hide the columns, right click on the column header of each column and click: *Hide* from the shortcut menu.

6   Create a pivot table from the Product table.

Normal pivot tables can only work with one table. Now that you have added a *Category Name* to the *Product* table, you can use a pivot table to analyze products by category name.

1. Click inside the table.

2. Click: Insert→Tables→PivotTable.

3. Click the *OK* button.

7   Use the pivot table to show the total units in stock by category.

Click the check boxes next to the *Category Name* and *UnitsInStock* fields in the *PivotTable Fields* task pane.

Take a moment to consider what you have just achieved.

You've just joined two related tables together via their primary and foreign keys using a VLOOKUP function to show the related categories in the *Product* table.

You then used the *Product* table to create a pivot table that reports the total units in stock analyzed by category.

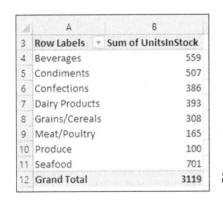

8   Save your work as *Primary and Foreign Keys-2.*

note

Views can contain calculated fields

A *View* is defined within a database using a powerful relational query language called SQL (Structured Query Language).

SQL isn't an Excel skill. Books of over 600 pages have been written that teach the SQL language.

Every professional DBA (database administrator) will have excellent SQL skills and will be able to create any view that you need in a few minutes.

You need to be aware that you can also ask your DBA to include calculated fields in a view.

The example view used in this lesson contains a simple primary key/foreign key lookup from the *Product* table to the *Category* table.

It is effectively doing what you did with a VLOOKUP in: *Lesson 10-27: Link primary and foreign keys using VLOOKUP*.

It only took me about 30 seconds to create this view using SQL.

Here's an example of a view that contains a calculated field:

Chai	$18.00	39 702.00
Chang	$19.00	17 323.00

In this example the *Product Name*, *Unit Price* and *Units In Stock* fields exist in the source table.

The right-hand field is a calculated field that shows the total inventory value (*Units in Stock* multiplied by *Unit Price*).

Lesson 10-28: Efficiently import data using a view

In: *Lesson 10-27: Link primary and foreign keys using VLOOKUP*, you had to add a related column to a table in order to make it suitable for a pivot table to analyze (as normal pivot tables can only work with one table of source data).

In a corporate setting the database is normally maintained by a data professional called a DBA (database administrator). Because relational table data is awkward for Excel (and other reporting tools) to analyze, database software (such as SQL Server, Oracle and Access) supports a concept called a *View*.

If you ask the DBA to create a *View* containing all of the information you need, you won't need to do any more work when you import the data.

A few minutes' work by the DBA might save you many hours of work if you have to work with raw tables.

Sometimes you'll have no choice other than to work with raw tables of course. This might be the case if you use an off-the-shelf package, if your company do not allow any changes to the database, or if it takes too long to get your IT department to respond to change requests.

1   Open a new blank workbook.

2   Import the *Products and Categories View* from the *With View* Access database in your sample files folder.

   1.   Click: Data→Get & Transform Data→Get Data→ From Database→From Microsoft Access Database.

   2.   Select the Access database file *With View* from your sample files folder.

   3.   Click the *Import* button.

      The *Navigator* dialog appears:

      Notice that this there's a different icon for a view.

   4.   Click on the *Products and Categories View* to select it.

   5.   Click: Load (drop-down arrow)→Load To…

      The *Import Data* dialog appears:

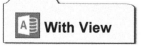

With View

6.   Click the *Table* option button (if it isn't already selected).

7.   Click the *OK* button.

A new table is added to a new worksheet. It already contains everything you need for the pivot table:

	A	B	C	D	E	F	G	H
1	ProductName	CategoryName	QuantityPerUnit	UnitPrice	UnitsInStock	UnitsOnOrder	ReorderLevel	Discontinued
2	Chai	Beverages	10 boxes x 20 bags	18	39	0	10	FALSE
3	Chang	Beverages	24 - 12 oz bottles	19	17	40	25	FALSE
4	Guaraná Fantástica	Beverages	12 - 355 ml cans	4.5	20	0	0	TRUE

note

You can also create the equivalent of a view outside the database

Later, in: *Lesson 10-31: Understand normal and de-normalized data,* you'll learn that a view is also referred to as *de-normalized data.*

Later, in: *Lesson 10-32: Create a simple two-table merged query,* you'll create a de-normalized data extract that is similar to the view used in this lesson.

In this way you can create something that is functionally equivalent to a view without having to bother your IT department.

You can now appreciate what a huge time saver views are when importing data from a relational database.

3   Rename the new worksheet: **Products and Categories**

4   Rename the table: **ProductsAndCategories**

This time Excel has given the table the name:

Products and Categories View

1.   Click inside the table.

2.   Click: Table Tools→Design→Properties→Table Name.

3.   Change the table name to: **ProductsAndCategories**

5   Create a pivot table from the *ProductsAndCategories* table.

1.   Click inside the table.

2.   Click: Insert→Tables→PivotTable.

3.   Click the *OK* button.

6   Change the pivot table worksheet's name to: **Pivot Table**

7   Use the pivot table to show the total units in stock by category.

Click the check boxes next to the *CategoryName* and *UnitsInStock* fields in the *PivotTable Fields* task pane.

8   Save your work as *With View-1.*

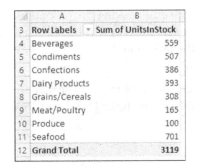

	A	B
3	Row Labels	Sum of UnitsInStock
4	Beverages	559
5	Condiments	507
6	Confections	386
7	Dairy Products	393
8	Grains/Cereals	308
9	Meat/Poultry	165
10	Produce	100
11	Seafood	701
12	**Grand Total**	**3119**

Lesson 10-29: Understand linked table and pivot table refresh

A linked table is an Excel table that was created by a Get & Transform query. The linked table is shaded green (instead of the normal default blue) to provide a visual clue that it is a linked table.

Linked tables can be refreshed at any time by re-running the Get & Transform query that they are linked to. In: *Lesson 10-28: Efficiently import data using a view* you also created a pivot table, using a linked Excel table as the pivot table's data source.

In: *Lesson 8-4: Understand the pivot table data cache,* you learned that a pivot table does not access its data source directly. Instead it creates a *pivot table data cache* from its own data source. It is also possible for the user to refresh the pivot table. In this case the pivot table cache will refresh from the linked table.

This diagram makes things clearer:

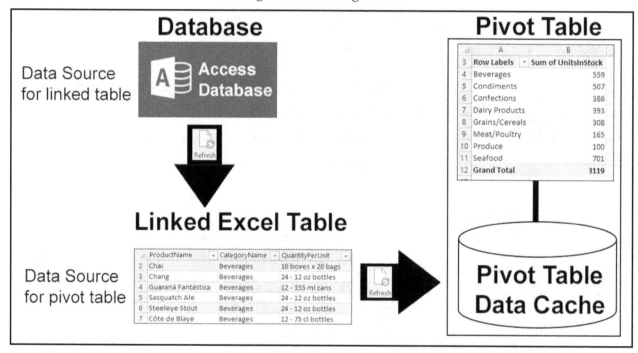

You can see that two refresh options are possible.

A linked table refresh can be done by right-clicking the table and then selecting *Refresh* from the shortcut menu. This refresh goes to the database and fetches the latest data from it.

A linked pivot table refresh can be done by right-clicking the pivot table and then selecting *Refresh* from the shortcut menu. A pivot table refresh goes to its own data source (in this case the linked table) and updates its *pivot table data cache* from the values found there.

You can see that in order to make sure that the pivot table is showing the very latest data you would have to first refresh the linked table and then refresh the pivot table.

With View-1

note

Unlinking a linked table

When you import a table from Access (or any other relational database), the table is linked to the source data.

You may, however, wish to break the link between the source data and the table.

To do this:

1. Right-click on the table.

2. Click:

Table→
Unlink from Data Source

… from the shortcut menu.

note

You can load the output of a Get & Transform query directly into the PivotTable data cache

When you have become more proficient with Get & Transform you will probably never load data into a worksheet table if you only want to create a pivot table from the data.

Later, in: *Lesson 10-30: Load a query directly into the PivotTable cache,* you'll load an Access database table directly into the PivotTable data cache using Get & Transform.

As you'll see, this approach has many advantages over using an intermediate Excel table (as you did in this lesson's example).

1 Open *With View-1* from your sample files folder (if it isn't already open).

2 Click on the *Pivot Table* worksheet and note that the total units in stock for the *Beverages* category is 559 units.

3 Change the value in cell E2 on the *Products and Categories* worksheet from 39 to 1,039.

Cell E2 contains the number of *Chai* units in stock. Note that *Chai* is in the *Beverages* category.

4 Select the *Pivot Table* worksheet. Notice that the total *Beverages* units in stock remains unchanged at 559 units.

The *Beverages* units have not updated because the pivot table gets its data from the *pivot table data cache*.

Because the *pivot table data cache* has not been refreshed, it does not yet know that its source data (the *ProductsAndCategories* table) has changed.

5 Refresh the pivot table. Notice that the total *Beverages* units in stock has increased to 1,559 units.

Right-click inside the pivot table and click: *Refresh* from the shortcut menu. The pivot table cache has now been refreshed to reflect the values displayed in its source data (the source data for the pivot table is the *ProductsAndCategories* table).

6 Refresh the *ProductsAndCategories* table. Notice that the Chai *UnitsInStock* (in cell E2) has decreased to 39 units.

Right-click inside the *ProductsAndCategories* table and click: *Refresh* from the shortcut menu.

The linked table has now been refreshed to show the values from its source data (the source data for the table is the *With View* Access database).

Because the values in the database have not changed, the linked table is updated to match the current values in the database.

In a real-world database, the values can be expected to constantly change as goods are sold or received and as prices and other data are changed.

7 Select the *Pivot Table* worksheet. Notice that the total *Beverages* units in stock remains unchanged at 1559 units.

The *Beverages* units have not updated because the pivot table gets its data from the *pivot table data cache*.

Because the *pivot table data cache* has not been refreshed, it does not yet know that its source data (the *ProductsAndCategories* table) has changed.

8 Refresh the pivot table. Notice that the total *Beverages* units in stock has decreased to 559 units.

Right-click inside the pivot table and click: *Refresh* from the shortcut menu. The pivot table cache has now been refreshed to reflect the values displayed in its source data (the source data for the pivot table is the *ProductsAndCategories* table).

important

Out of memory errors

To complete this lesson, the *PivotTable Data Cache* has to be loaded into memory.

If you only have a small amount of free memory on your computer, you may encounter out of memory errors.

note

What is big data?

In 2010 it was estimated that the world was generating 2.5 Exabytes of new data every day. An Exabyte is approximately one million Terabytes.

The amount of data generated today is far greater. In 2016 it was estimated that the Internet alone may now be generating more than a thousand Exabytes of new data every day.

Worrying though it sounds, every click you make, every e-mail you send and every telephone call you make is being stored somewhere.

This explosion of data is often referred to as *big data*. Big data doesn't mean any particular number but refers to data of such a size that analysis (with tools such as Excel) can be a problem.

Perhaps Excel would regard *big data* as being data with more than a million rows (an Excel worksheet cannot have more than 1,048,576 rows).

You may find that memory and speed constraints sometimes impose a far lower limit on the size of worksheet-based data you can usefully work with.

Big Data

Lesson 10-30: Load a query directly into the PivotTable cache

In *Lesson 10-28: Efficiently import data using a view,* you loaded data into a single Excel table and then created a pivot table from this table. There is absolutely nothing wrong with this approach and it is appropriate for many data analysis tasks. There are, however, three potential problems:

- You cannot analyze a data source that has more than approximately a million rows (1,048,576 to be precise) as that is the largest number of rows that a worksheet can contain. Very large data sets are often referred to as: *Big Data* (see sidebar).

- It can take a long time to create the *pivot table data cache* when working with large data sets stored in worksheets.

- Storing data in worksheets means that data is loaded into the computer's memory twice when you open the workbook. Once from the table in the workbook (the entire Excel workbook is held in the computer's memory) and again from the *pivot table data cache* (also held in the computer's memory). This means that you could start to see "out of memory" errors when working with very large data sets.

In this diagram you can see how Excel can be used to analyze big data:

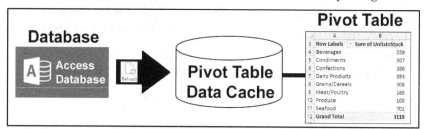

If the pivot table cache is created directly from the external data source, you can avoid all of the above three problems. There is a physical limit to the amount of data you can store in a *pivot table data cache,* but it is very large (theoretically 2.1 billion data items or individual values).

Later, in: *Session Eleven: Power Pivot, Data Modeling, OLAP and Business Intelligence,* you'll learn how to work with even bigger data (that can contain up to two thousand million rows – each of which can contain many data items).

1   Open a new blank workbook.

2   Import the *BigData* table from the *Big Data* Access database directly into a Pivot Table Data Cache.

   1. Click: Data→Get & Transform Data→Get Data→ From Database→From Microsoft Access Database.

   2. Navigate to the *Big Data* Access database in your sample files folder.

   3. Double-click on the *Big Data* Access database file.

      The *Navigator* dialog appears:

note

An Access database can't really handle big data

You're simulating big data techniques in this lesson using an Access database.

An Access database can only contain 2 Terabytes of data. That is still enough to store several million rows in one table.

SQL Server and Oracle databases can handle really big data with billions of rows.

note

The 64-bit version of Excel is best when working with big data

Both Windows and Excel are available in 32-bit and 64-bit editions.

If you work a lot with big data and are finding that you encounter *out of memory* errors, you should consider switching to the 64-bit version of Excel (to run this you must also have the 64-bit version of Windows).

The normal 32-bit version of Excel can only make use of 2 gigabytes of memory, but the 64-bit version can effectively use all of the memory installed on your computer.

You'll learn more about memory issues and how they can be overcome later, in: *Lesson 11-1: Understand data model memory requirements.*

4. Select the *BigData* table and click:

   Load (drop-down arrow)→Load To…

   The *Import Data* dialog is displayed.

5. Click the *PivotTable Report* option button and then click the *OK* button. A pivot table is created showing the fields in the *BigData* table.

   The *BigData* table in the sample file contains 1,301,840 rows of data. Because an Excel table can only contain 1,048,576 rows of data you clearly cannot load this data into an Excel table.

   If you had selected *Table* in the above dialog (and then clicked the *OK* button) the import would have failed, and you would have (eventually) have seen an error message.

3 Use the pivot table to show the total *InvoiceAmount* for each *ProductCode* for each *year*, *quarter* and *month*.

This is a very similar pivot table to the one you created in: *Lesson 8-19: Group by date.*

In order to make the *Big Data* sample Access database as small as possible, I have only included three fields:

InvoiceDate: The date the product was invoiced.
ProductCode: A number that identifies the product.
InvoiceAmount: The amount that was charged.

Drag the *ProductCode* to the *Rows* pane, the *InvoiceAmount* to the *Values* pane and the *InvoiceDate* to the *Columns* pane.

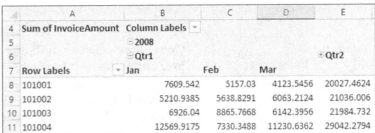

4 Save your work as *Big Data-1.*

trivia

Third normal form

This sidebar was also included in: Lesson 2-1: Split fixed width data using Text to Columns. I've also included it here as an overview of Third Normal Form is needed to understand the concept of normal and de-normalized data.

Dr E.F. Codd (1923-2003) is a cult figure to every database designer worthy of the name.

He was not only the inventor of the relational database (while working for IBM) but he also wrote the rulebook for excellence in database design.

Codd's books are essential (and even exciting) reading for anybody who designs relational databases for a living. I have read all of them and hung on every word!

Codd defined a set of rules that are collectively called third normal form (or 3NF for short).

Codd's rules are broken into three parts: First Normal Form, Second Normal Form and Third Normal Form.

Each set of rules builds upon the earlier set so that a database design cannot conform to 2NF unless it first conforms to 1NF (and a 3NF design must first conform to 2NF).

In theory, all of the corporate databases that you work with should be third normal form compliant. In practice you'll often find database design errors that may make some databases difficult to work with.

Lesson 10-31: Understand normal and de-normalized data

What is normal data?

Most relational databases conform to design rules that are collectively called *Third Normal Form* (often abbreviated to 3NF).

A data source that complies with these rules is said to contain normal (or normalized) data. Compliance with 3NF is a pre-requisite for an efficient relational database that can reliably allow rows to be added, edited or deleted.

What is de-normalized data?

Regular Excel pivot tables can only use a single table of source data.

When data is extracted from multiple tables (usually residing in a relational database such as SQL Server, Oracle or Access) and combined into a single table, the data in the single table is referred to as *de-normalized data*.

In: *Session Eleven: Power Pivot, Data Modeling, OLAP and Business Intelligence* you'll learn to build a relational (multi-table) in-memory construct called a *data model* that can be analyzed using a new type of pivot table (called an OLAP pivot table).

To create efficient OLAP data models you'll often need to de-normalize data (combine two or more related tables into a single de-normalized table).

De-normalizing by adding derived values

One of the most important normal form rules prohibits *derived* values in a relational database table. There are very good reasons for this (see facing page sidebar).

A *derived value* is a value that can be calculated from other columns in the same row. In: *Lesson 10-18: Create an aggregated data query*, you worked with this view:

	A	B	C	D
1	ProductName	CategoryNa	UnitsInStock	UnitPrice
2	Chai	Beverages	39	18.00
3	Chang	Beverages	17	19.00
4	Guaraná Fantástica	Beverages	20	4.50

One of the challenges in: *Lesson 10-18: Create an aggregated data query*, was to calculate the total *Inventory Value*. A correctly designed database cannot contain a column showing *Inventory Value* because it can be calculated by multiplying the *UnitsInStock* column by the *UnitPrice* column (in other words it would be a *derived value*).

You de-normalized the data by adding a custom column containing a calculated (derived) field to show the *Inventory Value*. Here is the de-normalized data that you created:

Add Custom Column

New column name

Inventory Value

Custom column formula:

= [UnitPrice]*[UnitsInStock]

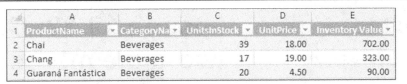

	A	B	C	D	E
1	ProductName	CategoryNa	UnitsInStock	UnitPrice	Inventory Value
2	Chai	Beverages	39	18.00	702.00
3	Chang	Beverages	17	19.00	323.00
4	Guaraná Fantástica	Beverages	20	4.50	90.00

note

Why are derived values a bad thing in a relational database?

The problem with a derived field is that it allows you to ask a database the same question in two different ways.

This often results in two different answers.

When a database can answer the same question with different results it is referred to as being corrupt.

Imagine that the database designer (in this lesson's example) had designed the *Product* table with an *Inventory Value* field.

Every time a programmer wrote code that updated the *UnitPrice* and *UnitsInStock* field it would be necessary to also remember to update the *Inventory Value* field.

At some point, a routine might be coded that "forgot" to update the *Inventory Value* field. This wouldn't really be the programmer's fault, as it shouldn't have been there in the first place.

Now imagine that the CEO asks two analysts to provide the total inventory value.

The first analyst computes the value by multiplying the *QuantityPerUnit* by the *UnitPrice* and sums the resulting values.

The second analyst sums the *Inventory Value* field.

The CEO, presented with two very different figures, asks which figure is correct.

The analysts advise that both of them are correct.

Perhaps the CEO would fire the analysts or programmer at this point, but really, he should fire the database designer.

Learning more about third normal form

Third normal form is a subject that sometimes even confuses specialized IT personnel. Apart from professional specialist database designers it is unusual to find IT workers who can create a correctly normalized database from a business requirement specification.

This lesson has only presented a simplified overview of third normal form, but it will be enough for your work with *Get & Transform*.

If you want to learn more about third normal form, an Internet search will uncover a huge amount of information upon this widely misunderstood subject.

De-normalizing by combining tables

In: *Lesson 10-26: Understand primary and foreign keys,* you learned about related tables. Here's the data that you worked with:

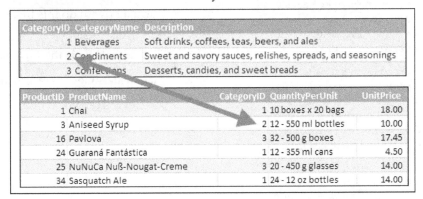

CategoryID	CategoryName	Description
1	Beverages	Soft drinks, coffees, teas, beers, and ales
2	Condiments	Sweet and savory sauces, relishes, spreads, and seasonings
3	Confections	Desserts, candies, and sweet breads

ProductID	ProductName	CategoryID	QuantityPerUnit	UnitPrice
1	Chai	1	10 boxes x 20 bags	18.00
3	Aniseed Syrup	2	12 - 550 ml bottles	10.00
16	Pavlova	3	32 - 500 g boxes	17.45
24	Guaraná Fantástica	1	12 - 355 ml cans	4.50
25	NuNuCa Nuß-Nougat-Creme	3	20 - 450 g glasses	14.00
34	Sasquatch Ale	1	24 - 12 oz bottles	14.00

An important normal form rule is that you cannot have information about more than one entity in the same table. Think of an entity as a noun (or thing). A *Category* is a noun and a *Product* is a noun.

Now consider the de-normalized version of the above tables that you worked with in: *Lesson 10-28: Efficiently import data using a view*:

	A	B	C	D
1	ProductName	CategoryName	QuantityPerUnit	UnitPrice
2	Alice Mutton	Meat/Poultry	20 - 1 kg tins	39.00
3	Aniseed Syrup	Condiments	12 - 550 ml bottles	10.00
4	Boston Crab Meat	Seafood	24 - 4 oz tins	18.40

You can see that this de-normalized view breaks normal form rules because the *Category Name* field rightly belongs in the *Category* table.

It is quite correct for a database administrator to create this type of de-normalized read-only view within a correctly designed relational database, as the view is only used for reporting purposes.

Later, in: *Lesson 10-32: Create a simple two-table merged query,* you'll learn how to create this type of de-normalized table using the *Get & Transform* tool.

note

What is a join?

When a relationship is defined within a query it is called a *join*.

There are different types of join that define the data that is returned when there is a missing foreign key in a foreign key column.

There is a drop-down list at the bottom of the *Merge* dialog used in this lesson, that allows you to specify a *Join Kind*.

Left Outer (all from first, matching from second)
Right Outer (all from second, matching from first)
Full Outer (all rows from both)
Inner (only matching rows)
Left Anti (rows only in first)
Right Anti (rows only in second)

The *Left Outer* join is the default join kind and it is the join type that you'll use nearly all of the time. In this lesson, imagine that there are some *Product* rows that have a missing (or invalid) *CategoryID*.

The *Left Outer* join will return all of the rows in the *Product* table. No category data is returned if there is a missing *CategoryID* (in other words the *Category* field will be left blank).

Sometimes you might want to only return *Product* records if the *Category ID* field is not blank and there is a matching *CategoryID* field in the *Category* table. This type of join is called an *Inner* join.

With this knowledge, you should be able to figure out (from the description provided in brackets) what the other four (lesser used) join types would return in different situations.

Two Tables-1

Lesson 10-32: Create a simple two-table merged query

In: *Lesson 10-27: Link primary and foreign keys using VLOOKUP,* you opened a worksheet that contained two related Excel tables. One table contained *Product* information and the other contained *Category* information.

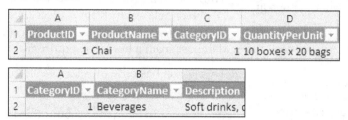

In: *Lesson 10-26: Understand primary and foreign keys*, you learned that the two tables had a relationship linking the *CategoryID* primary key (in the *Category* table) to the *CategoryID* foreign key (in the *Product* table).

1   Open *Merge-1* from your sample files folder.

2   Create two connection-only *Get & Transform* queries to extract all values from the *Product* and *Category* tables.

You learned how to do this in: *Lesson 10-20: Work with multiple queries.*

1.   Click anywhere in the *Product* table.

2.   Click: Data→Get & Transform Data→From Table/Range.

The Get & Transform query editor opens.

3.   Click the Expand button ⟩ in the left-hand *Navigator* Pane.

The *Product* query is now visible in the *Navigator* pane.

4.   Click: Home→Close→Close & Load→Close & Load To...

5.   Click the *Only Create Connection* option button and click OK.

6.   Click anywhere in the *Category* table.

7.   Click: Data→Get & Transform Data→From Table/Range.

The Get & Transform query editor opens.

8.   Click the Expand button ⟩ in the left-hand *Navigator* Pane.

9.   Both the *Product* query and the *Category* query are now shown in the Navigator pane (see sidebar).

3   Create a merged query to show the *Category* name in the *Product* query.

1.   Select the *Product* query in the left-hand *Navigator* pane.

2.   Click: Home→Combine→Merge Queries.

The *Merge* dialog appears.

note

VLOOKUP, View or de-normalized Get & Transform query?

You have now discovered three different ways to work with relational data.

You may wonder when to use each. Here are the advantages of each approach:

1. VLOOKUP

This is the most primitive way to create a de-normalized data extract from related tables. It may also be the one you see most often as it is the only method that most Excel users understand.

The VLOOKUP method is very slow and cumbersome to implement and maintain. It is the least preferred way to work with relational data.

2. View

A *View* is the best way to obtain a de-normalized data extract from a relational database.

While *Views* are wonderful, they can only be used with a relational database data source and can only be created by specialized IT staff.

3. Get & Transform Query

A de-normalized extract created by a *Get & Transform* query can be used as the data source of a linked table as well as a normal pivot table.

Get & Transform queries can be automatically refreshed at a timed interval (when used to populate a linked table).

Later, in: *Session Eleven: Power Pivot, Data Modeling, OLAP and Business Intelligence*, you'll learn yet another way (and the most powerful way of all) to work with relational data by creating an in-memory relational data model.

3. Click in the *CategoryID* (foreign key) column in the *Product* table shown at the top of the *Merge* dialog.

4. Select the *Category* table from the drop-down list in the middle of the dialog.

5. Click in the *CategoryID* (primary key) column in the *Category* table.

6. Click *OK* to merge the queries.

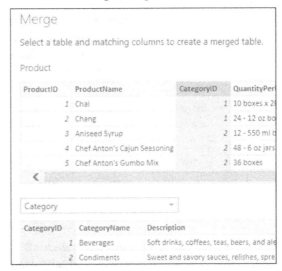

Notice that a new *Category* column has appeared on the right of the preview window.

4 Expand the new column to see the contents of the *Category* table.

1. Click the expand button on the right of the *Category* column header.

2. Click the *OK* button.

The *Category* names are now shown in the preview window.

5 Remove the *ProductID, CategoryID, Category.CategoryID and Category.Description* columns from the query.

You learned how to do this in: *Lesson 10-4: Move, remove, rename, filter and sort columns.*

6 Move the *Category.CategoryName* field so that it is next to the *ProductName* field.

You learned how to do this in: *Lesson 10-4: Move, remove, rename, filter and sort columns.*

7 Close the Power Query Editor, creating *Connection only* queries in the workbook.

You learned how to do this in: *Lesson 10-20: Work with multiple queries.*

8 Save your work as *Merge-2*.

Lesson 10-33: Create a five-table merged query

In this lesson you'll create a *Merge* query to extract data from five related tables and then combine them all into a single de-normalized table.

1   Open a new blank workbook.

Here is a diagram showing the tables and primary key/foreign key relationships used in this lesson. This type of diagram is often referred to as a *schema*:

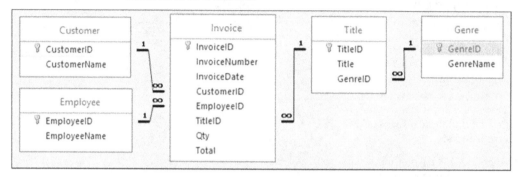

The challenge for this lesson will be to extract a single de-normalized table from the five related tables using *Get & Transform Merge Queries*. The single-table extract will merge the values of every field in the database (seventeen fields) into one table.

2   Create five queries containing all of the data from all five tables in the *Film Sales-1* Excel workbook.

Because all of these tables are contained in the same workbook, there's a really quick way to do this.

1.   Click: Data→Get & Transform Data→Get Data→ From File→From Workbook.

2.   Navigate to the *Film Sales-1* workbook and open it.

3.   Check the *Select multiple items* check box.

4.   Check the check boxes next to each of the five tables (see sidebar).

5.   Click the *Transform Data* button.

The Power Query Editor opens, and five queries are shown in the left-hand query list. There is one query for each table (see sidebar).

3   Merge the five queries together so that the Invoice query returns all of the data contained in the four related tables.

You learned how to do this in: *Lesson 10-32: Create a simple two-table merged query*.

1.   Select the *Title* query and then merge the *Genre* query into the *Title* query using the *GenreID* key to link the tables.

2.   Select the *Invoice* query and then merge the *Customer* query into the *Invoice* query using the *CustomerID* key to link the tables.

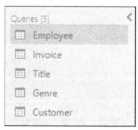

Film Sales-1

note

Merge queries are easier to create when using a relational database source

Later, in: *Lesson 11-9: Create a data model directly from a relational database,* you will use Get & Transform to import an entire relational database.

When Get & Transform imports data from a relational data source it also imports the relationships.

When Get & Transform is already aware of the relationships between tables a Merge button  is automatically displayed in related tables. This makes merging tables a lot easier.

The *Invoice* query should now return all fields from both the *Invoice* and *Customer* tables.

3. Select the *Invoice* query and then merge the *Employee* query into the *Invoice* query using the *EmployeeID* key to link the tables.

   The *Invoice* query should now return all fields from the *Invoice, Customer* and *Employee* tables.

4. Select the *Invoice* query and then merge the *Title* query into the *Invoice* query using the *TitleID* key to link the tables.

   Remember that the *Title* query is itself a merged query (that includes fields from the *Genre* table). By merging the *Title* query with the *Invoice* query, you have made both the *Title* and *Genre* table's data available within the *Invoice* query.

4 Select the Invoice query and expand all of the new columns.

You learned how to do this in: *Lesson 10-32: Create a simple two-table merged query.*

The new columns are those where every cell contains the word: *Table.*

The *Invoice* query should now return all seventeen fields from the *Invoice, Customer, Employee, Title* and *Genre* tables

5 Remove all of the primary and foreign key columns from the query (all of the fields that are suffixed with *ID*).

You learned how to do this in: *Lesson 10-4: Move, remove, rename, filter and sort columns.*

6 Close the Power Query Editor, creating *Connection only* queries.

You learned how to do this in: *Lesson 10-20: Work with multiple queries.*

7 Create a new linked table using the *Invoice* query.

1. Right-click on the *Invoice* query in the *Queries & Connections* task pane.

2. Select *Load to…* from the shortcut menu.

   The *Import Data* dialog appears.

3. Click the *Table* option button and the *Existing worksheet* option button.

4. Select cell A1 as the location for the linked table and click the *OK* button.

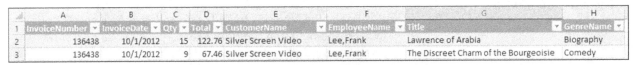

You could also have loaded the output of this query directly into the Pivot Table Data Cache (using the *PivotTable Report* option button) to further analyze the data.

8 Save your work as *Five Table Query-1.*

note

Fuzzy logic uses Jaccard similarity

Paul Jaccard (1868-1944) was a professor of botany at the *Swiss Federal Institute of Technology* in Zurich.

Jaccard published his paper on the Jaccard index of similarity (*coefficient de communauté*) in 1901.

Jaccard developed this technique to combine regional floras.

When comparing two sample sets Jaccard realized that similarity could be measured by considering the *intersection* and *union* of two sets. For example, consider these two sets:

- John Peter Travolta
- John Simon Travolta

Each word in each set is called a *token*.

Jaccard's *intersection* value would be 2 because two of the tokens (John and Travolta) are the same in each set.

Jaccard's *union* value would be 4 because there are four unique tokens (John Peter Simon and Travolta) in both sets.

This allows the *Jaccard Similarity* to be calculated using the formula: intersection/union, in this case 2/4=0.5.

As you will discover in: *Lesson 10-35: Improve fuzzy logic results using a custom transformation table*, Excel's fuzzy logic implementation is more sophisticated than the simple *Jaccard Similarity* method described above.

Lesson 10-34: Create a merged query using fuzzy logic

Computers like things to be very precise. While a human will instanty realize that *John Smith* and *Johnny Smith* are the same person, it is difficult for a computer to do this. Fuzzy logic is a type of artificial intelligence that allows you to work with data that imperfectly matches.

Artificial intelligence isn't perfect (as anybody who has had a conversation with Amazon's Alexa, Apple's Siri or Microsoft's Cortana will know) so use this feature with caution.

1 Open *Sales Performance-1* from your sample files folder.

You can see that this workbook contains two tables.

The *Salesman* table contains the correct spelling of each salesman's full name.

The *Sales* table contains details of each sale made. Unfortunately the staff who log the sales are not very consistent in how they name each salesman.

Salesman	Region		Salesman	Invoice Value
Tom Cruise	North		john travolta	$ 84.76
Johnny Depp	Midlands		Mr John Travolta	$ 106.73
John Travolta	South		John Travvolta	$ 118.93
			mr jonny depp	$ 121.56

In this lesson you'll use Excel's fuzzy logic feature to automatically match the different variations of each salesman's name.

2 Create two connection-only *Get & Transform* queries to extract all values from the *Salesman* and *Sales* tables.

You learned how to do this in: *Lesson 10-20: Work with multiple queries.*

3 Merge the *Sales* query into the *Salesman* query using fuzzy logic to match the *Salesman* field in each table.

1. Click: Data→Get & Transform Data→Get Data→ Combine Queries→Merge.

   The *Merge* dialog appears.

2. Select *Salesman* for the first (top) table. Select *Sales* for the second table.

3. Click inside the *Salesman* field in both of the tables displayed in the dialog to indicate which fields to join.

4. Change the *Join Kind* to *Full Outer (all rows from both)*. You learned about join types in: *Lesson 10-32: Create a simple two-table merged query* (sidebar).

5. Click the *Use fuzzy matching to perform the merge* check box.

   Your dialog should now look like this:

Sales Performance-1

trivia

How John Travolta and Johnny Depp got their nicknames

Johnny Depp is a member of the *Honorable Order of Kentucky Colonels.* His close friend Hunter S. Thompson nominated him for the honor and always refers to Johnny as "The Colonel".

John Travolta was nicknamed "Bone" when he was young because he was long and lean.

Salesman	Region
Tom Cruise	North
Johnny Depp	Midlands
John Travolta	South

Salesman	Invoice Value
john travolta	84.76
Mr John Travolta	106.73
John Travvolta	118.93
mr jonny depp	121.56
John Travolta Jr	121.02

Join Kind

Full Outer (all rows from both)

☑ Use fuzzy matching to perform the merge

▷ Fuzzy merge options

✓ The selection matches 3 of 3 rows from the first table, and 17 of 24 rows f...

Notice that Excel is only able to match 17 of the 24 salesman names.

6. Click on *Fuzzy merge options.*

   Notice the *Similarity threshold (optional)* box. This allows you to set the *Jaccard similarity* (see facing page sidebar). By default this is set to 0.8.

7. Set the *Similarity threshold* to 0.6. Note that Excel is now able to match 18 salesman names.

8. Set the similarity threshold to 0.5. Excel is now able to match 22 of the 24 salesman names.

9. Click the *OK* button.

10. Click the *Merge* button.

11. Click the *OK* button to merge all fields from both tables.

   You can see that Excel has done an almost perfect job in identifying all of the similar names (see sidebar).

   There are two names that cannot be matched. It is not possible to determine that *The Colonel* is a nickname for *Johnny Depp* and *Bone* is a nickname for *John Travolta* using *Jaccard similarity.* In the next lesson: *Lesson 10-35: Improve fuzzy logic results using a custom transformation table,* you'll learn how to overcome this problem.

4 Close the Get & Transform window saving the merge query as a connection only query.

5 Save your work as *Sales Peformance-2.*

Tom Cruise	Tom Cruise
Tom Cruise	tom cruise
Tom Cruise	Tom cruize
Tom Cruise	Mr tom cruise
Tom Cruise	tom cruise jr
Tom Cruise	Cruise
Johnny Depp	Johnny Depp
Johnny Depp	john depp
Johnny Depp	Johnny dep
Johnny Depp	jonny deppp
Johnny Depp	johnny Depp jr
Johnny Depp	Depp
Johnny Depp	mr jonny depp
John Travolta	john travolta
John Travolta	john Travolta
John Travolta	John Travolta
John Travolta	John Travvolta
John Travolta	Jon Travolta
John Travolta	Mr John Travolta
John Travolta	John Travolta Jr
John Travolta	Travolta
John Travolta	John Travolta-jr
null	Bone
null	The Colonel

note

Fuzzy logic uses token weighting, edit distance and transformations

Token weighting

Excel will look for tokens that appear frequently and those that are more novel.

For example, in a list of company names, *Corporation* might appear many times but a company name such as: *Amazon* might appear less frequently. A direct match on the word *Amazon* would then have more importance than a match on *Corporation*.

Edit distance

Edit distance counts the number of changes that need to be made to convert one word to another.

For example, when comparing *Jonny* with *Johnny* the edit distance is only 1. This would be considered a higher value match than comparing *Johnny* with *Jon* (edit distance 2).

Transformations

A transformation table allows tokens to be converted from one string to another before considering a match.

When a transformation table is defined, the original value will still be considered (along with the values defined in the transformation table).

For example, you may wish that Excel considers the token *Robert* to also have the values *Bob* and *Bobby*.

Lesson 10-35: Improve fuzzy logic results using a custom transformation table

In: *Lesson 10-34: Create a merged query using fuzzy logic* (sidebar), you learned that fuzzy logic uses Jaccard similarity to find similar (but not exact) matches between sets of data.

Excel's fuzzy logic feature uses more sophisticated techniques than simplistic Jaccard similarity. *Token weighting*, *transformations* and *edit distance* are also used to improve fuzzy matches (see sidebar if you are interested in how these work).

While you have no control over *token weighting* and *edit distance* you can improve Excel's fuzzy logic accuracy by defining a custom transformation table.

In: *Lesson 10-34: Create a merged query using fuzzy logic,* you matched some names using fuzzy logic. Excel was able to correctly match:

- *Tom Cruise* with *tom cruize*

- *Johnny Depp* with *Mr Jonny Depp*

There were two names that Excel was unable to pair. They were:

- *Johnny Depp* with *The Colonel*

- *John Travolta* with *Bone*

You can see that it is impossible to match the above names with their nicknames simply by applying logical rules to the text.

In order for Excel to regocnize similarity, in these cases, a custom transformation table is needed.

The transformation table is a table with two fields named *From* and *To*. When performing a fuzzy match Excel will convert the tokens using this table and also consider the converted values before establishing a match.

1 Open *Sales Performance-2* from your sample files folder.

This is the workbook you created in: *Lesson 10-34: Create a merged query using fuzzy logic.*

2 Add a custom transformation table to transform *John Travolta* to *Bone* and *Johnny Depp* to *The Colonel.*

Here is the table you need to create:

3 Name the new table: **Transform**

4 Create a connection-only *Get & Transform* query to extract all values from the *Transform* table

5 Open the *Merge1* query.

1. If the *Queries & Connections* task pane is not visible click:

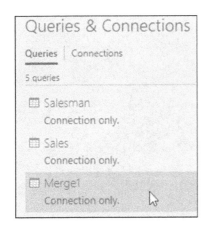

Data→Queries & Connection→Queries and Connections

Note the *Merge1* connection. This is the connection you saved in: *Lesson 10-34: Create a merged query using fuzzy logic.*

2. Double click on the *Merge1* connection to open the query.

Notice that there are two applied steps in this query.

3. Double click on the *Source* applied step.

The *Merge* dialog opens.

4. Click *Fuzzy merge options* to add merge options to the bottom of the dialog.

5. Select the *Transform* table in the *Transformation table (optional)* drop-down list.

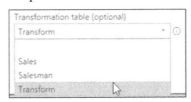

6. The *Merge* dialog should now look like this:

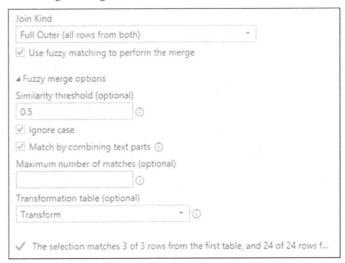

You can see that all 24 rows now match.

7. Click the *OK* button.

8. Click the *Expanded Sales* step in the *Query Settings* pane on the right of the *Power Query Editor*.

Notice that Excel has now matched every name (see sidebar).

9. Close the *Power Query Editor* keeping changes when prompted.

6   Save your work as *Sales Peformance-3.*

Session 10: Exercise

For this exercise there is an *Exercise* folder in your session ten sample files folder that contains three workbooks: *Customer-1, Order-1* and *Product-1*.

1   Open a new blank workbook.

2   The *Customer-1* workbook contains three tables called: *FranceTable, UKTable* and *USATable*. Create three *Connection only* queries that return the data from each table.

3   Create a new *Append* query called *AllCustomers* that will combine all of the rows contained in the other three queries into one query.

4   The *Order-1* and *Product-1* workbooks each contain a single table (*OrderTable* and *ProductTable*). Create two new *Connection only* queries that return the data from each table.

5   Add a *Custom Column* to the *OrderTable* query named *Total Price* that will calculate the total price of each row using the formula: **[Quantity]*[Unit Price]**

6   Set the data type of the new *Total Price* column to: *Currency*.

7   Load the *OrderTable* query results directly into a pivot table.

8   Use the pivot table to show total sales by year and month for each *Country*.

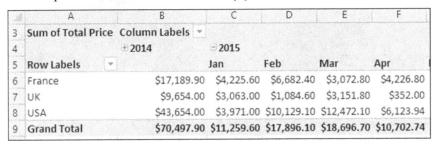

	A	B	C	D	E	F
3	Sum of Total Price	Column Labels				
4		+2014	-2015			
5	Row Labels		Jan	Feb	Mar	Apr
6	France	$17,189.90	$4,225.60	$6,682.40	$3,072.80	$4,226.80
7	UK	$9,654.00	$3,063.00	$1,084.60	$3,151.80	$352.00
8	USA	$43,654.00	$3,971.00	$10,129.10	$12,472.10	$6,123.94
9	Grand Total	$70,497.90	$11,259.60	$17,896.10	$18,696.70	$10,702.74

In the screen grab above the *Currency* number format has been applied to the values.

9   Save your work as: *Exercise 10-End*.

Customer-1, Order-1, Product-1

If you need help slide the page to the left

Session 10: Exercise Answers

These are the three questions that students find the most difficult to answer:

Q 5	Q 3	Q 2
1. Click: Add Column→ General→ Custom Column (from inside the Get & Transform editor). The *Custom Column* dialog appears. 2. Type: **Total Price** into the *New column name* box. 3. Click *Quantity* in the *Available columns* list and then click the << *Insert* button. 4. Type the multiplication operator <*>. 5. Click *Unit Price* in the *Available columns* list and then click the << *Insert* button. 6. Click the OK button. This was covered in: *Lesson 10-17: Add a custom calculated column.*	1. Click: Data→ Get & Transform Data→ Get Data→ Combine Queries→Append. The *Append* dialog appears. 2. Click the *Three or more tables* option button. 3. Select the three tables from the left-hand window and use the *Add >>* button to copy them to the right-hand window. 4. Click the *OK* button. A new query appears in the left-hand navigator pane called: *Append1.* 5. Double-click on the *Append1* query and type: **AllCustomers** 6. Press the <Enter> key. This was covered in: *Lesson 10-21: Create an append query.*	1. Click: Data→ Get & Transform Data→ Get Data→ Launch Power Query Editor… 2. Click: Home→ New Query→ New Source→File→Excel. 3. Select the *Customer-1* workbook from the *Exercise* folder beneath your *Session 10* sample files folder. 4. Check the *Select multiple items* checkbox. 5. Select the *FranceTable, UKTable* and *USATable* tables. 6. Click the *OK* button. The three queries appear in the left-hand navigaor bar. 7. Click: Home→Close→ Close & Load→ Close and Load To… 8. Click the *Only Create Connection* option button. 9. Click the *OK* button. This was covered in: *Lesson 10-20: Work with multiple queries.*

If you have difficulty with the other questions, here are the lessons that cover the relevant skills:

4   Refer to: *Lesson 10-20: Work with multiple queries.*

6   Refer to: *Lesson 10-11: Specify data types.*

7   Refer to: *Lesson 10-15: Transform date and time columns.*

8   Use these fields in your pivot table:

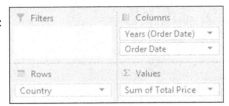

Introduction to the Data Modeling and Power Pivot sessions

The contents of the next two sessions will be challenging to most readers

Your Excel skills are now very advanced and would already be regarded as Expert level by any employer. The concepts presented in the next two sessions are not commonly understood by Excel users (even IT professionals often struggle with relational database and OLAP concepts).

Excel 365 (and Excel 2019) added Microsoft's powerful *Power Pivot* data modeling add-in to all versions of Excel. This new tool enables you to create sophisticated relational data models.

Power Pivot is only used to create OLAP data models

Excel users are often confused about exactly what Power Pivot does (especially if they have been browsing the Internet). Power Pivot is a very sophisticated data modeling tool that enables you to construct tabular data models (called *Relational OLAP tabular databases*) from multiple related data sources (whose data has been imported and prepared using *Get & Transform*).

When an OLAP data model has been constructed it is very easy (even for unsophisticated Excel users) to use a special new type of pivot table (called an OLAP pivot table) to quickly and efficiently create a huge variety of reports using the data contained in the model.

If you cannot understand the above two paragraphs don't worry. The following sessions will enable you to acquire all of the theory you need to make use of Power Pivot.

It has been estimated that only 10% of Excel users are able to use the regular pivot tables that you mastered in: *Session Eight: Pivot Tables*. It is likely that far less than 1% of Excel users (even those with expert skills) will venture into the bold new world of OLAP multidimensional analysis using Power Pivot.

The material that follows is of necessity more complex than in the previous sessions

To create efficient Power Pivot data models, you must first master relational database theory along with many DAX (Data Analysis eXpression) concepts.

By the end of the next two sessions, you will have mastered the core concepts needed to effectively create efficient OLAP data models using Get & Transform and Power Pivot. You'll also be able to include DAX expressions (referred to as *calculated measures*) in the data models you build.

Do not be discouraged if the material in the next two sessions proves difficult to understand upon first reading. It is unlikely that any reader will find the material easy to digest (unless you have existing relational database modeling skills).

Things will become a lot clearer upon a second or third read, as you put the entire subject of multidimensional analysis into a broader context.

11

Session Eleven: Power Pivot, Data Modeling, OLAP and Business Intelligence

> Any sufficiently advanced technology is indistinguishable from magic.
>
> *Sir Arthur C. Clarke, British Science Fiction Writer (1917 - 2008)*

This session will give you the data modeling skills that you need to build OLAP-friendly relational data models and to create OLAP pivot tables from them.

Later, in: *Session Twelve: An introduction to DAX*, you'll learn how to use DAX expressions to further refine your data model.

Session Objectives

By the end of this session you will be able to:

- Understand data model memory requirements
- Install the Power Pivot add-in
- Add tables to a data model
- Understand the Power Pivot window
- Add a relationship to a data model using Power Pivot
- Use an OLAP pivot table to analyze data residing in a data model
- Understand OLAP pivot tables
- Understand modern data analysis
- Understand many-to-many relationships
- Create a data model directly from a relational database
- Understand OLTP database design
- Understand OLAP database design
- Create a snowflake data model from a relational database
- Convert a snowflake data model into a star data model
- Hide, remove and rename data model columns
- Add a calendar table to a data model
- Format values in a data model
- Understand MDX queries and OLAP pivot table limitations
- Use the CUBEVALUE function to query a data model
- Convert CUBEVALUE functions to include MDX expressions
- Create an asymmetric OLAP pivot table using Named Sets

note

How to check how much memory you have available

Click in the Windows search box (at the bottom left of your screen) and type: **System Information** and then press the **<Enter>** key.

A screen appears showing how much memory is installed, and how much is currently available, for your computer.

Installed Physical Memory (RAM)	16.0 GB
Total Physical Memory	15.9 GB
Available Physical Memory	9.03 GB

The above grab was from my own computer, running the 64-bit version of Windows. On my computer I have 9.03 GB of memory available

If I ran the 32-bit version of Windows on the same computer I would only have 2GB of memory available.

You should also make sure that you are running the 64-bit version of Windows 10. Look for this item:

System Type	x64-based PC

x64 indicates that a 64-bit version of Windows 10 is installed.

note

SSAS version history

Microsoft's first OLAP product was released in 1998 as part of SQL Server 7. It was called *OLAP services*.

OLAP services could host an OLAP data model that could be accessed via the MDX query language.

In the year 2000, *OLAP services* was renamed *Analysis Services*. The current version is *Microsoft SQL Server 2019 Analysis Services* (usually referred to using the acronym: *SSAS*).

Lesson 11-1: Understand data model memory requirements

In this book's remaining sessions, you will create and use data models. The data models created in this book reside within the Excel workbook in which they are created. When you save the workbook you also save the data model and the data it contains.

For some of the lessons in this session you will need to open sample files. Though it is very unlikely, you may have a computer that has insufficient free memory to load the sample files into memory.

When you create your own real-world data models you may need to work with very large data sets. This may cause you to experience memory-related problems.

Why memory issues can occur

When a data model is hosted inside Excel, the Power Pivot engine must reside in your computer's memory, along with the data model you create. This can cause out-of-memory errors on computers running the 32-bit version of Windows or on computers with very little memory (RAM) installed.

Make sure you are using the 64-bit version of Windows

Even if you use the 32-bit version of Office (as users who installed Office before February 2019 may do) you will probably using the 64-bit version of Windows (as most users also do).

Microsoft still produce a 32-bit version of Windows 10, but this is only provided to support very old computer hardware (that cannot run a 64-bit operating system) or for companies that run very old software (that cannot run in a 64-bit environment).

The 32-bit version of Windows can only use up to 4GB of RAM (no matter how much memory you install in your computer).

See sidebar to find out how to check whether you are using the 32-bit or 64-bit version of Windows 10.

Solving memory issues with the 64-bit version of Excel

There are two versions of Office available and you have access to both with your 365 subscription:

- The 32-bit version (that most users install)

- The 64-bit version (that only power users typically install).

To discover the version of Office you are using:

1. Start Excel.

2. Click: File→Account→About Excel.

About Excel

Learn more about Excel, Support, Product ID, and Copyright information.

Version 1908 (Build 11929.20562 Click-to-Run)

Semi-annual Channel (Targeted)

You'll now see which version you are using.

note

Out of memory errors may crash or hang your computer

If your computer hangs or crashes when using an Excel workbook that contains a data model the cause could be a memory-related issue. You may have to do the following to close Excel:

1. Open the *Windows Task Manager* application (the easiest way to do this is to press the **<Ctrl>+<Alt>+<Delete>** keys) and then select *Task Manager* from the shortcut menu.

2. Click the *Processes* tab.

3. In the *Apps* list, right-click on *Microsoft Excel* and select *End Task* from the shortcut menu.

4. Restart Excel.

note

Some modern computers support an enormous amount of RAM

For example, the Hewlett Packard Integrity MC990X supports up to 6 Terabytes of RAM (though it does cost over $70,000).

About Microsoft® Excel® for Office 365

Microsoft® Excel® for Office 365 MSO (16.0.11929.20536) 64-bit

Until January 2019 the 32-bit version of Office was automatically installed by default. This was to avoid potential problems with older 32-bit items such as add-ins or embedded media. Since January 2019 the 64 bit version has been installed by default (a welcome change). If your copy of Office 365 was installed before February 2019 you may find that you are still using the 32-bit version.

The Excel 32-bit version can only utilize 2GB of memory while the Office 64-bit version can address up to 8 Terabytes. It is difficult to imagine any data analysis task that would need more memory than this.

Users of the 64-bit version of Excel can thus always overcome out-of-memory problems by installing more memory.

Solving memory issues by pre-compression

When a data model is loaded into memory it is compressed (by the Power Pivot engine) into a much more compact form. Compression can reduce the data model's size by as much as 90%.

In: *Appendix A: Power Pivot Rules*, you can find out how to make your data model compression-friendly so that Power Pivot can achieve optimal compression.

If you have access to a 64-bit version of Excel running on a machine with a lot of memory, you may be able to create a data model that can be used by 32-bit users with limited memory. When you create the data model and then save the workbook (that contains the data model) you may find that it opens without issues on computers that would have been unable to create the model themselves.

If you adopt this strategy be aware that users will be unable to refresh data models (from the original source data) on their machines.

Solving memory issues by hosting your data model on SSAS

Microsoft have a product called SSAS (SQL Server Analysis Services). A Power Pivot data model can be exported (including any DAX expressions it may contain), without modification, into a tabular model that can be hosted on an SSAS server (rather than in your computer's memory).

Out of memory problems can then be avoided (even by 32-bit users with modest hardware) as the data model is stored in the SSAS server's memory (and not in the user's own computer memory).

There are other advantages to hosting a data model on an SSAS server:

- **The ability to work with bigger data:** The size of the model is no longer limited by the size of your computer's memory.

- **Better security:** It is easier to restrict the data that the user of the data model is permitted to see.

- **Refresh scheduling:** SSAS allows the data model to be refreshed on a scheduled basis.

- **Centralized data:** The data model is held at one central location.

important

What to do if your Power Pivot tab disappears

Many users have reported that their *Power Pivot* tab disappears from time to time. When it disappears, nothing happens when you click:

Data→Data Tools→Manage Data Model

There is an easy work-around to this problem that will restore the Power Pivot tab and put everything back working as it should.

If you have this problem, here's what you need to do:

1. Click: File→Options→Add-ins.

2. At the bottom of the *Add-ins* dialog you'll see a *Manage: Excel Add-ins* drop-down list.

3. Select: *COM Add-ins* from the drop-down list and then click the *Go…* button.

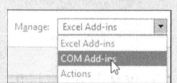

You'll now see a *COM Add-ins* dialog and you'll probably see that *Microsoft Power Pivot for Excel* is checked.

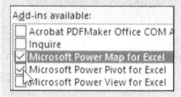

4. De-select the check box and click the *OK* button.

5. Repeat the whole procedure but this time check the check box to switch Power Pivot back on again.

Yes, it's that old favourite "switch it off and then switch it back on again" technique that solves so many computer problems.

Lesson 11-2: Install the Power Pivot add-in

Until the January 2020 Version 1908 release the Power Pivot add-in was not installed by default. If the Power Pivot add-in mis missing from your Ribbon you may need to install it to complete this session.

1   Open Excel and create a new blank workbook.

2   Install Power Pivot.

1.   Click Data→Data Tools→Manage Data Model.

If Power Pivot is already installed then the Power Pivot window will open. If this is the case you can close the Power Pivot window and move to the next lesson.

If Power Pivot is not already installed, a dialog may appear asking you to *Enable the Data Analysis add-ins.*

This is Excel's way of asking for permission to install the Power Pivot add-in.

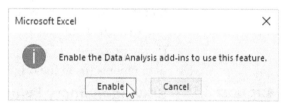

2.   Click the *Enable* button.

Power Pivot could take 30 seconds or more to install on a slower computer.

When the installation process is complete the Power Pivot application is opened:

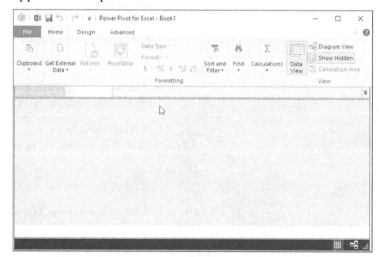

trivia

PowerPivot or Power Pivot (with a space)?

Between 2010 and 2013 Microsoft used the product name PowerPivot (without a space).

On July 8, 2013 Microsoft announced that PowerPivot would now form part of a new *Power BI* suite of self-service tools.

The suite comprised of:

- Power Pivot
- Power Query
- Power Maps
- Power View

PowerPivot had been renamed *Power Pivot* to maintain consistency with the naming convention of the other applications in the suite.

As you know from the earlier OLAP sessions, *Power Query* has now been renamed *Get & Transform* and *Power Maps* has now been renamed *3D Maps*.

Power View (now obsolete) was an early incarnation of the product Microsoft now call: *Power BI*.

Power BI is a fast-evolving stand-alone tool that aims to allow unsophisticated users to create visual representations of data from data models created by more sophisticated users (such as yourself when you have finished this book).

3. Close the *Power Pivot* window.

   Notice that a new *Power Pivot* tab has now appeared on the ribbon:

3 **Open the Power Pivot window.**

   Now that the Power Pivot add-in has been installed you can open the Power Pivot window in two ways:

   Either

   Click: Power Pivot→Data Model→Manage.

   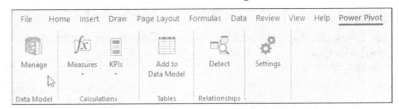

   Or

   Click: Data→Data Tools→Manage Data Model.

important

Do not use the Power Pivot ribbon to add tables to a data model

When you installed Power Pivot a new Power Pivot tab was added to the ribbon.

You may have noticed a *Tables* ribbon group:

If you select an Excel table and then click this button you will import the table directly into the *Power Pivot* data model.

This button is provided so that unsophisticated users who do not understand *Get & Transform* can create simplistic data models, but it is not best practice to import tables in this way. I advise that you never use this method.

You should always import tables into the data model using *Get & Transform* (as you do in this lesson). You'll then have access to a huge range of transformation features (that you may need in the future even if you don't at the time of import).

There are many other advantages of adding tables to the model via *Get & Transform* that will become apparent as you progress through this session.

The best-practice rule:

Do not use Power Pivot to import or transform data.

… is included in: *Appendix A: Power Pivot Rules.*

Lesson 11-3: Add tables to a data model

In this lesson you'll create your first data model using Get & Transform and Power Pivot.

A data model contains one or more tables and defines the (primary key/foreign key) relationships between them. (You learned about primary keys and foreign keys in: *Lesson 10-26: Understand primary and foreign keys.*)

It is possible to import data directly into a data model from many different data sources. In this lesson you will import data from two Excel tables.

1   Open *Stock List-1* from your sample files folder.

2   Select the *Product* worksheet.

3   Add the *Product* table to the data model.

   1. Click on any cell inside the *Product* table.

   2. Click: Data→Get & Transform Data→From Table/Range.

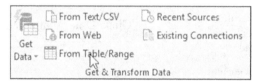

The Get & Transform editor opens. Note that the left-hand bar contains a new query called *Product*.

(You may have to click the *Expand* button [>] to expand the *Navigator Pane*).

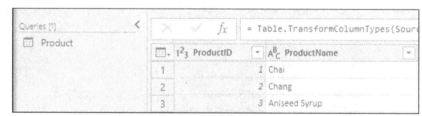

   3. Click: Home→Close→Close & Load→Close & Load To…

The *Import Data* dialog appears.

   4. Click the *Only Create Connection* option button.

   5. Check the *Add this data to the Data Model* check box.

Stock List-1

note

Data models that source data from Excel tables in the same workbook are inefficient

In this lesson's example, data is sourced from Excel tables that are in the same workbook that the data model resides in. This means that Excel must maintain two copies of the same data (one in the data model and one in the Excel tables). This is not best-practice when creating data models.

Both Excel and the data model must fit in the computer's available memory. When dealing with large data sets there is an increased risk of encountering out-of-memory errors when the data is duplicated in the way described above.

For this reason, importing data into a data model from a linked Excel table (in the same workbook) is not considered to be best-practice when creating data models.

The best-practice rule:

Do not use linked Excel tables.

... is included in: *Appendix A: Power Pivot Rules.*

6. Click: *OK.*

   You are returned to Excel with the *Queries & Connections* task pane visible. You cannot see the *Data Model* yet (the Data Model is an in-memory construct that is invisible within the Excel application).

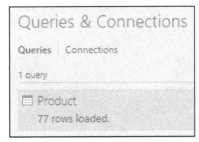

4 Add the *Category* table to the data model.

Do this in the same way you added the *Product* table.

Don't forget to check the *add this data to the Data Model* check box (as you did with the *Product* query).

You should now be inside Excel with two queries shown in the *Queries & Connections* task pane.

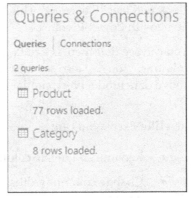

5 Save your work as *Stock List-2.*

Lesson 11-4: Understand the Power Pivot window

1   Open *Stock List-2* from your sample files folder.

2   Open the Power Pivot window.

Click: Power Pivot→Data Model→Manage.

The Power Pivot window opens.

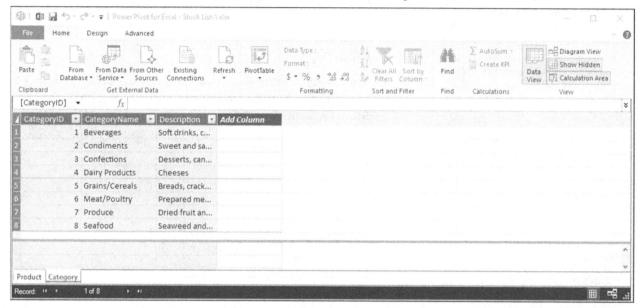

This is your first view of the Power Pivot application.

note

You can paste data directly into a new data model table

To do this:

1. Select and copy the range of data that you want to import into a new Power Pivot table.

2. Open the Power Pivot window.

3. Click: Home→Clipboard→ Paste (from within the Power Pivot window).

4. Provide a name for the new table when prompted.

The differences between the Power Pivot window and Excel

The Power Pivot window seems very similar to Excel but you are really looking at a completely different product that has been engineered to "look and feel" like Excel. This is intended to make you feel instantly at home with Power Pivot.

You can see that there is a data grid that is similar to Excel with rows and columns. You can also see tabs showing that there are two tables in the above data model (very similar to two worksheets in a workbook).

Just like Excel, you can:

- Rename and delete columns.

- Change column widths.

- Insert new columns.

- Click and drag columns to new locations.

- Rename and delete sheet tabs.

- Click and drag sheet tabs to re-arrange them.

- Use AutoSum to aggregate all of the values in a column.

note

If data in the workbook changes the data model will not automatically update

The data you are looking at is an independent copy of the data residing in the Excel *Product* and *Category* tables.

If the data in the *Product* and *Category* tables changes you will not see any change in the data model (unless you refresh the model from the original source data).

important

Do not import or transform data using Power Pivot

The Power Pivot application is a tool to construct and refine data models.

Power Pivot is not a good tool for importing data into the data model.

You should always import data into the data model using Get & Transform (in the way you did for this model in: *Lesson 11-3: Add tables to a data model*).

Using Get & Transform provides powerful data transformation features that enable you to edit and refine your data in the future.

The best-practice rule:

Do not use Power Pivot to import or transform data.

… is included in: *Appendix A: Power Pivot Rules.*

This creates a *calculated measure*. You'll learn how to use calculated measures later in: *Lesson 12-3: Create a DAX calculated measure.*

- Format cells.

- Sort columns.

Unlike Excel, you can't:

- Type a value into a cell or change any of the information you see displayed (although you can refresh the data from the original data source).

- Have more than one table in a sheet. A Power Pivot sheet contains a single table rather than a worksheet.

- Refer to a cell using A1 notation (A1 notation means cell references such as B12 or A1:C14). Power Pivot does not recognize letters to identify columns. Columns must be referred to by name.

- Assign different data types within a column. You cannot, for example, have text in some cells and numbers in other cells in the same column. You learned about data types in: *Lesson 10-6: Understand data types.*

- Have more than one formula in a column. When a formula is added to a Power Pivot column it always applies to every cell in that column. You'll learn more about calculated columns later, in: *Lesson 12-2: Add a DAX calculated column.*

Some things Power Pivot can do that Excel cannot

- Create relationships between tables.

- Assign a larger range of data types to columns.

- Use DAX functions (you'll learn about DAX later, in: *Session Twelve: An introduction to DAX*).

- Create calculated measures. You'll learn more about measures later, in: *Lesson 12-3: Create a DAX calculated measure.*

- Work with *Big Data*. An Excel worksheet can contain a maximum of just over a million rows. A Power Pivot table can contain a maximum of just over a thousand million rows.

- Produce extremely fast (often perceived as instant) results even when analyzing data sets containing many millions of rows. Power Pivot uses Microsoft's *xVelocity in-memory analysis engine*. This engine can scan billions of data rows per second and can produce reports in a tiny fraction of the time needed by Excel.

3 Close the Power Pivot window.

4 Close Excel without saving the workbook.

note

Classic Data Analysis and Modern Data Analysis

In: *Lesson 10-27: Link primary and foreign keys using VLOOKUP,* you effectively created a primary key/foreign key relationship using a simple VLOOKUP function.

This methodology is often described as belonging to *Classic Data Analysis.*

In this lesson you use Power Pivot to define a primary key/foreign key relationship within a data model without the use of any function.

This methodology is often described as belonging to *Modern Data Analysis.*

You'll discover more about the differences between Classic Data Analysis and Modern Data Analysis later, in: *Lesson 11-8: Understand modern data analysis.*

Lesson 11-5: Add a relationship to a data model using Power Pivot

In: *Lesson 11-3: Add tables to a data model,* you added two table to a data model.

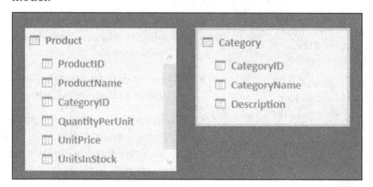

If you completely understood: *Lesson 10-26: Understand primary and foreign keys,* you will see at a glance that:

- *ProductID* is the primary key of the *Product* table.

- *CategoryID* is the primary key of the *Category* table.

- The *Product* table contains a single foreign key called *CategoryID.*

The data model is not yet aware that there is a relationship between the tables. In this lesson you'll add the relationship to the data model.

1   Open *Stock List-2* from your sample files folder.

2   Open Power Pivot.

Click: Power Pivot→Data Model→Manage.

3   Change the Power Pivot window view to *Diagram View*

In the Power Pivot window click:

Home→View→Diagram View

The window contents change to show a graphical representation of both tables. This type of graphical representation of tables (and their relationships) within a database is often referred to as a *Schema.*

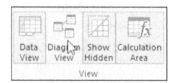

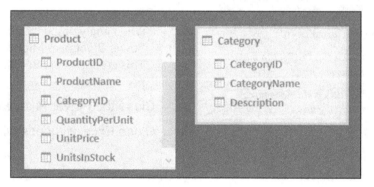

You can drag the tables around the window or click and drag the edge of a table to re-size it.

note

Before Power Pivot was added to Excel relationships had to be designed in a more cumbersome way

When Excel 365 was updated to *January 2019 semi-annual version 1808,* the Power Pivot add-in was made available to all Excel 365 subscribers.

The same add-in is also available in all Excel 2019 perpetual license versions.

You use the Power Pivot add-in's *Diagram View* in this lesson to easily define a primary key/foreign key relationship using drag-and-drop.

Before Power Pivot arrived, relationships had be defined in a far more cumbersome way using the *Manage Relationships* dialog.

The "old way" of defining relationships using the *Manage Relationships* dialog is still included on the ribbon.

A *Relationships* button is available when there are two or more tables within a workbook's data model.

The button can be found at:

Data→Data Tools→ Relationships

Some may argue that using the *Manage Relationships* dialog avoids the need to open the Power Pivot window and can be faster when modeling simple relationships.

My own view is that there are no circumstances when you would want to use this older (and less intuitive) method today.

4   **Add a Primary Key/Foreign Key relationship between the tables.**

Click on the *Category ID* primary key (in the *Category* table) and drag it on top of the *Category ID* foreign key (in the *Product* table).

It doesn't really matter which table you drag the key field from, and which you drag it to. Power Pivot is clever enough to figure out which table contains the primary key column and which table contains the foreign key (whichever direction you drag them in).

A relationship appears in the diagram window:

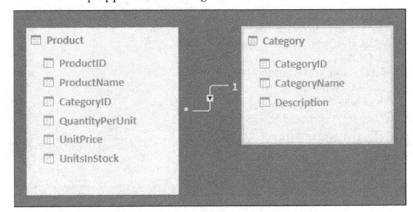

Notice the number **1** next to the *Category* table and the asterisk next to the *Product* table.

You can read this relationship as follows:

***One** Category can be associated with **Many** products, but each product can be associated with one (**and only one**) category.*

This type of relationship is called a one-to-many relationship and is the only relationship used in Power Pivot data models (often called OLAP databases).

Relational databases often contain a different (but rarer) relationship called a many-to-many relationship. You'll learn about this type of relationship in: *Lesson 11-10: Understand many-to-many relationships.*

5   **Close the Power Pivot window.**

6   **Save your work as** *Stock List-3.*

You've now created your very first data model.

In this very simple data model you imported data from two small Excel tables and then defined a relationship between them.

You can probably appreciate how you can use Power Pivot to create large data models that import table data from multiple sources with defined relationships between them.

The data model is invisible (unless you open Power Pivot). In the next lesson: *Lesson 11-6: Use an OLAP pivot table to analyze data residing in a data model,* you will make use of the data model by using it as the source data for a new type of Pivot Table (called an OLAP Pivot Table).

Microsoft's *Modern Data Analysis* vision will then become a little clearer.

important

Excel can add relationships automatically

In: *Lesson 11-5: Add a relationship to a data model using Power Pivot,* you manually created a relationship for the data model used in this lesson.

If you had not created the relationship and tried to create an OLAP pivot table from the data model, you would see this warning at the top of the *PivotTable Fields* pane:

You can see that Excel offers to automatically detect the relationships in the data model for you.

If you clicked the *Auto-Detect…* button, Excel would notice that there is only one field name that is common to both tables (*CategoryID*) so would correctly conclude that these fields are related and automatically create the relationship.

In the simple two-table data model used in this lesson *Auto-Detect* will work perfectly.

It is not a good ideal to rely upon this feature as Excel will get things wrong sometimes (especially when data originates from multiple sources).

If you use the Auto-Detect feature you should always examine the schema afterwards to confirm that Excel has created the correct relationships.

Stock List-3

Lesson 11-6: Use an OLAP pivot table to analyze data residing in a data model

In: *Lesson 11-3: Add tables to a data model* and *Lesson 11-5: Add a relationship to a data model using Power Pivot,* you created a very simple data model that contained two tables and one relationship.

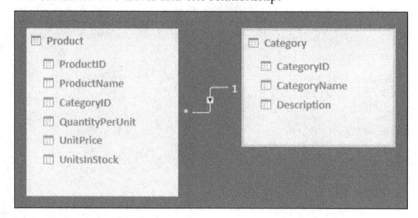

In this lesson you'll analyze the data contained in this model using an OLAP pivot table.

1   Open *Stock List-3* from your sample files folder.

2   Open Power Pivot.

Click: Power Pivot→Data Model→Manage.

3   Create an OLAP pivot table that uses the data model as source data.

1.   Click: Home→PivotTable→Pivot Table (in the Power Pivot window).

The *Create PivotTable* dialog appears.

2.   Click: OK.

A special type of pivot table is created that references the data model. While the pivot table looks almost the same as the pivot tables you worked with in: *Session Eight: Pivot Tables,* it is actually a completely new type of pivot table called an *OLAP pivot table.* OLAP is an acronym for *OnLine Analytical Processing.*

Later in this session you'll learn a lot more about OLAP pivot tables. OLAP pivot tables can do many things that regular pivot tables cannot do. Conversely, there are some features

available in a regular pivot table that are not supported (or needed) in OLAP pivot tables.

Notice that the *PivotTable Fields* pane is headed with two tabs: *Active* and *All* (although there are no active fields at present). This is one way to immediately identify OLAP pivot tables (as they look very similar to regular pivot tables).

4   Rename the pivot table worksheet tab: **Pivot Table**

5   Use the OLAP pivot table to show total units in stock for each category.

1. Click on the pivot table to activate it.

   In the *PivotTable Fields* pane, tables in the data model are shown with a orange icon on the bottom-right corner. Tables in the regular Excel workbook do not have this icon (see sidebar).

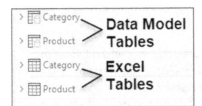

2. Click the fly out menu button next to the Data Model *Category* table and check the *CategoryName* check box.

3. Click the fly out menu button next to the Data Model *Product* table and check the *UnitsInStock* check box.

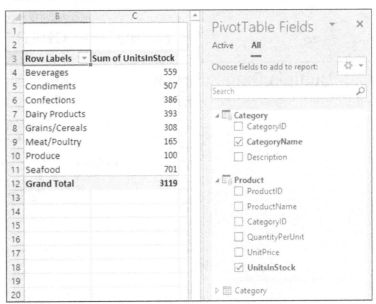

You have now created a single OLAP pivot table based upon a data model. The data model:

- Contains two tables (that were imported using *Get & Transform* queries).

- Contains a relationship (that was created using *Power Pivot*).

- Is being used by an OLAP Pivot Table (within *Excel.*)

In the lessons and sessions that follow you'll appreciate the huge advantages of assembling data into a data model prior to analysis with an OLAP pivot table.

6   Save your work as *Stock List-4.*

note

Another way to automatically detect and add relationships

On the facing page sidebar you learned that Excel can add relationships to a data model automatically – and that you should use this feature with caution.

You can also launch the Auto-Detect feature from the Power Pivot ribbon tab (within Excel).

1. Select a pivot table that uses the data model as its source:

2. Click: Power Pivot→ Relationships→Detect

The relationships will then be automatically detected and created.

Lesson 11-7: Understand OLAP pivot tables

In: *Lesson 8-4: Understand the pivot table data cache* you learned that a pivot table does not access the source data directly. Instead, a *pivot table data cache* is created from the data source. The pivot table then takes its data from the cache.

In: *Lesson 10-30: Load a query directly into the PivotTable cache*, you learned that a pivot table data cache doesn't need to use an Excel worksheet as its data source. It is possible to construct the cache directly from an external data source.

In: *Lesson 11-3: Add tables to a data model, Lesson 11-5: Add a relationship to a data model using Power Pivot* and *Lesson 11-6: Use an OLAP pivot table to analyze data residing in a data model*, you created a data model and then used it as the data source for a new type of pivot table called an OLAP pivot table.

You may wonder why a different type of pivot table is needed when you create a pivot table from a data model rather than a single Excel table.

Normal and OLAP Pivot Tables

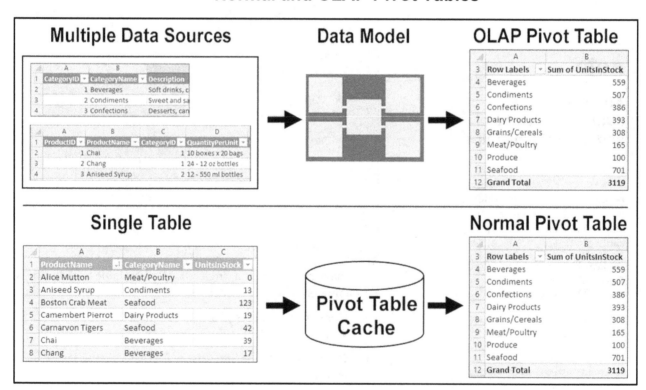

In the above diagram you can see that both the regular pivot table and the OLAP pivot table look identical.

The difference between them is that the *OLAP pivot table* obtains its data from a *Data Model* created from one or more related tables. The ability to select fields from more than one related table is one of the biggest advantages of working with OLAP pivot tables.

note

What is self-service BI?

In the recent past it was very expensive to implement a Business Intelligence solution using server-based products such as *Microsoft SQL Server Analysis Services.*

BI projects would often take many months to complete and involve large numbers of highly trained IT professionals to design (and extract and transform data into) an OLAP cube. An OLAP cube is the earliest implementation of an OLAP database – for more on this see: *Lesson 11-11: Understand OLTP database design (sidebar).*

The vision for the Excel data model is that ordinary Excel users can instantly and automatically create a ready-to-go data model (OLAP database).

An OLAP pivot table or OLAP pivot chart can then be used to analyze and present the contents of the data model. Microsoft sometimes call this concept: *Self Service BI.*

The *regular pivot table* obtains its data from a *pivot table data cache* created from a single table residing in an Excel worksheet or external data source.

OLAP pivot tables are standards-based

The *PivotTable data cache* can be thought of as a non-standard OLAP implementation that is restricted to a single table data source.

In contrast, when data resides in a data model it can be retrieved directly from the data model using an industry-standard query language called MDX (Multi-Dimensional eXpressions). You'll learn more about MDX queries later, in: *Lesson 11-19: Understand MDX queries and OLAP pivot table limitations.*

MDX is also used by many non-Microsoft products such as *Crystal Reports.*

An OLAP pivot table automatically generates the MDX queries it needs to return values to display in the OLAP pivot table.

OLAP pivot tables can work with big data

Excel worksheets are limited to approximately one million rows. OLAP pivot tables obtain their data from a Data Model. Data Models can contain about two thousand million data rows.

In: *Lesson 10-30: Load a query directly into the PivotTable cache,* you learned how a regular pivot table can work with big data by using Get & Transform to load data (from an external non-Excel data source) directly into the *PivotTable Data Cache.*

While it is true that a regular pivot table can also overcome the million-row limitation in this way, the *PivotTable Data Cache* is still restricted to 2.1 thousand million data items (rather than rows) and is unable to work with more than one table.

What is Business Intelligence?

Business Intelligence is a very broad term that was first used in 1865 to describe how the banker Sir Henry Furnese prospered by receiving and acting upon information before his contemporaries.

When IT professionals talk about Business Intelligence (BI) today, they usually mean the analysis and presentation of data sourced from an OLAP database (data model).

Dr E.F. Codd (the inventor of OLAP) wrote a paper in 1985 that proposed 12 rules for defining OLAP. Two of his rules were:

- *The tool (and not the user) should be concerned with where the physical data comes from.*

- *Reporting facilities should present information in any way the user wants to view it.*

You can see how Microsoft's BI solution complies with Codd's rules by separating the data modeling (difficult) and reporting (easy) tasks and by enabling complete reporting flexibility via the OLAP pivot table.

note

Power Pivot has been available for selected versions of Excel for a long time

Power Pivot was first released in May 2010 as part of the *SQL Server 2008 R2* product line. It was also possible to install Power Pivot onto any version of Excel 2010 as a free add-in.

For Excel 2013 and Excel 2016 the full Power Pivot add-in was only available for Pro Plus versions of Excel.

In the standard version of Excel 2013 it became possible to create a relational data model and analyze the model using an OLAP pivot table or chart. Without access to Power Pivot it wasn't possible to create DAX calculated fields or calculated measures or to display a schema. You'll learn more about DAX later, in: *Session Twelve: An introduction to DAX*.

Excel 2016 also added the *Get & Transform* tool (previously named Power Query) as an integral part of all Excel versions.

Excel 2019 (and the Jan 2019 semi-annual Excel 365 release) finally added Power Pivot to all Excel versions. It then became possible to realize the full *modern data analysis* vision using any Excel version.

Lesson 11-8: Understand modern data analysis

You now have an in-depth understanding of *Get & Transform*. You also have a limited understanding of relational database theory and Power Pivot. With this foundation knowledge you should now be able to understand how these tools and technologies work together to provide a new paradigm for data analysis using Excel that is often described as: *Modern Data Analysis*.

What does modern data analysis mean?

When the *Get & Transform* and *Power Pivot* tools were added to Excel (in the Excel 2019 perpetual licence version and the January 2019 Excel 365 semi-annual update) they enabled a new paradigm for data analysis.

The term: *Modern Data Analysis* is often used to describe the use of these new tools in their intended fashion. The term: *Classic Data Analysis* has been used to describe the "old way" of doing things.

The five steps in the modern data analysis workflow

Most data analysis tasks require five clearly defined steps: Get, Transform, Relate, Summarize and Visualize.

1. **Get** the data. This means importing data (that may be located in a database, Excel worksheet, CSV file or other source).

2. **Transform** the data. This might include removing unwanted columns, converting text fields to dates, rounding numeric values, filtering, sorting, renaming columns, adding calculated columns and other similar tasks.

3. **Relate** the data. If data resides in several different tables, there needs to be a method to either define the relationships between them or to consolidate the data into a single table.

4. **Aggregate** (summarize) the data. Values usually need to be aggregated (for example by creating grouped totals or averages) into a digestible form.

5. **Visualize** the data. This may involve adding charts, pivot charts, conditional formatting, sparklines and other visualizations.

How data analysis was done in the past (classic data analysis)

1. **Get** the data. This was traditionally done by importing data into a collection of Excel tables or ranges.

2. **Transform** the data. This might include removing unwanted columns from the worksheet, adding new calculated columns containing Excel functions and formulas, converting text fields to dates, rounding numeric values, renaming columns, formatting cells and other similar tasks.

note

Modern data analysis supports Big Data

One of the compelling reasons to move to modern data analysis is the increasing requirement to work with Big Data.

Excel worksheets theoretically support a little over a million rows of data (in reality the useful limit is far lower).

Power Pivot tables can contain up to approximately two thousand million rows, meaning that there is no imaginable data requirement that cannot be supported.

note

Modern data analysis is fast

Even when working with data tables containing many millions of rows most analysis actions will complete almost instantly.

Power Pivot uses Microsoft's *xVelocity in-memory analysis engine*. This engine can scan billions of data rows per second and can produce reports in a tiny fraction of the time that would be needed by Excel.

note

Modern data analysis performs most of the work outside Excel

Notice that, in modern data analysis, only Step 5 involves using Excel.

All of the actions that are used to create the data model are performed by the *Get & Transform* and *Power Pivot* applications.

3. **Relate** the data. Traditional (non OLAP) pivot tables can only summarize data from a single table so data from several different tables would often have to be consolidated into a single table. This was traditionally done with VLOOKUP, SWITCH, INDEX, MATCH, IF and IFS functions.

4. **Aggregate** the data. Excel contains many methods to summarize data. Popular methods include Automatic Subtotals, Data Tables, traditional (as opposed to OLAP) Pivot Tables and aggregation functions such as SUM, AVERAGE, MAX, MIN, COUNT and COUNTIF.

5. **Visualize** the data. This might involve summarizing data in a traditional pivot table or pivot chart, adding charts, conditional formatting, sparklines and other visualizations.

How modern data analysis achieves faster and better results

1. **Get** the data. This is done using the *Get and Transform* tool. Data can be imported from a huge range of data sources using this tool (including relational databases, Excel worksheets, CSV files and web pages). Get & Transform can work with very large data sets (often called *Big Data*) as it is not restricted to Excel's million row limitation (see sidebar).

2. **Transform** the data. This is also done using the *Get and Transform* tool. Unlike Excel, the transform actions are stored in PQFL (Power Query Formula Language) expressions. Both the connection details and the PQFL steps are stored in a query. This means that the query can be re-run, avoiding repetitive work in the future if the source data changes.

3. **Relate** the data. Power Pivot enables tables to be related in a *data model* using primary key/foreign key relationships. This provides huge flexibility and avoids the use of any Excel functions (such as VLOOKUP) to relate data.

4. **Summarize** the data. While a traditional pivot table can only access data residing in a single table, data models can be analyzed with a new type of pivot table (called an OLAP pivot table). The OLAP pivot table can do just about anything that a regular pivot table can do but can access data residing in multiple related tables.

   Power Pivot also enables DAX (Data Analysis Expressions) to be added to the data model. DAX enables calculated columns and calculated measures (aggregations) to be simply defined. You'll learn about DAX later, in: *Session Twelve: An introduction to DAX*.

5. **Visualize** the data. OLAP Pivot Tables and OLAP Pivot Charts provide the primary method of visualizing data residing in data models. It is also possible to use any of Excel's classic analysis and visualization features by using CUBEVALUE functions to extract data directly from a data model into Excel cells. You'll learn more about the CUBEVALUE function later, in: *Lesson 11-20: Use the CUBEVALUE function to query a data model.*

note

Relationships imported from a relational database are reliable

When you import data from a relational database (via Get & Transform) both tables and relationships are imported.

Get & Transform can then load both the tables and the relationships into a data model.

Note that this is very different to the auto-detect feature discussed in: *Lesson 11-6: Use an OLAP pivot table to analyze data residing in a data model*(sidebar).

When you import data from relational database there is no scope for error as the relationships defined by the database designer are also imported.

Lesson 11-9: Create a data model directly from a relational database

In: *Lesson 10-26: Understand primary and foreign keys,* you learned how a relational database consists of several tables linked by relationships.

In: *Lesson 10-30: Load a query directly into the PivotTable cache,* you created a *PivotTable data cache* directly from a single database table (without importing any data into a worksheet).

Of course, the *PivotTable data cache* doesn't understand the concept of multiple related tables. You can only create a *PivotTable data cache* from a single worksheet or single external table (or view). Data models don't have this limitation.

A relational database (such as Access, Oracle or SQL Server) already contains defined relationships between tables. When the data source has defined relationships, Get & Transform imports both the tables and the relationships. Get & Transform can then load both the tables and the relationships into a data model.

In this lesson you'll import a complete relational database (along with its relationships) into a data model. You won't need to define the relationships yourself. You'll then use the data model as the source for an OLAP pivot table.

1   Open a new blank workbook.

2   Import the *Categories* and *Products* tables from the *Two Related Tables* Access database in your sample files folder directly into a data model.

1.   Click: Data→Get & Transform Data→Get Data→
From Database→From Microsoft Access Database.

The *Import Data* dialog appears.

2.   Select the Access database file *Two Related Tables* from your sample files folder and click the *Import* button.

The *Navigator* dialog appears.

3.   Check the *Select multiple items* check box.

Check boxes appear next to each table.

4.   Check the check boxes next to the *Category* and *Product* tables.

5.   Click: Load (drop-down arrow)→Load To…

Two Related Tables

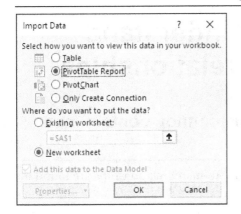

The *Import Data* dialog appears (sometimes this takes a few moments to appear).

6. Click the *PivotTable Report* option button. Notice that when you select this option the *Add this data to the Data Model* checkbox is automatically checked and cannot be changed. This happens because Get & Transform knows that the data source contains both tables and relationships.

7. Click the *OK* button.

When you click the OK button Excel uses the *Category* and *Product* tables from the Access database to create a new data model with primary key/foreign key relationships that match those defined in the database.

An empty OLAP pivot table is then created. *The PivotTable Fields* list references this data model. You can see that all of the fields from both the *Category* and *Product* tables are available.

Notice the small orange database symbols shown on each table. This indicates that the data source resides in the data model and not in an Excel worksheet.

3   View the relationships in the data model.

1. Click: Power Pivot→Data Model→Manage.

The Power Pivot window opens.

2. In the Power Pivot window, click: Home→View→ Diagram View.

The Schema is displayed.

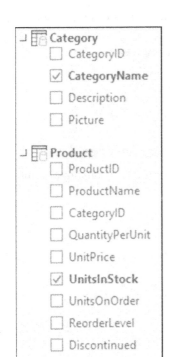

3. Click the relationship line between the tables.

The *CategoryID* field is highlighted in both tables, proving that the relationship between the *Category* and *Product* tables has been correctly applied:

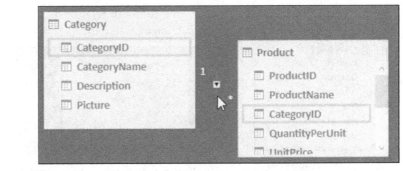

4   Close the Power Pivot window.

5   Use the OLAP pivot table to show the total *UnitsInStock* for each *CategoryName*.

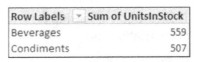

Row Labels	Sum of UnitsInStock
Beverages	559
Condiments	507

6   Save your work as *Two Related Tables-1.*

note

Even IT professionals often find many-to-many relationships difficult to understand

Unfortunately, database design is one of the least understood skills in the world of IT.

I have spent a great deal of my professional life implementing clumsy work-arounds to overcome badly designed databases (even when working on multi-million-dollar projects).

One of the most common errors I have encountered in corporate databases all over the world is the incorrect modeling of many-to-many relationships. Often a programmer that doesn't really understand database design will try to "muddle through".

The normal error is when the programmer didn't "get" many-to-many relationships and tried to model a series of one-to-many relationships instead.

If you see this type of table:

… you will know at once that the designer didn't understand many-to-many relationships.

The designer of the above table has tried to work-around their inability to model many-to-many relationships by defining three one-to-many relationships.

You are almost certain to encounter design errors like this if you work with corporate data.

Lesson 11-10: Understand many-to-many relationships

Power Pivot data models cannot contain many-to-many relationships

As you will learn in this lesson, many-to-many relationships are found in most commercial databases.

Later, in this session you'll discover that Power Pivot data models need to be designed in a different way to commercial databases as they cannot contain many-to-many relationships. You'll learn how to convert any many-to-many relationships in the source data into the one-to-many relationships needed in a correctly designed Power Pivot data model.

One-to-many relationships

Up until now you have only modeled a one-to-many relationship.

In: *Lesson 11-5: Add a relationship to a data model using Power Pivot,* you created a relationship between a *Product* table and a *Category* table. This defined the following relationship:

- Each Product can be associated with one, and only one, Category.

- *One* Category can potentially be associated with *Many* Products.

This type of relationship is called a *one-to-many* relationship, with the Category on the *One* side of the relationship and the Product on the *Many* side.

One-to-many relationships are by far the most common type of relationship.

A one-to-many relationship is displayed in the Power Pivot window's *diagram view* like this:

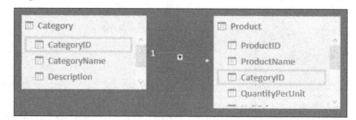

You can see how the *One* and *Many* sides of the relationship are marked.

Many-to-many relationships

This type of relationship is more difficult to model than a simple one-to-many relationship.

In the world of commerce, a many-to-many relationship that is often encountered is that between *Products* and *Invoices.*

- One *Invoice* can bill many *Products.*

- One *Product* can appear on many *Invoices.*

note

Many Power Pivot users never overcome the many-to-many issue

You can design a data model that can effectively analyse data that originated in a database containing many-to-many relationships.

To do this you'll need to convert those relationships into the one-to-many relationships needed by a correctly designed data model.

With the skills you've already acquired you can already do a lot of useful data analysis using Get & Transform and Power Pivot.

In the lessons that follow you'll learn why commercial (transactional) databases need to be designed differently to Power Pivot data models.

With this understanding you'll learn how to overcome the many-to-many issue and will be able to design data models that work perfectly with Power Pivot.

How many-to-many relationships are modeled

In: *Lesson 10-26: Understand primary and foreign keys,* you learned that a one-to-many relationship uses a primary key on the "one" side of the relationship and a foreign key on the "many" side.

For a many-to-many relationship, a link table is required. This sits between the tables on either side of the many-to-many relationship like this:

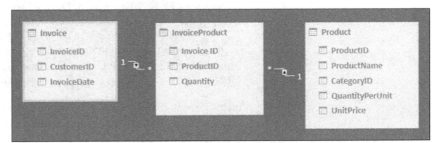

In the example above, the primary key of the link table (*InvoiceProduct*) is a concatenation of the primary keys found in the two related tables. Remember that you cannot use this type of relationship in a Power Pivot data model (though you will usually find them in commercial databases).

The Invoice table

This table contains information about the invoice as a whole.

Think of it as the invoice before any items have been added. In this simple example it only contains the *InvoiceDate* and the *InvoiceID.* You could also use this table to store information such as the ship-to address or due date. Notice that there is also a *CustomerID* foreign key. This identifies the customer to invoice in a separate *Customer* table (not shown in the schema above).

The Product table

This table contains information about each product. In this simple example it only contains *ProductName, QuantityPerUnit* and *UnitPrice* fields. Notice that there is also a *CategoryID* foreign key pointing to the category that the product belongs to (not shown in the above schema).

You could also use this table to store other information about the product such as the cost price or wholesale discount.

The InvoiceProduct table

This is the many-to-many link table. It is a good relational database naming convention to name link tables as a concatenation of the two tables on either side of the many-to-many relationship (in this case the *InvoiceProduct* table joins the *Invoice* and *Product* tables in a many-to-many relationship). The *InvoiceProduct* table has a row for each line item in the invoice.

Each row has a column that stores the number of units sold on each invoice line. The *ProductID* is a foreign key that identifies the row in the *Product* table that contains details of the product sold.

Lesson 11-11: Understand OLTP database design

OLTP databases

A database that is used by business to support day-to-day business transactions is called an OLTP (OnLine Transactional Processing) database.

OLTP relational databases are designed around the need to quickly perform four actions: *Create, Retrieve, Update* and *Delete*. The anagram CRUD is often used for these four requirements.

Imagine that your computer application manages employee records (stored in a database). If an employee's details change you would need to first *Retrieve* (find) the employee's record. You'd then have to *Update* the record with the new information.

If an employee left the company, you might want to *Delete* their record. If a new employee was then recruited, you'd need to *Create* a new employee record.

OLTP database schema example

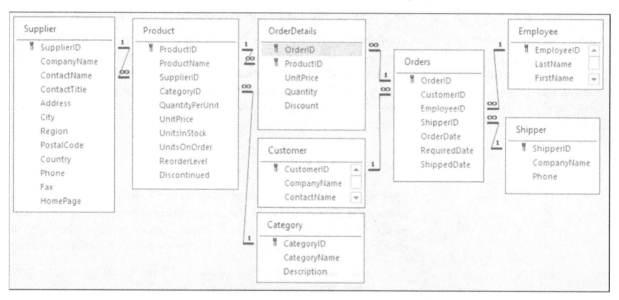

The above schema example comes from an OLTP database. You can see a many-to-many relationship between the *Orders* and *Product* tables (you learned about many-to-many relationships in: *Lesson 11-10: Understand many-to-many relationships*).

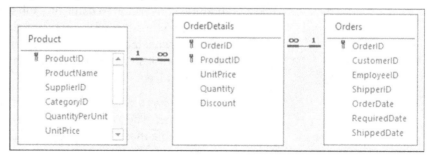

note

OLAP, MOLAP, HOLAP and ROLAP

You don't need to understand the difference between ROLAP, MOLAP and HOLAP to use Power Pivot. You may find this terminology used in articles about Power Pivot however, so I thought I'd give you an overview of what they mean.

Power Pivot uses a *tabular data model*. An SSAS (SQL Server Analysis Services) server supports three models: *tabular, multidimensional* and *hybrid*. The newer tabular model was introduced by Microsoft in 2012 (the multidimensional model is an older technology). Excel uses the newer tabular model (that can be simply exported to an SSAS server if required).

OLAP (*OnLine Analytical Processing*) is an acronym that is used to describe a database (data model) that is used to interactively analyze data from multiple perspectives. In the Excel implementation a tabular data model is analyzed using an OLAP pivot table.

To differentiate between the tabular and multidimensional models, the term ROLAP (Relational OLAP) and MOLAP (Multi-dimensional OLAP) can be used.

Another type of OLAP database is sometimes referred to as HOLAP (Hybrid OLAP). This refers to an OLAP database that combines ROLAP and MOLAP features.

So which OLAP model is best? IT professionals could spend hours arguing the answer, but Microsoft have stated:

"For new projects, we generally recommend tabular models".

In this book I use the more generic term: OLAP though it would also be correct to use the term ROLAP as Power Pivot uses the tabular model.

The *Orders* table contains values that relate to items you'd typically find in the header area of a paper order (such as *OrderDate*).

The *OrderDetails* table contains one row for each item ordered. These would be the values defined in the body area of a paper order (first order item, second order item, etc).

This schema describes a perfectly designed OLTP database, but it is not useful for an OLAP database (a Power Pivot data model is a type of OLAP database).

A Power Pivot data model is an OLAP database

The data model that you create in Power Pivot is a copy of data (from one or more data sources) at a given point in time. This is sometimes called a *Snapshot* of the data (as a photograph does not change after it has been taken).

The data model is a special type of database that has to be designed around the need to quickly analyze data. This type of database is called an *OLAP database* (OnLine Analytical Processing).

Terminology confusion

Current Excel documentation refers to an OLAP database hosted by Excel as a *Data Model*.

If the same model is created using Power Pivot, it is sometimes called a *Power Pivot Model*.

OLAP databases are also often referred to as an *OLAP data source*.

SSAS data models that use the Multidimensional Model (see sidebar) are often referred to as *OLAP Cubes*.

You'll also find the term *OLAP Cube* referred to extensively in OLAP-related discussions as multi-dimensional analysis concepts are often explained using the analogy of a three-dimensional cube (a little like a Rubik's cube) with aggregated values in each cell.

note

Fact and Dimension tables

A perfect OLAP data model contains one Fact table and several Dimension tables.

Fact table

The *Fact* table is the central table that (ideally) contains nothing but values and foreign keys (that are used to define relationships to the dimension tables).

The values in the fact table can be aggregated into the values displayed in the body of pivot tables.

The best-practice rule:

Only store numerical data and foreign keys in the fact table.

… is included in: *Appendix A: Power Pivot Rules.*

Dimension tables

Dimensions can be thought of as filters. They contain fields that will be used for the row, column, filter and slicer names in pivot tables.

Data models with many dimensions add more flexibility but increase the data model size.

There is always a trade-off between reporting flexibility and the data model size.

Lesson 11-12: Understand OLAP database design

OLAP databases and OLTP databases are designed differently

OLTP design criteria

In: *Lesson 11-11: Understand OLTP database design* you learned that an OLTP (On Line Transaction Processing) database is designed around the need to quickly perform four actions: *Create, Retrieve, Update* and *Delete.*

Well-designed OLTP databases must also conform to Third Normal Form (3NF) and are said to contain *Normalized Data.* A normalized database reduces the risk of data corruption during transactional processing. You learned a little about 3NF in: *Lesson 10-31: Understand normal and de-normalized data.* OLTP databases can contain one-to-many and many-to-many relationships. You learned about relationship types in: *Lesson 11-10: Understand many-to-many relationships.*

OLAP design criteria

The data model that you create in Power Pivot is an OLAP (On Line Analytical Processing) database. An OLAP database is read-only and has no need to *Create, Retrieve, Update* and *Delete* records. Instead it is designed around the need to quickly analyze data.

Data analysis is most easily performed using a special table and relationship arrangement called a *Star* or *Snowflake* schema that has a central *Fact* table surrounded by several *Dimension* tables.

OLAP databases used with Power Pivot cannot contain many-to-many relationships.

Because OLAP databases do not process transactions they have no need to conform to third normal form. For this reason several dimension tables are often de-normalized into a single dimension table.

Snowflake schema

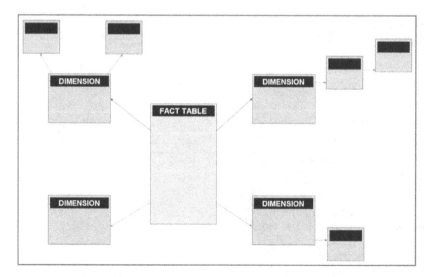

A Snowflake schema has a central *Fact* table surrounded by several *Dimension* tables.

Notice that some of the dimension tables have sub-dimensions giving the schema the appearance of a snowflake.

You can think of the dimension tables as filters that enable aggregations of the values in the fact table.

note

Other names for dimension and fact tables

Some users prefer the term *Lookup table* (for dimension tables) and *Data table* (for fact tables).

Star schema (the best choice for OLAP)

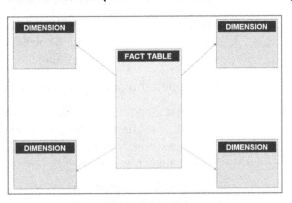

In the above diagram, you can see that a star schema has only one level of dimension tables, giving the schema the appearance of a star.

While Power Pivot will work with either a snowflake or star schema, Power Pivot works faster and better with a star schema. Star schemas are also easier for users to work with.

For these reasons the star schema is the recommended choice when working with Power Pivot.

The best-practice rule:

Use a star schema (rather than a snowflake schema) when constructing data models.

... is included in: *Appendix A: Power Pivot Rules.*

Creating a star schema from an OLTP database

To create an OLAP star schema database from an OLTP database it is first necessary to create a snowflake schema database by converting any many-to-many relationships into one-to-many relationships. You'll do this later, in: *Lesson 11-14: Create a snowflake data model from a relational database.*

The snowflake schema can then be converted into a star schema by de-normalizing any chains of dimension tables into single dimension tables. You'll do this later in: *Lesson 11-15: Convert a snowflake data model into a star data model.*

Lesson 11-13: Understand how to resolve many-to-many relationships

In: *Lesson 11-11: Understand OLTP database design,* you discovered that relational databases use a different type of schema to Power Pivot data models (also called OLAP databases).

When importing data from an OLTP database into a data model (OLAP database) the first problem to consider is the existence of many-to-many relationships in the source data.

1   Open the source OLTP database using Microsoft Access.

Not all editions of Office 365 include Microsoft Access (a tool that allows databases to be designed and used). Microsoft Access is often referred to as a desktop RDBMS (relational database management system).

If your edition of Office 365 includes Microsoft Access, open the *Orders* Access database from your sample files folder using Microsoft Access and then click:

Database Tools→Relationships→Relationships

The following schema will then be displayed:

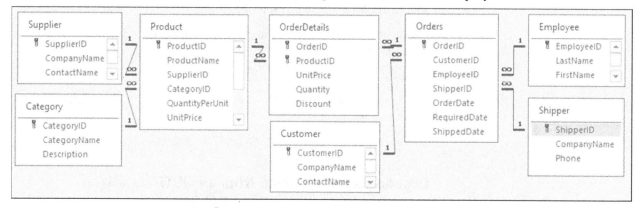

2   Identify any many-to-many relationships.

Microsoft Access makes it very easy for you to identify many-to-many relationships because it graphically represents primary keys with a small key symbol. .

You can see that all of the tables (except one) have a single primary key. The *OrderDetails* many-to-many link table has a compound primary key made from a concatenation of the OrderID and ProductID.

You can read this as:

- One *Product* may be related to many *Orders*
- One *Order* can be related to many *Products.*

Orders

3 **Understand how the many-to-many issue can be solved.**

In: *Lesson 11-12: Understand OLAP database design,* you learned that an OLAP database cannot contain a many-to-many relationship.

In: *Lesson 10-31: Understand normal and de-normalized data,* you learned that two tables can be merged together. The resulting table contains de-normalized data.

De-normalized data cannot be used in an OLTP database as it would break third normal form rules. (You learned a little about third normal form in: *Lesson 10-31: Understand normal and de-normalized data* - sidebar). It is, however, perfectly correct to include de-normalized data within an OLAP database.

In: *Lesson 10-32: Create a simple two-table merged query,* you learned how to use Get & Transform to merge two tables together.

If the *Orders* table and *OrderDetails* table are merged the database will consist only of one-to-many relationships. The model would then look like this:

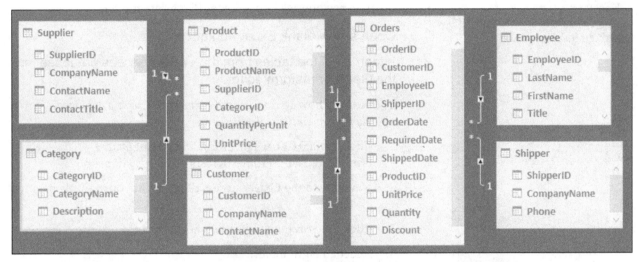

In: *Lesson 11-12: Understand OLAP database design,* you learned that correctly designed OLAP databases need to have a *Snowflake* or *Star* schema arrangement.

You may recognize that the above is a Snowflake schema. The Orders table is the *Fact* table and all other tables are *Dimension* tables.

In the next lesson: *Lesson 11-14: Create a snowflake data model from a relational database,* you'll create the OLAP database shown above.

4 **Close Microsoft Access (if it is open).**

important

In this lesson you never leave the "Power" environment

The Power tools (Power Pivot and Get & Transform) can work with Big Data containing billions of rows.

Excel can only deal with data that contains approximately a million rows. In this lesson you have never entered the Excel environment so do not have this restriction.

Data was imported and transformed using Get & Transform and then loaded directly into the data model without involving Excel.

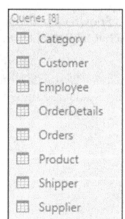

Orders

Lesson 11-14: Create a snowflake data model from a relational database

In: *Lesson 11-13: Understand how to resolve many-to-many relationships,* you developed a strategy to convert a many-to-many relationship into a one-to-many relationship by merging two tables together.

In this lesson you'll create a snowflake schema OLAP database (Power Pivot data model) from an OLTP database.

To do this you'll need to perform three operations:

- Create Get & Transform queries for each of the tables in the Orders database.

- Merge the *OrderDetails* query into the *Orders* query.

- Load all of the queries into a Power Pivot data model.

1   Open a new blank Excel workbook.

2   Import all of the tables from the *Orders* Access database into the Get & Transform editor.

> You learned how to do this in: *Lesson 11-9: Create a data model directly from a relational database.*

> 1. Click: Data→Get & Transform Data→Get Data→ From Database→From Microsoft Access Database.

> 2. Navigate to the *Orders* Access database in your sample files folder.

> 3. Click the *Select multiple items* checkbox.

> 4. Select all eight tables.

> 5. Click the *Transform Data* button

> The *Power Query Editor* window opens.

> You can see eight queries listed in the left-hand *Navigator Pane,* one for each table in the Orders database.

3   Merge the *ProductID, UnitPrice, Quantity* and *Discount* fields from the *OrderDetails* query into the *Order* query.

> You learned how to do this in: *Lesson 10-32: Create a simple two-table merged query.*

> 1. Select the *Orders* query in the left-hand *Navigator Pane.*

> 2. Click the expand button on the right of the *OrderDetails* column header.

> A dialog appears.

> 3. Make sure that the *Expand* option button is selected.

> 4. Select the *ProductID, UnitPrice, Quantity* and *Discount* fields.

5. De-select the *Use original column name as prefix* check box.

    Your dialog should now look like the one shown in the sidebar.

6. Click the OK button.

    You have now created a single de-normalized *Orders* table that includes data that was previously in the *Orders* and *OrderDetails* tables.

4   Delete the *OrderDetails* query from the query list.

1. Right-click on the *OrderDetails* query in the left-hand *Navigator Pane.*

2. Click *Delete* from the short cut menu.

5   Create Connection Only queries that will Load the output of all queries to the data model.

You learned how to do this in: *Lesson 11-3: Add tables to a data model.*

1. Click Close & Load→Close & Load To…

2. Select the *Only Create Connection* option button.

3. Check the *Add this data to the Data Model checkbox*.

4. Click the OK button.

    You will see the queries executing in the right-hand *Queries & Connections* task pane. It may take some time to import and transform all of the data in the database.

6   Open the Power Pivot window in *Diagram* view.

The model shows that you have created a snowflake schema from the OLTP relational database.

Notice how Get & Transform has automatically created the relationships for you to match those defined withing the source database.

You may wish to move the tables around in diagram view to match the arrangement shown below.

7   Close the Power Pivot window.

8   Save your work as *Orders-1*

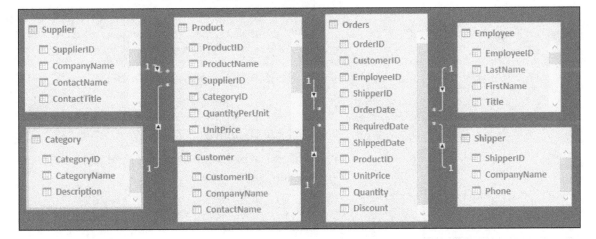

Lesson 11-15: Convert a snowflake data model into a star data model

1   Open *Orders-1* from your sample files folder.

2   Open the Power Pivot window in *Diagram View.*

You can see that the schema only deviates from being a star schema because of the *Product* table that has two sub-dimensions (the *Supplier* and *Category* tables).

3   Merge the Category table and Supplier table into the Product table using Get & Transform.

1.   Close the Power Pivot window.

2.   Click: Data→Get & Transform Data→Get Data→ Launch Power Query Editor.

3.   Select the *Product* query from the left-hand *Queries* bar.

4.   Scroll to the right until you see the *Category* and *Supplier* tables.

5.   Click the expand button on the right of the *Category* column header.

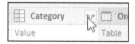

A dialog appears.

6.   Select the *CategoryName* and *Description* fields.

7.   Make sure that the *Use original column name as prefix* check box is checked.

Your dialog should now look like this:

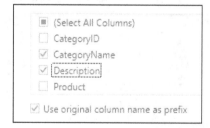

8.   Click the OK button.

9.   Click the expand button on the right of the *Supplier* column header.

Orders-1

A dialog appears.

10. Select all fields except the *SupplierID* and *Product*.

11. Make sure that the *Use original column name as prefix* check box is checked.

Your dialog should now look like the one shown in the sidebar.

12. Click the OK button.

4 Delete the *Category* and *Supplier* queries from the left-hand *Queries* bar.

1. Right-click on the *Category* query.

2. Select *Delete* from the shortcut menu.

3. Delete the *Supplier* query in the same way.

5 Close the Power Query editor and load the query results back into the data model.

Click: Home→Close→Close & Load→Close & Load.

6 Open the Power Pivot window in *Diagram View*

7 Refresh the data model.

Click: Home→Refresh→Refresh All.

You should now see a perfect star schema:

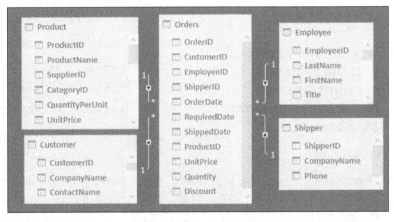

If you re-size the *Product* table, you will find that it now contains all of the information that was previously contained in the *Category* and *Supplier* tables (see sidebar).

While the data model could be used in its present form there are many fields that are of no interest to users (for example, most of the primary and foreign key fields).

You can also see that some of the field names do not conform to the naming conventions defined in: *Appendix A: Power Pivot Rules.*

Both of these issues will be dealt with in the next lesson.

8 Close the Power Pivot window.

9 Save your work as *Orders-2.*

Lesson 11-16: Hide, remove and rename data model columns

You have now created a good basic star schema from a relational database. In this lesson you'll refine the data model to make it more compact and easier to use.

1   Open *Orders-2* from your sample files folder.

2   Remove any columns from the data model that are not needed by your users.

Don't be tempted to bloat your data model by including columns just in case you might need them later. You know how easy it is to add and delete columns using Get & Transform should future requirements change.

When removing redundant columns, the most important table to consider is the fact table (the *Orders* table in this case). You need to particularly focus upon columns that contain unique values (such as dates) as power pivot will be unable to compress them (see: *Appendix A: Power Pivot Rules* for more information about making your tables file-compression friendly).

The sidebar shows the results of user feedback for this data model. Remove the columns that users have indicated are not required.

1.   Close the power pivot window if it is open.

2.   Click: Data→Get & Transform Data→Get Data→ Launch Power Query Editor…

3.   Select the *Orders* query from the left-hand *Queries* sidebar.

4.   Right-click on the *Required Date* column header.

5.   Select *Remove* from the shortcut menu.

6.   Do the same for the other fields in the *Orders* and *Product* tables that are listed in the sidebar.

3   Hide all primary and foreign key columns from your users.

Some columns are needed in the data model but are of no interest to users. For example, primary and foreign key columns are required to maintain relationships but of no interest for reporting purposes. These columns need to be hidden from end users.

1.   Click: Home→Close→Close & Load, to close the Get & Transform query editor and save your changes to the data model.

It may take some time for your updates to be applied.

2.   Open the Power Pivot window in data view.

3.   Click the *Customer* tab at the bottom of the Power Pivot window to view the contents of the Customer table.

4.   Right-click on the *CustomerID* column header.

---

important

Users have identified that the following columns are not required for reporting purposes

Orders Table

Required Date
Shipped Date

Product Table

Category.Description
QuantityPerUnit
Supplier.HomePage

Orders-2

---

important

Why not delete the OrdersID column?

It is normally best practice to remove the primary key from the fact table (in this model the Orders table is the fact table).

Normally the primary key is meaningless and is only used to create relationships between tables.

In this exceptional case the designer of the source database has broken normal design rules and used the *Order Number* as the primary key of the *Orders* table.

For this reason, the primary key column needs to be retained but renamed to a more descriptive name (*Order Number*).

5. Select *Hide from Client Tools* from the shortcut menu.

   Notice that the column is grayed out when hidden.

6. Do the same for all primary and foreign key columns in the model except the *OrderID* in the *Orders* table (see sidebar). The primary and foreign keys can be identified as they all have a suffix of *ID*.

4 **Correct all column names so that they adhere to the naming convention defined in:** *Appendix A: Power Pivot Rules.*

   1. Close the power pivot window if it is open.

   2. Click: Data→Get & Transform Data→Get Data→ Launch Power Query Editor…

   3. For each query, where required, rename field names, or add spaces to existing field names to conform with the naming conventions defined in: *Appendix A: Power Pivot Rules.*

5 **View the schema in Power Pivot.**

   1. Close Get & Transform and save your changes.

      Click: Home→Close→Close & Load.

      It may take some time for your changes to update.

   2. Open the Power Pivot window in diagram view.

      Your schema should now look like this:

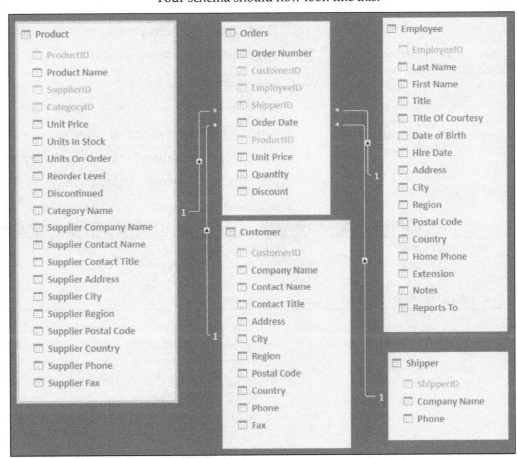

6 **Close the Power Pivot window and save your work as** *Orders-3.*

note

It is possible to update the range of dates in a Calendar table manually

In this lesson Power Pivot added a self-updating calendar table. Power Pivot established a date range for the calendar by looking at every table in the data model that contained dates.

The *Employee* table contained an employee with a date of birth in 1952 so Power Pivot used this as a starting date.

You could make the Calendar table more compact in two ways:

1. Remove the *BirthDate* column from the *Employee* table (by editing the Get & Transform query) and refresh the data model.

The query would then update the data model, causing Power Pivot to scan the tables once again (but this time the earliest date found would be in 2017).

2. Manually adjust the start date of the calendar table. This can be done by selecting the date table tab and then clicking:

Design→Calendars→Date Table→Update Range.

Lesson 11-17: Add a calendar table to a data model

Most fact tables (in this model the fact table can be identified by its plural name: *Orders*) will contain transactional data that includes a date field.

Many reporting requirements will include the need to aggregate values by time dimensions (such as week, month, quarter and year).

While it would be possible to add calculated columns to the fact table, or to create these aggregations inside a pivot table, best OLAP practice is to add a *Calendar* dimension table to the data model.

The best-practice rule: *Use a calendar table for date dimensions* is included in: *Appendix A: Power Pivot Rules.*

You'll only fully appreciate the advantages of using a calendar table later, in: *Lesson 12-4: Understand Implicit and Explicit measures.*

Power Pivot automates the process of creating a calendar table

In earlier versions of Power Pivot you had to do a lot of work to add a calendar table to a data model. Fortunately, Power Pivot has recently added a feature that enables you to add a self-updating calendar table with a single click.

1   Open *Orders-3* from your sample files folder.

2   Open the Power Pivot window.

3   Create a calendar table.

Click: Design→Calendars→Date Table→New

A new table is created named *Calendar*.

4   Inspect the contents of the new Calendar table.

1.   Click: Home→View→Data View.

2.   Select the *Calendar* tab.

Date	Year	Month Number	Month	MMM-YYYY	Day Of Week Number	Day Of Week
1/1/1952 12:00:00 AM	1952	1	January	Jan-1952	3	Tuesday
1/2/1952 12:00:00 AM	1952	1	January	Jan-1952	4	Wednesday
1/3/1952 12:00:00 AM	1952	1	January	Jan-1952	5	Thursday
1/4/1952 12:00:00 AM	1952	1	January	Jan-1952	6	Friday

Notice that the calendar contains several columns. Each column except the primary key column (the primary key is the *Date* column) contains a formula rather than a value. This keeps the table very compact as Power Pivot is easily able to compress the table.

Notice that the table contains sequential rows of dates that include a date for every date value found in any column, and in any table of your data model. This is an outstanding feature as it means that you don't have to update the calendar table

Orders-3

note

What is a hierarchy?

When you create a calendar table (as you do in this lesson), Power Pivot creates a hierarchy for you.

This appears in an OLAP pivot table like this:

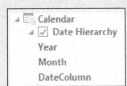

When you add the hierarchy field to a pivot table you can add the above three fields to a row or column with one click (instead of three).

You may think that the hierarchy is more confusing for users of the pivot table than it is worth. If you feel this way it is easily removed like this:

1. Open the data model in Diagram View.

2. Right-click on the *Date Hierarchy* column.

3. Click: *Delete* from the shortcut menu.

Creating a hierarchy is also very easy:

1. Open the data model in Diagram View.

2. Select the *Date, Year* and *Month* columns.

3. Right-click one of the selected fields and select: *Create Hierarchy* from the shortcut menu.

4. Right-click the hierarchy and select: *Rename* from the shortcut menu to give the hierarchy a meaningful name.

5. Click and drag the fields within the hierarchy to put them in the right order (*Year, Month, Date*).

when the model is refreshed (and new date rows may be needed).

The calendar begins in 1952 as this is the date of birth of the Vice President of Sales: Dr. Andres Fuller. It would be possible to adjust the date range manually to make the table more compact (see facing page sidebar).

You can add, delete or change any of the columns in the new Calendar table. There's also a *Set Default* option (Design→Calendars→Date Table→Set Default), to restore the table to its original form (if you have altered the columns and want to start again).

5 **Define a relationship between the *Calendar* table and the *Orders* table.**

1. The Calendar table's *Date* column is the Calendar table's primary key. You will need to relate this to the *Order Date* column in the fact (Orders) table.

2. Change the view to *Diagram* view.

   Click: Home→View→Diagram View.

3. Drag the *Order Date* field from the *Orders* table and place it on top of the *Date* field in the *Calendar table.*

6 **Hide the Order Date field from users.**

Having two different date fields visible in pivot tables may be confusing for users.

1. Right-click on the *Order Date* field in the *Orders* table.

2. Select: *Hide from Client Tools* from the shortcut menu.

7 **View the schema.**

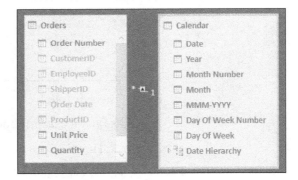

The calendar table's fields will now appear in the PivotTable fields list enabling values to be aggregated by many different time periods. Notice that Power Pivot has also created a *Date Hierarchy* for you (see sidebar).

The fields that are grayed out will not appear in the PivotTable

If a new time aggregation (such as quarter) was required, it would be a simple matter to add a new calculated column to the calendar table. You'll learn how to add calculated columns later, in: *Lesson 12-2: Add a DAX calculated column.*

8 **Close the Power Pivot window and save your work as *Orders-4.***

Lesson 11-18: Format values in a data model

If you format values inside the data model, you'll never have to re-format when you use a column within a pivot table. This makes the data model easier to use by untrained users (who may not even know how to format a value in a pivot table).

Remember that the data model may be used by many pivot tables. By formatting once in the data model, you avoid formatting many times each time you add the value to a pivot table.

1   Open *Orders-4* from your sample files folder.

2   Open the Power Pivot window.

3   View the data model in Data View.

     Click: Home→View→Data View.

4   Review the formatting of all values in the fact table.

     The fact table in this model is the *Orders* table. You learned about fact and dimension tables in: *Lesson 11-12: Understand OLAP database design.*

     If you have followed our naming convention detailed in: *Appendix A: Power Pivot Rules,* it is obvious that this must be the fact table as it is the only table named in the plural.

     The fact table usually contains all of the numeric fields in a data model.

     You can see that there are four value columns visible to users and that none of them have yet been correctly formatted:

     Format them as follows:

     1.   Click on the *Quantity* column header.

     2.   Click: Home→Formatting→Format.

     3.   Select: *Whole Number* from the drop-down list.

     4.   Format the other fields as follows:

         Discount: Percentage.

         Unit Price: Currency.

         Order Number: Whole number.

     The columns now display correctly in Power Pivot and, more importantly, will display correctly when used within a pivot table:

Orders-4

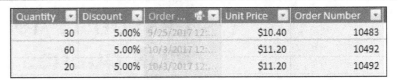

Quantity	Discount	Order ...	Unit Price	Order Number
30	5.00%	9/25/2017 12:...	$10.40	10483
60	5.00%	10/3/2017 12:...	$11.20	10492
20	5.00%	10/3/2017 12:...	$11.20	10492

5   Review the formatting of all values in the *Product* table.

The Product table is the only other table in this model that contains values.

You can see that there are four value columns and that none of them have yet been correctly formatted:

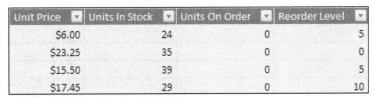

Unit Price	Units In Stock	Units On Order	Reorder Level
6	24	0	5
23.25	35	0	0
15.5	39	0	5
17.45	29	0	10

Format them as follows:

- **Unit Price:**   Currency.

- **Units In Stock:**   Whole Number.

- **Units On Order:**   Whole Number.

- **Reorder Level:**   Whole number.

The columns now display correctly:

Unit Price	Units In Stock	Units On Order	Reorder Level
$6.00	24	0	5
$23.25	35	0	0
$15.50	39	0	5
$17.45	29	0	10

6   Close the Power Pivot window.

7   Save your work as *Orders-5*.

Lesson 11-19: Understand MDX queries and OLAP pivot table limitations

How an OLAP pivot table obtains its data using MDX

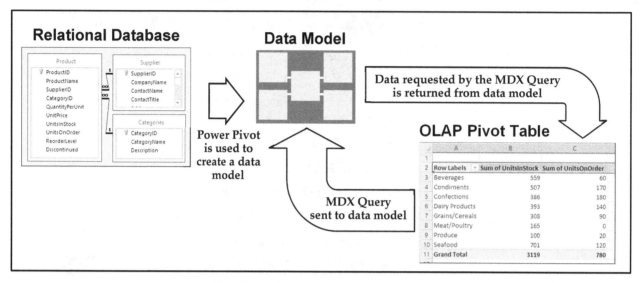

The above diagram shows a data model that has been created from a relational database using Get & Transform and Power Pivot.

When the OLAP pivot table needs to get information from the data model, it requests the information using an MDX query.

The OLAP pivot table creates the MDX query and submits it to the data model. This is done individually with a new MDX query for every value displayed in the pivot table. Each requested value is then returned to the pivot table.

In: *Lesson 11-21: Convert CUBEVALUE functions to include MDX expressions,* you'll get a glimpse of some MDX code that has been created by an OLAP pivot table.

What is MDX?

MDX (Multi-Dimensional eXpressions) is the standard query language used to request data that resides in an OLAP database (a data model is an OLAP database).

History of MDX

MDX was invented by Microsoft and was used as the query language for Microsoft's first OLAP product in 1998.

Even though MDX is owned by Microsoft, it has become the standard OLAP query language and has been adopted by a wide range of OLAP

info

Increasing the default drill-down items in an OLAP pivot table

By default, data models only include 1,000 rows from the source data that was used to aggregate totals.

This is a sensible restriction as it reduces the size of the data model.

If there is a special need to drill-down to more than the default 1,000 rows of source data, you can increase this limit in the connection properties.

1. Click:

Data→
Queries & Connections→
Queries & Connections

The *Queries & Connections* task pane appears.

2. Select *Connections* at the top of the *Queries and Connections* task pane.

3. Right-click on the *ThisWorkbookDataModel* connection.

4. Select *Properties* from the shortcut menu.

5. Click on the *Usage* tab.

You are now able to select a maximum number of rows to store (for drill-through purposes) within the data model:

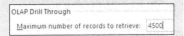

Note that (because drill-through items are shown on an Excel worksheet) this is restricted to a maximum of 1,048,576 items.

vendors including Oracle Corporation, SAP, Cognos and Business Objects.

You don't need to learn MDX to use OLAP pivot tables

Hand-crafting an MDX query is not an Excel skill. You don't have to know anything about the MDX query language to work with Excel's data model and OLAP pivot tables.

Some dedicated MDX books stretch to over 700 pages so, of course, this book will not attempt to teach you how to hand-craft an MDX query.

OLAP pivot table limitations

Because OLAP pivot tables can only retrieve data from an OLAP database (the data model is an OLAP database) using MDX, there are some features found in regular pivot tables that are not used in OLAP pivot tables

Here are some regular pivot table features that are not supported in OLAP pivot tables:

Show Report Filter Pages is not supported: The *Show Report Filter Pages* feature discussed in: *Lesson 8-10: Use report filter fields to automatically create multiple pages* cannot be used with OLAP pivot tables.

Drill-down is restricted (by default) to 1,000 items: In regular pivot tables you can double-click any pivot table aggregated value to "drill down" to the data source items that were used to calculate the value. When you drill down, Excel creates a new worksheet that contains every row of source data used for the aggregation (without restricting the number of rows available).

OLAP pivot tables (that are often used to analyze big data containing millions, or even billions of rows) could potentially be enormous if unlimited drill-down data was included. For this reason, drill down is limited (by default) to 1,000 rows. It is possible to manually increase this limit (see sidebar).

Calculated Fields and Calculated Items are not needed: You learned how to use these features in regular pivot tables in: *Lesson 8-16: Add a calculated field to a pivot table* and *Lesson 8-17: Add a calculated item to a pivot table*.

These features are not needed in OLAP pivot tables because any calculated fields that may be required should already exist in the data model (removing the need for the Pivot Table to calculate them).

You already know how to add calculated columns using Get & Transform so that calculated columns are added before data is exported to the data model. This is best practice.

Later, after you have completed: *Session Twelve: An introduction to DAX*, you'll discover that DAX also enables the addition of *calculated columns* to the data model. While you can do this, it is better practice to add calculated columns using Get & Transform (for the reasons explained in: *Appendix A: Power Pivot Rules*).

note

Why does the CUBEVALUE function have the prefix CUBE?

It is common to teach and visualize OLAP concepts in the context of an imaginary three-dimensional *OLAP Cube*.

The imaginary cube is a little like a Rubik's cube but contains a set of aggregated values in each cell.

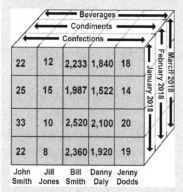

OLAP concepts are taught in the context of *Slicing, Dicing* and *Rotating* (Pivoting) the cube of data.

MDX queries (created by the CUBE functions) retrieve aggregated totals from specified cells (intersections of three values) from a cube of data.

Lesson 11-20: Use the CUBEVALUE function to query a data model

In: *Lesson 8-23: Use the GETPIVOTDATA function,* you discovered a way to reference data that is visible on the screen within a pivot table.

If you've completely understood this session so far, you'll now realize that an OLAP pivot table is simply a visual and user-friendly way to display, format and present the values stored in a data model.

The CUBEVALUE function enables you to obtain values directly from the data model without a pivot table. This opens up many new possibilities when presenting and formatting data.

1 Open *Stock List-4* from your sample files folder (if it isn't already open).

This workbook contains the pivot table that you created from a data model in: *Lesson 11-6: Use an OLAP pivot table to analyze data residing in a data model.*

	B	C
3	Row Labels	Sum of UnitsInStock
4	Beverages	559
5	Condiments	507
6	Confections	386
7	Dairy Products	393
8	Grains/Cereals	308
9	Meat/Poultry	165
10	Produce	100
11	Seafood	701
12	**Grand Total**	**3119**

2 Attempt to insert a column or row within the pivot table.

Notice that (as with all pivot tables) this isn't possible.

When you attempt to insert a row or column, a warning dialog is shown:

Microsoft Excel
⚠ We can't make this change for the selected cells because it will affect a PivotTable. Use the field list to change the report. If you are trying to insert or delete cells, move the PivotTable and try again.
OK

3 Convert the pivot table into a set of CUBEVALUE functions.

1. Click inside the pivot table to activate it.

2. Click:

PivotTable Tools→Analyze→Calculations→ OLAP Tools→Convert to Formulas

(This option is grayed out when working with regular pivot tables).

Notice that the OLAP pivot table no longer exists but the data previously displayed remains:

Stock List-4

note

The GETPIVOTDATA function is also supported by OLAP pivot tables

In: *Lesson 8-23: Use the GETPIVOTDATA function,* you learned how to use the GETPIVOTDATA function to access values in a regular pivot table from outside the pivot table.

The GETPIVOTDATA function can only be used to reference values *that are visible in a pivot table*.

This can be a huge problem, as a user may change the fields displayed in a pivot table, causing functions that use the GETPIVOTDATA function to fail.

If there were a function that directly accessed data from the *pivot table data cache* (that regular pivot tables use instead of the data model) this problem would be overcome.

Unfortunately, there is no way to do this in a regular pivot table.

The CUBEVALUE function has none of these problems as data is accessed directly from the data model without any interaction with a pivot table.

OLAP pivot tables still support the GETPIVOTDATA function but you'll probably prefer to use CUBEVALUE functions in their place when working with data that originates in a data model.

	B	C
3	Row Labels	Sum of UnitsInStock
4	Beverages	559
5	Condiments	507
6	Confections	386
7	Dairy Products	393
8	Grains/Cereals	308
9	Meat/Poultry	165
10	Produce	100
11	Seafood	701
12	Grand Total	3119

Each value is now directly accessed from the data model using CUBEVALUE functions.

4   Examine the CUBEVALUE function for the *Sum of UnitsInStock* column in the *Beverages* category.

1.   Click once in cell C4.

2.   Look at the function displayed in the formula bar:

```
=CUBEVALUE("ThisWorkbookDataModel",$B4,C$3)
```

The first argument identifies the name of the connection to the data model. In this case it is the data model that you defined in: *Lesson 11-3: Add tables to a data model* and *Lesson 11-5: Add a relationship to a data model using Power Pivot.*

The last two arguments are MDX expressions. You learned about the MDX query language in: *Lesson 11-19: Understand MDX queries and OLAP pivot table limitations.*

3.   Click on cell B4 and C3 to see how the MDX expressions have been created. With your understanding of data models, you should be able to broadly understand how the references work.

You have used an OLAP pivot table to automatically create the MDX code for you. This technique allows you to create CUBEVALUE functions without any understanding of the MDX language.

5   Insert a column before column C and a row before row 5.

	B	C	D
1			
2			
3	Row Labels		Sum of UnitsInStock
4	Beverages		559
5			
6	Condiments		507
7	Confections		386

There is now no barrier to inserting rows and columns, as each cell contains a normal function.

You can also format the values in any way you wish.

6   Save your work as *Stock List-5.*

note

The many ways to refresh data

There are many places within Excel and Power Pivot where you can refresh data.

The *Home* tab in the Power Pivot window

There are two options here:

1. Refresh: Only refresh the data shown in the currently selected table (when in Data View).

2. Refresh All: Refresh the entire data model.

When working with a Pivot Table

When working with a Pivot Table you can click:

PivotTable Tools→Analyze→Data→Refresh

You are then presented with the same two *Refresh* and *Refresh All* options discussed above.

Automatic refreshing

In: *Lesson 10-3: Understand queries and connections,* you learned how to configure a connection to automatically refresh at a specified time interval.

When a file is opened

By default data is not refreshed every time a file is opened. You are able to change this (so that data is refreshed upon opening a file) using the *Query Properties* dialog discussed in the facing page sidebar.

Stock List-5

Lesson 11-21: Convert CUBEVALUE functions to include MDX expressions

At the moment the CUBEVALUE functions (created in: *Lesson 11-20: Use the CUBEVALUE function to query a data model*) are not very transportable.

The CUBEVALUE functions reference MDX code contained in other cells. This creates two potential problems:

1. If you copy and paste a function to a different worksheet, the references to the MDX expressions may be adjusted to point to incorrect cells.

2. If the cells containing the MDX functions are deleted, the functions will fail.

The functions will be far more robust if they contain the actual MDX expressions rather than references to cells containing the MDX expressions.

1 Open *Stock List-5* from your sample files folder (if it isn't already open).

This workbook contains the CUBEVALUE functions that you created automatically from an OLAP pivot table in: *Lesson 11-20: Use the CUBEVALUE function to query a data model.*

	B	C	D
3	Row Labels		Sum of UnitsInStock
4	Beverages		559
5			
6	Condiments		507
7	Confections		386
8	Dairy Products		393
9	Grains/Cereals		308
10	Meat/Poultry		165
11	Produce		100
12	Seafood		701
13	Grand Total		3119

2 Convert the formula in cell D4 so that it contains no cell references.

1. Click in cell D4.

2. Look at the formula in the formula bar:

`=CUBEVALUE("ThisWorkbookDataModel",$B4,D$3)`

You can see that MDX expressions in cells B4 and D3 are being referenced.

3. Click in cell B4.

Look at the formula in the formula bar.

You can see that this cell is using the CUBEMEMBER function to access the data model:

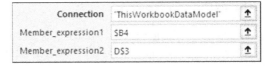

4. Select and copy all of the contents of the formula bar after the = sign.

5. Press the **<Escape>** key.

6. Click in cell D4.

7. Click the *Insert Function* button on the left of the formula bar.

   The *Function Arguments* dialog is displayed.

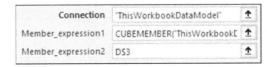

8. Click in the *Member_expression1* text box and delete the current contents.

9. Paste the CUBEMEMBER function into the text box.

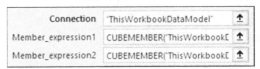

10. Press the **<Enter>** key.

11. Use a similar technique to copy the formula behind cell D3 into the *Member_expression2* box.

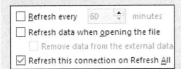

12. Click the *OK* button.

    The formula in cell D4 now directly references the data model without any references to other cells in the workbook.

3 Copy the formula in cell D4 to any other cell on any other worksheet in the workbook.

   You can see that you can now show the *Sum of UnitsInStock* for the *Beverages* category absolutely anywhere in the workbook.

   The value will update if any referenced value in a table within the data model changes.

4 On the *Product* worksheet, change the *UnitsInStock* value for any product in the *Beverages* category.

5 Refresh the data model.

   Click: Data→Queries & Connections→Refresh All.

   Notice that both cells showing *Sum of UnitsInStock* for the *Beverages* category have now updated.

6 Save your work as *Stock List-6*.

important

Why you may want to disable *Refresh All*

The facing page sidebar discusses the many ways that Excel and Power Pivot can refresh data.

You've probably already become a little impatient when refreshing the data model (even with the small database you've been working with in these lessons).

Imagine working with a billion-row data source and accidentally clicking one of the *Refresh All* buttons. You might have to wait a long time before you could resume work.

To avoid this problem you can use the *Query Properties* dialog to disable refreshing from the data source when the *Refresh All* button is clicked.

1. Open Excel.

2. Click:

Data→
Get & Transform Data→
Existing Connections.

The *Existing Connections* dialog appears.

3. Right-click the query (or connection) that you want to configure.

4. Select: *Edit Connection Properties…* from the shortcut menu.

The *Query Properties* (or *Connection Properties*) dialog opens.

Notice that there are two options available:

You can use these options to control when data is refreshed.

note

You could achieve a similar result by using CUBEVALUE functions

In: *Lesson 11-20: Use the CUBEVALUE function to query a data model,* you discovered how to obtain values directly from a data model. It would be easy to reproduce the solution described in this lesson using this technique. To do this you would proceed as follows:

1. Open *Americas and Europe-1* from your sample files folder.

2. Enable external data connections if necessary.

3. Click inside the pivot table to activate it.

4. Click:

PivotTable Tools→
Analyze→Calculations→
OLAP Tools→
Convert to Formulas

5. Delete rows 6, 9, 11, 13, 15, 16 and 17.

6. Delete the values in cells B4 and B9.

The worksheet would then look like this:

	A	B
3	Row Labels	Sum of InvoicePrice
4	2011	
5	Austria	70600.68
6	France	35654.88
7	Germany	109595.61
8	USA	130834.27
9	2012	
10	Brazil	41941
11	USA	114845.12
12	Venezuela	26404.77

To refresh the values displayed by the CUBEVALUE functions, click:

Data→Queries & Connections→
Refresh All

Americas and Europe-1

Lesson 11-22: Create an asymmetric OLAP pivot table using Named Sets

OLAP pivot tables have an interesting feature that is not available in regular pivot tables: the ability to create *Named Sets*. Named Sets are a little like filters in that they allow you to hide specific rows or columns from your pivot table. You can also implement named sets using CUBEVALUE functions (see sidebar) and many users may find this easier than using the Named Sets feature demonstrated in this lesson.

The sample file for this lesson contains a data model consisting of an *Invoice* table with over 1,400 rows and a related *Category* table.

The invoice table lists sales to all customers in 2011 and 2012. It is easy to generate a pivot table showing annual sales for each year by country like this:

	A	B
3	Row Labels	Sum of InvoicePrice
4	2011	475,836.30
5	Austria	70,600.68
6	Brazil	66,848.42
7	France	35,654.88
8	Germany	109,595.61
9	UK	31,897.11
10	USA	130,834.27
11	Venezuela	30,405.33
12	2012	430,332.72
13	Austria	57,402.38
14	Brazil	41,941.00
15	France	45,263.40
16	Germany	117,402.02
17	UK	27,074.03
18	USA	114,845.12
19	Venezuela	26,404.77

But imagine that management have requested a different report. They want to see sales to Europe (Austria, France, Germany and the UK) for 2011 followed by sales to the Americas (Brazil, USA and Venezuela) for 2012.

Here's the report they want:

	A	B
3	Row Labels	Sum of InvoicePrice
4	2011	
5	Austria	70,600.68
6	France	35,654.88
7	Germany	109,595.61
8	UK	31,897.11
9	2012	
10	Brazil	41,941.00
11	USA	114,845.12
12	Venezuela	26,404.77

You couldn't do this with a regular pivot table as regular pivot tables are always *symmetric*.

note

Named sets and MDX

As you know from: *Lesson 11-19: Understand MDX queries and OLAP pivot table limitations,* OLAP pivot tables use MDX to retrieve data from the data model.

Microsoft have designed their *named sets* feature to enable users to create and use named sets without needing to know anything about the MDX language.

Users who understand the MDX query language are able to create hand-crafted custom MDX code.

Click the *Edit MDX…* button on the *New Set* dialog to view (and even edit) the MDX code that the dialog has automatically generated.

With an in-depth understanding of MDX it is possible to implement more advanced requirements (such as adding subtotals by named set).

See also facing page sidebar for a more versatile solution using CUBEVALUE functions.

	A	B
3	Row Labels	Sum of InvoicePrice
4	2011	
5	Austria	70,600.68
6	France	35,654.88
7	Germany	109,595.61
8	UK	31,897.11
9	2012	
10	Brazil	41,941.00
11	USA	114,845.12
12	Venezuela	26,404.77

If you showed European sales for 2011 you'd also have to display European sales for 2012. The OLAP pivot table in the above screen grab is *asymmetric.* It displays just what you specify using *Named Sets.*

1 Open *Americas and Europe-1* from your sample files folder.

2 Enable external data connections if necessary.

You may see a security warning advising that external data connections have been disabled:

> ⚠ SECURITY WARNING External Data Connections have been disabled   Enable Content

Excel regards all OLAP data sources as external databases.

Click the *Enable Content* button to allow the OLAP pivot table in this worksheet to access the data.

This workbook contains two tables: An *Invoice* table and a related *Category* table. A data model has been created from these related tables and then used to create an OLAP pivot table summarizing sales by year and by country.

3 Create a named set to show sales for Europe in 2011 and for the Americas in 2012.

1. Click anywhere within the pivot table (in the *Pivot Table* worksheet).

2. Click: PivotTable Tools→Analyze→Calculations→ Fields, Items & Sets→Create Set Based on Row Items…

   The *New Set* dialog appears.

   You can see all countries that have sales in 2011 and 2012. It is possible to delete rows by selecting them and then clicking the *Delete Row* button.

3. Type the set name: **Americas and Europe** into the *Set Name* box.

4. Remove the 2011 *Americas* country rows (*Brazil, USA* and *Venezuela*).

5. Remove the 2012 *European* country rows (*Austria, France, Germany* and *UK*).

6. Remove the two rows that have *All* shown for the *Country.*

   These are the rows that listed total sales for each year. As you have removed some countries from each year, the totals will no longer show the correct value.

   In order to add subtotals for each named set you would need an advanced understanding of the MDX query language (see sidebar).

7. Click the *OK* button.

   The OLAP pivot table now lists European sales for 2011 and Americas sales for 2012.

4 Save your work as *Americas and Europe-2.*

Session 11: Exercise

1 Open *Film Sales-1* from your sample files folder.

This contains five tables detailing sales from a DVD film wholesaler.

2 Use Get & Transform and Power Pivot to create a snowflake data model containing all of the tables and relationships defined in the schema shown below.

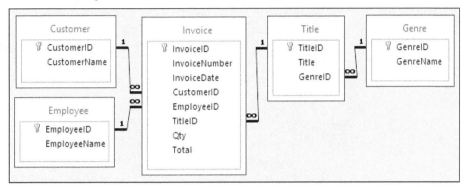

3 Add a *Calendar* table to the data model and create a relationship between the *Calendar* table and *Invoice* table.

4 Within the data model, format the *Invoice* Table's *Total* field as *Currency*.

5 Create an OLAP pivot table (in a new worksheet) from the data model.

6 Use the OLAP pivot table to report each customer's *Total* purchase value by *Genre*.

	B	C	D
2	Sum of Total	Column Labels	
3	Row Labels	Action	Adventure
4	Addison-Freelander Screen Agency	$2,961.43	$1,051.02
5	AV Supplies	$3,044.27	$438.40

7 Use the OLAP pivot table to report the total cash value of goods (*Sum of Total*) sold by each *Employee* during each *Month* and *Year*.

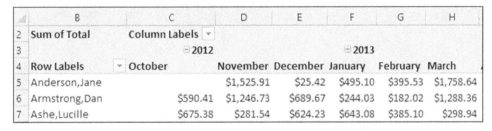

	B	C	D	E	F	G	H
2	Sum of Total	Column Labels					
3			2012		2013		
4	Row Labels	October	November	December	January	February	March
5	Anderson,Jane		$1,525.91	$25.42	$495.10	$395.53	$1,758.64
6	Armstrong,Dan	$590.41	$1,246.73	$689.67	$244.03	$182.02	$1,288.36
7	Ashe,Lucille	$675.38	$281.54	$624.23	$643.08	$385.10	$298.94

8 Save your work as *Film Sales-2*.

If you need help slide the page to the left

Film Sales-1

Session 11: Exercise Answers

These are the three questions that students find the most difficult to answer:

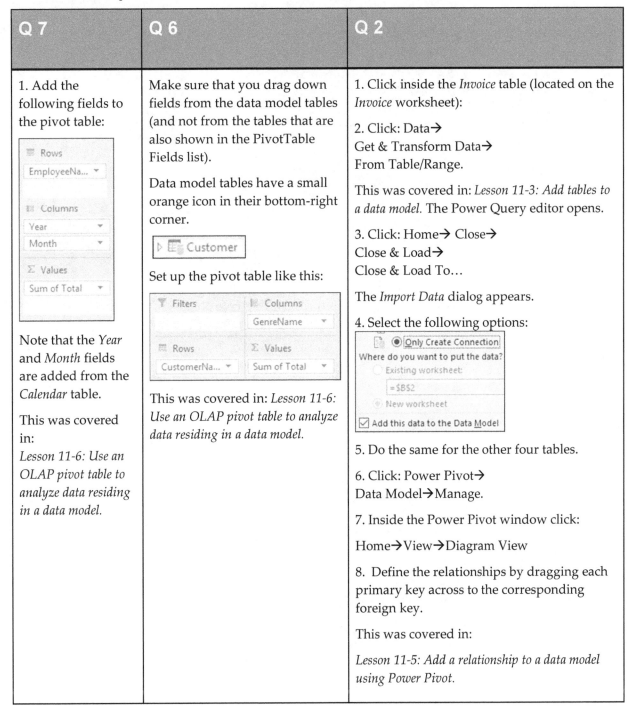

Q 7	Q 6	Q 2
1. Add the following fields to the pivot table:	Make sure that you drag down fields from the data model tables (and not from the tables that are also shown in the PivotTable Fields list).	1. Click inside the *Invoice* table (located on the *Invoice* worksheet):
		2. Click: Data→ Get & Transform Data→ From Table/Range.
	Data model tables have a small orange icon in their bottom-right corner.	This was covered in: *Lesson 11-3: Add tables to a data model.* The Power Query editor opens.
	Set up the pivot table like this:	3. Click: Home→ Close→ Close & Load→ Close & Load To...
		The *Import Data* dialog appears.
	This was covered in: *Lesson 11-6: Use an OLAP pivot table to analyze data residing in a data model.*	4. Select the following options:
Note that the *Year* and *Month* fields are added from the *Calendar* table.		5. Do the same for the other four tables.
This was covered in: *Lesson 11-6: Use an OLAP pivot table to analyze data residing in a data model.*		6. Click: Power Pivot→ Data Model→Manage.
		7. Inside the Power Pivot window click: Home→View→Diagram View
		8. Define the relationships by dragging each primary key across to the corresponding foreign key.
		This was covered in:
		Lesson 11-5: Add a relationship to a data model using Power Pivot.

If you have difficulty with the other questions, here are the lessons that cover the relevant skills:

3   Refer to: *Lesson 11-17: Add a calendar table to a data model.*

4   Refer to: *Lesson 11-18: Format values in a data model.*

5   Refer to: *Lesson 11-6: Use an OLAP pivot table to analyze data residing in a data model.*

12

Session Twelve: An introduction to DAX

> You can't build a great building on a weak foundation. You must have a solid foundation if you're going to have a strong superstructure.
>
> *Gordon B. Hinckley (1910-2008)*
> *American religious leader and author*

In: *Lesson 10-1: Understand Get & Transform and ETL* and *Session Eleven: Power Pivot, Data Modeling, OLAP and Business Intelligence* you learned how to create an efficient star schema data model.

The data model that you created can already support most reporting requirements (when used as the data source for an OLAP pivot table or chart), but you may encounter some reporting requirements that cannot be satisfied. In these cases, the DAX language will enable you to further refine the data model by adding *DAX calculated measures*.

The DAX language has over 200 functions and there are 500-page books published that are entirely devoted to the subject of DAX. The purpose of this session is to provide you with a solid grounding in key DAX concepts and to cover a few of the most widely used DAX functions.

In this session you'll create DAX measures that conform to the best-practice rules defined in: *Appendix A: Power Pivot Rules*. This will provide you with a solid foundation for future learning, enabling you to explore DAX in greater depth, when you apply your data modeling and DAX skills to solve real-world reporting problems.

Session Objectives

By the end of this session you will be able to:

- Understand the Power Pivot window
- Add a DAX calculated column
- Create a DAX calculated measure
- Understand Implicit and Explicit measures
- Understand row and filter context
- Create a calculated measure using the measure dialog
- Use a DAX DISTINCTCOUNT function
- Create a Key Performance Indicator
- Use a DAX CALCULATE function
- Use a DAX measure to calculate year-on-year growth
- Use a DAX ALL function

Lesson 12-1: Understand the Power Pivot window

1   Open *Orders-5* from your sample files folder.

This workbook contains a copy of the data model that you created in: *Session Eleven: Power Pivot, Data Modeling, OLAP and Business Intelligence.*

2   Click the Enable Content button if prompted to do so.

3   Open Power Pivot in data view.

You learned how to do this in: *Lesson 11-2: Install the Power Pivot add-in.*

4   Make sure that the Calculation Area is enabled.

If the calculation area is not visible (the area at the bottom of the window), click:

Home➔View➔Calculation Area

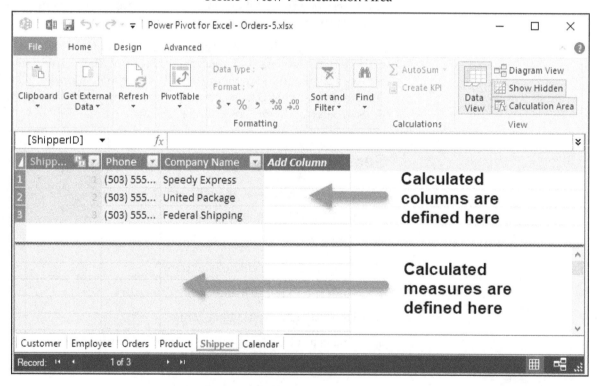

Power Pivot supports two very different types of calculated fields

Power Pivot enables you to create two different types of calculated fields: *Calculated Columns* and *Calculated Measures.*

Orders-5

Calculated Columns

In the screen grab on the previous page you can see can see that Calculated Columns are defined in the column headed *Add Column* within the Power Pivot data view window.

Calculated Columns are very easy to understand as they are very similar to the calculated fields that you created in: *Lesson 8-16: Add a calculated field to a pivot table.* You'll create a calculated column later, in: *Lesson 12-2: Add a DAX calculated column.*

Calculated Measures

In the facing page screen grab you can see can see that calculated measures are defined in the area beneath the table called the *Calculation Area.*

Calculated measures contain aggregations of data contained in one or more table columns.

Calculated measures are one of Power Pivot's most important features. Very complex business analysis scenarios can be delivered using a well-designed data model containing DAX calculated measures.

You'll create your first calculated measure later, in *Lesson 12-3: Create a DAX calculated measure.*

5   Keep the workbook open for the next lesson.

Lesson 12-2: Add a DAX calculated column

DAX enables you to create two different types of calculated fields: *Calculated Columns* and *Calculated Measures*.

In this lesson you'll create a *Calculated Column*. This is the simpler of the two types of DAX formula.

1   Open *Orders-5* from your sample files folder.

This workbook contains a copy of the data model that you created in: *Session Eleven: Power Pivot, Data Modeling, OLAP and Business Intelligence.*

2   Open the data model using Power Pivot.

Click: Power Pivot→Data Model→Manage.

3   Make sure that you are viewing the model in Data View.

Click: Home→View→Data View.

4   Add a calculated column to the *Orders* table that will show the *Order Value.*

Third normal form (3NF) is a set of rules that must be followed when designing OLTP databases. You learned about the difference between OLTP and OLAP databases in: *Lesson 11-11: Understand OLTP database design.*

One important 3NF rule is that a table cannot contain a value that can be calculated from other columns in the table. In the case of the *Orders* table, the order value can be calculated from other columns using this formula:

Order Value = Quantity * Unit Price * (1-Discount)

The final multiplication of (1-Discount) is needed because the discount values in the table are percentages. A 10% discount would have a value of 0.1.

If a 10% discount value is subtracted from 1 the result is 0.9. Multiplying by 0.9 will return 90% of the value (a discount of 10%).

Because this is an OLAP database it is perfectly correct (and desirable) to have calculated columns.

1.   Select the *Orders* table tab.

2.   Click anywhere in the rightmost column with the header *Add Column.*

3.   Press the <=> key to begin the formula (your keypresses will appear in the formula bar and not the column) .

4.   Click once anywhere in the *Quantity* column.

5.   Press the multiplication <*> key.

6.   Click once anywhere in the *Unit Price* column.

7.   The formula bar now contains this DAX formula:

Orders-5

fx =Orders[Quantity]*Orders[Unit Price]

8. Add the following to the DAX formula:

fx =Orders[Quantity]*Orders[Unit Price]*(1-

9. Click anywhere in the *Discount* column.

10. Finish the formula with a closing bracket.

The DAX formula should now look like this:

fx =Orders[Quantity]*Orders[Unit Price]*(1-Orders[Discount])

11. Press the <**Enter**> key.

After a short time, the column calculates and all of the calculated values are displayed.

Unit Price	Order Number	Calculated Column 1
$36.80	10294	552
$27.20	10294	571.2
$6.20	10294	37.2

Notice that Power Pivot calculated columns are shaded differently to regular columns.

5 **Change the name of the new calculated column to: Order Value**

Double-click in the column header and type the new name: **Order Value**

6 **Format the new calculated column as** *Currency.*

1. Click anywhere in the *Order Value* column.

2. Click: Home→Formatting→Format→Currency.

The calculated column should now look like this:

Quantity	Discount	Order ...	Unit Price	Order Number	Order Value
10	0.00%	1/9/2017 12:0...	$7.70	10250	$77.00
40	0.00%	1/10/2017 12:...	$27.20	10252	$1,088.00
20	0.00%	1/20/2017 12:...	$8.00	10261	$160.00

There is some debate amongst Power Pivot professionals regarding whether it is better to create a calculated column using *Get & Transform* or as a Power Pivot calculated column.

My own preference would be to create calculated columns as close to the source data as possible. For this reason, I would tend to do this using Get & Transform (though you could argue that it doesn't really matter).

The *Order Value* calculated column will now be available to your users in any OLAP pivot table that uses this data model.

7 **Save your work as** *Orders-6.*

note

You can also create a DAX formula using the keyboard

In this lesson you used the point-and-click method to add column references to the DAX formula.

You can also use the keyboard to add the references like this:

1. Click anywhere in the column headed: *Add Column*.

2. Press the <=> key to begin the DAX formula.

3. Type: <[> (a square opening bracket). A list drops down showing all available columns:

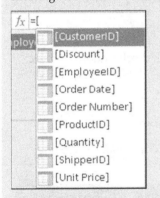

fx =[

| [CustomerID] |
| [Discount] |
| [EmployeeID] |
| [Order Date] |
| [Order Number] |
| [ProductID] |
| [Quantity] |
| [ShipperID] |
| [Unit Price] |

4. Press the <**Down Arrow**> key until the *[Quantity]* field is highlighted.

5. Press the <**Tab**> key to add the column name to the formula.

important

Terminology confusion

In the Excel 2010 version of the Power Pivot add-in, aggregations added to the calculation area were described as *Calculated Measures* (as they are today).

In the Excel 2013 version of the Power Pivot add-in, *Calculated Measures* were given the new name: *Calculated Fields*.

In the Excel 2016 and Excel 2019 versions of the Power Pivot add-in, *Calculated Fields* were renamed again and reverted to *Calculated Measures*.

If you read Excel 2013 Power Pivot books (or read online articles dating back to the 2013-2016 period) you'll often see the term *Calculated Field* used which causes some confusion. You may also encounter some users who still use the outdated term: *Calculated Field*.

In pure OLAP terms a *measure* is any value within a data model. The term *calculated measure* differentiates DAX measures from numeric values.

Lesson 12-3: Create a DAX calculated measure

In: *Lesson 12-2: Add a DAX calculated column* you added a calculated column to a data model.

Calculated columns are very easy to understand as each cell only references values that are in the same row. Calculated measures are more difficult to understand as they contain aggregations of data contained in one or more table columns.

In this lesson you'll create your first calculated measure.

1 Open *Orders-6* from your sample files folder.

2 Open the Power Pivot window.

3 Make sure you have *Data View* enabled.

Click: Home→View→Data View.

4 Select the Orders table (if it isn't already selected).

5 Use AutoSum to create a *Sum of Order Value* calculated measure.

Notice that the Power Pivot window is split into two panes. The lower pane is called the *Calculation Area.*

Calculated measures are created in the calculation area.

1. Click in the calculation area in the first cell underneath the *OrderValue* column (see facing page sidebar if this area is not visible).

2. Click: Home→Calculations→AutoSum. ∑ AutoSum ▾

A calculated measure called *Sum of Order Value* is created.

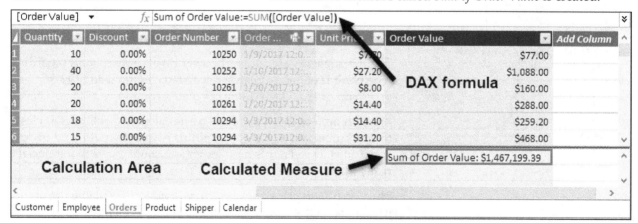

Notice the syntax of the DAX formula shown in the formula bar:

Sum of Order Value:=SUM([Order Value])

When you define a calculated measure, you begin with the measure name (in this case: **Sum of Order Value**), you then add a colon followed by an equals sign (:=) before creating the DAX formula: **SUM([Order Value])**.

Orders-6

note

If you don't see the calculation area

The calculation area is visible by default but can be toggled on and off.

If the calculation area is not visible on your computer click:

Home→View→ Calculation Area

… to bring it back.

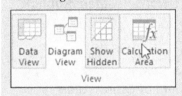

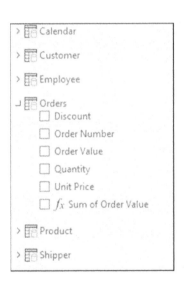

6   Correct the calculated measure formula to conform with naming convention rules.

AutoSum has done a good job in creating the DAX calculated measure. Unfortunately, AutoSum hasn't read this book so it doesn't know our naming convention rules.

One of the naming convention rules in: *Appendix A: Power Pivot Rules* is:

Include the table name when you reference a column.

There are two reasons for this rule:

- It is perfectly correct (in database design) to have the same field name in two different tables. By prefixing column names with table names, you will ensure that Power Pivot is always referencing the correct field.

- Because DAX formulas can include references to other measures, it can be difficult to identify which parts of a formula are column references and which are measure references. If you include the table name when you reference a column and do not include the table name when referencing a measure, it is always clear (when auditing a formula) where the values are coming from.

Edit the formula (in the formula bar) so that it reads as follows:

Sum of Order Value:=SUM(Orders[Order Value])

If a pivot table is created that references this data model, the calculated measure will appear in the PivotTable fields list in exactly the same way as the other fields (see sidebar).

Notice that the *Sum of Order Value* field (in the sidebar) is prefixed with *fx* to identify it as a calculated measure.

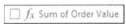

You may wonder why you would bother creating this calculated measure. You can, after all, sum the *Order Value* field in a pivot table simply by dragging it into the *Values* window.

The reason that calculated measures are better practice than simple pivot table aggregations will only be become clear later, in: *Lesson 12-4: Understand Implicit* and *Explicit measures.*

7   Rename the calculated measure from *Sum of Order Value* to: **CM – Sum of Order Value**

Edit the formula (in the formula bar) so that it reads as follows:

CM - Sum of Order Value:=SUM(Orders[Order Value])

You wouldn't normally rename the measure in this way. *Sum of Order Value* is a really great name for this field as users will instantly understand the value that the field is returning. The new name is being used only for the purpose of clarity in the next lesson: *Lesson 12-4: Understand Implicit and Explicit measures.*

8   Save your work as *Orders-7.*

Lesson 12-4: Understand Implicit and Explicit measures

1   Open *Orders-7* from your sample files folder.

2   Open the Power Pivot window.

3   Create a new OLAP pivot table in a new worksheet using the data model.

   1.   Click: Home→Pivot Table.

   2.   Click the OK button.

4   Name the new OLAP pivot table's worksheet tab: **Implicit and Explicit Measures**

5   Delete the *Sheet1* worksheet.

6   Use the OLAP pivot table to show *Sum of Order Value* by *Category Name* using the *CM - Sum of Order Value* calculated measure in the *Orders* table.

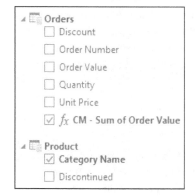

Rows	Σ Values
Category Name ▼	CM - Sum of Order Value ▼

Row Labels ▼	CM - Sum of Order Value
Beverages	$317,055.20
Condiments	$122,372.68
Confections	$186,880.13
Dairy Products	$273,542.81
Grains/Cereals	$105,933.41
Meat/Poultry	$191,412.40
Produce	$123,686.33
Seafood	$146,316.42
Grand Total	**$1,467,199.39**

7   Drag the *Order Value* field from the *Orders* table to the pivot table's *Values* pane.

Rows	Σ Values
Category Name ▼	CM - Sum of Order Value ▼
	Sum of Order Value ▼

Both the *CM - Sum of Order Value calculated measure* and the *Sum of Order Value measure* are returning exactly the same values.

Row Labels ▼	CM - Sum of Order Value	Sum of Order Value
Beverages	$317,055.20	$317,055.20
Condiments	$122,372.68	$122,372.68
Confections	$186,880.13	$186,880.13
Dairy Products	$273,542.81	$273,542.81
Grains/Cereals	$105,933.41	$105,933.41
Meat/Poultry	$191,412.40	$191,412.40
Produce	$123,686.33	$123,686.33
Seafood	$146,316.42	$146,316.42
Grand Total	**$1,467,199.39**	**$1,467,199.39**

It is important to appreciate the difference between them.

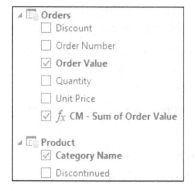

Orders-7

note

You cannot apply further aggregations to explicit measures

1. Click on *the CM – Sum of Order Value calculated measure* (in the Pivot Table's *Values* box).

2. Click *Value Field Settings…* on the pop-up menu.

3. Click the *Summarize Values By* tab.

Notice that the summation methods (for this explicit measure) are all disabled:

Summarize value field by

Choose the type of calcula
data from the selected fiel

Sum
Count
Average
Max
Min
StdDev

4. Now do the same thing for the *Sum of Order Value* measure.

Notice that the summation methods (for this implicit measure) are all enabled:

Summarize value field by

Choose the type of calcula
data from the selected fiel

Sum
Count
Average
Max
Min
StdDev

This is exactly what you would expect. Because the explicit measure only returned eight values to the pivot table it is not possible for the pivot table to apply any other summation method to the measure.

If your users needed several summation methods, you would need to provide several calculated measures in the data model.

The values returned by the *CM - Sum of Order Value calculated measure* column were explicitly calculated by Power Pivot before they were sent to the pivot table. This type of measure is called an *Explicit Measure.* This meant that only eight values had to be sent from the Power Pivot engine to Excel.

The regular *Order Value* PivotTable field returned 2,448 values from the Power Pivot engine to Excel. Excel's Pivot Table then calculated the *Sum of Order Value measure* by adding these values together. This type of measure is called an *Implicit Measure.*

8   Understand the advantages of using explicit measures.

- **Explicit measures calculate much faster than implicit measures:**

  Implicit measure values are calculated by the pivot table's own formula engine. Power Pivot explicit measures use Microsoft's *xVelocity in-memory analysis engine*. This engine can scan billions of data rows per second and can produce reports in a tiny fraction of the time needed by the Excel pivot table.

  Power Pivot's xVelocity engine produces extremely fast (often perceived as instant) results even when dealing with data sets containing many millions of rows.

- **Explicit measures are more sophisticated than implicit measures:**

  Implicit measures in the *Values* pane are aggregated using one of the pivot table's ten aggregation methods such as *Sum, Count* and *Average*. Sometimes your aggregation needs may go beyond what is possible using the pivot table's ten simple aggregation methods.

  Explicit measures are far more sophisticated than implicit measures as they can implement complex business logic using DAX functions.

- **Explicit measures are re-usable:**

  Explicit measures are defined within the data model. A single data model can be used by many pivot tables. Implicit measures are defined within (and can only be used by) one pivot table.

  For these reasons, it is best practice to always use explicit measures in your work.

The best-practice rule:

Always use explicit measures rather than implicit measures.

… is included in: *Appendix A: Power Pivot Rules.*

9   Save your work as *Orders-8*.

note

You wouldn't normally use a DAX aggregation function in a calculated column

In this lesson you discovered a key difference between DAX aggregation functions and their Excel namesakes. You used a DAX SUM aggregation function and found that it behaved differently to an Excel SUM function.

DAX aggregation functions always apply to an entire table column (they do not recognize the concept of a traditional Excel range).

For this reason, you would not normally use a DAX aggregation function (one whose Excel equivalent uses a range of cells as an argument) in a calculated column.

Non-aggregation functions (functions that require single cell arguments) work well in calculated columns.

For example, you'll find the LEFT, RIGHT and MID string manipulation functions and IF logical function useful in calculated columns. You'll find that these functions have the same syntax (and work in the same way) as their Excel equivalents.

Some DAX functions (such as CALCULATE and ALL) have no Excel equivalent. You'll learn how to use some of these functions later in this session.

Lesson 12-5: Understand row and filter context

When working with classic Excel data analysis you don't have to consider the issue of context.

When working with a data model and an associated OLAP pivot table an understanding of context (sometimes called *Evaluation Context*) is essential.

1 Open *Orders-8* from your sample files folder.

2 Open the Power Pivot window.

3 Make sure you have *Data View* enabled.

Click: Home→View→Data View.

4 Select the *Orders* table.

This table contains a calculated measure called: *CM – Sum of Order Value* that aggregates the sum of the total order value for all 2,448 rows in the table.

Order Value	CC - Sum of Order Value
$77.00	$1,467,199.39
$1,088.00	$1,467,199.39
$160.00	$1,467,199.39
CM - Sum of Order Value: $1,467,199.39	

You created this calculated measure in: *Lesson 12-3: Create a DAX calculated measure.* (All fields defined in the calculation area below the table are calculated measures).

Calculated measures always have *Filter Context*. (You'll discover how this differs from *Row Context* in a moment).

5 Add a new calculated column to show the total Order value.

To do this you'll use a DAX aggregation function. The DAX aggregation functions have familiar names (such as SUM and AVERAGE) but can sometimes behave differently to their Excel namesakes.

1. Click anywhere in the column that has the header: *Add Column.*

2. Add the following formula in the formula bar:

   =SUM(Orders[Order Value])

Aggregation functions (such as the SUM function) shouldn't normally be used in a calculated column (see sidebar). You are only doing this to illustrate the difference between row and filter context.

6 Rename the new calculated column to: **CC – Sum of Order Value**

You learned how to do this in: *Lesson 12-2: Add a DAX calculated column.*

Orders-8

7   Format the new calculated column as *Currency*.

You learned how to do this in: *Lesson 12-2: Add a DAX calculated column.*

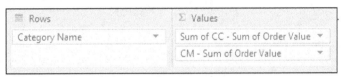

	$199.50	$1,467,199.39
	$1,064.00	$1,467,199.39
	$310.00	$1,467,199.39
CM - Sum of Order Value: $1,467,199.39		

Notice that, exactly as you would expect, the same value is shown in every row in the *CC – Sum of Order Value calculated column* and is exactly the same as the value returned by the *CM – Sum of Order Value calculated measure*.

The difference between the two is that calculated columns always have *Row Context* and calculated measures always have *Filter Context*. (You'll discover the difference between the two contexts in a moment).

8   Create a new OLAP pivot table from the data model on a new worksheet.

9   Rename the new worksheet: **Context**

10   Use the new pivot table to show *Sum of Order Value by Category* using both the *CM – Sum of Order Value calculated measure* and the *CC – Sum of Order Value calculated column*.

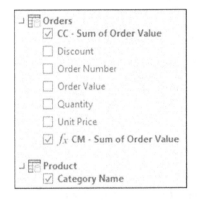

☰ Rows	Σ Values
Category Name ▼	Sum of CC - Sum of Order Value ▼
	CM - Sum of Order Value ▼

Row Labels ▼	Sum of CC - Sum of Order Value	CM - Sum of Order Value
Beverages	$689,583,714.79	$317,055.20
Condiments	$360,931,050.72	$122,372.68
Confections	$542,863,775.47	$186,880.13

The calculated measure has *filter context*. This means that the aggregated values respect the *context* of any row and column headers, slicers and report filters in the pivot table.

This means that the calculated measure is correctly returning the *Sum of Order Value by Category*.

The calculated column has row context. Row context does not respect the row and column headers so is showing incorrect results.

You may be curious about how these incorrect results have been calculated. The values have been calculated by multiplying the *Sum of Order Value* calculated column value ($1,467,199.39) by the number of orders in each category.

11   Save your work as *Orders-9*.

Lesson 12-6: Create a calculated measure using the measure dialog

In: *Lesson 12-3: Create a DAX calculated measure,* you created a calculated measure using the Power Pivot window's calculation area.

When working with OLAP pivot tables it is useful to be able to quickly create calculated measures without opening the Power Pivot window. This method creates the measure using the *Measure* dialog box rather than the calculation area.

1   Open *Orders-9* from your sample files folder.

2   Open the Power Pivot window.

3   Create a new pivot table on a new sheet in the workbook.

    1. Click: Home→PivotTable (from inside the Power Pivot window).

    2. Click OK.

4   Rename the new worksheet: **Measure Dialog**

5   Use the new pivot table to show the total *Quantity* (from the *Orders* table) sold by *Company Name* (from the *Customer* table).

    1. Check the box next to *CompanyName* in the *Customer* table.

    2. Check the box next to *Quantity* in the *Orders* table.

Row Labels	Sum of Quantity
Alfreds Futterkiste	264
Ana Trujillo Emparedados y helados	74
Antonio Moreno Taquería	359
Around the Horn	871
Berglunds snabbköp	1036

6   Change the *Sum of Quantity* field into an Explicit Measure using the *Measure* dialog.

The pivot table works perfectly but you have used an *Implicit Measure* (the *Sum of Quantity* field). *In: Lesson 12-4: Understand Implicit and Explicit measures,* you learned that it is better to use an *Explicit Measure.*

Explicit measures are created by defining a calculated measure in the data model.

In: *Lesson 12-3: Create a DAX calculated measure,* you did this using Power Pivot's calculation area. This time you will create the calculated measure directly from the pivot table.

    1. Right-click on the *Orders* table in the *PivotTable Fields* list.

Customer
- ☐ Address
- ☐ City
- ☑ Company Name
- ☐ Contact Name
- ☐ Contact Title
- ☐ Country
- ☐ Fax
- ☐ Phone
- ☐ Postal Code
- ☐ Region

> Employee

Orders
- ☐ CC - Sum of Order Value
- ☐ Discount
- ☐ Order Number
- ☐ Order Value
- ☑ Quantity

Orders-9

note

You can also open the Measure dialog from the Power Pivot ribbon tab

If you click:

Power Pivot→Calculations→
Measures→New Measure

... you will open exactly the same *Measure* dialog.

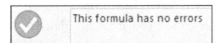

2. Select *Add Measure…* from the shortcut menu.

The *Measure* dialog appears.

3. Type: **Total Quantity** into the *Measure Name* box. (The *Value Description* is optional so leave this box blank).

4. Type this formula into the *Formula* box:

   =SUM(Orders[Quantity])

   You'll notice Excel offering to help you with drop-down lists as you type.

5. Click the *Check DAX Formula* button [Check DAX Formula] to make sure that your formula has no errors.

6. In the *Category* box click *Number* to apply a number format.

7. Use the values to the right of the *Category* box to set the number format to *Whole Number* with a thousand separator.

   The dialog should now look like this:

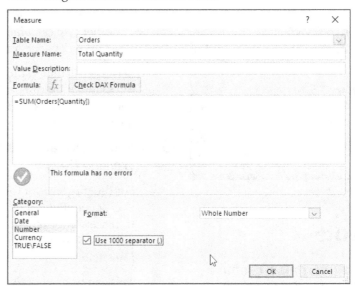

8. Click the *OK* button to create the calculated measure.

9. Remove the existing *Sum of Quantity* implicit measure from the *Values* box and replace it with the new *Total Quantity* explicit measure.

   The pivot table displays the same values but now uses an *Explicit* measure rather than an *Implicit* measure. The measure is pre-formatted (note the comma thousands separator) and will calculate large data sets much faster.

Row Labels	Total Quantity
Alfreds Futterkiste	264
Ana Trujillo Emparedados y helados	74
Antonio Moreno Taquería	359
Around the Horn	871
Berglunds snabbköp	1,036

7   Save your work as *Orders-10*.

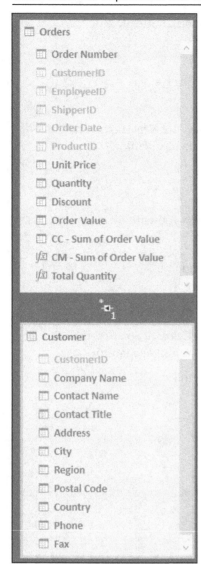

Lesson 12-7: Use a DAX DISTINCTCOUNT function

1 Open *Orders-10* from your sample files folder.

Inspect the workbook's schema using Power Pivot diagram view.

In this lesson you will work with the *Orders* and *Customer* tables. (You can see these two tables in the sidebar).

2 Understand the report specification.

Imagine that a manager has asked you for this report:

"I need to know average order value per working day. I'll need these figures summarized into years, months and days".

To produce this report, you will need to create three calculated measures:

1. The *Sum of Order Value* for all sales recorded in the *Orders* table (you have already created this calculated measure).

2. The *Count of Working Days* from the *Orders* table.

3. The *Average Order Value Per Working Day*. This will use the other two calculated measures to divide the *Sum of Order Value* by the *Count of Working Days*.

Because calculated measures will have *Filter Context*, the three new calculated measures will always calculate correctly within the *context* of any row and column headers, slicers and report filters in the pivot table.

3 Add a calculated measure that will calculate the *Count of Working Days.*

For the purposes of this calculation it is assumed that the business was never open for an entire day without taking at least one order. If this assumption is correct, the number of days upon which the business was open will be the total unique instances of the *Order Date* field.

This can be easily calculated using the DAX DISTINCTCOUNT function. DISTINCTCOUNT is an example of a DAX function that has no counterpart in Excel.

1. Change the Power Pivot view to: *Data View.*

2. Select the *Orders* table.

3. Click in any empty cell in the calculation area beneath the table.

4. Type this formula into any empty cell in the calculation area:

   fx Count of Working Days:=DISTINCTCOUNT(Orders[Order Date])

5. Press the **<Enter>** key.

   Count of Working Days: 516

note

You can also create a *Distinct Count* implicit measure

Unlike a traditional pivot table, an OLAP pivot table has a built-in implicit *Distinct Count* aggregation method but I don't recommend that you use it.

In: *Appendix A: Power Pivot Rules*, you'll find that I discourage the use of implicit measures, advising you to use explicit measures in every case.

Orders-10

trivia

Ad hoc and paper-based reporting

Many years ago, I was asked to implement a very early (not Excel) OLAP system for a large international company.

When I arrived, I was given a huge pile of paper reports from the legacy system to show the information that the business needed to function.

At a management meeting I was asked by a director how many of the paper reports were finished. I had to advise that the precise answer was "none of them". It was difficult to explain that there was no need to duplicate the old pre-defined reports individually. The information that the old paper reports contained could be assembled in seconds by untrained users using the new intuitive OLAP interface. My real task was to create the data models that users would need.

4 Add a calculated measure that will calculate the *Average Order Value per Working Day* from the *CM – Sum of Order Value* and *Count of Working Days* calculated measures.

A wonderful feature of calculated measures is the ability to use them within other calculated measures.

1. Type this formula into any empty cell in the Calculation Area:

fx Average Order Value per Working Day:= [CM - Sum of Order Value]/[Count of Working Days]

This formula demonstrates one of the advantages of the naming convention defined in: *Appendix A: Power Pivot Rules.*

Because you have adhered to the rules:

Include the table name when you reference a column.

Do not include the table name when you reference a measure.

…it is obvious that two calculated measures are being used in the above formula (rather than columns). This makes formulas (especially very complex ones) far simpler to work with.

2. Press the **<Enter>** key.

5 Format the new calculated measure as *Currency.*

Click: Home→Formatting→Format and select *Currency* from the drop-down list.

Average Order Value per Working Day: $2,843.41

6 Create a pivot table from the data model in a new worksheet and use it to report the *Average Order Value per Working Day* summarized by *Month and Year.*

Now that the data model is complete it is quite a trivial matter to create the report requested:

Row Labels	Count of Working Days	Average Order Value per Working Day
⊞ 2017	257	$1,893.85
⊞ 2018	259	$3,785.64
Grand Total	**516**	**$2,843.41**

The manager is also able to expand the left-most column from *Years* to *Months* and to *Days.*

7 Name the pivot table's worksheet: **DISTINCTCOUNT**

8 Save your work as *Orders-11.*

Calendar
  > ☐ Date Hierarchy
  ⌐ More Fields
      ☑ Date
      ☐ Day Of Week
      ☐ Day Of Week Number
      ☐ MMM-YYYY
      ☑ Month
      ☐ Month Number
      ☑ Year
> Customer
> Employee
⌐ Orders
      ☐ CC - Sum of Order Value
      ☐ Discount
      ☐ Order Number
      ☐ Order Value
      ☐ Quantity
      ☐ Unit Price
      ☐ fx CM - Sum of Order Value
      ☐ fx Total Quantity
      ☑ fx Count of Working Days
      ☑ fx Average Order Value per Working Day

Lesson 12-8: Create a Key Performance Indicator

The scenario used in this lesson is as follows:

The business has communicated their sales expectations to their employees:

- Your Sales Target is $2,000 per working day.

- If you exceed your sales target by 20% you will receive a bonus.

- If you consistently under-perform your sales target by 30% you may be re-assigned to a non-sales position.

Here is a pivot table with a KPI (Key Performance Indicator):

September	
Buchanan	$1,201.02 ●
Callahan	$2,622.69 ●
Davolio	$3,288.24 ●
Dodsworth	$1,409.00 ○
Fuller	$1,760.11 ○

The KPI status field provides the colored indicator shown next to each employee. You can see at a glance that, in September, *Davolio* and *Callahan* had excellent performance, *Dodsworth* and *Fuller* had acceptable performance, but *Buchanan* had unacceptable performance.

To create a KPI in Power Pivot three values are needed:

Base Value: In the above example the base value is the calculated measure: *Average Order Value per Working Day*.

Target Value: In the above example the target value is $2,000. In some scenarios this could reference a calculated measure rather than the absolute value ($2,000) used in this example.

Status Threshold: This consists of two values (a high and a low) that will define the color of the KPI indicator. In the above example this would be $2,400 (20% above target) and $1,400 (30% below target).

1 Open *Orders-11* from your sample files folder.

2 Create a KPI to the specifications shown above.

1. Open the Power Pivot window.

2. Make sure you are displaying *Data View*.

3. Select the *Orders* table.

4. Right-click on the *Average Order Value per Working Day* calculated measure.

5. Select *Create KPI...* from the shortcut menu.

   The *Key Performance Indicator (KPI)* dialog appears. Note that the KPI base field: *Average Order Value per Working Day* is pre-selected.

6. Click the *Absolute value* option button.

7. Type: **2000** into the *Absolute value* text box.

note

Other ways to open the KPI dialog

In this lesson I right-clicked on a calculated measure and then clicked: *Create KPI...* from the shortcut menu.

This is the method I prefer as the correct calculated measure is pre-selected, reducing the scope for error.

Excel provides several other ways to invoke the KPI dialog.

From the Power Pivot ribbon

1. Open the Power Pivot window.

2. Click on a calculated measure to select it.

3. Click: Home→Calculations→Create KPI.

Prom the Power Pivot tab in Excel

Click: Power Pivot→Calculations→KPIs→New KPI...

Note that you can also click:

Power Pivot→Calculations→KPIs→Manage KPIs...

... to edit the settings of an existing KPI.

Orders-11

This is the *Target Value*.

8. Click and drag the sliders to define a *lower status threshold* of **1400** and an *upper status threshold* of **2400.**

The dialog should now look like this:

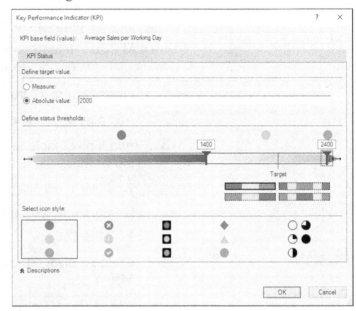

The icon style gallery at the bottom of the dialog can be used to choose from a range of visualizations.

9. Click the OK button.

3   Create a new OLAP pivot table on a new worksheet.

4   Rename the new worksheet: **KPI**

5   Use the new pivot table to show the *Average Sales per Working Day* (along with the KPI *Status*) achieved by each employee summarized by month and by year.

1. Notice that a special new KPI item has appeared in the *PivotTable Field List* within the *Orders* table (see sidebar).

2. Drag fields down to define the pivot table as follows:

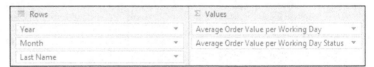

3. The pivot table now shows the sales performance for each employee:

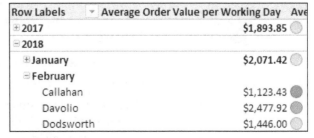

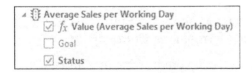

6   Save your work as *Orders-12*.

Lesson 12-9: Use a DAX CALCULATE function

The *CALCULATE* function is regarded by many Power Pivot experts as being the most important function in the vast DAX function library.

The CALCULATE function enables you to pre-filter a table (by adding one or more filters) prior to aggregating the values within it.

1   Open *Orders-12* from your sample files folder.

2   Add a new worksheet and name it: **CALCULATE**

3   Add a pivot table to the worksheet beginning in cell B3 using the workbook's data model as the data source.

   1.   Click in cell B3.

   2.   Click: Insert→Tables→Pivot Table.

   3.   Click OK.

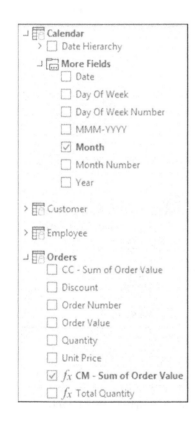

4   Create a pivot table to show the *Sum of Sales Value* by *Month*.

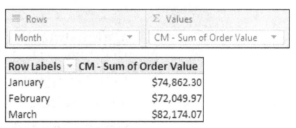

Row Labels	CM - Sum of Order Value
January	$74,862.30
February	$72,049.97
March	$82,174.07

This isn't a very useful pivot table. The January figure of $74,862.30 is actually the addition of the January 2017 and January 2018 sales.

5   Add a *Year* field (from the Calendar table) to the *Rows* window.

Row Labels	CM - Sum of Order Value
2017	
January	$27,219.69
February	$22,095.17
March	$30,125.70

The pivot table is now more useful as it shows sales by year and month.

6   Create a calculated measure to show the Sum of Sales Value in the year 2017 and format it as *Currency*.

You can address this requirement by pre-filtering the *Orders* table **before** any Pivot Table row and column headers, slicers and report filters are applied.

   1.   Create the following calculated measure in the *Orders* table:

Orders-12

Sum of 2017 Order Value:=CALCULATE(
[CM - Sum of Order Value],
YEAR(Orders[Order Date])=2017)

The second argument in the CALCULATE function pre-filters the value returned by the *CM - Sum of Order Value* calculated measure so that only sales occurring in 2017 are aggregated.

2. Format the calculated measure as *Currency*.

Sum of 2017 Order Value: $486,718.69

7   Add the new calculated measure to the pivot table.

Row Labels ▼	CM - Sum of Order Value	Sum of 2017 Order Value
⊞ 2017	$486,718.69	$486,718.69
⊞ 2018	$980,480.70	
Grand Total	$1,467,199.39	$486,718.69

You can see that the pre-filtered calculated measure results in the pivot table displaying no sales for 2018.

8   Create a Pivot table that shows monthly sales for 2017 and 2018 alongside each other.

1. Use the same technique you as you used to create the **Sum of 2017 Order Value** calculated measure to create a new calculated measure: **Sum of 2018 Order Value**

2. Set up the pivot table using these settings:

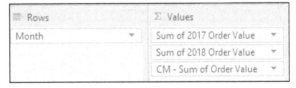

Row Labels ▼	Sum of 2017 Order Value	Sum of 2018 Order Value	CM - Sum of Order Value
January	$27,219.69	$47,642.61	$74,862.30
February	$22,095.17	$49,954.79	$72,049.97
March	$30,125.70	$52,048.37	$82,174.07

You may wonder what the point is of doing this.

You could have achieved exactly the same result by adding the *Year* PivotTable field to the *Columns* window and the *Month* PivotTable field to the *Rows* window.

You would not normally use a CALCULATE function that simply filtered a field that is already in the PivotTable field list. You've done it in this case merely as a simple example.

Later, in: *Lesson 12-10: Use a DAX measure to calculate year-on-year growth*, you'll use the two calculated measures that you created in this lesson to create a *Percentage Growth* calculated measure. This will enable you to create a useful OLAP pivot table that could not be easily created without the use of calculated measures.

9   Save your work as *Orders 13*.

Lesson 12-10: Use a DAX measure to calculate year-on-year growth

It is a very common business requirement to measure business growth by comparing a business metric (such as sales) with the same metric during a previous period.

In this example you will calculate the percentage growth of orders received in 2018 compared to orders received in 2017.

1   Open *Orders-13* from your sample files folder.

2   Add a new calculated field to calculate the percentage sales growth in 2018 compared to 2017.

This is quite easy using the formula:

(2018 Sales – 2017 Sales)/2017 Sales

You already have the calculated measures for both values.

1.   Open the Power Pivot window.

2.   Click inside any blank cell in the calculation area.

3.   Type this formula into the formula bar:

fx | Percentage Growth 2017/2018:=([Sum of 2018 Order Value]-[Sum of 2017 Order Value])/[Sum of 2017 Order Value]

3   Format the new calculated field as a percentage.

Click: Home→Formatting→Format→Percentage.

You can already see that sales in 2018 were just over double those in 2017.

Percentage Growth 2017/2018: 101.45%

4   Create a new pivot table on a new sheet in the workbook.

1.   Click: Home→PivotTable.

2.   Click OK.

5   Rename the new worksheet: **Year on Year**

6   Set up the pivot table to show three columns showing 2017 orders, 2018 orders and the percentage growth in 2018 (compared to 2017).

Add the following fields to the pivot table:

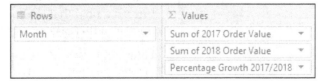

☰ Rows		Σ Values	
Month	▼	Sum of 2017 Order Value	▼
		Sum of 2018 Order Value	▼
		Percentage Growth 2017/2018	▼

Orders-13

Calendar
> Date Hierarchy
More Fields
  Date
  Day Of Week
  Day Of Week Number
  MMM-YYYY
  ☑ Month
  Month Number
  Year

> Customer

> Employee

Orders
  CC - Sum of Order Value
  Discount
  Order Number
  Order Value
  Quantity
  Unit Price
  fx CM - Sum of Order Value
  fx Total Quantity
  fx Count of Working Days
  ☑ *fx* Sum of 2017 Order Value
  ☑ *fx* Sum of 2018 Order Value
  ☑ *fx* Percentage Growth 2017/2018
  > Average Order Value per Working Day

Row Labels	Sum of 2017 Order Value	Sum of 2018 Order Value	Percentage Growth 2017/2018
January	$27,219.69	$47,642.61	75.03%
February	$22,095.17	$49,954.79	126.09%
March	$30,125.70	$52,048.37	72.77%
April	$28,236.30	$69,477.05	146.06%
May	$52,507.48	$46,007.83	-12.38%
June	$43,628.41	$60,688.96	39.10%
July	$56,619.44	$97,836.88	72.80%
August	$45,678.66	$108,474.59	137.47%
September	$36,839.31	$91,100.62	147.29%
October	$54,137.42	$135,026.86	149.42%
November	$52,824.70	$110,794.43	109.74%
December	$36,806.38	$111,427.71	202.74%
Grand Total	$486,718.69	$980,480.70	101.45%

In: *Lesson 12-4: Understand Implicit and Explicit measures* you learned the importance of explicit measures.

Because the pivot table only contains explicit measures, all calculation and aggregation has been done by the Power Pivot xVelocity engine. This means that results will be almost instantaneous (even when working with tables that contain millions of rows).

In: *Lesson 12-5: Understand row and filter context* you learned the importance of filter context.

Because the pivot table only contains calculated measures (that always have filter context) the pivot table can be used for many other year-on-year comparisons.

For example, here's how each employee performed:

Row Labels	Sum of 2017 Order Value	Sum of 2018 Order Value	Percentage Growth 2017/2018
Buchanan	$28,441.99	$42,821.79	50.56%
Callahan	$48,390.25	$114,223.05	136.05%
Davolio	$64,990.90	$144,682.65	122.62%
Dodsworth	$16,553.59	$70,384.27	325.19%
Fuller	$51,382.51	$155,599.24	202.83%
King	$46,778.42	$98,895.69	111.41%
Leverling	$80,918.95	$150,740.38	86.29%
Peacock	$114,914.01	$151,345.09	31.70%
Suyama	$34,348.05	$51,788.53	50.78%
Grand Total	$486,718.69	$980,480.70	101.45%

… and here are some sales changes for the best customers:

Row Labels	Sum of 2017 Order Value	Sum of 2018 Order Value	Percentage Growth 2017/2018
Save-a-lot Markets	$24,932.84	$98,181.85	293.79%
Ernst Handel	$35,001.82	$89,803.37	156.57%
QUICK-Stop	$42,784.81	$81,414.40	90.29%
Hungry Owl All-Night Grocers	$17,513.30	$33,160.10	89.34%
Hanari Carnes	$4,943.92	$30,130.15	509.44%
Folk och fä HB	$8,172.74	$26,678.07	226.43%
Rattlesnake Canyon Grocery	$26,964.03	$26,673.86	-1.08%

You can see that OLAP's other name: *Business Intelligence* is well deserved. Executives with very little training can make strategic decisions in moments based upon up-to-date data.

Of course, executives will need a data modeling expert with advanced Excel and Power Pivot skills to create easy-to-use and efficient data models.

7   Save your work as *Orders 14*.

Lesson 12-11: Use a DAX ALL function

The DAX *ALL* function cannot be used on its own (as it returns a table rather than an aggregation). It is very useful inside another function that requires a table as an argument.

In this lesson you will use the ALL function in conjunction with the CALCULATE function that you learned to use in: *Lesson 12-9: Use a DAX CALCULATE function.*

The ALL function is used to return a table containing all of the values from a table, single column or multiple columns, ignoring any filters that may have been applied.

In this lesson you'll use an ALL function to create a very useful report.

Consider this common business requirement:

Show me the total order value for each month in 2017 and, for each month, what percentage this is of the total order value for the entire year 2017.

You need these calculated measures to satisfy this requirement.

- Sum of order value for each month of 2017.

  You already have this calculated field (*Sum of 2017 Order Value*). Because the field has filter context it can easily be used to show order value by month.

- Sum of order value for the entire 2017 year. This value should remain constant even when filters are applied to the pivot table. This is the calculated field you'll create in this lesson that will require the DAX ALL function.

1   Open *Orders-14* from your sample files folder.

2   Add a new worksheet, name it: **ALL** and add a pivot table to cell B3 that references the data model.

3   Create a calculated measure named: **Sum of All 2017 Orders** that will calculate the total annual orders for 2017 (irrespective of any filters that may be applied).

    Create this calculated measure:

    fx | Sum of All 2017 Orders:=CALCULATE([Sum of 2017 Order Value], ALL(Orders))

4   Format the new calculated measure as currency.

    The calculated measure seems to return exactly the same value as the *Sum of 2017 Order Value* calculated measure:

    Sum of 2017 Order Value: $486,718.69

    Sum of All 2017 Orders: $486,718.69

    There is, however, an important difference between the values. The *Sum of All 2017 Orders* calculated measure will not be affected by any pivot table filter applied by a user.

    To see this in action, return to the *ALL* worksheet and create this pivot table:

Orders-14

Row Labels ▼	Sum of 2017 Order Value	Sum of All 2017 Orders
January	$27,219.69	$486,718.69
February	$22,095.17	$486,718.69
March	$30,125.70	$486,718.69

In: *Lesson 12-5: Understand row and filter context,* you learned that all calculated measures have *filter context.*

You might expect that even the *Sum of All 2017 Orders* column would show monthly sales because it has filter context (as do all measures). The reason that the *Sum of All 2017 Orders* column is unaffected by the monthly filter is a little difficult for some users to grasp.

The *ALL(Orders)* part of the DAX expression created a new (invisible) table in memory that was a duplicate of the *Orders* table. The CALCULATE function then used the existing *Sum of 2017 Order Value* calculated measure to calculate the total order value while referencing this duplicate (in memory) table.

Any filters applied to the *Orders* table will thus not affect the value returned because the filters are (correctly) not applied to this (invisible) duplicate table.

5 **Create a pivot table to show sales for each month in 2017 along with the percentage of annual sales this represents.**

You now have a calculated measure that returns the total annual orders for 2017 (*Sum of All 2017 Orders*). This calculated measure works as if it does not have filter context.

You also have a calculated measure for 2017 orders that does have filter context (*Sum of 2017 Order Value*).

You have a pivot table that shows these two calculated measures alongside each other. A simple division of *Sum of 2017 Order Value /All 2017 Orders* will return a percentage of the annual order value.

1. Create a new calculated measure as follows:

fx 2017 Sales as % of Annual Total:=[Sum of 2017 Order Value]/[Sum of All 2017 Orders]

2. Format the new calculated measure using the *Percentage* format.

3. Add the new calculated measure to the pivot table.

   Create this pivot table:

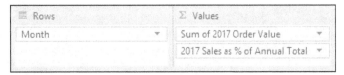

Row Labels ▼	Sum of 2017 Order Value	2017 Sales as % of Annual Total
January	$27,219.69	5.59%
February	$22,095.17	4.54%
March	$30,125.70	6.19%

6 Save your work as *Orders 15.*

Session 12: Exercise

1   Open a new blank workbook.

2   Use Get & Transform to import all seven tables from the *2018 Film Sales* Access database.

3   Close Get & Transform, loading the data from all tables into the Data Model.

4   Open the Power Pivot window and view the schema in *Diagram View*. Familiarize yourself with the data model's relationships (imported automatically from the Access database).

5   Switch from *Diagram View* to *Data View*. The *Orders* table has a *Qty* and *UnitPrice* column. Add an *Extended Price* calculated column to the *Orders* table by multiplying these two values together.

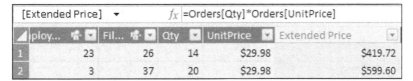

	[Extended Price] ▾			f_x =Orders[Qty]*Orders[UnitPrice]				
◢ploy...		Fil...		Qty	UnitPrice		Extended Price	
1	23		26	14	$29.98		$419.72	
2	3		37	20	$29.98		$599.60	

6   Use AutoSum to add two calculated measures to the *Orders* table that calculate the *Sum of Qty* and *Sum of ExtendedPrice*.

> Sum of Qty: 18409   Sum of Extended Price: $478,557.22

7   Rename the two calculated measures: **Qty Sold** and **Sum of Order Value**

> Qty Sold: 18409   Sum of Order Value: $478,557.22

8   Add a calculated measure to the *Orders* table that uses the calculated measures already defined to calculate the *Average Price Per Unit*.

> f_x Average Price Per Unit:=[Sum of Order Value]/[Qty Sold]

> Average Price Per Unit: 25.9958

9   Format the *Average Price Per Unit* calculated measure as *Currency*.

> Average Price Per Unit: $26.00

10   Add a KPI (Key Performance Indicator) to the *Average Price Per Unit* calculated measure that uses a *Target Value* of $26.00, a *Status Threshold (High)* of $27.00 and a *Status Threshold (Low)* of $25.00.

11   Create a pivot table that will show, for each *Employee*, the *Qty Sold, Sum of Order Value, Average Price Per Unit* and the KPI visual *Status* indicator.

Row Labels ▾	Qty Sold	Sum of Order Value	Average Price Per Unit	Average Price Per Unit Status
Anderson,Jane	993	$25,580.13	$25.76 ◯	
Armstrong,Dan	687	$17,174.05	$25.00 ●	
Ashe,Lucille	895	$23,556.94	$26.32 ◯	
Bell,Stephen	861	$23,588.72	$27.40 ●	
Bradshaw,John	608	$16,497.20	$27.13 ●	

12   Save your work as: *2018 Film Sales*.

2018 Film Sales

If you need help slide the page to the left ➡

Session 12: Exercise Answers

These are the three questions that students find the most difficult to answer:

Q 11	Q 5 & 6	Q 2 & 3
1. Click: Home→PivotTable (from the Power Pivot window). The *Create Pivot Table* dialog appears. 2. Click the OK button. You are taken back to an Excel worksheet containing an OLAP pivot table that references the data model. 3. Drag the following fields from the *PivotTable Fields* list to the lower panes: ☰ Rows EmployeeName ▾ Σ Values Qty Sold ▾ Sum of Order Value ▾ Average Price Per Unit ▾ Average Price Per Unit Status ▾ This was covered in: *Lesson 12-8: Create a Key Performance Indicator.*	1. Click: View→Data View (in the Power Pivot window). 2. Click the *Orders* tab. 3. Click anywhere inside the column headed: *Add Column.* 4. Type this formula into the formula bar: `=Orders[Qty]*Orders[UnitPrice]` 5. Press the **\<Enter\>** key. 6. Double-click the *Calculated Column 1* column header and type: **Extended Price** 7. Click in the first cell in the calculation area that is below the *Qty* column. 8. Click: Home→Calculations→Autosum. 9. Do the same thing for the *Extended Price* column. This was covered in: *Lesson 12-2: Add a DAX calculated column and Lesson 12-3: Create a DAX calculated measure.*	1. Click: Data→ Get & Transform Data→ Get Data→From Database→ From Microsoft Access Database. 2. Navigate to the *2018 Film Sales* Access database and open it. 3. Click the *Select multiple items* checkbox. 4. Select every table. 5. Click the *Load* button. This was covered in: *Lesson 11-9: Create a data model directly from a relational database.*

If you have difficulty with the other questions, here are the lessons that cover the relevant skills:

4   Refer to: *Lesson 11-5: Add a relationship to a data model using Power Pivot.*

7   Click on the *Sum of Extended Price* calculated measure and edit the text before the := operator.

8   Refer to: *Lesson 12-2: Add a DAX calculated column* and *Lesson 12-7: Use a DAX DISTINCTCOUNT function.*

9   Click on the *Average Price Per Unit* calculated measure (to select it) and then click: Home→Formatting→Format→Currency (from the Power Pivot window).

10   Refer to: *Lesson 12-8: Create a Key Performance Indicator.*

Appendix A: Power Pivot Rules

> Rules are for the obedience of fools and the guidance of wise men.
>
> *Douglas Bader (British World War II fighter pilot) 1910-1982*

When working with Power Pivot the very best practitioners are fanatical about rules.

Some rules are so self-evidently good and great that it's almost impossible to find anybody that could disagree with them.

Proposing some rules can cause debate, and even sometimes anger, amongst others who do not want to change the way they work. For this reason, whenever a team project is undertaken it is a good idea to publish the rules and spend the first morning in a meeting to ensure that everybody agrees with the rules and "buys into" them. During this meeting it must be made clear that all rules are entirely negotiable, providing that a case for changes can be logically argued. Some of our best rules have come from these brainstorming sessions.

The rules presented in this appendix include generally accepted best-practice as well as some of The Smart Method's own unique standards. Rules that apply to concepts not covered in this book are not included in order to avoid confusion.

You can use the "rule book" to QA your work prior to releasing the first version of your data model. All lessons in this book should conform to the rules (please let us know if you discover any that do not).

You don't need to adopt The Smart Method's rules, but they are a good starting point to derive your own rules.

Never be afraid to break the rules when you have good reason to. As Douglas Bader observed, they are only for guidance. When you do break the rules, however, make sure you can justify (to yourself at least) why you did it.

Never break the rules in a misguided attempt to save time by producing a "quick and dirty" data model. You'll waste far more time unravelling the mess than you'll ever save.

Adhere to the standard defined in this appendix (or your own derivative of it) and create beautiful, robust, extendable data models.

1: Get & Transform

1-1 When importing data from a database, transform data (as much as possible) with a View.

In an ideal world (when data resides in a database) your DBA would create a *View* for you that will remove a lot of transforming work (from Get & Transform).

A View can:

- Remove columns you don't need.

- Rename columns to the names you need (which are often different to the source data field names).

- De-normalize several source tables into a single View.

- Add calculated columns.

Because this is all done in the source database you have a flying start for your Get & Transform session and can re-use the View in any future Get & Transform queries.

You learned about Views in: *Lesson 10-28: Efficiently import data using a view.*

Because we do not live in an ideal world you may find resistance from your DBA when requesting views, or unacceptably long lead times to have them implemented. In this case you will need to use Get & Transform instead.

1-2 Do not use Power Pivot to import or transform data.

Get & Transform should be used to import and transform data before it is modeled using Power Pivot. You may have noticed that Power Pivot still retains limited direct import features. You should regard these as legacy features that date back to the days before Get & Transform was available.

1-3 Create compression-friendly columns with as few unique values as possible.

A Power Pivot data model contains compressed data.

How data compression works

You may be familiar with products such as WinZip that can compress a file so that it is many times smaller than the original file.

Compression is achieved using a lookup table.

For example, consider all the words in a novel stored as a text file. The word "and" takes up three characters (or three bytes) in the file. If you replaced all occurrences of the word: "and" with the number: 1 along with a lookup table defining that "1 = and" you would significantly reduce the size of the text file.

When you compressed the file, you'd substitute the number 1 (one byte) for every occurrence of "and" (3 bytes) and then do the reverse when you uncompressed the file.

This may be a slight over-simplification but it is essentially how Power Pivot compresses data.

How to make columns compression friendly

Here are some examples of how to reduce the unique values in a column.

If you had a column that contained date and time values, but you were only really interested in summarizing by date, you'd greatly reduce the number of unique values in the column by only storing the *date* part of the data in the model (removing the time component using Get & Transform). To take this further, if you were only interested in creating aggregations of monthly data, you'd make the column even more compression-friendly by converting the dates into month names.

If you had an address table with a column called *Location* (containing names such as *Orlando, FL)* you could reduce the size of the data model by splitting the column into two (*City* and *State*). This would work because there would be fewer unique values in each column. This is, of course, also better practice as it gives users more scope when filtering by dimension.

1-4 Only store numerical data and foreign keys in the fact table.

The central *fact* table in your star schema should not contain dimension columns. If any dimension columns exist, they should be split out into their own tables. Any correctly normalized relational database will already follow this rule.

Degenerate dimensions may break this rule

There are exceptions to this rule in respect of *degenerate dimensions*. These are dimensions that are so insignificant that there's no need to normalize the fact table column into its own dimension table. If a fact table column *could* be a foreign key (but there is no extra information about it that could appear in a separate dimension table) it would be correct to describe it as a *degenerate dimension*.

Here's a degenerate dimension example:

If an *Invoices* fact table had a field named *Discount Coupon Number,* it would be possible to regard it as a degenerate dimension but only if nothing else was known about the discount coupon in the data source. If there was extra data about each *Discount Coupon* within the data source (such as the *Issued Date* and *Expiry Date*) then *Discount Coupon Number* should be modeled as a foreign key (within the *Invoices* fact table) that relates to a *Discount Coupon* dimension table. The *Discount Coupon* dimension table would then contain the *Issued Date* and *Expiry Date* (and the primary key would contain the *Discount Coupon Number*).

1-5 When creating a fact table do not import the primary key.

It is necessary to have a primary key for each dimension table, but the primary key has no value in the fact table. Because the fact table's primary key consumes a substantial amount of space it should not be imported into the data model.

1-6 Remove redundant columns and tables.

There is often a huge amount of redundant data within a data source that is of little interest for reporting purposes. Don't be tempted to include all the source data tables and columns "just in case" they are needed in the future. It is easy to add tables and columns using Get & Transform if they are needed in the future.

You should pay particular attention to unnecessary columns in the fact table. Fact tables can contain millions of rows (while dimension tables are usually quite small). For this reason, an unnecessary column in a fact table can hugely impact upon the data model size.

There are many advantages in keeping your data models compact:

- The data model will use less memory.
- Reports (visualizations) will usually load faster.
- The Excel file size will be smaller.
- Users will find the model easier to use.

2: Data Modeling

2-1 Use a calendar table for date dimensions.

Whenever there is a date column in a fact table you should add a calendar dimension table.

Power Pivot makes it easy to add a self-updating calendar table with a single click. A calendar table opens many more possibilities when creating aggregations that use time dimensions.

2-2 Use a Star schema (rather than a Snowflake schema) when constructing data models.

A Snowflake schema is said to resemble a snowflake:

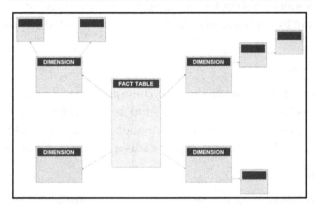

A Star schema de-normalizes the dimension tables into a single dimension:

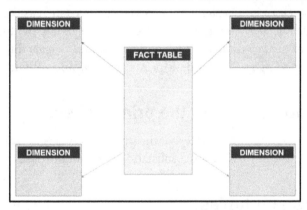

While Power Pivot will work well with either a Snowflake or Star schema, Power Pivot works faster and better with a Star schema. Star schemas are also easier for users to work with.

For these reasons the Star schema is the preferred choice when working with Power Pivot.

2-3 Do not model many-to-many relationships.

Many-to-many relationships (using a link table) are not supported in Power Pivot data models. In order to create accurate aggregations, Power Pivot needs a single path between tables.

Many-to-many relationships that exist in source data should be de-normalized to create a one-to-many relationship.

2-4 Do not use linked Excel tables.

If you import data into Get & Transform using a linked Excel table (in the same workbook) and then load it into Power Pivot you will create two copies of your data.

Data in Power Pivot is compressed in memory (and can shrink to as little as 10% of the source data size). For this reason, you may bloat the workbook's size by as much as 90% by duplicating data in both the data model and an Excel workbook linked table.

2-5 Always format columns inside the data model (and not in the Pivot Table).

If you format columns and calculated measures inside the data model, you'll never have to re-format when you use a column within a pivot table. This makes the data model easier to use by untrained users (who may not even know how to format a value in a pivot table).

Remember that the data model may be used by many pivot tables. By formatting once in the data model, you avoid formatting each time you add the measure to a pivot table.

3: Table, Column and Measure naming

3-1 Never use prefixes for table names.

You will often see star schemas with a fact table prefixed with *fact* (or sometimes *Fact* or *fct*) and dimension tables prefixed with *Dim* (or sometimes *dim*). This results in names such as: *FactOrders, fctOrders, Fact_Orders, DimProduct, dimProduct and Dim_Product.*

This convention originates in Ralph Kimball's *Business Dimensional Lifecycle* methodology.

While the Kimball naming convention works really well for data warehouses it is not a great fit for a Power Pivot data model. Data models are often used by ordinary, unsophisticated users to visualize their data (either using an OLAP pivot table or Microsoft's Power BI product).

Users reasonably expect a Product dimension table to have a plain English name such as *Product* rather than *DimProduct.*

Another advantage of using plain English nouns for tables is that the data model will work well with the Q&A tool in Microsoft's Power BI product. The Q&A tool enables users to type *natural language queries* such as: "List all Orders by Product and Month". A user would be unlikely to type "List all DimOrders by FactProduct and DimMonth".

Because many badly designed data models use cryptic names, Power Pivot allows you to define synonyms for table names (you can do this in Power Pivot by clicking: Advanced→Language→Synonyms). By avoiding prefixes, you will not have to define a synonym for each table.

3-2 Apart from acronyms, never use abbreviations for Table, Column, Measure (or any other) names.

A good yardstick for choosing a name is to try to imagine that there is an extraordinary reward for two programmers if they can independently come up with the same program text for the same problem. Both programmers know the reward but cannot otherwise communicate. Such an experiment would be futile, of course, for any sizable problem, but it is a neat goal. The reward of real life is that a program written by someone else, which is identical to what one's own program would have been, is extremely readable and modifiable.

Dr. Charles Simonyi (formerly Microsoft's Chief Architect)

Example: A dimension table contains Customer information. One of the fields in the table contains the Customer's first name. It was badly named in the source data as a table named *Cust* and a field named *CusFN*. How would you rename the field in Get & Transform?

If you were playing Charles Simonyi's game and you needed to guess which name another developer had come up with you'd probably win with:

Table Name: Customer
Field Name: First Name

A long time ago, when memory was a precious commodity, there was a small performance gain to be had by abbreviating names. There isn't any more (and hasn't been for many years). So why do 21st century developers still create cryptic, bug prone, and difficult-to-maintain data models by abbreviating names? It is one of the great mysteries of life!

Some data modelers might argue that you don't have to type as much if you use abbreviations. You may save a few keystrokes when you design the model, but you'll waste many hours later on when you have to consult documentation in order to establish what your cryptically named columns actually contain.

This rule can, of course, be sometimes waived in the case of commonly used acronyms. For example, if everybody in an organization refers to the *Gross Domestic Product* as the *GDP* it may be clearer to users if the abbreviation is used (though you'd probably define *Gross Domestic Product* as a synonym in this case by clicking: Advanced→Language→Synonyms).

3-3   Name dimension tables, fields, and everything else except the fact table, in the singular.

As previously noted, one of the goals of our naming convention is that you should be able to intuitively guess the correct name of any dimension table, column name or measure.

The use of plurals makes this goal more difficult. Consider a dimension table containing customer records. It would be difficult to guess whether the name of the table should be *Customer* or *Customers*.

This problem can be avoided by always using singular names for table names (except the fact table), column names and measure names.

You should be aware that some designers turn this convention upside down and make all dimension table names plural. It is (vastly) preferable to enforce an "everything in the singular" convention as column names are prefixed with the table name and may look confusing in the plural.

3-4   Name the fact table in the plural.

The fact table is the central table in a star schema. This table should be named in the plural because the table contains one-to-many relationships with the dimension tables. For example, an *Invoices* fact table contains many invoices, but each field only connects to one row in the *Customer* dimension table.

Using the "dimension table names singular/fact table name plural" convention provides several advantages:

- It is always apparent (at a glance) which table is the fact table in a star schema.

- Queries sound just like the spoken word:

    "Show me the Sales by Customer"

    … instead of:

"Show me the Sale by Customers" or "show me the Sale by Customer" or "Show me the Sales by Customers".

3-5 Use a single noun for table names whenever possible.

Most tables (such as Customer and Product) lend themselves to the use of a single noun. Where this is the case you should not use two words to describe the table.

3-6 Do not use spaces in table names.

There may be a very unusual case where you need to use two words to describe a table. When this is the case, use Upper Camel Case (also known as Pascal Case) with names such as *InternetSales* and *ProductSubcategory*, rather than spaces.

If you use spaces in table names you will need to enclose the table name in single quotation marks whenever you reference the table name in a formula.

3-7 Always use spaces in column names and measures.

Unlike table names, it is very common to need more than one word to clearly describe the data in a column. For example: *Company Name* and *Contact Name* (that might both appear in a *Supplier* table).

Unlike table names, you don't have to use quotation marks when referring to column names as they are always enclosed by square brackets such as: [Company Name] and [Contact Name].

Data models are often used by ordinary, unsophisticated users to visualize their data (either using an OLAP pivot table or Microsoft's Power BI product). They will find plain English column names (with spaces) easier to work with than underscores or camel case.

4: Creating DAX calculated measures

4-1 Place measures in the same table that they reference.

This is the most logical place for measures. The table in which the measure resides also determines where it will appear in the *Pivot Table Fields* list. It will be less confusing for users if the field appears in the correct table.

Power Pivot will allow you to place measures in any table but if you place measures in a different table than the one they reference, Power Pivot may become confused and trigger a relationship warning.

4-2 Always use explicit measures rather than implicit measures.

You learned about explicit and implicit measures in: *Lesson 12-4: Understand Implicit and Explicit measures*. Explicit measures have so many advantages over implicit measures that it is best practice to use them exclusively.

Make sure that you provide enough explicit measures for all likely reporting scenarios.

4-3 Use many simple measures rather than one complex measure.

Because measures can reference other measures it is better to create several interim measures and then to create a more complex measure by referencing the simpler measures that you have already defined.

4-4 Always format measures inside the data model (and not in the pivot table).

Just like columns, you should always format measures inside the data model and not in any pivot tables that are created from it.

4-5 Include the table name when you reference a column.

It is perfectly correct (in database design) to have the same field name in two different tables. By prefixing column names with table names, you will ensure that Power Pivot is referencing the correct field.

Good: =Product[FirstName] & " " & Product[LastName]
Bad: = [FirstName] & " " & [LastName]

4-6 Do not include the table name when you reference a measure.

Because DAX formulas can include references to other measures, it can be difficult to identify which parts of a formula are column references and which are measure references.

If you include the table name when you reference a column and do not include the table name when referencing a measure, it is always clear (when auditing a formula) where the values are coming from.

Appendix B: Skills Covered in the Essential Skills Course

You have to learn to crawl before you can walk.
You have to learn to walk before you can run.

Proverbs, unknown authors

In order to get the most out of this book you should already be very comfortable with Excel's main features. We also have an *Essential Skills* course for absolute beginners.

978-1-909253-42-1
386 pages

978-1-909253-43-8
(This book)

This (Expert Skills) book assumes that you have already mastered the skills taught in the *Essential Skills* book.

So how do you know if your skills are already advanced enough to tackle this book?

This appendix lists the objectives for each of the eight sessions in the *Essential Skills* course.

If you already have all (or at least most) of the skills taught in the *Essential Skills* course, you are ready to upgrade your skills to Expert level with this course.

Essential skills course outline

Session 1: Basic Skills

- Start Excel and open a new blank workbook
- Check that your Excel version is up to date
- Change between Touch Mode and Mouse Mode
- Change the Office Theme
- Maximize, minimize, re-size, move and close the Excel window
- Download the sample files and open/navigate a workbook
- Save a workbook to a local file
- Understand common file formats
- Pin a workbook and understand file organization
- View, move, add, rename, delete and navigate worksheet tabs
- Use the Versions feature to recover an unsaved Draft file
- Use the Versions feature to recover an earlier version of a workbook
- Use the Ribbon
- Understand Ribbon components
- Customize the Quick Access Toolbar and preview the printout
- Use the Mini Toolbar, Key Tips and keyboard shortcuts
- Understand views
- Hide and Show the Formula Bar and Ribbon
- Use the Tell Me help system
- Use other help features

Session 2: Doing Useful Work with Excel

- Enter text and numbers into a worksheet
- Create a new workbook and view two workbooks at the same time
- Use AutoSum to quickly calculate totals
- Select a range of cells and understand Smart Tags
- Enter data into a range and copy data across a range
- Select adjacent and non-adjacent rows and columns
- Select non-contiguous cell ranges and view summary information
- AutoSelect a range of cells
- Re-size rows and columns
- Use AutoSum to sum a non-contiguous range
- Use AutoSum to calculate average and maximum values

- Create your own formulas
- Create functions using Formula AutoComplete
- Use AutoFill for text and numeric series
- Use AutoFill to adjust formulas and use AutoFill options
- Speed up your AutoFills and create a custom fill series
- Understand linear and exponential series
- Use Flash Fill to split and concatenate text
- Analyze Data with the Ideas feature
- Use the zoom control
- Print out a worksheet

Session 3: Taking Your Skills to the Next Level

- Insert and delete rows and columns
- Use AutoComplete and fill data from adjacent cells
- Cut, copy and paste
- Cut, copy and paste using drag and drop
- Use Paste Values
- Increase/decrease decimal places displayed
- Transpose a range
- Use the Multiple Item Clipboard
- Use Undo and Redo
- Insert, View and Print cell notes and cell comments
- Understand absolute, relative and mixed cell references
- Understand templates and set the default custom template folder
- Create a template
- Use a template
- Add an Office Add-In to a workbook
- Freeze columns and rows
- Split the window into multiple panes
- Check spelling

Session 4: Making Your Worksheets Look Professional

- Format dates
- Understand date serial numbers
- Format numbers using built-in number formats
- Create custom number formats

- Horizontally and Vertically align the contents of cells
- Merge cells, wrap text and expand/collapse the formula bar
- Unmerge cells and Center Across Selection
- Understand themes
- Use cell styles and change themes
- Add color and gradient effects to cells
- Add borders and lines
- Create your own custom theme
- Create your own custom cell styles
- Use a master style book to merge styles
- Use simple conditional formatting
- Manage multiple conditional formats using the Rules Manager
- Bring data alive with visualizations
- Create a formula driven conditional format
- Insert a Sparkline into a range of cells
- Apply a common vertical axis and formatting to a Sparkline group
- Apply a date axis to a Sparkline group and format a single Sparkline
- Use the Format Painter
- Rotate text

Session 5: Charts and Graphics

- Understand chart types, layouts and styles
- Create a simple chart with two clicks
- Move, re-size, copy and delete a chart
- Create a chart using the Recommended Charts feature
- Add and remove chart elements using Quick Layout
- Apply a pre-defined chart style and color set
- Manually format a chart element
- Format 3-D elements and add drop shadows
- Move, re-size, add, position and delete chart elements
- Apply a chart filter
- Change a chart's source data
- Assign non-contiguous source data to a chart
- Understand data series and categories
- Add data series using the Select Data Source dialog tools
- Chart non-contiguous source data by hiding rows and columns
- Create a chart with numerical axes

- Deal with empty data points and add data labels to a chart
- Highlight specific data points with color and annotations
- Add gridlines and scale axes
- Emphasize data by manipulating pie charts
- Create a chart with two vertical axes
- Create a combination chart containing different chart types
- Work with trend lines and forecast sheets
- Add a gradient fill to a chart background
- Create your own chart templates
- Create a filled map chart

Session 6: Working with Multiple Worksheets and Workbooks

- View the same workbook in different windows
- View two windows side by side and perform synchronous scrolling
- Duplicate worksheets within a workbook
- Move and copy worksheets from one workbook to another
- Hide and unhide a worksheet
- Create cross worksheet formulas
- Understand worksheet groups
- Use find and replace

Session 7: Printing Your Work

- Print Preview and change paper orientation
- Use Page Layout view to adjust margins
- Use Page Setup to set margins more precisely and center the worksheet
- Set paper size and scale
- Insert, delete and preview page breaks
- Adjust page breaks using Page Break Preview
- Add auto-headers and auto-footers and set the starting page number
- Add custom headers and footers
- Specify different headers and footers for the first, odd and even pages
- Print only part of a worksheet
- Add row and column data labels and gridlines to printed output
- Print several selected worksheets and change the page order

- Suppress error messages in printouts

Session 8: Cloud Computing

- Understand cloud computing
- Save a workbook to a OneDrive
- Open a workbook from a OneDrive
- Understand operating systems and devices
- Understand Office versions
- Understand Excel Online
- Open a workbook using Excel Online
- Share a link to a workbook
- Understand OneDrive AutoSave and Version History
- Edit a workbook simultaneously with other users using Excel Online

Index

W

X

Y

Further Reading

The Essential Skills book isn't only for beginners! Experts find it useful too.

Many purchasers of *Expert Skills* also decide to purchase the *Essential Skills* book (the first book in this series). *Essential Skills* isn't only for Excel beginners. I often teach this course (as a classroom course) to professionals that have used Excel for over ten years and they *always* gain some fantastically useful skills from the course.

Essential Skills assumes no previous exposure to Excel and teaches all of the core skills. Charts and Graphics are extensively covered in a 30-lesson session and there's comprehensive coverage of Excel's cloud computing features (including collaborative working with Excel Online).

Available as both a printed paper book and e-book.

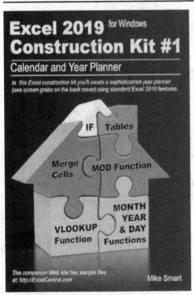

Learn how to apply your new Excel skills with a Smart Method construction kit.

For over 900 years craftsmen have traditionally taught their skills to an apprentice. In this model the apprentice learned his trade by observing how the master craftsman used his skills. This construction kit will teach you advanced Excel skills in the same way. Even if you only have basic Excel skills, the construction kit is designed in such a way that you'll be able to construct a complex, polished professional Excel application that would be well beyond the powers of most advanced Excel users. Available as both a printed paper book and e-book.

Preview the first chapter free at:

https://thesmartmethod.com

Excel Challenges.

Our Excel online challenges are a little like the exercises at the end of each session in this book. Unlike the exercises, the online challenges will test the application of many skills (covered in different sessions in the book).

We began trialling challenges in July 2018 and (at time of writing in July 2019) we'd published three challenges. By the time you read this book we may have produced more.

Access the challenges online at:

https://thesmartmethod.com/excel-challenges/

Use your new Excel skills to teach your own classroom courses

If you've worked through this book carefully you are now a true Excel expert. There is a huge demand, everywhere in the world, for Excel training at all levels. The skills you have learned in this book (and the preceding *Essential Skills* book) will enable you to teach Excel at all levels – from beginner to expert.

This book is available for all Excel versions in common use (Excel 2007, 2010, 2013, 2016, 2019 and 365 for Windows along with Excel 2016 & 2019 for Apple Mac). You can use the books as courseware during your classes and then give each student a copy of the book to take home as reference material when the course is over.

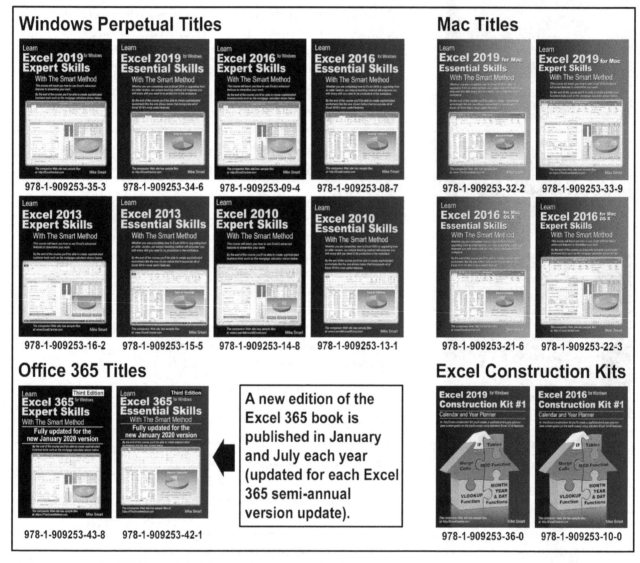

Windows Perpetual Titles

978-1-909253-35-3 | 978-1-909253-34-6 | 978-1-909253-09-4 | 978-1-909253-08-7

978-1-909253-16-2 | 978-1-909253-15-5 | 978-1-909253-14-8 | 978-1-909253-13-1

Mac Titles

978-1-909253-32-2 | 978-1-909253-33-9

978-1-909253-21-6 | 978-1-909253-22-3

Office 365 Titles

978-1-909253-43-8 | 978-1-909253-42-1

A new edition of the Excel 365 book is published in January and July each year (updated for each Excel 365 semi-annual version update).

Excel Construction Kits

978-1-909253-36-0 | 978-1-909253-10-0

You can quote the ISBN numbers shown above to any book retailer or wholesaler. All major distributors (in every country of the world) have our books in stock for immediate delivery.

Place a direct order for 5+ books for wholesale prices and free delivery worldwide

To place a publisher-direct order you only need to order five books or more (of the same title). To view wholesale prices, go to this web page:

https://thesmartmethod.com/wholesale-printed-books

CPSIA information can be obtained
at www.ICGtesting.com
Printed in the USA
LVHW061914031220
673319LV00011B/713

9 781909 253438